THE LAW
Analysis and Synthesis
(AN INTRODUCTION TO LAW)

BURTON ANDREWS, A.B., A.M., LL.B., J.D.
Albany Law School
Union University

CONTENTS

Published by Liberty Book Company
374 Morris Street
Albany, New York 12208

Library of Congress

Catalogue Card No.

68-2062

Classification No. KF
379
A5

TABLE OF CONTENTS

CHAPTER I

THE NATURE OF A CASE

CHAPTER II

THE SUBSTANTIVE LAW

CHAPTER III

THE ADJECTIVE LAW

CHAPTER IV

RES JUDICATA

CHAPTER V

THE JUDICIAL SYSTEM

CHAPTER VI

STARE DECISIS

CHAPTER VII

THE NATURE OF JUSTICE
(Lecture)

CHAPTER VIII

THE NATURE OF LAW
(Lecture)

CHAPTER IX

LEGISLATION

See Supplement at the back of this book. Various changes in this book are indicated in the Supplement.

TABLE OF CASES

Reference is to page numbers

Reference is to page numbers

PREFACE

Congratulations upon your desire to learn about The Law.

This is a casebook prepared to aid you in learning the nature of The Law and how it functions in human society. Being a casebook, it comprises reports of litigated cases by the judges who adjudicated them. This is deemed to be the best evidence available as to the nature and function of The Law.

As an introduction to The Law, the objectives have been: to indicate the comprehensive concepts of The Law in order to give a survey of the total area of The Law; to point out the relationship between the main features of the area; to make clear the nature of the adversary system inherent in Anglo-American Law; to give a method of study, and yet withal to maintain simplicity of organization and presentation so that you can synthesize your studies in The Law into a meaningful integrated whole.

The foregoing objectives necessarily required certain limitations as to what is presented. No aspect of The Law is developed in detail. Study in depth must come later in pursuit of particular subjects. Current law on particular points is not developed. Very few profound opinions of learned judges could be included. Reports have not been selected because of their social significance nor their importance in the development of national or political interests. Insofar as these aspects are included it is because the reports contribute to the objectives of this book.

The usual abbreviations are herein used for official and the unofficial reports of cases in Anglo-American courts and for law reviews and other legal publications. Punctuation for abbreviations is generally omitted. Abbreviations in titles of cases are usually obvious as to the full names. Omissions of material from reports of cases, irrelevant to the points herein presented, are indicated by a series of dots. Paragraphing in certain opinions has occasionally been changed with the intention of enhancing readability by the beginning student without in any instance, it is believed, affecting the continuity of thought or the meaning of the writer.

It is my earnest hope that you will develop an understanding and appreciation of The Law in human society.

Albany, New York
September 1, 1967

Burton Andrews

CHAPTER I

THE NATURE OF A CASE

OUTLINE OF CHAPTER I:

SUGGESTED READINGS:

Dowling, P. and P.: Legal Method
Ch. I, §2 "The Case Method of Studying Law", pp. 15-33

Fryer and Benson: Legal Method and System
Ch. I, §1 "Mechanics of Work", pp. 1-25

Karlen: Primer of Procedure
Appendix I, "Record of Trial", pp. 173-453

Morgan: The Study of Law
Ch. VII "How to Read and Abstract a Reported Case", pp. 151-165

The record below is part of the record in the Case of Owen v. Rochester Penfield Bus Co. (1952) 304 NY 457. It is set forth as an example of the steps taken in the course of an action tried before a jury.

(Cover Page)

STATE OF NEW YORK

Court of Appeals

MARY JANE LITTEER OWEN, 4216 Valley Road, Cleveland 9, Ohio,
Plaintiff-Appellant,

vs.

ROCHESTER-PENFIELD BUS COMPANY, INC., 60 River Boulevard, Rochester, New York,
Defendant-Respondent.

RECORD ON APPEAL

H. C. & H. B. HARPENDING and
F. M. HUNT,
Attorneys for Plaintiff-Appellant,
Office and Post Office Address,
Dundee, New York.

AUSTIN W. ERWIN and
AUSTIN W. ERWIN, JR.,
Attorneys for Defendant-Respondent,
Office and Post Office Address,
70 Main Street,
Geneseo, New York.

BATAVIA TIMES, LAW PRINTERS,
BATAVIA, N. Y.

INDEX

State of New York

SUPREME COURT

Appellate Division - Third Department

MARY JANE LITTEER OWEN, 4216 Valley Road, Cleveland 9, Ohio
Plaintiff-Respondent,

vs.

ROCHESTER-PENFIELD BUS COMPANY, INC., 60 River Boulevard, Rochester, New York,
Defendant-Appellant.

STATEMENT UNDER RULE 234.

This action was brought by the plaintiff against the defendant to recover damages for personal injuries alleged to have been sustained by the plaintiff on or about the first day of December, 1946, claiming that while a passenger on defendant's bus on said date riding from Bath to Rochester she sustained frozen feet. The action was tried before Hon. Riley H. Heath, Justice presiding, and a jury at a trial term of the Suprme Court held at the Court House in the Village of Watkins Glen commencing on the 8th day of June, 1949.

The jury rendered a verdict in favor of the plaintiff and against the defendant in the sum of $5,000.00 and judgment in the sum of $5,108.50 was entered in favor of the plaintiff and against the defendant in the Schuyler County Clerk's office on the 14th day of June, 1949.

This is an appeal from said judgment and from each and every part thereof and also from the denial of the defendant's motion for a new trial and for the setting aside of the verdict made on the minutes at the close of the case. The notice of appeal was served upon the attorneys for the plaintiff and filed in the office of the Clerk of the County of Schuyler on the 27th day of June, 1949.

Plaintiff duly appeared in this action by H. C. and H. B. Harpending and F. M. Hunt, attorneys, by Asbury Harpending of Counsel and the defendant appeared by Austin W. Erwin and Austin W. Erwin, Jr., by Austin W. Erwin of Counsel. There has been no change of parties or attorneys.

SUMMONS

STATE OF NEW YORK

SUPREME COURT—County of Schuyler

MARY JANE LITTEER, an infant, by
JOHN H. LITTEER, her Guardian
ad Litem,

Plaintiff,

against

ROCHESTER-PENFIELD BUS COMPANY, INC.,
Defendant.

To the above named Defendant:

YOU ARE HEREBY SUMMONED to answer the complaint in this action, and to serve a copy of your answer, or, if the complaint is not served with this summons, to serve a notice of appearance, on the Plaintiff's Attorney within twenty days after the service of this summons, exclusive of the day of service. In case of your failure to appear or answer, judgment will be taken against you by default for the relief demanded in the complaint.

Trial to be held in the County of Schuyler.

Dated: January 5, 1948.

H. C. & H. B. HARPENDING
and FREDERICK M. HUNT,
Attorneys for Plaintiff,
Office and Post Office Address,
Dundee, New York.

COMPLAINT

(Same Title)

Plaintiff complains of the defendant and for a cause of action alleges:

1. That plaintiff is an infant over the age of Fourteen years of age, and John H. Litteer was duly appointed her guardian ad litem for the purpose of bringing this action by an order of the County Court, County of Schuyler, duly made and entered on the 5th day of September, 1947, and he duly qualified and is now acting as such guardian.

2. Upon information and belief, that at all times hereinafter mentioned, the defendant, Rochester-Penfield Bus Company, Inc., was and still is a domestic corporation duly organized and existing under the laws of the State of New York, and was the owner of a motor bus

line operating buses in and about Western New York and particularly between the cities of Rochester, New York, and Bath, New York, and was a common carrier of passengers for hire from point to point and place to place.

3. That on the 1st day of December, 1946, the plaintiff was a passenger for hire on one of the motor busses of the defendant as such common carrier, then on a duly scheduled run; that on said date plaintiff was invited to and boarded said bus in the Village of Bath, New York, for the purpose of being conveyed as a passenger for hire to Rochester, New York; that the defendant sold to plaintiff the said passage and accepted the fare therefor, and the plaintiff thereby became entitled to be safely carried by the defendant in its said motor bus to her destination; that defendant owed the further duty to plaintiff to have the said bus operated carefully and prudently and to transport plaintiff in a safe, comfortable, careful and prudent manner, and to have proper automotive appliances and to have the same in proper working condition so that plaintiff might be carried safely as aforesaid.

4. That on said day and while plaintiff was being carried as aforesaid, defendant failed and neglected to safely carry plaintiff, but on the contrary permitted and caused improper, insufficient and faulty automotive heating appliances to be used therein, so that the interior temperature thereof decreased below the point of human safety and comfort, as a result of which plaintiff received and suffered serious first degree frost-bite on both her feet, and sustained other personal injuries, damaging her in the sum of Fifteen Thousand Dollars ($15,000.00).

5. That plaintiff's injuries were received without any fault, carelessness, or negligence, on the part of the plaintiff, but were due solely to the fault and negligence of the defendant and its servants and employees.

WHEREFORE, plaintiff demands judgment in the sum of Fifteen Thousand Dollars ($15,000.00), besides the costs and disbursements of this action.

H. C. & H. B. HARPENDING and
FREDERICK M. HUNT,
Attorneys for Plaintiff,
Office and Post Office Address,
Dundee, New York

ANSWER

(Same Title)

The defendant, answering the complaint herein:

FIRST: Admits the allegations contained in Paragraph "2" of the complaint.

SECOND: Denies the allegations contained in Paragraphs "4" and "5" of the complaint.

THIRD: Denies that it has knowledge or information sufficient to form a belief as to the allegations contained in Paragraphs "1" and "3" and therefore denies the same.

FOURTH: Denies each and every allegation in said complaint not heretofore specifically admitted or denied.

WHEREFORE, the defendant demands judgment for a dismissal of the complaint herein together with the costs and disbursements of this action.

AUSTIN W. ERWIN and
AUSTIN W. ERWIN, JR.,
Attorneys for Defendant,
104 Main Street
Geneseo, New York

DEMAND FOR BILL OF PARTICULARS.

(Same Title.)

Sirs:

PLEASE TAKE NOTICE, that the defendant, Rochester-Penfield Bus Company, Inc., demands that you serve upon its attorneys within ten days a verified bill of particulars specifying the following particulars of the said plaintiff's claim:

1. A detailed statement setting forth the personal injuries which the plaintiff alleges she received which comprise the injury damaging her in the sum of $15,000.00 as alleged in the complaint.

2. A detailed statement setting forth which of these injuries, if any of them, are permanent.

3. A statement setting forth the total amount of money which the plaintiff claims as damage for: (1) hospital expenses (2) physician's expenses (3) medical supplies (4) nurses services (5) any other expenses arising out of andas a result of the alleged injuries.

4. A detailed statement describing the employment engaged in at the time of the alleged injury by the plaintiff and the length of time lost by her in that employment as a result of the alleged injuries.

Yours, etc.,

AUSTIN W. ERWIN and
AUSTIN W. ERWIN, JR.,
Attorneys for Defendant,
70 Main Street
Geneseo, New York

To:
H. C. & H. B. Harpending and
Frederick M. Hunt,
Attorneys for Plaintiff,
Dundee, New York

BILL OF PARTICULARS

(Same Title.)

The plaintiff for her bill of particulars alleges:

1. That the personal injuries received by plaintiff at the time referred to in the complaint were severely frost bitten and frozen feet with resultant injuries to the tissues, blood vessels, nerves, flesh, muscles, tendons thereof resulting in pain, itching, cracking, swelling, bleeding, callouses, corns and other discomfort.

2. Plaintiff is advised and believes the aforesaid injuries are permanent, although there may be some improvement.

3. That a portion of the medical treatment furnished plaintiff was furnished by the school physician at the Rochester Institute of Technology where plaintiff was enrolled as a student at the time the injuries were received. That her other medical bills amount to $82.00 for medical treatment. That medical supplies and other treatment including medication, special shoes, special woolen stockings to be used in the inclement and cold weather approximate $35.00.

Dated: May 25, 1959.

Yours, etc.,

H. C. & H. B. HARPENDING and
Frederick M. Hunt, ESQS.,
Attorneys for the Plaintiff,
Office and P. O. Address,
Dundee, N. Y.

To:
Erwin & Erwin, Esqs.
Attorneys for the Defendant.

TESTIMONY

At a Trial and Special Term of the Supreme Court, held in and for the County of Schuyler, at the Courthouse in the Village of Watkins Glen, New York on the 8th day of June, 1949 with the Hon. Riley H. Heath, Justice Presiding,

STATE OF NEW YORK

SUPREME COURT—County of Schuyler

MARY JANE LITTEER, an Infant, by
JOHN LITTEER, her Guardian ad Litem,
Plaintiff,

vs.

ROCHESTER-PENFIELD BUS COMPANY, INC.,
Defendant.

Appearances:
H. C. and H. B. Harpending, and Frederick M. Hunt, by Asbury Harpending, attorneys for the Plaintiff.
Erwin and Erwin, by Austin W. Erwin, Sr., attorneys for the Defendant.
(This case was Number 3 on the June, 1949 General Calendar of Supreme Court for Schuyler County.)

K. E. WOOLSEY,
Stenographer

The trial of the above entitled action was commenced on June 8th, 1949 at ten A.M. and a Jury was selected and sworn at 10:45.
Court recessed from 10:50 to 11:05.

Mr. Harpending and Mr. Erwin opened their respective cases to the jury.

MARY JANE OWEN, being duly sworn, and called as a witness on behalf of the plaintiff, testified as follows:

Direct Examination by Mr. Harpending:

Mr. Harpending: I move at this time if the Court please, to amend the pleadings to change the name of the Plaintiff from Mary Jane Litteer to Mary Jane Owen.
The Court: Granted
Q. Mrs. Owen, what is your age now? A. I am twenty-one.
Mr. Harpending: And then, I don't, I am not sure if the Court please, the proper, but I would like to continue this action by Mrs. Owen as the Plaintiff and not the Guardian ad Litem.
The Court: That's right. We will dispense with the Guardian.
Q. That is, you are twenty-one years, as of the present date? A. Yes, I am.
Q. And when this action was started you were under twenty-one, and it was brought by your father, as your Guardian ad litem, is that right? A. Yes, it was.
Q. Now Mrs. Owen, in the fall and winter of '46, where were you, what were you doing? A. I was a student at Rochester Institute of Technology.
Q. Now you have to speak so we can hear you back here. And how long have you been a student there? A. That was my second year in school.
Q. You had gone to school in the winter of '45 and '46? A. Yes, I did.
Q. And late in the fall of '46? A. Yes.
Q. And were going through your second year? A. That's right.
Q. Is that right? How long a course were you taking? A. A three years' course.
Q. And what was the course? A. Retailing.
Q. Retailing? A. In merchandising.
Q. And that was a three year course given by that school, is that right? A. Yes, it was.
Q. And will you tell the Court and Jury the method of instruction there at the school, that is in the fall and winter of '46? A. (The witness did not answer).
Mr. Harpending: Repeat the question, will you please, Ken? (The question was re-read.) A. We went to school a month, and then worked a month. It was a course--.
Q. And that work would be in some merchandising establishment? A. Yes, it was.
Q. And on December 1st, 1946, what part of the course were you taking? A. I was on my work program and I was working at McCurdy's in Rochester.
Q. That is one of the large department stores? A. Yes, it is.
Q. Now over the Thanksgiving holidays what did you do, where did you go? A. I came to my parents in Weston.
Q. And they live at Weston and that is in the town of Tyrone in the County of Schuyler? A. That's right.

Q. And how did you come when you came there? A. I came by bus.
q. To Bath? A. Yes.
Q. And did your parents meet you? A. Yes, they did.
Q. Do you recall what day you came, what day of the week? A. I came Wednesday night.
Q. You came on Wednesday night. And did you come by a bus of this company? A. Yes, I did.
Q. And what was the weather? What were the weather conditions when you came home for the holiday? A. It was very mild. It was nice.
Q. Did you bring any overshoes with you? A. No, I didn't.
Q. Did you have overshoes? A. Yes, I did.
Q. And then coming down to the first of December, what day of the week was that please? A. The first of December?
Q. Yes. A. That was Sunday night.
Q. Sunday night. And who came home with you for the holidays? A. Well my brother-in-law and sister were there ahead of me, and they rode to Rochester with me.
Q. I see, and that is your sister there? (indicating). A. Yes, it is.
Q. And her name is Jean Perkins? A. That's right.
Q. And she and her husband were there at your parents', is that right? A. That's right.
Q. Now when you started to return how did you go? A. By bus from Bath.
Q. And where did you take the bus? A. From Bath.
Q. And that is the bus of this Defendant? A. Yes it is.
Q. And who took you to Bath? A. My brother-in-law.
Q. Now what were the weather conditions? A. Well it was snowy and cold, very cold.
Q. Now in relation to that brother-in-law, was it Jean's husband? A. No.
Q. That was Thelma's husband? A. That's right.
Q. And did he drive you there in his car? A. Yes, he did.
Q. And was the car heated? A. Yes, it was.
Q. And did you notice any discomfort at all going from your home to the bus terminal?

Mr. Erwin: I object to that as incompetent, improper, irrelevant-

The Court: Yes, I will sustain it.

Mr. Harpending: Exception, particularly in view of counsel's opening, if the Court please.

Q. Had you any discomfort to your feet prior to the time you got on the bus? A. No, I hadn't.
Q. Had you had, were your feet cold at any time that day, Sunday, before you got on the bus? A. No.
Q. Now what did you wear on your feet when you started back? A. I wore wool socks and my saddle shoes.
Q. And were these the only shoes you had with you? A. Well I had heels too, but that's all.
Q. Well now your overshoes you say were in Rochester? A. That's right.
Q. Well then what bus did you. I will withdraw that. Was there more than one bus of the Defendant there when you got there? A. Yes, there was two busses.
Q. And was it, the bus that went first, filled up? A. Yes.
Q. And you got on the second one, didn't you. A. That's right.
Q. Now where did you sit on the bus? A. We sat about half way back on the bus on the right hand side.
Q. And did you sit with either your sister or your brother-in-law or did you sit with some stranger? A. I sat with a stranger.
Q. Well which side of the seat did you sit on? A. I sat on the side of the window, on the inside.
Q. And where did your sister sit? A. She sat directly in front of me.
Q. And her husband sat with her? A. Yes, he did.
Q. Now were there any people in the aisles? A. Yes, there were.
Q. What did you notice about the temperature in the bus when you first go on? A. It was very cold.

Q. And as you proceeded from Bath towards Rochester, did it seem to get any warmer?
A. No, it didn't.
Q. And did there come a time when you noticed that your feet got cold? A. Yes.
Q. Was there some conversation that you had about that? A. Yes, I was talking with my sister--
Mr. Erwin: I object to any conversation with the sister.
The Court: Yes, sustained.
Q. Well, what did you do to protect your feet then? A. We had these mittens. First we put our feet under us and we rubbed them and then I finally took my shoes off and put them in these heavy mittens.
Q. What were the mittens? Describe them to the Jury? A. Well, they were very old-fashioned mittens, they were made out of horsehair I think on the outside. And they were wool-lined and they were very very warm and very large. And we had them on our hands, and my hands being warm, they were warm mittens, so I thought by putting them on my feet, I could keep my feet warm.
Q. Well did you do that? A. Yes, I did.
Q. And did there come a time when you did something else? A. Yes, my sister said her feet was very cold--
Mr. Erwin: I object to that and ask that it be stricken out.
The Court: Yes, that may go out, the Jury will disregard that.
Q. Jean will have to explain that herself. A. Oh.
Q. Well then did you turn the mittens over to her? A. Yes, I did.
Q. And go on Mary Jane, and tell us as you proceeded towards Rochester what you noticed now. A. Well my feet began getting colder and colder. Then they felt, they just didn't feel at all. I mean it just felt like I didn't have any feet.
Q. And then you reached the bus terminal in Rochester and what did you do?
A. Well, we were an hour late in Rochester and I had to hurry right back to the dormitory because we had check-in hours.
Q. What time was the bus due in Rochester that night? A. I think it was quarter of nine.
Q. What time did you get there? A. Around ten o'clock.
Q. And you went to the dormitory then? A. Yes, I did.
Q. You went how? A. By cab.
Q. When you got there what did you notice with reference to your feet? A. Well, I just didn't feel anything in them at all.
Q. Well now tell us this. Did you notice any difference in the feeling in your feet between the time you got off the bus and the time you got to the dormitory while you were riding in the cab? A. No, I guess not. No feeling at all there.
Q. This numbness came on while you were in the bus? A. That's right.
Q. Now after you got to the dormitory tell the Court and the Jury, what did you do? A. Well I checked in and I went to my room and I was, my feet were very numb. And I didn't know what it was and I took my shoes and socks right off, and my roommates were all becoming very alarmed. They were white--
Mr. Erwin: I object to what her roommates did or said.
The Court: Yes.
Q. Just tell how you felt? A. The feet were very white there almost to the ankles. And they were very hard and so I soaked them in the bathtub with ice water.
Q. And did somebody recommend that treatment? A. Yes.
Q. Who was that? A. Our residence nurse.
Q. And she was the nurse who took care of you girls at the dormitory? A. That's right.
Q. And did she come? A. Yes, she did.
Q. And go ahead and tell the Jury then what you did with reference to the bathtub? A. We put ice water in with ice cubes, and then sat there and let it cool gradually, and it was about three hours or a little more before the color had completely returned. And then my feet started swelling and were very very uncomfortable. I couldn't walk

on them. They were just like blisters, and I had to be carried to my bed that night.
Q. Who carried you? A. My roommates.
Q. Now how long did you stay in bed then? A. I was in bed the next day, all the next day.
Q. Then the next day what did you do? A. Well I was working. It was before Christmas. And they needed me at the store and I felt that I should go, so I went and tried to work but I had to return back to the dormitory.
Q. Do you remember how long you stayed at the store that day? A. It was, I left sometime in the morning, I don't know when.
Q. Well then what did you do the next day? A. The next day I tried to go to work again and had the same experience.
Q. Did you have some doctor look at you then, between the time that you got home that night and the time you went to work in the store? A. Yes, I did.
Q. Was that some doctor that was the school physician? A. Yes, he was our school physician.
Q. And did he recommend some method of treatment?

Mr. Erwin: I object to what he recommended. The doctor should be here.
The Court: I will overrule and give you an exception.
Mr. Erwin: Exception.

Q. You may answer? A. Well he said that the only treatment--

Mr. Erwin: If the Court please, I object to that, what the doctor said as incompetent.
The Court: Yes, that's right.

Q. Just say that, whether he recommended some treatment? A. Yes, he did.
Q. Did you follow it? A. Yes.

Mr. Erwin: I object to that, and ask that it be stricken out.
The Court: Overruled, and give you an exception, overruled.

Q. What did you do for your feet? A. Well I tried to be, I had to be very cautious to prevent further damage. He said once they would--
Q. No, you can't say what he said. A. No?
Q. What did you do for your feet? A. I had to wear heavy wool socks and my stadium boots on them even with no snow, just when it was cold.
Q. And go on through the winter and tell the Jury what you notice about your feet as time progressed. A. Well I had to be very, very careful, and then when they did get cold which once in a while I would be caught without my boots, why then they got very hard and white again and then they would bleed. They would crack open and bleed.
Q. Well about how many times did that happen during the winter? A. Only about twice. I was very careful.
Q. Now coming along to the warm months, what did you notice when the weather got warm? A. When the weather got warm my feet started to swell. And they would blister and bleed and crack and were most painful.
Q. And what did you do to prevent that? A. Well I changed my shoes very often. I had to have two or three pairs of shoes with me to change through the day. I couldn't wear rubber soles on my feet. And I had to be, I couldn't wear nylon stockings and of course I soaked them in water myself to bring the swelling down. I tried--
Q. Now tell us about the progress of that condition down to the present time, Mary Jane? On hot days what do you notice now and what have you noticed over the months? A. Well they still blister on hot days and burn and hurt.
Q. Now did there come a time when you consulted a nerve surgeon, a neural surgeon to see if anything could be done by surgery to help you? A. Yes I did.
Q. And who was that you consulted? A. Doctor Gibe of Rochester.
Q. G-i-b-e. Fred Gibe. And were you advised surgery could not help you?

Mr. Erwin: Now I object to that--
The Court: I assume the doctor will be here. I will sustain it.

Q. Anyways you have gone along and used the same treatment? A. Yes.
Q. That you originally used, and you have done that after consulting this surgeon, is that right? A. Yes, treatment was the only way I could cure them.

Q. And has the condition, this condition of cold and hot weather affecting your feet, continued down to the present time? A. Yes, it has.

Q. And do you have to yet, to protect your feet from the cold?

Mr. Erwin: I object to that as leading.

Q. Well what do you do now to protect your feet from the cold? A. We, I still have to be very, very careful, and I always wear my boots and wool socks in the winter time.

Q. Now had you ever been told, or did you know in any way prior to the first of December, 1946 that your system of circulation was such that you were more susceptible to freezing of the extremities?

Mr. Erwin: I object to that, your Honor, unless it is connected--

The Court: Well there is no foundation.

Mr. Harpending: I will prove it right after lunch by medical.

The Court: All right, I will leave it on the statement of counsel, if you connect it up.

Mr. Harpending: Will you catch me up please, Ken.

The last question was read by the stenographer as follows: Now had you ever been told, or did you know in any way prior to the first of December, 1946, that your system of circulation was such that you were more susceptible to freezing of the extremities?

Q. Than for instance, your sister Jean would be or one of your other sisters. A. No, I didn't know anything about that.

Q. Had you ever had frost bitten feet or frozen feet before December first, 1946? A. No. I hadn't.

Q. And had you ever ridden in a vehicle that was as cold as this bus was that night going into Rochester? No, I hadn't.

Q. And you did know did you not Mary Jane, or you had been told by your parents that you had a heart condition that existed since you were a baby? A. Yes.

Mr. Erwin: The same objection unless it is connected up.

The Court: Yes.

Mr. Harpending: Well--

The Court: I think I will sustain.

Mr. Harpending: All right.

Q. Mary Jane, from where you sat in the bus as you went towards Rochester, were you able to see the driver? A. No, I wasn't.

Q. Now after this, after you got your feet in this condition that you have described, what did you notice about how they were affected when you stood on the, on the floor of the store in the mercantile establishment. A. Well, they were very tender and I had to be on my feet all day working, and I just couldn't take it.

Q. And after that did you change your course that you were taking? A. I finished up my year and then I didn't go back, because I couldn't.

Q. And what did you do, did you, what did you notice, with reference to your feet when you would stand on them all day working on the floors of the store of that establishment? A. They would swell and they would be painful and of course if they cracked, the next day, it would be just that much worse.

Q. Now what then did you take up, what line of work? A. I went into office work.

Q. And did you take some studies, some course in that? A. No, I didn't.

Q. I see, but you are doing office work yet? A. Yes, I am.

Q. And have done since that time? A. Yes.

Q. And you did not finish your mercantile course? A. No, I didn't.

Q. What were your marks up to that time? What did they average?

Mr. Erwin: I object to that as incompetent, irrelevant and immaterial.

The Court: Well is there a claim here on that?

Mr. Erwin: No, there isn't.

The Court: I think I will sustain.

Mr. Harpending: Exception, please. That is all.

CROSS EXAMINATION by Mr. Erwin:

Q. Mary Jane, you say you wore wool socks when you left home on the first of December? A. Yes, I did.
Q. Good heavy wool socks? A. I think so, sir.
Q. You realized it was getting colder than when you left for Rochester? A. Yes.
Q. When you left Rochester prior to Thanksgiving Day it was mild? A. That's right.
Q. When did the cold weather start if you recall, Mary Jane? A. It was probably Sunday morning or Saturday night. I am not sure, sir.
Q. And December first is on Sunday? A. That's right.
Q. Do you know how cold it was that day? A. No, I don't.
Q. Do you know how cold it was that evening? A. I don't remember, sir.
Q. You didn't tlook at a thermometer anywhere? A. No.
Q. And when you went to your home in Dundee you wore your saddle shoes and what kind of stockings? A. I think when I went home I went from work and I wore nylons.
Q. Nylons? And were those wool socks or stockings that you wore? A. Socks.
Q. They were bobby socks? A. Yes, but I had wool slacks on.
Q. You had wool slacks on but you wore bobby socks. A. Yes, high ones.
Q. Pardon me? A. High ones.
Q. High bobby socks and they were good heavy socks? A. Uh-huh.
Q. So your foot fitted your shoe quite tightly. A. Well saddle shoes are plenty loose.
Q. Well they didn't wobble all over your feet though, did they, when you wore nylons on your way home? A. I think I wore heels down, probably, because I was at work.
Q. Well now did you or didn't you, Mary Jane? I don't care which way. I just want it one way or the other? A. I think I was dressed up when I came home.
Q. And did you take your saddle shoes with you? A. Yes.
Q. Did you wear them around home? A. Yes.
Q. Well when you were around the house you didn't wear wool socks on your feet did you? A. I don't recall.
Q. You don't always wear wool socks with them, do you? A. Not always.
Q. No? A. I usually wear heavy cottons.
Q. Heavy cotton, these wool socks you mentioned were heavier than the cotton you usually wear around, weren't they? A. I don't think so, sir.
Q. You can't remember that? A. That I remember that I was wearing socks.
Q. And the shoes were tight, weren't they? A. I don't think so, sir.
Q. Would you say they weren't with those heavy socks on your feet, or would you rather not say? A. I don't think they were tight.
Q. Well they fit snugly, didn't they? A. They were comfortable.
Q. What do you mean by comfortable? A. They were comfortable.
Q. Well you could get them on, couldn't you? A. Oh, easily.
Q. And it was wool socks that you had on? A. That's right.
Q. You usually wore cotton stockings? A. Yes.
Q. And they were snugger than the cotton stockings, weren't they? A. Just slightly.

Mr. Erwin: That's all.

Mr. Harpending: That's all.

JEANNE PERKINS, being duly sworn, and called as a witness on behalf of the plaintiff, testified as follows: (omitted)

RACHEL LONG, being duly sworn, and called as a witness on behalf of the plaintiff, testified as follows: (omitted)

CARTER PERKINS, being duly worn, and called as a witness on behalf of the plaintiff, testified as follows: (omitted)

The Court: All right, we will recess now until 1:30. Members of the Jury, don't talk about the case, that is, don't discuss it among yourselves or allow anyone to talk to you about it. Keep your minds open and we will recess until 1:30.

The Court recessed from 12 P.M. until 1:30.

WILLIAM C. STEWART, being duly sworn and called as a witness on behalf of the plaintiff, testified as follows:

DIRECT EXAMINATION by Mr. Harpending:

Q. Doctor Stewart, you are a practicing physician and surgeon? A. I am.
Q. And you practice your profession in Watkins Glen? A. I do.
Q. Have your ffice here. And Doctor, you are a graduate of what medical school? A. University of Buffalo.
Q. And when, please. A. 1924.
Q. And then Doctor, did you have subsequent hospital training? A. Yes, both in Syracuse and back in Buffalo.
Q. And an internship with those, and house physician? A. Yes.
Q. And then, when did you come here to practice in Schuyler County, Doctor? A. 1926.
Q. And have practiced here since? A. Yes.
Q. And you practice as a physician and surgeon doing general work, do you? A. Yes.
Q. And Doctor did you examine Mary Jane Litteer Owen, the plaintiff in this case? A. Yes.
Q. And when and where did you examine her, please? At my office yesterday morning.
Q. And will you go on and tell the Court and Jury the extent of your examination and what you found? A. Why, the examination showed a skin condition of both feet, about what you would expect to find after a history of severe freezing three years before. That is, the skin was red, swollen, hot to the touch, covered with little bits of fluid, and I think a history of tenderness, itching and burning.
Q. What was the temperature of your office, Doctor? A. About seventy degrees.
Q. And does temperature have an effect on that kind of a condition that you found on Mrs. Owen's skin at the examination? A. Yes it does, either cold or heat has an effect on it.
Q. And what effect does cold and heat have on that kind of condition? A. Cold blanches it out, makes it white and numb. And will sometimes, will even crack the skin.
Q. What does heat do? A. Heat produces the condition which I just described.
Q. And the more intense the heat, does that make it more severe, Doctor? A. I think so, yes.
Q. And could you tell from your examination what parts of the skin and the flesh were, had been and were affected? A. Yes, it was quite evident. It, the condition was similar apparently on both feet and the whole outer third of the foot towards the toes were affected with all of the top, and both the top and bottom of the foot, and then there was a rim along the outside of the foot back towards the heel, and then the greater part of the heel was affected again, including the bottom part of the heel.
Q. Doctor, assuming that on December 1st, 1946, Mrs. Owen had not had her feet frozen or frost bitten, and had not suffered from them, and that on that day she boarded a bus traveling between Bath and Rochester; that it was a cold day; that her feet became very cold; that she was wearing woolen bobby socks and saddle shoes, that she took off the shoes and rubbed the feet and tried sitting on them to protect them; and at times placed them in fur mittens that she was wearing on her hands but they continued to be cold and before she reached Rochester became numb from sensation; that she took a taxi from the bus station to her residence in Rochester and upon arriving there removed her shoes and

socks and found her feet to be white and somewhat frozen up nearly to the ankle; that with help she put water with ice cubes in it in the bathtub and sat for some three hours with her feet in that water, letting the water gradually cool, and at the end of the period, some three hours, the color came back to her feet and that thereafter her feet were swollen and sore and that she went to bed for a day; and that then during the period subsequent to that, during periods of cold weather her feet would become white and cracked and hard; and when hot weather came the next summer her feet would swell, become red, and sometimes bleed, have you an opinion formed with reasonable medical certainty, as to what condition she was suffering from, on the night of December 1st when she arrived at her residence in Rochester? A. That question is pretty involved but I would say, I think she has a severe freezing.

Q. Freezing? A. Yes, frostbite, either freezing or frostbite.

Q. And Doctor, assuming the facts assumed in that same question, and the facts that you have related here of having found in your examination yesterday, have you an opinion formed with reasonable certainty as to whether or not the condition of her feet which you have described here is permanent, and if not permanent can you say with a reasonable degree of medical certainty, the period of time over which you think, you feel it would exist? A. Well assuming that she had a severe frostbite which I am quite positive she did, the average person following that, or that will be the condition of the skin usually from ten to fifteen years. It is variable in different people and with different conditions and of course in different climates, but not here, and the main danger is the ease of which the feet will freeze again. But if she could go from twelve to fifteen years we will say, and not freeze her feet again there is a possibility she might be back to normal.

Q. Back to normal? A. Yes.

Q. Now Doctor, did you examine the plaintiff sufficiently to determine her circulatory system as to whether or not it was normal? A. Yes, I did.

Q. And did you examine her heart, Doctor? A. Yes, I did.

Q. Will you tell the Court and Jury what you found on that examination? A. Well, she was born with a heart condition which has a tendency to give them poor circulation. And she has at the examination yesterday, she had poor circulation. She had a low blood pressure.

Q. And does that, whether or not Doctor, that condition brings about more sensitivity to frostbite and freezing than someone with a good strong circulation? A. That is true.

CROSS EXAMINATION by Mr. Erwin

Q. Doctor, you say she has poor circulation and has had it according to your knowledge and and information, for a great many years? A. I never examined her before yesterday to my recollection, and she had poor circulation yesterday. And I am basing my answer on the history which she gave and the heart findings, and I believe she has had poor circulation.

Q. Did she tell you she was born with that condition? A. Yes.

Q. Did she tell you how long she had known it? A. She didn't, her mother did.

Q. And did they tell you how long they had known that she had that heart condition? A. Yes.

Q. How long? A. If I recollect right, it was discovered in the clinic when she was two years of age.

Q. She had a chronic valvular heart lesion with moderate enlargement of the heart, did you find that? A. No, she doesn't have it at present.

Q. She doesn't have it at present? A. She does have, you might say she has moderate, will you ask that question again, that part beginning--

Q. Did she have a chronic valvular heart lesion with moderate enlargement of the heart? A. She did on examination yesterday.

Q. And according to the information you got from the plaintiff and her mother, she has known that since she was about two years of age?

Mr. Harpending: I object to that, what the mother knew.

Mr. Erwin: He said the mother was present at the examination.

The Court: I will overrule.

Q. You said they had known that since she was about two years of age? A. According to the history given to me, yes.

Q. Doctor, a person having a poor circulation system, should wear heavier footwear and more protection on their feet in winter time, shouldn't they, than the ordinary person? A. I would think so, yes.

Q. Would it be advisable to wear overshoes in winter weather? A. Well I wouldn't say what, but in colder weather they should make proper provision, yes.

Q. To protect themselves against that? A. Yes.

Q. And it doesn't take as severe cold weather to bring that to a person with a poor circulation system as it does with a person who has a good system? A. No, the poorer the circulation, the more tendency there is to freezing.

Q. And that tendency towards freezing will come in much milder weather than it ordinarily will with a person with a good system? A. Yes, I think the frostbite would take place more readily.

Q. Around what temperature do you think frostbite would take effect in a person of that poor circulation? A. Well that would vary according to the circulation and any other condition. But we feel the average normal person is susceptible to frostbite at the point of ten degrees above zero.

Q. Ten degrees above zero? A. Yes.

Q. And from ten degrees above zero up they are not susceptible to it? A. Not the average normal person, no.

Q. Now what about a person with a poor circulatory system. When will they first be susceptible to freezing from the temperature? A. Well they will, anybody is freezing when the temperature of the skin becomes thirty-two degrees which is the freezing point.

Q. I am talking about a severe frostbitten foot or feet in a person with a poor circulatory system. When does that begin to take effect, about what degree? A. Well, if with the normal person it is possible to take effect at ten degrees above zero--

Q. Yes. A. --it would vary anywheres to 32 degrees above zero, according to your circulation.

Q. Well take this patient that you examined yesterday. According to her circulation when would it take effect on her? A. I couldn't say. It would be only a guess. I haven't any idea, but, except that I think she would freeze faster than the normal person with a normal circulation.

Q. And she would freeze much faster without artic shoes or overshoes on? A. Oh yes, with with less protection, the faster you will get frostbite.

Q. And she would freeze her feet, she would freeze her feet faster if her shoes were tight, wouldn't she? A. Yes, because that interferes with the circulation.

Q. Tight shoes interfere with the circulation, is that right? A. Yes.

Q. So if a person wore real heavy socks and shoes a little snug or tight, in her condition, that interferes with her circulation more than otherwise, doesn't it? A. I would think so if the tightness went to a certain degree.

Q. You don't know when she was frostbitten, do you, yourself? A. No.

Q. You have no idea whether it was on the bus of the defendant or somewhere else of your own knowledge? A. Well--

Q. Of your own knowledge? A. I think I am able to form some--

Q. Of your own knowledge, Doctor, of your own knowledge, Doctor, do you know when she was frostbitten? A. Well--

Q. Of your own knowledge?

Mr. Harpending: Well I object to that, he asked it, and let the witness answer.

Q. Of his own knowledge. I am not asking for an opinion now. A. I don't know how to answer that.

The Court: Well he means Doctor, were you there or do you know of your own knowledge. A. No, I am depending entirely on history.

Q. And you don't know how long ago she may have been frostbitten from your examination yesterday? A. No.

RE-DIRECT EXAMINATION by Mr. Harpending:

Q. Doctor, counsel has asked you about tight shoes. If you remove the shoes and rub the feet, that helps the circulation, doesn't it? A. Yes, indeed.

Q. And Doctor, counsel has asked you about a person with poor circulation being more susceptible to freezing, and more careful. If their feet are frozen once, do they have to be more careful? A. Yes, exceptionally careful.

Q. And careful for years? A. Yes, for years.

Q. And do you know whether all the tissues in the outer portion of the foot were involved in this process? A. Pardon me?

Q. Were all the tissues in the outer portion of the foot, involved in this freezing process? A. I didn't understand the question then.

Q. You mentioned to me about the capillaries being involved. Now were there nerve ends involved in this freezing process? A. Yes, of course when the tissue freezes, all the structure is involved, but the structure upon which the lasting effect is left from frostbite is particularly the blood capillaries and the fine nerve endings that go to them.

Q. And the blood capillaries are the fine little blood vessels that go to the surface, is that it? A. Yes.

Mr. Harpending: I think that is all.

RE-CROSS EXAMINATION by Mr. Erwin:

Q. Well another question, Doctor, if the girl's feet had been frozen sometime before this bus ride, they would have frozen easier the second time on the bus ride, wouldn't they, if they froze then? A. Yes.

Mr. Erwin: That's all.

Mr. Harpending: That's all.

RUTH LITTEER, being duly sworn, and called as a witness on behalf of the plaintiff, testified as follows: (omitted)

MOTION FOR DISMISSAL OF COMPLAINT AND NON-SUIT

The Court: Yes, do you want--

Mr. Erwin: I don't care which, if you want--

The Court: Do you want the Jury excused?

Mr. Erwin: Yes.

The Court: Members of the Jury. You may be excused. I guess we haven't any place to put you except out in the hall or downstairs. You may stand aside.

(The Jury was excused during the making of the motions).

Mr. Erwin: If your Honor please, I move for a dismissal of the complaint and a non-suit upon the ground that the plaintiffs have failed to prove the cause of action alleged in the complaint or any cause of action.

(There was argument by the attorneys on the motion.)

The Court: I deny the motion and give you an exception.

Mr. Erwin: Exception, all right.
(The Jury returned to the Courtroom).

ARTHUR J. FAULKNER, being duly sworn and called as a witness on behalf of the defendant, testified as follows:

DIRECT EXAMINATION by Mr. Erwin:

Q. Mr. Faulkner, where do you live, please? A. 95 Crittendon Boulevard, Rochester, New York.
Q. How long have you lived in Rochester? A. About twenty years.
Q. On December 1st, 1946, were you employed by the Rochester-Penfield Bus Company? A. I was.
Q. In what capacity? A. As a driver.
Q. Full time or extra driver? A. Full time.
Q. On December 1st, 1946 did you drive the second section of the Rochester-Penfield Bus Company from Bath to Rochester? A. Yes.
Q. What bus was that? A. Number 6, number 106.
Q. Number 106. What time was that scheduled, do you know, to leave Bath? A. I believe it was 6:10.
Q. Do you make a trip sheet when you get into Rochester? A. Yes.
Q. And did you make a trip sheet on that day? A. I did.
Defendant's Exhibit A marked for identification.
Q. I show you Exhibit A for identification, and ask you if that is the trip sheet for December 1st, 1946? A. Yes.
Q. Now do you recall what time you arrived in Rochester without referring to the trip sheet? A. We were late. I imagine it was around ten o'clock.
Q. Around ten o'clock. And do you recall how many passengers you carried? A. Well, there was quite a few.
Q. Do you know how many? A. Approximately forty.
Mr. Harpending: What did he say?
Mr. Erwin: Approximately forty.
Q. During your trip in on that bus did any one holler from anywhere in the bus to turn on the heat and did you reply in words or substance, the heating system is out of order? A. No.
Q. Was the heating system out of order? A. No.
Q. When there is any trouble with the bus, what report do you make and when? A. Well if the trouble is on the road, we always called in to the garage, and if it was important trouble we always had another bus sent out to us. We would stop the bus on the road and wait.
Q. And when you got in, if there was any minor trouble, what kind of a report did you make? A. We made out a red card and left it on the bus for the shop mechanic to see.
Q. A red card. I show you Exhibit B for identification---Defendant's Exhibit B, marked for identification.
Q. —I show you Exhibit B for identification, and ask you if that is the kind of card you used in connection with any trouble? A. Yes.
Q And if it is trouble that doesn't stop you from going in, you make out this card when you get there and hand it in? A. That's right.
Q. If it is trouble that does prevent your going in, you say you stop? A. We stop the bus and call in.
Q. If your heating system went bad would you continue to drive or what would you do?
Mr. Harpending: I object to that, if the Court please.

Mr. Erwin: All right, I will withdraw it.
Q. But on this occasion, no one complained to you that the heating was bad?
Mr. Harpending: I object to that as leading and repetitious.
The Court: Well, overruled.
Mr. Harpending: Exception.
Q. You say no one did? A. No.
Mr. Erwin: Your witness.

CROSS EXAMINATION by Mr. Harpending:

Q. Are you driving for them yet Mr. Faulkner? A. No, sir, I am not.
Q. How long did you drive for them after December 1st? A. I was through in, I left them in March of '47.
Q. And were you a regular driver up until that time? A. That's right.
Q. How many times a week would you make that trip? A. About three times a week.
Q. And did you drive for them continually then through the winter of '46 and '47? A. Yes.
Q. And drove that trip three times a week. A. Approximately three times a week, yes.
Q. And how long had you driven for the defendant before that night? A. I started in the spring of '45.
Q. So you had driven during the summer andfall and winter, the early winter of '45? A. Yes.
Q. During practically the entire year of '46? A. That's right.
Q. Before this happened? A. Yes, sir.
Q. And you continued to drive until March of '47? A. That's right.
Q. And over that entire period did you drive this trip about three times a week? A. No, sir.
Q. How many times a week did you drive it, say, during '46 before this evening in question? A. I would say about three to four months.
Q. Three to four months prior to that. How many times did you drive it a week? A. Well, prior you mean to Bath and from Bath?
Q. Up and from Bath. A. Well I went on there as an extra from Bath, after the Bath run started, but before that I was a regular driver out of Dansville, that is from Rochester to Dansville.
Q. The Bath run opened during your service with the company, is that right? A. Yes.
Q. Well now do you have an independent recollection of this evening in question? A. Not definitely, no, sir.
Q. You have to rely on Exhibit A, did you not, to refresh your recollection of that evening? A. Somewhat, yes.
Mr. Harpending: May I see Exhibit A please, Mr. Erwin?
Q. Is this Exhibit A something that you made out- A. It is.
Q. Mr. Faulkner, as the driver? A. That is my initials down in the bottom.
Q. Now, what are the little yellow stubs attached to Exhibit A? A. We always made those out in the machine they had on the bus with that stamp, and when that's fastened that gives us the total number of passengers.
Q. Is it something that is stamped? A. That's right.
Q. When the passenger pays? A. Yes.
Q. Well each stub doesn't indicate one passenger, does it? A. Yes, well not on that particular, no, we have the-
Q. This particular night you had forty passengers you say? A. Yes.
Q. This particular night? A. Yes.
Q. And you only have some six or seven stubs attached here, don't you. What happened? A. Some of those I believe are cash fares.
Q. Oh, who paid you in cash? A. Yes, we stamp the cash fares off.
Q. Well how many times during 1946 do you think you made out the red tag, Exhibit B, and left it in one of the busses? A. I wouldn't know, sir.
Q. Several times? A. Well I really couldn't say, I don't remember how many. I have made

them out, sir.
Q. You have made them out and left them in the bus? A. Yes.
Q. Now in the event your heater had been, had not been working sufficiently to heat the bus that night, where would you have indicated it on Exhibit A? A. Nowhere on Exhibit A.
Q. Nowheres at all? A. Not on the trip sheet. That is what the red cards are for.
Q. Well do you have an independent recollection of this trip now? A. Somewhat, yes.
Q. And, but you say you did have to refer to Exhibit A to refresh your recollection? A. Yes.
Q. Is that so? Now there is nothing on Exhibit A that says whether or not this heater was working, is there? A. No.
Q. Do you recall what kind of an evening December 1st was, 1946? A. It was snowy and the road was slippery. I know that.
Q. Where did you get that information from? A. The reason being--
Q. Where did you get that information from? A. We came in late, well because we came in late.
Q. Because you were late? A. On the trip, So--
Q. So because you were late you have concluded that it was an evening when the road was slippery and traveling hard, is that right? A. That's right.
Q. Now when you made out one of those red cards and left it with the bus, who picked that up? A. The night man.
Q. And you never had anything to do with it after that? A. That's right.
Q. It went into somebody else's hands? A. Yes.
Q. So you would have to rely on your independent recollection as to whether or not you ever put on a red card on a bus on a certain night, would you not? A. Yes.
Q. Either that or hearsay from somebody else? A. Yes.
Q. And you do know there were times when you did put on a red card on the bus? A. Absolutely.
Q. When something faulty occurred? A. Yes, sir.
Q. But what those nights were, you can't give the Jury the dates? A. No, I can't.
Q. And you have to rely on the fact that somebody who works for the bus company tells you that they didn't get a red card on a certain night? A. Well, it definitely would be in the red card.
Q. No, I mean you have to rely on what somebody else tells you? A. Oh, yes.
Q. You didn't keep a record of that? A. That's right.
Q. You drive a bus? A. That's right.
Q. And when you do have some kind of trouble you attach the red card to the bus when you leave it? A. Yes.
Q. And then it goes into somebody else's hands, is that right? A. Yes.
Q. Now are you testifying to anything else here this afternoon upon which you rely upon the records of the company, either Exhibit A, or any other record? A. I don't understand you, sir.

Mr. Harpending: Well read it to him Ken, and see if he gets it. Read it slowly to him.
(Stenographer re-read the question.)

Q. Do you understand it now Mr. Faulkner? A. I would say, no.
Q. You don't have an independent recollection of all that trip then, do you? A. No, I do not.
Q. In fact, if you didn't look at some record of the company, would you be able to tell this Jury that you drove the second bus that night? A. Not after this long period of time, no, I wouldn't.
Q. It's been two years and a half since then? A. Yes.
Q. And you have driven a great many trips since that time? A. Not too many with the bus company. I am in an entirely different line of work now.
Q. But you drove until March? A. That's right.
Q. And you drove a great many of trips before this? A. That's right.
Q. So until you went over some records of the company you couldn't have come in and told this Court and Jury that you drove Number One or Number Two bus that night, could

you? A. No, because I didn't---

Q. And you couldn't even have told them whether you drove a bus that night, could you, without checking the records? A. Well my, yes, because my recollection---

Q. Well what would you refer to to refresh your recollection two and a half years later that you drove a bus on the night of December 1st, 1946? A. Because that is what I was doing.

Q. Did you drive every night? A. All but my day off.

Q. Well I thought you told us you drove three times a week? A. To Bath, Yes.

Q. From Bath? A. To, from---?

Q. That's right, we are talking about this trip from Bath to Rochester? A. Well, my day off was generally Tuesday and I worked over the week ends, so it would have to be.

Q. But then you said you only drove from Bath, into Bath three times a week, didn't you? A. Either way.

Q. One way or the other? A. That's right.

Q. Then to find out whether or not you drove to Bath or from Bath to Rochester on December 1st, 1946, you would have to refer to some record, wouldn't you? A. At this time, yes.

Q. Was that, there is no question about that, is there? A. No.

Q. Do you know whether you drove to Bath or from Bath to Rochester on November 2nd, 1946 or not? A. No.

Q. You can't tell us that now without referring to a record, can you? A. No, not at the present time.

Q. And you don't know exactly what nights you turned in red cards, do you? A. Not presently, no.

Q. Without referring to some record of the company? A. No.

Q. And so in giving substantially all of your testimony here this afternoon you have to refer to the records of the company, have you not? A. Not actually the records. The only ones I have seen is the trip tickets, the trip sheet--

Q. And the Exhibit B, the red card? A. That's right.

Mr. Harpending: That's all.

RE-DIRECT EXAMINATION by Mr. Erwin:

Q. Did you leave the company of your own accord, Mr. Faulkner? A. Pardon me?

Q. Did you leave the employ of the company of your own accord? A. I did.

Q. Went to what you thought was a better job? A. That's right.

Q. Now if the heating system had gone wrong that night, would you have stopped and sent word or what? A. Definitely stopped.

Mr. Harpending: Just a minute. I object to that as the operation of this man's mind.

The Court: Overruled.

Mr. Harpending: Exception.

Q. What would you have done? A. I would have stopped and called.

Q. Called into Rochester? A. Yes, because that would have been better for the passengers. Anything affecting the passengers, they was very strict on that.

Mr. Harpending: Well then did you ever stop and call into Rochester when your heating system went wrong? A. That I can't say. I might have.

Mr. Harpending: You might have? A. I might have. I don't know.

Mr. Harpending: Now do you recall all the reasons why you were late that night? A. Well the only one that I recall, that it was slippery out.

Mr. Harpending: Well to refresh your recollection-- A. --and snowy

Mr. Harpending: Could you have come on to the scene of an accident that held you up that night? A. I don't remember that.

Mr. Harpending: You don't remember. So if you had come on the scene of an accident that night, you don't have any recollection of it now? A. Not at present, no.

Mr. Harpending: That is all.

Mr. Erwin: That is all

RAE BOARD, being duly sworn, and called as a witness on behalf of the defendant, testified as follows:

DIRECT EXAMINATION by Mr. Erwin:

Q. Mr. Board, where do you live? A. Rochester.
Q. How long have you lived in Rochester? A. About twenty-eight years.
Q. You are employed by whom? A. The Valley Bus Lines.
Q. The Valley Bus Lines is the operating name for the Rochester-Penfield Bus Company? A. That's right.
Q. So when you refer to the Rochester-Penfield Bus Company or the Valley Bus Lines, they are one and the same company? A. That's right.
Q. How long have you been employed by the Valley Bus Lines? A. I am on my seventh year.
Q. In what capacity are you employed? A. Garage foreman.
Q. Are you familiar with a bus, 106, that came into Rochester on the 1st day of December, 1946? A. I am.
Q. What kind of a heating system was there on the bus 106 on December 1st, 1946? A. It is a hot water system, forcing air through it.
Q. What? A little louder? A. It is a hot water system, with forced heat radiated with electric fans inside the bus.
Q. How many heaters are there? A. Three.
Q. You say a hot water system. Where does the hot water come from? A. It comes from your motor. The power heats the water and drives it through the bus, through the radiators.
Q. Well to your knowledge, was that heating system in the bus on December 1st, 1946, heating the bus within the rules of the public service commission? A. It was.
Mr. Harpending: I object to that as calling for a conclusion.
The Court: Sustained.
Mr. Erwin: If he knows of his own knowledge?
The Court: Sustained.
Q. Was the heating system in good condition?
Mr. Harpending: I object to that.
The Court: Overruled.
Mr. Harpending: Exception
A. It was.
Q. Was the bus periodically inspected by the public service commission? A. It was.
Q. And a certificate given for its operation?
Mr. Harpending: Just a minute, I object to that as not the best evidence, incompetent.
The Court: I will overrule.
Mr. Harpending: Exception.
Q. If the heating system goes bad can you tell me whether or not the bus will operate?
Mr. Harpending: I object to that as calling for a conclusion.
The Court: Overruled.
Mr. Erwin: He is a mechanic and an expert.
The Court: Overruled.
A. If anything happens to the water, the bus cannot move.
Q. Why? A. Because the water is forced from the motor through the heater in series. The heaters are hooked in series. It comes from the heaters through the radiators back to the motor.

Q. So if a motor is running the heating system is operating also? A. The water is passing through the heating system.
Q. And it must proceed through the heating system to go back into the motor? A. That's right.
Q. What inspection was made of your busses generally? A. The bus is inspected each one thousand or twelve hundred and fifty miles.
Defendant's Exhibit C marked for identification.
Q. I show you Defendant's Exhibit C for identification, and ask you what that is. A. It is a twelve hundred and fifty mile inspection tag.
Q. And to what particular bus does it refer? A. 106.
Q. What is the date of the inspection of 106? A. 11-28-46.
Q. That would be the 28th of November, 1946? A. That's right.
(Balance of testimony of R. Board omitted)

JOHN M. WILLIAMS, being duly sowrn, and called as a witness on behalf of the defendant, testified as follows: (omitted)

JEANNE PERKINS, being re-called as a witness on behalf of the plaintiff, testified as follows: (omitted)

MARY JANE OWEN, re-called by the plaintiff, testified as follows:

DIRECT EXAMINATION by Mr. Harpending:

Q. Do you recall the bus stopping that night, Mary Jane, some time in the road? A. Yes, I do.
Q. And do you recall the bus driver getting out? A. Yes, I do.
Q. And do you recall whether or not the door was open for a while? A. It was.
Q. And do you recall where it was? A. No, I don't.
Q. You don't know the localities there? A. I never pay any attention.
Q. Do you know how long it was open? A. I don't know that, sir. It was cold and it seemed like a long time.
Mr. Harpending: That is all.

CROSS EXAMINATION by Mr. Erwin:

Q. You say you remember the bus door was open? A. Yes, it was.
Q. Do you remember making a statement on January 31st, 1947 in which you said--
Mr. Harpending: Now just a minute, I object to that, if the Court please.
Mr. Erwin: Cross examination.
Mr. Harpending: Unless the witness is shown the statement.
Mr. Erwin: Let me see what she says about it first.
The Court: You are asking her if she remembers making an oral statement?
Mr. Erwin: A written statement.
The Court: Then I will sustain.
Q. Did you tell anyone that the bus stopped for an accident betwen Bath and Dansville, I think the bus door was kept closed, and the motor was running? Didn't you make that statement to anyone? A. Well I talked to someone.
Q. Yes, and did you make that statement, you think the bus door was kept closed and the

and the motor was running? A. I don't know. He cross-examined me.
Q. Will you say you didn't make that statement? A. No, but I won't say I did either.
Q. You won't say you didn't or did? You might have made it then? A. I could have, I doubt it.
Q. And if you made it on January 31st, 1947, it was true, wasn't it? A. I doubt, I mean I doubt if I made that.
Q. You said you might have made it? A. I don't remember.
Q. Will you say you didn't make it? A. No, I didn't say I did.
Q. Well was your recollection better then than it is today? A. Yes, but I didn't write that.
Q. I know you didn't write it, but you signed the original of it? A. Well he rushed me off.
Q. No, no, you signed the statement, didn't you on January, or about that time, January 31st, 1947. A. I signed something.
Q. And in that statement if you said that you didn't think that the door was left open and the motor kept running, it was true, wasn't it?

Mr. Harpending: I object to that this time.

The Court: Sustained, yes.

Mr. Erwin: I will produce the original statement. I haven't it here.

Q. But you might have said it? A. Well, I don't know.

Mr. Erwin: I assume then that I can get the original by tomorrow morning. I would like to offer that.

Mr. Harpending: She will be here.

RE-DIRECT EXAMINATION by Mr. Harpending:

Q. Then somebody was acting for this bus company, representing them, taking a statement for them last December, were they?

Mr. Erwin: No, January.

The Court: January

A. Uh-huh.

Q. Did some man come to you and question you about this? A. Before that they did.
Q. Before that? A. Uh-huh.
Q. How many times did they come to you and ask you questions about this trip? A. Well, there was this one gentleman before, and then he sent me down, I think to see a Mr. Stoll, I think that was the gentleman's name they wanted me to see, I am not sure.
Q. Well now this first man, when did first somebody come to you and ask you questions about your freezing your feet on this bus? A. Approximately two weeks after I wrote the company, I am not sure.
Q. And where did this man talk with you. A. At the dormitory.
Q. And then did he ask you to go to the office? A. Yes, he did.
Q. Did you go to the office? A. Yes, I did.
Q. And did some man there write something down and then-- A. Well he asked a whole bunch of questions and wrote on them and when he finished why he said, sign this.
Q. Now did you have either of your parents there with you? A. No, I didn't.
Q. Was anybody there representing you at all? A. No, there weren't.
Q. And this was in the office of the company? A. That's right.
Q. They asked you to come in there? A. That's right.
Q. And this man wrote things down as you talked with him? A. That's right, yes.
Q. And then handed you the paper and asked you to sign it? A. Uh-huh.

Mr. Harpending: That's all.

RE-CROSS EXAMINATION by Mr. Erwin:

Q. You told the truth didn't you, Mary Jane? A. Well I expect I did.
Q. Sure, you did, you intended to tell the truth didn't you? A. I did.

Q. And then did the man ask you to read it over?

Mr. Harpending: Just a minute, I object to that, it is leading.

Mr. Erwin: Let me ask her if this happened.

The Court: All right.

Q. And did they ask you to read it over and did it say at the bottom, I have read this statement over and it is true?

Mr. Harpending: I still object.

The Court: Yes, sustained.

Mr. Erwin: I will ask her this question, I thought I did but perhaps I didn't.

The Court: All right.

Q. Did they ask you to read it over, and did you read that part, I have read this over and it is true? A. I don't remember. I remember saying it and I signed it.

Q. You were nineteen years old then, weren't you? A. Yes.

Q. Or were you twenty? A. Yes.

Q. Your eye sight was perfectly good? A. My eyesight was good.

Q. And you could read, couldn't you? A. Yes.

Mr. Erwin: That's all.

Mr. Harpending: You say he asked you sign something and you signed it? A. I signed it.

The CROSS EXAMINATION by Mr. Erwin continued as follows:

Q. Did you sign it without knowing what it was, Mary Jane? A. I was in an awful--

Q. No, just a minute, just a minute. Did you sign it without knowing what was in it? A. He kept me a long--

Q. Did you sign that without knowing what was in it? A. Oh no, I just scanned it. I am not sure what was in there.

Q. Well I suppose you told him the truth anyways? A. Uh-huh.

Mr. Erwin: That's all.

Mr. Harpending: That's all.

The Court: Is that all for this afternoon?

Mr. Erwin: Just a moment.

The Court: All right, members of the Jury we are quitting. We are going to recess now until tomorrow morning for some medical evidence. Don't discuss the case, don't allow anyone to talk to you about it. Don't come to any conclusion about it until it is finally submitted to you. You are excused until, well I assume you would rather have it at ten o'clock. You wouldn't want to put it at 9:30 would you?

Mr. Erwin: No, that is rather early to get from Rochester.

The Court: Then come back at ten o'clock tomorrow morning. You are excused.

(Court recessed at 3:07 and reconvened the following morning June 9th, 1949 at 10:27).

STIPULATION

Mr. Erwin: That's all. I call Dr. Maggio.

Mr. Harpending: Just a minute. I understand this is part of the plaintiff's case yet?

The Court: Yes.

Mr. Harpending: Cross examination. I ask to call another witness.

Mr. Erwin: I object to it if the Court please. We adjourned for the purpose of swearing my doctor and cross examination of Mrs. Owen, if I could get the original statement.

The Court: Well, I don't know what the witness is about?

Mr. Harpending: Well the stipulation was medical testimony?

The Court: Yes.

Mr. Erwin: The stipulation was, I would like to have this in the record. Was for medical testimony for my doctor. It was talked over in chambers. He couldn't get here yesterday. It was definitely understood no other testimony would be offered today except my medical testimony and any rebuttal you might have on the medical testimony. And then cross examination of Mrs. Litteer if I could get that statement. That's all. I object to any other testimony on behalf of the plaintiff.

The Court: I want this to appear in the record. That what was said in chambers is not a part of this record, and if I am running into this difficulty in this case, I will take care of it in my own way. I am standing on the record here. That is all I intend to say now, counsellor.

Mr. Erwin: All right, exception.

Mr. Harpending: I will call Mrs. Pinder.

LOUISE PINDER, being duly sworn, and called as a witness on behalf of the plaintiff, testified as follows: (omitted)

CHARLES I. MAGGIO, being duly sworn, and called as a witness on behalf of the defendant, testified as follows:

DIRECT EXAMINATION by Mr. Erwin:

Q. Dr. Maggio, where do you reside? A. Rochester, New York.

Q. Practicing physician and surgeon? A. Yes, sir.

Q. Over how many years? A. Since 1917.

Q. Graduate of what medical school? A. University of Michigan.

Q. Served your internship where? A. At the Lee Private Hospital, Rochester.

Q. And have practiced your profession in Rochester since that time? A. I was in the medical corp in World War One for eight months and then returned to Rochester and have been practicing medicine since then.

Q. You are licensed to practice in the State of New York? A. Yes, sir.

Q. Do you specialize in anything particularly? A. Industrial medical, and minor traumatic surgery.

Q. Did you examine Mary Litteer on or about the third day of February, 1947, at the request of the representative of this defendant, the Rochester-Penfield Bus Company? A. Yes, I did.

Q. At the time of your examination on February the third, 1947, are you able to state an opinion with a reasonable degree of medical certainty whether or not she was suffering from any disability by reason of her feet? A. Yes, I am.

Q. What is your opinion? A. It is my opinion that she had no disability.

Q. Was there anything at all of a permanent nature indicating she might have had her feet frozen at some prior date, was there anything of a permanent nature that would indicate that? A. There was nothing present to indicate that.

Q. Did you find the condition of her heart? A. Yes, I did.

Q. What condition of her heart did you find? A. I found she had a chronic valvular heart lesion with a moderate enlargement. Her pulse was 76, which would indicate that although she had a valvular heart lesion, the heart was well compensated and functioning properly.

Q. Assuming Doctor, that she had poor circulation as has been testified to here, and assuming that she wore a pair of shoes over heavy wool socks that fitted snugly, can you state an opinion with a reasonable degree of certainty as to whether or not that might affect the circulation?

Mr. Harpending: I object to that, Counsel is assuming facts not in evidence here.
The Court: I will overrule.
Mr. Harpending: Exception.
A. Will you repeat that question?
(The last question was re-read by the stenographer.)
A. Yes, I can.

Q. And would that condition in your opinion make the feet get cold more easily?
Mr. Harpending: Now I certainly object to that if the Court please.
The Court: Well, I don't know what counsel means, what you mean by cold, but I think he means it in a colloquial sense?
Mr. Erwin: Cold.
The Court: Overruled, yes, sure.
A. Yes, if the circulation is interfered with, the feet would get colder quicker.

Q. Doctor, assuming that this young lady rode on a bus that she boarded at Bath at 6:10 and arrived in Rochester at 10:05 which would be three hours and 55 minutes; assuming that the bus was loaded with 40 people and assuming that the temperature outside at six o'clock was 26 degrees and gradually lowered to 17 degrees at ten o'clock when she left the bus and assuming that there was no heat at all in the bus, in your opinion, would her feet freeze during that period of time? A. No, sir.
Mr. Harpending: I move to strike out the answer if the Court please, it is not a proper subject of medical testimony, and assuming too many other factors, not specified.
The Court: I deny the motion.-
Mr. Harpending: Exception.
The Court: -and give you an exception.
Mr. Erwin: That is all.

CROSS EXAMINATION by Mr. Harpending:

Q. Doctor, during the course of your testimony, you have, you made reference to some paper you have in your hand? A. Yes, sir.
Q. May I see it please? A. Yes, sir.
(There was a brief pause while other jurors in the room were excused until a later time.)
Q. Doctor, this is a copy of your report you made to the people who hired you to conduct this examination? A. Yes, sir.
Q. And in this report you do say that there was some redness of the soles on both feet noted, particularly along the outer border of the heel, is that right? A. If it is down there, I said it, that's right.
Q. And in this, in conclusion, did you say, it would appear that this young woman suffered from frost bite of both feet, but it is difficult to conceive how this could have happened riding in the bus if there was any heat in the bus at all? A. That's right.
Q. This was the report you made at the time of your examination, is that right? A. That's right.
Q. Doctor, in the course of your work, you do a great many examinations in industrial cases? A. Yes, I do.
Q. And that is a great part of your work, is it not? A. Yes, sir.
Q. That is when an employee is injured or taken sick on the job, you examine him for the employer or for the, whoever carries the compensation? A. That's right.
Q. And you report to that person or company that retains you to examine them? A. That's right.
Q. And you frequently testify in Court for employers or for compensation carriers? A. Yes, I do.

Q. And is also a part of your work Doctor, to examine for the defense in negligence cases?
A. Yes, sir.
Q. And have you examined in other cases for the people who retained you to examine Miss Litteer here? A. Yes, I have.
Q. And have you ever testified for these people in any other case? A. I think just once.
Q. But you do frequently testify in Court for the defense in liability cases, do you not?
A. Yes, sir.
Q. Well Doctor, chilling, a general chilling of the body, would make freezing more likely, would it not? A. Chilling up to a certain point, yes it would.
Q. And that, so cases have been, I will withdraw that. There are medical cases on record where the extremities have been frozen at temperatures no lower than 23 degrees fahrenheit, are there not? A. I don't know from the records whether this is true or not. I can readily understand that in cases where the circulation is impaired considerably, that that might be possible.
Q. It would be possible in cases of weak circulation without any other factor entering into the impairment of the circulation, where the body has been chilled over a period of time?
A. I don't know what you mean by weak circulation.
Q. By circulation weakened because of a heart condition? A. Well, I would answer that the same way as I did the last one, that if the circulation were considerably impaired that that would be possible.
Q. Well, generally chilling of the body makes freezing more likely at a higher temperature, does it not? A. Under the circumstances of sluggishness of poor circulation, yes.
Mr. Harpending: I think that is all.

RE-DIRECT EXAMINATION by Mr. Erwin:

Q. Just one more question, Doctor. Counsel read from your report, there was some redness of the soles of both feet noted particularly along the outer border of the heel, more so on the right one. Could that come from something else outside of from freezing?
Mr. Harpending: I object to that if the Court please, incompetent----
Mr. Erwin: Do you know?
The Court: Overruled.
A. Yes, sir.
Q. What could it come from? A. A lot of things could cause redness of the feet.
Q. Tell me some of them? A. Increased circulation, that is from increased heat. Dermatitis will do it. A blow might cause redness. Rubbing against a shoe might cause a redness. There are many other conditions that could do that.
Q. It doesn't indicate then that the person who has that condition, must have suffered from frozen feet, does it? A. No, sir.

RE-CROSS EXAMINATION by Mr. Harpending:

Q. You reported frost bite here, right in your report, didn't you? A. I said that, yes, but---
Mr. Harpending: That's all
A. It doesn't necessarily mean in answer to Mr. Erwin's question that redness of the feet means frostbite.
Q. But you reported frostbite right in your report here? A. Yes, sir.
Mr. Erwin: But you did report that and it was based upon a history that you had of frozen feet.
A. That's right.

MOTIONS

Mr. Erwin: You had no knowledge her feet were frozen except what she told you?
A. That's right.
Mr. Harpending: Did you check with the school authorities at all?
A. I beg your pardon?
Mr. Harpending: You didn't check with the school authorities?
A. No, well, no. I think I talked with Dr. Powell.
Mr. Harpending: That's all.
Mr. Erwin: That is all.
Dr. Maggio: I apologize to the Court for not being able to come yesterday and for being late.
The Court: That is quite all right.
Mr. Erwin: If your Honor please, I now offer in evidence Exhibit D for identification.
Mr. Harpending: No objection.
The Court: Received.
Mr. Erwin: The defendant rests.
The Court: Evidence closed?
Mr. Harpending: Evidence closed.
(Court recessed from 11 to 11:10)

Mr. Erwin: I renew my motion made at the close of the plaintiff's case for a non-suit and a dismissal of the complaint on the same grounds therein stated, on the record as now presented.

The Court: Motion denied.

Mr. Erwin: And I move for a directed verdict in favor of the defendant of no cause for action.

The Court: I deny that.

Mr. Erwin: Exception to both.

Mr. Erwin, and Mr. Harpending summed up their respective cases to the jury.

Mr. Erwin: I take exception to counsel's statement that the defendants could have subpoenaed the personal physicians of the plaintiff and forced them to testify without a waiver from the plaintiff herself.

The Court: I give you an exception, counsellor. And I hold now that when a person brings a personal injury action of this character, they submit their condition to subpoena, that is not the way, may I, well leave it in. I mean to say, that they submit that physical condition to scrutiny and that the defendant could have subpoenaed any witness here, any doctor that the plaintiff had, and required him to testify.

Mr. Erwin: I take exception to that, if your Honor please.

CHARGE OF THE COURT

The Court: I am going to order, give you a dinner after this, after my charge is over, so you don't watch the clock. This is an action by Jane, Mary Jane Owen as she is now known since her marraige, as plaintiff, against the Rochester-Penfield Bus Company, Inc., as defendant. And it is a negligence action as we term it, and before you can render a verdict you will have to find that the defendant was guilty of negligence; that the plaintiff was free from negligence. Now on the first day of December, 1946, it seems the plaintiff claims that she was a passenger on a bus operated by the defendant that ran from Bath, New York, to Rochester. She says that she got on the bus at Bath on the evening of December first, 1946, and that the bus was so cold that she had frost bitten feet as a result of it and received injury that has continued to this time.

Now under the law it was the duty of the defendant bus company to furnish reasonable heat in its bus. The statute in that regard reads, that, "every omnibus corporation shall furnish and provide with respect thereto"--that means with respect to the omnibus--" such service and facilities as shall be safe and adequate and in all respects just and reasonable." Well that of course includes weather, weather includes reasonable heat. Now there is a direct dispute here in this case as to whether or not this bus did give reasonable heat, furnish reasonable heat as a facility, and that will be one of the things for you to determine in coming to a conclusion as to whether or not the defendant was guilty of any negligence.

The plaintiff claims that it did not have reasonble heat and that it was cold. That someone called to the bus driver and the bus driver said, well nothing can be done about it, something to that effect. Nothing can be done because the heating apparatus is out of order. And in that regard too, the plaintiff claims that some place along the line, the bus stopped because there was an accident ahead, and that the bus driver got out of the bus and left the door open for fifteen minutes and that that was negligence.

The test here is, Members of the Jury, whether or not this bus company failed to furnish reasonable heat to the plaintiff or whether or not it did. In other words, in some cases of negligence actions, we have a situation where you can't claim that anyone is deliberately lying, an accident happens for instance and whether a car did this or did that or just what caused the accident, people differ, naturally differ. But this is a little bit different sort of a case. The defendant disputes here that the bus was cold and that this plaintiff suffered frost-bitten feet as a result of her ride on the defendant's bus. And you will have to determine that question, as best you may. You and I weren't there. We are not always deciding cases to a certainty. You have to use your own good judgment. You have heard these witnesses. You have listened to this testimony and you will have to use your own good judgment in determining what the truth is as you have heard it in this trial.

Now while I am on the subject, something has been said about subpoenaing witnesses, about subpoenaing the plaintiff's doctors and so forth. Let me tell you a bit about that. I have said here that the plaintiff's doctors could have been sworn by the defendant and that is the law and you take it from me, of course, the law. But that doesn't necessarily mean that the defendant should have subpoenaed the doctors of the plaintiff. That is a matter of trial tactics and what you expect in a lawsuit, you know, what you expect to be confronted with. There isn't anything about calling a witness or failing to call a witness that is important unless the issue is clear cut, and you have a right to expect that that is going to be the issue, and then whether you call a witness or not is your own good judgment. I mean, not necessarily the young lady here, but her attorney's good judgment.

Now to get back to the real issue here. Was this defendant negligent? Did it fail to use such care as a reasonably prudent person would have used and did that failure cause the accident? That is the real issue here. The first issue that you will meet in your jury room--if you fail to find that the defendant was negligent and that this, in keeping this bus in a reasonably heated condition, then your verdict will be no cause of action in favor of the defendant. If you find that the defendant was negligent under the rule I have given you of reasonable care, using reasonable care, then you will pass to the second question, and that is whether or not the plaintiff herself was guilty of negligence that contributed to the condition of which she claims. If she were guilty of negligence, she cannot recover ever though you found the defendant guilty of negligence. She owed a duty of using reasonable care as a reasonably, prudent person would in being a passenger. She says that she was back in the bus quite aways, that there were people in the aisles. She says that she took off her shoes and manipulated her feet with her hands and that she put on mittens that she had with her. Did she do what a reasonably, prudent person would have done or did she fail to do what a reasonably prudent person would have done under like circumstances? That is a question for you to determine.

As I have said to you, even though you found the defendant guilty of negligence, she can't recover if she were guilty of negligence. Now if you find that the defendant was guilty of negligence here in furnishing reasonable heat, and you find that the plaintiff was free from negligence in that, in relation to what happened, then you will award a verdict for the plaintiff. If the plaintiff is entitled to recover here, she is entitled to be compensated for the actual injury that she received. It is for you to say the nature of it and the extent of it. There has been evidence here that this condition will continue for some time in the future and if you award this plaintiff a verdict, you will include any amount, what item you feel is proper for the future injury, that is for the future inconvenience and disability, if any, that she may suffer, and that you may find that she may suffer in the future.

There is no yardstick I can give you on such things. It is something for you to use your own good common sense about in determining what amount would adequately and fairly compensate the plaintiff, if you award her a verdict.

Now the burden of proof here is upon the plaintiff. That means, she has the burden of satisfying you by a fair preponderance of evidence that the defendant was negligent, that she was free from negligence and that burden applied to the damages. It doesn't mean the greater number of witnesses. We don't count noses to determine a lawsuit, but it does mean such evidence as to your minds, more nearly speaks the truth. And the burden in that regard is upon the plaintiff here. The case has been well tried. It has been speedily tried in Court. It is all within your mind and memory now, what has happened, what the evidence is, and I am sure you can arrive at a verdict that will be just and proper. It won't satisfy one side or the other. You and I are not concerned with that. What we are concerned with, is that our work, and you with your verdict, will maintain the standard of justice that is fair under the law and under the facts as you find them. I am sure you will have that in mind when you retire.

Now it requires ten of your number to agree. We like unanimous verdicts if we can have them but when there are ten who agree, you may return to Courth with your verdict. Requests and exceptions?

Mr. Erwin: No requests or exceptions.
Mr. Harpending: No requests or exceptions.
The Court: Swear an officer.

VERDICT
MOTION TO SET ASIDE VERDICT

(The jury retired at 12:15).

The Court: Counsellor, you are going to stay, are you?

Mr. Erwin: A little while, yes, I can't get home to do any work.

The Court: That is okay. Then if you do go, we will put a stipulation on the record, if you want to.

The jury returned to the Courtroom to report a verdict at 2:17.

The Court: All right, you can be seated. Members of the jury, have you agreed on a verdict?

Foreman: We have.

The Court: Will you report or recount to us what the verdict is?

Foreman: Your Honor, the jury decided unanimously to give the plaintiff, five thousand dollars.

Mr. Erwin: I move to set the verdict aside on all the grounds specified in section 549 of the Civil Practice Act.

The Court: Motion denied.

Mr. Erwin: And order a copy of the minutes at the present time.

The Court: All right, do you want any, I don't know? You don't need any bond or stay of execution?

Mr. Erwin: All right.

DEFENDANT'S EXHIBIT D

Rochester, New York, January 31, 1947

Statement of Mary Jane Litteer, 19 years old, single and living at 55 S. Washington Street, Rochester. My home address is Dundee, N.Y., R.D. #2 where my parents reside, John & Ruth Litteer. I am a student at R.I.T. This is a cooperative plan, work a month, school a month. I work at McCurdy's and lost three days because of this accident. I earn $24.00 per week. On Dec. 1, 1946 I was going from Bath to Rochester. I caught the bus at 6 P.M. and is due in at 9:20 P.M. I sat on the right side of the bus a little more than half way to the rear. When I first boarded the bus I didn't notice if it was cold although they usually aren't too warm when they start up. I had on wool socks and saddle shoes and was wearing slacks. I had no rubbers or galoshes. When I boarded the bus it was cold with a sleet-rain falling. I sat next to the window past N. Cohocton and then traded to an aisle seat on into Rochester, N.Y. I couldn't feel any heat all around my seat. The window was closed but cold air came in around it and on the floor. I don't know if the front heater was turned on. As I recall, the windows were frozen over, but I'm not sure whether inside or outside. The bus had to stop for an accident between Bath and Dansville and we had to wait quite awhile. I think the bus door was kept closed and the motor was running. This was a second section and the wind was blowing very hard which doesn't help any. I began to notice my feet hurting me then. I didn't speak to the driver at any time about the lack of heat. I don't know that anyone else mentioned it to the driver. M.J.L. Mr. and Mrs. Perkins of Fairport were on the bus with me and seated in front of me. They had said they were both cold during the trip. My feet got so cold finally that they stopped hurting me so I thought they were better. The bus was late getting in and when I got to the Dorm my feet were solid white. The next day I called Dr. Powell who said my feet had been frozen and I would have trouble with them for years.

I saw him only once and there was no charge as he is the school doctor. I lost no time from school. I have had no expense other than my lost time. I don't think my feet were cold when I got on the bus as I was brought to the terminal in a car and got right on the bus. I have read this statement and it is true to the best of my knowledge.

MARY JANE LITTEER.

Witness:
W. N. Tohl, Rochester, N.Y.

JUDGMENT.

(Same Title)

This action having been originally commenced against defendant above named by Mary Jane Litteer, an infant, by John H. Litteer, her Guardian ad Litem, and the issues in this action having been duly brought on for trial before Mr. Justice Riley H. Heath and a jury at a trial term of this court held on the 8th day of June 1949 at the court house in the Village of Watkins Glen, Schuyler County, New York, and the parties appearing by counsel and the plaintiff's attorney having suggested on the record in open court that the plaintiff had then reached her majority of 21 years and had taken the married name as given in the above title and the court having directed on the record that the Guardian ad Litem aforesaid be discharged and the action continued by the plaintiff as above entitled, and the issues having been duly tried and a verdict for the plaintiff having been duly rendered on the 9th day of June, 1949 for the sum of Five Thousand Dollars ($5000.00) and the costs of the plaintiff having been duly taxed at One Hundred Eight and 50/100 Dollars ($108.50),

Now, on the motion of H.C. & H.B. Harpending and Frederick M. Hunt, attorneys for the said plaintiff it is

ADJUDGED that the plaintiff, Mary Jane Litteer Owen, recover of the defendant, Rochester-Penfield Bus Company, Inc., the sum of Five Thousand Dollars ($5000.00), so found by the jury, together with One Hundred Eight and 50/100 Dollars ($108.50) costs as taxed, amounting in all to Five Thousand One Hundred Eight and 50/100 Dollars ($5108.50) and that plaintiff have execution therefor.

Judgment signed this 14th day of June 1949.

L. E. MORGAN,
Clerk.

NOTICE OF APPEAL

STATE OF NEW YORK

SUPREME COURT—COUNTY OF SCHUYLER

MARY JANE LITTEER OWEN, 4216
Valley Road, Cleveland 9, Ohio
Plaintiff-Respondent,

vs

ROCHESTER-PENFIELD BUS COMPANY, INC.,
60 River Boulevard
Rochester, New York
Defendant-Appellant.

PLEASE TAKE NOTICE that the defendant above named hereby appeals to the Appellate Division of the Supreme Court, Third Department, from the judgment entered herein in the office of the Clerk of this County on the 14th day of June, 1949, and from each and every part thereof, and from the denial of defendant's motion for a new trial made upon the minutes on the 9th day of June, 1949.

Dated: June

Yours, etc.,

AUSTIN W. ERWIN and
AUSTIN W. ERWIN, JR.,
Attorneys for Defendant-Appellant,
70 Main Street
Geneseo, New York.

To:
H. C. & H. B. Harpending and F. M. Hunt,
Attorneys for Plaintiff-Respondent,
Dundee, New York

L. E. Morgan
Clerk of the County of Schuyler,
Watkins Glen, New York.

AFFIDAVIT OF NO OPINION

(Same Title.)

STATE OF NEW YORK,) SS.:
Livingston County.)

AUSTIN W. ERWIN, being duly sworn, deposes and says:

That he is one of the attorneys for the defendant-appellant in the above entitled action;

that the court below rendered no opinion or memorandum in writing on the denial of the motion for new trial made on the minutes at the close of the said action.

AUSTIN W. ERWIN

Sworn to before me this
19th day of January, 1950.
Jessie M. Erwin,
Notary Public.

STIPULATION WAIVING CERTIFICATION
AND SETTLING CASE

(Same Title.)

IT IS HEREBY STIPULATED and agreed by and between the attorneys for the parties in the above entitled action pursuant to section 170 of the Civil Practice Act, that the foregoing copies of case and exceptions, judgment roll, notice of appeal, demand for bill of particulars and bill of particulars is a correct transcript of the originals thereof now on file in the office of the Clerk of the County of Schuyler and of the whole thereof and certification thereof by the Clerk pursuant to Section 615 of the Civil Practice Act is hereby waived:

IT IS FURTHER STIPULATED and agreed that the foregoing case and exceptions contain all the evidence and proceedings had upon the trial of this action material to the decision and the questions to be raised on this appeal and that an order may be entered upon this stipulation settling said case accordingly.

Dated, January 19, 1950

AUSTIN W. ERWIN and
AUSTIN W. ERWIN, JR.,
Attorneys for Defendant-Appellant.

To:
H. C. & H. B. Harpending and
F. M. Hunt,
Attorneys for Plaintiff-Respondent.

ORDER SETTLING AND FILING CASE

(Same Title.)

On the foregoing stipulation, the foregoing case on appeal, containing all the evidence, is hereby settled and ordered on file in the office of the Clerk of the County of Schuyler and the Clerk of the Appellate Division of the Supreme Court, Third Judicial Department.

Dated: February , 1950.

RILEY H. HEATH,
Justice Supreme Court

ADDITIONAL PAPERS TO COURT OF APPEALS

SUPPLEMENTAL STATEMENT UNDER RULE 234

COURT OF APPEALS

OF THE

STATE OF NEW YORK

(Same Title)

This action was commended in the Schuyler County Supreme Court by the Service of a summons and complaint on the defendant on or about January 12, 1948. The Defendant served its answer on or about February 21, 1948.

The action was tried before Hon. Riley H. Heath, Justice of the Supreme Court, and a jury on June 8 and 9, 1949, at the June Trial Term held at Watkins Glen, New York. The jury awarded the plaintiff a verdict of $5,000 damages. A judgment in the sum of $5,108.50 was entered in favor of the plaintiff and against the defendant in the Schuyler County Clerk's Office on June 14, 1949.

The defendant moved to set aside the verdict on all of the grounds specified in Section 549 of the Civil Practice Act. The motion was denied.

The defendant filed a notice of appeal from the judgment and from the denial of the motion on June 27, 1949. The appeal was argued before the Appellate Division of the Supreme Court, Third Judicial Department, on January 10, 1951, and on March 7, 1951, said court rendered a unanimous decision in which it reversed the judgment on the law and facts and dismissed the complaint without costs. An opinion was delivered. An order to this effect was entered in the Office of the Clerk of the Appellate Division, Third Department, at Albany, New York, on March 29, 1951.

This order was filed in the Schuyler County Clerk's Office on April 9, 1951, and judgment was entered on said order on April 9, 1951, reversing the judgment of June 14, 1949, on the law and facts and dismissing the complaint without costs. Notice of appeal by the plaintiff from this order and judgment was filed in the Schuyler County Clerk's Office on June 12, 1951.

There has been no change in the parties herein.

DECISION.

SUPREME COURT

Appellate Division — Third Judicial Department

Decision handed down March 7, 1951

(Same title)

Judgment reversed, on the law and facts, and complaint dismissed, without costs.

Opinion by Coon, J.

Foster, P. J., Heffernan, Brewster and Bergan, JJ., concur.

ORDER OF REVERSAL.

At a Term of the Appellate Division of the Supreme Court, of the State of New York, held in and for the Third Judicial Department of said State, at the Court House, in the City of Albany, commencing on the 8th day of January, 1951.

Present: Hon. Sydney F. Foster,
Presiding Justice.
Hon. Christopher J. Heffernan,
Hon. O. Byron Brewster,
Hon. Francis Bergan,
Hon. William H. Coon,
Associate Justices.
(Same title.)

The appeal from the judgment in the above entitled action having been duly brought before this Court during the above stated Term and having been argued for Appellant by Hon. Austin W. Erwin, Esq., of counsel, for Austin W. Erwin and Austin W. Erwin, Jr., Attorneys for Appellant and by Harold A. Jerry, Jr., of Counsel, for H. C. and H. B. Harpending and F. M. Hunt, attorneys for Respondent, and due deliberation having been had and decision thereon having been handed down March 7, 1951, it is

ORDERED, that the judgment so appealed from be and the same hereby is reversed on the law and facts and complaint dismissed without costs.

Opinion by Coon, J.

Foster, P. J., Heffernan, Brewster and Bergan, JJ., concur.

J. ROBERT LANNON,
Deputy Clerk.

A true copy:
J. Robert Lannon,
Deputy Clerk, Ent. 3/29/51

OPINION FOR REVERSAL

(Same title)

Argued January Term, 1951

Decided March , 1951

Before:
Hon. Sydney F. Foster,
Presiding Justice,
Hon. O. Byron Brewster,
Hon. Francis Bergan,
Hon. William H. Coon,
Associate Justices.

APPEAL by defendant from a judgment of the Supreme Court (Heath, J.), entered in the office of the Clerk of Schuyler County on June 14, 1949, in favor of the plaintiff upon a jury verdict after trial.

COON, J.:

Plaintiff, then 18 years of age, boarded defendant's bus at Bath, N.Y., and traveled thereon to Rochester, N.Y., on December 1, 1946. It is her contention that the defendant was negligent in that the bus was improperly heated and as a result she suffered frost-bitten feet. She has recovered a verdict and judgment on this theory, from which this appeal is taken.

Plaintiff was a student at a school in Rochester and lived in a dormitory there. She had spent Thanksgiving recess at her home in the Town of Tyrone and was returning to Rochester. She traveled by car from her home to Bath. She testified that the weather was cold and snowy and the bus was cold when she boarded it and remained cold throughout the trip. Upon arrival in Rochester she walked through snow, getting her feet wet, to a cab and traveled by cab to her dormitory, where she found that her feet were white and numb, and thereafter caused her severe discomfort. On the trip her feet were dressed in wool socks and saddle shoes without rubbers or overshoes. Her sister and brother-in-law, who were also on the bus, testified that "someone" on the bus told the driver to turn on the heat and that he replied that he could not because the heater was out of order. This is disputed by the driver and there is substantial evidence that the heaters were working. However, upon this conflict of testimony the jury could have found that the bus was cold and that the heaters were not working properly.

The plaintiff was and had been from early infancy afflicted with a chronic valvular heart lesion and enlargement accompanied by low blood pressure. This condition was known to plaintiff and her mother and had been for many years. This condition was not made known to the defendant or its driver, nor was it apparent. There is no evidence that the plaintiff or any one in her behalf complained to the driver of the cold, or that her feet were cold. There is no evidence that she requested any additional protection. There were approximately 40 passengers on the bus, some standing in the aisles. So far as appears, none of them suffered any ill effects from the trip. None of them were called as witnesses except the plaintiff's sister, her brother-in-law and the driver.

The bus was scheduled to leave Bath at 6:10 p.m., and was due in Rochester at 8:45 p.m. It was late and arrived at about 10:00 p.m. It is the undisputed evidence that the official U. S. Weather Bureau temperatures recorded at Rochester on that day were: 26 degrees above zero at 5:25 p.m.; 25 degrees at 6:26 p.m.; 24 degrees at 7:25 p.m.; 19 degrees at 8:25 p.m.; and 17 degrees at 9:25 p.m. It does not appear what the temperature was inside the bus, but common sense dictates that in an enclosed bus containing 40 people the temperature would be somewhat higher than out of doors, even without artificial heat.

It is likewise undisputed, and, in fact, is the testimony of plaintiff's doctor, that the average normal person is not susceptible to frost bite from ten degrees above zero upward, and that a person of poor circulation would be more susceptible. It necessarily follows that the plaintiff would not have suffered the injury from which she complains, or any injury, except for her own latent physical impairment.

Upon this state of facts the question is squarely presented whether a common carrier is liable in negligence for injuries to a passenger suffering from a secret impairment when no injury would have resulted except for such impairment. It is well established that a common carrier may be held to a higher degree of care to prevent injury to persons who are ill, aged or infirm of the infirmity is known or should have been known. "It would seem certain that this result would follow only where the one charged with negligence either had knowledge of the infirmity of the other or, in the exercise of due care, should have had such knowledge." (Warren's New York Negligence, Vol. 3 §137). American Jurisprudence, (Vo. 10, p. 184, §1273) says: "as a general rule a common carrier of passengers is under no duty to anticipate or guard against an injurious result which would only occur to a person of abnormal peculiar sensitiveness."

Plaintiff's injuries did not come within the realm of reasonable foreseeability. Defendant was under no legal duty to guard against dangers which could not reasonably be foreseen. In Lane v City of Buffalo, (232 A.D. 334), Mr. Justice Edgcomb says at page 338: "Negligence is to be gauged by the ability of one to anticipate danger. The test of actionable negligence is not what could have been done to have prevented a particular accident, but what a reasonable prudent and careful person would have done under the circumstances in the discharge of his duty to the injured party. Failure to guard against a remote possibility of accident, or one which could not, in the exercise of ordinary care, be foreseen, does not constitute negligence." As phrased by Chief Judge Cardozo in Palsgraf v Long Island R. R. Co., (248 NY 339): "The risk reasonably to be perceived defines the duty to be obeyed....." That no injury was sutained by other passengers demonstrates that there was no danger which could be reasonably apprehended. Had defendant been advised of plaintiff's condition it might well have afforded her some form of additional protection. There are doubtless passengers who suffer ill effects from too much heat. Some individuals might be allergic to the material from which the bus cushions are made or to innumerable conditions which exist from time to time on a bus. To hold a carrier liable for injuries or illness to all persons normal and abnormal, especially when the abnormality is not known, would make a carrier an insurer of the well being of all passengers. As yet the point has not been reached where such is the law.

A statute is involved here which we do not think affects liability. Public Service Law, §60 (a) (1), reads in part as follows: "Every omnibus corporation shall furnish and provide with respect thereto, such services and facilities as shall be safe and adequate and in all respects just and reasonable..... This statute deals with reasonableness, and as we interpret this language, it requires nothing more than reasonable facilities, safe for normal individuals.

The cases cited by respondent are readily distinguishable. They all deal with foreseeable danger to normal persons and acts which would constitute negligence to normal persons, and stand only for the proposition that a party once guilty of such negligence, cannot escape added consequences or damages because of a previously existing physical condition. Here plaintiff would not have been injured at all but for her previous physical condition.

The judgment should be reversed on the law and facts and the complaint dismissed, without costs.

JUDGMENT OF REVERSAL

(Same Title.)

An appeal having been taken to the Appellate Division of the Supreme Court for the Third Judicial Department from a judgment entered in the office of the Clerk of the County of Schuyler on the 14th day of June, 1949, in favor of the plaintiff and against the defendant in the sum of $5,000.00 with costs and said appeal having been heard and said Appellate Division having, by an order entered in the office of the Clerk of the Appellate Division, Third Department, at Albany, New York, on the 29th day of March, 1951, unanimously reversed the said judgment on the law and the facts and dismissing the complaint, without costs, and the said record of appeal, together with a certified copy of said order having been remitted to the office of the Clerk of the County of Schuyler, it is

On motion of Austin W. Erwin, one of the attorneys for the defendant,

ADJUDGED that the judgment of this court entered on the 14th day of June, 1949, in in favor of the plaintiff and against the defendant in the sum of $5000.00 and costs be, and the same hereby is reversed on the law and the facts and the complaint herein dismissed without costs.

Judgment signed this 9th day of April, 1951.

LAWRENCE E. MORGAN,
Clerk.

NOTICE OF APPEAL TO THE COURT OF APPEALS

STATE OF NEW YORK

SUPREME COURT — Schuyler County

(Same title)

PLEASE TAKE NOTICE that the above named plaintiff-respondent hereby appeals to the Court of Appeals from a judgment of affirmance herein entered in the office of the Clerk of the County of Schuyler on the 9th day of April, 1951, pursuant to order of the Appellate Division, Third Department, duly entered herein and which judgment unanimously reversed the judgment of the Supreme Court, Schuyler County, entered herein on the 14th day of June, 1949, in favor of the plaintiff and against the defendant in the sum of Five Thousand One Hundred Eight Dollars and Fifty Cents ($,108.50) total damages and costs, and this appeal is from each and every part of said judgment of reversal.

Dated: June 5, 1951.

Yours, etc.,
H. C. and H. B. HARPENDING and
FREDERICK M. HUNT,
Attorneys for the Plaintiff-Respondent,
Office and Post Office Address,
Dundee, New York.

To:
Austin W. Erwin and
Austin W. Erwin, Jr.,
Attorneys for Defendant-Appellant,
70 Main Street,
Geneseo, New York.
and
Clerk of the County of Schuyler

AFFIDAVIT OF NO OTHER OPINION BY THE APPELLATE DIVISION

(Same Title)

State of New York)
County of Chemung) ss.:

A. H. HARPENDING, Esq., being duly sworn, deposes and says: That he is a member of the firm of H. C. & H. B. Harpending & F. M. Hunt, attorneys for the plaintiff-appellant in this action; that no opinion was delivered by the Appellate Division at the time of the order of reversal and judgment thereon from which this appeal is taken other than the opinion printed herein.

A. H. HARPENDING

Sworn to before me this
31st day of July, 1951.
Nona Wombough
Notary Public

WAIVER OF CERTIFICATION

(Same Title)

IT IS HEREBY STIPULATED by and between the attorneys for the respective parties herein pursuant to Section 170 of the Civil Practice Act that the foregoing are true and correct copies of the judgment roll, the case and exceptions herein, the notice of appeal to the Court of Appeals, the order of reversal of the Appellate Division, the judgment entered thereon in the Office of the Clerk of Schuyler County, the opinion of the Appellate Division, and the record on appeal in the Appellate Division, Third Judicial Department, and the whole thereof, now on file in the Office of the Clerk of Schuyler County; and that certification thereof by the Clerk, pursuant to Section 616 of the Civil Practice Act, is hereby waived.

Dated: August , 1951.

H. C. & H. B. HARPENDING &
F. M. HUNT,
Attorneys for Plaintiff-Appellant.

ERWIN & ERWIN,
Attorneys for Defendant-Respondent.

No. 138 Form 6

COURT OF APPEALS

STATE OF NEW YORK, SS.:

PLEAS in the Court of Appeals, held at Court of Appeals Hall, in the City of Albany, on the 24th day of October in the year of our Lord one thousand nine hundred and fifty-two, before the judges of said Court.

Witness,
The Hon. John T. Loughran,
Chief Judge, Presiding.

Raymond J. Cannon, Clerk.

Remittitur October 24, 1952.

Mary Jane Litteer Owen,
Appellant

-against-

Rochester-Penfield Bus Company, Inc.
Respondent.

BE IT REMEMBERED, that on the 29th day of May in the year of our Lord one thousand nine hundred and fifty-two, Mary Jane Litteer Owen the appelant — in this cause, came here unto the Court of Appeals by H. C. and H. B. Harpending and Frederick M. Hunt, her attorneys, and filed in the said Court a Notice of Appeal and return thereto from the judgment of the Appellate Division of the Supreme Court in and for the Third Judicial Department. And Rochester-Penfield Bus Company, Inc., the respondent — in said cause, afterwards appeared in said Court of Appeals by Austin W. Erwin and Austin W. Erwin, Jr., its attorneys.

Which said Notice of Appeal and the return thereto, filed as aforesaid, are hereunto annexed.

WHEREUPON, the said Court of Appeals having heard this cause argued by Mr. Asbury H. Harpending, of counsel for the appellant, and by Mr. Austin W. Erwin, of counsel for the respondent, and after due deliberation had thereon, did order and adjudge that the judgments herein be and the same hereby are reversed and a new trial granted, with costs to abide the event.

And it was also further ordered, that the records aforesaid, and the proceedings of this Court, be remitted to the said Supreme Court, there to be proceeded upon according to law.

THEREFORE, it is considered that the said judgments be reversed and a trial granted, with costs &c, as aforesaid.

And hereupon, as well the Notice of Appeal and return thereto aforesaid as the judgment of the Court of Appeals aforesaid, be it given in the premises, are by the said Court of Appeals remitted into the Supreme Court of the State of New York before the Justices thereof, according to the form of the statute in such case made and provided, to be enforced according to law, and which record now remains in the said Supreme Court, before the Justices thereof, &c.

Raymond J. Cannon
Clerk of the Court of Appeals of the State of New York

COURT OF APPEALS, CLERK'S OFFICE,)
(
Albany, October 24, 1952)

I HEREBY CERTIFY, that the preceding record contains a correct transcript of the proceedings in said cause in the Court of Appeals, with the papers originally filed therein, attached thereo.

Raymond J. Cannon
Clerk

§1.2 REPORT OF THE CASE

MARY JANE L. OWEN, Appellant, v. ROCHESTER-PENFIELD BUS COMPANY, INC., Respondent.

(Argued October 7, 1952; decided October 24, 1952.)

Negligence--carriers--failure to heat bus--(1) action, based on asserted negligence of bus company, by passenger whose feet became frostbitten while riding in bus; evidence that bus was not heated (see Public Service Law, Sec. 60-a; Public Service Comm. Rules, rule 23); complaint improperly dismissed on ground injuries were not reasonably foreseeable--(2) although passenger was more susceptible than others to frostbite because of heart condition, under law of case she was not deemed abnormal--(3) passenger's low blood pressure and poor circulation foreseeable by common carrier--(4) court may take judicial notice of rule of Public Service Commission (Civ. Prac. Act, Sec. 344-a, subd. 4).

1. While plaintiff, eighteen years of age, was riding on defendant's bus, her feet were frozen. There was evidence that the bus was cold; that its heater was out of order; that during the course of the trip, the driver had stopped to investigate an accident and had left the bus door open for fifteen minutes; that plaintiff had been xposed to the cold for about four hours, and that the temperature had been as low as 17°. In accordance with the Public Service Law (§60-a, subd. 1), the court charged that it was the duty of defendant to furnish a reasonable amount of heat in the bus. Upon the established facts the jury had the right to find that defendant had failed to furnish a reasonable amount of heat to plaintiff, in consequence of which she had suffered frostbite. The complaint should not have been dismissed upon the ground that as matter of law her injuries did not come within the realm of reasonable foreseeability. A new trial should be granted.

2. There was also evidence that plaintiff was more susceptible to frostbite than the average person would be because she had been born with a heart condition which affected her circulatory system. However, both plaintiff and her mother stated that they did not know of this susceptibility, and the trial court made no reference thereto in its charge and did not state that the passenger should be deemed an abnormal person. In the absence of requests or exceptions, this charge became the law of the case. The only question presented to the jury, other than the issue of contributory negligence and damage, was whether defendant had been negligent in failing to furnish reasonable heat, and, if so, whether such failure had caused the injuries.

3. It is foreseeable by a common carrier that many people are subject to low blood pressure and poor circulation.

4. The court may take judicial notice of said rule of the Public Service Commission (Civ. Prac. Act. §344-a, subd. 4).

Owen v. Rochester-Penfield Bus. Co., 278 App. Div. 5 reversed.

APPEAL from a judgment in favor of defendant, entered April 9, 1951, upon an order of the Appellate Division of the Supreme Court in the third judicial department, which (1) reversed, on the law and facts, a judgment of the Supreme Court in favor of plaintiff, entered in Schuyler County upon a verdict rendered at a Trial and Special Term (HEATH, J.), and (2) dismissed the complaint.

Asbury H. Harpending for appellant. I. There is ample proof of negligence in the record to support the jury's finding that defendant violated its duty to plaintiff as a passenger as such duty was properly defined by the trial court. (Imbrey v. Prudential Ins. Co., 286 N.Y. 434; Kulch v. Kulch, 271 App. Div. 840; Walldorf v. Central Greyhound Lines, 256 App. Div. 854, 280 N.Y. 725.) II. The negligence of defendant having been established under the law of the case and to the satisfaction of the jury, defendant is liable to plaintiff for the injuries she sustained and the verdict is supported by the evidence. (Davis v. New York Central R. R. Co., 163 Misc. 710; Campbell v. Pullman Co., 182 App. Div. 931; Killeen v. U. S. Lines Operations 234 App. Div. 789; Poplar v. Bourjois, Inc., 298 N. Y. 62; McCahill v. New York Transp. Co., 201 N. Y. 221; Lang v. Stadium Purchasing Corp., 216 App. Div. 558.)

Austin W. Erwin and Austin W. Erwin, Jr., for respondent. I. There is no proof in the record of any negligence upon the part of defendant. (Churchill v. United Fruit Co., 294 F. 400; Laitenburger v. State of New York, 190 Misc. 633; Lane v. City of Buffalo, 232 App. Div. 334; Trapp v. McClellan, 68 App. Div. 362; Kingsland v. Erie Co. Agric. Soc. 298 N.Y.

409, Nuss v. State of New York, 195 Misc., 38; Radin v. State of New York, 192 Misc. 247; Payne v. City of New York, 277 N.Y. 393; Palsgraf v. Long Island R.R. Co., 248 N.Y. 339.) II. Recovery is allowed in cases of this type only where a dangerous condition due to weather is coupled with actual negligence on the part of the carrier. (Atlantic Coast Line v. Powell, 127 Ga. 805; Humphrey v. Stokes Bus Line, 199 S.C. 132; Ziccolillo v. Oregon Short Line R. Co., 53 Utah 39; Southern Pacific Co. v. Bunting, 54 Ariz. 180.)

FROESSEL, J. A jury has awarded plaintiff the sum of $5,000 by way of damages to compensate her for having suffered a severe frostbite of both feet. She claims these injuries were sustained as a result of defendant's negligence in failing properly to heat its bus while she was a passenger. The Appellate Division unanimously reversed the judgment on the law and facts and dismissed the complaint. In this state of the record, plaintiff is entitled to the benefit of every favorable inference which can reasonably be drawn from facts proven (De-Wald v. Seidenberg, 297 N.Y. 335, 336, 337; Betzag v. Gulf Oil Corp., 298 N.Y. 358).

Thus viewed, the jury had the right to find the following facts:

Plaintiff, then eighteen years of age, was a student at the Rochester Institute of Technology. She returned to her parents' home in the town of Tyrone, New York, where she remained over the 1946 Thanksgiving holidays. On Sunday evening, December 1st, she, together with her sister and brother-in-law, were driven to Bath, New York, in a heated car to catch a bus for Rochester leaving at 6:10 P.M. The bus was "very cold," "extremely cold," "awfully cold," not only for plaintiff but for her sister and brother-in-law as well, and for other passengers, who complained to the bus driver; he replied that the heater was out of order. In the course of the trip, he stopped to investigate an accident, during which time he left the bus door open for fifteen minutes. Plaintiff's feet became numb during the trip, and, after four hours of such exposure, she discovered on returning to her dormitory in Rochester that she had frozen feet. The jury also had the right to find, from evidence given by one Williams in charge of the United States Weather Bureau, that the temperature in Rochester during this period had descended to as low as 17°, and that it must have been freezing temperature or below in the bus in the light of a physician's testimony that no one could get frozen feet above 32°.

The evidence also disclosed that plaintiff was born with a heart condition that affected her circulatory system in such a manner as to make her more susceptible to frostbite than the average person, though both plaintiff and her mother stated they did not know of this susceptibility. Plaintiff had never had frostbite before. Her mother stated that they had ignored the heart condition; on medical advice she reared plaintiff with the other children; and plaintiff knew nothing whatever about it.

The Appellate Division took the view that as a matter of law defendant was not liable, inasmuch as plaintiff's poor circulation, attributable to the heart condition, rendered her more susceptible to frostbite than a person in normal health, and therefore her injuries did not come within the realm of reasonable foreseeability.

We do not agree with this view here. The trial court told the jury that it was the duty of defendant to furnish reasonable heat in its bus, and in that regard charged subdivision 1 of section 60-a of the Public Service Law, which reads in part as follows: "Every omnibus corporation shall furnish and provide with respect thereto, such services and facilities as shall be safe and adequate and in all respects just and reasonable." Under subdivision 4 of section 344-a of the Civil Practice Act we may take judicial notice of the then effective Public Service Commission rule adopted pursuant to subdivision 14 of section 61 of the Public Service Law: "23. Heating: Each omnibus shall be heated when reasonably required for the comfort and safety of passengers."

After pointing up the dispute between the parties and reviewing the evidence, the court further charged that the "test here is *** whether or not this bus company failed to furnish reasonable heat to the plaintiff or whether or not it did." Thus she was not deemed an abnormal person, and the court made no reference thereto in its charge. No requests were made or exceptions taken to this or any other part of the court's charge by either counsel, each one stating: "No requests or exceptions." Under these circumstances, the charge became the law of the case (Imbrey v. Prudential Ins. Co., 286 N.Y. 434, 440.)

Thus, without objection by either side, the only question presented to the jury, besides the issue of contributory negligence and damage, was whether defendant was negligent in failing to furnish reasonable heat, and if so whether that caused plaintiff's injuries. It is common knowledge that many people are subject to low blood pressure and poor circulation, and certainly this is foreseeable by a common carrier. We have held that "a defendant is chargeable for all the harm and suffering which his negligent act brought on even though the plaintiff's injuries were aggravated by his own predisposition or weakness (citing cases.)" Poplar v. Bourjois, Inc., 298 N.Y. 62, 67-68.) The jury here had the right to find upon the above-recited facts that defendant failed to furnish reasonable heat to plaintiff, in consequence of which she suffered frostbite.

In the circumstances disclosed, we cannot say as a matter of law, as did the Appellate Division, that plaintiff's injuries did not come within the realm of reasonable foreseeability.

The judgment should be reversed and a new trial granted, with costs to abide the event.

LOUGHRAN, Ch. J., LEWIS, CONWAY, DESMOND, DYKE and FULD, JJ., concur.

Judgments reversed, etc.

---

§1.3 How to Brief a Case

(Outline of a Brief of the Case)

MARY JANE L. OWEN, Appellant v. ROCHESTER-PENFIELD BUS COMPANY, INC., Repondent (1952) 304 NY 457, r278 AD 5, 103 S2d 137

PRINCIPLES: (1) The duty of a carrier to furnish a reasonable degree of heat for its passengers in its bus includes, as being reasonably foreseeable, a passenger subject to low blood pressure and poor circulation and more susceptible to frostbite than a person in normal health.

(2) The court's charge to the jury, not differentiating plaintiff as an abnormal person to which no objection is made by counsel, becomes the law of the case so that the verdict is valid when the facts are otherwise sufficient to support it.

FACTS: Plaintiff: Mary Jane Litteer Owen was a passenger on defendant's bus from Bath, N.Y., to Rochester, N.Y., in the evening on Sunday, Dec. 1, 1946, and the bus not being heated she suffered frostbite in her feet.

C/A (Cause of Action): To recover damages for personal injuries by reason of the defendant's negligence in failing to heat the bus.

Remedy: Action under N. Y. law (Civil Practice Act) for a judgment for damages. Court's charge to the jury did not differentiate plaintiff from a normal person as to blood pressure and susceptibility to frostbite.

Defendant: Rochester-Penfield Bus Company, Inc., a corporation operating a bus line between Bath, N.Y., and Rochester, N.Y., subject to the regulations of the Public Service Commission of N.Y., on whose bus plaintiff was riding when injuries were suffered.

Defense (or Motion or Demurrer): Answer alleged general denial and the evidence showed that the plaintiff suffered from chronic heart condition causing poor circulation and that normal persons did not suffer frostbite since 40 other passengers were on the bus but only plaintiff suffered frostbite.

LOWER COURTS: In trial court plaintiff obtained verdict and judgment for $5,000. Defendant moved to set aside the verdict but motion was denied and defendant appealed.

The Appellate Division (3rd Dept.) reversed on the ground that as a matter of law defendant was not liabile, inasmuch as plaintiff's poor circulation, attributable to the heart condition, rendered her more suceptible to frostbite than a person in normal health, and therefore her injuries did not come within the realm of reasonable foreseeability; plaintiff appealed.

ISSUES: (1) Does the duty of a carrier to furnish a reasonable degree of heat for its passengers in its bus include, as being reasonably foreseeable, a passenger subject to low blood pressure and poor circulation and more susceptible to frostbite than a person in normal health?

(2) Does a court's charge to a jury, not differentiating plaintiff as an abnormal person to which no objection is made by counsel, become the law of the case so that the verdict is valid when the facts otherwise are sufficient to support it?

HELD: (1) Yes (2) Yes — Reversed and new trial granted.

REASONS: A. (1) Defendant had the duty under §60-a of the Public Service Law to furnish "services and facilities as shall be safe and adequate and in all respects just and reasonable." Under §344-a, Subd. 4 of Civil Practice Act court took judicial notice of Rule 23 of Public Service Commission requiring "each omnibus shall be heated when reasonably required for comfort and safety of passengers."

(2) It is common knowledge that many persons are subject to low blood pressure and poor circulation which is foreseeable by a common carrier.

(3) A defendant is chargeable for all the harm and suffering which his negligent act brought on even though the plaintiff's injuries were aggravated by his own predisposition or weakness, citing: Poplar v Bourjois, Inc., 298 NY 62, 67-68.

Consequently, defendant's duty included plaintiff.

B. After pointing up the dispute and reviewing the evidence the court charged: "the test here is ... whether or not this bus company failed to furnish reasonable heat to plaintiff or whether or not it did." Plaintiff was not deemed an abnormal person and attorneys made no requests or exceptions to this or any other part of court's charge but stated they had no requests or exceptions so the charge became the law of the case, citing: Imbrey v Prudential Ins. Co., 286 NY 434, 440.

Consequently, the jury had the right to find upon the facts that defendant failed to furnish reasonable heat to plaintiff and as a result she suffered frostbite.

CONTRA: (1) Defendant was not informed of plaintiff's abnormal condition.

(2) There were 40 other passengers on the bus and only plaintiff suffered frostbite.

(3) Plaintiff's poor circulation was attributable to her heart condition and rendered her more susceptible to frostbite than a person in normal health and consequently her injuries were not reasonably foreseeable by the defendant, as held by the Appellate Division.

CLASS NOTES

CHAPTER II

THE SUBSTANTIVE LAW

OUTLINE OF CHAPTER II:

Introductory Concepts
Substantive Law vis-a-vis Adjective Law
Common Law, Equity, and Statutory Law

Sec. 2.1 Elements of a Cause of Action
Sec. 2.2 Examples of Causes of Action
Sec. 2.3 Evolution of a Cause of Action
Sec. 2.4 Analysis of a Cause of Action
Sec. 2.5 Nature of a Defense
Sec. 2.6 Juridical Persons and Their Substantive Law Capacities for Legal Interests: Rights and Duties

SUGGESTED READINGS:

Bowman: Elementary Law
Ch. 5 "The Subject-Matter of Law" pp 75-94
Ch. 6 "The Subject-Matter of Law (cont'd)" pp 95-110
Ch. 7 "The Divisions of Law" pp 111-124
Griffith: Outlines of the Law
Ch's II - XVIII (generally on substantive law) pp 4-566
Holdsworth: History of English Law
V's 4-9, "The Common Law and Its Rivals"
Kinnane: Anglo-American Law
Ch. XIX Sec's 181-182, pp 521-528
Maitland: "History of the Register of Original Writs"
3 Har. L.R., pp 97-115; 167-179; 212-225
2 Select Essays in Anglo-American Legal History, pp 549-596 (reprint)
Morgan: Study of Law
Ch. III "Main Topics of the Law" pp 50-56
Plucknett: History of the Common Law
Book II, Parts II-V, pp 392-635
Pollock and Maitland: History of English Law
Vol. II, Ch's IV-VIII (generally on substantive law)
Radin: Anglo-American Legal History
Ch's 21-35 (generally on substantive law)
Smith: Elementary Law
Ch's 8-20 (generally on substantive law) pp 95-340

Sec. 2.1 Elements of a Cause of Action, General Categories of the
Sec. 2.11 Legal Interest of Plaintiff (property, personal, or contract)
Sec. 2.12 Conditions Fulfilled as to the Cause of Action, such as
- a. Performance by Plaintiff of Conditions Precedent (if any)
- b. Demand, if necessary, by Plaintiff that Defendant Perform
- c. (other conditions, if any)

Sec. 2.13 Breach of Duty by Defendant, including when necessary
- a. Acts and Words of Defendant
- b. State of Mind of Defendant
- c. Refusal to Perform upon Plaintiff's Demand
- d. Injury to Plaintiff (loss or deprivation as to his legal interest)
- e. Legal Causation (defendant's breach as the legal cause, direct or proximate, of plaintiff's injury)
- f. Other required factors, if any

Sec. 2.14 Right to Relief
- a. to recover damages, or
- b. to recover possession of a chattel, or
- c. to recover possession of real property, or
- d. to have specific performance of a contract
- e. and others

Sec 2.1 Elements of a Cause of Action, General Categories of the
Sec. 2.11 Legal Interest of Plaintiff (property, personal, or contract)

ELTERMAN, Appellant v HYMAN, Respondent (1908) 192 NY 113, r117 AD 519

APPEAL from a judgement of the Appellate Division of the Supreme Court in the first judicial department, entered February 14, 1907, affirming a judgment in favor of defendant entered upon a dismissal of the complaint by the court on trial at Special Term.

This action was brought to recover the amount paid upon a contract for the purchase of land as well as the amount incurred for expenses in examining the title and to establish and enforce a lien therefor upon the ground that the plaintiff was ready and willing to perform while the defendant was not because the title was unmarketable. The answer admitted the contract and the payment made thereon, but denied the remaining allegations of the complaint. It alleged facts constituting a counterclaim and asked that the plaintiff be adjudged to specifically perform by paying the balance of the purchase price.

VANN, J. .... It is clear, therefore, that the facts found no not support the conclusion of law that the defendant "was in a position to convey to the plaintiff a good and marketable title to said premises in accordance with the terms of said contract." The question remains whether a vendee, not in possession and with no special equity, has a lien for the amount paid on a contract for the purchase of land that can be foreclosed upon the default of the vendor? The Appellate Division in the first department, after thorough discussion, two elaborate opinions having been written, one on either side, has held that a lien exists for the amount paid on the contract, but not for the expense of examining the title. (Occidental Realty Co.

v Palmer, 117 AD 505. The rule in the second department is that no lien exists even for the purchase money paid down, unless the vendee has taken possession. (Kilm v Sachs, 102 AD 44.) The subject was not considered at length in the case last cited, only three sentences being devoted to it; and while the judgement was modified by striking out the part giving a lien, it was affirmed as to the recovery of the sum paid on the contract although the action was in equity. This case was followed without discussion by the same court in Krainin v Coffey, (119 AD 516).

The right of a vendor to a lien for the purchase money unpaid is well established, and the courts of this state have uniformly recognized the right of a vendee to a lien when he was in possession, or had made improvements, or where special equities intervened. (Parks v Jackson, 11 Wend-(NY)442; Chase v Peck, 21 NY 581; Gilbert v Peteler, 38 NY 165 ...) In some cases in this state and generally other states which give a lien to the vendor, a lien has been decreed although there was no equity except that arising from payment on the land, pursuant to a contract for the land, provided the vendor made default. (Occidental Realty Co. v Palmer, supra...)

The question does not appear to have been before the Supreme Court of the United States, although it has declared that "the vendor is a trustee of the legal title for the vendee to the extent of his payments." (Jennisons v Leonard, 21 Wall(US) 302, 309.)

We find no well-considered case in any state that denies a lien to the vendee, even if payment is the only ground therefor, except such as withhold a lien from the vendor also. (Ahrend v Odiorne, 118 Mass 261...). The doctrine is well established in England where it is sometimes said to have originated as recently as 1855, but it was clearly announced nearly twenty years before the Revolutionary War by a court of which Lord Mansfield was a member. (Burgess v Wheate, 1 W. Blacks. 123, 150.) It was recognized by Lord St. Leonards in the first edition of his great work on Vendors and Purchasers, published in 1805 (p. 671), and three years later by Lord Eldon in Mackreth v Symmons, (15 Vesey, Jr. 329, 344). In 1855, however, the question arose directly and although the vendee was not in possession and there was no special equity in his favor he was held to have a lien both upon principle and authority. (Wythes v Lee, 3 Drewry's Ch. 396, 403).

In 1864 the question was fully discussed in the House of Lords and it was adjudged without dissent that the vendee has a lien, because every payment by him is pro tanto performance of the contract on his part and in equity transfers to him a corresponding portion of the estate. (Rose v Watson, 10 H.L. Cas. 672). The Lord chancellor in delivering the leading opinion said: "When the owner of an estate contracts with a purchaser for the immediate sale of it, the ownership of the estate is, in equity, transferred by that contract. Where the contract undoubtedly is an executory contract, in this sense, namely, that the ownership of the estate is transferred, subject to the payment of the purchase money, every portion of the purchase money paid in pursuance of that contract is a part performance and execution of the contract, and, to the extent of the purchase money so paid, does in equity, finally transfer to the purchaser the ownership of a corresponding portion of the estate. * * * In conformity, therefore, with every principle, the purchaser paying the money acquired an interest in the estate by force of the contract and of that part performance of the contract, namely, the payment of that portion of the purchase money. * * * It cannot be contested in this case that although the contract has failed of being performed completely, that failure of performance is attributable entirely to the vendor. * * * It has been contended at the bar, in words, that the contract has been rejected by the purchaser, and that, therefore, the purchaser ought not to have the benefit of lien, that is, of that partial ownership, that interest in the estate which is due to the purchase money which he has paid. It is quite a mistake and a misapplication of the word to say that the purchaser has rejected the contract, or put an end to the contract. The purchaser would have been willing to perform that contract if the vendor had performed those things which, in good faith, he was bound to do. And it is impossible to say, with any truth or accuracy of expression, that the purchaser has repudiated the contract, because the vendor has failed to redeem his own promise to which he had pledged his faith and in dependence upon which the purchaser entered into the contract."

LORD CRANWORTH, who delivered the other opinion, concurred with the Lord chancellor and added: "There can be no doubt, I apprehend, that when a purchaser has paid his purchase money, though he has got no conveyance, the vendor becomes a trustee for him of the legal estate and he is in equity considered as the owner of the estate. When, instead of paying the whole of his purchase money, he pays a part of it, it would seem to follow as a necessary corollary, that, to the extent to which he has paid his purchase money to that extent the vendor is a trustee for him; in other words, that he acquires a lien exactly in the same way as if upon the payment of part of the purchase money the vendor executed a mortgage to him of the estate to that extent."

Quite recently a case arose in the Chancery Division of the Court of Appeal where a contract for the purchase of land authorized the purchaser to rescind on the happening of a specified event and in due exercise of the power he rescinded the contract, but it was held that he had a lien on the land for the deposit which he had made. (Whitbread & Co., Limited v Watt, LR (1 Ch Div 1902) 835.)

In the case last cited the lien is spoken of as the invention of equity for the purpose of doing justice, but this is the foundation of all equitable liens. They did not exist at common law, but were created by courts of equity because required by natural equity. They do not depend upon express contract, but on the principle that one person has the legal title to something that another person has a natural and, hence, within well-guarded limits, a better right to, or to some part thereof.

In Rose v Watson and Whitbread & Co., Limited v Watt the vendor was insolvent, but in neither case did the decision turn on that fact, which apparently was regarded as of no importance.

The elementary writers from Sugden, who wrote more than a century ago with almost the force of judicial authority, to the latest authors, announce as an established rule that the lien exists in favor of a purchaser, if the vendor cannot make a title, even if there are no extraneous equities. (Sugden's, Vendors & Purchasers (1st ed.), 671.) In an edition, written fifty years later after the learned author had become Lord St. Leonards, he was more elaborate in statement and, among other things, said: "A deposit is part payment. Therefore, part payment to that extent constitutes the purchaser actually owner of the estate; consequently of the contract does not proceed without the fault of the purchaser, the seller, to recover the equitable ownership, must repay the deposit, which, representing a portion of the interest in the property, is a lien upon it." (Id. (13th ed.) 672.)

Judge Story, writing in 1835, declared "that from the time of the contract for the sale of the land the vendor, as to the land, becomes a trustee for the vendee, and the vendee, as to the purchase money, a trustee for the vendor, who has a lien upon the land therefor." Mr. Bigelow, the learned editor of the eighth American edition, adds in a note: "In the view of a court of equity the payment of the purchase money may well be deemed a loan upon the security of the land until it has been conveyed to the vendee. At least there is quite as much reason to presume it as there is to presume the land, when conveyed, to be still a security for the purchase money due to the vendor. In the latter case, though there is a debt due by the vendee, it does not follow that it is a debt due by the land. In the former, if the estate cannot be conveyed and is not conveyed, the money is really a debt due to the vendee. At all events in equity it is not very clear what principle is impugned by deeming the money a lien upon the ground of presumed intention." (2 Story's Eq. Jur. (8th Am. ed.) Sec. 789, 1217, note.)

Mr. Pomeroy, who ranks as an author with Judge Story, wrote: "The lien of the vendee under a contract for purchase of land for the purchase money paid by him before a conveyance is the exact counterpart of the grantor's--or, as it is commonly called, the vendor's--lien, described in the last section but one. In the latter case the legal title has been conveyed to the grantee, and yet the grantor retains an equitable lien upon the land as security for the purchase price agreed to be paid. In the former case the legal title remains in the vendor who has simply agreed to convey, while the vendee, although having as yet acquired no legal interest in the land by virtue of the contract does obtain a lien upon it as security for the purchase money he has paid and for the performance of the vendor's obligation to convey. In England, therefore, and in the American states where the grantor's lien has been adopted, the vendee's lien upon the lands contracted to be sold as a security for so much of the purchase price as he has paid prior to a conveyance and for the performace by the vendor of his obligation, exists to the same extent against the same classes of persons and is governed by the same rules as the corresponding lien of the grantor. The lien only arises, of course, when the vendor is in some default for not completing the contract according to its terms and the vendee is not in default so as to prevent him from recovering the purchase money paid." (3 Pomeroy's, Eq. Jur. (3rd ed.) Sec. 1263.)....

Whether the foundation of the lien is natural equity, imputed intention, partial ownership, the implication of a trust, or a blending of some of these sources, the authorities, almost without exception in those jurisdictions which give a lien to the vendor, are clear that one exists. As the vendor has a lien because he owned the the land but conveyed prematurely and the vendee ought not to keep it without paying for it, so, as it seems to me, the vendee has a lien because he has paid for the land pursuant to contract, and as he cannot get the land, he has a right to get out what he put in on the faith of the land. The lien springs from the trust under which the vendor, as the legal owner, holds the land for the vendee, the equitable owner. Part Payment creates partial ownership, and the vendee has an interest in the land itself to the extent of the payments made thereon. The contract and payment in full make him the equitable owner of all the land. The contract and payment in part make him the equitable owner pro tanto. When the vendor cannot convey, the equitable owner, wholly or in part, may assert his rights in a court of equity to get out of the land what he paid on it. If the vendor is not the absolute owner, the lien of the vendee "exists only to the extent of the vendor's interest," which in this case is only that of a sub-purchaser. (Aberaman Iron Works v Wickens, L.R. (4 ChApp.) 101; Fry on Specific Performance (3rd Am. ed.), 660.) The right is correlative to that of the vendor conveying without payment. In either case the res, or the subject of the contract, is the land, and whatever is paid on the land without corresponding conveyance, or conveyed without corresponding payment, is a lien on the land by virtue of parting with money on the faith of the land, or with land on the faith of the promise to pay for it. Payment is not made on the credit of the vendor, but on the credit of the land, and the purchaser's money, in equity, is converted into land, or attached to it as a lien. The equitable ownership, when specific performance cannot be had, is converted into money by a judicial sale of the vendor's interest, which in effect is the foreclosure of an equitable mortgage.

It is insisted that the whole agreement is to be taken together and completely performed or wholly rescinded, and that resicission by the vendee destroys the contract in toto and ab initio. The same argument was urged by counsel in Rose v Watson, and the complete answer of LORD WESTBURY has already been quoted. None of the authorities relating to the lien of a vendee, and we have cited but few out of many, seem to regard the doctrine of rescission as at all applicable to the subject. This is not an action at law resting on rescission by which an election is made to declare the contract void in its inception, but a suit in equity resting on the equitable principle that the vendee by the contract and payment acquired an interest in the land. Rescission was neither alleged nor found and as the affirmance was unanimous we cannot look into the evidence for further facts. The vendee does not elect to nullify the contract nor seek remission to his original rights when he asserts his acquired rights, depending wholly on the contract and his action thereunder. He recognizes the contract as a subsisting obligation, valid in its inception and still in force, and founds his entire claim for relief on the theory that because it is valid and he has made payments on it as required by it, he has become an owner of the land in equity to the extent of such payments. He accepts "the situation which the wrongdoing of the other party has brought about," and tries to get out of the land what he paid on it under the contract. The termination of a contract as to the future by one party owing to the default of the other is a rescission neither ab initio, nor in any true sense. (Hurst v Trow P. & B. Co., 2, 361, 366; 142 NY 637.) If it were, it would involve the surrender of possession taken pursuant to a provision authorizing it and the abandonment of all improvements made while in possession. The vendee does not rescind when without fault he goes into a court of equity and insists on a right springing from the contract and payment thereon pursuant to its terms. He does not repudiate the contract, but stands on it and affirms it as the foundation of the right he seeks to enforce, as fully as if he sought entire specific performance. He does not abandon his ownership by trying to assert it in the only way that it can be asserted. The contract has been performed by him, wholly it may be, or in part, as in the case before us, and as, owing to the fault of the vendor, he cannot have the full performance to which he is entitled, he asks for partial performance by the enforcement of the trust created by the contract and payment as provided thereby. He does not sue for money had and received, but to enforce a lien on land into which the money went. Nor does he rescind the contract, which is the source of his lien, but seeking to enforce it to the only extent now possible, owing to the breach by the vendor, but he demands that equity should give him the interest in the land that he acquired by the contract and payment. The denial of that right would be an encouragement to wrongdoing, and to hold that an attempt to foreclose the equitable lien is a rescission of the contract would deny the right in all cases, including those in which the vendee is in possession and has made improvements.

The analogy of personal property is suggested and it is argued that the purchaser may pay on potatoes the same as on land, but the rules applicable to real estate, which, as part of the soil earth, is immovable and indestructible, have never been applied and in the nature of things cannot be applied to movable property that can disappear in a moment, can be delivered from hand to hand and which usually is paid for on delivery. The anology, if logically and universally applied, would destroy many of the rules of equity, established after centuries of earnest thought by the most learned lawyers known to jurisprudence.

The judgement appealed from should be reversed and a new trial granted, with costs to abide the event.

....WILLARD BARTLETT, J., dissents solely on the ground that no action is maintainable to enforce a vendee's lien.

Judgment reversed, etc.

TAYLOR v KEEFE (1947) 134 Conn 156, 56 A2d 768

BROWN, J. This is an action on behalf of a minor son to recover of the defendant for the alienation of his mother's affections. The trial court sustained the defendant's demurrer to the complaint and, upon the plaintiff's failure to plead further, entered judgment for the defendant, from which the plaintiff has appealed. The following facts stand admitted upon the demurrer. For many years the plaintiff had been living happily with his mother. In 1943 the defendant by his arts, blandishments and seductions alienated her love and affection and destroyed the happiness of the plaintiff's home. In consequence, the plaintiff has suffered great distress of body and mind and has lost the love, affection and society of his mother. As a further result, he has lost much happiness, has been forced out of the home which he had with his mother, and has been denied her social and moral support, guidance and protection. It is also conceded that the plaintiff's father and mother are divorced and that custody of the plaintiff as a minor was awarded to the mother.

The sole question for determination is whether a minor child can maintain an action for alienation of affections against one who has alienated from him the affections of his mother. The question has never been passed upon by this court, and no appellate court of last resort has recognized a cause of action in the plaintiff under such circumstances. There appear to be but three reported decisions in which the question has been ruled upon. In two of these, relief was granted where a father's affections had been alienated, and in the other it was denied where those of a mother were in question. The plaintiff contends that although this court has never recognized such a cause of action the time has now come when it should do so. The defendant takes the position that a child's right to his mother's affection is a natural right only, as distinguished from the legal right which a spouse has to the love and affection of his mate by virtue of the marriage contract, and that the practical difficulties of extending the protection of the law to the former are the reason why courts have not recognized and should not recognize a right in the plaintiff to the relief which he seeks.

In considering the nature of the mutual right of husband and wife to enjoy the love and affection of the other, we have said: "The gist of an action for alienation of affections is the loss of consortium. 'This is a property right growing out of the marriage relation and includes the exclusive right to the services of the spouse, and these contemplate not so much wages or reward earned as assistance and helpfulness in the relations of conjugal life according to their station and the exclusive right to the society, companionship, and conjugal affection of each other.' Valentine v Pollak, 95 Conn 556, 561, 111 A 869, 872." Maggay v Nikitko, 117 Conn 206, 208, 167 A 816, 817. The concrete inquiry is whether, under the present conception of the family relationship, a minor child's natural right to the love and affection of his mother should be accorded by the law the same protection as a husband's or wife's property right of consortium. The nature of the question is well set forth in the editorial comment in 162 American Law Reports 825, where it is pointed out that the underlying problem is, in its last analysis, a sociological rather than a legal one; that a child has an interest in his parent's affection and company which the courts under our system of law have the power to "legalize" by recognizing a right of action for its protection; but that the vital query is whether it is wise for the courts to exercise their power of lawmaking in this particular instance.

Of the two decisions chiefly relied upon by the plaintiff, one is the case of Daily v Parker, 152 F2d 174, 162 ALR 819, decided by the Circuit Court of Appeals, Seventh Circuit, in 1945. There, four minor children sued a married woman for enticing their father to leave them and their home and go to live with her and to refuse to contribute further for their maintenance and support. The court, 152 F2d at page 177, held "that a child today has a right enforceable in a court of law, against one who has invaded and taken from said child the support and maintenance of its father, as well as damages for the destruction of other rights which arise out of the family relationship and which have been destroyed or defeated by a wrongdoing third party." The court, in the words of the American Law Reports note, supra, "based its conclusion on the change in the accepted view of the status of the wife and the children and their rights and obligations as members of the family, which, according to the court, lead from the old concept of the husband and father as the lord and master of his family to the recognition in modern times of mutual rights and obligations possessed by all the members of the family."

In the other case, Johnson v Luhman, 330 IllApp 598, 71 NE2d 810, five minor children sued a woman for alienating the affections of their father and depriving them of his support and society, including their rights to his paternal care and to the security of a family life. In upholding the right of action in the plaintiffs, the court cited with approval the reasoning and decision in the Daily case, decided a few months earlier. Referring to the change that has taken place in the conception of the family, it pointed out (330 IllApp at page 604, 71 NE2d at page 813) that under the early common law "The father spoke and acted for the family unit and the individual members thereof with no distinct identity. Hence, it was stated in 3 Blackstone's Commentaries 143 (1765), 'The child hath no property in his father.' It is common knowledge, however, that a transition has taken place in our conception of the family, and in the law which reflects, in a measure, our social standards. The family is now a cooperative enterprise with correlative rights and duties among all members thereof. * * * The children * * * are presently regarded more as responsible individuals than as subservient charges * * * they are entitled to both the tangible incidents of family life, such as food, clothing and shelter, and to the intangible, though equally significant elements of affection, moral support, and guidance from both of the parents." The court concluded that the nature of the present-day status of the child, so described, gave rise to a right in the plaintiff warranting the creation of the remedy sought, even though unsupported by binding precedent, since the defendant's conduct had destroyed "the children's family unit * * * and deprived them of * * * the security afforded by (their father's) affection and presence."

Morrow v Yannantuono, (152 M 134, 273 S 912) reaches a contrary result. In that case the infant plaintiff sued the male defendant for wrongfully depriving him of the affection, comfort and love of his mother by enticing her away and harboring her. The court, after stating the plaintiff's claim that, inasmuch as the family is a legal unit, when another by his wrongful act interferes with such unit each member sustains an injury for which he has a cause of action, pointed out the distinction between the claimed cause of action and that which a husband or wife has for the loss of consortium predicated on the marriage contract, and ruled that the plaintiff had stated no valid cause of action. Referring to the practical danger of holding to the contrary, the court said (152 M at page 135, 273 S at page 914): "I am convinced that to uphold this complaint would open our courts to a flood of litigation that would inundate them. It would mean that everyone whose cheek is tinged by the blush of shame would rush into court to ask punitive damages to compensate them for their distress of body and mind and the damage that their reputation suffered in the community." While the validity of the court's "so-called practical reasons" has been challenged (20 Corn. LQ 255), it has been cogently suggested that, notwithstanding there seems no theoretical reason for denying the relief claimed on the basis of a child's right to the "consortium" of his parents, "numerous practical obstructions * * * inhibit application of this reasoning." (83 U of Pa LR 276.) Among the difficulties enumerated are (1) possibility of a multiplicity of suits; (2) possibility of extortionary litigation by virtue of the relative tenuousness of the child's relationship; (3) inability to define the point at which the child's right would cease, inasmuch as the status itself hypothesizes mutability, for although a spouse is, barring extraordinary circumstances, always a spouse, the very nature of childhood implies an eventual change to adulthood; and (4) the inability of a jury to cope with the question of damages, particularly because damages thus asserted are apt to overlap, in view of the number and different ages of the children.

These difficulties suggest persuasive reason why as a matter of policy this court should not recognize the validity of the cause of action claimed. Reference to a specific situation may serve to illustrate the practical difficulty of carrying the "family unit" theory to its logical conclusion. Under it, the parent would have the same right of action for the alienation of the affection of the child which the plaintiff here claims for the alienation of that of his parent. Yet the marriage of a child might well give rise to a factual situation which a parent could utilize as the basis of an action against the child's spouse for alienating the child's affections. Such a possibility emphasizes the real distinction between permitting such an action in a case dependent upon the relationship of husband and wife, who have voluntarily created the unit status "for better or for worse" for life, and permitting it in a case dependent upon the relationship of parent and child, where in the course of nature the child is likely to substitute in large part for the family unit of the parents a family unit of his own. This distinction makes clear why the case of Foot v Card, (58 Conn 11, 18 A 1027...) does not constitute a controlling precedent for recognizing a cause of action in the present case. In that case the court recognized a cause of action not previously given judicial sanction and, having done so, held that the law would attach a remedy to it and afford relief to a wife for the alienation of her husband's affections. An action brought by a parent upon the facts suggested above would require a very careful differentiation of factual situations and strict limitation upon the granting of relief, if such a cause of action were allowed.

Our decision accords with the view expressed by the only authoritative writer who to our knowledge has specifically dealt with the subject (Prosser, Torts (1941 Ed.) p. 937); and it is worthy of note that the American Law Institute, Restatement of Torts, makes no mention of such right in the child and expressly negatives (3 Torts #699) liability to the parent for alienation of a child's affections. (See also Pyle v Waechter, 202 Iowa 695, 210 NW 926...) The following facts also tend to confirm our conclusion. First, so far as appears, only in the three cases mentioned has such a claim for relief ever been urged upon any court. Second, since 1935 at least twelve states, including our neighbors Massachusetts and New York, have by statute taken away the right of a husband or wife to bring an action for alienation of affections. (Keezer, Marriage and Divorce, 3d Ed., #191.) The former fact indicates the absence of any need for such relief sufficiently general to induce the bar to press for its recognition by the courts. The latter suggests widespread appreciation of the fact that the special advantages of granting the right claimed would be outweighed by the disadvantages. (See Fearon v Treanor, 272 NY 268, 273, 5 NE2d 815...) The refusal by the court to grant it does not violate article first, #12,, of the Connecticut constitution, guaranteeing redress "for an injury done" to the plaintiff for "injury" as there used means a legal injury, that is, one violative of established law of which a court can properly take cognizance. A like provision of the Montana constitution was so construed by its court (Stewart v Standard Publishing Co., 102 Mont 43, 49, 55 P2d 694); as was a similar provision in the constitution of Pennsylvania by its court in Jackson v Rosenbaum Co. (263 Pa 158, 168, 106 A 238).

There is no error.

In this opinion, the other Judges concurred.

BINGHAM v BOARD OF EDUCATION OF OGDEN CITY (1950) 118 Utah 582, 223 P2d 432

LATIMER, Justice. This is an action brought by Jack T. Bingham, individually and as guardian ad litem of his minor daughter, Marilyn Bingham, against the Board of Education of Ogden City, to recover damages flowing from an accident which injured Marilyn Bingham while she was playing on the school grounds of the Central Junior High School, in Ogden, Utah. The complaint attempts to state two causes of action; the first for injuries received by the minor, and the second reimbursement for hospital and medical expenses paid by the father. A general demurrer to both causes of action was sustained by the lower court, the plaintiffs elected to stand on the allegations of the complaint, and the action was therefore dismissed. On this appeal the parties are referred to as they appeared in the court below.

The material facts pleaded in the complaint are as follows: That the defendant is a body corporate and owns the premises upon which the accident occurred; and on the day of the accident, and for some time prior thereto, the defendant maintained an incinerator for the purpose of burning old books, papers, debris, and other rubbish collected on the school premises; that these materials were deposited in the incinerator located in an unguarded place adjacent to a playground area and were burned at regular periods; that hot debris, embers and ashes were discharged or removed and allowed to accumulate over an area of several feet; that on the day in question the plaintiff, Marilyn Bingham, a child of the age of three years, was riding a tricycle and fell into the burning embers, receiving severe injuries; and that the operation of the incinerator in the dangerous and hazardous manner alleged constituted a nuisance.

The Board of Education of Ogden City is an agency of the State of Utah, created by the legislature. Article X, Section 1, of the Constitution requires the legislature to provide for the establishment and maintenance of a public school system... In accordance with these requirements, the legislature of the State enacted legislation setting up school districts, creating boards of education, prescribing the functions and duties of such boards and granted to them the necessary powers and authority to carry out their required duties. (See Title 75, UCA 1943.)....

It frequently happens that the same act or omission may constitute negligence, and, at the same time, give rise to a nuisance. At times it is most difficult to determine whether an alleged state of facts establishes a nuisance or shows merely a lack of due care. Whether or not the allegations of this complaint picture a condition which in law, is a nuisance or show merely negligent conduct, is a question not free from difficulty. Accordingly, we dispose of the liability of the school board regardless of the characterization of the negligence.

If the facts alleged in this action show ordinary negligence then, under previous statements made by this court, it would appear the demurrer was properly sustained. In the case of Woodcock v Board of Education of Salt Lake City (55 Utah 458, 187 P 181) this court made mention of the lack of liability of a board of education for tort actions......

While law writers, editors and judges have criticized and disapproved the foregoing doctrine of governmental immunity as illogical and unjust, the weight of precedent of decided cases supports the general rule and we prefer not to disregard a principle so well established without statutory authority. We, therefore, adopt the rule of the majority and hold that school boards cannot be held liable for ordinary negligent acts.

Plaintiffs, however, contend that even if we follow the general rule they still have alleged a cause of action, as immunity from tort liability cannot be claimed when the act complained of reaches the level of a nuisance......

The reasons given by most courts in holding boards of education immune from liability for negligence center around the proposition that school boards act in connection with public education as agents or instrumentalities of the state, in the performance of a governmental function, and consequently they partake of the state's sovereignty with respect to tort liability. If this reason be good to relieve boards of education from tort liability, then it should apply with equal force in cases involving personal injury caused by nuisances. The latter may involve mere aggravated or continuous acts, but the right to recover should not be determined by the gradation of negligence or by the adjectives used in the complaint. If the strictness of the rule is to be relaxed in cases of nuisance, and if the schools are to be stripped of immunity, the stripping process should be by legislative enactment and not by court decree....

In the instant case, disposing of papers, rubbish and debris which collect daily on schoolgrounds and in classrooms is reasonably within the scope of the duties imposed upon boards of education by the legislature. The burning of such rubbish and debris is an essential part of the sanitation of the school building and grounds. Since the acts complained of were committed in the performance of a governmental function, the rule of immunity applies, even though the firing of the incinerator was performed in such a negligent manner as may be characterized as maintaining a nuisance. We are aware that the allegations of the complaint portray a tragic and unfortunate case, and we are not without sympathy for the little girl and her father. However, under our constitution, the power to make departments of the state respond in damages for torts rests with the legislature, and without legislative enactment we are unable to impose any liability or obligation upon school districts.

The decision of the trial court is affirmed, costs to respondent......

WOLFE, Justice. I dissent.

The court's opinion states: "While law writers, editors and judges have criticized and disapproved the foregoing doctrine of governmental immunity as illogical and unjust, the weight of precedent of decided cases supports the general rule and we prefer not to disregard a principle so well established without statutory authority. We, therefore, adopt the rule of the majority and hold that school boards cannot be held liable for ordinary negligent acts."

I prefer to regard said principle for the purpose of overruling it. I would not wait for the dim distant future in never never land when the legislature may act. During my six years on the bench, the principle of sovereign immunity and its cousin, non-liability of charitable institutions, specifically of hospitals, has come before this court at various times. We, as well as other courts of last resort, in various jurisdictions have had to face this problem of the principle of non-liability of the state and of municipal and quasi-municipal corporations which are said to have taken on the cloak of sovereignty because of their exercise of governmental functions which, it is claimed, insulates them from the doctrine of respondent superior. We have recognized that the state, which permits an action for damages against its citizens for injuries inflicted by their torts and the torts of their servants committed in the course of or in pursuance of the master's business, should not shield itself behind the immoral and indefensible doctrine that "the king (sovereign) can do no wrong": that neither should the sovereign take refuge in the doctrine that it's own agencies, the courts, must not be allowed to render judgment against their creator. This court, as have other jurisdictions has resorted to various devices to circumvent the injustices on sovereign immunity...:

Certainly we have duty here. There are cases where we are powerless to act because the remedy lies solely with the legislature. But in those cases where we still have control of a rule or doctrine because it was judge made and developed, we may act. Non-action here and "passing" the problem to the legislature is the easy way out. But I do not think it conscienable for us not to lift our hand when to do so would bring the law up to date and furnish remedies long over due opine that if we affirmatively acted, there would be those who would hasten to the legislature to advocate such limitations and conditions that they would be needed to give the state and now exempt bodies opportunity to make timely investigation and to prevent excessive judgments against these public bodies.

RHODES, Respondent v SPERRY & HUTCHINSON CO., Appellant (1908) 193 NY 223, a120 AD 467

Appeal from a judgment of the Appellate Division of the Supreme Court in the second judicial department, entered July 5, 1907, affirming a judgment in favor of plaintiff entered upon a decision of the court on trial at Special Term enjoining the defendant from using pictures or photographs of the plaintiff for purposes of trade or advertising and awarding damages to the plaintiff for injuries sustained by reason of such use of her portrait.

The action was brought under the second section of chapter 132 of the Laws of 1903. That statute reads as follows:

"An Act to prevent the unauthorized use of the name or picture of any person for the purposes of trade (Passed April 6 1903).

"Section 1. A person, firm or corporation that uses for advertising purposes, or for purposes of trade, the name, portrait or picture of any living person without having first obtained the written consent of such person, or, if a minor, of his or her parent or guardian, is guilty of a misdemeanor.

"Section 2. Any person whose name, portrait or picture is used within this State for advertising purposes of trade without the written consent first obtained as above provided may maintain an equitable action in the Supreme Court of this State against the person, firm, or corporation so using his name, portrait or picture, to prevent and restrain the use thereof; and may also sue and recover damages for any injuries sustained by reason of such use, and if the defendant shall have knowingly used such person's name, portrait, or picture in such manner as is forbidden or declared to be unlawful by this act, the jury, in its discretion, may award exemplary damages..."

WILLARD BARTLETT, J. In the case of Roberson v Rochester Folding Box Co. (171 NY 538) this court determined that in the absence of any statute on the subject the right of privacy as a legal doctrine enforcible in equity did not exist in this state so as to enable a woman to prevent the use of her portrait by others for advertising purposes without her consent. In the prevailing opinion in that case, however, Chief Judge Parker suggested that the right of privacy to that extent might properly be protected by an act of the legislature, saying: "The legislative body could very well interfere and arbitrarily provide that no one should be permitted for his own selfish purpose to use the picture or the name for advertising purposes without his consent."

Chapter 132 of the Laws of 1903 was passed at the very next session of the legislature after this judicial utterance was made public and there can be little doubt that its enactment was prompted by the suggestion which I have quoted. We are now asked to reverse the judgment in this action based on that statute on the ground that its enactment was not a valid exercise of the power of the legislature under the Constitution of the State of New York and on the further ground that it is violative of the Constitution of the United States.

It is contended that the act in question violates the State Constitution: (1) Because it deprives persons of liberty without due process of law.....

As to the first objection, it is to be observed that the statute does not deny the right of any person to make such use of his own portrait as he may see fit. The legislature has not undertaken to restrict his liberty in this respect to any extent whatever. It is only the use of his name or picture by others and by others for particular purposes that is affected by the Statute. Unless we are bound to assume that there is an inherent right in the public at large to use the names and portraits of others for advertising or trade purposes without their consent, the legislative restriction of their liberty imposed by his act is not an exercise of power which affords the basis of any valid objection in a court of justice. The statute merely recognizes and enforces the right of a person to control the use of his name or portrait by others so far as advertising or trade purposes are concerned. This right of control in the person whose name or picture is sought to be used for such purposes is not limited by the statute. The requirement of his written consent in order to effectuate a valid transfer of the privilege of thus using his name or portrait is not any more liable to constitutional objection than the requirement of the Statute of Frauds that an executory contract for the sale of personal property exceeding $50 in price must be made in writing in order to be enforcible.

The power of the legislature in the absence of any constitutional restriction to declare that a particular act shall constitute a crime or be actionable as a tort cannot be questioned, where the right established or recognized and sought to be protected is based upon an ethical sanction. Such is the character of the right of privacy preserved by legislation protecting persons against the unauthorized use of their names or portraits in the forms of advertisements or trace notices. It is a recognition by the law-making power of the very general sentiment which prevailed throughout the community against permitting advertisers to promote the sale of their wares by this method, regardless of the wishes of the persons thereby affected. There was a natural and widespread feeling that such use of their names and portraits in the absence of consent was indefensible in morals and ought to be prevented by law. Hence the enactment of this statute."

It is not a valid objection to the act of 1903 that it creates a right of action and imposes a liability unknown to the common law. There is no such limit to legislative power. The legislature may alter or repeal the common law. It may create new offenses, enlarge the scope of civil remedies and fasten responsibility for injuries upon persons against whom the common law gives no remedy." (Bertholf v O'Reilly, 74 NY 509, 524.) Nor can the statute be deemed unconstitutional because it converts what has heretofore been an innocent act into a criminal offense. "The power of the legislature to define and declare public offenses is unlimited, except in so far as it is restrained by constitutional provisions and guaranties." (People v West, 106 NY 293.) The Civil Damage Act of 1873 was held to be constitutional by this court, not withstanding the fact that it created a cause of action previously non-existent, and so far as I know no one has ever questioned the validity of Chapter 219 of the Laws of 1871, which provides that an action may be maintained by a female to recover damages for words spoken imputing unchastity to her, without the necessity of proving special damage, although no such action was maintainable prior to the enactment of that statute. But much the most notable instance of the legislative creation of a right of action non-existent at common law is the statute giving a cause of action to the personal representatives of a decedent for wrongfully causing his death. No such right existed under the common law or in England until the middle of the last century. Laws of this characted now exist in every state of the Union. The aggregate of the recoveries under these statutes must be enormous; yet their constitutionality has never been challenged.....

...In my opinion the statute is in all respects constitutional and the judgment should be affirmed, with costs....

Judgment affirmed.

IVES, Respondent v SOUTH BUFFALO RY CO., Appellant (1911) 201 NY 271, 140 AD 921

APPEAL from a judgment of the Appellate Division of the Supreme Court in the fourth judicial department, entered October 25, 1910, which affirmed a final judgment in favor of plaintiff entered upon a decision of the court at Special Term sustaining a demurrer to the answer.

This is an action brought by an employee against his employer to recover compensation under article 14-a of the Labor Law, being chapter 674 of the Laws of 1910, entitled "An act to amend the labor law, in relation to workmen's compensation in certain dangerous employments."

The complaint alleges, in substance, that on the second day of September, 1910, while the plaintiff was engaged in his work as a switchman on defendant's steam railroad, he was injured solely by reason of a necessary risk or danger of his employment; that at the time of the commencement of the action he had been totally incapacitated for labor for a period of three weeks, and that such incapacity would continue for four weeks longer, and demands judgment for compensation in accordance with the provisions of said act for a period of five weeks. The answer, after admitting all the allegations of the complaint, pleads as a defense the unconstitutionality of article 14-a of the Labor Law, upon the ground that it contravenes certain provisions of the Federal and State Constitutions. The plaintiff demurred to this defense on the ground that it was insufficient in law upon the face thereof. The issue of law thus presented was tried at Special Term, where the demurrer was sustained. Final judgment was entered upon this decision, and the defendant appealed to the Appellate Division, where the judgment was affirmed by a divided court....

WERNER, J. In 1909 the legislature passed a law (Chap. 518) providing for a commission of fourteen persons, six of whom were to be appointed by the governor, three by the president of the senate from the senate, and five by the speaker of the assembly from the assembly, "to make inquiry, examination and investigation into the working of the law in the State of New York relative to the liability of employers to employees for industrial accidents, and into the comparative efficiency, cost, justice, merits and defects of the laws of other industrial states and countries, relative to the same subject, and as to the causes of the accidents to employees." The act contained other provisions germane to the subject and provided for a full and final report to the legislature of 1910 if practicable, and if not practicable, then to the legislature of 1911, with such recommendations for legislation by bill or otherwise as the commission might deem wise or expedient. Such a commission was appointed and promptly organized by the election of officers and the appointment of sub-committees, the chairman being Senator Wainwright, from whom it has taken the name of the "Wainwright Commission," by which it is popularly known. No word of praise could overstate the industry and intelligence of this commission in dealing with a subject of such manifold ramifications and of such far-reaching importance to the state, to employers and to employees. We cannot dwell in detail upon the many excellent features of its comprehensive report, because the limitations of time and space must necessarily confine us to such of its aspects as have a necessary relation to the legal questions which we are called upon to decide. As the result of its labors the commission recommended for adoption the bill which, with slight changes, was enacted into law by the legislature of 1910, under the designation of article 14-a of the Labor Law. This act is modeled upon the English Workmen's Compensation Act of 1897, which has since been extended so as to cover every kind of occupational injury. Our commission has frankly stated in its report that the classification of the industries which will be immediately affected by the present statute is only tentative, and that other more extended classifications will probably be recommended to the legislature for its action.

The statute, judged by our common-law standards, is plainly revolutionary, its central and controlling feature is that every employer who is engaged in any of the classified industries shall be liable for any injury to a workman arising out of and in the course of the employment by "a necessary risk or danger of the employment or one inherent in the nature thereof; * * * provided that the employer shall not be liable in respect of any injury to the workman which is caused in whole or in part by the serious and willful misconduct of the workman." This rule of liability, stated in another form, is that the employer is responsible to the employee for every accident in the course of the employment, whether the employer is at fault or not, and whether the employee is at fault or not, except when the fault of the employee is so grave as to constitute serious and willful misconduct on his part. The radical character of this legislation is at once revealed by contrasting it with the rule of the common law, under which the employer is liable for injuries to his employee only when the employer is guilty of some act or acts of negligence which caused the occurrence out of which the injuries arise, and then only when the employee is shown to be free from any negligence which contributes to the occurrence. The judicial and statutory modifications of this broad rule of the common law we shall further on have occasion to mention. Just now our purpose is to present in sharp juxtaposition the fundamentals of these two opposing rules, namely, that under the common law an employer is liable to his injured employee only when the employer is at fault and the employee is free from fault; while under the new statute the employer is liable, although not at fault, even when the employee is at fault, unless this latter fault amounts to serious and willful misconduct. The reason for this departure from our long-established law and usage are summarized in the language of the commission as follows:

"First, that the present system of New York rests on a basis that is economically unwise and unfair, and that in operation it is wasteful, uncertain and productive of antagonism between workmen and employers.

"Second, that it is satisfactory to none and tolerable only to those employers and workmen who practically disregard their legal right and obligations, and fairly share the burden of accidents in industries.

"Third, that the evils of the system are most marked in hazardous employments, where the trade risk is high and serious accidents frequent.

"Fourth, that, as matter of fact, workmen in the dangerous trades do not, and practically cannot, provide for themselves adequate accident insurance, and, therefore, the burden of serious accidents falls on the workmen least able to bear it, and brings many of them and their families to want."

This indictment of the old system is followed by a statement of the anticipated benefits under the new statute as follows: "These results can, we think, be best avoided by compelling the employer to share the accident burden in intrinsically dangerous trades, since by fixing the price of his product the shock of the accident may be borne by the community. In those employments which have no so great an element of danger, in which, speaking generally, there is no such imperative demand for the exercise of the police power of the state for the safeguarding of its workers from destitution and its consequences, we recommend, as the first step in this change of system, such amendment of the present law as will do away with some of its unfairness in theory and practice, and increase the workman's chance of recovery under the law. With such changes in the law we couple an elective plan of compensation which, if generally adopted, will do away with many of the evils of the present system. Its adoption will, we believe, be profitable to both employer and employee, and prove to be the simplest way for the State to change its system of liability without disturbance of industrial conditions. Not the least of the motives moving us is the hope that by these means a source of antagonism between employer and employed, pregnant with danger for the State, may be eliminated."...

......The new statute, as we have observed, is totally at variance with the common-law theory of the employer's liability. Fault on his part is no longer an element of the employee's right of action. This change necessarily and logically carries with it the abrogation of the "fellow-servant" doctrine, the "contributory negligence" rule, and the law relating to the employee's assumption of risks. There can be no doubt that the first two of these are subjects clearly and fully within the scope of legislative power; and that as to the third, this power is limited to some extent by constitutional provisions.

The "fellow-servant" rule is one of judicial origin engrafted upon the common law for the protection of the master against the consequences of negligence in which he has no part. In its early application to simple industrial conditions it had the support of both reason and justice. By degrees it was extended until it became evident that under the enormous expansion and infinite complexity of our modern industrial conditions the rule gave opportunity, in many instances, for harsh and technical defenses. In recent years it has been much restricted in its application to large corporate and industrial enterprises, and still more recently it has been modified and, to some extent abolished, by the Labor Law and the Employer's Liability Act.

The law of contributory negligence has the support of reason in any system of jurisprudence in which the fault of one is the basis of liability for injury to another. Under such a system it is at least logical to hold that one who is himself to blame for his injuries should not be permitted to entail the consequences upon another who has not been negligent at all, or whose negligence would not have caused the injury if the one injured had been free from fault. It may be admitted that the reason of the rule is often lost sight of in the effort to apply it to a great variety of practical conditions, and that its efficacy as a rule of justice is much impaired by the lack of uniformity in its administration. In the admiralty branch of the Federal courts, for instance, we have what is known as the rule of comparative negligence under which, when there is negligence on both sides, it is apportioned and a verdict rendered accordingly. In many of the states contributory negligence is a defense which must be pleaded and proved by the defendant, and in some states it has been entirely abrogated by statute. In our own state the plaintiff's freedom from contributory negligence is an essential part of his cause of action which must be affirmatively established by him, except in cases brought by employees under the Labor Law, by virtue of which the contributory negligence of an employee is now made a defense which must be pleaded and proved by the employer; and under the Employer's Liability Act which provides that the employee's continuance in his employment after he has knowledge of dangerous conditions from which injury may ensue, shall not, as matter of law, constitute contributory negligence.

Under the common law the employee was also held to have assumed the ordinary and obvious risks incident to the employment, as well as the special risks arising out of dangerous conditions which were known and appreciated by him. This doctrine, too, has been modified by statute so that under the Labor Law and the Employers' Liability Act the employee is presumed to have assented to the necessary risks of the occupation or employment and no others; and these necessary risks are defined as those only which are inherent in the nature of the business and exist after the employer has exercised due care in providing for the safety of his employees, and has complied with the laws affecting or regulating the business or occupation for the greater safety of employees.

We have said enough to show that the statutory modifications of the "fellow-servant" rule and the law of "contributory negligence" are clearly within the legislative power. These doctrines, for they are nothing more, may be regulated or even abolished. This is true to a limited extent as to the assumption of risk by the employee. In the Labor Law and the Employers' Liability Act, which define the risks assumed by the employee, there are many provisions which cast upon the employer a great variety of duties and burdens unknown to the common law. These can doubtless be still further multiplied and extended to the point where they deprive the employer of rights guaranteed him by our Constitutions and there, of course, they must stop....

This legislation is challenged as void under the fourteenth amendment to the Federal Constitution and under section 6, article 1 of our State Constitution, which guarantee all persons against deprivation of life, liberty or property without due process of law. We shall not stop to dwell at length upon definitions of "life," "liberty," "property" and "due process of law". They are simple and comprehensive in themselves and have been so often judicially defined that there can be no misunderstanding as to their meaning. Process of law in its broad sense means law in its regular course of administration through courts of justice, and that is but another way of saying that every man's right to life, liberty and property is to be disposed of in accordance with those ancient and fundamental principles which were in existence when our Constitutions were adopted. "Due process of law implies the right of the person affected thereby to be present before the tribunal which pronounces judgment upon the question of life, liberty or property in its most comprehensive sense; to be heard by testimony or otherwise, and to have the right of controverting by proof every material fact which bears upon the question of right in the matter involved. If any question of fact or liability be conclusively presumed against him this is not due process of law." (Zeigler v S & N. Ala. R. R. Co., 58 Ala 594.) Liberty has been authoritatively defined as "the right of one to use his faculties in all lawful ways, to live and work where he will, to earn his livelihood in any lawful calling, and to pursue any lawful trade or avocation" (Matter of Jacobs, 98 NY 98, 106); and the right of property as "the right to acquire, possess and enjoy it in any way consistent with the equal rights of others and the just exactions and demands of the State." (Bertholf v O'Reilly, 74 NY 509, 515.)

The several industries and occupations enumerated in the statute before us are concededly lawful within any of the numerous definitions which might be referred to, and have always been so. They are, therefore, under constitutional protection. One of the inalienable rights of every citizen is to hold and enjoy his property until it is taken from him by due process of law. When our Constitutions were adopted it was the law of the land that no man who was without fault or negligence could be held liable in damages for injuries sustained by another. That is still the law, except as to the employers enumerated in the new statute, and as to them it provides that they shall be liable to their employees for personal injury by accident to any workman arising out of and in the course of the employment which is caused in whole or in part, or is contributed to, by a necessary risk of the employment or one inherent in the nature thereof, except that there shall be no liability in any case where the injury is caused in whole or in part by the serious and willful misconduct of the injured workman. It is conceded that this is a liability unknown to the common law and we think it plainly constitutes a deprivation of liberty and property under the Federal and State Constitution, unless its imposition can be justified under the police power which will be discussed under a separate head. In arriving at this conclusion we do not overlook the cogent economic and sociological arguments which are urged in support of the statute.

There can be no doubt as to the theory of this law. It is based upon the proposition that the inherent risks of an employment should in justice be placed upon the shoulders of the employer, who can protect himself against loss by insurance and by such an addition to the price of his wares as to cast the burden ultimately upon the consumer; that indemnity to an injured employee should be as much a charge upon the business as the cost of replacing or repairing disabled or defective machinery, appliances or tools; that, under our present system, the loss falls immediately upon the employee who is almost invariably unable to bear it, and ultimately upon the community which is taxed for the support of the indigent; and that our present system is uncertain, unscientific and wasteful, and fosters a spirit of antagonism between employer and employee which it is to the interests of the state to remove.

We have already admitted the strength of this appeal to a recognized and widely prevalent sentiment, but we think it is an appeal which must be made to the people and not to the courts. The right of property rests not upon philosophical or scientific speculations nor upon the commendable impulses of benevolence or charity, nor yet upon the dictates of natural justice. The right has its foundation in the fundamental law. That can be changed by the people, but not by legislatures. In a government like ours theories of public good or necessity are often so plausible or sound as to command popular approval, but courts are not permitted to forget that the law is the only chart by which the ship of state is to be guided. Law as used in this sense means the basic law and not the very act of legislation which deprives the citizen of his rights, privileges or property. Any other view would lead to the absurdity that the Constitutions protect only those rights which the legislatures do not take away. If such economic and sociologic arguments as are here advanced in support of this statute can be allowed to subvert the fundamental idea of property, then there is no private right entirely safe, because there is no limitation upon the absolute discretion of legislatures, and the guarantees of the Constitution are a mere waste of words (Wynehamer v People, 13 NY 378...)....

We conclude, therefore, that in its basic and vital features the right given to the employee by this statute, does not preserve to the employer the "due process" of law guaranteed by the Constitutions, for it authorizes the taking of the employer's property without his consent and without his fault.

So far as the statute merely creates a new remedy in addition to those which existed before it is not invalid. The state has complete control over the remedies which it offers to suitors in its courts even to the point of making them applicable to rights or equities already in existence.

It may change the common law and the statutes so as to create duties and liabilities which never existed before. It is true, as stated by Mr. Justice BROWN in Holden v Hardy (169 US 366, 385, 386), that "the law is, to a certain extent, a progressive science; that in some of the states methods of procedure, which at the time the Constitution was adopted were deemed essential to the protection and safety of the prople, or to the liberty of the citizen, have been found to be no longer necessary; that restrictions which had formerly been laid upon the conduct of individuals, or of classes of individuals, had proved detrimental to their interests; while, upon the other hand, certain other classes of persons, particularly those engaged in dangerous or unhealthful employments, have been found to be in need of additional protection. Even before the adoption of the Constitution, much had been done toward mitigating the severity of the common law, particularly in the administration of its criminal branch. * * * The present century has originated legal reforms of no less importance. The whole fabric of special pleading, once thought to be necessary to the illumination of the real issue between the parties, has crumbled to pieces. The ancient tenures of real estate have been largely swept away, and land is now transferred almost as easily and cheaply as personal property. Married women have been emancipated from the control of their husbands and placed upon a practical equality with them with respect to the acquisition, possession and transmission of property. Imprisonment for debt abolished. Exemptions from execution have been largely added to, and in most of the states homesteads are rendered incapable of seizure and sale upon forced process. Witnesses are no longer incompetent by reason of interest, even thought they be parties to the litigation. Indictments have been simplified, and an indictment for the most serious of crimes is now the simplest of all. In several of the state grand juries, formerly the only safeguard against a malicious prosecution, have been largely abolished, and in others the rule of unanimity, so far as applied to civil cases, has given way to verdicts rendered by a three-fourths majority."

The power of the state to make such changes in methods of procedure and in substantive law is clearly recognized. (Hurtado v California, 110 US 516...)....

***All that it is necessary to affirm in the case before us is that in our view of the Constitution of our state, the liability sought to be imposed upon the employers enumerated in the statute before us is a taking of property without due process of law, and the statute is therefore void.

The judgment of the Appellate Division should be reversed and judgment directed for the defendant, with costs in all courts....

Judgment reversed, etc.

CARLILL v CARBOLIC SMOKE BALL CO. (Ct of App 1893) 1 Q.B. 256.

Appeal from a decision of Hawkins, J., (1892) 2 Q.B. 484.

The defendants, who were the proprietors and vendors of a medical preparation called "The Carbolic Smoke Vall," inserted in the Pall Mall Gazette of November 13, 1891, and in other newspapers, the following advertisement:

"£100 reward will be paid by the Carbolic Smoke Ball Company to any person who contracts the increasing epidemic influenza, colds or any disease caused by taking cold, after having used the ball three times daily for two weeks according to the printed directions supplied with each ball. £1000 is deposited with the Alliance Bank, Regent Street shewing our sincerity in the matter.

"During the last epidemic of influenze many thousand carbolic smoke balls were sold as preventives against the disease, and in no ascertained case was the disease contracted by those using the carbolic smoke ball.

"One carbolic smoke ball will last a family several months, making it the cheapest remedy in the world at the price, 10s., post free. The ball can be refilled at a cost of 5s. Address, Carbolic Smoke Ball Company, 27 Princes Street, Hanover Square, London."

The plaintiff, a lady, on the faith of this advertisement, bought one of the balls at a chemist's and used it as directed, three times a day from November 20, 1891, to January 17, 1892, when she was attacked by influenza. Hawkins, J., held that she was entitled to recover the £100. The defendants appealed.

LINDLEY, L.J. ...We are dealing with an express promise to pay £100 in certain events. Read the advertisement how you will, and twist it about as you will, here is a distinct promise expressed in language which is perfectly unmistakable: "£100 reward will be paid by the Carbolic Smoke Ball Company to any person who contracts the influenza after having used the ball three times daily for two weeks according to the printed directions supplied with each ball."

We must first consider whether this was intended to be a promise to all, or whether it was a mere puff which meant nothing. Was it a mere puff? My answer to that question is "No," and I base my answer upon this passage: "£1000 is deposited with the Alliance Bank, shewing our sincerity in the matter." Now, for what was that money deposited or that statement made except to negative the suggestion that this was a mere puff and meant nothing at all? The deposit is called in aid by the advertiser as proof of his sincerity in the matter, that is, the sincerity of his promise to pay this £100 in the event which he has specified. I say this for the purpose of giving point to the observation that we are not inferring a promise; there is the promise, as plain as words can make it.

Then it is contended that it is not binding. In the first place, it is said that it is not made with anybody in particular. Now that point is common to the words of this advertisement and to the words of all other advertisements offering rewards. They are offers to anybody who performs the conditions named in the advertisement, and anybody who does perform the conditions accepts the offer. In the point of law this advertisement is an offer to pay £100 to anybody who will perform these conditions, and the performance of the conditions, is the acceptance of the offer. That rests upon a string of authorities, the earliest of which is Williams v Carwardine, 4 Barn. & Adol. 621, which has been followed by many other decisions upon advertisements offering rewards....

We, therefore, find here all the elements which are necessary to form a binding contract enforceable in point of law, subject to two observations. First of all it is said that this advertisement is so vague that you can not really construe it as a promise--that the vagueness of the language shows that a legal promise was never intended or contemplated. The language is vague and uncertain in some respects, and particularly in this, that the £100 is to be paid to any person who contracts the increasing epidemic after having used the balls three times daily for two weeks.... I do not think that business people or reasonable people would understand the words as meaning that if you took a smoke ball and used it three times daily for two weeks you were to be guaranteed against unfluenza for the rest of your life, and I think it would be pushing the language of the advertisement too far to construe it as meaning that. But if it does not mean that, what does it mean? It is for the defendants to shew what it does mean; and it strikes me that there are two, and possibly three, reasonable constructions to be put on this advertisement, any one of which will answer the purpose of the plaintiff. Possibly it may be limited to persons catching the "increasing epidemic" (that is, the then prevailing epidemic), or any colds or diseases caused by taking cold, during the prevalence of the increasing epidemic. That is one suggestion; but it does not commend itself to me. Another suggested meaning is that you are warranted free from catching the epidemic, or colds or other diseases caused by taking cold, whilst you are using this remedy after using it for two weeks. If that is the meaning, the plaintiff is right, for she used the remedy for two weeks and went on using it till she got the epidemic. Another meaning, and the one which I rather prefer, is that the reward is offered to any person who contracts the epidemic or other disease within a reasonable time after having used the smoke ball....

Then it is asked, What is a reasonable time? It has been suggested that there is no standard of reasonableness; that it depends upon the reasonable time for a germ to develop! I do not feel pressed by that. It strikes me that a reasonable time may be ascertained in a business sense and in a sense satisfactory to a lawyer, in this way; find out from a chemist what the ingredients are; find out from a skilled physician how long the effect of such ingredients on the system could be reasonably expected to endure so as to protect a person from an epidemic or cold, and in that way you will get a standard to be laid before a jury, or a judge without a jury, by which they might exercise their judgment as to what a reasonable time would be. It strikes me, I confess, that the true construction of this advertisement is that 100£ will be paid to anybody who uses this smoke ball three times daily for two weeks according to the printed directions, and who gets the influenza or cold or other diseases caused by taking cold within a reasonable time after so using it; and if that is the true construction, it is enough for the plaintiff.....

It appears to me, therefore, that the defendants must perform their promise, and, if they have been so unwary as to expose themselves to a great many actions, so much the worse for them.

BOWEN, L. J. I am of the same opinion....

Appeal dimissed.

STRANGBOROUGH AND WARNER CASE (King's Bench 1589) 4 Leonard 3, 74 Eng. Rep. 686

Assumpsit. Note, that a promise against a promise will maintain an action upon the case, as in consideration that you do give to me 10L on such a day, I promise to give you 10L such a day after.

SLADE'S CASE (King's Bench 1602) 4 Coke 92b, 76 EngRep 1074

John Slade brought an action on the case in the King's Bench against Humphrey Morley, (which plea began Hil, 38 Eliz. Rot. 305) and declared, that whereas the plaintiff, 10th of November, 36 Eliz. was possessed of a close of land in Halberton, in the county of Devon, called Rack Park, containing by estimation eight acres for the term of divers years then and yet to come, and being so possessed, the plaintiff the said 10th day of November, the said close had sowed with wheat and rye, which wheat and rye, 8 Maii, 37 Eliz., were grown into blades, the defendant, in consideration that the plaintiff, at the special instance and request of the said Humphrey, had bargained and sold to him the said blades of wheat and rye growing upon the said close, (the tithes due to the rector, etc., excepted,) assumed and promised the plaintiff to pay him 16 at the Feast of St. John the Baptist then to come: and for nonpayment thereof at the said Feast of John the Baptist, the plaintiff brought the said action: the defendant pleaded non assumpsit modo et forma; and on the trial of this issue the jurrors gave a special verdict, sc. that the defendant bought of the plaintiff the wheat and rye in blades growing upon the said close as is aforesaid, prout in the said declaration is alleged, and further found, that between the plaintiff and the defendant there was no other promise or assumption but only the said bargain; and against the maintenance of this action divers objections were made by John Dodderidge of counsel with the defendant.

That the plaintiff upon his bargain might have ordinary remedy by action of debt, which is an action formed in the register, and therefore he should not have an action on the case, which is an extraordinary action, and not limited within any certain form in the register;...

The second objection was, that the maintenance of this action takes away the defendant's benefit of wager of law, and so bereaves him of the benefit which the law gives him, which is his birthright. For peradventure the defendant has paid or satisfied the plaintiff in private betwixt them, of which payment or satisfaction he has no witness, and therefore it would be mischievous if he should not wage his law in such case. And that was the reason (as it was said) that debts by simple contract shall not be forfeited to the King by outlawry or attainder, because then by the King's prerogative the subject would be ousted of his wager of law, which is his birthright, as it is held in 40 E. 3, 5 a, 50 Ass. 1, 16E. 4, 4 b, and 9 Eliz. Dyer, 262, and if the King shall lose the forfeiture and the debt in such case, and the debtor by judgment of the law shall be rather discharged of his debt, before he shall be deprived of the benefit which the law gives him for his discharge, although in truth, the debt was due and payable; a fortiori in the case at Bar, the defendant shall not be charged in an action in which he shall be ousted of his law, when he may charge him in an action, in which he may have the benefit of it; and as to these objections the Court of King's Bench and Common Please were divided, for the Justices of the King's Bench held, that the action (notwithstanding such objections) was maintainable, and the Court of Common Please held the contrary. And for the honour of the law, and for the quiet of the subject in the appeasing of such diversity of opinions Quia nil in lege intolerabilius est eandem rem diverso jure censeri) the case was openly argued before all the Justices of England, and Barons of the Exchequer, Sir John Popham, Knt. C.J. of England, Sir Edm. Anderson, Knt, C.J. of the Common Please, Sir W. Periam, Chief Baron of the Exchequer Clark, Gewdy, Walmesley, Fenner, Kingmill, Savil, Warburton, and Yelverton, in the Exchequer Chamber by the Queen's Attorney General for the plaintiff, and by John Dodderidge for the defendant, and at another time the case was argued at Serjeant's Inn, before all the said justices and Barons by the Attorney General for the plaintiff, and by Francis Bacon for the defendant, and after many conferences between the justices and barons, it was resolved that the action was maintainable, and that the plaintiff should have judgment. And in this case these points were resolved:

1. That although an action of debt lies upon the contract, yet the bargainor may have an action on the case, or an action of debt at his election, and that for three reasons or causes: 1. In respect of infinite precedents, (which George Kemp, Esq., Secondary of the Prothonotaries of the King's Banch, shewed me,) as well in the Court of Common Pleas, as in the Court of King's Bench, in the reigns of

King H. 6, E. 4, H. 7, and H. 8, by which it appears, that the plaintiffs declared that the defendants, in consideration of a sale to them of certain goods, promised to pay so much money, etc. in which cases the plaintiffs had judgment. To which precedents and judgments being of so great number, in so many successions of ages, and in the several times of so many reverend judges, the justices in this case gave great regard; and so the justices in ancient times, and from time to time did as well in matters of form as in deciding of doubts and questions as well at the common law, as in construction of Acts of Parliament, and therefore in 11 E. 2, Formedon 32, it is held that the ancient forms and manner of precedents are to be maintained and observed; and in 34 Ass. 7, that which has not been according to usage shall not be permitted, and in 2 E. 3, 29, the ancient form and order is to be observed....

So, that in the case at Bar it was resolved that the multitude of the said judicial precedents in so many successions of ages, well prove that in the case at Bar the action was maintainable.

2. The second cause of their resolution was divers judgment and cases resolved in our books where such action on the case on Ass. has been mainable, when the party might have had an action of debt, 21 H. 6, 55 b, 12 E. 4, 13, 13 H. 7, 26, 20 H. 7, 4 b, and 20 H. 7, 8 b, which case was adjudged as Fitz James cites it, 22 H. 8, Dyer, 22 b; 27 H. 8, 24 and 25, in Tatam's case; Norwood and Read's case, adjudged Plowd. Com. 180.

3. It was resolved, that every contract executory imports in itself an assumpsit, for when one agrees to pay money, or to deliver anything, thereby he assumes or promises to pay, or deliver it, and therefore when one sells any goods to another and agrees to deliver them at a day to come, and the other in consideration thereof agrees to pay so much money at such a day, in that case both parties may have an action of debt, or an action on the case on assumpsit, for the mutual executory agreement of both parties imports in itself reciprocal actions upon the case, as well as actions of debt, and therewith agrees the judgment in Read and Norwood's case, Pl. Com. 128.

4. It was resolved, that the plaintiff in this action on the case on assumpsit sould not recover only damages for the special loss (if any be) which he had, but also for the whole debt, so that a recovery or bar in this action would be a good bar in an action of debt brought upon the same contract so vice versa, a recovery or bar in an action of debt, is a good bar in an action on the case on assumpsit. Vide 12 E, 4, 13a; 2 R. 3, 14; (32) 33 H. 8, Action sur le Case, Br. 105.

5. In some cases it would be mischievous if an action of debt should be only brought, and not an action on the case, as in the case inter Redman and Peck, 2 and 3 ph, and Mar., Dyer, 113, they bargained together, that for a certain consideration Redman should deliver to Peck twenty quarters of barley yearly during his life, and for non-delivery in one year, it is adjudged that an action well lies, for otherwise it would be mischievous to Peck, for if he should be driven to his action of debt, then he himself could never have it, but his executors or administrators, for debt doth not lie in such case, till all the days are incurred, and that would be contrary to the bargain and intent of the parties, for Peck provides it yearly for his necessary use; so 5 Mar. Br., Action sur le Case, 108, that if a sum is given in marriage to be paid several days, an action upon the case lies for non-payment at the first day, but no action of debt lies in such case till all the days are past. Also it is good in these days in as many cases as may be done by the law, to oust the defendant of his law, and to try it by the country, for otherwise it would be occasion of much perjury.

6. It was said, that an action on the case on assumpsit is as well a formed action, and contained in the register, as an action of debt, for there is its form: also it appears in divers other cases in the register, that an action on the case will lie, although the plaintiff may have another formed action in the register....

And therefore it was concluded, that in all cases when the register has two writs for one and the same case, it is in the party's election to take either. But the register has two several actions, sc. action upon the case upon assumpsit, and also an action of debt, and therefore the party may elect either. And as to the objection which has been made, that it would be mischievous to the defendant that he should not wage his law, forasmuch as he might pay it in secret: To that it was answered, that it should be accounted his folly that he did not take sufficient witnesses with him to prove the payment he made: but the mischief would be rather on the other party, for now experience proves that men's consciences grow so large that the respect of their private advantage rather induces men (and chiefly those who have declining estates) to perjury; ...and therefore in debt, or other action where wager of law is admitted by the law, the Judges without good admonition and due examination of the party do not admit him to it....

NICHOLS AND RAYNBRED (King's Bench 1615) 12 Jac. Rot. 131, Hobart 89, 80 EngRep 238

Assumpsit. Promise for promise. Nichols brought an assumpsit against Raynbred, declaring that in consideration, that Nichols promised to deliver the defendant to his own use a cow, the defendant promised to deliver him 50 shillings; adjudged for the plaintiff in both Courts, that the plaintiff need not to aver the delivery of the cow, because it is promise for promise. Note here the promises must be at one instant, for else they will be both nuda pacta.

WOOD, Appellant v DUFF-GORDON, Respondent (1917) 222 NY 88, r177 AD 624

Appeal from a judgment entered April 24, 1917 upon an order of the Appellant Division of the Supreme Court in the first judicial department, which reversed an order of Special Term denying a motion by defendant for judgment in her favor upon the pleadings and granted said motion.

CARDOZO, J., The defendant styles herself "a creator of fashions." Her favor helps a sale. Manufacturers of dresses, millinery and like articles are glad to pay for a certificate of her approval. The things which she designs, fabrics, parasols and what not, have a new value in the public mind when issued in her name. She employed the plaintiff to help her to turn this vogue into money. He was to have the exclusive right, subject always to her approval, to place her indorsements on the designs of others. He was also to have the exclusive right to place her own designs on sale, or to license others to market them. In return, she was to have one-half of "all profits and revenues" derived from any contracts he might make. The exclusive right was to last at least one year from April 1, 1915, and thereafter from year to year unless terminated by notice of ninety days. The plaintiff says that he kept the contract on his part, and that the defendant broke it. She placed her endorsement on fabrics and millinery without his knowledge, and withheld the profits. He sues her for the damages, and the case comes here on demurrer.

The agreement of employment is signed by both parties. It has a wealth of recitals. The defendant insists, however, that it lacks the elements of a contract. She says that the plaintiff does not bind himself to anything. It is true that he does not promise in so many words that he will use reasonable efforts to place the defendant's indorsements and market her designs. We think, however, that such a promise is fairly to be implied. The law has outgrown its primitive stage of formalism when the precise word was the sovereign talisman, and every slip was fatal. It takes a broader view to-day. A promise may be lacking , and yet the whole writing may be "instinct with an obligation," imperfectly expressed (Scott, J., in McCall Co. v Wright, 133 AD 62; Moran v Standard Oil Co., 211 NY 187, 198). If that is a contract.

The implication of a promise here finds support in many circumstances. The defendant gave an exclusive privilege. She was to have no right for at least a year to place her own indorsements or market her own designs except through the agency of the plaintiff. The acceptance of the exclusive agency was an assumption of its duties (Phoenix Hermetic Co. v Filtrine Mfg. Co., 164 AD 424; W.G.Taylor Co. v Bennerman, 120 Wis. 189; Mueller v Bethesda Mineral Spring Co., 88 Mich. 390). We are not to suppose that one party was to be placed at the mercy of the other (Hearn v Stevens & Bro., 111 AD 101, 106; Russell v Allerton, 108 NY 288). Many other terms of the agreement point the same way. We are told at the outset by way of recital that "the said Otis F. Wood possesses a business organization adapted to the placing of such indorsements as the said Lucy, Lady Duff-Gordon has approved." The implication is that the plaintiff's business organization will be used for the purpose for which it is adapted. But the terms of the defendant's compensation are even more significant. Her sole compensation for the grant of an exclusive agency is to be one-half of all the profits resulting from the plaintiff's efforts. Unless he gave his efforts, she could never get anything. Without an implied promise, the transaction cannot have such business "efficacy as both parties must have intended that at all events it should have" (Bowen, L. J., in The Moorcock, 14 PD 64, 68). But the contract does not stop there. The plaintiff goes on to promise that he will account monthly for all moneys received by him, and that he will take out all such patents and copyrights and trademarks as may in his judgment be necessary to protect the rights and articles affected by the agreement. It is true, of course, as the Appellate Division has said, that if he was under no duty to try to market designs or to place certificates of indorsement, his promise to account for profits or take out copyrights would be valueless. But in determining the intention of the parties, the promise has a value. It helps to enforce the conclusion that the plaintiff had some duties. His promise to pay the defendant one-half of the profits and revenues resulting from the exclusive agency and to render accounts monthly, was a promise to use reasonable efforts to bring profits and revenues into existence. For this conclusion, the authorities are ample (Wilson v Mechanical Orguinette Co., 170 NY 542....)

The judgment of the Appellate Division should be reversed, and the order of the Special Term affirmed, with costs in the Appellate Division and in this court.

Judgment reversed, etc.

MOSES v MACFERLAN (King's Bench 1760) 2 Burr 1005, 92 EngRep 676

Lord Mansfield delivered the resolution of the Court in this case, which stood for their opinion, "Whether the plaintiff could recover against the defendant, in the present form of action, (an action upon the case for money had and received to the plaintiff's use;) or whether he should be obliged to bring a special action upon the contract and agreement between them."

It was an action upon the case, brought in this Court, by the now plaintiff, Moses, against the now defendant, Macferlan, (heretofore plaintiff in the Court of Conscience, against the same Moses now plaintiff here,) for money had and received to the use of Moses and now plaintiff in this Court.

The case, as it came out upon evidence and without dispute, at nisi prius before Lord Mansfield at Guildhall, was as follows. It was clearly proved, that the now plaintiff, Moses, had indorsed to the now defendant, Macferlan, four several promissory notes made to Moses himself by one Chapman Jacob, for 30s, each, for value received, bearing date 7th November, 1758; and that this was done in order to enable the now defendant Macferlan to recover the money in his own name, against Chapman-Jacob. But previous to the now plaintiff's indorsing these notes, Macferlan assured him "that such his indorsement should be of no prejudice to him:" and there was an agreement signed by Macferlan, whereby he (amongst other things) expressly agreed "that Moses should not be liable to the payment of the money, or any part of it; and that he should not be prejudiced, or be put to any costs, or any way suffer, by reason of such his indorsement." Notwithstanding which express condition and agreement, and contrary thereto, the present defendant Macferlan summoned the present plaintiff Moses into the Court of Conscience, upon each of these 4 notes, as the indorser thereof respectively, by 4 separate summonses. Whereupon Moses, (by one Smith, who attended the Court of Conscience at their second Court, as Solicitor for him and on his behalf,) tendered the said indemnity to the Court of Conscience, upon the first of the said four causes; and offered to give evidence of it and of the said agreement, by way of defence for Moses in that court. But the Court of Conscience rejected this defence, and refused to receive any evidence in proof of this agreement of indemnity, thinking that they had no power to judge of it: and gave judgment against Moses, upon the mere foot of his indorsement, (which he himself did not at all dispute,) without hearing his witnesses about the agreement "that he should not be liable:" for the commissioners held this agreement to be no sufficient bar to the suit in their court; and consequently decreed for the plaintiff in that court, upon the undisputed indorsement made by Moses. This decree was actually pronounced, in only one of the 4 causes there depending: but Moses's agent, (finding the opinion of the commissioners to be as above mentioned,) paid the money into that court, upon all the four notes; and it was taken out of Court by the now defendant Macferlan, (the then Plaintiff, in that court,) by order of the commissioners.

All this matter appearing upon evidence before Lord Mansfield at nisi prius at Guildhall, there was no doubt but that, upon the merits, the plaintiff was entitled to the money: and accordingly, a verdict was there found for Moses, the plaintiff in this Court, for £6. (the whole sum paid into the Court of Conscience;) but subject to the opinion of the Court, upon this question, "Whether the money could be recovered in the present form of action; or whether it must be recovered by an action brought upon the special agreement only."

The Court, having heard the counsel on both sides, took time to advise.

LORD MANSFIELD now delivered their unanimous opinion, in favour of the present action.

There was no doubt at the trial, but that upon the merits the plaintiff was intitled to the money: and the jury accordingly found a verdict for the f6. subject to the opinion of the Court upon this question, "Whether the money might be recovered by this form of action," or "must be by an action upon the special agreement only."

Many other objections, besides that which arose at the trial, have since been made to the propriety of this action in the present case.

The 1st objection is, "That an action of debt would not lie here: and no assumpsit will lie, where an action of debt may not be brought:" some sayings at nisi prius, reported by note takers who did not understand the force of what was said, are quoted in support of that proposition. But there is no foundation for it.

It is much more plausible to say, "That where debt lies, an action upon the case ought not to be brought." And that was the point relied upon in Slade's Case, 4 Co. 92: but the rule then settled and followed ever since is, "That an action of assumpsit will lie in many cases where debt lies, and in many where it does not lie." A main inducement, originally, for encouraging actions of assumpsit was, "to take away the wager of law:" and that might give rise to loose expressions, as if the action was confined to cases only where that reason held.

2d Objection- "That no assumpsit lies, except upon an express or implied contract: but here it is impossible to presume any contract to refund money which the defendant recovered by an adverse suit."

Answer. If the defendant be under an obligation, from the ties of natural justice, to refund; the law implies a debt, and give this action, founded in the equity of the plaintiff's case, as it were upon a contract ("Quasi ex contractu,") as the Roman law expresses it. This species of assumpsit ("for money had and received to the plaintiff's use") lies in numberless instances, for money the defendant has received from a third person; which he claims title to, in opposition to the plaintiff's right; and which he had, by law, authority to receive from such third person.

3d Objection. Where money has been recovered by the judgment of a court having competent jurisdiction, the matter can never be brought over again by a new action.

Answer. It is most clear, "that the merits of a judgment can never be over-haled by an original suit, either at law or in equity." Till the judgment is set aside, or reversed, it is conclusive, as to the subject matter of it, to all intents and purposes. But the ground of this action is consistent with the judgment of the Court of Consicence: it admits the commissioners did right. They decreed upon the indorsement of the notes by the plaintiff: which indorsement is not now disputed. The ground upon which this action proceeds was no defence against that sentence. It is enough for us, that the commissioners adjudged "they had no cognizance of such collateral matter." We can not correct an error in their proceedings; and ought to suppose what is done by a final jurisdiction, to be right. But we think "the commissioners did right, in refusing to go into such collateral matter." Otherwise, by way of defence against a promissory note for 30s. they might go into agreements and transactions of a great value: and if they decreed payment of the note, their judgment might indirectly conclude the balance of a large account. The ground of this action is not, "that the judgment was wrong;" but, "that, (for a reason which the now plaintiff could not avail himself of against that judgment,) the defendant ought not in justice to keep the money." And at Guildhall, I declared very particularly, "that the merits of a question, determined by the commissioners, where they had jurisdiction never could be brought over again, in any shape whatsoever."

Money may be recovered by a right and legal judgment; and yet the iniquity of keeping that money may be manifest, upon grounds which could not be used by way of defence against the judgment. Suppose an indorsee of a promissory note, having received payment from the drawer (or maker) of it, sues and recovers the same money from the indorser who knew nothing of such payment. Suppose a man recovers upon a policy for a ship presumed to be lost, which afterwards comes home; or upon the life of a man presumed to be dead, who afterwards appears; or upon a representation of a risque deemed to be fair, which comes out afterwards to be grossly fraudulent.

But there is no occasion to go further; for the admission "that unquestionably, an action might be brought upon the agreement," is a decisive answer to any objection from the judgment. For it is the same thing, as to the force and validity of the judgment, and it is just equally affected by the action, whether the plaintiff brings it upon the equity of his case arising out of agreement, that the defendant may refund the money he received; or upon the agreement itself, that, besides refunding the money, he may pay the costs and expenses the plaintiff was put to.

This brings the whole to the question saved at nisi prius, viz. "Whether the plaintiff may elect to sue by this form of action, for the money only; or must be turned round, to bring action upon the agreement.

One great benefit, which arises to suitors from the nature of this action is, that the plaintiff needs not state the special circumstances from which he concludes "that ex aequo et bono, the money received by the defendant, ought to be deemed as belonging to him:" he may declare generally, "that the money was received to his use;" and make out his case at the trial. This is equally beneficial to the defendant. It is the most favourable way in which he can be sued: he can be liable no further than the money he has received; and against that may go into every equitable defence upon the general issue; he may claim every equitable allowance; he may prove a release without pleading it; in short, he may defend himself by every thing which shews that the plaintiff, ex aequo et bono, is not entitled to the whole of his demand, or to any part of it. If the plaintiff elects to proceed in this favourable way, it is a bar to his bringing another action upon the agreement; though he might recover more upon the agreement, than he can by this form of action. And therefore, if the question was open to be argued upon principles at large, there seems to be no reason or utility in confining the plaintiff to an action upon the special agreement only.

But the point has been long settled; and there may have been many precedents: I will mention to you one only, which was very solemnly considered. It was the case of Dutch v Warren, M. 7 G. I, C.B. An action upon the case, for money had and received to the plaintiff's use. The case was as follows-Upon the 18th of August, 1720, on payment of £262. 10s. by the plaintiff to the defendant, the defendant agreed to transfer him 5 shares in the Welsh copper mines, at the opening of the books; and for security of his so doing, gave him this note - "18th of August, 1720. I do hereby acknowledge to have received of Philip Dutch, £262. 10s. as a consideration for the purchase of 5 shares; which I do hereby promise to transfer to the said Philip Dutch as soon as the books are open; being 5 shares in the Welsh copper mines. Witness my hand, Robert Warren." The books were opened on the 22d of the said month of August; when Dutch requested Warren to transfer to him the said 5 shares; which he refused to do; and told the plaintiff "he might take his remedy." Whereupon the plaintiff brought this action, for the consideration-money paid by him. And an objection was taken at the trial, "that this action upon the case, for money had and received to the plaintiff's use, would not lie; but that the action should have been brought for the non-performance of the contract." This objection was overruled by the Chief Justice; who notwithstanding left it to the consideration of the jury, whether they would not make the price of the said stock, as it was upon the 22d of August, when it should have been delivered, the measure of the damages; which they did; and gave the plaintiff but £175. damages. And a case being made for the opinion of the Court of Common Pleas, the action was resolved to be well brought; and that the recovery was right, being not for the whole money paid, but for the damages, in not transferring the stock at the time; which was a loss to the plaintiff, and an advantage to the defendant, who was a receiver of the difference-money, to the plaintiff's use. The Court said, that the extending those actions depends on the notion of fraud. If one man takes another's money to do a thing, and refuses to do it, it is a fraud; and it is at the election of the party injured, either to affirm the agreement; by bringing an action for the non-performance of it; or to disaffirm the agreement ab initio, by reason of the fraud, and bring an action for money had and received to his use.

The damages recovered in that case show the liberality with which this kind of action is considered: for though the defendant received from the plaintiff £262. 10s. yet the difference-money only, of £175. was retained by him against conscience: and therefore the plaintiff ex aequo et bono, ought to recover no more agreeable to the rule of the Roman Law - "quod condictio indebiti non datur ultra, quam locupletior factus est, qui accepit." If the five shares had been of much more value, yet the plaintiff could only have recovered the £262. 10s. by this form of action.

The notion of fraud holds much more strongly in the present case, than in that: for here it is express. The indorsement, which enabled the defendant to recover, was got by fraud and falsehood, for one purpose, and abused to another.

This kind of equitable action, to recover back money, which ought not in justice to be kept, is very beneficial, and therefore much encouraged. It lies only for money which, ex aequo et bono, the defendant ought to refund: it does not lie for money which, ex aequo et bono, the defendant ought to refund: it does not lie for money paid by the plaintiff which is claimed of him as payable in point of honour and honesty, although it could not have been recovered from him by any course of law; as in payment of a debt barred by the statute of limitations, or contracted during his infancy, or to the extent of principal and legal interest upon an usurious contract, or for money fairly lost at play; because in all these cases the defendant may retain it with a safe conscience, though by positive law he was barred from recovering. But it lies for money paid by mistake; or upon a consideration which happens to fail; or for money got through imposition (express or implied;) or extortion; or oppression; or an undue advantage taken of the plaintiff's situation, contrary to laws made for the protection of persons under those circumstances.

In one word the gist of this kind of action is that the defendant, upon the circumstances of the case, is obliged by the ties of natural justice and equity to refund the money.

Therefore we are all of us of opinion. That the plaintiff might elect to waive any demand upon the foot of the indemnity, for the costs he had been put to; and bring this action, to recover the £6 which the defendant got and kept from him iniquitously.

Rule - That the postea be delivered to the plaintiff.

PEASE PIANO CO., Respondent v TAYLOR, Appellant (1stDept 1921)197 AD 468, 189 S 425

From an order denying defendant's motion for judgment on the pleadings, defendant appeals.

PAGE, J. ... The action is brought to recover from a salesman the difference between the amount paid him on a drawing account and the amount of commissions earned and credited to him on such account. The complaint does not allege an agreement to repay any excess of advances over commissions earned. Annexed to the bill of particulars served by the plaintiff is a copy of the contract of employment. This contract can be considered on the motion. As the plaintiff has stated this to be the contract upon which the action is predicated, the legal effect of which is alleged in the complaint, we can treat it as if a copy were annexed to the complaint and referred to and made a part thereof. (cases)

This contract, so far as pertinent to the question under consideration, is as follows:

"Compensation will be based upon the net business done by me at the following rates: (Schedule of rates) payable as follows: A drawing account of $35 per week to be charged against commissions earned by me, and a quarterly settlement of any commissions standing to my credit on the 1st day of September, December, March and June of each year; but it is expressly understood that the Pease Piano Company are to retain, to offset charge backs, 20 per cent of the commissions earned by me during the quarter given me in settlement. It is further understood that the Pease Piano Company may reduce the drawing account above mentioned, should I fail to earn sufficient commissions during the quarter to cover."

There is no agreement to pay back any excess of payments on the drawing account over commissions earned. The sole right that the plaintiff reserved was to reduce the drawing account, should the defendant fail to earn sufficient commissions during any quarter to cover the amount paid. There is no personal liability of the defendant to repay the sum, and the same is payable out of commissions, and not otherwise. It is well settled that without an agreement, express or implied, to repay the excess of a drawing account over and above commissions earned, the employer cannot recover such excess from the employee. (North Western Mutual Life Ins. Co. v Mooney, 108 NY 118, 15 NE 303.)

The facts alleged in the complaint, with the contract set forth in the bill of particulars, are insufficient to constitute a cause of action. The order will therefore be reversed, with $10 costs and disbursements, and the motion for judgment in favor of the defendant, dismissing the complaint, granted, with $10 costs. All concur.

Sec. 2.12 Conditions Fulfilled as to the Cause of Action, such as
a. Performance by Plaintiff of Conditions Precedent (if any)
b. Demand, if necessary, by Plaintiff that Defendant Perform
c. (other conditions, if any)

WOOD & SELICK, Appellant v BALL, Respondent (1907) 190 NY 217, a114 AD 743

This action was commenced on the 28th of November, 1904, in the County Court of Jefferson county for goods sold and delivered to the value of $97.44.

The answer contained a partial denial and a counterclaim for breach of warranty, to which a reply was served. There was no allegation in any pleading, nor any evidence, that the plaintiff either had or had not complied with section fifteen of the General Corporation Law.

Upon the trial plaintiff produced evidence tending to support every allegation of the complaint. It was also proved without objection that the plaintiff is a stock corporation. The defendant put in no evidence but moved for a nonsuit and the court granted the motion upon the ground that the complaint did not set forth a cause of action, in that it contained no allegation of compliance by the plaintiff with section fifteen of the General Corporation Law. Upon appeal to the Appellate Division the judgment was affirmed, one of the justices dissenting. The plaintiff appealed to this court.

VANN, J. The question presented by this appeal has led to some conflict of opinion. (Fuller v Schrenck, 58 AD 222...) While we regard the conflict as now settled, a few words may remove a doubt which has arisen because we have held that the failure of the plaintiff to allege compliance with section fifteen of the General Corporation Law renders a complaint demurrable, and have also held that the failure to allege compliance with section 181 of the Tax Law does not render a complaint demurrable. (Welsbach Co. v Norwich Gas & Electric Co., 180 NY 533; Parmele Co. v Haas, 171 NY 579.)

These decisions are not in conflict. Each rests upon a statute peculiar to itself, which differs so essentially from that governing the other as to effect a different purpose and call for the application of a different rule in pleading. An examination of the decisions, the one rendered with an opinion and the other by simply answering questions certified, without comparing the statutes upon which they are founded, has led to some confusion which we now hope to dispel.

In the Parmele case we had before us the Tax Law, which is a revenue act. As written when that case was decided it provides that "Every foreign corporation," with certain exceptions not now material, "authorized to do business under the General Corporation Law, shall pay to the state treasurer, for the use of the state, a license fee of one-eighth of one per centum for the privilege of exercising its corporate franchises or carrying on its business in such corporate or organized capacity in this state, to be computed upon the basis of the capital stock employed by it within this state, during the first year of carrying on its business in this state; and if any year thereafter any such corporation shall employ an increased amount of its capital stock within this state, the same license fee shall be due and payable upon any such increase. The tax imposed by this section on a corporation not heretofore subject to its provisions shall be paid on the first day of December, 1901, to be computed upon the basis of the amount of capital stock employed by it within the state during the year preceding such date, unless on such date such corporation shall not have employed capital within the state for a period of thirteen months in which case it shall be paid within the time otherwise provided by this section. No action shall be maintained or recovery had in any of the courts in this state by such foreign corporation without obtaining a receipt for the license fee hereby imposed within thirteen months after beginning such business within the state, or if at the time this section takes effect such a corporation has been engaged in business within this state for more than twelve months, without obtaining such receipt within thirty days after such tax is due." (L. 1896, ch. 908, sec. 181; L. 1901, ch. 558 sec. 1.)

In the Welsbach case we had before us the General Corporation Law, which is not a revenue act, but is designed to regulate domestic corporations of all kinds and to prescribe the conditions upon which foreign stock corporations may do business in this state. It provides that "No foreign stock corporation other than a monied corporation, shall do business in this state without having first procured from the secretary of state a certificate that it has complied with all the requirements of law to authorize it to do business in this state, and that the business of the corporation to be carried on in this state is such as may be lawfully carried on by a corporation incorporated under the laws of this state for such or similar business * * *. No such corporation now doing business in this state shall do business herein after December 31st, 1892, without having procured such certificate from the secretary of state, but any lawful contract previously made by the corporation may be performed and enforced within the state subsequent to such date. No foreign stock corporation doing business in this state shall maintain any action in this state upon any contract made by it in this state unless prior to the making of such contract it shall have procured such certificate." (L. 1892, ch. 687, sec. 15; L. 1901, ch. 538, sec. 1.)

The provision of the Tax Law, which led to the result reached in the Parmele case, is a condition subsequent. There is a command to pay a license fee for the privilege of carrying on business in this state, but not until business has been carried on for a longer or shorter period, varying according to circumstances. The amount is to be fixed by the comptroller, who is authorized to examine books, records and employees for the purpose. (L. 1895, ch. 240) It cannot be said in advance, for it must first be computed and the computation is made on the basis of the capital stock employed in this state, which cannot be known in advance. When computed on that basis it is to be paid "within thirty days after such tax is due." Unless it is paid within thirteen months after the commencement of business in this state, or if the corporation has already carried on business in this state for a certain length of time, within thirty days after the tax is due, no action can be maintained in our courts by the corporation in default. There is no express prohibition against doing business without a license, but a penalty is imposed through the withholding of the right to sue, unless a license fee is paid within the period prescribed. We, therefore, held that a complaint which did not allege compliance with this section was not defective for that reason, but that non-compliance was a matter of defense, to be availed of by answer. This is in accordance with the general rule that performance of a condition subsequent, which continues in force a right already acquired, need not be pleaded, while performance of a condition precedent, by which the right itself is acquired in the first instance, must be pleaded.

On the other hand, the requirement of section 15 of the General Corporation Law, which led to the result in the Welsbach case, is a condition precedent to the right of a foreign stock corporation to lawfully do business in this state. The procuring of a license must precede the transaction of business or the contracts of the corporation are not lawful. Aside from the provision withholding legal remedies, no such corporation can lawfully make contracts in this state without obtaining the certificate in advance....

The Welsbach case came before us upon a certificate of the Appellate Division, presenting the following questions for decision:

"1. Was the complaint demurrable upon the ground that it appears upon the face thereof that the plaintiff did not have legal capacity to sue?

"2. Was the complaint demurrable on the ground that facts are not therein stated sufficient to constitute a cause of action?"

We affirmed the order appealed from and answered both questions in the affirmative. The only defect claimed to exist in the complaint in that case was the omission to allege compliance with section 15 of the General Corporation Law. The same defect exists in the complaint now before us. There is no allegation, either general or specific, that the condition precedent in the statute has been performed. (Code Civ. Pro. Sec. 533.) Such an allegation is essential in order to set forth a cause of action, and the objection that the complaint does not state facts sufficient to constitute a cause of action is not waived by the failure to raise it by demurrer or answer. (id. Sec. 499.)

It is suggested that a recovery ought to be permitted, if possible, because the defendant had the goods, and it is equitable that she should be compelled to pay for them, but that which a statute prohibits is not equitable, and, as was said below, "the logic of that suggestion might do away with the statute in every instance."

We think that compliance with section 15 of the General Corporation Law should be alleged and proven by a foreign corporation such as the plaintiff, in order to establish a cause of action in the courts of this state. The cases holding otherwise should be regarded as overruled and the conflict of authority ended.

O'BRIEN, J. (Dissenting.) (omitted.)

RUTHERFORD v HAVEN & CO. (1861) 11 Iowa 587

(Vendor of real estate filed a bill for specific performance of the contract. Vendee's demurrer, on ground that vendor did not allege his tender of a deed, was sustained by the trial court. Vendor appealed.)

WRIGHT, J. The leading question in this case is, whether in equity the vendor of real estate who seeks a performance and foreclosure of a contract containing mutual and dependent covenants, is required, as at law, to tender a deed to the vendee before filing his bill. None of the cases cited by appellees sustain the affirmative of this proposition. They were all actions at law, except that of Barron v Easton, et al., (3 Iowa 76), and what is said in that case may be well understood as applying to an action at law for the purchase money. And in our opinion the reason for the rules in a law action, does not apply in a court of equity. At law, if the vendor recovers his judgment for the purchase money, it must necessarily, from the nature of the tribunal, be unconditional or without terms. In equity the chancellor has full power to protect the vendee, and to make the execution and deposit of the deed with the clerk or other person to be named, a condition precedent to the enforcement of the decree.

This view is in principle sustained in the reasoning used in Young v Daniels (2 Iowa 135), and we deem it just and equitable. And especially is this so in view of the fact that the chancellor, is justified in awarding any costs against the complainant, which it shall appear might have been avoided by a prior offer to perform on his part.

The other points made by the demurrer to the bill, are not strongly urged and are not of such weight as to require specific attention. None of them impress us as being well made.

Decree reversed.

DOWNS v THE PHOENIX BANK OF CHARLESTOWN (1844) 6 Hill(NY) 297

Assumpsit brought against the defendants as a foreign corporation, by attachment. The defendants appeared and pleaded non assumpsit, and the cause was tried at the New York circuit before Kent, C. Judge, in April, 1843. The plaintiff gave in evidence his deposit or bank book of account with the defendants' bank, on which there stood to the plaintiff's credit the sum of $496.09, being a balance struck on the 1st of October, 1842, in the handwriting of a clerk of the bank. The defendants moved for a nonsuit on two grounds, viz: 1. That the suit was commenced by attachment against a foreign corporation, and the plaintiff was bound to prove he was a resident of this state at the time it was commenced; and 2. That he was bound to prove a demand of the money deposited with the defendants before the suit was commenced. The judge overruled the motion, and instructed the jury to find a verdict for the plaintiff. Verdict accordingly. The defendants now moved for a new trial on a case, with leave to turn it into a bill of exceptions.

BRONSON, J. Actions against foreign corporations may be commenced by attachment, by a resident of this state. (2 R.S. 459, @ 15.) The objection is, that the plaintiff did not prove that he was a resident. In the circuit and district courts of the United States, the facts upon which their jurisdiction depends must be alleged in the declaration, and proved on the trial. But these are courts of limited jurisdiction. The rule is otherwise in courts of general jurisdiction. There as a general rule, the defendant must plead to the jurisdiction. A plea in bar of the action admits that the court may take cognizance of the cause. The objection on the trial went to the ability of the plaintiff to sue by attachment. That might, perhaps, have been pleaded in abatement; and if so, the objection was lost by pleading in bar. A motion to set aside the attachment for irregularity would have been the best mode of raising the question. But clearly, after appearing and pleading in bar, it is too late to make the objection that the suit was not properly commenced.

This is the common case of an account between a bank and one of its dealers. The usual course of such business is, for the dealer to deposit his money with the bank, to be repaid upon his checks or drafts, or in taking up his notes or acceptances made payable at the bank. It is not strictly a deposit, nor a bailment of any kind; for the same thing is not to be returned, but another thing of the same kind and of equal value. In the civil law it is called a mutuum, or loan for consumption. Except where the deposit is special, the property in the money deposited passes to the bank, and the relation of debtor and creditor is created between the parties. (Commercial Bank v Hughes, 17 Wend(NY) 94.) Still, the commonly received opinion is, that the banker cannot be sued for the money until after the customer has drawn for it, or in some other way required its repayment. Mr. Justice Story says, the bank is to restore the money "whenever it is demanded." (Story on Bailm. 66, @ 88; and see Marzetti v Williams, 1 Barn. & Ad. 415; Chit. On Bills, 547, ed. of 1839; Chit. Jr. On Dills, 44.) Judging from the ordinary course of this business, I think the understanding between the parties, is that the money shall remain with the banker until the customer, by his check, or in some other way, calls for its repayment: and if such be the nature of the contract, the banker is not in fault, and no action will lie, until payment has been demanded. No one could desire to receive money in deposit for an indefinite period, with a right in the depositor to sue the next moment, and without any prior intimation that he wished to recall the loan. I do not find that the point has ever been decided; but it may be that this is the first case where a man has sued his banker without first drawing on him for the money.

We are reminded that, where the promise is to pay on demand, the bringing of the action is a sufficient request. If that were a new question I think the courts would not again fall into the absurdity of admitting that there must be a demand, and still holding that a suit may be commenced without any prior request. They would either say that no demand was necessary, or else that it was a condition precedent to the right of action. It is an anomaly in the law that the breach of the defendant's contract should be made out by the very fact of suing him upon it. In all other cases there must be a breach before suit brought. The rule ought not to be extended to cases which do not fall precisely within it. Here, the contract to be implied from the usual course of the business is, that the banker shall keep the money until it is called for. Although it is not strictly a bailment, it partakes in some degree of that character. That is enough to distinguish it from the ordinary case of a debt payable on demand, though it must be admitted that the distinction is not a very strong one.

Some stress has been laid upon the fact that a balance had been struck upon the plaintiff's bankbook by one of the clerks in the bank. That was but the ordinary transaction of writing up the customer's book; or, in other words, setting the debits, or sums which had been paid upon his checks, against the credits which were given in the book at the time the deposits were made. It only rendered the account complete up to the time when the balance was struck. It furnished no evidence of a change of the contract upon which the money was received in deposit.

New trial granted.

WHEELER, Respondent v WARNER, Appellant (1872) 47 NY 519, 19 S 374

Action against makers on a promissory note of $500 payable on demand, with interest. Defense, statute of limitations. Judgment for plaintiff and defendant appealed.

PECKHAM, J. The decision in Merrit v Todd, 23 NY 28, 80 AmDec 243, seems to have caused some disturbance in the law as to the right of parties upon demand notes. That case simply decided that an indorser on such a note bearing interest was not discharged, though no demand was made upon the maker until some three and a half years after the making of the note. That as between holder and indorser, such a note was not due until demand made. This rule, by the decision itself, was confined to that particular case, and did not apply, nor was it claimed to apply, to the rights of holders of such paper as against the maker. We are not disposed to extend the rule there laid down.

There is no divided opinion here or in England that upon such a note, with or without interest, an action may be maintained against the maker without any demand because it is due. No demand can be sued before due; no action will lie upon any claim of any description arising upon contract before it is due. To say that the suit is the demand is to repeat an unmeaning phrase as thus used, which no number of repetitions can make sensible. A demand note is due forthwith, and hence may be sued without demand, nor until this decision of Merrit v Todd has there been any difference of opinion as to the time when such a note is barred by the statute. But that decision does not settle this question.

There is really no reason why the statute should not run, and that it does run, both here and in England, is settled beyond all doubt.

If Merrit v Todd, in its reasoning, can be regarded as impugning this doctrine, it has been distinctly decided again in this court since that decision. (Howland v Edmonds, 24 NY 307.) In that case the point was whether the note sued upon was sustantially a demand note. The court held it was and therefore barred. In this case Merrit v Todd, although just decided by the same court, was not alluded to or regarded as having any legitimate bearing upon the question. In Herrick v Woolverton, 41 NY 581; 1 AmRep 461, originally tried before me and reversed by my brethren of the Supreme Court, this point was discussed, and all the judges who delivered opinions agreed that a note like this is due forthwith so far as regards the statute. See the authorities cited; and see Ang. Lim. 89, Sec. 95, and authorities cited in note; also an English elementary work, Darby & Bosang Stat. of Lim. 20, and cases cited.

This rule is not affected by any decision to the contrary in this court.

The judgment must be reversed and a new trial ordered.

Judgment reversed.

PEASE et al, Respondents v SMITH et al, Appellants (1875) 61 NY 477, a5 Lans. 519

APPEAL from judgment of the General Term of the Supreme Court in the third judicial department, affirming a judgment in favor of the plaintiffs entered upon a verdict, and affirming an order denying a motion for a new trial.

The action was brought for the alleged conversion by the defendant of a quantity of law blanks belonging to the plaintiffs.

Plaintiffs were book-sellers and stationers in the city of Albany. The defendants dealt largely in materials used in the manufacture of paper. Their course of business was to purchase from junk shops and small dealers rags, old paper, etc., in bales, and to sell to the manufacturers. They bought, among others, from Moses K. Perry, a junk dealer in Albany. The evidence upon the trial tended to show that among the materials purchased from Perry were law blanks belonging to the plaintiffs, which had been stolen from them by one Frank Mason, who was a porter in their employ. He lived in the building occupied by plaintiffs as a store, had the key to it, and it was his business to open it in the morning. He delivered packages and parcels of books, and went upon errands, etc., but was never authorized to sell their goods. Certain bales of paper materials containing these blanks were shipped after purchase by the defendants from Perry's store to Allen Brothers, paper manufacturers at Sandy Hill. The defendants paid five cents per pound for the materials bought from Perry. Mason was detected in carrying away blanks by Pease, one of the plaintiffs. The plaintiffs opened several bales of paper materials at Perry's and took out of each some law blanks, amounting to 237 pounds. They also obtained from Allen Brothers 700 or 800 pounds of blanks, paying five cents a pound for them. Evidence was offered tending to show that blanks with the names of the plaintiffs upon them had been used in manufacturing by Allen Brothers. The good faith of the defendants was not questioned. It was shown that a demand was made of the defendants for the value of the blanks before the commencement of the action, and soon after the discovery of the loss payment was refused by the defendants. A motion for a nonsuit was made and denied, defendant's counsel duly excepting, and the jury rendered a verdict for the plaintiffs.

DWIGHT, C. There are several objections raised by the defendants on this appeal.

It is claimed that the judge erred at the trial in refusing to grant a nonsuit, because the defendants bought the goods in controversy in the course of trade, and had sold them before any claim was made by the owners. It is insisted by the appellant that it is a prerequisite to a valid claim for conversion, in such a case, that a demand should have been made for the goods while they were in the defendant's possession, and before their sale, and that there can be no conversion, unless control over the property was exercised with knowledge of the plaintiffs' rights. This proposition is untenable. The assumed sale by the porter of the plaintiffs to Perry was wholly nugatory, and conveyed no title. (Saltus v Everett, 20 Wend.(NY) 267...) On like grounds, the sale by Perry to the defendants was without effect. They were constructively in possession of the plaintiffs' property without the consent of the latter. They even sent their own carts to transfer the goods when sold to Allen Brothers. This exercise of an act of ownership or dominion over the plaintiffs' property, assuming to sell and dispose of it as their own, was, within reason and the authorities, and act of conversion to their own use. The assumed act of ownership was inconsistent with the dominion of the plaintiffs, and this is of the essence of a conversion. Knowledge, and intent on the part of the defendants, are not material. So long as the defendants had exercised no act of ownership over the property, and had acted in good faith, a demand and refusal would be necessary to put them in the wrong and to constitute conversion. Until such demand, there is no apparent inconsistency between their possession and the plaintiffs' ownership. After a sale has been made by the defendants, they have assumed to be the owners, and will be estopped to deny, in an action by the lawful owner, the natural consequences of their act, and to resist an action for the value of the goods. The principle is well stated by Alderson, B., in Fouldes v Willoughby (8 M&W, 540): "Any asportation of a chattel for the use of the defendant or a third person amounts to a conversion for this simple reason, that it is an act inconsistent with the general right of dominion which the owner of a chattel has in it, who is entitled to the use of it at all times and in all places." In the same spirit, "conversion" is defined, in a very recent case, to be an unauthorized act which deprives another of his property permanently or for an indefinite time. (Hiort v Bott, L R (9 ex.), 86(AD 1874).) So, it is said in Boyce v Brockway (31 NY 490), that a wrongful intent is not an essential element in a conversion. It is enough that the rightful owner has been deprived of his property by some unauthorized act of another assuming dominion or control over it. No manual taking, on the defendants' part, is necessary. (Bristol v Burt, 7 JR, 254...) The case of Harris v Saunders (2 Strobh. Eq., 370), resembles closely the case at bar. The defendant having the property of the plaintiff in his own hands by purchase from one who had no title, sold it to another who carried it beyond the plaintiff's reach, and received the purchase-money. These acts were held to amount to a conversion, though the defendant was not aware of the plaintiff's title. As, according to these views, the conversion took place at the moment of the unauthorized sale by the present defendants, no demand was necessary, the sole object of a demand being to turn an otherwise lawful possession into an unlawful one, by reason of a refusal to comply with it, and thus to supply evidence of a conversion. (Esmay v Fanning, 9 Barb.(NY) 176...) After a wrongful taking and carrying away of the property, the cause of action has become complete without further act on the plaintiff's part. (Brewster v Silliman, 38 NY 423...)

Judgment affirmed

KNIGHT v POWERS DRY GOODS CO., INC. (1948) 225 Minn 280, 30 NW2d 536

Action by Mary E. B. Knight against Powers Dry Goods Company, Inc., for injuries sustained when the plaintiff was knocked down by an escaping shoplifter in defendant's store. From an order denying defendant's motion for judgment notwithstanding the verdict for plaintiff or for a new trial, the defendant appeals.

MAGNEY, J.... Lyman Newlin is a bookstore operator in Minneapolis. Formerly he had been employed in a similar store in Chicago. On or about February 2, 1945, he saw one Vancil Ingall standing on a street corner. He was bareheaded and carrying with one finger a box 18 to 24 inches long and about 10 inches wide and high. Newlin recognized him, having seen him in the Chicago store, and thought he was a book thief. The next day Ingall stepped into Newlin's store. He had his box with him. Newlin told his assistant to watch him, "because he is a slick operator." She watched him and "made herself almost obnoxious to him, asking could she help him." Ordinarily, prospective buyers are not pestered, the rule being that a man who buys books likes to browse. The assistant made it so uncomfortable for him that in about ten minutes he left. Newlin then called up every bookseller in the Twin Cities whom he knew, including defendant, the owner and operator of a large department store, giving them a description of the man....

The two women house detectives of defendant, one of whom was deputized by the city of Minneapolis, were notified that same day that there was a book thief in town. They had received such warnings several times before. No further information was given. Late in the afternoon they were called to the book department, and Ingall was there... One of the detectives remained inside, and the other went outside to watch him through the window. They saw him stack the books on the floor and then shove them into the opening of his trick box. It was like watching a slight-of-hand performance. Then he went out the door. He was stopped on the sidewalk. Mrs Augar said to him: "Pardon me, sir, but don't you think you had better pay for those books?" He said, "I guess I will" in a very gentle, soft voice. He turned around and calmly walked ahead of her through the door into the store, showing no violence or attempt to get away, and started to turn into the book department. Every indication was that he was going back to that department to pay for the books. Mrs. Augur then took hold of his arm and said to him: "There are too many people here. Let's go to the office, it will be less conspicuous." They walked along the aisle toward the elevator. The other detective took hold of his other arm. According to Mrs. Augur, Ingall looked "rather chagrined," but walked along quietly to the front of the elevator. While they were waiting for the elevator, Ingall suddenly threw the box and started to run. That was the first indication that he was going to be violent and the detectives stated that they had no idea he was a vicious character. Some men employees were standing at a freight elevator near by. Mrs. Augur called out to them once to stop him. She did not call out again, and no one else did.

Mrs. Augur, one of plaintiff's witnesses, testified that as Ingall was running down an aisle plaintiff, 67 years old, ran toward him several steps, swinging a cane at him and trying to hit him. In order to get away and protect himself, he pushed her aside with his hand. She was the only obstacle in his way. "She made herself a nuisance because she was right in everybody's way when we were trying to hold him." She fell to the floor. She was taken to the coffee shop....

Dr. Harvey Nelson, plaintiff's physician, testified that plaintiff, in giving her history stated "that she noticed a number of people chasing the thief in the bookstore in Powers. * * * and she attempted to stop him with a ski pole, and the thief grabbed her wrist with such force that it apparently fractured it. * * * My recollection is that she either tried to strike him or tried to trip him with it."

On this evidence, a verdict was rendered for plaintiff.

The court charged the jury: "* * *The defendant in this case was bound to use reasonable care to protect plaintiff as its customer from injury at the hands of vicious or lawless persons who it might bring in to its store."

This instruction made it the duty of defendant to use reasonable care to protect plaintiff from the hands of a vicious person whom it might bring into the store, irrespective of whether defendant knew or should have known that the person so brought in was vicious. Until Ingall started to run, there is no evidence that defendant knew or should have known that he was vicious. The court instructed the jury, therefore, upon an issue upon which there was no evidence and, in addition thereto, made it defendant's bounden duty to use reasonable care to protect plaintiff, whether at the time prior to his starting to run it knew or should have known that Ingall was vicious. In our opinion, the error in giving this instruction was so material and prejudicial that a new trial should at least be granted.

Defendant urges that the evidence does not support the verdict and therefore it is entitled to judgment notwithstanding. If defendant was negligent, that negligence must have taken place before Ingall started to run. All the testimony covering the events up to the time Ingall started to run was given by witnesses produced by plaintiff, and there is no conflict in that evidence. We have stated it in considerable detail. The question, then, is whether on this undisputed evidence a verdict for plaintiff can be sustained.

Newlin, the only witness who had known Ingall prior to this day, thought, from observations he had made in Chicago, that he was a book thief. He said that he was a "big fellow, heavy set"; seemed well-bred and looked like an educated man; that he represented himself to be a literary critic and looked the part' that he did not exhibit any violent propensities nor did he have the appearance of a thug or a criminal, and that he acted the part of a perfect gentleman. In fact, when Ingall appeared in his store in Minneapolis, Newlin permitted his assistant, a "very diminutive" girl, to watch him and to interfere with his browsing to such an extent that he left in a few minutes. Another of the plaintiff's witnesses, Mrs. Augur, one of the store detectives, said he looked like a rather distinguished businessman, a rather interesting looking person. She said there was nothing about him that looked like a vicious individual. She was asked if he appeared to be a violent sort, and she answered: "Far from it." Opal Daggett, another witness for plaintiff, said he looked more like a retired minister than anything else. There is no evidence to the contrary. When Newlin called up defendant to tell it that there was a book thief in town, he gave a description of the man. He did not say that Ingall was a vicious character, and he gave no advice on how to proceed with him. When Mrs. Augur stopped him on the sidewalk and asked him if he did not think he ought to pay for the books, he said in a soft, gentle voice, "I guess I will," walked calmly back into the store, and proceeded quietly until he reached the elevator. Shoplifters, according to one witness, are rather sneaky shy sort of persons. Another one stated that "They are very quiet, inconspicuous people mostly, to mingle in with a crowd or to appear inconspicuous in the store"; that sometimes, when first stopped, they will try to run.

It is evident from the above that defendant's employees did not know they were dealing with a vicious or violent person, and there is nothing in the record to indicate that they should have so known. The undisputed evidence in the case, in our opinion, does not spell out a case of negligence. Knowledge of the fact that Ingall was a shoplifter, a type of sneak thief, was not knowledge that he was vicious, or dangerous as well.

In Christianson v C., St. P., M. & O. Ry. Co., 67 Minn 94, 97, 69 NW 640, 641, Mr. Justice Mitchell states the rule: "* * * If a person had no reasonable ground to anticipate that a particular act would or might result in any injury to anybody, then, of course, the act would not be negligent at all;*** Otherwise expressed, the law is that if the act is one which the party ought, in the exercise of ordinary care, to have anticipated was liable to result in injury to others, then he is liable for any injury proximately resulting from it, although he could not have anticipated the particular injury which did happen."

In Seward v Minneapolis St. Ry. Co., 222 Minn 454, 25 NW2d 221, adherence to this rule was stated. In view of all the circumstances disclosed by the evidence, it cannot be said that defendant's employees had any reasonable ground to anticipate that the act of taking Ingall over to the elevator would or might result in any injury to anybody. Consequently their act would not be negligent.

Order reversed and judgment ordered for defendant.

Sec. 2.13 Breach of Duty by Defendant, including when necessary:

a. Acts and Words of Defendant
b. State of Mind of Defendant
c. Refusal to Perform upon Plaintiff's Demand
d. Injury to Plaintiff (loss or deprivation as to his legal interest)
e. Legal Causation (defendant's breach as the legal cause, direct or proximate, of plaintiff's injury)
f. Other required factors, if any

SMITH v STATE (1846) 26 Tenn 30, 7 Humph. 43

Rogers, with horse and carryall, was carried over the Chucky river by Smith in his ferryboat. Smith was the keeper of a public ferry. When over Smith demanded ferriage, which Rodgers said was already paid: on this a dispute occurred, and Smith told him he should not go on till he paid the ferriage. Some other conversation ensued, when Rodgers paid the ferriage demanded. Rodgers was detained ten or fifteen minutes. An indictment was found against Smith for an assault and false imprisonment.

Rogers stated on the trial before R. M. Anderson, presiding judge, and a jury of Cooke County, that Smith had not touched his bridle or his horse, and that he made no threats of personal violence, but that he was afraid of a difficulty with Smith. Smith told Rodgers after he had paid the charge, that if he had not paid it he had determined to have put his carryall and horse back into the boat, and to have carried them back. A verdict and judgment were rendered for the State, and defendant appealled.

GREEN, J. The plaintiff in error was indicted for an assault and false imprisonment of Mark H. Rodgers. The court charged the jury, "That to make out the offense as charged, no actual force was necessary, but that a man might be assaulted by being beset by another; and if the opposition to the prosecutor's going forward was such as a prudent man would not risk, then the defendant would, in contemplation of law, be guilty of false imprisonment."

This charge is correct in all parts, and the facts were fairly left to the jury. A verdict of guilty has been pronounced, and we do not feel authorized to disturb it. The prosecutor and defendant disputed about the ferriage defendant claimed. Smith insisted upon this demand, and said he did not choose to sue every man that crossed at his ferry. Although he did not take hold of the prosecutor, or offer violence to his person, yet his manner may have operated as a moral force to detain the prosecutor.

And this appears the more probable, as after the affair was settled, the prosecutor inquired what defendant would have done if he had not paid the ferriage demanded, to which the defendant replied, "he would have put his carryall and horse back into the boat and taken them across the river again." As this determination existed in his mind, it doubtless was exhibited in the manner of the defendant, and thus operated upon the fears of the prosecutor.

Judgment affirmed.

SWEATT, Petitioner v PAINTER, et al, Texas Board of Regents, Respondent (1950) 339 US 629, 94 LEd 1114, r210 SW2d(Tex) 442

Mr. Chief Justice VINSON:.... In the instant case, petitioner filed an application for admission to the University of Texas Law School for the February, 1946 term. His application was rejected solely because he is a Negro. Petitioner thereupon brought this suit for mandamus against the appropriate school officials, respondents here, to compel his admission. At that time, there was no law school in Texas which admitted Negroes.

The State trial court recognized that the action of the State in denying petitioner the opportunity to gain a legal education while granting it to others deprived him of the equal protection of the law guaranteed by the Fourteenth Amendment. The court did not grant the relief requested, however, but continued the case for six months to allow the State to supply substantially equal facilities. At the expiration of the six months, in December, 1946, the court denied the writ on the showing that the authorized university officials had adopted an order calling for the opening of a law school for Negroes the following

February. While petitioner's appeal was pending, such a school was made available, but petitioner refused to register therein. The Texas Court of Civil Appeals set aside the trial court's judgment and ordered the cause "remanded generally to the trial court for further proceedings without prejudice to the rights of any party to this suit."

On remand, a hearing was held on the issue of the equality of the educational facilities at the newly established school as compared with the University of Texas Law School. Finding that the new school offered petitioner "privileges, advantages, and opportunities for the study of law substantially equivalent to those offered by the State to white students at the University of Texas," the trial court denied mandamus. The Court of Civil Appeals affirmed. (TexCivApp) 210 SW2d 442 (1948). Petitioner's application for a writ of error was denied by the Texas Supreme Court. We granted certiorari, 338 US 865, ante, 530, 70 SCt 139 (1949), because of the manifest importance of the constitutional issues involved.

The University of Texas Law School, from which petitioner was excluded, was staffed by sixteen full-time and three part-time professors, some of whom are nationally recognized authorities in their field. Its student body numbered 850. The library contained over 65,000 volumes. Among the other facilities available to the students were a law review, moot court facilities, scholarship funds, and Order of the Coif affiliation. The school's alumni occupy the most distinguished positions in the private practice of the law and in the public life of the State. It may properly be considered one of the nations's ranking law schools.

The law school for Negroes which was to have opened in February, 1947, would have had no independent faculty or library. The teaching was to be carried on by four members of the University of Texas Law School faculty, who were to maintain their offices at the University of Texas while teaching at both institutions. Few of the 10,000 volumes ordered for the library had arrived; nor was there any full-time librarian. The school lacked accreditation.

Since the trial of this case, respondents report the opening of a law school at the Texas State University for Negroes. It is apparently on the road to full accreditation. It has a faculty of five full-time professors; a student body of 23; a library of some 16,500 volumes serviced by a full-time staff; a practice court and legal aid association; and one alumnus who has become a member of the Texas Bar.

Whether the University of Texas Law School is compared with the original or the new law school for Negroes, we cannot find substantial equality in the educational opportunities offered white and Negro law students by the State. In terms of number of the faculty, variety of courses and opportunity for specialization, size of the student body, scope of the library, availability of law review and similar activities, the University of Texas Law School is superior. What is more important, the University of Texas Law School possesses to a far greater degree those qualities which are incapable of objective measurement but which make for greatness in a law school. Such qualities, to name but a few, include reputation of the faculty, experience of the administration, position and influence of the alumni, standing in the community, traditions and prestige. It is difficult to believe that one who had a free choice between these law schools would consider the question close.

Moreover, although the law is a highly learned profession, we are well aware that it is an intensely practical one. The law school, the proving ground for legal learning and practice, cannot be effective in isolation from the individuals and institutions with which the law interacts. Few students and no one who has practiced law would choose to study in an academic vacuum, removed from the interplay of ideas and the exchange of views with which the law is concerned. The law school to which Texas is willing to admit petitioner excludes from its student body members of the racial groups which number 85% of the population of the State and include most of the lawyers, witnesses, jurors, judges and other officials with whom petitioner will inevitably be dealing when he becomes a member of the Texas Bar. With such a substantial and significant segment of society excluded, we cannot conclude that the education offered petitioner is substantially equal to that which he would receive if admitted to the University of Texas Law School.

It may be argued that excluding petitioner from that school is no different from excluding white students from the new law school. This contention overlooks realities. It is unlikely that a member of a group so decisively in the majority, attending a school with rich traditions and prestige which only a history of consistently maintained excellence could command, would claim that the opportunities afforded him for legal education were unequal to those held open to petitioner. That such a claim, if made, would be dishonored by the State, is no answer. "Equal protection of the laws is not achieved through indiscriminate imposition of inequalities." (Shelley v Kraemer, 334 US 1, 22, 92 LEd 1161, 1185, 68 SCt 836, 3 ALR2d 441 (1948).

It is fundamental that these cases concern rights which are personal and present. This Court has stated that "The State must provide (legal education) for (petitioner) in conformity with the equal protection clause of the Fourteenth Amendment and provide it as soon as it does for applicants of any other group." (Sipuel v Board of Regents, 332 US 631, 633, 92 LEd 247, 249, 68 SCt 229 (1948). That case "did not present the issue whether a state might not satisfy the equal protection clause of the Fourteenth Amendment by establishing a separate law school for Negroes." (Fisher v Hurst, 333 US 147, 150, 92 LEd 604, 606, 68 SCt 389 (1948). In Missouri ex rel Gaines v Canada, 305 US 337, 351, 83 LEd 208, 214, 59 SCt 232 (1938), the Court, speaking through Chief Justice Hughes, declared that "petitioner's right was a personal one. It was as an individual that he was entitled to the equal protection of the laws, and the State was bound to furnish him within its borders facilities for legal education substantially equal to those which the State there afforded for persons of the white race, whether or not other Negroes sought the same opportunity." These are the only cases in this Court which present the issue of the constitutional validity of race distinctions in state-supported graduate and professional education.

In accordance with these cases, petitioner may claim his full constitutional right: legal education equivalent to that offered by the State to students of other races. Such education is not available to him in a separate law school as offered by the State. We cannot, therefore, agree with respondents that the doctrine of Plessy v Ferguson, 163 US 537, 41 LEd 256, 16 SCt 1138 (1896), requires affirmance of the judgment below. Nor need we reach petitioner's contention that Plessy v Ferguson should be reexamined in the light of contemporary knowledge respecting the purposes of the Fourteenth Amendment and the effects of racial segregation. (See supra, p 1118.)

We hold that the Equal Protection Clause of the Fourteenth Amedment requires that petitioner be admitted to the University of Texas Law School. The judgment is reversed and the cause is remanded for proceedings not inconsistent with this opinion.

Reversed.

LILLIE v THOMPSON, Trustee for St Louis-San Francisco Ry Co. (1947) 332 US 459, 92 LEd 73, r162 F2d 716

PER CURIAM. Petitioner sued for damages under the Federal Employers' Liability Act.[1] The essence of her claim was that she was injured as a result of the respondent's negligence in sending her to work in a place he knew to be unsafe without taking reasonable measures to protect her.

The district court dismissed the complaint for failure to state a cause of action and entered summary judgment for the respondent. The Circuit Court of Appeals affirmed without opinion.

There is thus a single issue in the case: Could it be found from the facts alleged in the complaint, as supplemented by any uncontroverted allegations by the respondent, that petitioner's injuries resulted at least in part from respondent's negligence?[2]

Petitioner's allegations may be summarized as follows: Respondent required her, a 22-year-old telegraph operator, to work alone between 11:30 p.m. and 7:30 a.m. in a one-room frame building situated in an isolated part of respondent's railroad yards in Memphis. Though respondent had reason to know the yards were frequented by dangerous characters, he failed to exercise care to light the building and its surroundings or to guard or patrol it in any way. Petitioner's duties were to receive and deliver messages to men operating trains in the yard. In order for the trainmen to get the messages it was necessary for them to come to the building at irregular intervals throughout the night, and it was petitioner's duty to admit them when they knocked. Because there were no windows in the building's single door or on the side of the building in which the door was located, petitioner could identify persons seeking entrance only by unlocking and opening the door. About 1:30 a.m. on the night of her injury petitioner responded to a knock, thinking that some of respondent's trainmen were seeking admission. She opened the door, and before she could close it a man entered and beat her with a large piece of iron, seriously and permanently injuring her.

In support of his motion for summary judgment respondent alleged, and petitioner did not deny, that the assailant was not an employee of the respondent and that the attack was criminal.

The district court stated, in explanation of its action, that there would be no causal connection between the injury and respondent's failure to light or guard the premises, and that the law does not permit recovery "for the intentional or criminal acts" of either a fellow-employee or an outsider.

We are of the opinion that the allegations in the complaint, if supported by evidence, will warrant submission to a jury. Petitioner alleged in effect that respondent was aware of conditions which created a likelihood that a young woman performing the duties required of petitioner would suffer just such an injury as was in fact inflicted upon her. That the foreseeable danger was from intentional or criminal misconduct is irrelevant; respondent nonetheless had a duty to make reasonable provision against it. Breach of that duty would be negligence, and we cannot say as a matter of law that petitioner's injury did not result at least in part from such negligence. The cases cited by the district court, we believe, do not support the broad proposition enunciated by it, and do not cover the fact situation set forth by the pleadings in this case.

Certiorari is granted, and the judgment is reversed and the case remanded to the district court.

Reversed.

---

1 45 USCA Sec. 51, 10A FCA title 45, Sec. 51.

2 "Every common carrier by railroad...shall be liable in damages to any person suffering injury while he is employed by such carrier...for such injury....resulting in whole or in part from the negligence of any of the officers, agents, or employees of such carrier..." ibid.

It is not questioned that respondent was engaged in interstate commerce and that petitioner was injured while employed in such commerce.

HELEN PALSGRAF, Respondent, v THE LONG ISLAND RAILROAD COMPANY, Appellant (1928) 248 NY 339, r222 AD 166

APPEAL from a judgment of the Appellate Division of the Supreme Court in the second judicial department, entered December 16, 1927, affirming a judgment in favor of plaintiff entered upon a verdict.

CARDOZO, CH. J. Plaintiff was standing on a platform of defendant's railroad after buying a ticket to go to Rockaway Beach. A train stopped at the station, bound for another place. Two men ran forward to catch it. One of the men reached the platform of the car without mishap, though the train was already moving. The other man, carrying a package, jumped aboard the car, but seemed unsteady as if about to fall. A guard on the car, who had held the door open, reached forward to help him in, and another guard on the platform pushed him from behind. In this act, the package was dislodged, and fell upon the rails. It was a package of small size, about fifteen inches long, and was covered by a newspaper. In fact it contained fireworks, but there was nothing in its appearance to give notice of its contents. The fireworks when they fell exploded. The shock of the explosion threw down some scales at the other end of the platform, many feet away. The scales struck the plaintiff, causing injuries for which she sues.

The conduct of the defendant's guard, if a wrong in its relation to the holder of the package, was not a wrong in its relation to the plaintiff, standing far away. Relatively to her it was not negligence at all. Nothing in the situation gave notice that the falling package had in it the potency of peril to persons thus removed. Negligence is not actionable unless it involves the invasion of a legally protected interest, the violation of a right. "Proof of negligence in the air, so to speak, will not do" (Pollock, Torts (11th ed.), p. 455; Martin v Herzog, 228 NY 164, 170; cf. Salmond, Torts (6th ed.), p.24). Negligence is the absence of care, according to the circumstances" (Willes, J., in Vaughan v Taff Vale Ry Co., 5 H&N 679, 688; 1 Beven Negligence (4th ed.), 7; Paul v Consol. Fireworks Co., 212 NY 117; Adams v Bullock, 227 NY 208, 211; Parrott v Wells-Fargo Co., 15 Wall.(US) 524). The plaintiff as she stood upon the platform of the station might claim to be protected against intentional invasion of her bodily security. Such invasion is not charged. She might claim to be protected against unintentional invasion by conduct involving in the thought of reasonable men an unreasonable hazard that such invasion would ensue. These, from the point of view of the law, were the bounds of her immunity, with perhaps some rare exceptions, survivals for the most part of ancient forms of liability, where conduct is held to be at the peril of the actor (Sullivan v Dunham, 161 NY 290). If no hazard was apparent to the eye of ordinary vigilance, an act innocent and harmless, at least to outward seeming, with reference to her, did not take to itself the quality of a tort because it happened to be wrong, though apparently not one involving the risk of bodily insecurity, with reference to some one else. "In every instance, before negligence can be predicated of a given act, back of the act must be sought and found a duty to the individual complaining, the observance of which would have averted or avoided the injury" (McSherry, C.J., in W.Va. Central R. Co. v State, 96 Md 652, 666; cf. Norfolk & Western Ry. Co. v Wood, 99 Va 156, 158, 159; Hughes v Boston & Maine R.R. Co., 71 NH 279, 284; U.S. Express Co. v Everest, 72 Kan 517; Emry v Roanoke Nav. Co., 111 NC 94, 95; Vaughan v Transit Dev. Co., 222 NY 79; Losee v Clute, 51 NY 494; DiCaprio v N.Y.C.R.R.Co., 231 NY 94; 1 Shearman & Redfield on Negligence, Sec.8, and cases cited; Cooley on Torts (3d ed.), p. 1411; Jaggard on Torts, vol. 2, p. 826; Wharton, Negligence, Sec.24; Bohlen, Studies in the Law of Torts, p. 601). "The ideas of negligence and duty are strictly correlative" (BOWEN, L. J., in Thomas v Quartermaine, 18 QBD 685, 694). The plaintiff sues in her own right for a wrong personal to her, and not as the vicarious beneficiary of a breach of duty to another.

A different conclusion will involve us, and swiftly too, in a maze of contradictions. A guard stumbles over a package which has been left upon a platform. It seems to be a bundle of newspapers. It turns out to be a can of dynamite. To the eye of ordinary vigilance, the bundle is abandoned waste, which may be kicked or trod on with impunity. Is a passenger at the other end of the platform protected by the law against the unsuspected hazard concealed beneath the waste? if not, is the result to be any different, so far as the distant passenger is concerned, when the guard stumbles over a valise which a truckman or a porter has left upon the walk? The passenger far away, if the victim of a wrong at all, has a cause of action, not derivative, but original and primary. His claim to be protected against invasion of his bodily security is neither greater nor less because the act resulting in the invasion is a wrong to another far removed. In this case, the rights that are said to have been violated, the interests said to have been invaded, are not even of the same order. The man was not injured in his person nor even put in danger. The purpose of the act, as well as its effect, was to make his person safe. If there was a wrong to him at all, which may very well be doubted, it was a wrong to a property interest only, the safety of his package.

Out of this wrong to property, which threatened injury to nothing else, there has passed, we are told, to the plaintiff by derivation or succession a right of action for the invasion of an interest of another order, the right to bodily security. The diversity of interests emphasizes the futility of the effort to build the plaintiff's right upon the basis of a wrong to some one else. The gain is one of emphasis, for a like result would follow if the interests were the same. Even then, the orbit of the danger as disclosed to the eye of reasonable vigilance would be the orbit of the duty. One who jostles one's neighbor in a crowd does not invade the rights of others standing at the outer fringe when the unintended contact casts a bomb upon the ground. The wrongdoer as to them is the man who carries the bomb, not the one who explodes it without suspicion of the danger. Life will have to be made over, and human nature transformed, before prevision so extravagant can be accepted as the norm of conduct, the customary standard to which behavior must conform.

The argument for the plaintiff is built upon the shifting meanings of such words as "wrong" and "wrongful", and shares their instability. What the plaintiff must show is "a wrong" to herself, i.e., a violation of her own right, and not merely a wrong to some one else, nor conduct "wrongful" because unsocial, but not "a wrong" to any one. We are told that one who drives at reckless speed through a crowded city street is guilty of a negligent act and therefore, of a wrongful one irrespective of the consequences. Negligent the act is, and wrongful in the sense that it is unsocial, but wrongful and unsocial in relation to other travelers, only because the eye of vigilance perceives the risk of damage. If the same act were to be committed on a speedway or a race course, it would lose its wrongful quality. The risk reasonably to be perceived defines the duty to be obeyed, and risk imports relation; it is risk to another or to others within the range of apprehension (Seavey, Negligence, Subjective or Objective, 41 HarLRv 6; Boronkay v Robinson & Carpenter, 247 NY 365). This does not mean of course, that one who launches a destructive force is always relieved of liability if the force, though known to be destructive, pursues an unexpected path. "It was not necessary that the defendant should have had notice of the particular method in which an accident would occur, if the possibility of an accident was clear to the ordinarily prudent eye" (Munsey v Webb, 231 US 150, 156; Condran v Park & Tilford, 213 NY 341, 345; Robert v U.S.E.F. Corp., 240 NY 474, 477). Some acts such as shooting, are so imminently dangerous to any one who may come within reach of the missile, however unexpectedly, as to impose a duty of prevision not far from that of an insurer. Even today, and much oftener in earlier stages of the law, one acts sometimes at one's peril (Jeremiah Smith, Tort and Absolute Liability, 30 HarLR 328; Street, Foundations of Legal Liability, vol. 1, pp. 77, 78). Under this head, it may be, fall certain cases of what is known as transferred intent, an act willfully dangerous to A resulting by misadventure in injury to B (Talmage v Smith, 101 Mich. 370, 374). These cases aside, wrong is defined in terms of the natural or probable, at least when unintentional (Parrot v Wells-Fargo Co. (The Nitro-Clycerine Case), 15 Wall.(US) 524). The range of reasonable apprehension is at times a question for the court, and at times, if varying inferences are possible, a question for the jury. Here, by concession, there was nothing in the situation to suggest to the most cautious mind that the parcel wrapped in newspaper would spread wreckage through the station. If the guard had thrown it down knowingly and wilfully, he would not have threatened the plaintiff's safety, so far as appearance could warn him. His conduct would not have involved, even then, an unreasonable probability of invasion of her bodily security. Liability can be no greater where the act is inadvertent.

Negligence, like risk, is thus a term of relation. Negligence in the abstract, apart from things related, is surely not a tort, if indeed it is understandable at all (BOWEN, L. J., in Thomas v Quartermaine, 18 QBD 685, 694). Negligence is not a tort unless it results in the commission of a wrong, and the commission of a wrong imports the violation of a right, in this case, we are told, the right to be protected against interference with one's bodily security. But bodily security is protected, not against all forms of interference or aggression, but only against some. One who seeks redress at law does not make out a cause of action by showing without more than there has been damage to his person. If the harm was not willful, he must show that the act as to him had possibilites of danger so many and apparent as to entitle him to be protected against the doing of it though the harm was unintended. Affront to personality is still the keynote of the wrong. Confirmation of this view will be found in the history and development of the action on the case. Negligence as a basis of civil liability was unknown to mediaeval law (8 Holdsworth, History of English Law, p. 449; Street, Foundations of Legal Liability, vol. 1, pp. 189, 190). For damage to the person, the sole remedy was trespass, and trespass, did not lie in the absence of aggression, and that direct and personal (Holdsworth, op. cit. p. 453; Street, op. cit. vol. 3, pp. 258, 260, vol. 1, pp. 71, 74.) Liability for other damage, as where a servant without orders from the master does or omits something to the damage of another, is a plant of later growth (Holdsworth, op. cit. 450, 457; Wigmore, Responsibility for Tortious Acts. vol. 3, Essays in Anglo-American Legal History, 520, 523, 526, 533).

When it emerged out of the legal soil, it was thought of as a variant of trespass, an offshot of the parent stock. This appears in the form of action, which was known as trespass on the case (Holdsworth, op.cit. p. 449; cf. Scott v Shepard, 2 Wm. Black. 892; Green, Rationale of Proximate Cause, p. 19). The victim does not sue derivatively, or by right of subrogation, to vindicate an interest invated in the person of another. Thus to view his cause of action is to ignore the fundamental difference between tort and crime (Holland, Jurisprudence 112th ed. 1, p. 328). He sues for breach of a duty owing to himself.

The law of causation, remote or proximate, is thus foreign to the case before us. The question of liability is always anterior to the question of the measure of the consequences that go with liability. If there is no tort to be redressed, there is no occasion to consider what damage might be recovered if there were a finding of a tort. We may assume, without deciding, that negligence, not at large or in the abstract, but in relation to the plaintiff, would entail liability for any and all consequences, however novel or extraordinary (Bird v St. Paul F. & M. Ins. Co., 224 NY 47, 54; Ehrgott v Mayor, etc., of N.Y., 98 NY 264; Smith v London & S.W. Ry. Co., L.R. 6 C.P. 14; 1 Beven, Negligence, 106; Street, op. cit. vol. 1, p. 90; Green, Rationale of Proximate Cause, pp. 88, 118; cf. Matter of Polemis, LR 1921, 3 KB 560; 44 Law Qr 142). There is room for argument that a distinction is to be drawn according to the diversity of interests invaded by the act, as where conduct negligent in that it threatens an insignificant invasion of an interest in property results in an unforseeable invasion of an interest of another order, as, e.g., one bodily security. Perhaps other distinctions may be necessary. We do not go into the question now. The consequences to be followed must first be rooted in a wrong.

The judgment of the Appellate Division and that of the Trial Term should be reversed, and the complaint dismissed, with costs in all courts.

ANDREWS, J. (dissenting). Assisting a passenger to board a train, the defendant's servant negligently knocked a package from his arms. It fell between the platform and the cars. Of its contents the servant knew and could know nothing. A violent explosion followed. The concussion broke some scales standing a considerable distance away. In falling they injured the plaintiff, an intending passenger.

Upon these facts may she recover the damages she has suffered in an action brought against the master? The result we shall reach depends upon our theory as to the nature of negligence. Is it a relative concept--the breach of some duty owing to a particular person or to particular persons? Or where there is an act which unreasonably threatens the safety of others, is the doer liable for all its proximate consequences, even where they result in injury to one who would generally be thought to be outside the radius of danger? This is not a mere dispute as to words. We might not believe that to the average mind the dropping of the bundle would seem to involve the probability of harm to the plaintiff standing many feet away whatever might be the case as to the owner or to one so near as to be likely to be struck by its fall. If, however, we adopt the second hypothesis we have to inquire only as to the relation between cause and effect. We deal in terms of proximate cause, not of negligence.

Negligence may be defined roughly as an act or omission which unreasonably does or may affect the rights of others, or which unreasonably fails to protect oneself from the dangers resulting from such acts. Here I confine myself to the first branch of the definition. Nor do I comment on the word "unreasonable." For present purposes it sufficiently describes that average of conduct that society requires of its members.

There must be both the act or the omission, and the right. It is the act itself, not the intent of the actor, that is important. (Hover v Barkhof 44 NY 113; Mertz v Connecticut Co., 217 NY 475.) In criminal law both the intent and the result are to be considered. Intent again is material in tort actions, where punitive damages are sought, dependent on actual malice--not on merely reckless conduct. But here neither insanity nor infancy lessens responsibility. (Williams v Hays, 143 NY 442.)

As has been said, except in cases of contributory negligence, there must be rights which are or may be affected. Often though injury has occurred, no rights of him who suffers have been touched. A licensee or trespasser upon my land has no claim to affirmative care on my part that the land be made safe. (Meiers v Koch Brewery, 229 NY 10.) Where a railroad is required to fence its tracks against cattle, no man's rights are injured should he wander upon the road because such fence is absent. (Di Caprio v N.Y.C.R.R., 231 NY 94.) An unborn child may not demand immunity from personal harm. (Drobner v Peters, 232 NY 220.)

But we are told that "there is no negligence unless there is in the particular case a legal duty to take care, and this duty must be one which is owed to the plaintiff himself and not merely to others." (Salmond, Torts (6th ed.), 24.) This, I think too narrow a conception. Where there is the unreasonable act, and some right that may be affected there is negligence whether damage does or does not result. That is immaterial. Should we drive down Broadway at a reckless speed, we are negligent whether we strike an approaching car or miss it by an inch. The act itself is wrongful. It is a wrong not only to those who happen to be within the radius of danger but to all who might have been there--a wrong to the public at large. Such is the language of the street. Such the language of the courts when speaking of contributory negligence. Such again and again their language in speaking of the duty of some defendant and discussing proximate cause in cases where such a discussion is wholly irrelevant on any other theory. (Perry v Rochester Lime Co., 219 NY 60.) As was said by Mr. Justice Holmes many years ago, "the measure of the defendant's duty in determining whether a wrong has been committed is one thing, the measure of liability when a wrong has been committed is another." (Spade v Lynn & Boston R.R. Co., 172 Mass 488.) Due care is a duty imposed on each one of us to protect society from unnecessary danger, not to protect, A, B or C alone.

It may well be that there is no such thing as negligence in the abstract. "Proof of negligence in the air, so to speak, will not do." In an empty world negligence would not exist. It does involve a relationship between man and his fellows. But not merely a relationship between man and those whom he might reasonably expect his act would injure. Rather, a relationship between him and those whom he does in fact injure. If his act has a tendency to harm some one, it harms him a mile away as surely as it does those on the scene. We now permit children to recover for the negligent killing of the father. It was never prevented on the theory that no duty was owing to them. A husband may be compensated for the loss of his wife's services. To say that the wong-doer was negligent as to the husband as well as to the wife is merely an attempt to fit facts to theory. An insurance company paying a fire loss recovers its payment of the negligent incendiary. We speak of subrogation--of suing in the right of the insured. Behind the cloud of words is the fact they hide, that the act, wrongful as to the insured, has also injured the company. Even if it be true that the fault of father, wife or insured will prevent recovery, it is because we consider the original negligence not the proximate cause of the injury. (Pollock, Torts (12th ed.), 463.)

In the well-known Polemis case (1921, 3 KB 560), SCRUTTON, L.J., said that the dropping of a plank was negligent for it might injure "workmen or cargo or ship." Because of either possibility the owner of the vessel was to be made good for his loss. The act being wrongful the doer was liable for its proximate results. Criticized and explained as this statement may have been, I think it states the law as it should be and as it is. (Smith v London & Southwestern Ry. Co., (1870-71) 6 CP 14; Anthony v Slaid, 52 Mass 290; Wood v Penn. R.R. Co., 177 PennSt 306; Trashansky v Hershkovitz, 239 NY 452.)

The proposition is this. Every one owes to the world at large the duty or refraining from those acts that may unreasonably threaten the safety of others. Such an act occurs. Not only is he wronged to whom harm might reasonably be expected to result, but he also who is in fact injured, even if he be outside what would generally be thought the danger zone. There needs be duty due the one complaining but this is not a duty to a particular individual because as to him harm might be expected. Harm to some one being the natural result of the act, not only that one alone, but all those in fact injured may complain. We have never, I think, held otherwise. Indeed in the Di Caprio case we said that a breach of a general ordinance defining the degree of care to be exercised in one's calling is evidence of negligence as to every one. We did not limit this statement to those who might be expected to be exposed to danger. Unreasonable risk being taken, its consequences are not confined to those who might probably be hurt.

If this be so, we do not have a plaintiff suing by "derivation or succession." Her action is original and primary. Her claim is for a breach of duty to herself--not that she is subrogated to any right of action of the owner of the parcel or of a passenger standing at the scene of the explosion.

The right to recover damages rests on additional considerations. The plaintiff's rights must be injured, and this injury must be caused by the negligence. We build a dam, but are negligent as to its foundations. Breaking, it injures property down stream. We are not liable if all this happened because of some reason other than the insecure foundation. But when injuries do result from our unlawful act we are liable for the consequences. It does not matter that they are unusual, unexpected, unforeseen and unforseeable. But there is one limitation. The damages must be so connected with the negligence that the latter may be said to be the proximate cause of the former.

These two words have never been given an inclusive definition. What is a cause in a legal sense, still more what is a proximate cause, depend in each case upon many considerations, as does the existence of negligence itself. Any philosophical doctrine of causation does not help us. A boy throws a stone into a pond. The ripples spread. The water level rises. The history of that pond is altered to all eternity. It will be altered by other causes also. Yet it will be forever the resultant of all causes combined. Each one will have an influence. How great only omniscience can say. You may speak of a chain, or if you please, a net. An analogy is of little aid. Each cause brings about future events. Without each the future would not be the same. Each is proximate in the sense it is essential. But that is not what we mean by the word. Nor on the other hand do we mean sole cause. There is no such thing.

Should analogy be thought helpful, however, I prefer that of a stream. The spring, starting on its journey , is joined by tributary after tributary. The river, reaching the ocean, comes from a hundred sources. No man may say whence any drop of water is derived. Yet for a time distinction may be possible. Into the clear creek, brown swamp water flows from the left. Later from the right comes water stained by its clay bed. The three may remain for a space, sharply divided. But at last, inevitably no trace of separation remains. They are so commingled that all distinction is lost.

As we have said, we cannot trace the effect of an act to the end, if end there is. Again, however, we may trace it part of the way. A murder at Serajevo may be the necessary antecedent to an assassination in London twenty years hence. An overturned lantern may burn all Chicago. We may follow the fire from the shed to the last building. We rightly say the fire started by the lantern caused its destruction.

A cause, but not the proximate cause. What we do mean by the word "proximate" is, that because of convenience, of public policy, of a rough sense of justice, the law arbitrarily declines to trace a series of events beyond a certain point. This is not logic. It is practical politics. Take our rule as to fires. Sparks from my burning haystack set on fire my house and my neighbor's. I may recover from a negligent railroad. He may not. Yet the wrongful act as directly harmed the one as the other. We may regret that the line was drawn just where it was, but drawn somewhere it had to be. We said the act of the railroad was not the proximate cause of our neighbor's fire. Cause it surely was. The words we used were simply indicative of our notions of public policy. Other courts think differently. But somewhere they reach the point where they cannot say the stream comes from any one source.

Take the illustration given in an unpublished manuscript by a distinguished and helpful writer on the law of torts. A chauffeur negligently collides with another car which is filled with dynamite, although he could not know it. An explosion follows. A, walking on the sidewalk nearby, is killed. B, sitting in a window of a building opposite, is cut by flying glass. C, likewise sitting in a window a block away, is similarly injured. And a further illustration. A nursemaid, ten blocks away, startled by the noise, involuntarily drops a baby from her arms to the walk. We are told that C may not recover while A may. As to B it is a question for court or jury. We will all agree that the baby might not. Because, we are again told, the chauffeur had no reason to believe his conduct involved any risk of injury either C or the baby. As to them he was not negligent.

But the chauffeur, being negligent in risking the collision, his belief that the scope of the harm he might do would be limited is immaterial. His act unreasonably jeopardized the safety of any one who might be affected by it. C's injury and that of the baby were directly traceable to the collision. Without that, the injury would not have happened. C had the right to sit in his office, secure from such dangers. The baby was entitled to use the sidewalk with reasonable safety.

The true theory is, it seems to me, that the injury to C, if in truth he is to be denied recovery, and the injury to the baby is that their several injuries were not the proximate result of the negligence. And here not what the chauffeur had reason to believe would be the result of his conduct, but what the prudent would foresee, may have a bearing. May have some bearing, for the problem of proximate cause is not to be solved by any one consideration.

It is all a question of expediency. There are no fixed rules to govern our judgment. There are simple matters of which we may take account. We have in a somewhat different connection spoken of "the stream of events." We have asked whether that stream was deflected--whether it was forced into new and unexpected channels. (Donnelly v Piercy Contracting Co., 222 NY 210). This is rather rhetoric than law. There is in truth little to guide us other than common sense.

There are some hints that may help us. The proximate cause, involved as it may be with many other causes, must be, at the least, something without which the event would not happen. The court must ask itself whether there was a natural and continuous sequence between cause and effect. Was the one a substantial factor in producing the other? Was there a direct connection between them, without too many intervening causes? Is the effect of cause on result not too attentuated? Is the cause likely, in the usual judgment of mankind, to produce the result? Or by the exercise of prudent foresight could the result be foreseen? Is the result too remote from the cause, and here we consider remoteness in time and space. (Bird v St. Paul F. & M. Ins. Co., 224 NY 47, which we passed upon the construction of a contract--but something was also said on this subject.) Clearly we must so consider, for the greater the distance either in time or space, the more surely do other causes intervene to affect the result. When a lantern is overturned the firing of a shed is a fairly direct consequence. Many things contribute to the spread of the conflagration--the force of the wind, the direction and width of streets, the character of intervening structures, other factors. We draw an uncertain and wavering line, but draw it we must as best we can.

Once again, it is all a question of fair judgment, always keeping in mind the fact that we endeavor to make a rule in each case that will be practical and in keeping with the general understanding of mankind.

Here another question must be answered. In the case supposed it is said, and said correctly, that the chauffeur is liable for the direct effect of the explosion although he had no reason to suppose it would follow a collision. "The fact that the injury occurred in a different manner than that which might have been expected does not prevent the chauffeur's negligence from being in law the cause of the injury." But the natural results of a negligent act--the results which a prudent man would or should foresee--do have a bearing upon the decision as to proximate cause. We have said so repeatedly. What should be foreseen? No human foresight would suggest that a collision itself might injure one a block away. On the contrary, given an explosion, such a possibility might be reasonably expected. I think the direct connection, the foresight of which the courts speak, assumes prevision of the explosion, for the immediate results of which, at least, the chauffeur is responsible.

It may be said this is unjust. Why? In fairness he should make good every injury flowing from his negligence. Not because of tenderness toward him we say he need not answer for all that follows his wrong. We look back to the catastrophe, the fire kindled by the spark, or the explosion. We trace the consequences--not indefinitely, but to a certain point. And to aid us in fixing that point we ask what might ordinarily be expected to follow the fire or the explosion.

This last suggestion is the factor which must determine the case before us. The act upon which defendant's liability rests is knocking an apparently harmless package onto the platform. The act was negligent. For its proximate consequences the defendant is liable. If its contents were broken, to the owner, if it fell upon and crushed a passenger's foot, then to him. If it exploded and injured one in the immediate vicinity, to him also as to A in the illustration. Mrs. Palsgraf was standing some distance away. How far cannot be told from the record--apparently twenty-five or thirty feet. Perhaps less. Except for the explosion, she would not have been injured. We are told by the appellant in his brief "it cannot be denied that the explosion was the direct cause of the plaintiff's injuries." So it was a substantial factor in producing the result--there was here a natural and continuous sequence--direct connection. The only intervening cause was that instead of blowing her to the ground the concussion smashed the weighing machine which in turn fell upon her. There was no remoteness in time, little in space. And surely, given such an explosion as here it needed no great foresight to predict that the natural result would be to injure one on the platform at no greater distance from its scene than was the plaintiff. Just how no one might be able to predict. Whether by flying fragments, by broken glass, by wreckage of machines or structures no one could say. But injury in some form was most probable.

Under these circumstances I cannot say as a matter of law that the plaintiff's injuries were not the proximate result of the negligence. That is all we have before us. The court refused to so charge. No request was made to submit the matter to the jury as a question of fact, even would that have been proper upon the record before us.

The judgment appealed from should be affirmed, with costs.

Judgment reversed, etc.

Sec. 2.14 Right to Relief
a. to recover damages, or
b. to recover possession of a chattel, or
c. to recover possession of real property, or
d. to have specific performance of a contract
e. and others

GUMB, Respondent v TWENTY-THIRD STREET R. CO., Appellant (1889) 114 NY 411, r21 J&S 466

APPEAL from judgment of the General Term of the Superior Court of the City of New York, entered upon an order made July 2, 1886, which affirmed a judgment in favor of plaintiff, entered upon a verdict, and affirmed an order denying a motion for a new trial.

FOLLETT, Ch. J. At the intersection of Sixth Avenue and Twenty-third Street the tracks of the defendant and of the Sixth Avenue Railroad cross each other nearly at right angles. On February 12, 1883, a Sixth Avenue car was moving north on the east track of that line, closely followed (from Carmine Street to Twenty-third Street) by a butcher's wagon, with its wheels on the rails, drawn by one horse, driven by the plaintiff, who owned horse and wagon. This car stopped to receive and discharge passengers at the north crosswalk of Twenty-third Street. The plaintiff stopped his horse immediately behind the car. As this occurred one of defendant's cars approached from the west on the north track of its line, collided with the hind wheels of plaintiff's wagon, overturned, broke it, and, as it is asserted, injured the plaintiff's left leg. The plaintiff testified that the head of his horse was close to the rear end of the Sixth Avenue car, with the hind wheels of his wagon standing midway between the rails of the north track of defendant's line, and that defendant's car was driven against the hind end of his wagon. Foley, plaintiff's witness, testified that the rims of the hind wheels stood over the north rail of the north track. Edwards, defendant's driver, testified that the hind wheels stood far enough north of the north rail to have permitted the car to pass without touching; but that as the car was passing the plaintiff's wagon was backed in the way of the car. This and the rate of speed of the defendant's car were the principal facts in dispute. The plaintiff testified that he saw the defendant's car approaching rapidly; but he did not explain why he made no attempt to turn to the right or left of the Sixth Avenue car, and leave the track. There is no evidence that anything prevented him from doing this.

The plaintiff was permitted to testify, over defendant's objection, that the evidence was not within the issue; that while suffering from his injury he employed two men to work in his place, paying them $12 and $15 per week each, ($135 in the aggregate. When a plaintiff alleges that his person has been injured and proves the allegation, the law implies damages, and he may recover such as necessarily and immediately flow from the injury (which are called general damages) under a general allegation that damages were sustained; but if he seeks to recover damages for consequences which do not necessarily and immediately flow from the injury (which are called special damages) he must allege the special damages which he seeks to recover. It is not alleged in the complaint that the plaintiff expended money in hiring others to work in his place; the defendant had no opprotunity of contradicting the evidence, and its reception was error. (Cases).

The plaintiff was permitted to testify that he had paid seventy dollars for the reparation of his wagon. The defendant objected to this evidence upon the ground that it did not establish the extent of the injury or the value of the repairs. The objection was overruled and the defendant excepted. In the absence of evidence that the repairs were proper, or worth the sum paid, it was error to hold that the sum paid could be recovered. This error was repeated. The plaintiff, under a like objection, was permitted to show how much this physician charged him, without giving evidence of payment or any evidence of the value of the services, except the incidental remark of the physician, who testified, "Seventy-five dollars is the amount of my bill now; that is very small, too."

The judgment should be reversed and a new trial granted, with costs to abide the event...

Judgment reversed.

WALLINGFORD, Respondent v KAISER, Sheriff of Erie Co., Appellant (1908) 191 NY 392, a118 AD 918

WILLARD BARTLETT, J. The only question which we consider it necessary to discuss in passing upon this appeal relates to the measure of damages adopted by the trial court. The action was for the conversion of a number of horses which were seized by the defendant assuming to act under a warrent of attachment issued to him as sheriff of Erie County, the animals having been taken from a railroad train at East Buffalo while in course of transportation from Chicago, Illinois, to Liverpool, England. The learned trial judge instructed the jury that if the plaintiff was entitled to recover at all he was entitled to recover the value of the horses in Liverpool, less the expense of transporting them and putting them on the market in Liverpool for sale and selling them. No exception was taken to this instruction; but counsel for the appellant had previously disputed the correctness of the rule thus laid down for ascertaining plaintiff's damages by objecting to a question as to the value of one of the horses in Liverpool at the time that it would have arrived there in due course of transportation and taking exception to the decision of the court in overruling that objection; the court having stated at the time that one objection to like questions was sufficient and that the defendant need not object to each like question.

In actions for conversion, and actions of a similar character, the general rule is that the value of the property at the place of conversion is the correct measure of damages. (2 Sedgwick on *Damages* (8th ed.). Sec. 496; *Tiffany v Lord*, 65 NY 310...) But this rule is subject to important qualifications and exceptions. Among these may be mentioned (1) cases where there is no market value for such or like property at the place of conversion. In that event resort is had to evidence of market value at the nearest place where there is a market. (*Keller v Paine*, 34 Hun. 167, 176.) This may be as far removed as San Francisco is from the Isthmus of Panama (*Harris v Panama R. R. Co.*, 58 NY 660) or half way around the earth. (*Bourne v Ashley*, 1 Lowell 27.) The case last cited was a libel in admiralty by the owners of one whaling ship against the owners of another, both vessels hailing from New Bedford, for the conversion of a whale in the Okhotsk Sea. There being no market price for whales at the place of conversion, the court held that the libelants were entitled to the value of the oil and bone at New Bedford, which was the controlling market of the country as well as the home port of both the whalers, less the expenses of taking the oil and bone out of the whale and getting it to such port. (2) A second class of cases, constituting an exception to the rule that the value of the converted article at the place of conversion is ordinarily the true measure of damages, are actions against common carriers, where the goods are lost, destroyed or damaged in transit, in which the damages recoverable against the carrier are based on the market value at the point of destination. (2 Sedgwick on *Damages* (8th ed.), Sec. 844; Mayne on *Damages*, 285; *Sturgess v Bissell*, 46 NY 462...)

So far as I have been able to ascertain, the precise questions presented by this appeal does not appear to have been determined in this state; that is, whether where property in the custody of a common carrier in the course of transportation is converted by a stranger, the owner's right of recovery is limited to the market value at the place of conversion or nearest market, or may be measured by the market value at the place of destination, less the cost of conveyance thither and the selling expenses. That the latter is the only just rule was strongly suggested in *Suydam v Jenkins* (3 Sandf. Superior Ct. 614, 622) by Duer, J., in the course of what was pronounced an "extremely able opinion" by Rapallo, J., in *Baker v Drake* (53 NY 211, 224). Judge Duer said: "When the market price is justly assumed as the measure of value, there are numerous cases in which the addition of interest would fail to compensate the owner for his actual loss. It may be shown that had he retained the possession, he would have derived a larger profit from the use of the property than the interest upon its value; or that he had contracted to sell it to a solvent purchaser at an advance upon the market price; *or that when wrongfully taken or converted, it was in the course of transportation to a profitable market where it would certainly have arrived*; and in each of these cases the difference between the market value when the right of action accrued and the advance which the owner had he retained possession, would have realized, ought plainly to be allowed as compensatory damages, and as such be included in the amount for which judgment is rendered."

The view of Judge Duer, as expressed in the passage which I have emphasized by italics, was adopted by the Supreme Court of Missouri in a well-considered case decided in 1960. (*Farwell v Price*, 30 Mo 587.) Referring to the rule as to which some doubt then existed, but which is now well established, that the measure of damages in the case of a conversion by the common carrier is the market value at the point of delivery, the court went on to say: "And where the wrongdoer is a mere stranger, a trespasser, it is not easy to see upon what ground he can insist that the value of the property at the place where the conversion occurred shall be the measure of damages to which the owner is entitled. Such a rule would in effect force the owner to dispose of his property in a market not of his own selection, and one where perchance the property might be valueless." In that case the property consisted of flour consigned from St. Louis to Boston, and was converted en route by the forwarding agent at New Orleans. "Going no further, for illustration than the case under consideration, we see, as a matter of fact, that the market value of flour at New Orleans is not at all times the same as at Boston, minus the cost of transporting it from one point to the other, though doubtless any considerable disparity could not long continue. Scarcity of capital or other circumstances may depress the price of an article in one market below its value in another, after deducting the expense of removing the article, though in the present condition of trade this could not continue long. But as the price of an article must mainly be regulated by its value for home consumption, and must be so altogether if there is no capital engaged in its removal to other places, the price at the place of conversion would in most instances prove an inadequate compensation for the loss sustained by the owner."

This last proposition seems strictly correct as applied to the proof in the case at bar, which showed that the horses taken from the railway train by the sheriff had been selected at great pains and with special care in reference to the demand in the Liverpool market.

As may be inferred from what has already been said, I think there is and ought to be an exception to the general rule in trover that the value of the property at the place of conversion is the owner's measure of damages, in the case of goods converted by a stranger at an intermediate point while in the course of transportation; and that where the property when wrongfully taken is on the way to a profitable market where it would certainly have arrived, the owner is entitled to recover the value of the goods at the place of destination, less the cost of carriage and the cost of effecting a sale in that market. The purpose of the law is to afford just and reasonable compensation to the injured party for the natural and proximate consequences of the wrongful act; and this can hardly otherwise be accomplished in such a case as that which we have presented for our consideration here. The special damage which the plaintiff claimed to have sustained by reason of his inability to sell the horses in Liverpool was distinctly alleged in the complaint and the defendant's lack of information as to the particular destination of the animals is not available to him in mitigation. (See Lathers v Wyman, 76 M 616). The circumstances under which the horses were taken constituted notice that they were destined for some point beyond East Buffalo.

The appellant relies upon the cases of Brizsee v Maybee (21 Wend(NY) 144) and Spicer v Waters (65 Barb(NY) 227), but in neither of those cases was the property converted while in the course of transportation. The Brizsee case was an action of replevin for a quantity of saw logs which were replevied at the mills of the defendant in Niagara County. The defendant was allowed to prove what would have been the value of the stuff made from the logs in the Albany and Troy markets at the time it would in the ordinary course of business have reached those cities. The old Supreme Court, per Cowen, J., held that the ultimate value at Albany or Troy when in the ordinary course of business the boards would reach there, deducting the expense of manufacturing and the price of transportation, was a proper topic of inquiry, with a view of ascertaining the value of the saw logs at the place where they were replevied, but not for any other purpose. In the Spicer case there was a conversion of lumber in Lewis County and the trial judge charged the jury that if the lumber was to be taken thence to the Troy market and there to be held in the plaintiff's lumber yard, they were entitled to recover its market value in Troy, less the cost and risk of transportation. The General Term of the fifth district (Mullin and Morgan, JJ., Bacon, J., dissenting, held that this charge was erroneous in view of the general rule that in an action for the conversion of personal property the measure of damages was the market value at the time and place of conversion, with interest up to the time of trial. The prevailing opinion shows that the court deemed the decision in Brizsee v Maybee(supra) controlling on the question, although, as already suggested, that was not a case of the conversion of goods in transit.

I find nothing in the reasoning or decision of these cases in conflict with the conclusion that the present judgment should be affirmed, with costs.

VANN, J. (dissenting). When a sheriff is sued, as such, for an official act done in his own county, and damages are assessed against him for the conversion of a common kind of property, they should not be measured by the market price at a place three thousand miles away, but by the market price in the locality where the act of conversion took place. That is the general rule, and there is no occasion for an exception, for there was a home market and the defendant was not a common carrier. A public officer who makes a mistake in an effort to discharge an official duty and is required to pay damages in consequence, should not be compelled to visit foreign countries and import witnesses therefrom in order to keep the damages within reasonable limits. No authority requires us to sanction proof of the market price at a remote place, on another continent, and it is against public policy to establish a rule that may call a sheriff far from the county and even the state where his official duties are to be performed. Evidence of the market price at no place outside of the state where the owner was deprived of his property should be allowed, and I regret that a rule is about to be laid down which will not only be inconvenient in practice, but will frequently lead to injustice. As the question is open in this state, why should we go abroad for a market price when we have one at home? If we can go to England we can go to Russia, China or Australia, and to points where local conditions may temporarily raise the price, and where tariff regulations may hamper investigation and complicate the question. In laying down a rule to govern our own citizens the market price established by themselves should be sufficient to measure the value of property converted in this state. I apprehend that no other rule will be welcome to them or regarded by them as just or right. Simple rules are the best, and no exception should be made except to prevent injustice.

Even where the property is on the way to a better market, if the act is neither vindictive nor a violation of contract, future profits, although reasonably certain, should not be awarded when the owner could purchase similar property at the place of conversion and thus save prospective profits for himself and the defendant from serious loss. Under such circumstances the home market price and interest is enough without profits, cases against common carriers excepted, because the law is loath to allow them any excuse for non-delivery.

American horses, raised, purchased and converted in America, should be valued according to the American markets rather than the English, even if they are on their way to England when converted.

Judgment affirmed.

HADLEY et al v BAXENDALE et al. (Court of Exchequer, 1854) 9 Exch 341, 156 Eng Rep 145

This was an action of contract against a carrier. At the trial before COMPTON, J., at the Gloucester Assizes the following facts appeared.

The plaintiffs carried on an extensive business as millers at Gloucester, and on the 11th of May their mill was stopped by a breakage of the crank shaft, by which the mill was worked. The steam engine was manufactured by Messrs. Joyce & Co., the engineers, at Greenwich, and it became necessary to send the shaft as a pattern for a new one to Greenwich. The fracture was discovered on the 12th, and on the 13th the plaintiffs sent one of their servants to the office of the defendants, who are well-known carriers trading under the name of Pickford & Co., for the purpose of having the shaft carried to Greenwich. The plaintiffs' servant told the clerk that the mill was stopped, and that the shaft must be sent immediately; and in answer to the inquiry when the shaft would be taken the answer was that if it was sent by twelve o'clock any day it would be delivered at Greenwich on the following day. On the following day the shaft was taken by the defendants, before noon, for the purpose of being conveyed to Greenwich, and the sum of L2. 4s. was paid for its carriage for the whole distance. At the same time the defendants' clerk was told that a special entry, if required, should be made, to hasten its delivery. The delivery of the shaft at Greenwich was delayed by some neglect, and the consequence was that the plaintiffs did not receive the new shaft for several days after they would otherwise have done, and the working of their mill was thereby delayed and they thereby lost the profits they would otherwise have received.

On the part of the defendants it was objected that these damages were too remote, and that the defendants were not liable with respect to them. The learned judged left the case generally to the jury, who found a verdict with L25, damages beyond the amount paid into court by defendant, which was L25.

A rule nisi for a new trial was obtained by defendant.

ALDERSON, B. We think that there ought to be a new trial in this case; but in so doing we deem it to be expedient and necessary to state explicitly the rule which the judge, at the next trial, ought, in our opinion, to direct the jury to be governed by when they estimate the damages.

It is, indeed, of the last importance that we should do this; for, if the jury are left without any definite rule to guide them, it will, in such cases as these, manifestly lead to the greatest injustice. The courts have done this on several occasions; and in Blake v Railway Co., 21 L.J.Q.B. 237, the court granted a new trial on this very gound, that the rule had not been definitely laid down to the jury by the learned judge at nisi prius. "There are certain established rules," this court says, in Alder v Keighley, 15 Mess. & W. 117, "according to which the jury ought to find." And the court in that case adds: "And here there is a clear rule that the amount which would have been received if the contract had been kept is the measure of damages if the contract is broken."

Now, we think the proper rule in such a case as the present is this: Where two parties have made a contract which one of them has broken, the damages which the other party ought to receive in respect of such breach of contract should be such as may fairly and reasonably be considered either arising naturally--i.e., according to the usual course of things, from such breach of contract itself--or such as may reasonably be supposed to have been in the contemplation of both parties at the time they made the contract, as the probable result of the breach of it. Now, if the special circumstances under which the contract was actually made were communicated by the plaintiffs to the defendants, and thus known to both parties, the damages resulting from the breach of such a contract, which they would reasonably contemplate, would be the amount of injury which would ordinarily follow from a breach of contract under these special circumstances so known and communicated. But, on the other hand, if these special circumstances were wholly unknown to the party breaking the contract, he, at the most, could only be supposed to have had in his contemplation the amount of injury which would arise generally, and in the great multitude of cases not affected by any special circumstances, from such a breach of contract. For, had the special circumstances been known, the parties might have specially provided for the breach of contract by special terms as to the damages in that case; and of this advantage it would be very unjust to deprive them. Now, the above principles are those by which we think the jury ought to be guided in estimating the damages arising out of any breach of contract.

It is said that other cases, such as breaches of contract in the nonpayment of money, or in the not making a good title to land, are to be treated as exceptions from this, and as governed by a conventional rule. But as, in such cases, both parties must be supposed to be cognizant of that well-known rule, these cases may, we think, be more properly classed under the rule above enunciated as to cases under known special circumstances, because there both parties may reasonably be presumed to contemplate the estimation of the amount of damages according to the conventional rule.

Now, in the present case, if we are to apply the principles above laid down, we find that the only circumstances here communicated by the plaintiffs to the defendants at the time the contract was made were that the article to be carried was the broken shaft of a mill, and that the plaintiffs were the millers of that mill. But how do these circumstances show reasonably that the profits of the mill must be stopped by an unreasonable delay in the delivery of the broken shaft by the carrier to the third person? Suppose the plaintiffs had another shaft in their possession, put up or putting up at the time, and that they only wished to send back the broken shaft to the engineer who made it, it is clear that this would be quite consistent with the above circumstances, and yet the unreasonable delay in the delivery would have no effect upon the intermediate profits of the mill. Or, again, suppose that, at the time of the delivery to the carrier, the machinery of the mill had been in other respects defective, then, also, the same result would follow. Here it is true that the shaft was actually sent back to serve as a model for a new one, and that the want of a new one was the only cause of the stoppage of the mill, and that the loss of profits really arose from not sending down the new shaft in proper time, and that this arose from the delay in delivering the broken one to serve as a model. But it is obvious that in the great multitude of cases of millers sending off broken shafts to third persons by a carrier under ordinary circumstances, such consequences would not, in all probability, have occurred; and these special circumstances were here never communicated by the plaintiffs to the defendants. It follows, therefore, that the loss of profits here cannot reasonably be considered such a consequence of the breach of contract as could have been fairly and reasonably contemplated by both the parties when they made this contract. For such loss would neither have flowed naturally from the breach of this contract in the great multitude of such cases occuring under ordinary circumstances, nor were the special circumstances, which perhaps, would have made it a reasonable and natural consequence of such breach of contract, communicated to or known by the defendants. The judge ought, therefore, to have told the jury that upon the facts then before them they ought not to take the loss of profits into consideration at all in estimating the damages. There must therefore be a new trial in this case.

IVES v SOUTH BUFFALO RY. CO. (1911) 201 NY 271, r140 AD 921

(This case appears p. 12, supra.)

SHEARING et al v CITY OF ROCHESTER (Sp Ct Monroe Co 1966) 51 M2d 436, 273 S2d 464

Action by homeowners against city seeking an injunction to restrain city from continued burning of rubbish and for damages claimed to have been suffered to real and personal property and to homeowners' health.

CHARLES LAMBIASE, Justice. Plaintiffs are owners of premises at #1748 Lexington Avenue, Rochester, New York, which they purchased in 1958 as a recently built house. At the time of their said purchase, the defendant City of Rochester owned and now owns a considerable acreage in the general locality known as the "Emerson Street Landfill Area" hereinafter referred to as "landfill" for the purposes of convenience.

Upon a portion of this area the City of Rochester, New York now operates and at all times herein mentioned operated in one phase of its refuse disposal program, an incerator for the burning of rubbish and the like accumulated from ordinary household collections from the inhabitants of the city, said incinerator, at all times herein mentioned, though in the general area of the aforementioned landfill, being some considerable distance from plaintiffs' house. Plaintiffs do not complain about the operation of the incinerator.

In another phase of its disposal operations, the city has since about 1955 done so-called "open burning" on the subject landfill site...

The "open burning" operation has been conducted there by the City since 1955 and fires have burned at the site since then continuously, and were burning there at the time of the trial. These fires burn often at night producing quantities of smoke, odors, and resultant soot, soot which has collected on the outside of plaintiffs' house covering the aluminum siding installed in 1965, and gathering on curtains and furniture inside of plaintiffs' dwelling and of adjoining neighbors' homes. Plaintiffs observed smoke there shortly after they moved into their home. However, the "open burning" operation was much farther removed then and did not cause too much concern. It has been since 1964 and thereafter that the situation has become particularly alarming to plaintiffs, during which period of time said operation has been carried on at intervals as close as about 800 yards from plaintiffs' property and that of adjoining neighbors.

Plaintiffs and their neighbors have attempted to have the matter corrected by the city, but the city had not done so or had not been able to do so up to the time of the trial although it has tried to find other areas upon which to dispose of its rubbish through appropriately reasonable and proper methods and to serve as part of its general refuse disposal and landfill operations.

The instant action has been brought by plaintiffs for (1) an injunction against the city to enjoin and to restrain it from continuing its burning of rubbish and of other materials in the open in the area known as the Emerson Street Landfill Area set out in the notice of claim and more particularly hereinbefore described; and for (2) judgment for damages claimed to have been suffered by them to their property, real and personal, and to their health by reason of said "open burning" operations.

We find the record before us of "open burning" operations of defendant in the so-called Emerson Street Landfill Area to be a state of facts constituting a nuisance to the plaintiffs and to their property, and, in our opinion, such a finding is amply sustained in said record. Therefore, it is the duty of this court as a court of equity to grant relief, it being found that plaintiffs have no adequate remedy at law...

Therefore, plaintiffs are entitled to a permanent injunction against the City of Rochester enjoining and restraining it from continuing to dispose of rubbish and other material by "open burning" in the area known as the Emerson Street Landfill Area. However, in view of the fact that the City of Rochester at the time of the trial was and for some appreciable time prior thereto had been actively engaged in attempting to find other methods of disposal of the refuse now being burned in the open in the area involved herein, and in attempting to find an alternate landfill site for use by the city other than the one involved herein, and in view of the further fact that evidence offered by the city indicates that there are other methods and incinerator-type instrumentalities now available in refuse disposal operations which are capable of disposing by burning materials of large size that cannot be burned in the type of incinerator such as is being used by the City of Rochester, New York, the injunction shall be so framed that it shall not be operative for the period of four months from the date of service of a copy of the decree or judgment to be entered herein with notice of entry thereof upon the defendant City of Rochester, and shall contain the further provision that this court or any justice thereof sitting at special term, upon due notice of application therefor, shall have the right upon proper showing to postpone the effective date of said injunction for a reasonable time beyond said four months period as in the Court's discretion shall seem necessary for finding another area or other areas on which to lawfully carry on its refuse disposal operations or to adopt available methods which will serve for the purpose of disposing of its rubbish in such a reasonable and proper manner as the necessities of the case demand, including, if necessary, the obtaining of appropriate authorization for instituting proceedings for the condemnation by defendant of a right to utilize plaintiffs' property in a manner now or in such a manner as may hereafter be employed. Sammons v City of Gloversville, 175 NY 346, 67 NE 622; Pendorf v City of Rome, 203 NY 645, 97 NE 1111, aff'g without opinion, 138 AD 913, 123 NYS 1133.

We consider now the cause of action as to damages which had been joined with the prayer for equitable relief and has thereby become an incident to said relief.

As to any alleged damage to the health and to any other item other than to the house which we discuss hereinafter separately, there is no proof whatsoever in the record and, therefore, there is a failure of proof with reference thereto.

In our opinion plaintiffs have proceeded upon the wrong theory in connection with the alleged damage to the house. It seems quite clear to us that plaintiffs have proceeded in connection therewith upon the assumption that the invasion of their rights effected by the acts found herein of the City of Rochester is permanent. This is an erroneous assumption under the circumstances prevailing. The invasion of plaintiffs' rights is not necessarily permanent. The offending situtation may be remedied, and the plaintiffs' land may be restored to its former condition. There is no presumption that the City of Rochester will persist in its course of conduct, but, on the contrary, plaintiffs' damages are to be assessed on the assumption that the City of Rochester will right the wrong and, therefore, plaintiffs are limited to the injury which they had sustained to their house, exterior and interior, and furnishings therein to the time of the filing of their claim. Uline v New York Central and Hudson River R. R. Co., 101 NY 98, 4 NE 536. We, therefore, cannot and do not allow any recovery on the basis of a permanent damage to the premises as borne out by the evidence adduced by plaintiffs of market value before and market value after of the premises demanding the difference between the two figures as the damages to be awarded. No other measure of damages was proved on this item. It would seem under the circumstances herein the damages would be the diminished rental value of the premises (Francis v Schoelkopf, 53 NY 152; Bly v Edison Electric Illum. Co., 172 NY 1, 64 NE 745).

In respect to other items of damage, it would seem that the proper measure thereof would be the reasonable expense of cleaning the aluminum siding and other items in the house allocating so much thereof as the contribution of the conditions complained of could be connected therewith, a matter which we do not consider to have been accomplished by the proof. Upon this record plaintiffs have failed to give evidence as to these items of loss founded upon the true measure of damages. Under the circumstances herein where the loss is pecuniary and actual and can be measured, but no evidence is given showing its extent or from which it can inferred, the jury can allow nominal damages only. Leeds v Metropolitan Gas Light Co., 90 NY 26, 29. Also, in equity, a judgment awarding nominal damages has been granted when it was necessary to preserve rights and to prevent subsequent possible breaches in the future. Skinner v Allison, 54 AD 47, 66 NYS 288; Henry Hof, Inc. v Noll 273 AD 361. 77 NYS 2d 484, affd. 299 NY 588, 86 NE2d 108.

Our findings herein indicate an award of nominal damages which are damages in name only having no substance but which nevertheless vindicate the plaintiffs' rights. The usual amount awarded as such damages in this state is six cents, and accordingly we award said amount and direct entry of judgment in favor of plaintiffs and against the defendant, City of Rochester, in said sum. In addition we award costs and disbursements to the plaintiffs against the defendant to be taxed by the Clerk of this court.

Sec. 2.2 Examples of Causes of Action

I. Examples of Causes of Action at Common Law

A. Criminal Causes of Action

1. Arson
2. Assault
3. Bigamy
4. Burglary
5. Forgery
6. Larceny
7. Manslaughter
8. Mayhem
9. Murder
10. Rape
11. Suicide
12. (and others)

B. Contractual Causes of Action

1. To recover damages for breach of a covenant or contract under seal (Covenant)
2. To recover a certain specific sum of money (Debt)
3. To recover damages for non-performance of a special contract not under seal (Special Assumpsit)
4. To recover damages (1) for a claim growing out of a breach of contract; or (2) for non-performance of a duty implied in law to pay for a benefit conferred; quasi-contract (General Assumpsit)

C. Tortious Causes of Action

1. Assault, to recover damages for (Trespass vi et armis)
2. Unlawfully carrying away goods or property, to recover damages for (Trespass de bonas asportatis)
3. Unlawful entry upon land, to recover damages for (Trespass quare clausum fregit)
4. Conversion by an unlawful use, to recover damages for (Trover)
5. Spoil or destruction as to real property, to recover damages for (Waste)
6. To recover possession of real property (Ejectment)
7. To recover goods unlawfully taken (Replevin)
8. To recover possession of Chattels unlawfully detained (Detinue)
9. Causes of Action in Trespass on the Case - To recover damages for:

   (a) Abuse of Process
   (b) Alienation of Affections
   (c) Deceit
   (d) Libel
   (e) Malicious Prosecution
   (f) Malpractice
   (g) Negligence
   (h) Nuisance
   (i) Slander
   (j) and others

SOCONY-VACUUM OIL CO., INC. v BAILEY (Sp Ct Cattaraugus Co 1952) 109 S2d 799

Trespass action by Socony-Vacuum Oil Company, Inc., against Gerald L. Bailey.

WARD, Justice. This is an action tried at a trial term before a jury in which the plaintiffl seeks to recover damages for injury to its oil pipe line resulting from an alleged trespass by the defendant.

The essential facts, as proved on the trial, are simple and generally conceded by both parties. The plaintiff, a producer and distributor of oil and petroleum products, is the owner of an easement to maintain and operate and has, in fact, for a long period of time operated a pipe line across certain rural property in Cattaraugus County now owned by the Vacuum Gas Burner Company. At the time involved herein, the pipe line was being operated by the plaintiff in accordance with the provisions of the easement. It appears that under these conditions, the defendant, pursuant to a contract with the Vacuum Gas Burner Company to level the latter's property, operated a bulldozer in such a manner that he ran into and broke the plaintiff's pipe line. The instrument creating the easement was duly recorded but there is no proof that the defendant had actual knowledge of the location or even the existence of the line.

At the end of the plaintiff's case, the defendant moved for a dismissal of the complaint, which motion was renewed and a motion for a directed verdict also made at the close of the evidence. At the time, the plaintiff also moved for a direct verdict. Decision on all motions was reserved. The court submitted only the question of the amount of damages to the jury which returned a verdict of $100. The defendant thereupon moved to set aside the verdict and renewed his motion for a directed verdict dismissing the complaint. The plaintiff then moved for the entry of judgment in accordance with the finding of the jury. Decisions of these motions were likewise reserved.

The issue presented in this case should be spelled out at the outset. From an analysis of the pleadings and briefs, it appears that the plaintiff seeks to recover on the theory that the defendant committed a trespass to its easement and to its pipe line. If this court understands correctly the substance of the plaintiff's position, it attempts to claim an actionable wrong by the defendant against its easement of a type which might have been covered at common law by an action of trespass on the case and further, a wrong against its personalty, i.e., the pipe line, as a trespass to chattels, which might have been founded at common law on the ancient actions of trespass vi et armis or de bonas asportatis. It does not seek to recover on the theory of a trespass quare clausum fregit to its easement. Because of the requirement that trespass quare clausum fregit must be against a possessory estate in real property, it was well established at common law that an easement, being an incorporated hereditament was not such an interest as would support the action. (Pollock's Law of Torts, 14th ed. 1939, p. 299; Tiffany, Law of Real Property, 3rd ed. 1939, vo. 3, sec. 814; cf. First Baptist Church v Witherell, 1832, 3 Paige(NY) 296 and Shaw v Boveridge, 1842, 3 Hill 26 (in which trespass was held to lie for interference with right of owner of church pew on theory such right was not an easement but a property right and therefore "real estate".) In fact, on page 6 of its brief, plaintiff admits ejectment or trespass quare clausum fregit would not have been a proper common0law action for the interference alleged herein. It is equally clear that the plaintiff does not seek to recover on the theory of negligence and, in fact, the evidence would sustain no such claim. If it is to be successful, the plaintiff must recover upon a theory of liability not based on negligence.

It is true that under the common law the action of trespass on the case was not limited to situations where negligence was involved. Its purpose was to supply a remedy where the other forms of actions were not applicable. (Kukek v Goldman, 1896, 150 NY 176, 44 NE 773, 34 LRA 156.) It was employed where the damage suffered was consequential or indirect and not the direct result of the act constituting the trespass as was required in the older form of actions of trespass quare fregit, trespass vi et armis and trespass de bonis asportatis. Thus under the early law, there could be a negligent harm by direct contact remediable by trespass vi et armis or de bonis asportatis, Percival v Hickey, 1820, 18 John 257, or a harm not based on negligence for which case was the proper action, the distinguishing factor being whether the harm was immediate and direct or consequential and indirect.

It is important to analyze the act which constitutes the alleged trespass before it can be found to be actionable under the principles underlying any of the common-law actions of trespass. In the absence of any question of negligence, the requisites were the same whether the act was to be remedied by an action of trespass to chattels or an action on the case. Before the act was actionable, it was necessary that it be voluntary. (Smith v Stone, 1647, Style 63 (King's Bench).) There is no question that in the instant case the defendant was acting voluntarily when he operated the bulldozer in such a manner as to strike the plaintiff's pipe line. It must, however, have been more than just a voluntary act. The act must also have been intentional except in a case of negligence which it has already established is not involved herein. It was not necessary, however, that the trespasser intend to commit a trespass or even that he knew that his act will constitute a trespass, Winteringham v Lafoy, 1827, 7 Cow 735. The actor may be innocent of moral fault, but there must be an intent to do the very act which results in the immediate damage. In other words, trespass requires an intentional act. Harper on Torts, (1932)Sec. 27. Applying this requirement to the case at bar, it is difficult to find the defendant's act in striking the pipe to be an actionable trespass. There is no proof that the defendant intended to strike the pipe and, in fact, it is clearly established to the contrary, for he did not know the existence or location of the line, nor is he charged with such knowledge for purposes of determining whether his action was intentional. Without an intentional act, the defendant's conduct cannot give rise to a trespass and, therefore, the plaintiff's cause of action based on the theory of trespass must fail.

The Court has carefully considered the cases cited by the plaintiff and does not find them determinative of the subject matter. New York Steam Co. v Foundation Co., 1909, 195 NY 43, 87 NE 765, 21 LRA, NS, 470 is distinguishable. There the court rested its decision on the fact that the work undertaken by the defendant inevitably injured the plaintiff's pipes and, since the defendant took its license from the city, subject to the burden of paying for the injury caused by its work, it must respond in damages for the injury. The court pointed out that any other rule "might result in the utter destruction of public utility lines without liability", 195 NY at page 52, 87 NE at page 768, indicating it was influenced by the public purpose of the plaintiff therein. The doctrine of the New York Steam Co. case has not been extended nor, in fact, has it been relied on in later cases. See Town of Greenburgh v J. F. Shea Co., Sup., 1944, 48 S2d 69, affirmed without opinion, 2dDept 1944 268 AD 998, 51 S2d 862, also cited by plaintiff which rests on contract and not on the absolute rule of liability inherent in trespass. The rule applicable to the public utility conduits has now developed in the direction of liability based on negligence where there is no actual knowledge of the existence or location of the lines. (Frontier Telephone Co. v Hepp, 1910, 66 M 265, 121 S 460.) Certainly, no stricter rule can be applied to the defendant's conduct in a rural area under the facts in the case at bar than applicable to conduits in city streets.

Based upon the above, the motion of the defendant for a non-suit and dismissal of the complaint made at the end of the plaintiff's case, his motion for a directed verdict and his motion to set aside the verdict of the jury are hereby granted. All other motions upon which decision was reserved are hereby denied.

Enter judgment in accordance with this decision.

II. Examples of Causes of Action in Equity

1. To Have an Accounting
2. To Cancel an Instrument
3. To Reform a Writing
4. To Rescind a Transaction
5. To Quiet Title
6. To Partition Real Property
7. To Remove a Cloud on Title
8. To Set Aside a Fraudulent Conveyance
9. To Have Specific Performance of a Contract
10. To Recover Possession of a Unique Chattel
11. To Have Restitution as a Constructive Trust
12. To Have Another Stop His Breach, or Threatened Breach, of Contract
13. To Have Another Stop His Trespass to Real Property
14. To Have Another Stop His Waste of Real Property
15. To Have Public Officers Stop Violating Private Property Rights
16. To Have Another Stop His Unfair Competition
17. and Others.

ELTERMAN v HYMAN, supra p. 2
RUTHERFORD v HAVEN & CO., supra p. 27
BIANCHI v LEON, infra p. 61
COATSWORTH v LEHIGH VALLEY R. CO., infra p. 88

III. Examples of Causes of Action Under Statute

JORDAN v DIXIE CHEVROLET, INC. (1950) 218 SCar 73, 61 SE2d 654

TAYLOR, Justice. This appeal comes to this Court from an order of the Resident Judge of the Twelfth Judicial Court, dated February 9, 1950, affirming an opinion and award of the South Carolina Industrial Commission, dated March 7, 1949, wherein claimant was denied compensation for injuries sustained by him which were alleged to have arisen out of and in the course of his employment.

From this order, exceptions were taken which present the question of whether or not the injuries received by appellant were the result of an accident which arose out of and in the course of his employment, appellant contending that under the facts, as found by the Industrial Commission, claimant is entitled to compensation as a matter of law.

The testimony reveals that three persons were employed by respondent in its paint and body repair shop at the time in question and for several months prior thereto. The foreman having been discharged some time prior to the accident, an arrangement had been entered into whereby the three employees were to work together, with Mr. W. O. Turner being in charge of repair orders and parceling out the work equally so that one would not be called upon to do more than his share of the work. This arrangement was to be in force unless the manager should call upon one of the employees to do some specific job.

A Florence, South Carolina, Police car was brought in some two or three days prior to the accident and turned over to Mr. Turner by Mr. Smith, the manager, with instructions to weld the holes in the body where the radio aerial had been previously installed and had at that time been removed, and to have the police signs removed from the doors. Turner assigned the work to one of the employees named B. G. Game, who was engaged in this operation at the time claimant was injured.

On June 3, 1948, the day in question, claiment, having no work assigned to him by his employer, had been idle all day and at about 4 p.m. was sitting in the front seat of the car on which Game was working, when he took from the glove compartment a tear gas bomb. Not knowing what the object was, he pulled the cotter pin, thereby releasing the contents of the bomb, which he then threw to the floor where it exploded, as a result of which the tear gas injured claimant's eyes and impaired his sight.

The Hearing Commissioner found that "Jordan was undoubtedly on the job at the time of the accident in the sense that it was during his work hours and at a time his employer could command his services, but a careful and painstaking consideration of the entire convinces me that he had no duties to perform in or about the Chevrolet Police car at the time of the injury and that his handling of the tear gas bomb was merely to pass the time and his pulling of the cotter pin thereof was in pursuit of natural curiosity which resulted so unfortunately to himself."

The case therefore falls within that class where one, while awaiting a work assignment during working hours at his place of employment in idle curiosity tampers with a strange object which is present by reason of the nature of the employer's business, is injured, bearing in mind that negligence and contributory negligence are of no consequence in Workmen's Compensation cases. Allsep v Daniel Construction Co., 216 SC 268, 57 SE 2d 427...

This being the first "curiosity" case to come before this Court, we have looked to other jurisdictions for guidance and quote quite extensively therefrom....

In Derby v International Salt Co., 233 AD 15, 251 S 531, "The claimant was engaged in moving salt in a hand cart. He placed the cart in position where it would be filled from a chute and, while waiting for this he exercised by walking about, as the weather was cold. He received serious injuries to each hand from the explosion of a dynamite cartridge or cap. He describes the happening: "I saw something across a long board that was lying there. It was shining. It was in a little box and I picked it up and looked at it and in the left hand I held it and * * * I pulled that wire and it exploded.' The claimant had not abandoned his employment. It was his duty to wait until the cart was filled, and observing the interesting looking box or device he picked it up to investigate. Except for the dangerous character of his find, this act would not have lessened the amount of labor which he would do. It was a peril arising because of his employment at the salt works. The principle does not differ from Miles v Gibbs & Hill, Inc., 250 NY 590, 166 NE 335, where an employee walking along a railroad track struck, with a long-handled hammer which he was carrying, a small object on the rail which proved to be a torpedo."....

Frequently quoted in our decisions and by other courts has been the early (1913) Massachusetts McNicol's Case, cited as Re Employers' Liability Assurance Corporation, 215 Mass 497, 102 NE 697, LRA 1916A, 306, wherein Chief Justice Rugg undertook to define the troublesome phrase, "arising out of." 6 Schneider 8 discusses the subsequent development and broadening of the view and states: "But the more adaptable rule is that an injury may be said to arise out of the employment when it arises out of the nature, condition, obligation or incident of the employment, and it is enough if there be a causal connection between the injury and the business, a connection substantially contributory though it need not be the sole or proximate cause." The author further remarks that the Massachusetts court, which decided McNicol, supra, years before, recognized and gave effect to the more modern and liberal view in 1940 in Caswell's Case, 305 Mass 500, 26 NE2d 328, 330, and said: "An injury arises out of the employment if it arises out of the nature, conditions, obligations or incidents of the employment; in other words, out of the employment looked at in any of its aspects."

Comment upon Caswell's Case is found in 3 NACCA Law Journal 39, as follows: "This case is a landmark in Massachusetts law as it avoided the paralyzing effect of the earlier decision in McNicol's Case requiring 'peculiar' exposure, and denial of compensation for common risks." That author further says on the same page: "Under such a broad definition, as well as under narrower rules, it is not necessary that the injury be one which ought to have been foreseen or expected. Even unusual or extraordinary consequences of the employment may well be compensable. The risk insured is not only the foreseeable one, but the risk which, after the event, can be seen to have its origin in the nature, conditions, obligations, or incidents of the employment.

"A slight deviation, caused by curiosity or other natural human act, is not necessarily a bar to compensation. Although the older cases used the strict common-law theories to bar even compensation claims, the modern theory is to permit an award where an instrumentality of the employer, or a risk incidental to the employment, in fact combined with the act of curiosity or other reasonably natural acts, and produced the injury. Furthermore, the defense of 'deviation' or 'curiosity' is borrowed from the common law, and workmen's compensation meant to discard narrow common-law theories. The defense, therefore, should rarely be upheld and must be limited to acts so foreign to the employment (used in its widest sense) and not to 'arise out of' even a reasonable incident thereof." (4 NACCA Law Journal 23...)

The Circuit Judge, feeling that he was bound by the findings of the fact-finding body, which is well-established law, affirms the findings of the Industrial Commission, but we are of the opinion that, under the facts as heretofore determined, the claimant is entitled to compensation as a matter of law and that the order appealed from should be reversed, the case remanded to the Circuit Court with instructions that it be remanded to the Industrial Commission for the purpose of making an award commensurate with claimant's injuries, and it is so ordered.

Sec. 2.3 Evolution of a Cause of Action

ROGERS v BREWSTER (1809) 5 Johns(NY) 125

ON certiorari from a justice's court.

The plaintiff brought an action on the case, against the defendant, for maliciously distraining a valuable horse out of his team, for a militia fine, and refusing to take other property, by reason whereof, a great sacrifice of the plaintiff's property was made. The defendant justified under a warrant from the president of a court-martial, and called for a jury. Upon the trial, it was proved that the defendant required of the president of the court martial the warrant against the plaintiff, and said he would collect it in such a manner, that the plaintiff would remember it, and he would take the property nearest to his heart; and that when he called on the plaintiff, he set his eye on the horse, as he thought the taking of it would most touch the plaintiff's feelings; that when he took the horse, the plaintiff showed to him six or seven large swine, and requested the defendant to take them and leave the horse; but the defendant replied, that he would take that which would most touch the feelings of the plaintiff. The justice gave his opinion, at the trial that if an officer wilfully and maliciously took an unreasonable distress, an action would lie. It appeared that the defendant was a constable, and had the warrant for the collection of the fine. He had previously called twice on the plaintiff for the fine. After taking the horse, he offered to redeliver him on receiving the fine. On the next day, the horse was returned to the plaintiff on his engaging to produce him at the date of sale, which was done. The justice decided, that the act concerning distresses (11 Sess. ch. 36 Sec. 3. . .) applied; and that it was unlawful for the defendant to levy on a horse, or beast of the plough, while other property could be found. The jury found a verdict for the plaintiff, for five dollars damages, on which judgment was entered by the justice. On these facts, as stated in the return to the certiorari, the case was submitted to the court without argument.

PER CURIAM. The statute concerning distresses, & c. does not apply to the case of a levy upon personal property, by an officer, by warrant, in the nature of an execution. But the constable appears to have executed the warrant in an unreasonable and oppressive manner, and with the avowed and malicious design to vex and oppress the plaintiff below. When the oppression and malice are thus charged as the gist of the action, and are clearly made out, an action on the case will lie. The oppression of officers, in the execution of process, is indictable; (T. Raym. 216. . .) and a great abuse of the powers of a sheriff, on execution, has been held sufficient to make him a trespasser, (Noy, 59. . .) or to bring him into contempt. (2 Shaw. 87.) If he be charged with a malicious and oppressive proceeding, the proper remedy for this abuse of power, is a special action on the case, in which the malice and the oppression must both be made manifest. In Sutton v Johnstone, (1 Term Rep. 503.) Baron Eyre, in giving the opinion of the Court of Exchequer, laid down this general principle, that where it could be shown that one man had causelessly and maliciously exercised over another, to his damage, powers incident to his situation of superior, a special action on the case lay. The judgment in that case was afterwards reversed; but the reversal did not affect the solidity of this principle, in cases not arising under the exercise of military or naval authority. The seizing and selling the horse, in the case before us, was without any just cause, so long as other property was shown, which would have raised the money with equal facility. It was, therefore, a causeless and malicious proceeding. Where a ministerial officer does anything against the duty of his office, and damage thereby accrues to the party, an action lies. The judgment must be affirmed.

Judgment affirmed.

BALDWIN v WEED (1837) 17 WEND(NY) 225

This was an action for malicious prosecution, tried at the Saratoga circuit, in May 1835, before the Hon. Esok Cowen, then one of the circuit judges.

The plaintiff charged the defendant with having maliciously and without probable cause, procured him to be indicted for obtaining goods by false pretences from one James Sowden on which indictment the plaintiff was tried and acquitted. It was also stated in the declaration, that the defendant had procured the plaintiff to be arrested in Vermont, on the requisition of the governor of this state, and to be brought here for trial. On the trial of this cause, the following facts appeared: The plaintiff, the defendant and one Wood, had been partners in the business of making and vending blacking, and transacted such business under the name of "J. Wood & Co." In the spring of 1833, the partnership was dissolved, though it was agreed between the parties that the materials on hand should be made up and vended by the plaintiff, who was also authorized to collect the debts due the firm. In September 1833, the plaintiff called upon James Sowden to obtain a quantity of stocks and moccasins to sell on commission, with which he was accordingly furnished, and for which he gained an accountable receipt, signing thereto the partnership name of J. Wood & Co., and immediately afterwards absconded. Sowden testified that at the time of obtaining the goods, the plaintiff made no representation whatever as to his being a member of the firm of J. Wood & Co., and that he let him have the goods on information obtained from Wood about three weeks previous to the transaction, that the plaintiff was a member of the firm; he further testified, that previous to the indictment of the plaintiff, he informed both Weed and Wood that he would not have parted with his goods, but for the information so received from Wood, that the plaintiff was a member of the firm. The defendand appeared as a witness against the plaintiff before the grand jury, but previous to doing so, he had called upon the district attourney of Saratoga, and stated to him that the plaintiff had obtained the goods from Sowden by representing himself a partner of the firm of J. Wood & Co. and giving an accountable receipt in the name of the firm. . . It was prayed on the trial, that Weed procured a requistion from the governor of this state for the arrest of the plaintiff in Vermont, that he was present at his arrest, and when he got him into this state, caused him to be fettered and manacled with irons and chains, and to be thus transported from Crown Point to Ballston. It also appeared that the sole object of the proceeding on the part of Weed, was to secure two small debts amounting together to less than $100; that the plaintiff, to obtain his liberattion fromprison, executed a bond to the defendant for the delivery of property and payment of money to the amount $700, and the defendant then procured bail for the plaintiff, and promised that he would not appear as a witness against him, and would use his influence to have the prosecution dropped. . . .

The jury found a verdict for the plaintiff for $500, which the defendant moved to set aside.

By the Court, NELSON, C. J. The material question here is, whether want of probable cause in the criminal proceedings against the plaintiff was sufficiently established on the trial of this cause. The leading principles involved in actions for malicious arrest and prosecution, have been so often and ably discussed both in England and this country, that they are extremely well settled. When there is no dispute as to the facts relied on, the question of want of probable cause is for the determination of the court; when they are controverted, or the preponderance of the testimony doubtful it belongs to the jury under proper advice as to the law. 1 T. R. 545. . .and cases there cited. The want of probable cause is the essential ground of the action, and must be substantially and satisfactorily proved and cannot be implied. (1 T. R. 545. . .)

As to the offense of obtaining goods by false pretences: By the 2Revised Statutes, 677, #53, every person who, with intent to cheat or defraud another, shall designedly by color of any false token in writing, or by any other false pretence, & c. obtain from any person any money, personal property, or valuable thing, upon conviction, & c. . . The materiality of the pretences which are laid in the indictment, and the necessity of proving on the trial that they influenced the mind of the person to part with his property, clearly show that he must be defrauded to bring the case within the statute. (11 Wendell(NY)557. . .) The testimony of Sowden, therefore, necessarily produced an acquittal on the indictment found against the plaintiff. . .

Not that there was no attempt to commit the offense by the plaintiff - for that was clearly undertaken- but that it so happened, the person upon whom the attempt was made, having a previous knowledge of the false fact or pretence, was not therefore influenced by it when used by the prisoner; or rather, he assumed a fact to be true, by means of this previous knowledge, which the prisoner knew to be false, and the falsehood of which he intended to communicate, and did so, by signing the receipt in the partnership name. As the false pretence was not, however, necessary under the circumstances, it did not have the effect required by the statute, and therefore the offence was not technically committed. The party acted upon his previous knowledge, and not upon the representations or conduct of the plaintiff.

Upon this view of the case, I confess I am unable to say there was a want of probable cause, assuming all the facts to have been known to the prosecutor which were disclosed upon the trial. Here is moral guilt enough, and an exemption from legal guilt only upon a very nice and accurate discrimination of the facts and the law - such as cannot be expected or required of a layman. I cannot say there was no reasonable foundation for the prosecution. The goods were obtained by the false representation and conduct of the plaintiff by a suppression of the truth, and therefore not exactly within the statute, but so near to it that there existed a reasonable and well grounded suspicion of guilt. . .

But while I am of opinion this action for a malicious prosecution cannot be maintained upon the safe and established principles which govern it, I should regret if the defendant should escape without proper responsibility for the cruel, unnecessary and oppressive manner in which he caused the execution of the warrant of the governor of Vermont. This feature in the case has undoubtedly imparted much of the importance that has been justly attached to the suit; for without it, I cannot think an action for a malicious prosecution would have been thought of. An action for trespass, assault and false imprisonment should have been brought, and was the appropriate remedy for the excess of authority and abuse of the process. (1 Chitty 185. . .) If any doubt has heretofore existed whether case might not also be sustained, it is, I apprehend, removed by the revised statutes. (2 R.S. 553 #16). The case of Rogers v Brewster (5 Johns R.

125), seems also an authority independently of the revised statutes. The declaration should have contained a count for the abuse of the process, and which would have reached this particular objectionable conduct of the defendant, so highly outrageous and indefensible. The court would probably yet permit a count to be added covering this ground of action.

On the whole, I am of opinion that a new trial should be granted; the costs to abide the event.

Mr. Justice BRONSON (dissenting opinion omitted)

Whereupon the court ordered a new trial; costs to abide the event.

GRAINGER v HILL (1838) 4 BingNC 212, 132 EngRep 769

TINDAL, C. J. This is a special action on the case, in which the plaintiff declares that he was the master and owner of a vessel which, in September, 1836, he mortgaged to the Defendants for the sum of 80L, with a covenant for repayment in September 1837, and under a stipulation that, in the mean time, the plaintiff should retain the command of the vessel, and prosecute voyages therein for his own profit: that the defendants, in order to compel the plaintiff through duress to give up the register of the vessel, without which he could not go to sea, before the money lent on mortgage became due, threatened to arrest him for the same unless he immediately paid the amount; that, upon the plaintiff refusing to pay it, the defendants knowing he could not provide bail, arrested him under a capias, indorsed to levy 95L 17s. 6d., and kept him imprisoned, until, by duress, he was compelled to give up the register, which the defendants then unlawfully detained; by means whereof the plaintiff lost four voyages from London to Caen. There is also a count in trover for the register. The defendants pleaded the general issue; and, after a verdict for the plaintiff, the case comes before us on a double ground, under an application for a non-suit, and in arrest of judgment.

The first ground urged for a non-suit is, that the facts proved with respect to the writ of capias do not amount to an arrest. It appears to me that the arrest was sufficiently established. The facts are, that the sheriff's officer comes with a capias to the plaintiff, when he is ill in bed, and tells him that, unless he delivers the register or finds bail, he must either take him or leave a man with him. Without actual contact, the officer's insisting that the plaintiff should produce the register, or find bail, shows that the plaintiff was in a situation in which bail was to be procured; that was a sufficient restraint upon the plaintiff's person to amount to an arrest...

The second ground urged for a nonsuit is, that there was no proof of the suit commenced by the defendants having been terminated. But the answer to this, and to the objection urged in arrest of judgment, namely, the omission to allege want of reasonable and probable cause for the defendants' proceeding is the same: that this is an action for abusing the process of the law, by applying it to extort property from the plaintiff, and not an action for a malicious arrest or malicious prosecution, in order to support which action the termination of the previous proceeding must be proved, and the absence of reasonable and probable cause be alleged as well as proved. In the case of a malicious arrest, the sheriff at least is instructed to pursue the exigency of the writ: here the directions given, to compel the plaintiff to yield up the register, were no part of the duty enjoined by the writ. If the course pursued by the defendants is such that there is no precedent of a similar transaction, the plaintiff's remedy is by an action on the case, applicable to such new and special circumstances; and his complaint being that the process of the law has been abused, to effect an object not within the scope of the process; it is immaterial whether the suit which that process commenced has been determined or not, or whether or not it was founded on reasonable and probable cause. . .

PARK, J. I am of the same opinion. According to the authority in Buller's Nisi Prins this was a good arrest.

The argument as to the omission to prove the termination of the defendant's suit, and to allege want of reasonable and probable cause for it, has proceeded on a supposed analogy between the present case and an action for a malicious arrest. But this is a case primae impressionis, in which the defendants are charged with having abused the process of the law, in order to obtain property to which they had no colour of title; and, if an action on the case be the remedy applicable to a new species of injury, the declaration and proof must be according to the particular circumstances. I admit the authority of the cases which have been cited, but they do not apply to the present.

VAUGHAN, J. I think that in law this was clearly an arrest. If the party is under restraint, and the officer manifests an intention to make a caption, it is not necessary there should be actual contact. With respect to the termination of the defendants' suit, all the facts in the declaration were proved. The termination of that suit is not alleged, nor was it necessary, because what the plaintiff complains of is an abuse of the process of law, for the purpose of extorting property to which the defendants had no claim: that abuse having been perpetrated, and the defendants having attained their end by it, it is immaterial whether their suit was terminated or not. The case is altogether distinct from cases of malicious prosecution or arrest, in which it is always the course to allege and prove that the former proceeding is at an end.

So, with respect to the argument in arrest of judgment, this case stands on its own peculiar circumstances. It is an action for abusing the process of law, by employing it to extort property to which the defendants had no right: that is of itself a sufficient cause of action, without alleging that there was no reasonable or probable cause for the suit itself. . .

BOSZNQUET, J. I thought at the trial, and am still of the same opinion, that these circumstances amounted to an arrest. The plaintiff resigned his personal liberty under the authority of the writ: and actual contact was not necessary to complete the arrest.

Then, as the record stands, it was not necessary to prove, and I think, under the circumstances of this case it was not necessary either to allege or prove the termination of the defendants' suit. This is not an action for a malicious arrest or prosecution, or for maliciously doing that which the law allows to be done: the process was enforced for an ulterior purpose; to obtain property by duress to which the defendants had no right. The action is not for maliciously putting process in force, but for maliciously abusing the process of the Court. And that distinction is an answer as well to the argument in arrest of judgment, as to the argument in support of a nonsuit. . .

And as it is clear that the register was illegally obtained by duress, under an abuse of the process of this Court, this rule must be

Discharged.

DISHAW v WADLEIGH (3dDept.1897) 15 AD 285, 44 S 207

Action by Frank W. Dishaw aginst L. Ogden Wadleigh. From a judgment entered on a verdict in favor of plaintiff for $500, and from an order denying a motion for a new trial, made on the minutes, defendant appeals. Reversed.

HERRICK, J. This case is somewhat novel in its character, and, owing to its peculiar features, my associates have thought that, while this appeal might perhaps be determined upon some of the rulings made upon the trial, yet it would be well to express our opinion upon the questions as to whether such an action is maintainable, and also give expression to our views upon the practice indulged in which led to this litigation, and by such expression perhaps relieve the court from resorting to harsher measures to cause a cessation of such practice in this department.

The appellant, as one of the reasons for asking for a reversal of the judgment against him, contends that the facts proved are insufficient to constitute a cause of action. He asserts that every step taken by him was authorized in law. It is true that Tucker had a legal right to assign his account to Woodard; that Woodward had a legal right to bring an action thereon in his own name, in the town where he lived; it is true that a party plaintiff has a right to subpoena the defendants as a wtiness; it is true, also, that where a witness does not obey a subpoena, it is legal to issue an attachment for him; and all these things can be done, or advised to be done, by an attorney for his client. Still, proceedings that are authorized by law may be made use of for an improper purpose, and acts which separately are legal may be so combined together for an illegal purpose as to constitute a single act that is obnoxious to the law. The facts here disclose a disreputable method of practice, degrading to an honorable profession, and well calculated to bring the administration of justice into reproach and contempt; and it cannot be upheld or justified under the plea that each step taken was one authorized by law, for "the law is just and good, and entitled to the obedience of all, the strong as well as the weak, and cannot sustain the perversion of its process to shield lawlessness and wrong, or permit it to be made the tool of trickery and cunning." (Sneeden v Harris, 109 NC 349, 13 SE 920.)

strong as well as the weak, and cannot sustain the perversion of its process to shield lawlessness and wrong, or permit it to be made the tool of trickery and cunning." (Sneeden v Harris, 109 NC 349, 13 SE 920.) Here it was sought by trickery and cunning to pervert the processes of the law from their proper use and design, in order to reach a result which it was thought could not be arrived at by the ordinary and legitimate procedure of the courts. The action here under review is not one for false imprisonment malicious prosecution, or the special action authorized by section 1900, of the Code of Civil Procedure, although it possesses some of the features of each of these actions. It is one, I think, for an abuse of process; something rarely brought to the attention of the courts, except in connection with actions for false imprisonment or malicious prosecution, but for which a separate action will lie, and the attorney guilty of it may be suspended from practice.

Counsel have not referred to, nor have I, after a somewhat careful examination, been able to find, any reported case in this state where an attorney has been held liable in damages for an abuse of process; but, if such an action can be maintained against any one, there is no reason why an attorney should not be held liable, and many why he should. Here the acts complained of were the direct personal acts of the atorney, not dependent upon any evidence or representation of his client or of any third person, as in most cases of malicious prosecution or false imprisonment, but wholly instigated and carried on by the attorney. The action for abuse of process is one well defined at common law.

Cooley, in his work on Torts (page 199), lays down the following rule: "If process, either civil or criminal, is willfully made use of for a purpose not justified by the law, this is an abuse for which an action will lie;" and the author proceeds to give some illustrations of such abuses. The leading English case upon the subject is that of Grainger v Hill (4 BingNC 212), where the owner of a vessel was arrested on civil process, and the officer, acting under the direction of the plaintiffs in the suit, used the process to compel the defendant therein to give up his ship register, to which they had no right. He was held entitled to recover damages, not for maliciously putting the process in force, but for maliciously abusing it to effect an object not within its proper scope. In this country it is a well-recognized form of action. "The common-law action for abusing legal process is confined to a use of process for the purpose of compelling the defendant to do some collateral thing which he could not lawfully be compelled to do." (Johnson v Reed, 136 Mass 421.) In that case it was held no abuse of process was alleged.

If process is willfully made use of for a purpose not justified by the law, this is an abuse for which an action will lie. (Antcliff v June, 81 Mich 477, 45 NW 1019.) It is not necessary, as in cases of malicious prosecution, to allege or prove that the proceeding complained of has been terminated. Where process is used to compel a party to do a collateral thing, or to accomplish an ulterior purpose, an action for malicious abuse of process may be maintained, without alleging or proving that the process improperly employed is at an end. (Sneeden v Harris, 109 NC 349, 13 SE 920.) It has also been held, where a person maliciously and without probable cause procured an attachment as auxiliary to his suit, that an action would lie, and that it was not necessary to allege or prove the termination of the first suit, upon the principle that when the termination of the former suit can neither tend to establish nor invalidate the plaintiff's cause of action, it is not necessary to allege its termination. (Fortman v Rettier, 8 OhioSt 548...)

From the evidence in this case the jury could have found that the defendant caused the subpoena to be issued for the plaintiff in the action against him in the justice's court, and the subsequent attachment to be issued against him, not for the purpose of procuring his attendance, and securing him as a witness in the case, but for the purpose of coercing payment of the claim against him, with the idea, the claim being small, that, rather than submit to the discomfort, inconvenience, and expense of attending court at so great a distance, he would pay the claim. A subpoena is for the purpose of compelling the attendance of a person whom it is desired to use as a witness. Its use for any other purpose is a perversion and abuse of the process of the court. And it seems to me that, within the principle and cases I have referred to, the action is well brought; and, if there is no precedent for it in this state, the facts in this case demonstrate that it is time that one was made. But, while the action is well brought, it is incumbent upon the plaintiff to establish his case by proper evidence. Upon the trial, the plaintiff was allowed to prove orally, by the witness Woodward, the arrangement between the defendant and the witness Woodward for the assignment of the claim against the plaintiff, and also of other assignments of claims, and of the reasons for making such claims in the village of Gouverneur. These arrangements were made, and the reasons therefor given, by letter. No sufficient foundation was laid for giving secondary evidence. The witness said: "I can't tell where the letter is. Don't know where it is. Don't think I could find it. I think it has been destroyed, but I am not sure." And again: "I have not been asked to produce these letters here. I have destroyed some of the letters, and som I have not." This evidence does not show that any effort whatever was made to produce the letters, or ascertain that they could not be found. I think it was error to receive such evidence, and error not to have stricken it out upon the defendant's motion. (Kearney v Mayor, etc., 92 NY 617.)

The evidence gave color to the transaction in controversy, and was well calculated to influence the jury, and for such error the judgment and order should be reversed, and a new trial granted, with costs to abide the event. All concur.

FOY v BARRY (1stDept 1903) 87 AD 291, 84 S 335

Action by Frank Foy against Thomas Barry and others. Motion by plaintiff for a new trial on exceptions ordered to be heard by the Appellate Division in the first instance.

HATCH, J. When this case was called for trial the defendants' counsel made a motion that the complaint be dismissed upon the ground that it did not state facts sufficient to constitute a cause of action. The court granted the motion, and plaintiff's counsel excepted to the dismissal as to the defendants Soper and James Barry. The plaintiff then moved for a new trial, which motion was denied, to which the plaintiff excepted, and the court ordered the exceptions to be heard by the Appellate Division in the first instance.

The complaint averred that the defendant Soper is a constable of Essex county, in the state of New York; that on the 10th day of May, 1899, the defendant Soper and James Barry arrested plaintiff while he was doing business in the city of New York, by virtue of an alleged criminal warrant issued by a justice of the peace of Essex county upon the affidavit of Thomas Barry; that upon said arrest being made the defendants held plaintiff in custody in his place of business, during which time the defendants James Barry and Soper told plaintiff that if he would get his (plaintiff's) father to withdraw a claim which he had made against Thomas Barry, and which was then in litigation, and in addition pay their expenses on the warrant from Essex county to New York, amounting to $60, they would release him, otherwise they would take him back to Essex county with them under the warrant; that the plaintiff, being in fear, explained the situation to his brother, James Foy, for whom he was working, and said James Foy gave to said Soper and Barry $60 in cash and a release from plaintiff's father, which said Soper and Barry accepted, and then informed plaintiff that he was at liberty.

The complaint in this action cannot be said to be a model pleading, but we are of opinion, nevertheless, that it states a good cause of action for an abuse of process. It avers facts showing and where use was made of the warrant, and from the facts thus averred is conveyed with considerable clearness that the defendant Soper, the constable, and James Barry made use of the warrant to compel the defendant therein to procure to be withdrawn a claim of his father against Thomas Barry, who made the affidavit upon which the warrant was issued, which claim was then in litigation, and in addition thereto to deliver a release thereof, and to pay Soper and Barry the sum of $60. It would be difficult to state a clearer case of abuse of process than these acts constituted. Cooley on Torts (2dEd) p. 189, defines what constitutes an abuse of process in these words: "If process, either civil or criminal, is wilfully made use of for a purpose not justified by the law, this is an abuse for which an action will lie." In Dishaw v Wadleigh (15 AD 205, 44 S 207), the Appellate Division in the Third Department, speaking through Mr. Justice Herrick, quotes the definition by Mr. Cooley with approval. Therein all the leading authorities bearing upon the subject are collected and commented upon. The case contains an elaborate and satisfactory discussion of the subject. Adopting its doctrine, as we do, without hesitation, it leaves no room for doubt but that a good cause of action for an abuse of process is stated in the present complaint. So far as appears from the record, no authority was shown to execute any warrant in the county of New York. It was issued by a magistrate in Essex county, and, in order to authorize its execution in New York county, proof would be required of the genuineness of the signature of the magistrate issuing the same before a magistrate in the county of New York, and authority for its execution is required to be indorsed thereon. (Code Cr. Proc. Sec. 156, 157).

But whether properly indorsed so as to authorize its execution in this county or not does not affect the cause of action stated in the complaint, even though it was used with such authority, if in fact it was used for the purpose averred therein. If executed without authority it would only accentuate the abuse, and, if the facts are established as averred in the complaint, the abuse of process, very gross in its character, will have been made out. The ground stated by counsel for the dismissal of the complaint was that there was no averment that the warrant was taken out willfully and intentionally for an improper purpose, or that it was wrongfully and willfully used for such purpose. It was not necessary that it should contain such averment. (Grainger v Hill, 4 BingNC 212.) In an action for malicious prosecution it is a part of the cause of action that there was no probable cause for the prosecution, and that its institution was malicious; consequently these facts must be averred and proved. (Cousins v Swords, 14 AD 338, 43 S 907), affirmed on the opinion below 162 NY 625, 57 NE 1107.) In the action for abuse of process the graveman of the complaint is the using of the process for purpose not justified by law, and to effect an object not within its proper scope; and in such action the facts may appear from which is fairly deducible the inference of wrongful and malicious use, and the pleading is sufficient if it aver facts out of which the inference arises. So far as Thomas Barry is concerned, the only averment of the complaint as to him is that he made the affidavit upon which the warrant was issued, and it is to be presumed that they acted within legal authority in so doing. There is no charge that he either instigated or had cognizance of the acts averred in the complaint, or that the warrant was to be used for such purposes; consequently no cause of action was stated as against him.

It follows from these views that the exceptions should be sustained, and the motion for a new trial granted, as to the defendants Soper and James Barry, with costs to the plaintiff to abide the event. All concur.

BIANCHI, Respondent v LEON AND TERRY, Appellants (1stDept 1910) 138 AD 215, 122 S 1004, r63 M 73, 118 S 386

Plaintiff's husband, who had obtained $600 from defendant by fraud, was arrested in a civil suit therefor; the order of arrest fixing bail at $500. At the time of the arrest, the officer told the husband the amount of bail fixed, and offered to go with him to any friends who might assist him. Instead of that, he asked to be taken to defendant's attorney and had his wife meet him there. Plaintiff requested the attorney to release her husband without bail, promising that the debt would be paid the next day; but the attorney refused to consent to the release unless plaintiff would secure other debts due to defendant by plaintiff and her husband amounting to $6,500. Plaintiff was entirely familiar with the facts, and was offered an opportunity to obtain independent legal advice, and was told that her husband could be released on only $500 bail. Instead of doing this, she gave a deed of her lands to the attorney as trustee to secure all the debts owing to defendant, amounting to $7,100. (Facts cited in headnote.)

CLARKE, J. This is a suit in equity to set aside a conveyance of certain land in Amherst, Mass., executed and delivered by the plaintiff to the defendant Leon for the purpose of securing payment to the defendant Terry of certain sums amounting to $7,100 claimed to be due and owing to her, $3,500 by the plaintiff, $600 jointly by the plaintiff and her husband, and $3,000 by her husband. The complaint alleges that the conveyance was obtained through false representations, threats, fear, and duress. The judgment of the court is based upon an abuse of process, and grants the relief prayed, except insofar as the conveyance is security for $600....

The findings and conclusion (by trial court) in their omissions, as well as in what they find, exclude fraud, false representations, and duress alleged in the complaint: First, because they are not found; and, second, because the conveyance could not have been sustained as security to the amount of $600 if the court had found fraud or duress. Further there is nothing in the case which would sustain a finding or an inference of fraud or misrepresentation. The judgment stands, then, absolutely upon the findings, as well as upon the opinion, upon the ground of abuse of process. That being based upon the fact that the security was given for other amounts conceded to be due, with the qualifications that if payments could be proved to have been made applicable either to interest or principal, such payments should be credited in the final settlement.

Can abuse of process be predicated upon the facts shown? It appears that plaintiff had full knowledge of the facts, that the order of arrest was valid, that she was more or less connected with the incurring of the other debts, and that she knew that bail for $500 would release her husband from custody. Did she desire to save her husband from being locked up under the order of arrest, under the circumstances disclosed, make her act in executing and delivering the conveyance of no effect? Can she now, the consideration therefor, the release of her husband, having passed, avoid her deed?

I have reached the conclusion, from the careful examination of this record and the principles of law which would govern, that the findings of fact negative the conclusion of law of abuse of precess. There is no suggestion of a conspiracy between Leon and the deputy by which the arrest was to be made use of as a lever to procure a general settlement. There is no proof that Leon had given any directions to have Bianchi brought to his house or had any idea of seeing him as a result of the arrest. Every step in these proceedings, after the arrest of Bianchi, was taken upon the initiative of Bianchi or his wife. The deputy sheriff told him he could confer with his friends. Instead, he asked to be taken to Miss Terry's attorney, and all the telephoning and all the engagements and all the talk and all the offers came from the Bianchis. It is conceded that the deputy's conduct was beyond reproach. He informed plaintiff of the small amount of bail. He said arrest under civil process involved no disgrace. He suggested consultation with friends. So there was neither an unlawful and ulterior purpose in the issuance of process, nor an unreasonable and oppresive execution thereof.

In Am.& Eng. Enc. of Law, vol. 1, p. 222, the definition is given: "A malicious abuse of legal process is where the party employs it for some unlawful object, not the purpose which it is intended by the law to effect."

This process was intended to effect the arrest of the defendant Bianchi and the keeping of him in custody until he gave bail, in order to secure by legal duress the payment of the money which he had fraudulently obtained. This security was given by the plaintiff for the purpose of avoiding the legal custody of her husband under the legal order of arrest. It was her initiative, and not that of Leon or Terry, which produced it. All she had to do was to let him go to jail or give bail. For reasons of her own she agreed to pay debts, some of which she had incurred herself, and all of which she had participated in, and none of which have been paid to this day.

In 32 Cyc 541, under Abuse of Process, it is said: "(b) Elements. It has been said that two elements are necessary, an unlawful and ulterior purpose and also an act done in the use of the process not proper in the regular prosecution of the proceeding. But it seems doubtful whether both of these elements must always be present. - - - It has been held that a malicious abuse of legal process consists in the malicious misuse or misapplication of that process to accomplish some purpose not warranted or commanded by the writ. And it has also been said that whoever makes use of the process of the court for some private purpose of his own, not warranted by the exigency of the writ or the order of the court, is answerable to an action for damages for an abuse of the process of the court. Similar expressions occur in many cases. None of these statements include the second element above set forth. On the other hand, the second element alone has been held sufficient to impose liability, as where a writ is executed against property in an unreasonable and oppressive manner; where, after arrest upon civil or criminal process, the party arrested is subject to unwarrantable insult or indignities, is treated with cruelty, is deprived of proper food or shelter, or is otherwise treated with oppression and undue hardships; or where a summons is served in an unreasonable, cruel, and oppressive manner."....

In Adams v Irving National Bank, 116 NY 606, 23 NE 7, 6 LRA 491, 15 Am StRep 447, and in many cases cited therein, a settlement was set aside as having been brought about by threat of criminal prosecution. There can be no doubt that these cases were correctly decided, for the obtaining of a settlement under a threat of criminal prosecution is blackmail, as defined by sections 856, 857 and 858 of the penal law (Consol. Laws, c.40): the cases relating thereto having been examined by us in People v Wickes, 112 AD 39, 98 S 163.

In Van Campen v Ford, 15 NYStRep 310, Van Brunt, P.J., speaking for the General Term, said:

"This action was brought to set aside a note and a mortgage made by the plaintiff to secure the note upon the ground that the note and mortgage were obtained by duress, and that the same was given to secure a debt of her husband and was without consideration. * * * It is claimed by the defendant that the note and mortgage was given by the plaintiff to relieve her husband from arrest in an action brought by the defendant's testator against him, and that in consideration of the note and mortgage he released the husband from arrest and refrained from prosecuting the suit against him. If this claim had been sustained by the evidence, a consideration for the note and mortgage would have been made out."

This case was a second time before the Supreme Court in Van Campen v Ford 53 Hun (NY) 636, 6 S 139. The evidence tended to show that while under arrest Van Campen requested his wife to relieve him from such arrest by settling the claim in an action then pending against him, and that at his request plaintiff made to defendant's attorney the proposition of settlement which was to give the note and to execute the mortgage involved in this suit in consideration of which was the release from arrest of Van Campen and the discontinuance of the suit against him. Barrett, J., with whom sat Van Burnt, P. J., and Daniels, J.:

"When this case was previously before the General Term, it was held that the instruments in question were free from the taint of duress, and that the plaintiff had fully recognized their validity. The same conclusion was arrived at upon the present trial, and the evidence again amply supports it. The new trial was ordered upon the sole ground that the case showed a want of consideration for the original note and mortgage renewed by the instruments in suit. This consideration was clearly shown upon the trial now under review. There was sufficient evidence, both direct and circumstantial, of the arrest of the plaintiff's husband. The surrounding circumstances, too, all point in that direction. The arrest was lawful, and the defendant's testator was guilty of no impropriety with regard to it. The plaintiff was not appealed to by the defendant's testator to secure her husband's release, nor was she subjected to anything in the nature of duress or threat. On the contrary, she voluntarily requested Mr. Ford's attorney to accept her obligation in settlement of the suit. This was acceded to; the consideration being the release of her husband and the discontinuance of the suit. The attorney, in compliance with this agreement, filed a consent of discontinuance with the clerk, and the plaintiff's husband was released from any restraint attaching to the order of arrest."

We are of the opinion that none of the elements necessary to constitute an abuse of process exist in the case at bar, and that, therefore, the judgment appealed from should be reversed, and a new trial ordered, with costs to the appelants to abide the event. All concur.

DEAN, Appellant v KOCHENDORFER, Respondent (1924) 237 NY 384, r206 AD 777

Appeal from a judgment of the Appellate Division of the Supreme Court in the second judicial department, entered July 6, 1923, affirming a judgment in favor of defendant entered upon a dismissal of the complaint by the court at a Trial Term.

POUND, J. The action is for malicious prosecution and malicious abuse of process. On the trial plaintiff was nonsuited. Judgment was affirmed by a divided court. Plaintiff is a lawyer and defendant is a city magistrate. The controversy arose over the conduct of plaintiff at the Town Hall in Jamaica on April 25, 1921, where the Magistrate's Court is held. While plaintiff was in the hallway, awaiting the arrival of a witness in a case set for trial on that day, he was ejected from the building by O'Leary, a police officer, who charged him with "loitering," against his protest that he was there in the proper discharge of his duty to his client in the regular administration of justice. It appears that defendant with a desire to check the soliciting of business about the hall, had made a rule against the practice. Plaintiff at once began a civil action against O'Leary to recover damages for assault and false arrest. O'Leary then brought to the attention of the magistrate the fact that a summons had been served on him and told him "that is what I get for my good work in the Hall." On the 26th of April defendant told Louis Cohen, a lawyer, that he would like to see plaintiff about the matter; that the police officer was simply carrying out his orders and it looked to him as if he (defendant) would have to stand the expense of his defense. Plaintiff declined to respond and defendant on the following day, on being told by Cohen that plaintiff did not propose to come over, said he would issue a warrant for his arrest; "Give him thirty days in the cooler and see if that will bring him over." On a charge preferred by O'Leary, plaintiff was on April 28th brought before the defendant as city magistrate, charged with disorderly conduct, "loitering in the hall, refusing to move and talking in a loud manner," and after a hearing was found guilty. Defendant said on the examination of plaintiff: "You are not brought here for the purpose of harassing or annoying you, but more for the purpose that I desire all lawyers to uphold the law." And, at the close of the hearing, said: "I feel more hurt than I do angry to think that a member of the bar is the first to refuse to uphold me" (in respect to the rule above referred to). Sentence was suspended. An appeal was allowed by the county judge and the judgment of conviction was reversed by the County Court of Queens county on the law and the facts.

The first question is whether plaintiff made out a prima facie case of malicious prosecution. Did plaintiff's testimony tend to show that defendant instituted the prosecution and instituted it in malice, without probable cause to believe that it could succeed and simply to harass and oppress the plaintiff? (Burt v Smith, 181 NY 1, 5.)

O'Leary, called as a witness for the plaintiff on the trial of this action, gave inconsistent testimony. He testified that he turned over to defendant the summons in the action against him at defendant's request, and that defendant said in substance that he would send for plaintiff to come down and see him and settle it out of court if he could; also that he (O'Leary) afterwards said to defendant, not in connection with the civil suit, that he wanted to charge plaintiff with disorderly conduct and that defendant told him to wait until he sent for plaintiff, because he didn't want a lawyer summoned into court on a charge of disorderly conduct without seeing him first. He thus presented two views of defendant's conduct: First, as that of one who would fix the matter up by interceding with plaintiff in O'Leary's behalf, and second, as that of a judicious magistrate who would not have a lawyer arrested on charge of disorderly conduct before he was given an opportunity to make his explanation.

Defendant contends that the only possible inference from the evidence is that O'Leary instituted the prosecution of plaintiff; not only that defendant did not instigate the prosecution, but also that he acted on O'Leary's complaint in good faith, with probable cause and without malice.

Plaintiff contends that the inference was permissible that defendant willfully issued the process of his court to accomplish his private purpose of compelling plaintiff to settle the action against O'Leary, and also to punish plaintiff for his refusal to come over to discuss the case with him.

Judgment of conviction might be used as a justification or bar in plaintiff's civil action against O'Leary whom defendant was trying to protect. The intimate relations between defendant and O'Leary are significant in this connection. Considering such relations and the fact that defendant took it amiss because plaintiff objected to O'Leary's conduct in carrying out the magistrate's order against "loitering", plaintiff made out a prima facie case of malicious prosecution.

If the magistrate and O'Leary acted together to institute the prosecution against plaintiff, the other elements of malicious prosecution may fairly be evolved from the evidence. The jury might say that defendant instigated the prosecution and was the direct agent in effecting the arrest. O'Leary, although plaintiff's witness, was hostile and the jury was not bound to give credence to the version of his evidence most favorable to defendant. Cohen says defendant told him that if plaintiff would not come voluntarily to see him, he would issue a warrant for his arrest; "give him thirty days in the cooler and that will bring him over." No very violent inference from the facts would be drawn if the jury found that he meant thereby that he would have a warrant issued against plaintiff to punish him for his refusal to come voluntarily to see the magistrate. The magistrate in substance admitted that it was he who brought the plaintiff before him. That defendant acted without probable cause might be inferred from the evidence that he relied on a rule which he had made that no person shall speak to another in the hallway adjacent thereto to solicit business and that under that rule it was the duty of plaintiff to move on when the officer told him to do so. He had no probable cause to regard as disorderly conduct such a legitimate assertion of plaintiff's right to be in the Town Hall about his business as an attorney. That defendant acted maliciously might be inferred from the evidence that he said in substance that he would issue his warrant to punish plaintiff for his contumacy.

Want of probable cause and malice are seldom established by direct evidence of an ulterior motive. They often rest upon circumstances such as the relation of the parties and the object sought or accomplished. Where malice or any improper or wrongful motive, or lack of probable cause exists it may be inferred that the act was malicious. Defendant might have acted in the honest and reasonable belief that plaintiff was guilty of disorderly conduct, but his good faith would not exonerate him if the facts themselves as presented to him did not constitute disorderly conduct. (Carl v Ayers, 53 NY 14, 17.)

O'Leary testified before the magistrate on the charge against plaintiff merely that plaintiff was in the hall and was put out when he refused to go, because O'Leary was acting on the judge's orders. This was the basis of the charge of disorderly conduct and was the magistrate's conception of disorderly conduct on which he issued his warrant and found plaintiff guilty.

The action is one for abuse of process as well as for malicious prosecution. The gist of the action for abuse of process lies in the improper use of process after it issued. To show that regularly issued process was perverted to the accomplishment of an improper purpose is enough. (Rogers v Brewster), 5 Johns(NY) 125). If a magistrate instigates a prosecution before himself without probable cause and deliberately uses the process issued by him therein, not for the legitimate purpose of hearing the case, but to show his authority and to gratify his personal feelings of importance, the act savors of oppresssion (Penal Law Sec. 854) and constitutes an illegal abuse of process. If it may be inferred that the warrant was issued by defendant merely to bring plaintiff into the presence of the magistrate in order that defendant might lecture and chide him under the guise of judicial action, a prima facie case of abuse of process is well made out.

Considering defendant's statement on the hearing that plaintiff was brought before him for the purpose of making him realize that "I desire all lawyers to uphold the law" (meaning his rule), and the other evidence in the case, it follows that this question was also presented.

The judgment should be reversed and a new trial granted with costs to abide the event.

Judgment reversed, etc.

KELLER, Appellant v BUTLER, Respondent (1927) 246 NY 249, 158 NE 510, r220 AD 212, 221 S 323

Appeal from a judgment, entered June 2, 1927, upon an order of the Appellate Division of the Supreme Court in the second judicial department, which reversed an order of Special Term denying a motion for a dismissal of the complaint and granted said motion.

CRANE, J. No cause of action, it is said, has been stated in the complaint, which has been dismissed. In effect this means that an action for damages cannot be maintained against one who falsely and maliciously and without probable cause procures the arrest of another as a fugitive from justice until a determination of the criminal proceeding instituted in the foreign State. According to the complaint, the defendant charged the plaintiff in the State of Florida with having committed larceny. Through the action of the defendant, the Governor of Florida made requisition upon the Governor of the State of New York for the extradition of the plaintiff who was in New York. The plaintiff was arrested upon the process of a magistrate issued in New York State under our procedure and brought before the Governor who determined that the prisoner was not a fugitive and should not be surrerndered. Thereupon, the plaintiff was discharged from arrest. The plaintiff brings this action against the defendant for falsely and maliciously and without probable cause accusing him of being a fugitive from justice, whereby he was arrested in New York State as a fugitive and imprisoned. By the motion to dismiss the complaint, all these facts are conceded, yet it has been held that the plaintiff has no remedy for this malicious arrest or abuse of process until the charge pending in the Florida courts has been determined in his favor.

We do not take this view of the law. The guilt or innocense of the defendant of the crime committed according to the laws of Florida may be - in this case was - an altogether different matter from the extradition proceedings in the State of New York, which depended entirely upon the identity of the defendant and his flight from Florida, taking New York as his asylum. Unless the plaintiff was in the State of Florida at the time of his commission of the crime, he could not be extradited under the Constitution and laws of the United States... Therefore, when this plaintiff was arrested in New York State, the question was not one of his guilt or innocence - that could not be inquired into - rather it was the question of his presence - in Florida at the time of the commission of the alleged crime, and his flight therefrom. Was he a fugitive? The complaint alleges that the defendant, knowing that the plaintiff was not a fugitive, maliciously caused his arrest under the extradition laws in the State of New York, and that after a hearing the plaintiff was released....

The complaint alleges that the plaintiff in this case was arrested upon the warrant of a magistrate before whom he was taken, and after some hours of confinement released on bail. This is the procedure outlined in section 828 of the Code of Criminal Procedure. In order to hold a prisoner until there can be a hearing, the magistrate may issue a warrant as a preliminary proceeding to the issuing of a requisition by the Governor of another State. An exemplified copy of an indictment found or other judicial proceeding in the State in which he is charged to have committed the offense may be received as evidence before the magistrate upon which to issue his warrant. The magistrate upon the arrest of the prisoner may hold him to await the warrant of the Governor, not to exceed thirty days. He may bail him in the meantime. This is the meaning of the allegations of the complaint in this case. The plaintiff was arrested in extradition proceedings through and by reason of the charge of the defendant pending the issuance of the warrant by the Governor of this State. He was brought before the magistrate and admitted to bail. Thereafter the Governor held his hearing as he was authorized to do (Code CIV. Pro. sec. 827); and refusing his warrant the magistrate subsequently released the bail and discharged the prisoner.

Here was a proceeding in this State instituted by the defendant resulting in the arrest of the plaintiff his commitment by the magistrate, his subsequent release and discharge on the ground that he could not legally be extradited. The wrong complained agaist is that the defendant instituted this proceeding maliciously, knowing that the plaintiff was not a fugitive and without any probable cause to believe him to be subject to extradition. This proceeding is terminated in favor of the plaintiff. These matters constitute all the elements necessary to make out a cause of action for malicious prosecution....

Even if this were not so, surely there must be some remedy afforded by the law for the willful and malicious arrest of another as a fugitive from justice when the charge is known to be false. Names and classifications of remedies are not indispensable to a court, although they may be convenient and necessary for the student. Justice may not tarry to tabulate. The fact is, such a wrong must have a remedy. It is provided either in the action for malicious prosecution or in an action for abuse of process. In the case of Johnson v Corrington (7 Ohio Decisions, Reprint, 572), an action upon such a state of facts as we have here was maintained as one for malicious prosecution. In Malone v Belcher (216 Mass 209) the defendant was sued for malicious abuse of process in causing the property of the plaintiff to be maliciously attached for the purpose of preventing a sale. The court in that case stated: "It was not necessary in order to maintain the action to show a termination of the action in which the attachment was made, as it would have been in a case of malicious prosecution. The attachment for the purpose of preventing the sale to Peterson was a perversion of the object which the writ was intended by law to effect, and it was therefore immaterial whether the action in which the attachment was made had been terminated or not. But as to malice and want of probable cause the case stood differently." As to these - malice and want of probable cause - the two actions are the same; that is, both in malicious prosecution and in the malicious abuse of process, malice and want of probable cause must be shown according to many authorities, the difference being that in the one the initial litigation must be terminated, while in the other it is the abuse of an incidental process which has caused the unjustifiable damage and the initial proceedings need not be terminated to give a cause of action. (See Cardival v Smith, 109 Mass 158.) Actions in the nature of malicious prosecutions have been maintained for the abuse of a search warrant (Boeger v Langenberg, 97 Mo 390); of injunction (Powell v Woodbury, 85 Vt 504); of attachment (Lawrence v Hagerman, 56 Ill 68.) Termination of the main proceeding is not always essential for the maintenance of these actions. (See Spangler v Booze, 103 Va 276.)

If, therefore, we should consider, as we do not, the requisition proceedings in the State of New York as incidental and not independent, an action should and would lie before the termination of the criminal action for the malicious abuse of the process of arrest in the State of New York under extradition proceedings...

For these reasons the judgment of the Appellate Division should be reversed and the order of the Special Term affirmed, with costs in this court and in the Appellate Division.

Judgment accordingly.

HAUSER, Appellant v BARTOW, Respondent (1937) 273 NY 370, a248 AD 712

APPEAL, by permission, from a judgment, entered June 25, 1936, upon an order of the Appellate Division of the Supreme Court in the first judicial department which unanimously affirmed an order of Special Term granting a motion by defendant for a dismissal of the complaint.

HUBBS, J. This is an action to recover damages for malicious abuse of process. The lower courts have dismissed the complaint on the ground that it fails to state a cause of action. The complaint alleges that respondent conspired with others "maliciously and wilfully, and without a legal cause or warrant" to have appellant declared incompetent so that she might control his property and prevent his executing a new will; that without the knowledge of appellant, respondent commenced a proceeding in the Supreme Court to have herself appointed committee of his person and property, and falsely and maliciously represented in that proceeding that he was violent and that it would endanger his life to appear in court and thereby induced the court to issue its process; that she was thereafter appointed committee of his person and property; that she caused him to be removed as an officer and director of a company in which they were each stockholders, sold certain securities and otherwise managed his property; that appellant was unaware of these proceedings until some time thereafter when respondent threatened to deprive him of his liberty; that he then applied to the Supreme Court, a jury trial was had on the issue of his competency, resulting in a verdict to the effect that appellant was then competent and an order was entered discharging respondent as committee and ordering her to account, and that she accounted and allowances were made to her for commissions, attorneys' fees and other expenses.

The sole question before the court is: Do the facts so pleaded constitute a good cause of action?

The legal purpose of appointing a committee of one's person and property is to conserve the property of the incompetent and to look after, care for and protect the person.

The complaint in effect alleges that such was not the purpose of the respondent, but that knowing that he was not incompetent, she conspired with others to have him wrongfully declared to be incompetent for a wrongful and ulterior purpose; that the apparently lawful act was unlawful because done untruthfully and maliciously with the sole purpose of injuring and damaging the appellant in order to bring about a financial benefit to herself. Assuming, as we must, that the allegations of the complaint are ture, if it alleges a cause of action it should not have been dismissed because it was given a wrong label. If it sets forth facts which constitute a legal wrong which the law recognizes, it is sufficient as a pleading.

"The gist of the action for abuse of process lies in the improper use of process after it is issued. To show that regularly issued process was perverted to the accomplishment of an improper purpose is enough." (Dean v Kochendorfer, 237 NY 384, 390). "The action is not for the wrongful bringing of an action or prosecution, but for the improper use, or rather "abuse" of process in connection therewith - as the Pennsylvania court has aptly put it, for a perversion of legal process. The process of law must be used improperly and this means something more than a proper use from a bad motive.* * *If the process is employed from a bad or ulterior motive, the gist of a wrong is to be found in the uses which the party procuring the process to issue attempts to put it. If he is content to use the particular machinery of the law for the immediate purpose for which it was intended, he is not ordinarily liable, notwithstanding a vicious or vindictive motive. But the moment he attempts to attain some collateral objective, outside the scope of the operation of the process employed, a tort has been consummated. * * * The tortious character of the defendant's conduct consists of his attempt to employ a legitimate process for a legitimate purpose in an improper manner, and this point must be clearly shown by the plaintiff to entitle him to maintain his action." (Harper on The Law of Torts, Sec. 272, pp. 593-595.)

It is not enough that the actor have an ulterior motive in using the process of the court. It must further appear that he did something in the use of the process outside of the purpose for which it was intended. (Cf. note 27 Har LR p. 594.) Every one has a right to use the machinery of the law, and bad motive does not defeat that right. There must be a further act done outside the use of the process - a perversion of the process. If he uses the process of the court for its proper purpose, though there is malice in his heart, there is no abuse of the process. He may be liable for malicious prosecution, but the distinction between these two wrongs must be kept in mind. As soon as the actor uses the process of the court, not to effect its proper function, but to accomplish through it some collateral object, he commits this tort. A concrete example may make this more intelligible. If one resorts to legal process to have another declared incompetent, and uses it for the purpose, he does not commit the wrong, though he may be guilty of another wrong, no matter what his motives, hopes or expectations may be. But if he makes use of that process, not for the purpose of attaining its proper end, but to extort money, or to coerce action, that is a perversion of process.

In this case, whatever may have been respondent's motives, she used the process of the court for the purpose for which the law created it. She used it, and she did not abuse it. Nowhere in the complaint can there be found any allegation that respondent did any act by virtue of the order adjudging the appellant incompetent and appointing her as committee of his person and property which was not within the scope of her duties as such committee or was in excess of the powers granted to her as such committee. The complaint, therefore, fails to state a cause of action for abuse of process.

It is urged that the complaint may be sustained as a complaint in an action for malicious prosecution. It appears, however, that the former proceeding has not been determined in appellant's favor. That it has been so determined is a necessary allegation in an action for malicious prosecution. If the rule were otherwise there might exist at the same time two judgments between the same parties directly in conflict upon the same issue. True it is that there are cases to the effect that the action will lie without such allegation where the original proceeding was without personal service and the defendant therein had no opportunity to defend. (Bump v Botts, 19 Wend(NY) 421...)

Assuming, however, that even though the order appointing the committee may have been jurisdictionally void, and that it would furnish no bar to an action for malicious prosecution of the incompetency proceedings, nevertheless the alleged incompetent thereafter appeared in the proceeding and, after his appearance, there was a conclusive adjudication of the validity of the original order.

The complaint alleges:

"Nineteenth. That immediately upon the discovery by the plaintiff of the fact of the appointment of the defendant as committee, the plaintiff began an investigation of such appointment, and in and about the month of March, 1935, caused an application to be made to the Supreme Court of the State of New York Westchester County, to set aside said appointment, which application resulted in an order of said Supreme Court directing a trial by jury of the issue of his competency.

"Twentieth. That thereupon a jury trial of said issue was had in the Supreme Court, Westchester County, which resulted in a verdict by said jury that the plaintiff was competent both as to person and property.

"Twnety-first. That thereupon an order was entered in said court discharging the defendant as such committee, and directing her to account for her acts as such, and thereupon the defendant accounted and allowances were made to her both for commissions, attorneys' fees and other expenses which she had incurred in and about the management of said property belonging to the plaintiff, and the defendant accepted such commissions and made such expenditures."

The proceedings upon that application are a part of the record in this appeal. In March, 1935, the plaintiff obtained orders to show cause "why an order should not be made vacating and setting aside the order of this court adjudging said Emil Hauser an incompetent and appointing Augusta M. Bartow as committee of his person and property." The petition upon which this order was presented shows that shortly after the defendant was appointed committee of the plaintiff's person and property, the plaintiff was informed that she "was perfectly willing to return the control of his property to him by the fall of 1934 as she felt that the treatments which he was getting would put petitioner in good physical condition, for which reason your petitioner took no further steps in the matter." The petition concludes with these words: "Wherefore, your petitioner prays that the order of this court made the first day of August, 1934, appointing your petitioner's half-sister his committee should be set aside and vacated and an opportunity be given to your petitioner to defend the question of competency before a jury so that this Honorable Court may make an order removing said committee and restoring his property to the petitioner." Upon the return of the order to show cause the motion was granted to the extent of ordering "that the competency of the incompetent be tried at the trial term of this court to be held," etc. The plaintiff here might have contested, upon the return of the order to show cause, the validity of the original order made without notice to him. (Matter of Blewitt, 131 NY 541.) Instead, he availed himself of the practice, also approved in that case, of showing that he was not incompetent at that time.

After the defendant was discharged as committee she filed her account and upon that accounting she was allowed commissions in the sum of $2,133.94.

Under those circumstances there has been a conclusive adjudication that the original order was valid; that is issued upon sufficient cause. Indeed, since the petition of the appellant herein prays for the discharge of the committee of his person, and alleges, in effect, that for months after he knew of the appointment of the committee, he acquiesced therein, it is too late now to urge that the proceeding was initiated without cause. The appellant had his day in court and failed in his effort to have respondent's original appointment revoked. It stands, therefore, as an adjudication after trial which bars an action for malicious prosecution.

It follows that no cause of action is stated and the judgment dismissing the complaint should be affirmed.

The judgment should be affirmed, with costs.

CRANE, Ch. J. (dissenting). One who has been wrongfully declared insane without notice or hearing at the instance of another, acting maliciously, knowing the allegations of insanity to be false, must have some remedy for such justice. It cannot be that the form of action or the name we give it fails to arouse the court.

The complaint in this action has been held to be insufficient as not stating a cause of action for an abuse of process. In my opinion it is entirely immaterial whether it be called such or an action of malicious prosecution; it states a grievance recognized by law. (Keller v Butler, 246 NY 249, 254.) In that case the court said: "Names and classifications of remedies are not indispensable to a court, although they may be convenient and necessary for the student. Justice may not tarry to tabulate. The fact is, such a wrong must have a remedy. It is provided either in the action for malicious prosecution or in an action for abuse of process." Continuing, we cited cases in the nature of malicious prosecutions for abuse of process. That insanity proceedings may be the basis for malicious prosecutions, see Harper on The Law of Torts (#268)...Even a civil proceeding brought to harass and oppress may give rise to such a remedy. (Burt v Smith 181 NY 1.)

Says Harper in his Law of Torts (#268): "Even under the narrow English rule, the action may be brought for insolvency or bankruptcy proceedings, since the reputation and credit of the plaintiff have sustained direct, pecuniary loss, and in most jurisdictions the action will lie for civil proceedings accompanied by arrest, attachment, or injunction. The institution of lunacy or insanity proceedings also comes within the principle since the liberty of the person charged is involved."

Where the alleged insane person has had no notice or hearing the decision of the court finding him incompetent is not such determination as bars the action for malicious prosecution. (Bump v Betts, 19 Wend(NY) 421...) In Swensgaard case it was said; "The general rule, making the right to maintain an action of this nature (malicious prosecution) to depend upon the fact that the prosecution complained of has resulted in a determination in favor of the accused, is applicable only when the course of the prosecution has been such that the accused had the opportunity to controvert the facts alleged against him, and to secure a determination in his favor."

Taking the essential allegations in the complaint we find them to set forth: The defendant maliciously and wilfully and without legal cause or warrant, sought to have the plaintiff declared incompetent, so as to procure his property. That in July, 1934, the defendant, without the knowledge of the plaintiff, began a proceeding in the Supreme Court to have herself appointed committee of the plaintiff's person and property, and caused such proceedings to be taken without notice to the plaintiff and without his knowledge and she falsely and maliciously represented in said proceedings that the plaintiff was violent, and that it would endanger his life to appear in court; and she thereby induced the court to issue process and to appoint the defendant committee of the plaintiff's person and property. The plaintiff was entirely unaware of these proceedings until late in 1934 when defendant threatened to deprive him of his liberty; that immediately after discovering what had been done the plaintiff applied to the Supreme Court to set aside the appointment. The application was granted after a jury on a hearing had declared the plaintiff competent.

The complaint then sets forth the following: "That at all times the defendant knew that the plaintiff was not incompetent, insane or a lunatic."

Here, in my opinion, we have pleaded a sufficient and complete cause of action for malicious prosecution. The judgment below should be reversed, with costs, and the motion to dismiss the complaint denied, with costs.

What a trial of this action may show we cannot tell; the plaintiff may not sustain his case. Now, however, we are dealing solely with his broad allegations as if they were true.

The judgment should be reversed.

Judgment affirmed.

MILLER v STERN (1stDept 1941) 262 AD 5, 27 S2d 374

Action for abuse of process by Robert Thomas Miller against Walter T. Stern and another. From an order denying his motion to dismiss the complaint for insufficiency under Rule 106 of the Rules of Civil Practice and from an order granting reargument but adhering to the original decision, named defendant appeals.

COHN, Justice. This is an action for abuse of process brought against Walter T. Stern, an attorney, and Marguerite Kirmse Cole, his client. It arises out of a previous suit for conversion brought by Marguerite Kirmse Cole through her attorney Walter T. Stern against Alexander Crane and the plaintiff herein.

The complaint in the present action alleges that Cole was the client of defendant Stern and that Crane was plaintiff's client; that notwithstanding the fact that defendant Stern knew that plaintiff's only connection with the controversy involved in the Cole suit was that of attorney for Crane, said defendant, acting in conspiracy with his client, Cole, made this plaintiff a defendant in the Cole suit and obtained therein an ex parte order for this plaintiff's examination before trial, pursuant to Section 1094-a of the Civil Practice Act for the following purposes: (a) To obtain confidential matters and communications which had been revealed to plaintiff by his client, this confidential information being sought by the defendant Stern for use in the controversy between Cole and Crane; (b) to harass the plaintiff and coerce him into recommending to his client, Alexander Crane, an unjust settlement of the litigation; (c) to destroy plaintiff's usefulness as attorney for his client and his usefulness as an officer of this court. The manner in which it is claimed that plaintiff was damaged as a result of the alleged wilfull misuse of the legal process by defendants is as follows: (1) Plaintiff was compelled to retain counsel to defend the action; (2) he was compelled to retain other counsel for his client Alexander Crane; (3) he was compelled to reveal privileged communications made to him by his client; (4) his usefulness as an attorney for his client and as an officer of the court in defense of his client was destroyed; (5) he was compelled to spend time and effort to resist an unfounded claim, and (6) he was put to great trouble and expense and was humiliated and force to submit to a lengthy examination before trial, all to his damage in the sum of $10,000.

That plaintiff was compelled to retain counsel to defend the action and to retain counsel for his own client; that he was put to trouble and expense in resisting and unfounded claim; that his usefulness as an attorney for his client and as an officer of the court in defense of his client was destroyed, were all incidents and annoyances which frequently accompany the ordinary law suit. It has repeatedly been held that the mere institution of a civil action which has occasioned a party trouble, inconvenience and expense of defending, will not support an action for abuse of process. (Lichter v Interwoven Stocking Co., 234 AD 204, 254 S 375...) Public policy requires that parties be permitted to avail themselves of the courts to settle their grievances and that they may do so without unnecessary exposure to a suit for damages in the event of an unsuccessful prosecution. "The costs awarded to a successful defendant in a civil action are the indemnity which the law gives him for a groundless prosecution." (Ferguson v Arnew, 142 NY 580, at page 583, 37 NE 626...).

The only alleged element of damage which remains to sustain the tort of abuse of process is that plaintiff was compelled to reveal privileged communications made to him by his client. This allegation is a pure conclusion of law. If the communications were privileged and were not germane to the law suit in which plaintiff was made a party, there appears to be no valid reason why the privilege could not have been asserted by plaintiff at the time when questions which might violate the confidential relationship between the plaintiff and his client were propounded to him (Sec. 353, Civil Practice Act.) An attorney may not be compelled at the instance of a hostile litigant to disclose his retainer or the nature of the transactions to which it related when such information could be made the basis of a suit against his client. (Matter of Shawmut Mining Co., 94 AD 156, 163, 87 S 1059).

The Special Term has sustained the complaint upon the theory that it alleges that plaintiff was joined in the Cole suit for the purpose of abusing the right of examination conferred by Section 1094-a of the Civil Practice Act in that defendant by joining plaintiff as a party in the Cole suit was thereby enabled to obtain an exparte order for his examination for the purpose of obtaining information with reference to the location of the chattels. Indeed, plaintiff states that the gravemen of the tortious conduct of the defendant is "abusing the right of examination." Subjection to an examination before trial, however, is one of the incidents of any civil action. A defendant is always subject to an examination before trial. (Civil Practice Act, Sec. 288.) By express language of Section 1094-a of the Civil Practice Act, all the provisions of Article 29, Sec. 288 et seq., of the Act and the Rules of Civil Practice relative to testimony by deposition apply to such order and to the taking of such deposition wherever the provisions of Article 29 are consistent with the requirements of Section 1094-a.

There is an obvious deficiency in the challenged pleading. Substantially, it sets forth the issuance of the process and the plaintiff's wrongful motives. This, however, is not enough to constitute a cause of action for abuse of process. If defendant used the process of the court for its proper purpose, though there was malice in his heart, there was no abuse of process. The tort is not committed until defendant uses or attempts to use the process of the court, not to effect its proper function, but to accomplish through it some collateral object. (Hauser v Bartow, 273 NY 370, 374, 7 NE2d 268...) "The gist of the action for abuse of process lies in the improper use of process after it is issued." (Dean v Kochendorfer, 237 NY 384, 390, 143 NE 229, 231.) In his pleading, plaintiff has failed to set forth how process of the court was abused after it had been issued.

In effect, plaintiff is complaining of the institution of former action against him and not of any wrong committed in the execution of process during the course of the Cole suit. The cause of action, if any, would fall within the category of malicious prosecution, i.e., maliciously causing process to issue, and could be upheld upon a showing that there had been interference with person or property and that the prior action had terminated favorably to plaintiff....

Orders unanimously reversed with $20 costs and disbursements, and motion to dismiss the complaint as against the defendant-appellant granted, with leave to the plaintiff to serve an amended complaint within ten days after service of order on payment of said costs. All concur.

GENERAL MOTORS ACCEPTANCE CORPORATION v DAVIS (1931) 151 Okla 255, 7 P2d 157

HEFNER, J. This is an action by John W. Davis against General Motors Acceptance Corporation to recover damages for conversion of an automobile and for malicious prosecution because of the unlawful use of criminal process in obtaining possession thereof.

In his first cause of action plaintiff claims damages in the sum of $1,000 because of conversion of his automobile, and $500 punitive damages; and in his second cause of action claims $1,000 actual damages and $500 punitive damages.

The jury returned a verdict in his favor for $545 actual damages and $500 punitive damages on his first cause of action and $1,000 actual damages and $500 punitive damages on his second cause of action, and judgment was entered in accordance with the verdict.

Defendant contends that the evidence is insufficient to sustain the judgment, and that the court erred in overruling its motion for a directed verdict.

The evidence offered on behalf of plaintiff discloses facts substantially as follows: On the 24th day of July, 1927, he purchased an automobile from the Underwood Motor Company of Pampa, Tex., and made a cash payment thereon in the sum of $800, and executed installment notes and a mortgage on the automobile to secure the payment of the balance of the purchase price. The notes and mortgage were thereafter transferred by the motor company to defendant. With the consent of the motor company, he removed the car to the State of Oklahoma and procured employment in an oil field at St. Louis, Okl. He defaulted on the payment of the installment notes due December, 1927, and January, 1928. In February, 1928, R. E. Limbecker made some inquiry of him relative to the location of the automobile, and a few days thereafter, L. G. Thomas, defendant's agent, and Limbecker demanded that the notes be immediately paid or the automobile be surrendered to defendant. He at that time advised them where the automobile was, but refused to surrender it, and stated to them that, if given a few days' time, he could get the money from his employer to take up the past-due installments. On the following day he was arrested on the charge of concealing mortgaged property, on complaint sworn to by Limbecker. He was arrested by a deputy sheriff and taken before a justice of the peace in Seminole and placed in his charge overnight. While under arrest, Limbecker told him that a warrant was also sworn out against him in the State of Texas for removing mortgaged property, and that a sheriff from Texas was then on his way to Oklahoma to arrest him on the warrant, and that, unless he surrendered the car before the sheriff arrived from Texas, he would be taken to that state to answer the charge. Under this threat he agreed to deliver the automobile to Limbecker. Under the direction of Thomas he delivered the car at Seminole the next morning and it was there placed in a garage and the criminal case against him was dismissed. He thereafter communicated with his employer and obtained the money from him to pay all pastdue notes, but was unable to locate the automobile. He made inquiry of defendant's agent relative thereto, but obtained no satisfaction...

Defendant contends that the evidence is insufficient to establish the fact that it was instrumental in taking possession of plaintiff's car and causing his arrest. If Limbecker was acting as agent for defendand in doing what he did, defendant would undoubtedly be liable...

We think the evidence sufficient to take the case to the jury on the question as to whether Limbecker was acting as agent for defendant in procuring plaintiff's arrest and taking possession of the automobile.

Defendant further contends that plaintiff cannot recover because he agreed to return the automobile in consideration of the dismissal of the criminal prosecution. The evidence is conflicting on this question. Plaintiff testified that he returned the automobile because of threats made that he would be arrested and taken to the State of Texas to answer a charge of removing mortgaged property unless he immediately surrendered possession thereof. Defendant offered evidence that he did agree to return the automobile in consideration of the dismissal of the criminal charge. The court charged the jury that the plaintiff could not recover in the event the criminal case was dismissed by his procurement and consent. The jury found this issue against defendant. There is sufficient evidence to sustain this finding, and we are bound thereby.

Defendant further contends that plaintiff's first cause of action pleaded an action in replevin, and at the close of the evidence requested the court to direct a verdict in its favor on that cause of action for the reason the evidence disclosed that it did not have possession of the car at the time the action was brought.

Plaintiff then asked and was granted permission to amend the prayer of his petition, and defendant's motion was overruled. Plaintiff in his original petition prayed for the return of the car or for the sum of $1,000, the value thereof, in case a return thereof could not be had.

The prayer of the petition was amended, praying damages in the sum of $1,000 for conversion of the car. When defendant filed its answer showing that it did not have possession of the car at the time the action was brought, plaintiff, in his reply, pleaded a conversion of the automobile. The case was tried on the theory that the pleading stated a cause of action in conversion.

Moreover, the original petition sufficiently alleged a cause of action in conversion. There was no error in permitting the prayer to be amended.

Defendant excepted to instruction No. 14 where in the court instructed the jury that in the event it found for plaintiff on his second cause of action, if he was so injured, in such sum as would fairly compensate him for the injury. The instruction is excepted to on the ground that there is no evidence upon which to base it. Plaintiff testified that he had a good credit prior to his arrest, that his credit was ruined thereby. That it was generally known in the community that he had been arrested. That after his arrest he was unable to get credit. We think this evidence sufficient upon which to base the instruction as to damages to reputation. The element of damage for injury to plaintiff's business should have been omitted. There was no evidence on this question. We do not, however, think that the jury was misled by the insertion of the word "business" therein. The verdict does not appear to be excessive. The error in this respect is harmless...

Defendant next contends that the evidence fails to establish a conversion under plaintiff's theory of the case and his evidence, this issue was properly submitted to the jury...

"Under section 7423, Compiled Oklahoma Statutes 1921, a person holding a lien on personal property extinguishes the lien by wrongfully converting said property to his own use."

Under the evidence offered by plaintiff, defendant obtained possession of the automobile by the unlawful use of criminal process and threats of further prosecution. In so doing it extinguished the mortgage lien and became guilty of conversion.

It is also urged that there is no competent evidence to support the verdict of the jury as to the value of the automobile. Plaintiff testified without objection that its value at the time of the conversion was $1,000. This evidence is sufficient to support the verdict.

It is finally contended that the damages awarded are excessive. That exemplary damages should not have been allowed on both causes of action. With this contention we are inclined to agree. While the wrongful act of defendant gave rise to different causes of action, the right to recover exemplary damages grows out of a single wrongful act, the unlawful use of criminal process to obtain possession of the automobile. In our opinion the allowance of exemplary damages on both causes of action constituted double punishment to defendant for a single wrongful act.

The judgment is therefore modified to the extent of disallowing exemplary damages on the first cause of action, and, as so modified, the judgment is affirmed.

Sec. 2.4 Analysis of a Cause of Action
a. Unitary Nature and Differentiation

REILLY v SICILIAN ASPHALT PAVING CO. (1902) 170 NY 40, r31 AD 302

Appeal from a judgment of the Appellate Division of the Supreme Court in the first judicial department, entered July 28, 1898, affirming a judgment in favor of defendant entered upon a dismissal of the complaint by the court at a Trial Term.

CULLEN, J. The appellant claimed that while driving in Central Park in the city of New York both his person and his vehicle were injured in consequence of collision with a gravel heap placed on the road through the negligence of the defendant. Thereupon he brought an action against the defendant in the Court of Common Pleas to recover damages for the injury to his person. Subsequently he brought another action in one of the District Courts in the city of New York to recover for the injury to his vehicle. In this last action he obtained judgment, which was paid by the defendant. Thereafter the defendant set up by supplemental answer the judgment in the District Court suit and its satisfaction as a bar to the further maintenance of the action in the Common Pleas. On the trial of the case in the Supreme Court (to which under the Constitution the action was transferred), it was held that the plaintiff's right of action was merged in the judgment recovered in the District Court and his complaint was dismissed. The judgment entered upon this direction was affirmed by the Appellate Division and an appeal has been taken to this court by allowance.

The rule is that a single or entire cause of action cannot be subdivided into several claims and separate actions maintained thereon. (Secor v Sturgis 16 NY 548; Nathans v Hope 77 NY 420.) As to this principle there is no dispute. Therefore, the question presented by this appeal is whether from the defendant's negligence and the injury occasioned thereby to the plaintiff in his person and his property there arose a single cause of action or two causes of action, one for injury to his person and the other for injury to his property. The question is not determined by the Code of Civil Procedure, for though in section 484 it prescribes what separate causes of action may be joined in the same complaint, it nowhere assumes to define what is a single cause of action. Nor is there any controlling decision of this court on the point. In Mulligan v Knickerbocker Ice Company (affirmed without opinion, 109 NY 657) the question discussed in the opinion of the learned court below and necessarily involved in the decision of this court was the effect of a release which the plaintiff asserted was intended to cover only the injuries to his property but was fraudulently prepared so as to embrace his whole cause of action. The case is doubtless authority for the proposition that a voluntary settlement between the parties of part of a claim does not satisfy or discharge the whole claim. But the principle that the parties may, by voluntary agreement, sever or split up a single cause of action, though a plaintiff cannot of his own violation do the same, seems to be generally recognized even in those jurisdictions where the rule is held most firmly that a single tort gives rise but to a single cause of action. (O'Beirne v Lloyd, 43 NY 248; Bliss v N.Y.C. & H.R.R.R. Co., 160 Mass 447.)

The question now before us has been the subject of conflicting decisions in different jurisdictions. In England it has been held by the Court of Appeal, Lord Coleridge, Chief Justice, dissenting, that damages to the person and to property though occasioned by the same wrongful act give rise to different causes of action (Brunsden v Humphrey, (LR (14 QBD) 141); while in Massachusetts, Minnesota and

Missouri the contrary doctrine has been declared. (Doran v Cohen, 147 Mass 342; King v Chicago, M. & St. P. Ry. Co., 82 NW 1113; Von Fragstein v Windler, 2 MoApp 598.) The argument of those courts which maintain that an injury to person and property creates but a single cause of action is that as the defendant's wrongful act was single, the cause of action must be single and that the different injuries occasioned by it are merely items of damage proceeding from the same wrong, while that of the English court is that the negligent act of the defendant in itself constitutes no cause of action and becomes an actionable wrong only out of the damage which it causes. "One wrong was done as soon as the plaintiff's enjoyment of his property was substantially interfered with. A further wrong arose as soon as the driving also caused by injury to the plaintiff's person." (Brundsen v Humphrey, supra.) I doubt whether either argument is conclusive. If, where one person was driving the vehicle of another, both the driver and the vehicle were injured, there can be no doubt that two causes of action would arise, one in favor of the person injured and the other in favor of the owner of the injured property. On the other hand, if both the horse and the vehicle being the property of the same person, were injured, there would be but a single cause of action for the damage to both. If, while injury to the horse and vehicle of a person gives rise to but a single cause of action, injury to the vehicle and its owner gives rise to two causes of action, it must be because there is an essential difference between an injury to the person and an injury to property that makes it impracticable, or, at least, very inconvenient in the administration of justice to blend the two. We think there is such a distinction. Different periods of limitation apply. The plaintiff's action for personal injuries is barred by the lapse of three years; that for injury to the property not till the lapse of six years. The plaintiff cannot assign his right of action for the injury to his person, and it would abate and be lost by his death before a recovery of a verdict, and if the defendant were a natural person, also by his death before that time. On the other hand, the right of action for injury to property is assignable and would survive the death of either party. It may be seized by creditors on a bill in equity (Hudson v Plets, 11 Paige(NY) 180), and would pass to an assignee in bankruptcy. Possibly the difficulties arising from the difference in the periods of limitation and the differences in the rule of survival between a personal injury and a property injury might be obviated in practice by holding the statute a bar to that portion of the damages, a claim for which would have been outlawed, had it been a separate cause of action, and by permitting, in case of death, the action to be revived so far as it relates to property. We do not see, however, how it would be practicable to deal with a case where the right of action for injury to the property had passed to an assignee in bankruptcy or to a receiver on a creditor's bill without treating it as an independent cause of action. Though, as we have already said, section 484 of the Code does not expressly determine the point in issue, still it is not without much force in the argument that the two injuries constitute separate causes of action. Under the old Code of Procedure, at the time of its original enactment, injuries to person and injuries to property were separately classified as as causes of action, and it was not permitted to join those of one class with those of another. (Code of Procedure Sec. 167.) By an amendment in 1852, injuries to persons and property were put in the same class. But by section 484 of the Code of Civil Procedure they are again placed in distinct classes and cannot be united. If the plaintiff's cause of action is single, into what class does it fall? Is it for an injury to the person which may be united with other causes of action for personal injuries, or is it for injury to property which may be joined with claims of the same nature, or is it sui generis, a nondescript which must stand alone?

While some of the difficulties in the joinder of a claim for injury to the person and one for injury to the property in one cause of action are created by our statutory enactments, the history of the common law shows that the distinction between torts to the person and torts to property has always obtained. Lord Justice Bowen in the Brunsden case has pointed out that there is no authority in the books for the proposition that a recovery for trespass to the person is a bar to an action for trespass to goods or vice versa. It is true that at common law the necessity of bringing two suits could at the election of the plaintiff be obviated in some cases, as, for instance, by declaring for trespass on the plaintiff's close and alleging in aggravation thereof an assault upon his person. (See Waterman on Trespass, 205, 406.) Still, in such case there would be but a single cause of action, to wit, the trespass upon the close, and if the defendant justified this trespass it would be a complete defense to the action, the personal assault being merely a matter of aggravation. (Carpenter v Barber, 33 Vt 441.)

Therefore, for reason of the great difference between the rules of law applicable to injuries of the person and those relating to injuries to property we conclude that an injury to person and one to property, though resulting from the same tortious act, constitute different causes of action.

The judgment appealed from should be reversed and a new trial granted, costs to abide the event.

Judgment reversed, etc.

PAYNE v N.Y., S.& W. R. R. Co. (1911) 201 NY 436, r141 AD 833

Appeal, by permission, from an order of the Appellate Division of the Supreme Court in the second judicial department, entered December 14, 1910, which purported to modify and as modified to affirm an order of Special Term denying a motion to cause the complaint to be made more definite and certain.

WERNER, J. The learned Appellate Division of the second department has certified to us the following questions: 1. "In an action for damages for personal injuries by a servant against a master, is it proper for the plaintiff to plead in his complaint as one cause of action facts constituting negligence under the common law; facts constituting negligence under the Employers' Liability Act of the State of New Jersey; and facts constituting negligence under the act of Congress known as the Federal Employers' Liability Act, or any two of said grounds of liability?" 2. "Should a plaintiff be compelled to separate the facts constituting liability under the aforesaid acts, and plead them as separate causes of action?" 3. "Under the complaint in this case, was it proper to direct the plaintiff, in case he desired to rely upon any except the common-law liability of defendant, to separately state the facts constituting the statutory liability and plead them as separate causes of action?"

The complaint upon which these questions arise is simple and precise. It alleges that the defendant is a railroad corporation, operating a line of railroad within certain parts of this state and within parts of the state of New Jersey; that on April 13th, 1910, the plaintiff was a brakeman employed by the defendant on a freight train which was being operated in the vicinity of Little Ferry Junction, in the State of New Jersey; that while the plaintiff in the exercise of his duties, and of due care, was standing upon one of the cars of said train, he was thrown therefrom by the sudden and violent movement thereof and sustained serious bodily injuries; that said injuries were caused by the improper movement of the train upon which the plaintiff was employed, by the person in charge of the locomotive engine attached thereto by the negligent direction of the conductor or other person in control of signals directing the movement thereof, and of some person who at the time had charge or direction of the movement of said train and was acting as superintendent with the authority and consent of the defendant; that there were defects in the brakes or coupling apparatus upon said train which could have been discovered by the use of ordinary care; that the caboose or car upon which plaintiff was stationed had no platform or guardrail, and that the grab-irons thereon were defective and improperly and inadequately secured, which was due to the neglect of some person in the employ of the defendant intrusted with the duty of seeing that the cars and appurtenances were in proper and safe condition, which defects are also referred to as causes of the accident. Continuing, the complaint proceeds to allege that the train was being used by defendant as a common carrier between the states of New York, New Jersey and elsewhere, and that the plaintiff was engaged in such commerce when he was injured, and this is followed by a recital of the provisions of the Employers' Liability Act of the state of New Jersey, and an averment of the service of a notice in accordance with its provisions. These several allegations are set forth in the order in which we have stated them, without being specified or numbered as separate causes of action.

The defendant moved at Special Term that the complaint be made more definite and certain in the following particulars: 1...2. "So that it will set forth plainly either a cause of action based on defendant's common-law liability, upon the New Jersey Employers' Liability Act, or one upon the Employers' Liability Act passed by the Congress of the United States in 1908." 3. "Or if plaintiff desires to set forth three causes of action, that plaintiff separately state and number such causes of action."

The Court at Special Term denied the defendant's motion. An appeal was taken to the Appellate Division, where an order was made which purports to modify, but in fact reverses, the order of the Special Term. The order of the Appellate Division directs the plaintiff to separate and number the causes of action, if he intends to set forth a cause of action other than under the common law; and since the order of the Special Term flatly denied the defendant's motion, it is apparent that there was in fact a reversal although it was called a modification...

There are times when nothing is more troublesome than the simplicity of our Code pleading, although in the main it works out for good. The question in this case is whether the plaintiff has pleaded a single cause of action, or several distinct and separate causes of action. The Code of Civil Procedure (Section 481) directs that a complaint shall contain a plain and concise statement of the facts constituting each cause of action without unnecessary repetition; and that when a complaint sets forth two or more causes of action the statement of facts constituting each cause of action must be separate and numbered. (Section 483). The Code contains no definition of what constitutes a single or separate cause of action, and we must, therefore, draw upon other sources of inspiration for the solution of the question. The term "cause of action" is one which has a technical and primary definition, although in practice it has also acquired a much wider secondary and colloquial meaning. In its simplest analysis the term "cause of action" is synonymous with "the right to bring suit," and that right is based upon the ground or grounds on which an action may be maintained.

There is a more technical and scientific definition which is well stated by Pomeroy, in his standard work on Code Pleading, as follows: "If the facts alleged show one primary right of the plaintiff, and one wrong done by the defendant which involves that right, the plaintiff has stated but a single cause of action. *** On the other hand, if the facts alleged in the pleading show that the plaintiff is possessed of two or more distinct and separate primary rights, each of which has been invaded, or that the defendant has committed two or more distinct and separate wrongs, it follows inevitably, from the foregoing principle, that the plaintiff has united two or more causes of action."

Every lawyer knows that for practical and colloquial uses these terms are frequently given a much broader significance. One has only to scan the judicial opinions in cases arising out of personal injuries to employees, to appreciate that they are frequently used interchangeably with the expressions "remedies" or "liabilities." In cases like the one at bar this is doubtless due to the fact that there are many instances in which the employer may be liable under the common law, and also under one or more statutes which have extended his liaility for reasons not cognizable at common law. In such cases the different grounds of liability have sometimes been referred to as "causes of action" when in fact there has been but a single "cause of action" which could be established by evidence appropriate to each of the grounds upon which the employer's liability is predicated, either under the common law or under the statutes.

There are other instances in which the statutes have created a new or extended liability not known at common law. In such cases it is quite accurate to say that the statute which establishes a new liability also creates a new "cause of action", for without the statute none would exist. In one case the right, the wrong, and the "cause of action" may all depend upon the language of the statute, and in another there may be separate and distinct grounds of liability under the common law, and under one or more statutes, which may be so pleaded as to entitle a plaintiff to recover under one or all. Thus, although there may be various grounds of liability, there can be but one cause of action and one recovery.

The complaint before us fairly illustrates the difference between a case wholly dependent upon one or more provisions of specified statutes, and one where the defendant's liability may be predicated either upon the common law, the statutes, or both. It sets forth facts which render the defendant liable at common law; it contains other allegations which tend to support a claim under the Employers' Liability Act which is pleaded; and it pleads still other averments which bring the case within the rule of the Federal statute. Suppose the plaintiff proves them all. Does that establish three distinct rights in the plaintiff, or three independent wrongs against the defendant, or support three separate recoveries? Obviously there is but one primary right, one primary wrong, and one liability. The single wrong has given rise to a single right, which may be established by as many different facts as the nature of the case may justify or demand...We think such a complaint pleads but a single cause of action, although it may specify different acts of negligence, some of which create a liability only under the common law and others of which create a liability only under the statute.

This view of the subject is entirely consistent with the statement that the statute may have given an additional or new cause of action, for that is literally true in all cases where the common law affords no relief, and where the only right to recovery is created by the statute. In the Uss case Mr. Justice Clarke argued, with much force, that the combination of several grounds of liability in a single count of a complaint may prevent a defendant from demurring to such parts thereof as would be plainly open to attack if separately numbered. That may be the result in some cases, but we think it can do little practical harm, since a defendant always has the power to limit the issues and to ascertain what he must meet by demanding a bill of particulars. We are convinced, moreover, that the occasional inconvenience in such instances will be more than offset by a general and consistent adherence to the simpler forms of pleading.

The order of the Appellate Division should be reversed and that of the Special Term affirmed, with costs to the appellant in both courts. The first question certified to us is answered in the affirmative; the second and third in the negative.

Orders reversed, etc.,

HEARN v STATE (1951) 55 So2d 559, 28 ALR2d 1179

James E. Hearn, and others, were convicted in the Circuit Court, Walton County, for the larceny of eight cows and two calves and they appealed.

DICKINSON, Associate Justice. This is a companion case to the case of Hearn v State, Fla., 54 So2d 651.

In the other case the defendants were accused and convicted of the larceny of one cow, the property of one M. M. Adkinson. In this case the defendants are accused and have been convicted of the larceny of eight cows and two calves, the property of one J. A. Ganey.

The defendants in this case filed a plea of former jeopardy averring that the larceny of the nine cows and two calves occurred at the same time, at the same place, and under the same circumstances, even though the cattle were the property of different owners, and that thus there was only one larceny involved for which they could be tried.

The State filed a demurrer to the plea of former jeopardy, which demurrer was sustained and the trial had which resulted in a conviction of the defendants of the larceny of these eight cows and two calves, the property of said Ganey. Thus the only question involved is whether or not the defendants had been placed in fromer jeopardy by the trial of the case above mentioned, that is, the case involving the larceny of the cow belonging to Adkinson.

The facts in the two cases are identical; the nine cows and the two calves were all on the same open range, were rounded up at the same time, were placed in the same truck by the defendants at the same time from the same loading pen. The cattle were all grazing in and around the same area, and apparently were not too far separated by distance, because the act of rounding up, loading, etc., consumed only a few minutes of time. All of the cattle were transported in the same truck to Selma, Alabama, and sold at the same time, or attempted to be sold as a single lot when the defendants were apprehended.

The defendants were convicted in the morning of the larceny of the one cow belonging to Adkinson, and placed on trial in the afternoon for the larceny of the Ganey cows and calves. Thus the only question posed is whether or not two offenses are committed when separate objects are stolen at the same time, from the same place, under the same circumstances and as part of the same act, although the objects of the larceny belong to two separate individuals, or whether or not such constitutes a single larceny.

So far as we can determine this is a case of first impression in this State, although the converse thereof, that is that where property is stolen from the same owner or from different owners at different times or places or as a result of a series of acts, separated in either time, place or circumstances, one from the other each taking is a separate and distinct offense has been established as the law of this State since the case of Green v State, 134 Fla 216, 183 So 728. If the converse is true, then it should follow that where several articles are taken at the same time and place as one continuous act, though owned by different people, the offense is a single larceny.

Each case of this nature must be determined by the facts and circumstances of the particular case. There is some conflict in the cases, but the clear weight of authority is to the effect that the stealing of several articles at the same time and place as one continuous act or transaction is a single offense, even though the property belongs to different owners, for the reason that it is only a single act or taking.

Some courts hold, however, that the prosecuting authorities may elect to try the larceny from each owner in such case as a separate and distinct offense and still others hold that they are necessarily separate and distinct, because of the separate trespass to the person or property of each owner; but this reasoning has been criticized on the ground that it ignores the character of the offense as one against the public and treats it as simply a trespass against the individual owner, 32 Am. Jurisprudence, Subject: Larceny, Article IX, page 895.

Larceny is an offense against the public, that is against the State, and the offense is the same whether the property stolen belongs to one person or several persons each owning separate parts thereof. The names of the owners of the stolen property constitute no part of the offense. They are stated in the information primarily as a matter of description for the purpose of identification and to show ownership in a person or persons other than the accused.

We will align ourselves with the majority rule in this country because we feel that to permit the dividing into several larcenies of objects which are the subject of larceny, although belonging to separate owners, when stolen at the same time, from the same place, and under the same circumstances with the same intent, would be violative of the spirit of the Constitution of the United States and the State of Florida that a man should not be put in jeopardy twice for the same offense. (See also Notes in 31 LRA, NS, 723, and 42 LRA, NS, 967.)

The State relies very strongly on the case of State v Akers (106 Mont 105, 76 P2d 638), wherein the Supreme Court of the State of Montana in a divided opinion held that in that case there were two separate thefts or larcenies of two separate animals, but a careful reading of the opinion leads us to the conclusion that the evidence showed that the animals were taken near the same time but at places a mile or so distant from each other. That space or distance distinguishes the case from the case at bar, where everything occurred at the same time, at the same place, and under the same circumstances.

Accordingly, it is our opinion that the learned Circuit Judge was in error in sustaining the State's demurrer to the plea of former jeopardy and that in fact the facts and circumstances of this case are identical with the other case for the larceny of which the defendants were convicted, all occurring at the same time and arising out of the same transaction, under the same circumstances and with the same intent, thus constituting this act a single larceny.

The judgment of conviction and the order sustaining the State's demurrer to the plea of former jeopardy interposed by the defendants, is therefore reversed.

GREEN v STATE (1938) 134 Fla 216, 183 So 728

A. D. Green was convicted of stealing seven hogs, and he brings error.

BUFORD, Justice. To an information, which was as follows:

"John H. Carter, Jr., as State Attorney for the 14th Judicial Circuit of the State of Florida, prosecuting for said State, in the County of Jackson, under oath information makes that A. D. Green on August 20, 1937, in said County and State , unlawfully did steal, take and carry away seven hogs, the property of Elijah Tyus, with the intent to deprive the owner of his property therein; contrary to the statute in such case made and provided, and against the peace and dignity of the State of Florida;"

The defendant plead not guilty and on trial was convicted and adjudged to be guilty and thereupon sentenced to serve two years in the State Prison at hard labor.

The record shows that of the seven hogs alleged to have been stolen two of them were found in possession of one Carlton Conrad and five were found in possession of one Paul Hall.

The record shows that two of the hogs came from a bunch that were "raised" about one place and that the others were raised about another place. In other words, the two hogs found in possession of Conrad were out of one bunch of hogs and the five found in possession of Hall were out of another bunch of hogs.

The record shows that the two hogs found in possession of Conrad were found by the alleged owner on September 19, 1937, and that the five hogs found in possession of Paul Hall were located by the owner in Hall's possession on October 1, 1937. Neither transaction appears to have had anything to do with the other.

The record shows that if larceny was committed of the seven hogs it was committed by asportation of two hogs from one place and five hogs from another place. When this developed in the record defendant, through his counsel, moved the court to require the states attorney to elect which transaction he would rely on for conviction. The court denied the motion.

In the light of the record this became a matter of paramount importance in this case.

The rule appears to be well settled that where property is stolen from the same owner from the same place by a series of acts, if each taking is a result of a separate independent impulse it is a separate crime. (See 36 C. J. 798, and cases cited; also Hamilton v State, 129 Fla 219, 176 So 89, 112 ALR 1013). It is also settled that if articles belonging to different owners are taken at different times or from different places it must be held that each taking is a distinct and independent larceny. (36 CJ 800, and cases there cited...)

The reason for the rule is demonstrated in the instant case.

There is no evidence to show that the alleged five stolen hogs found in possession of Hall were ever in the possession of the defendant or that he ever claimed ownership, possession or right of possession of the hogs. His connection with that transaction at most, as is shown by the record, was that Hall told Green, the defendant, that he wanted to buy some hogs. A negro owed the defendant some money. The defendant told the negro that Hall wanted to buy some hogs and the negro took the hogs to Hall's place and left them there. Green then went to see Hall to find out whether or not the negro had sold him the hogs. Hall told Green, the defendant, that the negro had left some hogs at his place but, in effect, that they had not agreed on a price. Green looked at the hogs but did not claim to know anything about them. He told Hall that he held a note secured by a lien on some hogs and he supposed those were the same hogs. The entire evidence in regard to this transaction is totally insufficient to constitute the basis of a conviction of the defendant Green. Therefore, if the State had relied upon that transaction, the trial judge should have, on timely motion made, directed a verdict because of the insufficiency of the evidence to establish any proof that would sustain a verdict of guilty.

Now, as to the two hogs found in possession of Conrad, the defendant admitted that he sold these two hogs to Conrad. He testified, as did several other witnesses, that he had raised those two hogs; that they had been in his mark since they were pigs and that they had never been the property of Tyus from whom they were alleged to have been stolen. Tyus and one other witness testified identifying the two hogs as the property of Tyus and Tyus claimed that the marks on them had been changed.

The record shows that these two hogs were delivered to Conrad at or near the time that Tyus claimed he missed his two hogs. Conrad testified that the hogs were not freshly marked when he bought them.

So if the State had elected to stand upon the transaction involving the two hogs, it is at least doubtful that a jury would have found the defendant guilty.

Under this state of facts, we must hold that the trial judge committed reversible error in not requiring the State's Attorney on motion of defendant timely made to elect as to which transaction he would stand upon for conviction.

The judgment is reversed.

BEBINGER v SWEET (1876) 1 AbbNC(NY) 263

George Bebinger sued Benjamin A. Sweet, and alleged by his complaint, that he was led into the execution of a hard contract for the occupation and working of defendant's farm, pledging certain personal property for the full performance of his agreements; that in pursuance of said contract, he entered upon said farm and expended his money in the cultivation of the farm, and in putting in crops thereon; that on or about July 3, thereafter, and after such crops had been put in, the defendant turned the plaintiff and his family off said farm, and refused to let him perform his contract as he was in good faith proceeding to do; that such conduct of the defendant was with the purpose of getting without compensation the avails of plaintiff's labor and expenditures upon the farm; that in furtherance of said purpose the defendant procured the arrest of the plaintiff for embezzlement, maliciously, in bad faith, and without probable cause, with intent to drive plaintiff to an abandonment of his rights; that in further pursuance of his wrongful acts, defendant took possession of the pledged property, and of other property belonging to the plaintiff, and has wrongfully refused to give the same up, after a demand; that the plaintiff fully, and in all things performed his contract until he was prevented by the defendant; and, finally, that all this conduct and these acts on the part of the defendant to cheat and defraud the plaintiff, and were all parts of one and the same transaction.

The defendant, by his answer, alleged that plaintiff broke his contract, and left his employ without his consent. The answer also set up a counter-claim for property used by plaintiff; denied all fraud or design to cheat, and denied the wrongful taking or retaining of plaintiff's property, or turning plaintiff off his premises.

Plaintiff replied denying the counter-claim.

Upon these pleadings a trial was had, and plaintiff recovered $600.

On the trial the court, against objection, admitted evidence that plaintiff was arrested and gave bail; that a lawyer, as defendant's counsel, was present at the police court, and advised plaintiff to settle, or defendant would send him to State Prison.

Defendant moved unsuccessfully for a new trial, and appealed from the judgment and order.

BY THE COURT - BOARDMAN, J. - An objection strenuously insisted upon by the defendant is, that several causes of action are improperly joined...

The cause of action is one and entire; it is not an action for malicious prosecution, nor for breach of contract, nor for recovery of damages for the conversion of personal property. It sets forth these facts, as elements of damage, and also as evidence of the fraudulent plan and design of defendant, and means used by him for accomplishing his purpose of cheating and defrauding plaintiff out of his property, and rights. It was not, therefore, necessary to set out those facts with the same particularity as if relying solely upon them for a cause of action.

The action being such as I have indicated, it was not necessary to allege the prosecution had ended. It is essentially an action against the defendant for an abuse of the process of the law, in order illegally, and wrongfully, by that means, to compel plaintiff to surrender up his property and rights to the defendant. In such a case, it is unnecessary to allege or prove the termination of the prosecution. The action may be maintained without it (2 Greenl. Ev. Sec. 452; Grainger v Hill, 4 BingNC 212.)

This renders it unnecessary to consider whether the prosecution was ended in fact...

No error is discovered to the prejudice of the defendant for which, in our judgment, a new trial should be granted.

The judgment and order are therefore affirmed with costs.

---

b. Continuing Cause of Action

BEACH v CRAIN (1842) 2 NY 86

The declaration averred that the plaintiff, on the 25th day of August, 1845, erected a gate at the place indicated in the instrument, and in pursuance of the covenant on his part. The breach complained of was that the defendants did not, after the erection of the gate, and while it was the pleasure of the plaintiff to have a gate continued at that place, make the necessary repairs thereto, but, on the contrary, on the 19th of October, 1846, suffered the gate to become dilapidated, broken down and nearly destroyed, and to remain in that condition until the 30th of November, 1846, by means of which the plaintiff had suffered great damage by cattle, &c.

The defendants pleaded the general issue, and gave notice therewith that they would prove that the gate was removed about the 22d of June, 1846, and had not since that time been rebuilt; that the defendants had refused to replace the gate after it was so removed, and that nothing had been done to it since; that the plaintiff, on the 29th of September, 1846, sued the defendants in a justice's court and declared upon the same covenant above set forth, alleging as a breach thereof that after the erection of the gate in question, and while it was the pleasure of the plaintiff to continue it, the defendants did not keep the same in good repair and condition, but suffered it to become dilapidated, destroyed and removed, and would not replace the same by the erection of a new one or otherwise, whereby the plaintiff was damaged by reason of cattle grazing on his land, &c.; that the defendants pleaded in that suit the general issue, and gave notice therewith that they would prove that the gate had been wholly removed, that they had never refused to repair it, and that the plaintiff had not kept a gate as he was bound to do; that on the 19th of October, 1846, the said former suit was tried, and judgment rendered on the same day in the plaintiff's favor for one dollar damages, and costs of suit.

On the trial of the present action, it was admitted that the parties executed the covenant above set forth; that soon after the execution thereof the plaintiff erected a gate at the place specified therein; that such gate was removed about the 23d of June, 1846, by some person unknown, and had never been found; that the gatepost and two iron staples remained; that before the 1st of September, 1846, the plaintiff requested the defendants to replace the said gate, which they refused to do; and that the cost of rebuilding said gate would be one dollar, besides lumber. It was also admitted that a former suit was brought, and that the proceedings and judgment therein were truly stated in the defendants' notice above set forth; and that on the trial of such former suit the same facts were proved which were admitted on the trial of this cause. It was further admitted that this suit was brought to recover damages on account of the gate remaining unrepaired or not rebuilt from the 19th of October, 1846, to the 30th of November, 1846, as alleged in the declaration.

Upon the above pleadings and admissions the cause was submitted to the justice, the parties agreeing that if he found for the plaintiff he might assess such damages as he should think just. The justice decided in favor of the defendants, and his judgment was removed by certiorari into the common pleas of Herkimer county, and was affirmed by that court. The supreme court sitting in the fifth district, on error brought, reversed the judgments of the common pleas and of the justice and the defendants thereupon brought error into this court...

WRIGHT, J., delivered the opinion of the court. This case involves the consideration of two questions, either of which, if determined against the defendant in error, would defeat his recovery. 1st. Whether, under their covenant to make all necessary repairs to the gate, the duty of rebuilding or replacing it devolved in law upon the Beaches. 2d. Whether the former suit is a good bar to the present action.

1. It is to be observed that the Beaches covenant in express terms to make all necessary repairs to the gate, and in passing and repassing it to use common care in having it shut after them. In the contemplation of the parties, the gate was to be erected and maintained for the protection of Crain, whilst the Beaches enjoyed the right of way across his lands. It is a familiar principle that in determing the meaning of a contract the subject matter, and the situation and true intention of the parties, are to be considered. In this case, Crain released to the Beaches and one Van Horn, and to their heirs and assigns, a right of way or road forever through his lands: and as a part of the agreement to be performed by him, it was provided that he should erect a good and substantial gate at the terminus of such road. As I read the contract, Crain bound himself no farther; but it was obviously the intention of the parties that the gate so erected should be maintained and kept up during the enjoyment and use of the road unless Crain should assent to its discontinuance or removal. To effectuate this intention, the Beaches covenanted that "all the repairs necessary to be made to said gate should be made by them, and that in passing and repassing it they should use common care to shut it after them." They covenanted therefore generally to repair; and I think the reasonable construction of the contract is, that they are to make not only ordinary repairs, but all that are necessary to maintain and keep up the gate fit for use, and for the purpose intended, during the pleasure of Crain, and that should it be removed without the knowledge or agency of Crain, or destroyed in whole or in part by dilapidation or accident, they are to replace or repair it. This construction seems to be in accordance with the intent and spirit of the contract, and is in harmony with the construction placed upon similar covenants in numerous adjudged cases. Indeed, it has always been adjudged that upon a covenant to repair the covenantor is bound to rebuild a house accidentally destroyed by fire or thrown down by enemies during his term. (cases) It was contended on the argument however, that these were cases between landlord and tenant, and that the reason alleged for the construction was only applicable to that peculiar relation; but the principle was applied in the case of the Breckrock Company v Pritchard, (6 T.R. 750) where the defendant on a covenant to keep a bridge in complete repair for seven years, was held liable to rebuild, the bridge having been washed away by an extraordinary and unusual flood of water.

Should we hold that the Beaches were not bound to rebuild or replace the gate, we would necessarily overrule a long line of adjudged cases.

2. Is the present action barred by a former recovery? The covenant of the Beaches is a continuing covenant. Their obligation is to repair the gate as often as repairs are needed, and they cannot discharge themselves from the effect of their contract, or change the rights of the parties, by a mere refusal to perform. In other words, they cannot by such refusal put at an end, for all future time, the duty imposed upon them by their covenant. Indeed, the counsel for the plaintiff in error admits, that if Crain should replace the gate, the covenant of his clients may again become operative; thus, by his admission, negativing the idea that the refusal to rebuild or replace, worked, under the circumstances of this case, a total and final breach of the covenant, insomuch that the measure of damages in the former suit was, or should have been, the cost of erecting a new gate, and such sumas would be necessary to keep it in repair during the period. Crain should desire it to be kept up. Neglecting, at any time, to make necessary repairs to the gate or to shut it in passing or repassing, would have been a partial breach of their covenant, and Crain could have recovered damages for any injury necessarily resulting therefrom. So for a like neglect, damages might be recovered, for injuries accruing subsequently to the former action. It is not perceived, therefore, how a refusal to repaid could change the obligations or rights of the parties, or introduce a new and different rule of damages. To constitute an effectual bar, the cause of action in the former suit should be identical with that of the present. It is the same cause of action when the same evidence will support both the actions, although they happen to be grounded on different writs. (Rice v King 7 Johns(NY) 20). But the evidence in both actions may be in part the same; yet the subject matter essentially different, and in such case there is no bar. For example, if money be awarded to be paid at different times, assumpsit will lie on the award for each sum as it becomes due. So, on an agreement to pay a sum of money by installments, an action will lie to recover each instalment as it becomes due. In covenant for non-payment of rent, or of an annuity payable at different times, the plaintiff may bring a new action toties quoties as

often as the respective sums become due and payable; yet in each of these examples, the evidence to support the different actions is in part the same. In this case the same covenant was the foundation of both actions; the same evidence, therefore, in part, is alike common to both; but there is this difference: in the former suit the breach was assigned, and the actual damages laid as having accrued prior to the commencement thereof; on the present, damages are sought to be recovered for a breach subsequent to such former action. In the present action, the plaintiff could not have recovered for damages that had accrued prior to the first suit, for he is not permitted to split up an entire demand, and bring several suits thereon; but he may show a breach subsequent to the former suit, and recover the actual damages arising from such subsequent breach. On the last trial, a breach of the covenant to repair subsequently to the former action was admitted and for this Crain was entitled to recover nominal damages, with such actual damages as could be shown to have accrued from such breach since the former recovery. This must necessarily be the effect of a continuing covenant. The former recovery, therefore, could be no bar to the present suit.

The plaintiffs in error insist that Crain did recover, or legally should have recovered, in the first suit, a sum sufficient to enable him to replace the gate. But this argument supposes that upon the Beaches' refusing to repair, there was a total breach of their covenant, and that they could relieve themselves from subsequent obligation by the payment of a gross sum in damages. If this were so, Crain's recovery should also have embraced a sum sufficient to keep the gate in necessary repair whilst it was his pleasure that it should remain: a sum that I imagine there would be insuperable difficulty to estimate. Whilst the obligation of the plaintiffs in error continued, and it was entirely practicable for them to perform, I do not well see how the value of a new gate could have legitimately formed a part of the damages to be recovered under the pleadings and evidence in the first suit. It is possible, that if Crain, for the protection of his lands, and with the view of making the default of the Beaches the least expensive to them, had, prior to such suit, rebuilt or replaced the gate, he might have recovered the cost thereof in the shape of damages. But it is enough to say that no such thing was done; neither did the law devolve upon him a duty which the plaintiffs in error had covenanted to perform, and which in its performance was neither difficult nor impracticable. As a matter of fact, it is obvious from the pleadings and evidence in the first suit, and the amount of the judgment therein, that the cost of erecting a new gate was not recovered; as a matter of law, under the circumstances of this case, it ought not to have been.

I am of the opinion that the judgments of the justice and common pleas should be reversed, and that of the supreme court affirmed.

Judgment affirmed.

---

c. Divisible Cause of Action

PAKAS, Appellant v HOLLINGSHEAD, et al, Respondents (1906) 184 NY 211, a99 AD 472

APPEAL from a judgment of the Appellate Division of the Supreme Court in the first judicial department, entered January 3, 1905, affirming a judgment in favor of defendants entered upon a dismissal of the complaint by the court at a Trial Term without a jury.

O'BRIEN, J. On the 30th day of August, 1898, the defendants, by an executory contract in writing, agreed to sell and deliver to the plaintiff fifty thousand pairs of bicycle pedals, the goods to be delivered and paid for in installments, as specified in the contract. It has been found by the trial court that the defendants delivered two thousand six hundred and eight pairs of pedals under the contract, and refused to make further deliveries. When the fact is established that the seller of goods to be delivered and paid for in installments, as in this case, refuses to deliver the goods, that amounts to a repudiation of the contract and a breach of it, for which the buyer may recover damages. So we start in this case with a breach of a contract on the part of the defendants by their refusal to be bound by its obligation.

It is found that on the 15th of March, 1899, the plaintiff commenced an action against the defendants in the City Court of New York for breach of this contract, in that they failed to deliver to the plaintiff the pedals which, by the terms of the agreement, the defendants were bound to deliver up to the first of March, 1899, to wit, nineteen thousand pair, of which the defendants had delivered only the two thousand six hundred and eight pairs, and had failed to deliver sixteen thousand eight hundred and ninety-two pairs, which were to be delivered up to the first of March, 1899. This action was put at issue, and after a trial the plaintiff recovered judgment against the defendants for the full amount claimed in the complaint in the action as damages for the breach of the contract, which judment has been paid by the defendants in full.

Subsequently and in February, 1900, the plaintiff commenced the present action to recover damages for a failure to deliver the balance of the goods, and both parties have pleaded the former suit and judgment. The plaintiff claims that it is conclusive evidence in his favor with respect to the existence, validity, terms and breach of the contract, while the defendants interpose it as a bar to the present action. This situation presents the question of law involved in the case. Judgment was given at the trial court in favor of the defendants and this judgment was affirmed on appeal. The question of law arising upon these facts is whether the former judgment concludes the plaintiff and is a bar to a second action to recover damages on the same contract. There can be no doubt that the contract was entire. It could not be performed on the part of the defendants without delivery of the property stipulated in the contract and the whole of it. As was said by Judge Bradley in Brock v Knower (37 Hun(NY) 609), the fact that the property was deliverable and the purchase money payable at different times in the future did not necessarily deprive the contract of the character of entirety or make it other than a single one in respect to all the goods embraced in its terms. The learned counsel for the plaintiff contends that the former judgment did not constitute a bar to the present action, but that the plaintiff had the right to elect to waive or disregard the breach, keep the contract in force and maintain sucessive actions for damages from time to time as the installments of goods were to be delivered, however, numerous these actions might be. It is said that this contention is supported in reason and justice, and has the sanction of authority at least in other jurisdictions.

We do not think that the contention can be maintained. There is not, as it seems to us, any judicial authority in this state that gives it any substantial support. On the contrary, we think that the cases, so far as we have been able to examine them, are all the other way, and are to the effect that inasmuch as there was a total breach of the contract by the defendants' refusal to deliver, the plaintiff cannot split up his demand and maintain successive actions, but must either recover all his damages in the first suit or wait until the contract matured or the time for the delivery of all the goods had arrived. In other words, there can be but one action for damages for a total breach of an entire contract to deliver goods, and the fact that they were to be delivered in installments from time to time does not change the general rule...

The English cases point to but two alternative remedies open to the buyer upon a breach of contract for the sale of goods to be delivered in installments. One is to sue upon repudiation for a total breach before the time for performance has arrived and the other is to await the time for full performance and then sue for the damages. No suggestion is to be found in any of the cases that I have observed, to the effect that the buyer had an option to bring successive actions as the time for the delivery of each installment matures. It is said in many of the cases that the injured party had an option but the option was not to bring several successive actions, but to elect whether, upon a breach, he shall proceed to recover all his damages or to await the time for full performance. The cases in the English courts on this question are very numerous, but they were all reviewed and the rule approved and followed in the case of Roehm v Horst (178 US 1), where it was held that the English rule was reasonable and just...

It was admitted upon the argument of this case, and is admitted upon the brief of plaintiff's counsel, that the plaintiff could have recovered all his damages for a breach of the whole contract in the first action. The only contention is that he was not obliged to do so but could maintain as many other actions as there were deliveries provided for in the contract in case of default. It does not seem to us that this proposition can be supported in reason or upon authority. The plaintiff claims in this action that the former judgment was conclusive as to him, that is, that it cuts off the defendants from any defense which they might originally have made, and thus it is sought to make this case an exception to the general rule that estoppels must be mutual; that is, that in general if the judgment is binding on one party it is equally binding in its effect upon the other. I think it would not be wise to engraft such a distinction upon the law of this state as was said in the case of Sykes v Gerber, (98 PennSt 179); "The law does not tolerate a second judgment for the same thing between the same parties, whether the claim is upon a contract or tort. * * * The general rule is that it is against the policy of the law to permit a plaintiff to prosecute in a second action for what was included in and might have been recovered in the first, because it would harass the defendant and expose him to double costs." (Guernesey v Carver, 8 Wend(NY) 492.)

We think the judgment below was right and should be affirmed, with costs.

CULLEN, Ch. J. (dissenting). I dissent from the decision about to be made. I concede to the fullest extent the principle that the plaintiff cannot split up a single cause of action and that if he does a recovery on any part of the cause of action bars a suit for the remainder. I also concede the principle that in an executory contract for the sale of a number of articles or a quantity of material, to be delivered in installments and payment made therefore as delivered, in the case of a breach by either party as to one of the installments the other party may elect to treat the default as complete breach of the contract, and maintain a suit for all his damages. I further concede that where there have been several breaches of a single contract the plaintiff must include in his action all breaches which have occurred prior to the commencement of the action.

But I insist that none of these principles controls the question before us, which is not whether the plaintiff upon the default in the delivery of the first installment of pedals should rescind the contract as having been abrogated by the act of the defendant, reserving his right to recover damages, but whether he was obliged to adopt that course. Had he not as the aggrieved party the option to treat the contract as still continuing in force and, therefore, assert his right to recover damages for each default as it might occur? There can be no question that there may be a continuous agreement or covenant for every breach of which a new cause of action arises. Such is a covenant to maintain and repair a gate across a right of way. (Beach v Crain, 2 NY 86.) There it was held that a recovery for one breach did not bar an action on a subsequent breach, and it was said that the defendants could not relieve themselves from subsequent obligations by payment of a gross sum as damages. There are many cases of a similar character.

Where the obligation is for the payment of money in installments the obligee has not, on default in the payment of one installment, even a right to elect to treat the contract as entirely broken, but must sue for the installments as they become due, unless the contract gives him the right of election. Where such an election is given by the contract, as is now quite common in the case of bonds and mortgages, the obligee is not bound to exercise it, but may do as he pleases. Therefore, to hold that the aggrieved party to a contract of the character of the one before us is not bound to accept a single breach of the contract as a total repudiation of its obligations, but can sue for each breach as it occurs, creates no anomaly in the law, and I can find no case where it has directly been held that he cannot. As I read them, in none of the cases cited by my brother O'Brien, except those relating to contracts of employment, was the question before us involved. They all present the question as to the right of an aggrieved party on a single breach to recover as for a total abrogation of the contract, not the question whether he is obliged so to do. In fact, in most of the cases it is said that the aggrieved party may elect to treat the contract as abrogated. An election necessarily imports a right of choice. The question not being settled by authority should be determined on principle.

Why should it be within the power of a party to a contract which may last over a long term of years, and the items or obligations of which are easily severable, to transmute by his own wrong his contract obligations into an unliquidated claim of damages against him, damages which as far as the future obligations of his contract are concerned are necessarily speculative. A person being about to contract for the construction of some work the execution of which will require a long period of time needs, to carry out the contract, brick, stone or steel, and to secure himself against subsequent fluctuations in the market price of these articles, which he may believe will be greatly enhanced in price in the future, contracts with a materialman for their delivery installments. It is by no means improbable that he has paid more than the present market price solely by reason of the uncertainty of the market price in the future. Under the decision about to be made he must either sue at the time of the first breach, when his damages will be necessarily be speculative, a speculation it was the very object of the contract to avoid, or perhaps wait till the time for the last delivery has passed, when it may be that under the doctrine now declared his cause of action would be barred by the Statute of Limitations...

The judgment appealed from should be reversed and a new trial granted, costs to abide the event.

Judgment affirmed.

KENNEDY, Appellant v CITY OF NEW YORK, Respondent (1909) 196 NY 19, r127 AD 89

The plaintiff is the owner of certain premises situated in that part of the city of New York formerly known as Long Island City. These premises had been leased to the latter city by one of the plaintiff's predecessors in title for a term of five years from January 1st, 1891. The lease was in writing and the rent reserved was $5,000 a year, payable monthly in advance. At the expiration of the term in January, 1896, the original lessee and its successor in interest, the city of New York, held over and continued in possession of the premises until some time in the year 1899, when the premises were abandoned.

On account of the defendant's holding over into the month of January, 1899, the plaintiff elected to treat it as a tenant for that year, and commenced two actions against it to recover the rent for that period. These two actions were commenced in 1905, and they were consolidated by order of the court. The present appeal is from the judgment rendered in the consolidated action.

Prior to the commencement of the two actions thus consolidated, and in 1904, the plaintiff had instituted another action against the defendant to recover the rent of the same premises for certain months of the year 1898. That first action, it will be observed, was instituted long after the rent for both the years 1898 and 1899 had accrued. In that first action the defendant made an offer of judgment, which offer was accepted and upon which a judgment was entered in February, 1905.

After the entry of judgment upon that offer the defendant interposed answers in the actions which had been commenced to recover the rent for the year 1899, setting up the judgment for the rent of 1898 as a bar to any recovery in the actions for the rent of 1899, and alleging that as the rent for both the years 1898 and 1899 was due at the time the judgment for the rent of 1898 was entered, the plaintiff was bound to unite in one action all its claims then due. The trial court overruled this defense and directed the jury to bring in a verdict for the plaintiff. Upon appeal the Appellate Division sustained the defense of the former recovery as a bar, reversed the judgment and dismissed the complaint. From that judgment the plaintiff now appeals to this court...

WERNER, J. The question to be decided is whether the defendant's liability for the rent of the years 1898 and 1899 arose out of a single contract or out of two distinct contracts, and that depends upon the underlying question whether a holding over from year to year, after the expiration of a definite term, is merely an extension or enlargement of the original term, or whether such a holding over constitutes a new term for each year that it continues.

In this jurisdiction it is the rule, settled by long acquiesence, that where several sums or installments are due upon a single contract, they must all be united in one action; and if several suits are brought upon such an indivisible contract, for separate installments after all are due, a recovery upon one will be a bar as to the others. The reason for the rule lies in the necessity for preventing vexatious and oppressive litigation, and its purpose is accomplished by forbidding the division of a single cause of action so as to maintain several suits when a single suit will suffice. (Perry v Dickerson 85 NY 345, 347; Lorillard v Clyde, 122 id. 41; Pakas v Hollingshead, 184 NY 211.) It is to be emphasized, however, that the rule applies only to such claims as are single, entire and indivisible. (Secor v Sturgis, 16 NY 548, 554.)

The Appellate Division had held that the balance of rent due for the year 1898, and the whole of the rent due for the year 1899 were parts of a single or indivisible demand; that although separate actions might have been maintained for each of the monthly installments as they became due, no such procedure was permissible after they all became due; that the same rule applies to the rent for the years 1898 and 1899 where no action was brought to recover either amount until after all was due; and that the judgment for the rent of 1898, was, therefore, a bar to the action to recover the rent of 1899. The correctness of this reasoning cannot be successfully challenged if the defendant's occupation of the premises during 1898 and 1899 was nothing more than an extension or prolongation of the original term; and it is palpably unsound if the holding over during these years constituted two separate and distinct terms. We must decide, therefore, which of these conditions existed.

A tenant who holds over after the expiration of a definite term for a year or years may be treated by his landlord as a trespasser, or as a tenant from year to year. If the landlord elects to treat the tenant as holding over for another year, the conditions of the original lease apply, except as to duration (Haynes v Aldrich, 133 NY 287; Adams v City of Cohoes, 127 id. 175.) Under such a holding over a tenant is bound for another year, not by virtue of an express contract but by implication of law springing from the circumstances. (Herter v Mullen, 159 NY 28, 43.) The only logical deduction from the choice thus given to the landlord of treating a holdover tenant either as a trespasser or as a tenant for another year is that each holding over, where acquiesced in by the landlord, constitutes a new term separate and distinct from those which preceded it, and related to each other only in the conditions of the original lease which the law reads into the new tenancy. Some of the text writers and a few of the earlier decisions seem to have confused the subject by referring to tenancies from year to year, arising by operation of law, as continuations of the original terms, when it would have been more correct to characterize them as new tenancies subject to the original conditions. The later decisions in this court have, however, defined this species of tenancy with a precision that admits of no misunderstanding...

Upon principle and authority we conclude that a tenancy from year to year, created by the tenant's holding over after the expiration of his original term, is a new term for each year of such holding over, upon the terms of the original lease so far as they are applicable to the new relation. It follows that a claim for unpaid rent of each year of such a holding over creates a separate and distinct cause of action. That such separate cause of action may be joined in one suit cannot be doubted, but it is equally clear that each may be made the subject of an independent action. The plaintiff might have grouped his several causes of action in a single suit, but he was not obliged to do so, and in bringing separate suits he was strictly within his rights.

The order of the Appellate Division should be reversed, and judgment of the Trial Term affirmed, with costs to the appellant in all courts.

EDWARD T. BARTLETT, J. (dissenting). (opinion omitted)

Order reversed

COATSWORTH v LEHIGH VALLEY R. CO. (1898) 156 NY 451, a24 AD 273, 48 S 511

MARTIN, J. This an appeal allowed by the Appellate Division of the Supreme Court from an interlocutory judgment overruling a demurrer to the complaint. The sole ground of demurrer was that the complaint did not state facts sufficient to constitute a cause of action.

...At the time, and prior to the construction of the bridge and super-structures mentioned in the complaint, the plaintiff or his grantors were, and he now is, the owner in fee simple and possessed of the premises in the city of Buffalo, which are also described therein. A portion of the premises is within the bounds of Alabama street, and is subject to an easement or right of way over it for the purpose of a public street. The Lehigh Valley Railway Company, without the consent of the plaintiff or the owners of the land, erected a bridge upon and across the premises lying within the bounds of such street, which is placed upon abutments of solid masonry, one on the easterly and the other on the westerly side, and upon iron pillars resting upon the street between the abutments. The bridge is solid and premanent in character and is a part of the real estate of the plaintiff. That company, in connection with the bridge, constructed and maintains a line of railroad immediately in front and on the northerly side of that portion of the plaintiff's premises which lie westerly of Alabama street and easterly of Louisiana street, and continues and maintains its railroad easterly and westerly from Alabama street for several thousand feet. A portion of its road is in front of plaintiff's premises, and is upon an embankment from four to fifteen feet above the level of the plaintiff's land, and the bridge across Alabama street is about twelve feet above the level of the plaintiff's premises and the grade of the street. The abutments, posts and bridge were erected and are maintained by the Lehigh Valley Railway Company without the consent or permission of the plaintiff. Their erection and maintenance and the erection of the elevated railroad bed have depreciated the value of the plaintiff's premises at least one-half, have depreciated their rental value about one-half, and as a consequence several building lots situated thereon cannot be rented and have been and are tenantless. The erection of the abutments and posts, the construction of the bridge and superstructure thereon, and their maintenance have caused the plaintiff continuous damage. The defendants have been and are guilty of numerous trespasses upon his land by running locomotives and cars over it each day. A multiplicity of actions would be necessary to recover for such trespasses, and the plaintiff has no adequate remedy at law to redress them. Subsequently to the construction of such road and bridge by the Lehigh Valley Railway Company, by some arrangement or agreement with the Lehigh Valley Railroad Company, it leased and licensed of the latter the right to use and occupy its line of railroad, including such bridge and superstructure. The two railroad companies are continuously maintaining such posts, abutments and bridge, and continuously trespassing upon the property of the plaintiff.

The foregoing is a brief synopsis of the material facts alleged in the complaint. The relief sought was a judgment adjudging and determining: 1. That the construction of the bridge was illegal, and became a part of the property of the plaintiff and that he was entitled to remove it; 2. That it was illegal, and its maintenance was a public nuisance from which the plaintiff suffered special injury; 3. That the running of locomotives and cars across the plaintiff's premises within the line of the street constituted trespass for which no adequate remedy at law is available, and that the plaintiff is entitled to an injunction restraining the defendants from trespassing upon such lands and property with in the bounds of the street; 4. That the plaintiff is at liberty to remove so much of such superstructure as is within the lines of the street and that the defendants be enjoined from interfering with the plaintiff in removing them and to recover the expense thereof from the defendants in this action; 5. That the plaintiff have damages; and 6. That he have costs and such other relief as may be just.

The facts stated are admitted by the demurrer. Hence, the only question is whether a cause of action is alleged or can be fairly gathered from all the averments contained in the complaint. A demurrer upon that ground can be sustained only when it appears that, after admitting all the facts alleged or that can by reasonable and fair intendment be implied from them, the complaint fails to state a cause of action. (Marie v Garrison, 83 NY 14...)

Under the more recent authorities, pleadings are not to be construed strictly against the pleader, but averments which sufficiently point out the nature of the pleader's claims are sufficient, if under them he would be entitled to give the necessary evidence to establish his cause of action. (Rochester R'way Co. v Robinson, 133 NY 242, 246.)

The alleged facts being admitted, it becomes obvious that the plaintiff was entitled to recover in this action. He was the owner in fee simple of the land where the bridge, or at least a portion of it, was placed, subject only to the right of way of the public over it. If the street should be discontinued or abandoned, he would have the entire and exclusive title and right of possession to the property within its bounds. Therefore, notwithstanding the right of the public to an easement in the street, he, as the owner of the soil, possessed an interest which would entitle him to remove any unauthorized erection upon his premises. (Eels v American Telephone & Tel. Co., 143 NY 133...)

Where trespasses upon land are continuous, the owner has a right to invoke the power of a court of equity to restrain such trespasses, and thus prevent a multiplicity of suits. That doctrine is fully sustained by the cases cited. Hence, it is clear that the complaint stated a cause of action, and the judgment of the Special Term overruling the demurrer was properly affirmed.

Judgment affirmed.

---

d. Accrual of a Cause of Action

IMIOLA v ERIE-LACKAWANNA RAILROAD COMPANY (SpCtSpTmErieCo. 1965) 257 S 2d 195

Action under Federal Employers' Liability Act for injuries as result of exposure to carbon tetrachloride. The defendant moved for summary judgment.

MATTHEW J. JASEN, Justice. Plaintiffs allege in their complaint that the decedent Richard J. Imiola, was injured while working for the defendant as a result of exposure to carbon tetrachloride prior to and on March 26, 1961. On said date it is alleged that the exposure caused him to become ill and as a result thereof he was hospitalized. On April 4, 1961 the decedent died.

This action was commenced pursuant to CPLR 203 (b) 4 on April 1, 1964 by delivery of the summons to the Sheriff of the County of Erie. The complaint alleges that the action arises out of and under the Federal Employers' Liability Act, 45 U.S.C. Sec. 51 et seq. and seeks damages for the "injuries" the pain and suffering and the death of plaintiff's intestate.

Pursuant to CPLR 3212, defendant moves for summary judgment dismissing that part of the complaint which claims damages for the pain and suffering of plaintiff's intestate on the grounds that said claim is barred by the statute of limitations.

It is the defendant's contention that the cause of action "accrued" no later than the date on which decedent was last employed by it (March 26, 1961) and that accordingly, as the present action was not commenced until April 1, 1964, it is barred by the statute.

In support of its position defendant cites Section 56 of Title 45 of the U.S.C.A., which states in regard to actions brought under the Federal Employers' Liability Act that:

"No action shall be maintained under this chapter unless commenced within three years from the date the cause of action accrued".

In opposition to this motion, plaintiffs state that the exact cause of the illness and death of the decedent was not known or discovered until the autopsy findings were made available after the death of said decedent and therefore the cause of action did not accrue until the date of death April 4, 1961.

The question submitted to the court is, under the Federal Employers' Liability Act, when does a cause of action for personal injuries accrue?

It is well settled law that a cause of action accrues on the date of the injury. In this category are personal injuries of such a character that the symptoms become immediately detectable, for example, burns, cuts, bruises, lacerations, fractured bones, etc. Practically from the moment that such injury is inflicted, the victim is aware of his condition and the wrongful act which caused it. Although he may not always know the extent of his disability or damages, he is in no doubt that he was injured. Where such knowledge exists upon the occurrence of the injury, there is an immediate accrual of the cause of action and the statute of limitations begins to run at that time.

However, we have other types of injuries which are not immediately detectable. In this category would fall many of the occupational diseases, such as silicosis. Ordinarily, these types of injuries do not manifest themselves when the disease is contracted or when the wrongful act which caused the injury was done, but usually a considerable time later.

Upon the facts and circumstances presented in this case, the court is of the opinion that an action under the Federal Employers' Liability Act for injuries sustained by virtue of an occupational hazard or condition, accrues at the time that the injury (disease) is discovered. (See Urie v Thompson, 337 US 163, 69 SCt 1018, 93 LEd 1282.)

The Urie case clearly demonstrates that when the nature of the injury is such that it does not manifest itself immediately, the determination of when the cause of action accrued does not depend on when the injury was inflicted. The court there held, that the cause of action accrues at such time as the victim has reason to know he has been injured and the wrongful act which caused it.

It is the opinion of this court that under the circumstances in this case, the personal representative of the decedent had three years from the date of the discovery of the occupational disease brought about by the alleged exposure to carbon tetrachloride to commence the action for the alleged injuries. The cause of action did not accrue until the results of the autopsy upon said decedent were made known, which from the facts presented here, the court finds to be April 4, 1961, the day of death of said intestate.

Motion for summary judgment is denied.

---

e. Co-Owners vis-a-vis a Cause of Action

MOORE LUMBER CO., INC., v BEHRMAN (MunCtBoroManhattan 1932) 144 M 291, 259 S 248

Action on contract for labor performed and materials furnished.

PRINCE, J., This action is brought by the plaintiff for labor performed and materials furnished to the premises 241 East Thirty-fifth street, New York City, pursuant to a contract between plaintiff and one Maz J. Belmont. Prior to the making of the contract, the premises were owned by the Alil Realty Corporation, in which Mr. Belmont was the principal officer and in charge of the premises. The Alil Realty Corporation thereafter conveyed a one-half undivided interest in the property to this defendant. Thereafter the plaintiff, pursuant to its contract with Mr. Belmont, performed the work and furnished the materials for which this defendant is sued.

I find as a fact that the plaintiff fully and competently performed the work and furnished the materials in the amount of $600, the claim for extra work having been withdrawn, and that the only question remaining in issue is one of law.

There was no evidence of any authority from the defendant to the plaintiff to do the work. The defendand contends that he is a tenant in common of the premises, and therefore, he is not liable unless it is shown that he authorized the plaintiff to do the work. The plaintiff concedes that a tenant in common is not liable for the unauthorized acts of his cotenant, but contends that this defendant is a joint tenant. It would seem that the plaintiff is mistaken.

"The essence of a joint tenancy is that the joint tenants take and hold as though they together constituted one person***. The four unities of (1) time - that they acquire their interests at the same moment, (2) title - that they acquire their interests by the same deed or will, (3) interest - that each have an interest identical with the interest of each of the other contenants, and (4) possession - that they each be entitled to the common possession of the entire property, grow out of this one essential, the fictitious unity of the tenants, they holding together as though they were one." (Walsh, Law of Real Prop. p. 345.)

"The four unities may all be present in a tenancy in common, and all except the unity of possession may be absent. They must all be present in a joint tenancy." (Walsh, Law of Real Prop. p. 354.)

It is evident that in the case at bar the first two elements of a joint tenancy are absent.

Furthermore, a corporation cannot hold as a joint tenant, either with an individual or another corporation. (2 Black. Comm. 148; Law Guarantee & Trust Soc. v Governor, etc., of Bank of England, 24 QBD 406.)

The judgment must, therefore, be for the defendant.

---

f. Termination of a Cause of Action:
Abatement (Lapse), Extinguishment, Merger,
Barring, of a Cause of Action

LAUDERDALE v SMITH (EDArk 1960) 186 FS 958

YOUNG, District Judge. This is an action for alleged violation of plaintiff's civil rights. (Rev.Stat. Sec. 1979 (1875); USCA Sec. 1938 (1958).)

At the time of commencement of this action the defendant was Chief of Police of the City of Little Rock, Arkansas. After the complaint was filed the defendant died.

The administrator of the estate of defendant has filed a motion suggesting the death of Smith and moving to dismiss the action, while plaintiff has moved to revive the action against the administrator of the defendant's estate.

The Motion to Dismiss is granted.

The plaintiff's cause of action is based upon alleged due process violations incident to his arrest for dynamiting a public building in the City of Little Rock. He seeks to recover for improper arrest, for detention without right to see counsel, for detention for an unreasonable time before being charged with an offense, and for the setting of excessive bail -- all alleged to have occurred at the direction of defendant acting under color of State law.

He asserts that the actions of defendant harmed his reputation and standing in the community, caused injury to his business, brought embarassment, humiliation and grief to his family and himself. It is clear that any possible damage to plaintiff's business was incidental to any damage to his reputation and standing in the community and was not the direct result of any action of defendant, lawful or otherwise, complained of in this action.

In other words, his action is for vindication of rights personal to himself. These violations of plaintiff's civil rights, if true, are in the nature of personal wrongs, similar to tort actions for slander, false imprisonment, malicious prosecution, and invasion of privacy. The question before the court is whether such alleged violations of plaintiff's civil rights survive the death of defendant. It is my conclusion that they do not, and that the action must abate.

The right of action plaintiff seeks to enforce was created by Congress and is governed by federal substantive law. (See Nelson v Knox, 6Cir, 1956, 230 F2d 483.) In the absence of Congressional provision for the survival of such cause of action we must resort to the common law, as developed in the federal courts. As so developed, the rule is said to be that causes of action akin to contract actions or to tort actions affecting property rights survive, while those akin to tort actions in the nature of personal wrongs abate, the reason for redressing purely personal wrongs ceasing to exist when the person inflicting the injury cannot be punished. (Barnes Coal Corp. v Retail Coal Merchants Ass'n. 4Cir, 1942, 128 F2d 645.)

This federal rule, though contrary to the Arkansas legislation upon the subject -- see ArkStats 1947, Sec. 27-901, 27-902 (wrongs to person, other than slander and livel, survive death of wrongdoer)--controls this case. The gravamen of plaintiff's allegations being for the vindication of wrongs to his person, I hold that his cause of action abated upon the defendant's death.

SCHULER v ISRAEL (1887) 120 US 506, 120 LEd 707

This was an action at law, in the nature of assumpsit, commenced in a state court against defendant in error...Judgment for defendant...Plaintiff sued out this writ of error. The case is stated in the opinion of the court.

MILLER, J.: The plaintiff in error, who was plaintiff below, brought two separate suits in the Circuit Court of the city of St. Louis, Missouri, on the same day, against C. W. Israel and J. N. Israel, as partners in the banking business. One case was brought upon a note for the sum of $10,000, and the other upon a draft made by C. W. Israel & Co., for $11,250 on the Laclede Bank, on which payment was refused when presented at the bank and the draft duly protested...

J. N. Israel appeared and filed an answer for himself alone in which he made no defence to the suit on the check, but set up as a defence to the suit on the note, that before the institution of the present suit in the Missouri court the plaintiff had commenced an action on the same note in the Circuit ccourt of the United States for the Northern District of Texas, and had at the time of the plea filed, recovered a judgment against the defendant, J. N. Israel, on said note, wherby he claimed that the note was merged in said judgment, and no judgment could be rendered on it in this action. Judgment was rendered in favor of plaintiff for the amount of the check. The suit was dismissed by plaintiff before hearing as to C. W. Israel...

The plaintiff demurred to the answer of the defendant Israel, setting up the judgment recovered in the United States Court for the Northern District of Texas on the note, and he demurred also to the answer of the Laclede Bank -- and the case was submitted to the court on these demurrers. The court rendered a judgment overruling both demurrers, finding for the defendant Israel in the suit upon the note and rendering judgment against him in the suit on the check...

The plaintiff brings this case here by writ of error, and the two questions presented are: first, as to the sufficiency of the answer of J. N. Israel setting up the judgment in the action on the same note in Texas.

While it is certainly true that the pendency of a suit in one court is not a defence, though it may sometimes be good in abatement, to another suit on the same cause of action in another court of concurrent jurisdiction, it may be considered as established that when a judgment is recovered against the defendant in one of those courts, if it is a full and complete judgment on the whole cause of action, it may be pleaded as a defence to the action in that court where it is pending and undecided. Neither court would be bound to take notice of the judgment in the other court judicially, but when the matter is pleaded in due time and it is made to appear that a judgment on the same cause of action has been recovered and is in full force and effect, that judgment must be held to merge the evidence of the debt, whether that evidence be parol or written, in the judgment first recovered. Freeman on Judgments, Sec. 221; Barnes v Gibbs, 2 Vroom (31 NJ Law), 317; McGilvray & Co. v Avery, 30 Vt 538; Rogers v Odell, 39 NH 452; Bank of North America v Wheeler, 28 Conn 433 (S.C. 73 Am Dec 683); Eldred v Bank, 17 Wall. 545. The court below was right, therefore, in overruling the demurrer to the plea and rendering judgment for the defendant.

The judgment of the Circuit Court is affirmed.

---

g. Survival and Revival of a Cause of Action

MANCHESTER et al, Respondents v BRAEDNER, Appellant (1887) 107 NY 346, 70 S 340

APPEAL from judgment of the General Term of the Supreme Court in the first judicial department, entered upon an order made January 9, 1885, which affirmed a judgment in favor of plaintiff entered upon the report of a referee.

This action was commenced June 20, 1882, to recover for building materials furnished and delivered by plaintiffs to defendant. The defense was the statute of limitations.

It appeared that defendant in February, 1876, entered into an agreement with one Hoover, who was engaged as contractor in building certain houses, to do all the plastering for a sum agreed upon, payable in installments as the work progressed. Plaintiffs agreed to furnish the materials, defendant agreeing to pay therefore in cash as wanted. In pursuance of this agreement plaintiffs furnished, between March 1 and June 12, 1876, materials from time to time as ordered. About that time Hoover became embarrassed and abandoned the work. The sub-contractors, and among them defendant, entered into an arrangement with Hoover to continue the work, and defendant delivered to plaintiffs three orders on Hoover, dated June 21, 1876, for sums aggregating the amount of their bill, payable, as the work progressed, from the sums coming to him under his contract. Defendant resumed his work, but in a few days abandoned it and refused to go on with the same.

ANDREWS, J. When one delivers to another an order on a third person to pay a specified sum of money to the person to whom the order is given, the natural import of the transaction is, that the drawee is indebted to the drawer in the sum mentioned in the order, and that it was given to the payee as a means of paying or securing the payment of his debt. In other words, it implies the relation of debtor and creditor between the parties to the extent of the sum specified in the order and a willingness on the part of the debtor to pay the debt. The transaction may be consistent with a different relation and another purpose, but in the absence of explanation, that is its natural and ordinary meaning. (See Bogert v Morse, 1 NY, 377)

The oral evidence shows that the defendant was owing the plaintiffs the amount specified in the several orders of June 21, 1876, and that they were given to secure the payment of the debt, thus fully corroborating the inferences deducible from the orders themselves. We think the orders constituted an acknowledgment in writing of the debt, within section 110 of the Code, and continued the debt for the period of six years from their date.

The decisions as to what is a sufficient acknowledgment of a debt, to take it out of the statute are very numerous and not altogether harmonious. It seems to be the general doctrine that the writing, in order to constitute an acknowledgment, must recognize an existing debt, and that it should contain nothing inconsistent with an intention on the part of the debtor to pay it. But oral evidence may be resorted to, as in other cases of written instruments, in aid of the interpretation. Consistently with this rule, it has been held that oral evidence is admissible to identify the debt and its amount, or to fix the date of the writing relied upon as an acknowledgment, when these circumstances are omitted, (Kincaid v Archibald, 73 NY 189; Lechman v Fletcher, 3 Tyrw. 450; Bird v Gammon, 3 Bing(NC) 883), or to explain ambiguties, (1 Smith's Lead. Cas. 960, and cases cited.) The promise to be inferred from the order was not conditional in the sense that the debt was to be paid only out of the fund in the hands of the drawee. At most, there was an appropriation of that fund for the payment of the debt, but the language of the orders did not import that the debt was to be paid only out of the fund against which they were drawn. (See Winchell v Hicks, 18 NY 558; Smith v Ryan, 66 id. 352.) The defendant by his own act in abandoning the contract with Hoover, the drawee, prevented the payment of the orders and left him subject to the general obligation of payment resting upon all debtors. The judgment should be affirmed.

All concur. Judgment affirmed.

Sec. 2.5 Nature of a Defense on the Merits and of a Defense Not on the Merits
Sec. 2.50 Defenses on the Merits - Examples

A. General Denial or Partial Denial:
at Common Law, in Equity, or under Statute

B. New Matters as Defenses - Examples at Common Law
1. Defenses to Assault Causes of Actions
   a. Abatement of substantive rights by death of Plaintiff
   b. Abatement of substantive rights by death of Defendant
   c. Self Defense
   d. Defense of a third person who has a right to defend himself
   e. Defense of Defendant's property
   f. Consent of Plaintiff
   g. Provocation by Plaintiff
   h. and other defenses
2. Defenses to Negligence Causes of Action
   a. Contributory Negligence
   b. Assumption of Risk
   c. Fellow Servant Rule
   d. Act of God
   e. and other defenses
3. Defenses, by Justification, to Certain Causes of Action
   a. Necessary Force (assault)
   b. Privilege (libel and slander)
   c. Truth (libel and slander)
   d. Probable Cause (false imprisonment, malicious prosecution)
   e. and other defenses
4. Defenses to Contract Causes of Action
   a. Incapacity of Plaintiff to have substantive right
   b. Incapacity of Defendant to have substantive duty
   c. Prior Breach by Plaintiff
   d. Condition Precedent Not Performed by Plaintiff
   e. Fraud of Plaintiff
   f. Impossibility of Performance
   g. Accord and Satisfaction
   h. Custom and Usage
   i. General Release
   j. Res Judicata
   k. and other defenses
5. Defenses to Other Types of Causes of Action
   a.

C. New Matters as Defenses - Examples in Equity
1. Defense of Clean Hands Doctrine
2. Defense of Laches
3. Defense of Equitable Estoppel
4. and other defenses

D. New Matters as Defenses - Examples Under Statute
1. The Statute of Frauds
2. The Statute of Limitations
3. Discharge in Bankruptcy
4. and other defenses

Sec. 2.5 Nature of a Defense on the Merits and of a Defense Not on the Merits (cont'd.)
Sec. 2.51 Defenses on the Merits
A. General Denial or Partial Denial: at Common Law, in Equity, or under Statute

SCHWARZ et al., Appellants v OPPOLD et al., Respondents (1878) 74 NY 307, a7 Daly 121

This action was upon a promissory note alleged in the complaint to have been made by defendant Wilhelm Oppold, payable to the order of defendant Joseph Letz, on demand, "with interest", and to have been indorsed by defendant Louisa Oppold, as follows:

"For value received, I hereby promise to pay the within note and charge my separate and individual property and estate with the payment thereof, and waive notice of presentment and nonpayment and protest."

"LOUISA OPPOLD.""

The defendants answered separately, Wilhelm Oppold by a general denial, and Louisa Oppold by admitting the making and indorsement of her name upon the note, setting up her coverture, and that she indorsed the note under coercion from the other defendants impleaded with her; that such indorsement was not made for the benefit of her separate estate, but in payment of a debt of her husband, and substantially denying the contents of the memorandum preceding her indorsement, or that the plaintiffs are holders for value before maturity.

REPALLO, J...The exception mainly relied upon was to the admission of the evidence of the defendant Wilhelm Oppold to the effect that the words "with interest" which appear at the end of the note given in evidence were not there when he signed it. The objection taken was that no such defense was pleaded.

The complaint set forth a note payable on demand with interest. The answer of the maker, Wilhelm Oppold contained a general denial. The note put in evidence purported to be payable with interest as alleged in the complaint. It was clearly competent for the defendant under his general denial to controvert this proof by showing that the note had been altered since its execution by adding the words "with interest." This alteration, which was established by the finding of the jury, clearly destroyed the effect of the note as evidence, and precluded any recovery thereon in the absence of sufficient explanation of the alteration.

The defendants also gave evidence to the effect that the special indorsement by which the defendant Louisa Oppold charged her separate estate, had been added after she had signed. A general objection was taken to the question put to her whether the writing above her signature was there when she signed. The question was material, and admissible as against a general objection. If it was intended to raise any question as to its admissibility under her answer, the objection should have been specifically taken, and in that case it could have been obviated by amendment. No such objection was interposed. The only question raised with respect to the answer of the defendant Louisa Oppold was that it had not been properly verified. That objection was not a proper one to be raised at the trial.

The questions of fact whether the note and indorsement had been altered after the defendants had affixed their respective signatures, were submitted to the jury on conflicting evidence, and they found for the defendants...there being no valid exception in the case the judgment must be affirmed.

Judgment affirmed.

ROGERS, Respondent v VOSBURGH, Impleaded, Appellant (1881) 87 NY 228

This is an appeal from a judgment of the General Term of the Supreme Court in the second judicial department, entered on an order made February 10, 1880, affirming a judgment in favor of the plaintiff, and also from the portion of that order which affirmed Special Term order, striking out defendant's answer as frivolous and sham.

This was an action on a promissory note. The defendants in their answer admit the making and delivery of the note, dated April 1, 1872, but allege that thereafter, without their knowledge and consent, and before the commencement of this action, plaintiff had materially altered the note by changing the date to April 1, 1873; by which act, defendants claim they were discharged from all liability...

MILLER, J. The order of the General Term, affirming the order of the Special Term, and striking out the defendants' answer as frivolous and sham and affirming the judgment was erronerous. The defendants' answer set up a defense, that after the making and delivery of the note the same was materially altered by the plaintiff without the knowledge of the defendants, by changing the date thereof from April 1, 1872, to April 1, 1873. If this was a material alteration, then the defense interposed was valid and legal. It is not necessary to cite authorities to sustain the proposition that an alteration of a note which postpones the time of payment for a year, is a vital one. The question of ratification of the alteration by a subsequent payment is not now before us, and did not arise upon the hearing of the motion. As there is no proof upon the subject, we are not called upon to consider whether, if the alleged alteration was made after April 1, 1875, it could have affected the liability of the defendants under the statute of limitations. The answer was neither frivolous nor sham, and it was not the province of the court, without proof, to decide the question of fact raised by the answer upon a mere inspection of the note upon which the action was brought. The order and judgment should be reversed and the motion denied, with ten dollars costs of opposing the same, and costs of appeal to the General Term and of this court.

Order and judgment reversed, and motion denied.

GRIFFIN, Receiver, Respondent v LONG ISLAND RAILROAD CO., Appellant (1886) 101 NY 348, r31 Hun 173

Appeal from a judgment of the Supreme Court at General Term in the second department, affirming a judgment for plaintiff in an action to recover personal property.

EARL, J. This action was brought to recover the possession of two railroad cars. The plaintiff in his complaint alleged that he was the receiver of the Southern Hempstead Branch Railroad Company, and that he as such became entitled to the two cars; that some time between the 1st of July, 1875, and the 1st of July, 1878, the defendant took from the possession of his railroad company the two cars, then the property of that company; that the cars were in the possession of the defendant and had been for several years, but that the defendant refused to deliver the same to the plaintiff, although before this action was commenced he made a demand in writing upon it so to do, and that it unjustly detained them from him. There is no allegation in the complaint that the defendant wrongfully took possession of the cars or wrongfully became possessed of them. The only wrong alleged is the refusal of the defendant to deliver the cars to the plaintiff upon his demand and the detention of them from him after that. The defendant in its answer alleged that it had no knowledge or information sufficient to form a belief as to the truth of the allegations containea in the complaint of the appointment of the plaintiff as receiver; admitted that the plaintiff had made a demand in writing of it to deliver the cars, and that it had not delivered them; denied on information and belief each and every allegation of the complaint not before admitted or controverted; alleged on information and belief that the cause of action set forth in the complaint did not accrue within six years before the commencement of the action, and that the property referred to in the complaint had been in possession of the Southern Railroad Company of Long Island, and its assigns, claiming title thereto for more than six years prior to the commencement of this action.

Upon the trial the plaintiff gave evidence tending to show that the Southern Hempstead Branch Railroad Company owned the cars and that the title to them came to him as receiver of that company; and he proved the value of the cars and then rested. The defendant offered to show a sale of the two cars to the Southern Railroad Company of Long Island by the persons who owned them before they were claimed to have been sold to the plaintiff's railroad company. The plaintiff objected to the evidence and the objection was sustained, the court ruling that the question of title in a third party was not raised by the pleadings, and the defendant excepted to the ruling. Later in the progress of the trial, the defendant offered to prove title in the Southern Railroad Company, of Long Island, and its successor, the Brooklyn and Montauk

Railroad Company, and that it was the lessee of the latter company and as such in possession of all its property. The evidence was objected to by the plaintiff, and the objection sustained on the ground that the title had not been set up in the answer, and the defendant excepted to the ruling. In these rulings excluding evidence of title to the cars of the plaintiff, we think the court erred.

The action to recover a chattel, as regulated by the Code of Civil Procedure, is substantially a substitute for the action of replevin as it had previously existed. At common law and under the Revised Statutes there were two actions of replevin, one in the cepit and one in the detinet. In replevin in the cepit the general issue was tendered by the plea of non cepit, and that put in issue only the taking at the place stated in the declaration. That rule of the common law was copied into the Revised Statutes. (2 R. S. 528 #39.) Under that plea the defendant could not show title in himself or in a stranger. As it was necessary in such an action for the plaintiff only to show that he was in possession of the property, and that the defendant wrongfully took it from his possession, the plea put in issue all plaintiff was, in the first instance, bound to prove. Without more, property in a third person could be no defense to such an action. Therefore, in order to defend such an action, the defendant was bound to prove either property in himself, or property in a third person with which he was in some way connected and under which he could justify, and the facts he was bound specially to allege.

But in an action of replevin in the detinet, the general issue was tendered by the plea of non detinet, and that plea at common law put in issue, as well the plaintiff's property in the goods as the detention thereof by the defendant. And it was provided in the Revised Statutes (2 R.S. 529, #40), that "when the action is founded on the wrongful detention of the goods, and the original taking is not complained of, the plea of the general issue shall be, that the defendant does not detain the goods and chattels specified in the declaration, or any part thereof, in manner and form as therein alleged; and such plea shall put in issue, not only the detention of such goods and chattels, but also the property of the plaintiff therein." It was also provided by the Revised Statutes (2 R.S. 528 #36), that the action of replevin might be founded upon both the wrongful taking and the detention of the property, in which case it was necessary that the declaration should allege the wrongful taking and also allege that the defendant continued to detain such property.

It cannot be doubted that this complaint contained all the allegations requisite to show a wrongful detention of the cars. By a liberal construction it might be held to be framed in a double aspect, both for the wrongful taking and the wrongful detention. Upon the trial there was no proof offered or given to show the wrongful taking of the cars, but the plaintiff simply gave proof to show the wrongful detention. Therefore, we think the action should have been treated as if it had been brought for a wrongful detention of the cars. It was necessary, therefore, for the plaintiff to show his title to the cars; and what it was necessary for him to show to maintain his action the defendant had the right to controvert by proof under its general denial. The general denial put in issue, not only the wrongful detention, but plaintiff's title, and upon that issue it had the right to show, not only title in itself, but title out of the plaintiff and in a stranger. The plaintiff, seeking to take property out of the possession of the defendant, was bound to show title in himself, and the defendant could defend itself by showing that he did not have title, and thus did not have the right to take from it the possession which it had acquired. (Caldwell v Bruggerman, 4 Minn 270...) In Kennedy v Shaw, decided under a system of pleading similar to our own, it is said: "Where the general denial is pleaded to a complaint in an action to recover the possession of personal property, the plaintiff must show his right to the possession of the property as against anybody else. He must recover upon the strength and validity of his own title and right to the possession of the property, and if the defendand can show the property, and right to the possession of the property to be in himself or in a third person, he may do so under the general denial and thus defeat the action." This broad and general statement of the rule, however, would not enable one who had taken property from the actual possession of another to justify the taking by the allegation and proof of title in a third person with which he did not connect himself.

There is nothing in the case of Stowell v Otis (71NY 36) in conflict with these views; but regarding this as an action for the wrongful detention of the cars, that case is an authority for the views we have expressed.

Under our system of practice, and under every rational, logical system of pleading, the defendant must, under a general denial be permitted to controvert by evidence everything which the plaintiff is bound in the first instance to prove to make out his cause of action. (Robinson v Frost, 14 Barb(NY) 536).

The denial in this answer of "each and every allegation of the complaint not hereinabove admitted or controverted is a good general denial. What had been before admitted and controverted was clearly specified, and hence there was no doubt or confusion as to the application of this general denial; and this answer is not, therefore, condemned by the decision in Clerk v Dillon, (97 NY 370).

The appellant also makes a point as to the statute of limitations. Upon the new trial it should be permitted to prove all the facts bearing upon that defense, and then the application of the law to the facts will probably not be difficult. We do not deem it our duty to say more about it now.

The judgment should be reversed and a new trial granted, costs to abide events.

Judgment reversed.

PORTER v AMERICAN TOBACCO CO. (2dDept 1910) 140 AD 871, 125 S 710

WOODWARD, J. The plaintiff brings this action to secure a perpetual injunction forbidding the defendant to make use of the plaintiff's name and picture for business purposes, and for damages for such use. The complaint alleges that the defendant "willfully, knowingly, and without the written or oral consent of plaintiff, used the name and picture or portrait of plaintiff, a living person, for advertising purposes and for the purposes of trade in the state of New York and elsewhere from the year 1909 to the present time, and still continues to so use plaintiff's name and picture"; and this is the gravamen of the action, though other matters are alleged in support of the claim for damages. The defendant denies the material allegations above quoted and sets up a separate and distinct defense, "that on or about the 5th day of July, 1909, and prior to the use by this defendant of the name, portrait, or picture of the plaintiff for advertising purposes, or for the purposes of trade, the plaintiff made, executed, and delivered a consent in writing as follows, "setting out a written consent without date. The plaintiff did not reply to this alleged defense, and the defendant moved the court for an order directing the plaintiff to reply, under the provisions of section 516 of the Code of Civil Procedure. The learned justice before whom the motion was made denied the same; the defendant appealing from such order.

Section 516 provides that, where "an answer contains new matter, constituting a defense by way of avoidance, the court may, in its discretion, on the defendant's application, direct the plaintiff to reply to the new matter." The matter is one going peculiarly to the discretion of the court which entertains the motion, and, while it is not beyond the power of this court to interfere, we apprehend that a clear case should be presented to warrant this court in overruling an order of this character. In the case now before us the statute, which alone gives the right of action, for none existed at common law (Roberson v Rochester Folding Box Co. 171 NY 538, 64 NE 442, 59 LRA 478, 89 AmStRep 828), provides that:

"Any person whose name, portrait or picture is used within this state for advertising purposes or for the purposes of trade without the written consent first obtained as above provided may maintain an equitable action in the Supreme Court of this state against the person, firm or corporation so using his name, portrait or picture, to prevent and restrain the use thereof." Section 51, Civil Rights Law (Laws 1909, c.14, Consol Laws, c.6).

The action is statutory, and the plaintiff must, by pleading and proof, bring the action within the terms and conditions of the statute. (Lewis v Howe, 174 NY 340, 343, 66 NE 975, 1101, and authorities there cited.) He must therefore plead and prove that the defendant is making use of his name or picture for advertising or business purposes without having first procured the written consent of the plaintiff to make such use of the same. The plaintiff had no cause of action whatever, unless he proves that the defendant is making use of his name or picture for advertising or trade purposes without his written consent. That is an essential part of his cause of action, and it may be questioned whether the alleged written consent of the plaintiff to the American Lithographing Company and its customers is "new matter, constituting a defense by way of avoidance."

An "avoidance" in pleading is defined to be the introduction of new or special matter, which, admitting the premises of the opposite party, avoids or repels his conclusions. 3Am. & Eng. Ency. of Law 523, and authorities cited in notes. Here the defendant denies that it has made use of the plaintiff's name or picture without his written consent. It raises an issue as to the facts alleged, and places the burden of establishing the fact upon the plaintiff. Its alleged new matter does not avoid the plaintiff's right to recover. It takes from him his cause of action, and that can all be fully and fairly brought out upon the trial of the issue of whether the defendant had made use of the plaintiff's name or picture without his written consent. The plaintiff must affirmatively prove his case, subject to the defendant's right of cross-examination; and it is difficult to see how any end of justice would be promoted by forcing the plaintiff to reply to matter which does not constitute a defense by way of avoidance, but by way of destroying absolutely the cause of action.

The order appealed from should be affirmed.

Order affirmed, with $10 costs and disbursements.

Sec. 2.51 Defenses on the Merits (continued)

B. New Matters as Defenses - Examples at Common Law
C. New Matters as Defenses - Examples in Equity
D. New Matters as Defenses - Examples under Statute

(See list of examples supra p. 95)

LAUDERDALE v SMITH (EDArk 1960) 186 FS 958

(The case appears supra, p. 92)

Sec. 2.52 Defenses not on the Merits - Examples
(New Matters of an Adjective Law Nature - see Ch. III, infra)

Sec. 2.521 No jurisdiction territorially venue
Sec. 2.522 No jurisdiction of the person of defendant or of the res
Sec. 2.523 No jurisdiction of the cause of action
Sec. 2.524 No jurisdiction of the remedy
Sec. 2.525 Incapacity of plaintiff to sue i.e., to act as a party in litigation
Sec. 2.526 Incapacity of defendant to be sued i.e., to act as a party in litigation
Sec. 2.527 Abatement of the action by death of plaintiff
Sec. 2.528 Abatement of the action by death of defendant
Sec. 2.529 Adequate remedy at law
Sec. 2.5210 Nonjoinder of necessary party
Sec. 2.5211 Misjoinder of party plaintiff or defendant
Sec. 2.5212 Misjoinder of Causes of Action
Sec. 2.5213 Another action pending for same cause
Sec. 2.5214 Election of remedies
Sec. 2.5215 Discharge in bankruptcy
Sec. 2.5216 Statute of frauds
Sec. 2.5217 Laches
Sec. 2.5218 Statute of limitations
Sec. 2.5219 Others

CHORNEY v CALLAHAN (DCtMass 1955) 135 FS 35

Action by motorist for injuries received in accident involving deceased. Deceased's administrator moved to be allowed to file a motion to dismiss late, to amend answer and for summary judgment.

FORD, District Judge. Plaintiff brings this action to recover for personal injuries suffered in a motor vehicle accident on March 17, 1952, allegedly caused by the negligence of Charles E. Callahan. The action was commenced by the filing of a complaint in this court on March 13, 1953, in which said Callahan was named as defendant. Service upon the named defendant was attempted but never made, since he had in fact died on January 11, 1953.

On April 1, 1953, plaintiff filed a suggestion of death of defendant and a motion to amend by substituting Charles E. Callahan, Jr., administrator of the estate of Charles E. Callahan, as defendant. This motion was allowed, without opposition, on April 13, 1953. Charles E. Callahan, Jr., had been appointed and qualified as such administrator in the Norfolk County Probate Court on February 4, 1953. Summons in this action was served upon him on April 24, 1953. Defendant-administrator appeared and filed an answer to the complaint. He now moves to be allowed to file a motion to dismiss late, to amend his answer to set up the defenses that the action is premature and a nullity, and for summary judgment.

As originally filed, this action was brought against a named defendant who was already dead. At that point the purported action was a nullity, for a dead man obviously cannot be named party defendant in an action. (Chandler v Dunlop, 311 Mass 1, 5, 39 NE2d 969. Cf. Pasos v Eastern S.S.Co., D.C., 9 FRD 279 (named plaintiff dead when complaint was filed).) Hence the attempted substitution of the administrator was ineffective as such. There was no action really existent in which he could be substituted. Rule 25 (a) (1) of the Federal Rules of Civil Procedure, 28 U.S.C.A., provides:

"(1) If a party dies and the claim is not thereby extinguished, the court within 2 years after the death may order substitution of the proper parties. ***"

This clearly contemplates substitution for a party, i.e., for someone who had been made a party to the action before his death. Cf. Chandler v Dunlop, supra, where a similar result was reached under Mass. G.L. ch. 228, Sec. 4. The amendment allowed on April 13, 1953 was not a substitution of a successor defendant, but the naming for the first time of a legally existent defendant. It was in effect the commencement of a new action against defendant-administrator.

The capacity of defendant to be sued is to be determined in accordance with Massachusetts law. (Federal Rules of Civil Procedure, Rule 17 (b).) Mass. G.L. ch. 197, Sec. 1 provides:

"Executor, etc., not liable to action for six months after giving bond.

"An executor or administrator shall not be held to answer to an action by a creditor of the deceased commenced within six months after his giving bond for the performance of his trust, unless such action is brought for the recovery of a demand which would not be affected by the insolvency of the estate or, after the estate has been represented insolvent, for the purpose of ascertaining a contested claim."

The defendant qualified as administrator on February 4, 1953. Whether this action is regarded as being commenced against him at the time he was made a defendant by the allowance of the amendment on April 13, 1953 or whether the amendment is regarded as dating back to the filing of the original complaint on March 13, 1953, the action was clearly begun within the six month period when no action could be brought against him. The case is clearly governed by Gallo v Foley, 296 Mass 306, 5 NE2d 425. That was also a personal injury action arising out of an automobile accident in which the action against the administrator was begun within six months after his qualification. Judgment was ordered for defendant on the ground that the suit was prematurely brought. A similar result was reached in White v Cormier, 311 Mass 537, 42 NE2d 256.

Plaintiff contends that since defendant did not raise these matters in his original answer or otherwise until the one-year statute of limitations on actions against an administrator had run, Mass.G.L. ch. 197, Sec. 9, he should not be allowed to amend his answer and should be estopped from setting up the defenses relied upon in his present motion. This contention must be rejected. In Gallo v Foley, supra, it was held that defendant was properly allowed to set up a similar defense by an amendment filed more than two years after the original answer. Garber v Hirsh, 225 Mass 422, 114 NE 670, cited by plaintiff presented a different situation. In that case it was held that the administrators of the original defendant, who appeared voluntarily to suggest defendant's death and asked to be allowed to defend, could not later defeat plaintiff's right by withdrawing after the statute of limitations had run.

Defendant's motions to amend his answer and for late filing of his motion to dismiss are allowed. Defendant's motion for summary judgment is allowed, and the action is dismissed.

In re HARLEM RIVER DRIVE. ISRAEL LEWIS, Appellant; KEARSE et al, Respondents (1stDept 1951) 278 AD 122, 103 S2d 695

Proceeding in the matter of the application of the City of New York relative to acquiring title where not heretofore acquired, to the real property required for the opening and extending of Harlem River Drive--Israel Lewis, mortgagee, make application for payment of award made for Damage Parcel No. 102H on the Damage Map, etc.; opposed by Josephine Kearse and others. The Supreme Court, New York County, entered an order amending the final decree in the condemnation proceeding by expunging therefrom the provision that the award was subject to a mortgage, and the petitioner appealed.

PER CURIAM. The City of New York was authorized by order dated April 17, 1947 to condemn certain property in the Borough of Manhattan which included a parcel upon which appellant held a mortgage. The City gave due notice for the filing of claims and the submission of proof of title. In the condemnation proceeding, appellant seasonably presented his proof of claim in which he set forth that he was the owner of a mortgage covering the plot in question and asking that he be awarded the amount due on the mortgage. He retained a real estate expert who gave evidence as to the value of the damage parcel. The Court, by final decree dated April 17, 1950, awarded $9,123 as compensation for the taking of the mortgaged premises to owners unknown, subject to appellant's mortgage. Respondents, who claim to be the holders of the equity in the property, did not appear in the condemnation proceeding, and failed to claim any interest in the award prior to the date of the final decree. No question was raised by anyone as to the enforcibility of appellant's mortgage or as to whether it was barred by the applicable statute of limitations.

We are of the view that there was here no authority to amend the final decree so as to delete therefrom the portion thereof which subjected the award to the mortgage, presumably upon the ground that the mortgage had been barred by the statute of limitations.

Concededly appellant was the mortgagee of record of the parcel at least from February 19, 1947. He was openly in possession of the mortgaged premises thereafter and respondents impliedly consented to such possession. According to respondents, the last payment made on account of the mortgage indebtedness was for interest which became due on July 6, 1941. A right to relief accrued to the mortgagee in February, 1942 because of the default in payment of interest due on January 6, 1942. The period of limitations under Sec. 47-a, Civil Practice Act*, is computed by respondents from the date in February 1942 when the aforementioned right of the mortgagee to relief accrued.

The record discloses that appellant appeared in the condemnation proceeding on May 1, 1947 claiming to be the owner of the mortgage. By serving his notice of appearance, appellant thus asserted his claim as mortgagee to any award that might be made therein. (Sec. 11, C.P.A.) Appellant, therefore, must be held to have interposed his claim as an owner of the mortgage in a special proceeding and to have done so within six years from the date his claim accrued in February, 1942.

Moreover, the statute of limitations does not discharge a debt but simply bars the remedy thereon. (Hulbert v Clark, 128 NY 295, 28 NE 638, 14 LRA 59.) It is an affirmative defense which to be availed of must be pleaded. (Nasaba Corp. v Harfred Realty Corp., 287 NY 290, 39 NE 2d 243...) Appellant concededly held a mortgage which was not void but which at most was unenforcible if the defense of the statute of limitations had been asserted. No such defense was raised. It would also seem that since respondents failed to appear in the condemnation proceeding they could not in the circumstances here obtain a modification of the final decree. (Merriman v City of New York 227 NY 279, 125 NE 500...)

Order unanimously reversed with $20 costs and disbursements to the appellant and an order is directed to be entered in accordance with the opinion herein. Settle order on notice.

*N.Y.Civil Practice Act Sec. 47-a. "1. An action upon a bond, the payment of which is secured by a mortgage upon real property, or upon a bond and mortgage so secured, or upon a mortgage of real property, or any interest therein, must be commenced within six years after the cause of action has accured...." (footnote added.)

NEWMAN v CHRISTENSEN (1948) 149 Neb 471, 31 NW2d 417

Action for personal injuries by Hillis C. Newman against Paul Christensen. From a judgment entered upon a directed verdict in favor of defendant, plaintiff appeals.

PAINE, Justice. This is an action for personal injuries suffered by the plaintiff by reason of his foot being suddenly jerked up by defendant, throwing him backward out of his chair, by which act he was injured. At the close of the plaintiff's evidence, the defendant moved to dismiss plaintiff's cause of action on the ground that it was barred by the statute of limitations. The court thereupon instructed the jury that it had become a legal question, which the court had determined, and instructed the jury to return a verdict for the defendant. Plaintiff appealed.

The evidence in the bill of exceptions discloses that the plaintiff was at the time of trial 54 years old. He was a traveling salesman for a Minneapolis firm, covering western Iowa, southern Minnesota, and a part of Nebraska, and had followed that occupation for 19 years.

At about 8:30 on the evening of March 18, 1945, the plaintiff, defendant, and two other friends were playing pitch in the Elks Club at Fremont. At the completion of a game two one-dollar bills were left lying on the corner of the table, which the plaintiff in a playful spirit said if the defendant did not want to get them off the table, the plaintiff thereupon pushed the money off the table. The plaintiff was sitting in a bentwood chair, with gliders under the legs, the linoleum on the floor being highly waxed. The defendant stooped down to get the money, grabbed plaintiff's right foot, and gave it a sharp jerk upward. The chair spun away and plaintiff fell over backward, with his feet in the air, striking the middle of his back. However, while he continued the same that evening, yet from the fall he allegedly suffered serious injuries to his back and spine. He charged in his petition that he was unable to do any work for a period approximately 38 weeks thereafter and will hereafter be partially disabled, decreasing his earning capacity at least 50 percent, the injury to his eighth dorsal vertebra causing great pain, and that the injuries are permanent.

The answer admitted the occurrence, which it claimed was "horse play," and charged that the cause of action, if any, was barred by the statute of limitations.

The two assignments of error are that the trial court erred in sustaining the defendant's motion to dismiss at the conclusion of the plaintiff's evidence, and erred in overruling the plaintiff's motion for a new trial.

The sole question involved is whether the action was governed by section 25-208, R.S. 1943, which provides that actions for assault and battery must be brought within one year, or by section 25-207, which provides that actions for tort can be brought within four years. The petition in this case was filed over a year and a half after the action arose.

If the act of the defendant was a battery, the Nebraska law requires that it should be filed within one year, and on that point alone the trial judge dismissed plaintiff's action....

...Although it may be true that every personal injury committed through negligence is, strictly speaking, a "battery," within the common-law definition, it does not follow that the word "battery," as used in section 25-208, R.S. 1943, is to be construed to include all personal injury actions. The action for a battery, brought within the one-year limitation, is proper if founded upon an intentionally administered injury to the person. But there is another class of cases in which the personal injury occured through the negligent act of one person, and such negligent acts do not come within the definitions of assault and battery heretofore set out, for the intention to inflict the injury is entirely lacking. 4 Am.Jur., Assault and Battery, Sec. 3, p. 126...

"The fact that a practical joke is the cause of an injury to a person does not excuse the perpetrator from liability in damages for the injury sustained." (52 Am.Jur., Torts, Sec. 90, p. 436.)

In the case of Great Atlantic & Pacific Tea Co. v Roch, 160 Md 189, 153 A 22, where a deat rat was substituted for a loaf of bread in a package which caused plaintiff such fright when she opened the package that she became a nervous wreck, the verdict for plaintiff was sustained. It was held that damages may be recovered for physical injuries caused by shock or fright....

It is a general rule that, when one does an act which proves injurious to another, civil liability usually follows from the existence of a right in the injured person. Although the act was done without malice, and no mischief was intended, he may be held answerable for the injuries which follow. (See 26 RCL, Torts, Sec. 6, p. 759....)

In the case at bar, we have reached the conclusion that, while actions for assault and battery, under section 25-208, R.S. 1943, must be brought within one year, this action is one for negligence, being an act which an ordinarily prudent man would not have done, and therefore, being in tort, may be brought within four years, as provided in section 25-207, R.S.1943.

Having reached this conclusion, it follows that the trial court erroneously directed a verdict for the defendant. The judgment is hereby reversed and the cause is remanded for a new trial.

MROWIEC v POLISH ARMY VET. ASSN. (SpCtOnondagaCo. 1947) 73 S2d 361

Action by John Mrowiec against the Polish Army Veterans Association of America, Post 124 of Syracuse, N.Y., Inc., to recover money lost in slot machines kept upon the defendant's premises, wherein the defendant filed a motion for an order striking out certain allegations of the complaint, requiring the plaintiff to separately state and number each alleged cause of action, and dismissing the complaint because the cause of action did not accrue within three months.

SEARL, J. This motion seeks an order (a) striking out certain allegations of the complaint, (b) requiring the plaintiff to separately state and number each alleged cause of action, (c) dismissing the complaint for the reason that the alleged cause of action did not accrue within three months, as provided by Section 995 of the Penal Law, after the payment of money claimed to have been placed in slot machines (Rules Civil Practice, rule 107, subd. 6), and (d) that the complaint does not state facts sufficient to constitute a cause of action. Rules Civil Practice, rule 106.

The complaint alleges defendant is a membership corporation, that its officers, agents or servants permitted slot gambling machines to be kept upon its premises, that plaintiff was invited to frequent the premises, and between the dates of April 1, 1946, and September 30, 1946, he lost at gambling on the machines the sum of $13,500.

It will be necessary to examine only objection (c), whether the action is barred by a statute of limitations, and (d), whether the complaint states a cause of action. If the motion be granted on either of these two grounds, decision on other grounds becomes purely academic.

Section 980, Penal Law, provides that "a person, who persuades another to visit any building or part of a building, or any vessel or float, occupied or used for the purpose of gambling, in consequence whereof such other person gambles therein, is guilty of a misdemeanor...."

Section 982 relates to "keeping slot machines or devices," and provides that it is unlawful to store, keep, possess, or to permit the operation of "any slot machine." It is unnecessary to be more explicit as to the definition of a "slot machine" as set forth in the section....

Approaching new consideration of the two sections of the law most directly affecting the determination of the instant motion, we find first:

"Section 994. Property staked may be recovered

"Any person who shall pay, deliver or deposit any money, property or thing in action, upon the event of any wager or bet prohibited , may sue for and recover the same of the winner or person to whom the same shall be paid or delivered, and of the stakeholder or other person in whose hands shall be deposited any such wager, bet or stake, or any part thereof, whether the same shall have been paid over by such stakeholder or not, and whether any such wager be lost or not."

This is followed immediately by:

"Sec. 595. Losers of certain sums may recover them

"Every person who shall, by playing at any game, or by betting on the sides or hands of such as do play, lose at any time on sitting, the sum or value of twenty-five dollars or upwards, and shall pay or deliver the same or any part thereof, may within three calendar months after such payment or delivery, sue for and recover the money or value of the things so lost and paid or delivered, from the winner thereof.

"In case the person losing such sum or value shall not, within the time aforesaid, in good faith and without collusion, sue for the sum or value so by him lost and paid or delivered, and prosecute such suit to effect without unreasonable delay, the overseers of the poor of the town where the offense was committed, may sue for and recover the sum or value so lost and paid, together with treble the said sum or value, from the winner thereof, for the benefit of the poor."

Peculiarly, the leading case that has been followed for many years arose in Syracuse in 1864. (Langworthy v Broomley, 29 HowPrac(NY) 92. Sections 994 and 995, above quoted, were then and had been since the year 1830, couched in substantially the same language as exists today. Justice Morgan, writing in the Langworthy case, pointed out that by the different sections the legislature had made provision for two classes of cases "one where parties bet or wager a sum of money upon some contingent event, and the other, where the parties play at a game, or bet on the sides or hands of such as do play." The court pointed out that the provisions as now contained in Sec. 994 pertained to a wager upon some contingent event, such as the result of a horse race or a presidential election, whereas the provisions of the latter section, now Sec. 995, related to gambling at cards, dice, or some other game.

In the Langworthy case, supra, as in Meech v Stoner, 19 NY 26, therein cited, the loser lost while playing the game of "faro."

Both cases sustain the conclusion that if the loser in a game of chance is to recover, he must by his complaint bring himself within the provisions of the statute. In other words, he must allege that the action is commenced within three calendar months after payment or delivery of his loss, also that the sum or value of twenty-five dollars or upwards was lost at the particular sitting. (See also Fowler v Van Surdam, 1 Denio(NY) 557...)

Our courts have followed the common law of England to effect that the loser at gambling is "an equal sharer" in the offense, that the loser is unworthy to be heard, and "thus the parties are left where the law finds them." When Section 995 was enacted, the loser was afforded a remedy, provided he acted diligently to recover his loss.

The right to recover under both sections 994 and 995 are remedial and not penal. This question was answered when Lord William Blackstone wrote in the case of Bones v Booth, 2 Bl. Wm. 1226, in the year 1783. The English statutes were similar in most respects to our own Sections 994 and 995. A verdict has been rendered in favor of the defendant. Counsel for the latter argued that a new trial could not be granted as the law was penal in its nature. The Appellate Court held the statute to be remedial only, as the provisions of the statute did not provide that the defendant could be placed in the pillory in event the verdict was against him.

Another interesting feature of this old decision is that it interprets our modern statute wherein our statute uses the expression "lose at any time on sitting." In the English case the gaming participants gambled at the game of "all fours" in the City of Bristol at two guineas a game from Monday evening continuously through until Tuesday evening, with the exception of one or two hours for dinner. The expression at "any one sitting" was interpreted by the Justice to mean as long as the gaming participants were in each other's company, although they took an hour or two out for dinner.

The plaintiff in the instant case raises the question seemingly thus far judicially undetermined. He urges that this action is brought under the provisions of Section 994 relating to a prohibited "wager or bet," wherein the time to commence an action to recover has not expired. Was this $13,500 sought to be recovered lost by placing it in slot machines maintained by defendant a "wager or bet," or was it lost by "playing at any game," and included within the purview of Section 995, which provides that plaintiff's action must be instituted within three months?

We must start with the premise that the claimed loss, being at gambling, places both winner and loser in pari delicto.

Thus, the use or maintenance of slot machines being unlawful (Penal Law, Sec. 982), the plaintiff would have no remedy by way of recovery of loss except as specifically provided by either Section 994 or 995. If plaintiff did not deposit and lose this considerable sum of $13,500, or 54,000 quarters, providing he only deposited a quarter of a dollar at each play, as a "wager or bet," or by "playing," he has no remedy.

Many authorities hold that Section 994, in relating to bets or wagers, pertains to the commonly accepted wagers on races or election bets; in other words, the result is a contingency. True, the placing of a quarter in a slot machine would create a contingency as to whether the slot machine would win. However, the same contingency would exist between any two or more players at cards, dice, faro, roulette, dominoes or scores of other games that afford an element of chance and equally an opportunity to gamble.

In coming to a conclusion, we must take the common and accepted use of the words as gleaned from a dictionary definition, and from their use in opinions taken from reported cases. Webster's International Dictionary (1940) gives: "Games of Chance include all games in which chance is the sole or a considerable factor in determining the outcome, as in dice and most card games." Wager is: "To hazard on the issue of a contest, or on some question that is to be decided, or on some casualty, to risk; venture; also to stake; bet; to lay as a gamble."

Searching for light in opinions of our court involving questions touching the law relating to slot machines, we find Judge Crane using the expression "played" in People v Jennings (257 NY 196, 198, 177 NE 419). Relating to a slot machine affording free games to the winner, we find the statement of the State Reporter in People v Swartz, 282 NY 596, 597, 25 NE 2d 386, making this reference: "he then played these free games." Again, the Second Department in People v Raziano (268 AD 798, 799, 49 S2d 236), refers to "winning players." In People v Boxer (SpSess, 24 S2d 628, 631), the court refers to "play the game."

A case most nearly in point is that of Foley v Whelan (219 Minn 209, 17 NW 2d 367, 370). The Minnesota Statutes, 1941, Sec. 614.09, MSA, provided that the loser might recover from the winner any money lost "by playing at cards, dice, or other game." Plaintiff maintained that playing a slot machine for money was playing a game within the meaning of the statute. Defendant argued that as the words "cards" or "dice" preceded, the statute did not contemplate nor include slot machines, entirely different instrumentalities. The court held that similar statutes in other states held that the word "game" included dog fighting and other similar types of gambling, that the words, "gamble," "game," "gambling" and "gaming" are all derived from the Anglo-Saxon word "gamen" - "which means to play," citing People v Todd (51 Hun 446, 4 S 25). The court, therefore, held, that "money lost by playing a slot machine is lost at playing a 'game'," and that "playing a slot machine is in principle the same kind of a game as playing at cards or dice."

This court can come to but one conclusion, namely, that the plaintiff, when playing the slot machine, was playing a game. He came within the provisions of Section 995. In fact, the language of his own complaint states: "the users thereof were playing a game of chance in that the machine would pay a certain percentage in kind that the player used, provided that certain numerals, figures or designs would appear on the machine." Such is not termed by the plaintiff, nor can it be construed by this court, to be a bet or wager. The play on the machines is alleged to have occurred between April 1, 1946, and September 30, 1946. The summons is dated April 16, 1947, more than three months after the last date of play.

The complaint is clearly defective in another respect. The Legislature has seen fit to afford no cause of action for losses at one time for sums less that $25. The complaint alleges loss of $13,500 between the two dates referred to. As each loss in excess of $25 at any one time constitutes a separate cause of action, it would be necessary for plaintiff to separately number such causes of action and allege dates and amounts claimed to be lost at each time.

An order may issue dismissing the complaint.

Sec. 2.6 Juridical Persons and Their Substantive Law Capacities for Legal Interests: Rights and Duties

Sec. 2.61 Natural Persons
A - Those sui juris
B - Those of limited capacity
1. Married Women
2. Minors
3. Incompetents
4. Aliens
5. Convicts
6. and Others

Sec. 2.62 Representative Persons
1. Administrator
2. Executor
3. Guardian
4. Committee for an Incompetent
5. Receiver
6. Trustee
7. Public Officer
8. Agents
9. and Others

Sec. 2.63 Collective Persons
1. Partnerships
2. Corporations
3. Unicorporated Associations
4. A State in the U.S.
5. The U.S.
6. A Foreign State
7. and Others

Sec. 2.64 Artificial Persons
1. A Res e.g. a boat
2. and Others

Sec. 2.61 Natural Persons
A - Those sui juris
B - Those of limited capacity
1. Married Women
2. Minors
3. Incompetents
4. Aliens
5. Convicts
6. and Others

WOOD v LANCET (1951) 303 NY 349, r278 AD 913

APPEAL from a judgment of the Appellate Division of the Supreme Court in the first judicial department, entered July 3, 1951, affirming, by a divided court, an order of the Supreme Court at Special Term (Hammer, J.) in favor of defendant, entered in Bronx County, granting a motion by defendant for a dismissal of the complaint for failure to state a cause of action.

DESMOND, J. The complaint served on behalf of this infant plaintiff alleges that, while the infant was in his mother's womb during the ninth month of her pregnancy, he sustained, through the negligence of defendant, such serious injuries that he came into this world permanently maimed and disabled. Defendant moved to dismiss the complaint as not stating a cause of action, thus taking the position that its allegations, though true, gave the infant no right to recover damages in the courts of New York. The Special Term granted the motion and dismissed the suit, citing Drobner v Peters, (232 NY 220.) In the Appellate Division one Justice voted for reversal with an opinion in which he described the obvious injustice of the rule, noted a decisional trend (in other States and Canada) toward giving relief in such cases, and suggested that since Drobner v Peters (supra) was decided thirty years ago by a divided vote, our court might well re-examine it.

The four Appellate Division Justices who voted to affirm the dismissal below, wrote no opinion except that one of them stated that, were the question an open one and were he not bound by Drobner v Peters (supra), he would hold that "when a pregnant woman is injured through negligence and the child subsequently born suffers deformity or other injury as a result, recovery therefor may be allowed to the child, provided the causal relation between the negligence and the damage to the child be established by competent medical evidence." (278 AD 913.) It will hardly be disputed that justice (not emotionalism or sentimentality) dictates the enforcement of such a cause of action. The trend in decisions of other courts, and the writings of learned commentators, in the period since Drobner v Peters was handed down in 1921, is strongly toward making such a recovery possible. The precise question for us on this appeal is: shall we follow Drobner v Peters, or shall we bring the common law of this State, on this question, into accord with justice? I think, as New York State's court of last resort, we should make the law conform to right.

Drobner v Peters (supra), like the present case, dealt with the sufficiency of a complaint alleging prenatal injuries, tortiously inflicted on a nine-month foetus, viable at the time and actually born later. There is, therefore, no material distinction between that case and the one we are passing on now. However, Drobner v Peters must be examined against a background of history and of the legal thought of its time and of the thirty years that have passed since it was handed down. Early British and American common law gives no definite answer to our question, so it is not profitable to go back farther than Dietrich v Northampton (138 Mass 14), decided in 1894, with an opinion by Justice Holmes, and apparently, the first American case. Actually that was a dealth case, since the five-month infant, prematurely born, survived for a few minutes after birth. The principal ground asserted by the Massachusetts Supreme Court (138 Mass., at p. 17) for a denial of recovery was that "the unborn child was a part of the mother at the time of the injury" and that "any damage to it which was not too remote to be recovered for at all was recoverable by her" (the mother). A few years later (1890), in Ireland, the Queen's Bench Division, in a very famous holding refused to allow a suit to be brought in behalf of a child born deformed as the result of an accident in defendant's railway coach, two of the Justices taking the ground that the infant plaintiff was not in esse at the time of the wrong, and the other two regarding the suit as one on the contract of carriage with no duty to care owing by the carrier to the unborn infant whose presence was unknown to defendant (Walker v Great Northern Ry of Ireland, 29 IRIr 69). A similar complaint was dismissed for similar reasons, and the dismissal affirmed by the Appellate Division, Second Department, in Nugent v Brooklyn Heights RR Co. (154 AD 667, appeal dismissed 209 NY 515). It is significant that the Appellate Division's opinion in the Nugent case (supra) indicates that, had it not been for the contract-of-carriage theory and its supposed consequences, the writer of the opinion would have favored recovery. Other strong support for just treatment of prenatal wrongs (of another kind) is found also in the 1893 opinion of Justice Haight (later of this court) in Quinlen v Welch (69 Hun 584); however, on appeal, this court found it unnecessary to pass on the point (141 NY 158). There were, in the early years of this century, rejections of such suits by other courts, with various fact situations involving before birth traumas (see Allaire v St. Luke's Hosp., 184 Ill 359...) and, quite recently, Massachusetts has reaffirmed the Dietrich rule (Bliss v Passanesi, 326 Mass 461). The movement toward a more just treatment of such claims seems to have commenced with the able dissent in the Allaire case (supra), which urged that a child viable but in utero, if injured by tort, should, when born, be allowed to sue; and the movement took impetus from the Wisconsin court's statement in the Lipps opinion (supra), that it was restricting its holding (of nonrecovery) to a nonviable child. Thus, when Drobner v Peters came to this court in 1921, there had been no decisions upholding such suits, although the two New York lower court rulings above cited (Nugent and Quinlen cases, supra), were favorable to the position taken by plaintiff here.

In Drobner v Peters (supra), this court, finding no precedent for maintaining the suit, adopted the general theory of Dietrich v Northampton (supra), taking into account, besides the lack of authority to support the suit, the practical difficulties of proof in such cases, and the theoretical lack of separate human existence of an infant in utero. It is not unfair to say that the basic reason for Drobner v Peters was absence of precedent. However, since 1921, numerous and impressive affirmative precedents have been developed. In California (Scott v McPheeters, 33 CalApp2d 629) the Court of Appeals allowed the suit - reliance was there put on a California statute but that statute was not directly in point, since it directed only that "a child conceived, but not yet born, is to be deemed an existing person, so far as may be necessary for its interests in the event of its subsequent birth." That California statute merely codified an accepted and ancient common-law rule (see Stedfast v Nicoll, 3 JohnsCas 18, 23, 24) which, for some reason, has not, at least in our court, been applied to prepartum injuries tortiously inflicted. In 1949, the Ohio Supreme Court (Williams v Marion R.T., Inc., 152 Ohio St 114, rule reaffirmed by the same court in Jasinsky v Potts, 153 Ohio St 529) and Minnesota's highest tribunal (Verkennes v Corniea, 229 Minn 365, and in 1951, the Court of Appeals of Maryland (Damasiewica v Gorsuch, ___ Md ___, 79 A2d 550) and the Supreme Court of Georgia (Tucker v Carmichael, 208 Ga 201) upheld the right of an infant to bring an action like the one we are here examing, without statutory authorization. The Supreme Court of Canada had announced the same rule in 1933 (Montreal Tramways v Leveille, (1933) 4 DomLRep 337). In New Jersey a strong five-to-ten dissent (written by the Chief Justice unsuccessfully urged the same view (Stemmer v Kline, 128 NJL 455(1942)). In England there seems to be no controlling precedent (see Professor Winfield's comprehensive article in 4 U. of Toronto L.J. (1941-1942) 285 et seq.). Of law review articles on the precise question there is an ample supply (see 20 Minn. LR (Feb. 1936) 321-322; 34 Minn LR (Dec., 1949) 65066; 48 Mich. LR (Feb., 1950) 539-541; 35 Cornell LQ (Spring, 1950) 648-654; 1951 Wis LR (May) 518-528; 50 Mich. LR (Nov., 1951) 166-167). They justify the statement in Prosser on Torts, at page 190, that: "All writers who have discussed the problem have joined in condemning the existing rule, in maintaining that the unborn child in the path of an automobile is as much a person in the street as the mother, and urging that recovery should be allowed upon proper proof."

What, then, stands in the way of a reversal here? Surely, as an original proposition, we would, today, be hard put to it to find a sound reason for the old rule. Following Drobner v Peters (supra) would call for an affirmance but the chief basis for that holding (lack of precedent) no longer exists. And it is not a very strong reason, anyhow, in a case like this. Of course, rules of law on which men rely in their business dealings should not be changed in the middle of the game, but what has that to do with bringing to justice a tort-feasor who surely has no moral or other right to rely on a decision of the New York Court of Appeals? Negligence law is common law, and the common law has been molded and changed and brought up-to-date in many another case. Our court said, long ago, that it had not only the right, but the duty to re-examine a question where justice demands it (Rumsey v New York & N. E. R. R. Co. 133 NY 79, 85, 86, and see Klein v Maravelas, 219 NY 383). That opinion notes that Chancellor Kent, more than a century ago, had stated that upwards of a thousand cases could then be pointed out in the English and American reports " 'which had been overruled, doubted or limited in their application' ", and that the great Chancellor had declared that decisions which seem contrary to reason " 'ought to be examined without fear, and revised without reluctance, rather than to have the character of our law impaired, and the beauty and harmony of the system destroyed by the perpetuity of error.' " And Justice Sutherland, writing for the Supreme Court in Funk v United States (290 US 371, 382), said that while legislative bodies have the power to change old rules of law, nevertheless, when they fail to act, it is the duty of the court to bring the law into accordance with present day standards of wisdom and justice rather than "with some outworn and antiquated rule of the past". No reason appears why there should not be the same approach when traditional common-law rules of negligence result in injustice (see Hagopian v Samuelson, 236 AD 491, 492, and see Justice Stone's article on "The Common Law in the United States", 50 HarLR (1936), pp. 4-7).

The sum of the argument against plaintiff here is that there is no New York decision in which such a claim has been enforced. Winfield's answer to that (see U. of Toronto L. J. article, supra, p. 29) will serve: "If that were a valid objection, the common law would now be what it was in the Plantagenet period." And we can borrow from our British friends another mot: "When these ghosts of the past stand in the path of justice clanking their mediaeval chains the proper course for the judge is to pass through them undeterred" (Lord Atkin in United Australia, Ltd., v Barclay's Bank, Ltd. (1941) AC 1, 29). We act in the finest common-law tradition when we adapt and alter decisional law to produce common-sense justice.

The same answer goes to the argument that the change we here propose should come from the Legislature, not the courts. Legislative action there could, of course, be, but we abdicate our own function, in a field peculiarly nonstatutory, when we refuse to reconsider an old and unsatisfactory court-made rule. Perhaps, some kinds of changes in the common law could not safely be made without the kind of factual investigation which the Legislature and not the courts, is equipped for. Other proposed changes require elaborate research and consideration of a variety of possible remedies - such questions are peculiarly appropriate for Law Revision Commission scrutiny, and, in fact, the Law Revision Commission had made an elaborate examination of this very problem (1935 Report of N. Y. Law Revision Commission, pp. 449-476). That study was made at the instance of the late Chief Judge Pound of this court and was transmitted to the Legislature by the commission. Although made before the strong trend in favor of recovery had clearly manifested itself, the Law Revision Commission's comments were strongly in favor of the position taken in this opinion. The report, itself, contained no recommendations for legislation on the subject but that apparently was because the commission felt that it was for the courts to deal with this common-law question. At page 465, for instance, the report said: "The common law does not go on the theory that a case of first impression presents a problem of legislative as opposed to judicial power."

Two other reasons for dismissal (besides lack of precedent) are given in Drobner v Peters (supra). The first of those, discussed in many of the other writings on the subject herein cited, has to do with the supposed difficulty of proving or disproving that certain injuries befell the unborn child, or that they produced the defects discovered at birth, or later. Such difficulties there are, of course, and, indeed, it seems to be commonly accepted that only a blow of tremendous force will ordinarily injure a foetus, so carefully does nature insulate it. But such difficulty of proof or finding is not special to this particular kind of lawsuit (and it is beside the point, anyhow, in determining sufficiency of a pleading). Every day in all our trial courts (and before administrative tribunals, particularly the Workmen's Compensation Board) such issues are disposed of, and it is an inadmissible concept that uncertainty of proof can ever destroy a legal right. The questions of causation, reasonable certainty, etc., which will arise in these cases are no different, in kind, from the ones which have arisen in thousands of other negligence cases decided in this State, in the past.

The other objection to recovery here is the purely theoretical one that a foetus in utero has no existence of its own separate from that of its mother, that is, that it is not "a being in esse". We need not deal here with so large a subject. It is to be remembered that we are passing on the sufficiency of a complaint which alleges that this injury occurred during the ninth month of the mother's pregnancy, in other words, to a viable foetus, later born. Therefore, we confine our holding in this case to prepartum injuries to such viable children. Of course such a child, still in the womb is, in one sense, a part of its mother, but no one seems to claim that the mother, in her own name and for herself, could get damages for the injuries to her infant. To hold, as matter of law, that no viable foetus has any separate existence which the law will recognize is for the law to deny a simple and easily demonstrable fact. This child, when injured, was in fact, alive and capable of being delivered and of remaining alive, separate from its mother. We agree with the dissenting Justice below that "To deny the infant relief in this case is not only a harsh result, but its effect is to do reverence to an outmoded, timeworn fiction not founded on fact and within common knowledge untrue and unjustified."(278 AD 913, 914.)

The judgments should be reversed, and the motion denied, with costs in all courts.

LEWIS, J. (dissenting). I agree with the view of a majority of the court that prenatal injury to a child should not go unrequited by the one at fault. If, however, an unborn child is to be endowed with the right to enforce such requital by an action at law, I think that right should not be created by a judicial decision on the facts in a single case. Better, I believe, that the right should be the product of legislative action taken after hearings at which the Legislature can be advised, by the aid of Medical science and research, not only as to the stage of gestation at which a foetus is considered viable, but also as to appropriate means - by time limitation for suit and otherwise - for avoiding abuses which might result from the difficulty of tracing causation from prenatal injury to postnatal deformity.

When, in England, the right - unknown to the common law - was created which permitted suit to recover damages for negligently causing the death of a human being, it was accomplished by legislative action. In our own jurisdiction a similar right of action - carefully limited as to time and by other measures to prevent abuse - has long been the subject of statute law adopted by the process incident to statutory enactment. That same process, in my opinion, is peculiarly appropriate for the solution of the problem now before us where unknown factors abound.

Accordingly, I dissent and vote for affirmance.

Judgments reversed, etc.

BINGHAM v BOARD OF EDUCATION OF OFDEN CITY (1950) 118 Utah 582, 223 P2d 432

(The case appears supra, p. 8)

Sec. 2.62 Representative Persons

1. Administrator
2. Executor
3. Guardian
4. Committee for an Incompetent
5. Receiver
6. Trustee
7. Public Officer
8. Agent
9. and Others

BUCKLAND v GALLUP (1887) 105 NY 453, a40 Hun 61

APPEAL from order of the General Term of the Supreme Court in the fifth judicial department, made April 23, 1886, which reversed an order of Special Term, setting aside a judgment for costs against plaintiff, individually, and amending the judgment so as to direct costs to be paid out of any assets in his hands as administrator.

DANFORTH, J. The plaintiff, describing himself both in the title and body of the complaint as "administrator, etc., of Warren Buckland, deceased, "demanded judgment against the defendant for the sum of $2,000 and costs of the action. The defendant answered, denying the material allegations of the complaint, and upon trial before a referee, had judgment dismissing the complaint, with costs against the plaintiff in his individual capacity. Upon the plaintiff's application the Special Term ordered an amendment so that the judgment should direct the costs of the action "to be paid out of any assets in his hands as administrator." Upon appeal to the General Term this order was reversed, and from the order of reversal the plaintiff appeals to this court.

The Special Term regarded the question as controlled by section 1814 of the Code of Civil Procedure, which declares that an action by an executor or administrator "upon a cause of action belonging to him in his representative capacity * * *must be brought by him in his representative capacity," while the General Term looking at the cause of action as one arising out of a transaction which occurred after the testator's death, held that it did not belong to the plaintiff in his representative capacity within the meaning of that section. This difference of opinion necessarily leads to an inquiry whether the cause of action upon which the plaintiff sues is, within the meaning of the Code, one "belonging to him in his representative capacity." That capacity was created by statute to carry into effect the wishes of the decedent, and by virtue of it an executor takes as of the time of the death of the testator, and as it were from his hands, his personal property, so that there is no interval of time when it is not the subject of ownership, by the testator up to the time of his death, and from that moment by the person named, not as an individual, but as a representative. The statute characterizes the property received as assets, requires it to be inventoried, and for those assets so inventoried and for any increase, the executor is to account. It includes, among other things, debts secured by mortgage, bonds, notes and things in action. He and his sureties are liable for the full value of all such property of the deceased, received by the executor and not dully administered, and if the cause of action accrued in the lifetime of the testator, any suit respecting it must be in the name of the executor as such. He then sues in the right of the testator, and can bring such actions only as the testator himself might have maintained.

On the other hand, if an injury to the property, or its conversion happens after the death of the decedent, although before letters are actually issued, or if a contract is made with an executor or an administrator personally, in regard to the effects or money belonging to the decendent, received by a third person after the death, the administrator might sue in his own name, and if in any of these cases he may also sue in his representative character, he is not required to do so. (Valentine v Jackson, 9 Wend(NY) 302...) When he sues in the right of the testator he pays no costs, because the law does not presume him to be sufficiently cognizant of the nature and foundation of the claims he has to assert, and in all these cases it is necessary for him to sue in his representative character, and expressly to name himself executor. (Toller's Law of Exrs., 438.) But if he may bring the action in his private capacity, then if he fails he is liable for costs....

The inquiry then is as to which of these two classes the cause of action in the present case belongs. As already stated, the action is to recover a sum certain. The right to such or any judgment depended upon the following facts: William Buckland died in 1873, leaving real estate worth about $4,000 and a small amount of personal property, all of which he gave, by will, to his wife, Matilda, and appointed her his executrix. She received letters, reduced the estate to possession, paid the testator's debts, sold the real estate, taking in payment one bond and mortgage of $1,000 and one of $4,437.50. The $1,000 bond and mortgage she delivered to the defendant about the time it was executed "in order that he might collect the interest for her and for safekeeping." She sold the other bond and mortgage, and of its proceeds loaned the firm of William Gallup & Co., $2,600, taking the note of that firm therefor. At the time of Matilda's death the note was in the possession of her sister, and she subsequently delivered it to the defendant Gallup, the brother of Matilda. The bonds, mortgages and note were payable by their terms to Matilda Buckland personally and individually. The defendant had no other property in his hands belonging to Matilda, and no property in which the estate of Warren Buckland ever had any interest, unless it was said note and bond and mortgage. These were the plaintiff's facts. He alleged, however, that the property belonged to the estate of Warren Buckland, that the legacies remain unpaid, that after the death of Matilda he was appointed administrator de bonis non with the will annexed of Warren Buckland, and demanded the above property of the defendant, who refused to deliver it. The referee held and decided that the note and bond and mortgage belonged to the estate of Matilda Buckland, and not to the estate of Warren Buckland.

If there is disclosed a cause of action belonging to the plaintiff in his representative capacity, then the order below is wrong, for the conditions do not exist which make him chargeable for mismanagement or bad faith. (Code, Sec. 3246). But on the other hand, merely describing himself as executor, either in the summons or complaint, or both, or saying that he sues in that capacity, will not relieve him from costs incident to an unsuccessful litigation. If on the facts stated in support of the motion there was anything for him to do in his official capacity it was because his predeceddor, Matilda, left some part of the estate of Warren Buckland unadministered. He succeeded to her power and duties only. The course of administration was merely interrupted by her death, and upon his appointment, while he became the legal representative of Warren Buckland, he could only take the estate in the condition in which the executrix left it. So far as any of the goods or effects of the testator remained in specie he, as administrator de bonis non, could take them, but this rule applies to such only as are distinguishable. He was bound by her contracts, and if he sues for the proceeds, or upon any promise made to her, he can occupy no different position. She sold the property and loaned a portion of the proceeds, and as to another part she put it in the hands of the defendant, as her agent, in each case, upon the plaintiff's construction of the will, necessarily remaining liable to the estate she represented and liable to account for the whole. I am unable to see that the case differs at all from the one cited. (Thompson v Whitmarsh, supra 100 NY 35).

The learned counsel concedes that had an action been commenced by Matilda "it must of course have been commenced in her own name," but he puts this admission upon the fact that she, "in her own right and as an individual, owned the property." If she did, and such is indeed the plain reading of the will, as well as the judgment of the court, obviously the plaintiff could have no right of action in any capacity. It is only on the supposition that it was part of the estate of Warren Buckland that he has any standing in the litigation. But confessedly the property, as it came from Buckland's estate, was changed in form, converted into money and transferred by the act and agreement of his then executrix, the plaintiff's predecessor. She converted the assets, and had become (if any liability at all was created) personally liable for them. She stood exactly in Thompson's position in the case referred to, and reached that position by the same method of business. In no view can the cause of action then created or as it is stated in the complaint, be said to be one belonging to the plaintiff in his representative capacity. It did not come to him by devolution from the testator. As the plaintiff, therefore, need not have sued in his representative character, and has failed, he is personally liable to pay costs.

The order appealed from is to that effect and should be affirmed.

Order affirmed.

Sec. 2.63 Collective Persons

1. Partnerships
2. Corporations
3. Unincorporated Associations
4. A State in the U.S.
5. The U.S.
6. A Foreign State
7. and Others

McMAHON v RAUHR (1871) 47 NY 67, r3 Daly 116

The plaintiffs and their assignors, together with the defendants herein, were members of an unincorporated association, known as the "Mutual Plaesure Club," a voluntary association for mutual recreation in boating and yachting. The club contracted with the defendant, Rauhr, who was its commodore, for a pleasure boat, which Rauhr agreed to build for $1,000. The boat was built, and $500 paid by the club to Rauhr on account thereof. After the boat was launched it was found defective, and Rauhr, on being informed of this, agreed to build the club a new boat. He did not build the new boat. This action was brought in the Marine Court of the city of New York, to recover back the $500, in the names of the present plaintiffs, as members of the club, and as assignees of all its other members, except the four defendants, Rauhr, McGrady, Richardson and Haviland, the last three of whom were made defendants because they refused to join in the assignment to the Plaintiffs, or in the suit as plaintiffs.

The defendant, in his answer and on the trial, objected that the action could not be maintained by the plaintiffs against the defendant, Rauhr, on the ground that the defendant was equally interested in the subject-matter of the action with the plaintiffs and their assignors, and was their co-partner in respect to said subject-matter, and that the defendants McGrady, Richardson and Haviland, should have been joined as plaintiffs in the action. The court overruled the objection, and on the conclusion of the trial the jury, under the charge of the court, found a verdict for the plaintiffs, against the defendants, for $500, the entire amount paid by the club to Rauhr....

FOLGER, J. The parties to this action are members with other persons of a voluntary association not incorporated. The object of the association is innocent pleasure, and not trade buisness adventure or profit. It is not strictly a copartnership, for it does not in its objects fall within the definition of one. (3 Kent, 23; Collyer, 263.) But the rights of the associates in the property, and the modes of enforcing them are not materially different from those of partners in the partnership property. (Beaumont v Meridith, 3 Vesey & Beames, 180.) Prima facie the interest of each associate in the property and effects of the association is equal or proportionate. No associate has an interest therein which can be separated and taken out of the whole for his sole use, until the joint affairs are settled, the association dissolved, the mutual rights of the members adjusted, and the ultimate share of each determined. It follows then that in any agreement made by a contracting party with the association as such, and in any right of action arising thereon, each associate has an interest, but no associate has an interest which he can so transfer, as that an action can be maintained by his assignee in his own name against the contractor with the association. The agreement and the right of action upon it, and the result of an action are the property of the association as such, and there is no separate ownership by an individual associate, save in the residuum after the liabilities of the association are discharged. The right of action claimed in this case was upon an express agreement of the defendant Rauhr, with the association as a body. The plaintiffs claimed to have the right of action, as original owners of four interests therein; and as the assignees of others of the associates, of whom the defendant Rauhr was not one. The association did not as a body, through any officers or agents thereto authorized, assign and transfer to the plaintiffs, nor did all the associates as individuals assign and transfer. The four interests which the plaintiffs owned, and the greater number which were assigned to them, were not so many parts of the agreement and right of action upon it nor of the results of the action. All which they owned, and all that which they got by the assignment was something indefinite and unascertained, and not to be ascertained until the affairs of their association were closed. It was nothing which they could enforce as plaintiffs in an action on this agreement against the defendant Rauhr. It is evident then, that the plaintiffs had no right of action which they could enforce in their own behalf against the defendant Rauhr. Nor can the judgment be upheld as one in an action to enforce, in behalf of the association against Rauhr, the agreement made with it by him. Such an action cannot be maintained in a court not of jurisdiction in equity. For no number of members short of the whole, can sue on a cause of action belonging to it. (Habict v Pemberton, 4 Sandf., S.C., 658.) Still less can they at law sue another member. The defendant Rauhr has as great an interest in the subject-matter as any other of the associates. On this theory of the action, he is one of those in whose behalf it is brought. And yet it is brought against him, and the judgment is against him, and in favor of four in their own right.

The judgment is erroneous. The nonsuit should have been granted on the ground stated in the motion therefor, that the defendant Rauhr was equally interested in the subject-matter with the plaintiffs. A court of equitable jurisdiction with all the parties before it might have granted appropriate relief...

Judgment reversed.

SAXER v DEMOCRATIC COUNTY COMMITTEE (SpCtErie Co. 1936) 161 M 35, 291 S 18

Supplementary proceedings by John P. Saxer and another against the Democratic County Committee of Erie County, wherein Edward C. Dethloff and another filed a motion for an order quashing subpoenaes on them.

MALONEY, Justice. Edward C. Dethloff and George F. Pfeiffer, individually and as chairman and treasurer respectively of the Democratic County Committee of Erie County, move this court for an order vacating, quashing, and setting aside subpoenaes served herein upon them. The chairman and treasurer aforesaid were duly elected April 8, 1936, at a meeting of the County Committee chosen at the primary election held April 2, 1936.

Frank J. Carr and Charles F. Boine were elected respectively chairman and treasurer of the predecessor County Committee at a meeting of said committee held following the primary election of September, 1934.

A judgment was obtained and entered and docketed in the office of the clerk of the county of Erie, N.Y., in favor of John P. Saxer and Raymond F. Pfeiffer against the Democratic County Committee of Erie County in the sum of $3,319.62 on the 6th day of May, 1936. Service of the summons and complaint was made April 8, 1936, upon Charles F. Boine, treasurer of the Democratic County Committee of Erie County prior to the organization meeting of the present County Committee. Admittedly the judgment was obtained against the County Committee for work, labor, services, and materials furnished to the then County Committee prior to December 1, 1935. Neither Mr. Dethloff nor Mr. Pfeiffer was an officer of the County Committee at the time.

The subpoenaes herein are directed to the judgment debtor the Democratic County Committee of Erie County in the matter of supplementary proceedings as provided in the Civil Practice Act, Art. 45, Sec. 775, and served upon Edward C. Dethloff and George F. Pfeiffer, directing each of them to appear and be examined on October 22, 1936, before a justice of the Supreme Court at a Special Term of said court held in and for the county of Erie.

The summons and complaint as shown by the judgment roll is entitled as follows: "State of New York, Supreme Court, County of Erie. John P. Saxer and Raymond F. Pfeiffer, Plaintiffs, vs. Frank J. Carr, Chairman, Phillip J. Barr, Secretary, Charles F. Boine, Treasurer, and Daniel J. Sweeney, Chairman of the Board of Governors of the Democratic County Committee of Erie County, and The Democratic County Committee of Erie County, Defendants."

Article 2 of the Election Law, Sec. 10-17, provides for the creation and existence of party committees of political organization. Section 10 defines the membership of such committees and that committee membership shall continue until their successors are chosen as therein provided. Section 13 provides that members of the County Committee shall be elected annually at primary elections except that if the rules so provide they may be elected biennially. Section 15 provides the time that officers of a county committee shall be elected.

A county committee created as provided in the Election Law is an unincorporated association. Cabana v Carr, etc., opinion by Larkin, J., not reported. An unincorporated association is not a legal entity and has no existence independent of the associates who are members. Ostrom v Greene, 161 NY 353, 361, 55 NE 919. At common law an unincorporated association cannot maintain an action in its name, but must sue in the names of all the associates as party plaintiff. McMahon v Rauhr, 47 NY 67, 71. At common law an unincorporated association cannot be sued in its name, but all the associates must be made parties defendant. (Sander v Edling, 13 Daly(NY) 238...)

Section 12 of the General Associations Law, formerly the Joint Stock Association Law, provides that the president or treasurer of an unincorporated association may maintain an action to recover upon any cause of action for or upon which all the associates may maintain such an action.

Section 13 provides that an action may be sustained against the president or treasurer of an unincorporated association to recover upon any cause of action for or upon which the plaintiff may maintain such action against all the associates.

Section 12 and 13 aforesaid are the same as former section 1919 of the Code of Civil Procedure except that chapter 609 of the Laws of 1932 effective April 2, 1932, struck out the words "consisting of seven or more members" which were originally contained in section 1919 of the Code, and in the General Associations Law as originally enacted by chapter 915 of the Laws of 1920. Cases decided prior to the enactment of the General Associations Law are authorities on the construction and interpretation of that statute.

The Democratic County Committee of Erie County is not and cannot legally be a party defendant. If action be brought as it may be against all of the associates, each of them is a defendant. If action be brought as it may be under section 13, supra, against the president or treasurer of such committee, the defendant is not the committee but is the officer named as such in the summons as the party defendant, in this case the officer served is Charles F. Boine, as treasurer of the Democratic County Committee of Erie County. In the instant case it is sought to have an examintation of the defendant committee. Where an examination of the defendant was sought before trial as an adverse party in an action brought against the president of an unincorporated association, it was held that only the president may be so examined, and not any of the other officers or any of the associates. (McGuffin v Dinsmore, 4 Abb NC(NY) 241...

"Any question as to the right to take the testimony * * * may be raised by a motion to vacate or modify the notice. * * * If the taking of the testimony be not authorized by the provisions of article 29 the court shall vacate the notice." (Civil Practice Act, Sec. 291...)

The subpoenaes served upon Messrs. Dethloff and Pfeiffer are directed to the Democratic County Committee of Erie County as judgment debtor. The subpoeneas are not directed to, nor do they name Mr. Dethloff or Mr. Pfeiffer individually or officially. The subpoenaes are invalid and not merely informal or irregular. The legal judgment debtor is Charles F. Boine, as treasurer of the Democratic County Committee of Erie County. A subpoena to examine the legal judgment debtor may be legally issued. A subpoena directed to the judgment debtor County Committee may not be legally issued and is therefore invalid.

The motion to quash, set aside, and vacate the subpoenaes served on Edward C. Dethloff and George F. Pfeiffer is granted without costs.

Sec. 2.64 Artificial Persons
1. A Res e.g. a boat
2. and Others

PEOPLE v THREE BARRELS FULL (1923) 236 NY 175, r203 AD 577

APPEAL, by permission, from a judgment of the Appellate Division of the Supreme Court in the first judicial department, entered December 7, 1922, unanimously affirming a judgment entered upon an order of the court at a Trial Term dismissing the above-entitled proceeding.

CARDOZO, J. The controversy before us has to do with an award of costs.

A peace officer of the city of New York seized intoxicating liquors, held, as he charged, in violation of law. He made return of his proceedings in accordance with the statute to a judge who was authorized to issue a warrant (Code Crim. Pro. Sec. 802-b, subd. 6). Thereupon demand for the return of the property was made by the owner, one Russato, who served an answer denying the legality of the seizure. "If such answer is interposed, the issue thus framed shall be deemed an action pending in the court of the judge or justice who issued the warrant, between the people of the State of New York and the liquor so seized and maybe entitled in the name of the said State and against the liquor so seized, adding for identification the name of the person or persons interposing such answer and claiming or defending the liquor so seized, and shall be tried in said court as other issues of fact are tried therein" (Code Crim. Pro. Sec. 802-b, subd. 2). Upon the determination of the issue in favor of the claimant, the liquors are to be returned. Upon its determination in favor of the people, the liquors are to be destroyed, or, in the discretion of the judge, may be sold for restricted purposes, in which event the proceeds of the sale are to be "paid over and accounted for to the treasurer of the county" (Code Crim. Pro. Sec. 802-b). In this case, the issue was determined in favor of the claimant. The charge was dismissed, and costs were awarded against the People of the state. A controversy ensued between the state and the county, each insisting by its representative that the burden of the costs should be borne by the other. The Appellate Division, concurring with the trial judge, held in favor of the county. The case comes to this court after the allowance of an appeal.

We find it unnecessary to choose between the contention of the state and that of its civil subdivision. Our judgment is that costs are not chargeable against either of them. The proceeding is in rem, not against the owner or possessor, but against the thing itself, which is treated as the real offender (People v Diamond, 233 NY 130, 135; Goldsmith-Grant Co. v U.S., 254 US 505). The section of the Code of Criminal Procedure which creates the remedy and defines it, is a section of part VI, entitled "Special Proceedings of a Criminal Nature." Costs are not awarded in actions or proceedings conducted under the Criminal Code (People ex rel. N.Y. Society, etc., v Gilmore, 88 NY 626). Even in actions or proceedings strictly civil, they owe their origin to statute, and do not exist without it (Cassidy v McFarland, 139 NY 201, 208). This statute does not give the right to costs in terms. We see no reason to believe that the right exists by implication. A special proceeding of a criminal nature (Code Crim. Pro. Sec. 950), initiated by the issue of a warrant, or by search and seizure, ripens, upon the service of an answer, into something which is to be tried after the manner of a civil action (Lilienthal's Tobacco v U.S., 97 US 237, 267; U.S. v Regan, 232 US 37). The trial over, it is to be the criminal code that we must look to ascertain the nature of the relief and the provisions of the judgment. Looking there (Code Crim. Pro. Sec. 802-b), we find minute directions as to what the judgment shall contain. We find nothing to the effect that it shall embody an award of costs. The owner would not have been chargeable with costs if he had lost. He may not charge them on his adversaries now that he has won.

The judgment of the Appellate Division and that of the Trial Term should be reversed.

Judgment reversed.

CHAPTER III

THE ADJECTIVE LAW

SUGGESTED READINGS:

Bowman: Elementary Law
- Ch. 7, Sec. 60-64 "Adjective Law", pp. 116-118
- Ch. 10, "Beginnings of the Common Law," pp. 152-169
- Ch's. 11-12, "Development of the Common Law," pp. 170-193
- Ch. 13, "Maturity of the Common Law," pp. 194-204
- Ch. 14, "The Common Law in the United States," pp. 205-216
- Ch's. 16-17, "The Common Law Actions," pp. 239-274
- Ch. 18, "Equity", pp. 275-297

Dowling, P. and P.: Legal Method
- Ch. II Sec. 3, "Procedure and Its Importance"

Fryer and Benson: Legal Method and Systems
- Ch. 2, "Actions at Law," pp. 143-210

SUGGESTED READINGS - Cont'd.

Gavit: Introduction to Study of Law
- Ch. VII, "Procedure", pp. 254-315
- Ch. VIII, "Common Law Forms of Action and Equity", pp. 316-370

Griffth: Outlines of the Law
- Ch. XIX, "Civil Procedure", pp. 567-637
- Ch. XX, "Criminal Procedure", pp. 638-657
- Ch. XXI, "Evidence", pp. 658-695

Karlen: Primer of Procedure
- Ch. I-XV (generally on Adjective Law) pp. 1-172
- Appendices pp. 175-516

Kinnane: Anglo-American Law
- Part II, Ch's. 7-15, Origin and Development, pp. 166-442
- Ch's. 19-21, "The...Lawsuit", pp. 520-607
- Ch. 22, "The Common Law Actions and Remedies", pp. 608-639
- Ch. 23, "...Equitable Remedies", pp. 640-660
- Ch. 24, "Extraordinary and Statutory Remedies", pp. 661-689

Maitland: "History of the Register of Original Writs"
- 3 Har. L.R., pp. 97-115; 167-179; 212-225
- 2 Select Essays in Anglo-American Legal History, pp. 549-596 (reprint)

Morgan: Study of Law
- Ch. IV, "Procedure", pp. 57-58
- Ch. V, "Forms of Action", pp. 79-115
- Ch. VI, "Pleadings", pp. 116-150
- Appendix - (forms) pp. 327-343

Plucknett: Concise History of the Common Law
- Book II, Part I, "Procedure", pp. 317-369
- Book II, Part II, Ch. 1, "Criminal Procedure", pp. 377-391

Radin: Anglo-American Legal History
- Ch. 15, "The System of Writs", pp. 179-189
- Ch. 16, "The Growth of Procedure", pp. 190-203
- Ch. 17, "The Jury Inquest", pp. 204-218
- Ch. 18, Sec. A, "Criminal Procedure", pp. 219-234

Smith: Elementary Law
- Ch. 21, "Remedies", pp. 341-362
- Ch. 23, "Procedure", pp. 384-414
- Ch. 24, "Trials", pp. 415-421

Sec. 3.10 CONSTITUTIONAL and STATUTORY provisions

N.Y. CONSTITUTION

Article VI - Judiciary (Unified court system for state established; organizations; courts of record; service and execution of process.)

Sec. 1. a. There shall be a unified court system for the state. The statewide courts shall consist of the court of appeals, the supreme court including the appellate divisions thereof, the court of claims, the county court, the surrogate's court and the family court, as hereinafter provided. The legislature shall establish in and for the city of New York, as part of the unified court system for the state, a single, city-wide court of civil jurisdiction and single, city-wide court of criminal jurisdiction, as hereinafter provided, and may upon the request of the mayor and the local legislative body of the city of New York, merge the two courts into one city-wide court of both civil and criminal jurisdiction. The unified court system for the state shall also include the district, town, city and village courts outside the city of New York, as hereinafter provided.

b. The court of appeals, the supreme court including the appellate divisions thereof, the court of claims, the county court, the surrogate's court, the family court, the courts or court of civil and criminal jurisdiction of the city of New York, and such other courts as the legislature may determine shall be courts of record.

c. All processes, warrants and other mandates of the court of appeals, the supreme court including the appellate divisions thereof, the court of claims, the county court, the surrogate's court and the family court may be served and executed in any part of the state. All processes, warrants and other mandates of the courts or court of civil and criminal jurisdiction of the city of New York may, subject to such limitation as may be prescribed by the legislature, be served and executed in any part of the state. The legislature may provide that processes, warrants and other mandates of the district court may be served and executed in any part of the state and that processes, warrants and other mandates of town, village and city courts outside the city of New York may be served and executed in any part of the county in which such courts are located or in any part of any adjoining county.

(Court of Appeals continued; organization; judges.)
Sec. 2. a. The court of appeals is continued. It shall consist of...
Sec. 3. a. The jurisdiction of the court of appeals shall be limited to the review of questions of law except...

(Judicial departments; appellate divisions continued; jurisdiction; justices.)
Sec. 4. a. The state shall be divided into four judicial departments...

(Judicial districts; composition; supreme court cont'd; justices of sup.ct.)
Sec. 6. a. The state shall be divided into eleven judicial districts. The first judicial district shall consist of the counties of Bronx and New York. The second judicial district shall consist of...

(Supreme court; jurisdiction.)
Sec. 7. a. The supreme court shall have general original jurisdiction in law and equity and the appellate jurisdiction herein provided. In the city of New York...

(Court of claims continued; judges; jurisdiction.)
Sec. 9. a. The court of claims is continued. It shall consist of...

(County court continued; judges.)
Sec. 10. a. The county court is continued in each county outside the city of New York. There shall be...

(County court; jurisdiction.)
Sec. 11. a. The county court shall have jurisdiction over the following classes of actions and proceedings which shall be originated in such county court in the manner provided by law, except...

(Surrogate's court continued; judges; jurisdiction.)
Sec. 12. a. The surrogate's court is continued in each county in the state. There shall be...

(Family court established; judges; jurisdiction.)
Sec. 13. a. The family court of the state of New York is hereby established. It shall consist of...
b. The family court shall have jurisdiction over the following classes of actions and proceedings...

(New York city; city-wide courts established; merger; judges; jurisdiction.)
Sec. 15. a. The legislature shall by law establish a single court of city-wide civil jurisdiction and a single court of city-wide criminal jurisdiction in and for the city of New York and the legislature may...

(District courts; establishment; jurisdiction; judges; Nassau co.dist.ct.cont'd)
Sec. 16. a. The district court of Nassau county may be continued under existing law and the legislature may, at the request of the board of supervisors or other elective governing body of any county outside the city of New York, establish the district court for the entire area of such county or for a portion of such county...

(Town, village and city courts; jurisdiction; regulation; judges.)
Sec. 17. a. Courts for towns, villages and cities outside the city of New York are continued and shall have the jurisdiction prescribed by the legislature but not...

(Administrative supervision of court system.)
Sec. 28. The authority and responsibility for the administrative supervision of the unified court system for the state shall be vested in the administrative board of the judicial conference. The administrative board shall consist of the chief judge of the court of appeals, as chairman, and the presiding justices of the appellate divisions of the four judicial departments. The administrative board, in consultation with the judicial conference, shall establish standards and administrative policies for general application throughout the state. The composition and functions of the judicial conference shall be as now or hereafter provided by law. In accordance with the standards and administrative policies established by the administrative board, the appellate divisions shall supervise the administration and operation of the courts in their respective departments.

(Power of legislature respecting jurisdiction and proceedings.)
Sec. 30. The legislature shall have the same power to alter and regulate the jurisdiction and proceedings in law and in equity that it has heretofore exercised. The legislature may, on such terms as it shall provide and subject to subsequent modification, delegate, in whole or in part, to a court, including the appellate division of the supreme court, to the administrative board of the judicial conference, or to the judicial conference, any power possessed by the legislature to regulate practice and procedure in the courts. Nothing herein contained shall prevent the adoption of regulations by individual courts consistent with the general practice and procedure as provided by statute or general rules.

N.Y. JUDICIARY LAW

Article 2. General Provisions Relating to Courts and Judges
Sec. 2. Courts of record
Each of the following courts of the state is a court of record:
1. The court for the trial of impeachments.
2. A court on the judiciary.
3. The court of appeals.
4. The appellate division of the supreme court in each department.

5. The supreme court.
6. The court of claims.
7. A county court in each county, except the counties of New York, Bronx, Kings, Queens and Richmond.
8. The family court.
9. A surrogate's court in each county.
10. The city courts of the cities of Albany, Mt. Vernon, Rochester, Schenectady, Syracuse, Troy, Utica and Yonkers.
11. The district court in each county or portion thereof in which such court shall be established.
12. The civil court of the city of New York and the criminal court of the city of New York.

All courts other than those specified in this section are courts not of record.

Sec. 2. a. Jurisdiction and powers of courts continued.
Each court of the state shall continue to exercise the jurisdiction and powers now vested in it by law, according to the course and practice of the court, except as otherwise prescribed by statute or rules adopted in conformance thereto.

Sec. 2. b. General powers of courts of record
A court of record has power
1. to issue a subpoena requiring the attendance of a person found in the state to testify in a cause pending in that court, subject, however, to the limitations prescribed by law with respect to the portion of the state in which the process of the local court of record may be served;
2. to administer an oath to a witness in the exercise of the powers and duties of the court and;
3. to devise and make new process and forms of proceedings, necessary to carry into effect the powers and jurisdiction possessed by it.

Article 3. Court of Appeals (Sec. 50-62 omitted)

Article 4. Appellate Division.
Sec. 70. Judicial departments. The state is hereby divided into four judicial departments. The first department shall consist of...(Sec. 71-108 ommitted)

Article 4-A Official Referees (Sec. 114-126 omitted)

Article 5 Supreme Court
Sec. 140. Division of state into judicial districts.
The state is hereby divided into (11) judicial districts, pursuant to...

Sec. 140.b. General jurisdiction of supreme court
The general jurisdiction in law and equity which the supreme court possesses under the provisions of the constitution includes all the jurisdiction which was possessed and exercised by the supreme court of the colony of New York at any time, and by the court of chancery in England on the fourth day of July, seventeen hundred seventy-six, with the exceptions, additions and limitations created and imposed by the constitution and laws of the state. Subject to those exceptions and limitations the supreme court of the state has all the powers and authority of each of those courts and may exercise them in like manner. (Sec. 140-c-175 omitted)

Article 6 The Surrogates' Courts (Sec. 178-181 omitted)

Article 6-A County Judges and Surrogates (Sec. 182-189-g omitted)

Article 7 County Court
Sec. 190 Jurisdiction of county court
The jurisdiction of each county court, except the county courts of counties within the city of New York, extends to the following actions and special proceedings, in addition to the jurisdiction, power and authority conferred upon a county court in a particular case by...(Sec. 193-208 omitted)

Article 7-A Judicial Administration

Sec. 210 Administrative board

1. The administrative board of the judicial conference shall consist of the chief judge of the court of appeals and the presiding justices of the appellate divisions of the four judicial departments. The chief judge of the court of appeals shall also be the chief judge of the state of New York and shall be the chief judicial officer of the unified court system established by article six of the constitution. He shall be the chairman of the administrative board and chairman of the judicial conference.

2. The members of the administrative board shall serve without compensation but shall be reimbursed for their traveling and other expenses...

Sec. 211 State administrator

1. Administrative board shall appoint upon the nomination of the chairman, and at pleasure may remove, a state administrator and fix his compensation within the appropriation made available therefor. Such state administrator, subject to the supervision and control of the administrative board shall exercise such duties as may be assigned to him by the administrative board. The state administrator shall act as secretary to the adminstrative board and secretary to the judicial conference.

2. The state administrator, with the approval of the administrative board, shall appoint and may at pleasure remove such deputies, assistants, counsel and employees as may be deemed necessary and fix their salaries within the appropriation made available therefor.

Sec. 212 Functions of the administrative board (Sec. 212-235 omitted)

Article 8 Clerks (Sec. 250-288 omitted)
Article 9 Stenographers (Sec. 290-319 omitted)
Article 10 Attendants, Officers and Messengers (Sec. 340-355 omitted)
Article 11 Criers (Sec. 360-367 omitted)
Article 12 Interpreters (Sec. 380-391 omitted)
Article 13 Sheriffs and Constables (Sec. 400-413 omitted)
Article 14 Law Reporting (Sec. 430-456 omitted)
Article 15 Attorneys and Counsellors (Sec. 460-480 omitted)
Article 16 Jurors in counties of less than one hundred thousand population (Sec. 500-531 omitted)
Article 17 Jurors in counties within cities having a population of one million or more (Sec. 590-609 omitted)
Article 18 Jurors in counties outside cities having a population of one million or more (Sec. 650-686 omitted)
Article 19 Comtempts (750-781 omitted)
Article 20 Collection of Fines (Sec. 790-797 omitted)
Article 20-A Remission of Fines and Forfeitures (798-799 omitted)
Article 21 Court and Law Libraries (Sec. 810-848 omitted)

COURT OF CLAIMS ACT

Article 1 The Court, Judges and Officers (Sec. 1 omitted)

Sec. 2 The court of claims is hereby continued. Such court shall consist of... (Sec. 3-7 omitted)

Article 2 Jurisdiction

Sec. 8 Waiver of immunity from liability

The state hereby waives its immunity from liability and action and hereby assumes liability and consents to have the same determined in accordance with the same rules of law as applied to actions in the supreme court against individuals....

Sec. 9 Jurisdiction and powers of the court

The court shall have jurisdiction:

1. To hear and determine all matters now pending in the said court of claims.
2. To hear and determine a claim of any person, corporation.... (Sec. 10-30 omitted)

SURROGATE'S COURT ACT

Article 1 The Surrogate and Acting Surrogate (Sec. 1-20 omitted)
Article 2 Officers of the Surrogate's Court (Sec. 21-33 omitted)
Article 3 The Surrogate's Court and Its General Jurisdiction (Sec. 34-39 omitted)
Sec. 40 General jurisdiction of surrogate's court

Each surrogate must hold, within his county, a court, which has, in addition to the powers conferred upon it, or upon the surrogate, by special provision of law, jurisdiction, as follows: To administer justice in all matters relating to the affairs of decendents, and upon the return of any process to try and determine all questions, legal or equitable, arising between any or all of the parties to any proceeding, or between any party and any other person having any claim or interest therein who voluntarily appears in such proceeding, or is brought in by supplemental citation, as to any and all matters necessary to be determined in order to make a full, equitable and complete disposition of the matter by such order or decree as justice requires.... (Sec. 41-47 omitted)
Articles (4-19 omitted)

FAMILY COURT ACT

Article 1 Family Court Established
Sec. 111 Title of act

The title of this act is "the family court act of the state of New York." It may be cited as "The Family Court Act."

Sec. 112 Applicability

The family court act applies in all counties of the state of New York.

Sec. 113 Establishment of court

The family court of the state of New York is established in each county of the state as part of the unified court system for the state.

Sec. 114 "Exclusive original jurisdiction"

When used in this act "exclusive original jurisdiction" means that the proceedings over which the family court is given such jurisdiction must be originated in the family court in the manner prescribed by this act. The provisions of this act shall in no way limit or impair the jurisdiction of the supreme court as set forth in section seven of article six of the constitution of the state of New York.

Sec. 115 Jurisdiction of family court

(a) The family court has exclusive original jurisdiction over

(i) neglect proceedings, as set forth in article three;

(ii) support proceedings, as set forth in article four;

(iii) proceedings to determine paternity and for the support of children born out-of-wedlock, as set forth in article five;

(iv) proceedings permanently to terminate custody of a child by reason of permanent neglect, as set forth in part one or article six;

(v) proceedings concerning juvenile delinquency and whether a person is in need of supervision, as set forth in article seven; and

(vi) family offenses proceedings, as set forth in article eight. (Sec. 116-1076 omitted)

Articles 2-10 (omitted)

UNIFORM DISTRICT COURT ACT

Article 1 Organization

Sec. 101 Short title. This act shall be known as the uniform district court act, and may be cited as "UDCA".

Sec. 102 Application of UDCA; court of record; seal

The jurisdiction of and practice and procedure in each district court governed by the UDCA shall be as prescribed herein, and such court shall be a court of record and a part of the unified court system for the state. Such court in each county shall have an official seal to be furnished by the county upon which shall be engraved the words "District Court of (insert name of county), New York, Seal".

Sec. 103 Judges (a) In each judicial district there shall be elected such number of judges as may be provided by law... (Sec. 105-106 omitted)

Article 2 Jurisdiction

Sec. 201 Jurisdiction; in general.

The court shall have jurisdiction as set forth in this article and as elsewhere provided by law. The phrase "$6,000", whenever it appears herein, shall be taken to mean "$6,000 exclusive of interest and costs". (Sec. 202-2103 omitted)

(Articles 3-22 omitted)

Article 23 Application (to counties Nassau and Suffolk) (Sec. 2300-2613 omitted)

UNIFORM JUSTICE COURT ACT

Article 1 - Organization	(Sec. 101-111 omitted)
Article 2 - Jurisdiction	(Sec. 201-213 omitted)
Article 4 - Summons	(Sec. 401-411 omitted)
Article 7 - Mandates	(Sec. 701 omitted)
Article 8 - Provisional Remedies	(Sec. 801 omitted)
Article 9 - Pleadings	(Sec. 901-910 omitted)
Article 10 - Motions	(Sec. 1001-1004 omitted)
Article 11 - Disclosure	(Sec. 1101-1102 omitted)
Article 12 - Subpoenas	(Sec. 1201 omitted)
Article 13 - Trial	(Sec. 1301-1307 omitted)
Article 14 - Judgment	(Sec. 1401-1403 omitted)
Article 15 - Execution	(Sec. 1501-1507 omitted)
Article 17 - Appeals	(Sec. 1701-1706 omitted)
Article 19 - Costs and fees	(Sec. 1900-1913 omitted)
Article 20 - Criminal Jurisdiction and procedure	(Sec. 2001-2020 omitted)
Article 21 - General	(Sec. 2101-2104 omitted)
Article 22 - Transition	(Sec. 2203-2204 omitted)
Article 23 - Application	(Sec. 2300-2301 omitted)

N.Y. CITY CIVIL COURT ACT

Article 1 Organization

Sec. 101 Short title. This act shall be known as the New York city civil court act, and may be cited as "CCA".

Sec. 102 Court established. The civil court of the city of New York is hereby established as a single city-wide court... (Sec. 103-109 omitted)

Article 2 Jurisdiction

Sec. 201 Jurisdiction; in general

The court shall jurisdiction as set forth in this article and as elsewhere provided by law. The phrase "$10,000" whenever it appears herein, shall be taken to mean "$10,000" exclusive of interest and costs." (Sec. 202-2300 omitted)

N.Y. CITY CRIMINAL COURT ACT

Article 1 Short Title; Definitions (Sec. 1-2 omitted)

Article 2 Organization and Administration

Sec. 20 The court constituted. The criminal court of the city of New York is hereby established as a single, city-wide court... (Sec. 21-23 omitted)

Article 3 Jurisdiction and Powers

Sec. 30 Judges are magistrates. The judges of the court are magistrates and shall have and exercise all the jurisdiction and powers, not inconsistent with this act, which are conferred by law upon magistrates...

Sec. 31 Jurisdiction. The court and the judges thereof, except as otherwise provided in this act, shall have jurisdiction with respect to crimes and offenses committed within the city of New York, as follows:

1. To hear, try, and determine all charges of misdemeanor, except charges of libel;
2. To hear, try, and determine all offenses of a grade less than misdemeanor. (sec. 32-102 omitted)

CIVIL PRACTICE LAW AND RULES

Article 1 Short Title; Applicability and Definitions

Sec. 101 Short title application. This chapter shall be known as the civil practice law and rules and may be cited as "CPLR"...

Sec. 102 Amendment, rescission or adoption of rules.

The civil practice rules are herein designated "rule". Any rule in this chapter may be amended, or rescinded, or additional civil practice rules may be adopted, not inconsistent with the constitution or statutes, pursuant to subdivision three of section two hundred twenty-nine of the judiciary law, or by act of the legislature. No rule so amended, rescinded or adopted shall abridge or enlarge the substantive rights of any party.

Sec. 103 Form of civil judicial proceedings

(a) One form of action. There is only one form of civil action. The distinctions between actions at law and suits in equity, and the forms of those actions and suits, have been abolished.

(b) Action or special proceeding. All civil judicial proceedings shall be prosecuted in the form of an action, except where prosecution in the form of a special proceeding is authorized. Except where otherwise prescribed by law, procedure in special proceedings shall be the same as in actions, and the provisions of the civil practice law and rules applicable to actions shall be applicable to special proceedings.

(c) Improper form. If a court has obtained jurisdiction over the parties, a civil judicial proceeding shall not be dismissed solely because it is not brought in the proper form, but the court shall make whatever order is required for its proper prosecution. (Sec. 104-106 omitted)

Article 5-Venue (Sec. 501-512 omitted)

(Articles 2-100 omitted)

CODE OF CRIMINAL PROCEDURE

Preliminary Provisions (Sec. 1-10-h omitted)

Part I - Of The Courts Having Original Jurisdiction in Criminal Actions Titles I-VI, (Sec. 11-77 omitted)
Titles I-VI, (Sec. 11-78 omitted)

Part II - Of the Prevention of Crime
Titles I-II, (Sec. 79-117-f omitted)

Part III- Of Judicial Proceedings for the Removal of Public Officers, By Impeachment, or Otherwise
Titles I-II, (Sec. 118-132 omitted)

Part IV - Of the Proceedings in Criminal Actions Prosecuted by Indictment
Titles I-XII, (Sec. 133-698 omitted)

Part V - Of proceedings in Courts of Special Sessions and Police Courts
Titles I -III, (Sec. 699-772 omitted)

Part VI - Of Special Proceedings of a Criminal Nature
Titles I-XIV, (Sec. 773-952-y omitted)

General Provisions and Definitions Applicable to This Code (Sec. 953-963 omitted)

REAL PROPERTY ACTIONS AND PROCEEDINGS LAW

Article 1 Short title; Definitions; Jurisdiction of Certain Actions; Construction of Act (Sec. 101-131 omitted)
Article 2 General Provisions Governing Real Property Actions (Sec. 201-241 omitted)
Article 3 Provisions Relating to Evidence (Sec. 301-351 omitted)
Article 4 Valuing Interests in Real Property (Sec. 401-406 omitted)
Article 5 Adverse Possession (Sec. 501-551 omitted)
Article 6 Action to Recover Real Property (Sec. 601-661 omitted)
Article 7 Summary Proceeding to Recover Possession of Real Property (Sec. 701-767 omitted)
Article 8 Waste and Other Actions and Rights of Action for Injury to Real Property (Sec. 801-871 omitted)
Article 9 Action for Partition (Sec. 901-992 omitted)
Article 10 Action for Dower (Sec. 1001-1093 omitted)
Article 11 Proceeding to Discover the Death of a Tenant for Life (Sec. 1101-1143 omitted)
Article 12 Other Actions and Proceedings Between Co-Owners or Owners of Successive Interests (Sec. 1201-1221 omitted)

Article 13 Action to Foreclose a Mortgage (Sec. 1301-1391 omitted)
Article 14 Foreclosure of Mortgage by Advertisement (Sec. 1401-1461 omitted)
Article 15 Action to Compel the Determination of a Claim to Real Property (Sec. 1501-1551 omitted)
Article 16 Judicial Authorization of Sale, Lease, Mortgage, Acquisition, Exchange or Voluntary Partition (Sec. 1601-1651 omitted)
Article 17 Special Proceedings for Disposition of Real Property of Infant or Incompetent (Sec. 1701-1766 omitted)
Article 18 Enforcement of Covenants and Easements; Recovery of Damages for Breach of Covenant or Injury to Easements (Sec. 1801 omitted)
Article 18 Special Proceeding for Release of Claims against State of Infant or Incompetent for Appropriation of Real Property (Sec. 1801-1808 omitted)
Article 19 Discharge or Extinguishment of Encumbrances, Claims and Interests (Sec. 1901-1955 omitted)
Article 21 Effective Date; Laws Repealed (Sec. 2101-2111 omitted)

DOMESTIC RELATIONS LAW

Article VII Adoption
Title 1 Adoptions generally (Sec. 109-111 omitted)
Title 2 Adoption from an authorized agency
Sec. 112 General provisions relating to adoption from authorized agencies (omitted)

Sec. 113 Special provisions relating to adoption from authorized agencies. An authorized agency may consent to the adoption of a minor in its lawful custody. The agreement of adoption shall be executed by such authorized agency. The proceeding shall be instituted in the county where the foster parents reside or, if such foster parents do not reside in this state, in the county where such authorized agency has its principal office. Neither such authorized agency nor any officer or agent thereof need appear before the judge or surrogate. The judge or surrogate in his discretion may accept the report of an authorized agency verified by one of its officers or agents as the report of investigation hereinbefore required. In making orders of adoption the judge or surrogate when practicable must give custody only to persons of the same religious faith as that of the foster child in accordance with article six of the social welfare law.

UNIFORM CITY COURT ACT

Article 1	Organization	(Sec. 101-105 omitted)
Article 2	Jurisdiction	(Sec. 201-213 omitted)
Article 4	Summons	(Sec. 401-411 omitted)
Article 7	Mandates	(Sec. 701 omitted)
Article 8	Provisional remedies	(Sec. 801-802 omitted)
Article 9	Pleadings	(Sec. 901-910 omitted)
Article 10	Motions	(Sec. 1001-1004 omitted)
Article 11	Disclosure	(Sec. 1101-1102 omitted)
Article 12	Subpoenas	(Sec. 1201 omitted)
Article 13	Trial	(Sec. 1301-1307 omitted)
Article 14	Judgment	(Sec. 1401-1403 omitted)
Article 15	Execution	(Sec. 1501-1509 omitted)
Article 17	Appeals	(Sec. 1701-1706 omitted)
Article 18	Small claims	(Sec. 1801-1809 omitted)
Article 19	Costs and fees	(Sec. 1900-1913 omitted)
Article 20	Criminal jurisdiction and procedure	(Sec. 2001-2020 omitted)
Article 21	General	(Sec. 2101-2103 omitted)
Article 22	Transition	(Sec. 2203-2204 omitted)
Article 23	Application	(Sec. 2300-2301 omitted)

U.S. CONSTITUTION

Article III (Federal Courts and Jurisdiction.)

Sec. 1. The judicial Power of the United States, shall be vested in one supreme Court, and in such inferior Courts as the Congress may from time to time ordain and establish. The Judges, both of the supreme and inferior Courts, shall hold their Offices during good Behaviour, and shall, at stated Times receive for their Services a Compensation which shall not be diminshed during their Continuance in Office.

Sec. 2 The judicial Power shall extend to all Cases, in Law and Equity, arising under this Constitution, the Laws of the United States, and Treaties made, or which shall be made, under their Authority; - to all Cases affecting Ambassadors, other public Ministers and Consuls; - to all Cases of admiralty and maritime Jurisdiction; - to Controversies to which the United States shall be a Party; - to Controversies between two or more States; - between a State and Citizens of another State; - between Citizens of different States; - between Citizens of the same State claiming Lands under Grants of different States, and between a State, or the Citizens thereof, and foreign States, Citizens or Subjects.

In all Cases affecting Ambassadors, other public Ministers and Consuls, and those in which a State shall be Party, the supreme Court shall have original Jurisdiction. In all the other Cases before mentioned, the supreme Court shall have appellate Jurisdiction, both as to Law and Fact, with such Exceptions, and under such Regulations as the Congress shall make.

The trial of all Crimes, except in Cases of Impeachment, shall be by Jury; and such Trial shall be held in the State where the said Crimes shall have been committed; but when not committed within any State, the Trial shall be at such Place or Places as the Congress may by Law have directed. . . .

U.S. CODE

Title 28 - Judiciary and Judicial Procedure

Part I - Organization of Courts

Ch.1., Sec. 1. The Supreme Court of the United States shall consist of a Chief Justice of the United States and eight associate justices, any six of whom shall constitute a quorum.

Ch.3., Sec. 41. The eleven judicial circuits of the United States are constituted as follows:

Circuits	Composition
District of Columbia. . .	District of Columbia.
First.	Maine, Massachusetts, New Hampshire, Puerto Rico, Rhode Island.
Second.	Connecticut, New York, Vermont
. . . .	. . . .

Sec. 43 (a) There shall be in each circuit a court of appeals, which shall be a court of record, known as the United States Court of Appeals for the circuit.

Ch.5., Sec. 81-131 (these omitted sections set up 89 federal judicial districts in the 50 states and certain territories of the U.S., each state and territory having one or more districts.)

Ch.14., Conferences and Councils of Judges

Sec. 331 Judicial Conference of the United States. - The Chief Justice of the United States shall summon annually the chief judge of each judicial circuit, the chief judge of the Court of Claims, the chief judge of the Court of Customs and Patent Appeals, and a district judge from each judicial circuit to a conference....

Sec. 332 Judicial councils. - The chief judge of each circuit shall call....a council of the circuit judges for the circuit, in active service, at which he shall preside....

Sec. 333 Judicial conferences of circuits. - The chief judge of each circuit shall summon annually the circuit and district judges of the circuit, in active service and residing within the continental United States, to a conference....

Ch.41., Administrative Office of the United States Courts

Sec. 601 The Administrative Office of the United States Courts shall be maintained at the seat of government. It shall be supervised by a Director and an Assistant Director appointed and subject to removal by the Supreme Court.

Sec. 604 (a) The Director shall be the administrative officer of the courts, and under the supervision and direction of the Judicial Conference of the United States, shall:

(1) Supervise all administrative matters relating to the offices of clerks....

Part II - U.S. Attorneys and Marshals (Sec. 501-556 omitted)

Part III - Court Officers and Employees (Sec. 601-963 omitted)

Part IV - Jurisdiction and Venue

Ch.81., Sec. 1251 (a) The Supreme Court shall have original and exclusive jurisdiction of:

(1) All controversies between two or more States;....

Sec. 1252 Any party may appeal to the Supreme Court from an interlocutory or final judgment, decree or order of any court of the United States...holding an Act of Congress unconstitutional in any civil action, suit, or proceeding to which the United States... is a party....

Sec. 1254 Cases in the courts of appeals may be reviewed by the Supreme Court by the following methods:

(1) By writ of certiorari...
(2) By appeal...
(3) By certification...

Sec. 1257 Final judgments or decrees rendered by the highest court of a State in which decision could be had, may be reviewed by the Supreme Court as follows:....

Ch. 83., Sec. 1291. The courts of appeals shall have jurisdiction of appeals from all final decisions of the district courts of the United States....

Ch. 85., Sec. 1331. Final question; Amount in controversy. The district courts shall have original jurisdiction of all civil actions wherein the matter in controversy exceeds the sum or value of $10,000, exclusive of interest and costs and arises under the Constitution, laws or treaties of the United States.

Sec. 1332. Diversity of citizenship; Amount in controversy.

(a) The district courts shall have original jurisdiction of all civil actions where the matter in controversy exceeds the sum or value of $10,000 exclusive of interest and costs, and is between:

(1) Citizens of different States;....

Sec. 1333. The district courts shall have original jurisdiction, exclusive of the courts of the States, of:

(1) Any civil case of admiralty or maritime jurisdiction, saving to suitors in all cases all other remedies to which they are entitled....

Sec. 1334. The district courts shall have original jurisdiction, exclusive of the courts of the States, of all matters and proceedings in bankruptcy.

Sec. 1335. Interpleader (omitted)
Sec. 1336. Interstate Commerce Commission's orders (omitted)
Sec. 1337. Commerce and anti-trust regulations (omitted)
Sec. 1338. Patents, copyrights, trade-marks, and unfair competition (omitted)
Sec. 1339. Postal matters (omitted)
Sec. 1340. Internal revenue; customs duties (omitted)
Sec. 1341. Taxes by States (omitted)
Sec. 1342. Rate orders of State agencies (omitted)
Sec. 1343. Civil rights and elective franchise (omitted)

....

Ch. 87., Sec. 1391. Venue generally (a) A civil action wherein jurisdiction is founded only on diversity of citizenship may, except as otherwise provided by law, be brought only in the judicial district where all plaintiffs or all defendants reside. (b) A civil action wherein jurisdiction is not founded solely on diversity of citizenship may be brought only in the judicial district where all defendants reside, except as otherwise provided by law. (c) A corporation may be sued in any judicial district in which it is incorporated or licensed to do business or is doing business, and such judicial district shall be regarded as the residence of such corporation for venue purposes. (d) An alien may be sued in any district....

Federal Rules of Civil Procedure (FRCP)

I. Scope of Rules - One Form of Action

Rule 1. These rules govern the procedure in the United States district courts in all suits of a civil nature whether cognizable as cases at law or in equity, with the exceptions stated in Rule 81. They shall be construed to secure the just, speedy, and inexpensive determination of every action.

Rule 2. There shall be one form of action to be known as "civil action".

II. Commencement of Action; Service of Process, Pleadings, Motions, and Orders (Rules 3-6 omitted)
III. Pleadings and Motions (Rules 7-16 omitted)
IV. Parties (Rules 17-25 omitted)
V. Depositions and Discovery (Rules 26-37 omitted)
VI. Trials (Rules 38-53 omitted)

VII. Judgment (Rules 54-63 omitted)
VIII. Provisional and Final Remedies and Special Proceedings (Rules 64-71A. omitted)
IX. Appeals (Rules 72-76 omitted)
X. District Courts and Clerks (Rules 77-80 omitted)
XI. General Provisions (Rules 81-86 omitted)
Appendix of Forms (Forms 1-32 omitted)

U.S. CRIMINAL CODE OF 1948

Part I.	Crimes Ch. 1-117,	(Sec. 1-2424 omitted)
Part II.	Criminal Procedure	
	Ch. 201 General Provisions	(Sec. 3001-3012 omitted)
	Ch. 203 Arrest and Commitment	(Sec. 3041-3060 omitted)
	Ch. 205 Searches and Seizures	(Sec. 3101-3116 omitted)
	Ch. 207 Bail	(Sec. 3141-3145 omitted)
	Ch. 209 Extradition	(Sec. 3181-3195 omitted)
	Ch. 211 Jurisdiction and Venue	(Sec. 3231-3243 omitted)
	Ch. 213 Limitations	(Sec. 3281-3290 omitted)
	Ch. 215 Grand Jury	(Sec. 3321-3328 omitted)
	Ch. 217 Indictment and Information	(Sec. 3361-3367 omitted)
	Ch. 219 Trial by Commissioners	(Sec. 3401-3402 omitted)
	Ch. 221 Arraignment, Pleas and Trial	(Sec. 3431-3446 omitted)
	Ch. 223 Witnesses and Evidence	(Sec. 3481-3499 omitted)
	Ch. 225 Verdict	(Sec. 3531-3532 omitted)
	Ch. 227 Sentence, Judgment, and Execution	(Sec. 3561-3574 omitted)
	Ch. 229 Fines, Penalties and Forfeitures	(Sec. 3611-3618 omitted)
	Ch. 231 Probation	(Sec. 3651-3656 omitted)
	Ch. 233 Contempts	(Sec. 3691-3693 omitted)
	Ch. 235 Appeal	(Sec. 3731-3741 omitted)
	Ch. 237 Rules of Criminal Procedure	(Sec. 3771-3772 omitted)

Part III. Prisons and Prisoners (Chs. 301-317 Sec. 4001-4321 omitted)
Part IV. Correction of Youthful Offenders (Chs. 401-403, Sec. 5001-5037 omitted)

Federal Rules of Criminal Procedure

I. Scope, Purpose, and Construction:

Rule 1. These rules govern the procedure in the courts of the United States and before United States commissioners in all criminal proceedings, with the exceptions stated in Rule 54.

Rule 2. These rules are intended to provide for the just determination of every criminal proceeding. They shall be construed to secure simplicity in procedure, fairness in administration and the elimination of unjustifiable expense and delay.

II. Preliminary Proceedings (Rules 3-5 omitted)
III. Indictment and Information (Rules 6-9 omitted)
IV. Arraignment, and Preparation for Trial (Rules 10-17 omitted)
V. Venue (Rules 18-22 omitted)
VI. Trial (Rules 23-31 omitted)
VII. Judgment (Rules 32-36 omitted)
VIII. Appeal (Rules 37-39 omitted)
IX. Supplementary and Special Proceedings (Rules 40-42 omitted)
X. General Provisions (Rules 43-60 omitted)
Appendix of Forms (Forms 1-27 omitted)

Sec. 3.1 ORIGINAL JURISDICTION delegated by CONSTITUTION and STATUTE (cont'd)
Sec. 3.11 Territorially including Venue
Sec. 3.12 Of Parties and their Adjective Law Capacities: Rights and Duties
Sec. 3.13 Of Causes of Action and of Defenses
Sec. 3.14 Of Remedies and their Elements

Sec. 3.11 Territorially including Venue

DORAN v BUSSARD (2dDept 1899) 38 AD 30, 55 S 987

Appeal from city court of Yonkers.

GOODRICH, P.J. The action was originally commenced in a justice's court in the city of Yonkers, and removed to the city court of that city, pursuant to chapter 186 of the Laws of 1878, entitled "An act in relation to the city court of Yonkers," as amended by chapter 416 of the Laws of 1893. The plaintiff contends that the act violates article 3, Sec. 18, of the constitution, which forbids the legislature to pass a local bill "providing for change of venue in civil or criminal cases." The question is first raised on this appeal. We are clearly of opinion that the act in question is not in conflict with the constitution. The constitutional inhibition does not relate to a removal of a cause from one court to another. The same provision appears in the amendments of the constitution which took effect in January, 1875. There have been numerous acts of the legislature before and since that time providing for the removal of causes from inferior to superior courts. Familiar instances of such removals can be found in the statutes authorizing the removal of causes from the district courts of the city of New York to the common pleas of the city and county of New York, and from the common pleas and the superior courts of the cities of New York and Buffalo and the city court of Brooklyn to the supreme court. I can find no case which holds that such removal is a change of venue. On the contrary, it is a change of forum. This distinction is clearly recognized in section 319 of the Code of Civil Procedure, which provides for the removal of causes from the city court of New York to the supreme court, for the very purpose of changing the place of trial to some other county, and such legislation remains unchallenged.

The action was brought to recover broker's commissions and the vital question was whether the plaintiff was the procuring cause of the sale. There was evidence which justified the submission of this question to the jury, and we see no reason to interfere with the verdict. We do not find that the other exceptions in the case require discussion.

The judgment must be affirmed, with costs. All concur.

Sec. 3.1 ORIGINAL JURISDICTION delegated by CONSTITUTION and STATUTE (cont'd)

Sec. 3.12 Of Parties and their Adjective Law Capacities: Adjective Rights and Adjective Duties
Sec. 3.121 Natural Parties
- A - Those sui juris
- B - Those of limited capacity
  1. Married Women
  2. Minors
  3. Incompetents
  4. Aliens
  5. Convicts
  6. and Others

Sec. 3.122 Representative Parties
1. Administrator
2. Executor
3. Guardian
4. Committee for an Incompetent
5. Receiver
6. Trustee
7. Public Officer
8. Agent
9. and Others

Sec. 3.123 Collective Parties
1. Partnerships
2. Corporations
3. Unincorporated Associations
4. A State in the U.S.
5. The U.S.
6. A Foreign State
7. and Others

Sec. 3.124 Artificial Parties
1. A Res e.g. a boat
2. and Others

Sec. 3.12 (Original Jurisdiction) Of Parties and Their Adjective Law Capacities: Adjective Rights and Duties

Sec. 3.121 Of Natural Parties

RALLI v EQUITABLE MUT. FIRE INS. CORP. OF NEW YORK (SpCtAppTm 1896) 16 M 357, 38 S 87

Action by Pandia C. Ralli and others against the Equitable Mutual Fire Insurance Corporation of New York. From a judgment of the general term (35 S 1115, mem.) affirming a final judgment entered on an order overruling a demurrer to the complaint, interposed on the ground of insuffiency in substance, defendant appeals...

BISCHOFF, J. The complaint alleged a cause of action in various parties, other than the plaintiffs, against the defendant, upon certain contracts of insurance, and the only manner in which the plaintiffs were sought to be connected with the transaction was through the allegation that "the said plaintiffs in respect to the policies above mentioned, and to the receipt of said unearned premiums, are trustees of an express trust, each of the said insured, above mentioned, in the said policies, have authorized and requested the said plaintiffs to collect and receive from the said defendant all of the said unearned portions of the said surrendered policies."

We are not advised by the record as to the grounds upon which the court below became satisfied with the sufficiency of this complaint, and, in our opinion, there can be no doubt that the pleading is fatally defective, if not, indeed, frivolous. Failing privity of contract or title in the plaintiffs to the demand in suit, the complaint did not state facts sufficient to constitute a cause of action (Bliss, Code Pl. Sec. 234; Mosselman v Caen, 1 Hun 648...) And the argument that the objection should have been taken to the capacity to sue is unfounded. As natural persons, the plaintiffs of course had capacity to sue, in the absence of affirmative allegations to the contrary; and, if the demurrer had been placed upon the ground noted, it would have, of necessity, been overruled. (Bank v Donnell, 40 NY 412; Insurance Co. v Baldwin, 37 NY 651.)

The allegation of trusteeship was merely a conclusion of law, and not alone thus objectionable; moreover, an erroneous conclusion, from the attendant averment upon which it appears to have been based. The fact that a person is constituted a collection agent does not authorize him, as trustee of an express trust, to bring an action upon the claim to be collected, in his own name. (Pom. Rem. & Rem. Rights, Sec. 174, and cases cited.) The plaintiffs were obviously not parties with whom the contracts in suit were made for the benefit of others, nor were they persons having title to the demand as the real parties in interest. (Code Civ. Proc. Sec. 449*).

The judgments of the court below must be reversed, and the demurrer sustained, with costs to the appellant. All concur.

---

*Sec. 449 became in the Civil Practice Act Sec. 210: "Every action must be prosecuted in the name of the real party in interest, except..." which is omitted in the Civil Practice Law and Rules but the intent of several sections, e.g. Sec. 1001, 1002, 1004 and perhaps others in the CPLR, would seem to be to broaden the concept of the legal interest required in a plaintiff; cf. N.Y., CPLR, Article 10 -Parties Generally, Sec. 1001-1025.

Rule 17 of the Federal Rules of Civil Procedure reads "(a) Real Party in Interest. Every action shall be prosecuted in the name of the real party in interest; but..."

MIDDLETON v WOHLGEMUTH (2dDept 1910) 141 AD 678, 126 S 734

Action by William Middleton against William Wohlgemuth. From a judgment for plaintiff, defendant appeals.

JENKS, J. This is an appeal from a judgment of the Municipal Court. The plaintiff sues for $140. He was the agent of a motor car manufacturer, entitled to a fixed commission on the sale of each car. He sold a motor car to the defendant. The regular price of it was $740, but he accepted $600 on the express agreement that the defendant would sell for him two motor cars within a definite period, and, if not, then the defendant would pay $740. The said regular price included the fixed commission of the plaintiff, which was $140. The action in effect, then, is to recover the full price of the car in order that the plaintiff may gain the commission which was due to him thereon by his agreement with his principal, and which the defendant in effect agreed to pay provided he did not carry out his said agreement. The defense is a general denial together with a plea of misjoinder of plaintiff, defect of parties plaintiff, no capacity to sue, and failure to state facts sufficient to constitute a cause of action, all of which rests upon the proposition that the plaintiff was an agent.

In the course of the trial the plaintiff testified directly that he sued as agent. I think this action can be maintained upon the theory that the plaintiff is the trustee of an express trust under section 449 of the Code of Civil Procedure. I think we may glean from the complaint that such is the theory of the action, and this was expressly avowed by the plaintiff in his testimony. In Stanley v Chappell, (8Cow(NY) 235), it was held that when the plaintiff declares in a special character, beginning his declaration by showing that character, he may by subsequent parts of the declaration refer to himself as the said plaintiff without adding his special character. Whether or not the contract was made and carried out with the plaintiff or with the principal was a question of fact in the case on which the finding of the court should not be disturbed. .. The written exhibits of the defendant are not conclusive, inasmuch as, although the check which represents the first payment was made out to the principal, examination shows that it was indorsed by the principal and subsequently indorsed by the plaintiff, and the receipt is nothing more than a formal statement that an amount of money had been received by the principal, the disposition of which was indicated by the said check.

The judgment is affirmed, with costs. All concur.

CITY OF BUFFALO v HAWKS et al. (4thDept 1929) 226 AD 480, 236 S 89

Appeal from Erie County Court.

Action by the City of Buffalo against Amanda Hawks and others, as executors of the last will and testament of Lydia Cox, deceased, County of Erie, and others. From an order denying its motion to vacate and set aside service of summons and complaint on it, defendant County of Erie appeals.

EDGCOMB, J. This action is brought by the city of Buffalo to foreclose several tax certificates of sale covering certain real property, and to sell the land against which the tax was assessed, and apply the proceeds of sale to the payment of the liens in the order of their priority. No personal judgment is demanded against any defendant.

The summons and complaint herein were served upon the defendants, pursuant to the provisions of section 643-a of the charter of the city of Buffalo, by mailing a copy thereof in a postpaid wrapper, addressed to each defendant at Buffalo, N.Y., and by publishing a copy of the summons, a notice of the object of the action, and a brief description of the property affected, in the official publication of the city of Buffalo, and in a daily newspaper published in that municipality. No order was ever granted permitting service to be made in such manner...

The county of Erie, one of the defendants herein, appeared specially, and moved to vacate and set aside the service of the summons, upon the ground that the same was not made personally, nor pursuant to any order of the court or to the provisions of the Civil Practice Act, and that the above-mentioned statute, authorizing service in the manner in which it was made, is unconstitutional, in that it is violative of the "due process" clause of both the federal and state Constitutions.

The only question presented upon this appeal is the constitutionality of this new provision of the Buffalo charter. We are not concerned with the wisdom or expediency of the statute, nor is it within our province to inquire into the motives which actuated its passage. Such questions are addressed solely to the Legislature which passed, and the Governor who signed, the act.

The right to private property is secured to its owner by the provisions of Section 1 of the 14th Amendment to the Federal Constitution, which was added to that remarkable document in 1868, and which prohibits any state from depriving a person of life, liberty or property without due process of law, and by section 6 of article 1 of the state Constitution, which declares that no person shall be divested of his property without due process of law.

It is asserted by the appellant that the commencement of an action in the manner provided by the statute in question makes it possible for the property of a defendant to be seized and confiscated without giving him his day in court, and that it is therefore contrary to the fundamental law of the land.

The phrase "due process of law" is not defined in either the Federal or State Constitution. Neither is it susceptible of an exact or comprehensive definition. (People v Adirondack Ry. Co., 160 NY 225, 236 54 NE 689, aff'd Adirondack R.Co. v New York, 176 US 335, 20 SCt 460, 44 LEd 492; Bertholf v O'Reilly, 74 NY 509, 519, 30 AmRep 323.)

It is well settled, however, that the "due process" clause in the two Constitutions assures to every person his day in court, and an opportunity to be heard, and defend and preserve his rights, by establishing any fact which, under the law, would be a protection to him or his property. (Stuart v Palmer, 74 NY 183, 191, 30 AmRep 289.)

One cannot be guaranteed a hearing, if he is not informed that one is to be had. The Constitution, however, does not require that personal notice of a proceeding be given to one whose property, situated within this commonwealth, is sought to be affected, and when no personal judgment against him is sought. Substituted notice in such a case is sufficient, if it be reasonably probable that it will reach the person interested, and apprise him of what is going on, and will afford him an opportunity to come in and defend his property. (Vatable v New York, L.E.&W.R.Co., 96 NY 50 62; Stuart v Palmer, 74 NY 183, 30 AmRep 289; Happy v Mosher, 48 NY 313; Ballard v Hunter, 204 US 241, 27 SCt 261, 51 LEd 461; Bowling v U.S. (CCA) 299 F 438, 443.

The state has power to regulate the method by which the process of its courts may be set in motion, provided, of course, that the procedure adopted is not repugnant to the fundamental law of the land.

There are many instances where personal service would be impracticable; others where it would be impossible. If a court could not obtain jurisdiction of a defendant except by personal service, one could easily defeat the administration of justice by keeping his whereabouts unknown, or by absenting himself from the state.

The guarantee of the Constitution was never intended to perpetuate any particular method of bringing a party into court. So long as his substantial rights are preserved, the Legislature may make such changes in the manner of the service of the process of the courts as it deems proper. (People v Board of Supervisors of Essex County, 70 NY 228.

Constructive service of the process of the court was not unknown to the common law; it was an authorized method by which the English courts, both of law and equity, acquired jurisdiction of defendants.

It has long been the practice in this state to permit a summons to be served by publication or by substituted service in certain specified instances, where an order authorizing such service has been granted. Neither method is repugnant to the provisions of the Constitution. (Coffin v Lesster 36 Hun 347, 350, aff'd 110 NY 645, 17 NE 873; Continental Nat, Bank v Thurber, 74 Hun 632, 26 NY S 956; aff'd sub non. Continental Nat. Bank of Boston v United States Book Co., 143 NY 040, 37 NE 000.)

The method of service specified in the statute here under consideration is practically the same as that provided by section 232 of the Civil Practice Act, when a summons is served by publication. The mere fact that in one case the court has ordered the service of process to be made in this particular manner, and in the other the service is made without the order, but by direction of the statute, can have no possible bearing on the probability of the defendant actually receiving notice of the commencement of the action. The likelihood of actual notice is the same in both cases.

Every intendment is in favor of the constitutionality of a legislative enactment. If a reasonable doubt as to its validity exists, it should be upheld. Kerrigan v Force, 68 NY 381; Ogden v Saunders, 12 Wheat 213, 270, 6 LEd 606.

For the reasons above stated, and under the authorities cited, I think that the court below was right in holding that the act in question did not violate the provisions of either the United States or state Constitution. The order appealed from should be affirmed.

Order affirmed without costs of this appeal to either party. All concur, except CROUCH, J., who dissents and votes for reversal.

SEARS, P. J. (concurring). (omitted).

FREEMAN v ALDERSON (1886) 119 US 185, 30 LEd 372

This was an action of trespass to try the title to certain land in Texas. It is the form in use to recover possession of real property in that State.

The plaintiffs (defendants in trial court) claimed the land under a deed to their grantor, executed by the sheriff of McLennan County, in that State, upon a sale under an execution issued on a judgment in a state court for costs, rendered against one Henry Alderson, then owner of the property, but now deceased.

The defendants (plaintiffs in trial court) asserted title to the land as heirs of Alderson, contending that the judgment under which the alleged sale was made was void, because it was rendered against him without personal service of citation, or his appearance in the action...

Mr. Justice FIELD: Actions in rem, strictly considered, are proceedings against property alone, treated as responsible for the claims asserted by the libellants or plaintiffs. The property itself is in such actions the defendant, and - except in cases arising during war, for its hostile character - its forfeiture or sale is sought for the wrong, in the commission of which it has been the instrument, or for debts or obligations for which by operation of law it is liable. The court acquires jurisdiction over the property in such cases by its seizure, and of the subsequent proceedings by public citation to the world, of which the owner is at liberty to avail himself by appearing as a claimant in the case.

There is, however, a large class of cases which are not strictly actions in rem, but are frequently spoken of as actions quasi in rem, because, though brought against persons, they only seek to subject certain property of those persons to the discharge of the claims asserted. Such are actions in which property of non-residents is attached and held for the discharge of debts due by them to citizens of the State, and actions for the enforcement of mortgages and other liens. Indeed, all proceedings having for their sole object the sale or other disposition of the property of the defendant, to satisfy the demands of the plaintiff, are in a general way thus designated. But they differ, among other things, from actions which are strictly in rem, in that the interest of the defendant is alone sought to be affected, that citation to him is required, and that judgment therein is only conclusive between the parties.

The State has jurisdiction over property within its limits owned by non-residents, and may, therefore, subject it to the payment of demands against them of its own citizens. It is only in virtue of its jurisdiction over the property, as we said on a former occasion, that its tribunals can inquire into the nonresident's obligations to its own citizens; and the inquiry can then proceed only so far as may be necessary for the disposition of the property. If the nonresident possesses no property in the State, there is nothing upon which its tribunals can act. (Pennoyer v Neff, 95 US 723 (Bk. 24, LEd 569)). They cannot determine the validity of any demand beyond that which is satisfied by the property. For any further adjudication the defendant must be personally served with citation or voluntarily appear in the action. The laws of the State have no operation outside of its territory, except so far as may be allowed by comity; its tribunals cannot send their citation beyond its limits and require parties there domiciled to respond to proceedings against them; and publication of citation within the State cannot create any greater obligation upon them to appear. (Id. p. 727 (570)). So, necessarily, such tribunals can have no jurisdiction to pass upon the obligations of nonresidents, except to the extent and for the purpose mentioned.

This doctrine is clearly stated in Cooper v Reynolds (10 Wall. 308 (77US bk. 19, LEd 931)), where it became necessary to declare the effect of a personal action against an absent party without the jurisdiction of the court, and not served with process or voluntarily appearing in the action, and whose property was attached, and sought to be subjected to the payment of the demand of the resident plaintiff. After stating the general purpose of the action and the inability to serve process upon the defendant, and the provision of law for attaching his property in such cases, the court, speaking by Mr. Justice Miller, said: "If the defendant appears, the cause becomes mainly a suit in personam, with the added incident that the property attached remains liable, under the control of the court, to answer to any demand which may be established against the defendant by the final judgment of the court. But if there is no appearance of the defendant, and no service of process on him, the case becomes in its essential nature a proceeding in rem, the only effect of which is to subject the property attached to the payment of the demand which the court may find to be due to the plaintiff. That such is the nature of this proceeding in this latter class of cases is clearly evinced by two well established propositions: First, the judgment of the court, though in form a personal judgment against the defendant, has no effect beyond the property attached in that suit. No general execution can be issued for any balance unpaid after the attached property is exhausted. No suit can be maintained in such a judgment in the same court, or in any other; nor can it be used as evidence in any other proceeding not affecting the attached property; nor could the costs in that proceeding be collected of defendant out of any other property than that attached in the suit. Second, the court, in such a suit, cannot proceed unless the officer finds some property of defendant on which to levy the writ of attachment. A return that none can be found is the end of the case, and deprives the court of further jurisdiction, though the publication may have been duly made and proven in court." (Id. p. 318 (932).)

To this statement of the law may be added what, indeed, is a conclusion from the doctrine that whilst the costs of an action may properly be satisfied out of the property attached, or otherwise brought under the control of the court no personal liability for them can be created against the absent or nonresident defendant; the power of the court being limited, as we have already said, to the disposition of the property which is alone within its jurisdiction.

The pleadings in the case in which judgment was rendered for costs against Alderson are not before us. We have only the formal judgment, from which it should seem that the action was to recover an undivided interest in the property, and then to obtain a partition of it, and have that interest set apart in severalty to the plaintiffs - a sort of mixed action to try the title of the plaintiffs to the undivided half of the property, and to obtain a partition of that half. Such action, though dealing entirely with the realty, is not an action in rem in the strict sense of the term; it is an action against the parties named, and, though the recovery and partition of real estate are sought, that does not change its character as a personal action; the judgment therein binds only the parties in their relation to the property. The service of citation by publication may suffice for the exercise of the jurisdiction of the court over the property so far as to try the right of its possession, and to decree its partition; but it could not authorize the creation of any personal demand against the defendant, even for costs which could be satisfied out of his other property.

The judgment is for all the costs in the case, and no order is made that they be satisfied out of the property partitioned. Had satisfaction been thus ordered, no exectuion would have been necessary. The execution, also, is general in its direction, commanding the sheriff to make the costs out of any property of the defendant.

The judgment, as far as the costs are concerned, must therefore be treated as a judgment in personam, and, for the reason stated, it was without any binding obligation upon the defendant; and the execution issued upon it did not authorize the sale made, and, of course, not the deed of the sheriff. Were the conclusion otherwise, it would follow, as indeed it is claimed here, that a joint owner of real property might sue a nonresident cotenant for partition, and, having had his own interest set apart to himself, proceed to sell out on execution the interest of his cotenant for all the costs.

The judgment of the court below must be affirmed; and it is so ordered.

McDONALD v MABEE (1917) 243 US 90, 61 LEd 608, r175 SW(Tex) 676

Mr. Justice HOLMES: This is a suit upon a promissory note. The only defense now material is that the plaintiff had recovered a judgment upon the same note in a previous suit in Texas which purported to bind the defendant personally as well as to foreclose a lien by which the note was secured. When the former suit was begun, the defendant, Mabee, was domiciled in Texas, but had left the state with intent to establish a home elsewhere, his family, however, still residing there. He subsequently returned to Texas for a short time and later established his domicil in Missouri. The only service upon him was by publication in a newspaper once a week for four successive weeks after his final departure from the state, and he did not appear in the suit. The supreme court of the state held that this satisfied the Texas statutes, and that the judgment was a good personal judgment, overruling the plaintiffs contention that to give it that effect was to deny the constitutional right to due process of law.

The foundation of jurisdiction is physical power, although in civilized times it is not necessary to maintain that power throughout proceedings properly begun, and although submission to the jurisdiction by appearance may take the place of service upon the person. (Cases). No doubt there may be some extension of the means of acquiring jurisdiction beyond service or appearance, but the foundation should be borne in mind. Subject to its conception of sovereignty even the common law required a judgment not to be contrary to natural justice. (Cases). And in states bound together by a Constitution and subject to the 14th Amendment, great caution should be used not to let fiction deny the fair play that can be secured only by a pretty close adhesion to fact. (Baker v Baker, E.&Co. Jan. 8, 1917 (242 US 394, ante, 386, 37 Sup Ct Rep 152)).

There is no dispute that service by publication does not warrant a personal judgment against a nonresident. (Pennoyer v Neff, 95 US 714, 24 LEd 565. Riverside & D. River Cotton Mills v Menefee, 237 US 189, 59 LEd 910, 35 SCt 579.) Some language of Pennoyer v Neff would justify the extension of the same principle to absent parties, but we shall go no farther than the precise facts of this case require. When the former suit was begun, Mabee, although technically domiciled in Texas, had left the state, intending to establish his home elsewhere. Perhaps in view of his technical position and the actual presence of his family in the state, a summons left at his last and usual place of abode would have been enough. But it appears to us that an advertisement in a local newspaper is not sufficient notice to bind a person who has left a state, intending not to return. To dispense with personal service the substitute that is most likely to reach the defendant is the least that ought to be required if substantial justice is to be done. We repeat, also, that the ground for giving subsequent effect to a judgment is that the court rendering it had acquired power to carry it out; and that it is going to the extreme to hold such power gained even by service at the last and usual place of abode...

...The personal judgment was not merly voidable, as was assumed in the slightly different case of Henderson v Staniford, (105 Mass 504, 7 AmRep 551), but was void.

Judgment reversed.

Sec. 3.122 Of Representative Parties

LEAVITT, as EXECUTRIX OF J. B. F. v SCHOLES CO. (1913) 210 NY 107, 148 AD 78

CHASE, J. The plaintiff's testator died May 10, 1901, leaving a will, which was duly probated, and she has been duly appointed sole executrix thereof. After the death of the testator she continued as sole executrix of his will and in his name, and for the benefit of his estate to conduct and manage the business theretofore conducted and managed by him.

The defendant is a corporation, and on May 20, 1906, pursuant to an agreement with the plaintiff as such executrix, undertook to remove certain glass from railroad cars in the borough of Brooklyn, city of New York, to the plaintiff's place of business in the borough of Manhattan in said city, but in doing so, pursuant to said agreement with plaintiff, it is alleged was careless and negligent and broke certain of the glass. This action is brought to recover the plaintiff's damages by reason of such alleged carelessness and negligence. The trial resulted in a verdict for the plaintiff of $754.80. An appeal from a judgment entered upon said verdict was taken to the Appellate Division, but the only question presented for review was the ruling of the trial court in refusing to dismiss the complaint because, as is claimed by the defendant, "the action should have been brought by the plaintiff in her individual capacity instead of as executrix." The Appellate Division by a divided court reversed the judgment and granted a new trial. (Leavitt v Scholes Co., 148 AD 78.) An appeal is taken to this court from such order of reversal.

To avoid confusion in the consideration of reported cases involving the estate of a deceased person and the acts and contract of a person duly appointed an executor or an administrator of the estate of such deceased person, it is necessary to ascertain in each case whether the action was brought by or against such person individually or in his representative capacity, and also whether the court in each case is considering a permissible or essential form of action or course of procedure.

In Schutz v Morette (146 NY 137, 140) this court, considering an action brought on an account against an executor as such, say: "When the account relates to transactions between the executor or administrator and another party, upon claims not existing at the death of the decedent, although they grow out of matters connected with administration, the action lies only against the executor or administrator personally. In the one case the judgment is de bonis testatoris, and in the other de bonis propriis. (Reynolds v Reynolds, 3 Wend.(NY) 244; Gillet v Hutchinson's Admrs., 24 id. 184.)"

This court, again referring to contracts by executors and administrators in O'Brien v Jackson (167 NY 31, 33) say: "The general rule is well settled in this state that executors or trustees cannot, by their executory contracts, although made in the interest and for the benefit of the estate they represent if made upon a new independent consideration, bind the estate and thus create a liability not founded upon the contract or obligation of the testator." In that case the reason for the rule and an exception to it are stated in language quoted from Ferrin v Myrick (41 NY 315), as follows: "While as between the executor and the person with whom he contracts the latter may rely on the contract, the beneficiaries are not concluded by the executor's act, but the propriety of the charge and the liability of the estate therefor must be determined in the accounting of the executor. In an action at law against the executor, the legatees and persons interested in the estate have no opportunity to be heard. To the general rule there are exceptions, and an equitable action can be maintained against the estate on behalf of a creditor in case of the fraud or insolvency of the executor, or when he is authorized to make an expenditure for the protection of the trust estate, and he has no trust fund for the purpose. In the latter case, if unwilling to make himself personally liable he may charge the trust estate in favor of any person who will make the expenditure. Charges against the trust estate in such cases can be enforced only in an equitable action brought for the purpose. To that action the beneficiaries and cestuis que trust are necessary parties. The trust estate cannot be depleted or swept away except in an action which they may defend."

Where a cause of action accrues after the death of a decedent and in the conduct of an estate and a recovery if had must be accounted for by the executor or administrator, and an action is brought thereon by such executor or administrator, the reason for enforcing the rule above stated in actions against an executor or administrator does not apply. We quote with approval from the dissenting opinion of Justice Laughlin of the Appellate Division in this case (148 AD 78): "Although the proper form of action on a cause of action arising out of the administration of the estate is by the personal representative individually, basing his right and title on his letters of administration or letters testamentary, yet it is well sustained by authority that, with the exceptions already stated, he may sue either individually or in his representative capacity, and this for the reason that no matter in which capacity a recovery is had the recovery becomes assets of the estate for which he is accountable, and it does not concern the defendant, whose liability is individual in any event so that the form of judgment is necessarily the same, and the same defenses and remedies are available to the defendant whose liability will be discharged by the satisfaction of the recovery no matter in which form it may be had. (Moss v Cohen, 158 NY 240...)

Where a cause of action accrues to the personal representatives of the decedent, as distinguished from a cause of action which accrued to the decedent, whether the personal representative prosecutes the action in his name individually or in his representative capacity, it is to be deemed, for the purpose of the taxation of costs, an action by him individually, and if the action be brought in his representative capacity, and he be unsuccessful, the costs may be taxed against him individually without an application to the court. (Dunphy v Callahan, 126 AD 11; affd. on the prevailing opinion in the Appellate Division, 194 NY 587.)

The order of the Appellate Division should be reversed and the judgment of the Trial Term affirmed, with costs in both courts.

Order reversed, etc.

Sec. 3.123 Of Collective Parties

TRUSTEES OF UNION COLLEGE v COUGHLIN (SpCtGenTm 1895) 89 Hun(NY) 171, 35 S 25

APPEAL from judgment on report of referee.

Actions by the trustees of Union College against Dennis Coughlin and others, as school trustees of the First ward of Long Island City. From a judgment for plaintiffs, defendants appeal.

BROWN, P. J. The plaintiffs have recovered a judgment against the defendants upon three separate causes of action: First, for unpaid rent upon a lease for a lot of land and buildings thereon used for school purposes; second, for the use and occupation of said premises for one year following the termination of said lease; and, third, for damages for breach of a covenant in said lease whereby the leasees agreed to surrender the demised premises at the expiration of the term in as good condition as reasonable use and wear thereof would permit, damages by the elements excepted. The lease was under seal, and was executed by and between the plaintiffs and the defendants' predecessors in office (the board of education of Long Island City consenting to the same), and bears date November 1, 1876, and was for the term of 15 years, at an annual rent of $2,347, the lessees agreeing to pay taxes and water rates as they became due. On May 1, 1877, by a further agreement, the lessees, in consideration of the lessor making certain alterations in the building, agreed to pay $66 additional rent for each year of the unexpired term.

The provisions of the charter of the city (chapter 461, Laws 1871) relating to public instruction therein are not very intelligible, and it is difficult to determine with entire satisfaction the powers of the several officers. It provides that each ward of the city shall be a school district, and that there shall be elected therein three trustees, who hold office for three years, one of whom shall be elected each year. The mayor of the city is authorized to appoint a commissioner of public instruction in each ward, who serve as school commissioners for their respective wards. These commissioners constitute the board of education for the city. The statute enumerates the powers of the board of education and of the school trustees...

The testimony is that the demised premises had been used as a school by the city for many years prior to the date of the lease, and in April, 1876, the board of education appointed a committee to act with the trustees of the ward in reference to improved school accommodations for the ward, and on May 23rd the board adopted a resolution that the total annual rent for that ward should not exceed $3,000. Negotiations appear to have been had with the plaintiffs in reference to improving the school building, with the result that a resolution was finally unanimously adopted that the commissioner and trustees of the ward were empowered to complete the negotiations on the basis of 10 per cent, upon the outlay to be made by plaintiffs, in addition to $1,400 annual rent then being paid for the buildings, and thereafter the lease in suit was executed.

...The board of education is by the charter made the responsible body for all expenses of public instruction within the city. For educational purposes, it is declared to be a corporation and is charged with the management and control of the schools. Its members are not servants or agents of the city, but public officers exercising such powers as are prescribed by statute, and the city is not liable for its acts. (Ham v Mayor, etc., of New York, 70 NY 459.) To it the ward trustees must annually report. It may remove the trustees from office, establish new schools, employ and discharge teachers, designate their duties and fix their salaries, furnish supplies for the schools and school buildings, and no expense in excess of $25 per month can be paid by the trustees without authorization. The money necessary to meet the expenses of public instruction in the city must be raised by the common council, upon the certificate of the board, by a tax on the property within the city. The amount necessary for each school is apportioned to it by the board, and no expenses can be paid by the ward trustees except upon the audit of the commissioner for such ward, and the money can be drawn from the treasurer only upon drafts of the board, signed by its president and countersigned by the clerk and the commissioner for the ward for which the money is to be paid.

These provisions show the controlling character of the board of education over all matters relating to public instruction within the city; and, while I am inclined to the opinion that the contract sued upon was, with the assent of the board of education, properly made in the name of the ward trustees, I think it was in law, and must be treated as, the contract of the board of education. Certainly, that body was the only one against whom it could be enforced, and in an action upon the contract the board has a clear right to be heard. The whole responsibility, from the inception of the contract to the final payment of the rent, rests upon that body. But if an action can be sustained against the ward trustees, the right to a hearing would be denied to the board; and, as the judgment recovered against the trustees would be conclusive as to the plaintiff's right to recover, its payment might enforced by mandamus against the board, and it would be denied a hearing upon all questions involved in the judgment.

We are of the opinion that the ward trustees are officers charged solely with the duty of supervising the ward schools. They are a sort of an adjunct to the board of education. They have no independent power to contract, except as to small amounts, and are not liable to be sued for the expenses of the schools. All contracts in reference to the public instruction within the city, lawfully made, and debts and liabilities lawfully incurred, are the contracts, debts and liabilities of the board of education, which body in its corporate capacity is liable therefor. Our conclusion is that this action should have been brought against the board of education, and that it cannot be maintained against the defendants. We therefore refrain from expressing any opinion upon the merits of the controversy. The judgment must be reversed, and the complaint dismissed.

Sec. 3.1 Original Jurisdiction delegated by Constitution and Statute (continued)

Sec. 3.124 Of Artificial Parties

PEOPLE v THREE BARRELS' FULL (1923) 236 NY 175, r203 AD 577

(The case appears supra, p.)

Sec. 3.1 Original Jurisdiction delegated by Constitution and Statute (continued)

Sec. 3.13 Of Causes of Action and of Defenses

FIELD v TRUE COMICS, INC. (SpCtNYCo. 1949) 89 S2d 35

Action by Rudolph Field against True Comics, Inc., for copyright infringement. On defendant's motion to dismiss the complaint for want of jurisdiction.

ROCH, J. This is a motion to dismiss the complaint upon the ground that this court has no jurisdiction of the subject of the action. The only alleged wrongdoing charged to the defendant is that it distributed a magazine containing material copied from a book copyrighted by one who granted and assigned to plaintiff the sole and exclusive right to publish, print and market the book. No acts of unfair competition are alleged. As well stated in Nims on Unfair Competition and Trademarks, 4th Edition, Vol. 2, p. 900:

"The unfair competition lies in copying features which identify the origin of the literary property. In so far as the literary property itself has been copied, redress can be had only under the Copyright Law."

If mere copying of copyrighted matter were to constitute unfair competition, almost every copyright owner could resort to the courts of this state for relief by calling his cause of action one for unfair competition rather than one for infringement of copyright. Although state courts do possess jurisdiction of actions for unfair competition, something more must be alleged than acts which amount merely to infringement of copyright. That the remedy for infringement of copyright in the Federal courts may be limited to the owner of the copyright and may not be available to plaintiff, if that be the law, does not alter the conclusion reached that the courts of this state do not possess jurisdiction of the present action because it is nothing more or less than an action for infringement of copyright. If the owner of the copyright may not sue in our state courts it would seem to follow a fortiori that an assignee of the owner's rights may not sue here.

The motion to dismiss the complaint is accordingly granted.

SOUTHERN LEASING CO. v LUDWIG (1916) 217 NY 100, r168 AD 233

APPEAL, by permission, from an order of the Appellate Division of the Supreme Court in the first judicial department, entered June 1, 1951, which reversed an order of Special Term denying a motion for an injunction pendente lite.

The following questions were certified: "1. Does the complaint state facts sufficient to constitute a cause of action? 2. Can the plaintiff as a taxpayer and without alleging special damage maintain an action to enjoin the defendant Alfred Ludwig, as superintendent of buildings, from permitting the sign or structure described in the complaint from being erected, or the other defendents from erecting the same? 3. Did the adoption of the ordinance of May 29, 1914, as recited in the complaint, render it unlawful thereafter to erect the skysign for which the defendant Ludwig, as superintendent of buildings, had theretofore issued a permit?"....

CARDOZO, J. This is a taxpayer's action under section 51 of the General Municipal Law (Cons. Laws, ch. 24). The Mecca Realty Company is the lessee of a building in the city of New York. In February, 1914, it filed a plan for the erection on the roof of a sign 141 feet high. The plan was approved by the superintendent of buildings and a permit granted. Before anything was done under this permit, the board of aldermen, in May, 1914, adopted an ordinance limiting the height of signs on the roofs of buildings to 75 feet. The Mecca Realty Company afterwards and in December, 1914, leased the roof of the O.J. Gude Company, which had commenced the erection of the sign in accordance with the plans. The superintendent of buildings has refused to revoke his permit or to interfere with the work of construction. The plaintiff alleges that the sign, if built, will be dangerous to life and limb. This action is brought to compel the superintendent of buildings to revoke his permit, and to enjoin him from permitting the work to proceed.

The first question is whether a taxpayer's action is the appropriate remedy. The statute says that an action may be maintained against officers of a municipal corporation to "prevent any illegal official act" (General Municipal Law, section 51). Is this action one to prevent an illegal official act within the meaning of that statute? The superintendent of buildings has already issued the permit. He issued it long before the adoption of the ordinance. If the effect of the ordinance is to nullify the permit, no other revocation is necessary. This was conceded by the Appellate Division. A majority of that court thought, however, that the taxpayer might enjoin the superintendent of buildings from inaction as well as action. He was not commanded to abate the nuisance, but he was restrained from not abating it. The distinction between these two remedies is verbal only. In effect, therefore, it has been held that an action in equity may be maintained by a taxpayer, not merely to restrain a public officer from acting, but to compel him to act. The remedy in equity has thus been made a substitute for the legal remedy by mandamus. Whether an illegal "act" in the sense in which that word is used in the General Municipal Law may under some conditions be an act of omission as well as one of commission, we are not required at this time to decide. It is enough to say that mere inaction will not justify the intervention of a court of equity where the legal remedy by mandamus is available and adequate. The equitable remedy of an injunction under the General Municipal Law is to be granted or withheld in accordance with the general principles which govern the exercise of equitable jurisdiction (People v Canal Board 55 NY 390, 394; Schieffelin v

Komfort 212 NY 520, 535.) This was clearly recognized by Judge Seabury writing for the court in Altschul v Ludwig (216 NY 459), the more recent case in which the subject has been considered. A fundamental principle governing the exercise of equitable jurisdiction is, however, that equity will not act where the remedy at law is adequate; and the remedy at law is adequate where a full measure of relief is available through mandamus. (Cases)...The public officer whose conduct is assailed has not threatened to act. He has threatened to refuse to act. The permit has already been granted; the sign is in course of construction; and, if the superintendent of buildings wrongfully refuses to remove it, the remedy for mandamus is available to any citizen to hold him to the performance of his duty (People ex rel. Pumpyansky v Keating, 168 NY 390; People ex rel. Cross Co. v Ahearn, 124 AD 840, 845.)

We are persuaded that a taxpayer's suit in equity cannot be extended to such conditions without a perversion of the purpose of the statute. To extend it to this case would be to confer upon courts of equity a power to supervise and correct the conduct of public officers coextensive with the supervisory and corrective jurisdiction that has been heretofore exercised by courts of law. If a highway commissioner, for illustration, permits a highway to be obstructed or to fall into decay, he may be compelled by mandamus to abate the nuisance. But unless special circumstances make the remedy of mandamus inadequate, he will not be enjoined by a court of equity at the instance of a taxpayer from refusing to abate it. The statute was designed to redress a substantial grievance. It was designed to give a taxpayer a remedy under conditions where none had been available before. It was not designed to reach conditions and correct evils where the existing law gave an effective remedy at the instance of any citizen.

The conslusion to which we are thus led makes the consideration of other questions needless.

The order should be reversed, with costs; the first and second questions should be answered in the negative; and it is unnecessary to answer the third question.

Order reversed, etc.

Sec. 3.1 Original Jurisdiction delegated by Constitution and Statute (continued)

Sec. 3.14 Of Remedies

MONTANA STATE BD OF EXAMINERS v KELLER (1947) 120 Mont 364, 185 P2d 503.

GIBSON, J. This action is brought as a suit in equity in behalf of the Montana State Board of examiners in photography, the appellant here, against the respondent, to enjoin him from "practicing the profession of photography within the state of Montana without having received a license from the said board as provided in Chapter 37 of the Session Laws of 1937."

The complaint alleges that at the time it was filed, February 3, 1947, respondent was a non-resident of Montana, engaged in taking photographs of the pupils in the various schools in the city of Butte and selling them to the pupils so photographed; that he has not applied for a license from the board to engage in the practice of photography and does not hold such a license. The appellant further states in the complaint that the criminal proceedings authorized by said Chapter 37 do not afford an adequate remedy to the board of examiners in photography nor to the licensed photographers of Montana and that unless (sic) the respondent will continue to practice the profession of photography in Butte and other cities of the State, even though a criminal prosecution be brought against him. It is also stated that the respondent has no property or visible means from which an execution could be satisfied in case of the rendition of a judgment against him and that it would be difficult to ascertain the amount of compensation which would afford adequate relief.

An order to show cause was issued upon the complaint and a temporary restraining order included therein. To the complaint the respondent interposed a general demurrer... The district court made and entered its judgment in which is sustained the demurrer, granted the motion to dissolve the temporary restraining order and dismissed the action. The appeal is from the judgment.

Chapter 37 of the Laws of 1937 defines photography and declares the "practice of photography" to be "the business or profession, occupation or avocation of taking or producing photographs, or any part thereof, for hire." It establishes a board of examiners in photography, provides for the organization of the board, authorizes it to give examinations and to issue licenses to those who pass the examination, specified an examination fee and a license fee, exempts photographers in business at the time the Act takes effect from the requirement of an examination, and provides in section 13 of the Act as follows: "Any person who shall practice, or attempt to practice, photography in the state, without first having complied with the provisions of this act, or who shall violate any provisions of this act, shall be guilty of a misdemeanor, and upon conviction thereof shall be punished by a fine for each offense, of not less than fifty (50) nor more than two hundred (200) dollars, or by punishment in the county jail not less than thirty (30) days nor more than six (6) months, or by both such fine and imprisonment. Each sale shall be a separate offense."....

The action was brought in Silver Bow county district court, by the appellant board to secure an injunction, an equitable remedy termed in practice and by Montana statutes "preventive relief." The statutes provide and specify the cases in which the courts may grant such relief. One statute provides that "specific and preventive relief may be given in no other cases than those specified in this part of the Civil Code." (Sec. 8657, Rev. Codes 1935.) Section 8710, Revised Codes, provides that "Neither specific nor preventive relief can be granted to enforce a penal law, except in a case of nuisance, nor to enforce the penalty or forfeiture in any case."

The district court was asked by appellant board to enjoin respondent from practicing the profession of photography without a license. The act under which the appellant claims authority provides that such practice is a crime punishable by fine, or imprisonment, or both. Unless such practice constitutes a nuisance the court could not grant the preventive relief asked.

...Is such taking of photographs a nuisance? We look to the statute which defines nuisances for answer. The statute says: "Anything which is injurious to health, or is indecent or offensive to the senses, or an obstruction to the free use of property, so as to interfere with the comfortable enjoyment of life or property, or unlawfully obstructs the free passage or use, in the customary manner, of any navigable lake, or river, bay, stream, canal, or basin, or any public park, square, street, or highway, is a nuisance." (Sec. 8642, Rev. Codes 1955.)

It seems most clear that taking pictures, either with or without a license, comes not within any of the things enumerated....

While the facts stated in the complaint are to be taken as true and appellant therein avers that "The said board of examiners in photography is authorized by said Act to take appropriate steps to prevent a violation of the provision of said Act," this is but a conclusion of the pleader. The Act does not give the board of examiners any power concerning the enforcement of the Act other than the right to revoke licenses of photographers under certain circumstances. Subdivision (e) of section 3 of the Act creates the photographers' license fund "to be used only in defraying the expenses of the board and in the prosecution of violations of this Act." This does not confer authority on the board to prosecute violations of the Act. The prosecution of violations of the Act refers to the criminal prosecutions that may be brought under section 13 of the Act. The Act does not give the board of examiners any power over unlicensed photographers. It is given some disciplinary authority over its licensees, to revoke their licenses. Its field is limited to photographers who have licenses and those who are applicants for licenses. The ones who practice without a license are to be dealt with, if at all by the criminal law. That is what Chapter 37 provides.

So that status of the case before the district court was this: The appellant board's complaint alleged that respondent was taking photographs of school children and selling them to the children photographed and that he had no license from the board. There was no element of nuisance alleged, nothing injurious to health, nothing indecent or offensive to the senses averred, no obstruction to the free use of property so as to interfere with the comfortable enjoyment of life or property asserted, no other of the acts denominated "nuisance" by section 8642 set forth. The fact that respondent did not have a license from the board was relied upon to justify the issuance of injunction. The Act declares the violation complained of to be a crime and fixes penalties for the violation. The Act does not declare the violation to be a nuisance. It gives the appellant board no power of enforcement of the Act either in equity or by criminal prosecution as against non-licensed photographers. The only method of enforcement in the Act mentioned is by criminal prosecution. This is an adequate remedy for such violations.

By reason of the prohibition of section 8710, the injunctive relief could not be granted. That remedy was, under the case made by the complaint, withheld from use by the court. Lacking the authority to enjoin the respondent, it could only refuse the preventive relief asked by appellant, sustain the demurrer to the complaint and dismiss the action...

The judgment of the court was correct and it is affirmed.

EXAMPLES OF REMEDIES

Sec. 3.2 Examples of Remedies: Actions, Proceedings etc.

Sec. 3.21 At Common Law - Examples of Actions and Proceedings:

Actions at Common Law:

1. Trespass vi et armis (an action for a judgment for damages for assault)
2. Trespass de bonis asportatis (an action for a judgment for damages for unlawfully carrying away goods or property)
3. Trespass quare clausum fregit (an action for a judgment for damages for unlawful entry upon land)
4. Ejectment (an action for a judgment for repossession of real property and for damages for unlawful detention of its possession)
5. Waste (an action for a judgment for damages for spoil or destruction as to real property)
6. Trover (an action for a judgment for damages for conversion of personal property by an unlawful use)
7. Replevin (an action for a judgment for repossession of goods unlawfully taken)
8. Detinue (an action for a judgment for repossession of chattels unlawfully detained)
(9. Trespass on the Case (an action for a judgment for damages for: (a) abuse of process; (b) alienation of affections; (c) deceit; (d) libel; (e) malicious prosecution; (f) malpractice; (g) negligence; (h) nuisance; (i) slander; (j) etc.)
10. Covenant (an action for a judgment for damages for breach of a covenant or contract under seal)
11. Debt (an action for a judgment for a certain specific sum of money)
12. Special Assumpsit (an action for a judgment for damages for nonperformance of a special contract not under seal)
13. General Assumpsit (an action for a judgment for damages: (a) for a claim growing out of a breach of contract; or (b) for non-performance of a duty implied in law to pay for a benefit conferred, quasi-contract)
14. and others.

Proceedings at Common Law:

A. Quo warranto (a proceeding for an order determining by what warrant the respondent exercises a franchise or office)
B. Certiorari (a proceeding for an order directing an inferior court or official to certify or to return the record or proceedings in a cause for the purpose of a judicial review of their action)
C. Mandamus (a proceeding for an order commanding that an inferior court or officer or a corporation or its officer perform an official or ministerial duty)
D. Prohibition (a proceeding for an order prohibiting an inferior court from assuming jurisdiction it doesn't have or from going beyond its legitimate powers in a matter within its jurisdiction)
E. and others.

Sec. 3.22 In Equity - Examples of Suits and Proceedings:

Suits in Equity

1. Specific Performance (a suit for a decree to compel performance of a contract by a party bound to fulfill it)

2. Injunction (a suit for a decree or order forbidding a party to do some act which he is threatening or attempting to do or to restrain him in the continuance thereof)
3. Accounting (a suit for a decree requiring defendant to account to plaintiff as to his transactions in matters of fiduciary nature)
4. Cancellation (a suit for a decree canceling instruments void or voidable to prevent vexatious use against the person apparently bound by them)
5. and others.

Proceedings in Equity:

A. Discovery (a proceeding for an order to disclose facts in the knowledge of respondent or of documents in his custody)
B. Contempt (a proceeding for an order imposing a fine as indemnity to petitioner for a failure by respondent to perform a mandate of the court)
C. Sequestration (a proceeding for an order directing the taking into custody of the law of the property of a party who is in contempt and holding same until he shall comply)
D. and others.

Sec. 3.23 Under Statute - Examples of Actions or Suits and Special Proceedings

Actions Under Statutes:

New York Civil Practice Law and Rules

Sec. 103. Form of civil judicial proceedings. (a) One form of action. There is only one form of civil action. The distinctions between actions at law and suits in equity, and the forms of those actions and suits, have been abolished.

(b) Action or special proceeding. All civil judicial proceedings shall be prosecuted in the form of an action, except where prosecution in the form of a special proceeding is authorized. Except where otherwise prescribed by law, procedure in special proceedings shall be the same as in actions, and the provisions of the civil practice law and rules applicable to actions shall be applicable to special proceedings.

(c) Improper form. If a court has obtained jurisdiction over the parties, a civil judicial proceeding shall not be dismissed solely because it is not brought in the proper form, but the court shall make whatever order is required for its proper prosecution.

Sec. 105. Definitions. (a) Applicability. Unless the context requires otherwise, the definitions in this section apply to the civil practice law and rules.

(b) Action and special proceeding. The word "action" includes a special proceeding; the words "plaintiff" and "defendant" include the petitioner and the respondent, respectively, in a special proceeding; and the words "summons" and "complaint" include the notice of petition and the petition, respectively, in a special proceeding...

Examples of C's/A and of Actions authorized by statute.

1. Sec. 994. of N.Y. Penal Law (an action for a judgment for damages for a lost wager) (see p. 188 supra)
2. Sec. 995 of N.Y. Penal Law (an action for a judgment for damages for a loss suffered in a gambling game) (see p. 188 supra)
3. Sec. 51 of N.Y. Civil Rights Law (L. 1903, c. 132, Sec. 2) (an action for a judgment for damages for an invasion of the "right of privacy") (see pp. 72 & 182)
4. Sec. 51 of N.Y. Civil Rights Law (L. 1903, c. 132, Sec 2.) (an action for a judgment enjoining an invasion of the "right of privacy") (see pp. 72 & 182)
5. Sec. 51 of N.Y. General Municipal Law (an action for a judgment enjoining an illegal official act) (see p. 140 supra)
6. and others (see NY CPLR and the NY Consolidated Laws)

Suits under Statute

In N.Y. State there are technically no statutory suits since all suits, just as all common law actions, have been converted into one type of statutory civil action by Sec. 103 (quoted supra) of the N.Y. CPLR. In some other jurisdictions the distinction between statutory actions and statutory suits, based upon similarities to the common law actions and the equity suits, may continue. Under the Federal Rules of Civil

Procedure, common law actions and equity suits have been merged into one form of action to be known as a "civil action" (FRCP, Rule 2 supra).

Special Proceedings under Statute:

New York Civil Practice Law and Rules(N.Y. CPLR)
ARTICLE IV. Special Proceedings.

Sec. 401 Parties. The party commencing a special proceeding shall be styled the petitioner and any adverse party the respondent. After a proceeding is commenced, no party shall be joined or interpleaded and no third-party practice or intervention shall be allowed, except by leave of court.

Sec. 402 Pleadings. There shall be a petition, which shall comply with the requirements for a complaint in an action, and an answer where there is an adverse party. There shall be a reply to a counterclaim denominated as such and there may be a reply to new matter in the answer in any case. The court may permit such other pleadings as are authorized in an action upon such terms as it may specify. Where there is no adverse party the petition shall state the result of any prior application for similar relief.

Sec. 403 Notice of petition; service; order to show cause. (a) Notice of petition. A notice of petition shall specify the time and place of the hearing on the petition and the supporting affidavits, if any, accompanying the petition.

(b) Time for service of notice of petition and answer. A notice of petition, together with the petition and affidavits specified in the notice shall be served on any adverse party at least eight days before the time at which the petition is noticed to be heard. An answer and supporting affidavits, if any, shall be served at least one day before such time. A reply, together with supporting affidavits, if any, shall be served at or before such time. An answer shall be served at least five days before such time if a notice of petition served at least ten days before such time so demands; whereupon any reply shall be served at least one day before such time.

(c) Manner of service. A notice of petition shall be served in the same manner as a summons in an action.

(d) Order to show cause. The court may grant an order to show cause to be served, in lieu of a notice of petition at a time and in a manner specified therein.

Sec. 404 Objections in point of law...
Sec. 405 Correction of defects in papers...
Sec. 406 Motions...
Sec. 407 Severance...
Sec. 410 Trial...
Sec. 411 Judgment. The court shall direct that a judgment be entered determining the rights of the parties to the special proceeding.

Examples of Special Proceedings:

A. Sec. 4-27 of N.Y. Condemnation Law (a Special Proceeding for an order to take property for a public purpose by condemnation)
B. Sec. 802-b of N.Y. Code of Criminal Procedure (a Special Proceeding for an order to seize and destroy intoxicating beverage)Repealed L. 1923, c. 871
C. Sec. 3101-3126 of N.Y. CPLR (a Special Proceeding for Disclosure)
D. Provisional Remedies, N.Y.CPLR, Articles 60-64
   (1) Arrest Sec. 6101-6118 (3) Attachment Sec. 6201-6226
   (2) Injunction Sec. 6301-6315 (4) Receivers Sec. 6401-6405
E. and others (see N.Y. CPLR; N.Y. Code of Criminal Procedure,Part VI; and the N.Y. Consolidated Laws)

Sec. 3.24 Self-Help Remedies: Examples

At Common Law:

1. Foreclosure of Artison's Lien
2. and others.

In Equity:

1.

Under Statute:

1. Sec. 200-204 of N.Y. Lien Law (Procedure for holder of lien to sell personal property to satisfy his lien)
2. Sec. 1401-1461 of N.Y. Real Property Actions and Proceedings (Procedure for foreclosure of a real property mortgage by the mortgagee, known as "Foreclosure by Advertisement")
3. and others (see Uniform Com'l Code Sec. 9-502 -- 9-507)

APPLICATION OF CALLAHAN
PEOPLE v CALLAHAN (3dDept 1941) 262 AD 398, 28 S2d 980

Proceeding in the matter of the application of Maurice Callahan and others, a copartnership trading as the Raquette Lake Supply Company, to perpetuate the testimony of named persons, proposed by the People of the State of New York. From so much of an order granting the relief sought as granted costs against the People of the State of New York, the People of the State of New York appeal.

HEFFERNAN, Justice. The only question involved on this appeal, and in the companion case of St. Williams Church, Raquette Lake, New York, 262 AD 931, 28 S2d 983, submitted to the court at the same time and decided herewith, is the allowance of costs.

Respondents presented to the Supreme Court a petition to perpetuate the testimony of certain persons therein named relative to the title and possession of real estate therein described pursuant to the provisions of Article 31 of the Civil Practice Act, Sec. 313 et seq. A like petition in the companion case was presented at the same time.

The petition, in each instance, alleged that respondents had been in possession of such real estate for one year preceding the institution of the proceeding. Upon the presentation of the petitions the court made an order directing that notice of the time and pgace when the applications would be heard should be given to the Attorney General of the State.

Upon the return day the appellants appeared by the attorney general and filed affidavits denying that respondents are the owners, or in possession, of the premises described in the petitions, denied the right of respondents to perpetuate the testimony of the proposed witnesses and also asserted that appellants are the owners of the premises in dispute. The court thereupon appointed a referee to take and report the testimony on the issues raised by the petitions and affidavits.

The appellants reviewed in this court the orders appointing a referee, contending that the court below had no authority to make them. This court (258 AD, 766, 14 S2d 720) unanimously affirmed the orders in question.

After proof was taken before the referee the court determined the issues raised in favor of respondents, made orders permitting the perpetuation of the testimony desired and awarded costs and disbursements to respondents as in an action. The appeal is only from so much of the orders as grants costs.

Appellants contend that a proceeding to perpetuate testimony is neither an action nor a special proceeding and that consequently the court was without power to award costs against them.

The term "action" is not synonymous with the term "proceeding" nor are the terms convertible.

The Civil Practice Act (sections 4 and 5) provides that an ordinary prosecution in a court of justice by one person against another for the enforcement or protection of a right, the redress or prevention of a wrong, or the punishment of a public offense is an action, and that every other prosecution by a party for any of the purposes above specified is a special proceeding. Section 46-a of the General Construction Law provedes that every prosecution by a party against another party in a court of justice which is not an action is a special proceeding.

A civil action is commenced by the service of a summons. Civil Practice Act, Sec. 218. A special proceeding is instituted by petition and notice of motion on a notice of eight days unless a shorter time is prescribed by an order to show cause which rests in the discretion of the court. A special proceeding and a motion have sometimes been confused. The difference between them is that the one is an application in a proceeding already pending or about to be commenced, on which it depends for jurisdiction, while the other is an independent prosecution of a remedy, in which jurisdiction is obtained by original process. A motion is not a remedy but is based upon some remedy and is always connected with and dependent upon the principal remedy.

Remedies are divide d by the Civil Practice Act into actions and special proceedings. The proceeding before us clearly is not an action, nor is it claimed to be; neither is it a motion. Therefore, what is it? It has all the elements of a litigation in a court of justice. It is a proceeding in court by which respondents are pursuing a remedy which the law affords them. We entertain not the slightest doubt that it must fall into the category of a special proceeding and that costs were properly allowed.

Article 31 of the Civil Practice Act makes no specific provision for costs. Section 1492 of the same Act however provides that costs in a special proceeding in a court of record, where the costs thereof are not specially regulated in the act, may be awarded to any party, in the discretion of the court, at the rates allowed for similar services in an action in the same court.

In the orders appealed from the court exercised its discretion in favor of respondents and awarded them costs at the rates allowed for similar services in an action.

In Matter of Durey, 223 AD 70, 227 S 580, aff'd 248 NY 594, 162 NE 538, a proceeding instituted for the identical relief sought here, this court and the Court of Appeals awarded the respondent costs against the same appellants. On the prior appeal to this court from the orders appointing a referee we awarded costs to respondents on the affirmance of the orders. (258 AD 766, 14 S2d 720.)

There is another consideration which confirms our view that this is a special proceeding. An appeal may be taken to this court only from a judgment or order in an action or a special proceeding. Civil Practice Act, Sec. 608-611, 631. Concededly the proceeding before us is not an action. Therefore, if it is not a special proceeding, as appellants contend, this court has no jurisdiction to review the determination of the court below, and the final order is binding upon them. To adopt that view would be to hold that this court and the Court of Appeals usurped jurisdiction in Matter of Durey, supra.

On the hearing before the referee the parties stipulated in open court that the referee should engage the services of a stenographer and that the fees of the latter should be added to those of the referee and taxed accordingly. Stenographers' fees are taxable when the parties have agreed that they may be taxed as disbursements. (Matter of French et al., 181 AD 719, 168 S 988, aff'd 224 NY 555, 120 NE 863.) The deputy attorney general who appeared for appellants now seeks to avoid the effect of this stipulation on the ground that it is not in writing. The stipulation was made in open court and may not now be repudiated.

The order appealed from should be affirmed with $50 costs and disbursements.

Order affirmed with fifty dollars costs and disbursements.

IN RE McDEVITT (SpCtKingsCo 1917) 101 M 558, 168 S 433.

Habeas corpus proceeding by Kathleen L. McDevitt for permission to see her children, who had been duly adopted by respondent.

CALLAGHAN, J. This is a proceeding by way of a writ of habeas corpus by a mother for permission to see her children, who have been duly adopted by the respondent.

One's natural impulses are in sympathy with the petitioner's contention; but, as I view the controlling authorities, the relief asked here cannot be granted in a proceeding of this nature. Section 70 of the Domestic Relations Law provides for proceedings by way of habeas corpus to procure custody of children when they are unlawfully restrained by one not entitled to their custody, but it is obvious that that provision of the Domestic Relations Law does not apply to this situation. The respondent in this proceeding is entitled to the legal custody of the children, and all natural rights of the parents have ceased. Matter of MacRae, 189 NY 142, 81 NE 956, 12 AnnCas 505. Therefore the respondent would be in a position to maintain such a proceeding against the petitioner, if the situation were reversed.

A writ of habeas corpus is a common-law proceeding. It was under the common law "a writ in behalf of liberty, and its purpose was to deliver a prisoner from unjust imprisonment and illegal and improper restraint." People ex rel Pruyne v Walts, 122 NY 238, 25 NE 266; People ex rel Keator v Moss, 6 AD 414, 39 S 690. The theory of such proceeding is, of course, that one is illegally restrained of his liberty as against one entitled to the custody. It is very true that habeas corpus may be resorted to for the purpose of determining the right of custody of children. The proceeding, however, is one of law and not in equity. When, therefore, one has the actual custody and the admitted legal right to the custody, the court cannot, on habeas corpus, upon equitable principles determine that the welfare of the child requires a temporary interference with such legal custody. It seems to me that an application for the relief here sought might be addressed to the equity side of the court, where the court would have full power, in its discretion, to do what is for the best interests of the children. That practice was followed in Matter of Knowack, 158 NY 482, 53 NE 676, 44 LRA 699, Wilcox v Wilcox, 14 NY 576, and Matter of Tierney, 128 AD 835, 112 S 1039. And that such is the correct theory for such proceeding is strongly suggested in Matter of Stewart, 77 M 524, 137 NY S 202, and People ex rel Keator v Moss, supra.

It follows, therefore, that the writ must be dismissed and the children remanded to the custody of their foster parent, without prejudice, however, to any proceeding which the mother may bring for the relief sought herein.

Ordered accordingly.

Sec. 3.3 Motions, Demurrers, etc.

APPLICATION OF BURGE (NYCo 1952) 118 S2d 23

Ex Parte petition of stockholder of foreign corporation to have appointment made of special receiver for certain assets of corporation was granted. Thereafter corporation made motion to have order set aside, on ground that court was without power to make appointment.

EDER, Justice. In March, 1952, one Henry Burge, a resident of this state and a stockholder of Oceanic Trading Co., Inc., a foreign corporation, filed with this court his ex parte petition praying for the appointment of a special receiver for certain assets in this state alleged to belong to it, said to consist of causes of action against one David C. Milton and one Ellery C. Huntington. The petition averred that said named persons were residents of this state and had offices here; that they jointly had and have working control of the corporation. By the allegations of the petition they were charged with breaches of fiduciary duties, with waste, mismanagement and with improper diversion of funds of the corporation in a sum in excess of $1,000,000. ...

The court being satisfied from the facts set forth that prima facie there existed against such persons a cause of action in equity to impress a trust and to require them to account as fiduciaries and that in the situation described an imperious necessity appeared requiring the appointment of a special receiver to secure and preserve said assets granted the application and by an order made on April 1, 1952, appointed a special receiver to take possession of said assets and hold the same subject to the further orders of the court;...

It appears that after his appointment the special receiver commenced an action in this court in which said Milton and Huntington are named as defendants, the summons being served upon them, personally, in this state. It is to be observed that they do not move to vacate or set aside the order as against them personally, nor do they assail its validity in any manner.

Rather, it is Oceanic Trading Co. Inc., over whom it is alleged they jointly have working control, who now moves to set aside the order, asserting the court was without power to make the appointment. ...

Movant's postulate that the order was made in a "special proceeding" is an erroneous one. The order appointing the special receiver was not made in a special proceeding. Nor was it made in an action. It was made on an ex parte motion anterior to the formal commencement of an action, upon a petition, the allegations of which disclosed that it was imperatively necessary that a receiver be appointed to protect and preserve the said causes of action as assets of the corporation, as an essential step preliminary to the formal institution of the action....

The ex parte application for the appointment of a special receiver did not involve the determination of or affect the substantive rights of the parties, a basic factor with which an action or special proceeding is identified and which is its purpose in either respect. That ex parte application was not an action since there were no parties plaintiff and no parties defendant; there were no pleadings; no summons was served; there was no trial; there was no determination made; no judgment was rendered.

Similarly, it was not a special proceeding, which is more analogous in its purpose and scope to an action, the difference being that the parties prosecuting are named as petitioner or relator instead of plaintiff, and the party proceeded against is named respondent instead of defendant. As to pleadings there is a petition in place of a complaint; the answer is sometimes called a return; as to process no summons is served; in its stead a notice or order to show cause initiates the proceeding; the procedure as to trial is somewhat summary in character; affidavits may be employed on either side to make the issue between the parties. Matter of Jetter, 78 NY 601, 605; Matter of Rensselaer & S.R.R.Co. v Davis, 55 NY 145, 148; Matter of Levine v Lending, 176 M 462, 26 S2d 775.

Unlike a motion, a special proceeding has all the elements of a litigation in a court of justice; it is not an ordinary litigation because the proceeding is special as prescribed by statute; and while it is not an action, it is a remedy, and is therefore a special proceeding. Jetter case, supra, 78 NY at page 604. Remedies are divided by the Civil Practice Act into actions and special proceedings. Secs. 4 and 5, Civ. Prac. Act; also, Secs. 11-a, 46-a, Gen. Construction Law. An action is an ordinary prosecution in a court of justice by a party against another for the enforcement or protection of a right, or the redress or prevention of a wrong, Sec. 4, Civ.Prac.Act; Sec. 11-a, Gen. Constr. Law, commenced by the service of a summons, Sec. 218, Civ.Prac.Act. Every other prosecution by a party in a court of justice which is not an action, is a special proceeding, Sec. 5, Civ.Prac.Act; Sec. 46-a, Gen. Constr. Law, and is commenced by the service of a notice or order to show cause, Sec. 1289, Civ.Prac.Act.

A motion is not a remedy in the sense of the Civil Practice Act but in general relates to some incidental matter collateral to the main object of an action. Jetter and Rensselaer cases, supra. Motions relate generally to matters of procedure or to matters which do not finally determine substantive rights. Actions or special proceedings relate to and affect substantive rights of the parties. The former, viz., motions, deals with adjective law; the latter, viz., actions or special proceedings, deal with substantive law. The distinction is both apparent and real.

The procedure here employed appointing the special receiver not being by way of action or special proceeding it constitutes a motion. Jetter and Rensselaer cases, supra. (Cf. State ex rel Ashley v Circuit Court of Milwaukee County, 219 Wis 38, 261 NE 737, 740. An application for an order is a motion, Sec. 113, Civ Prac Act).

The basal point then is whether a court of equity in the absence of express statutory authorization possesses inherent power, in an emergency, and prior to the formal commencement of an action by service of summons, to appoint a special or temporary receiver for a corporation to take possession of certain particular assets, to secure and preserve them to prevent their loss to the corporation and to hold them until the further orders of the court as to their ultimate disposition.

Inherent power is that which is necessary to a court for the proper and complete administration of justice and which is resident in all courts of superior jurisdiction and essential to their existence. In this connection it is recognized that the right of a court of equity to appoint a receiver ex parte for the preservation of property is an inherent part of its equity powers....(Citations and discussions omitted).

For the foregoing reasons and those set forth in the opinion filed on the ex parte motion for the appointment of the special receiver, the motion to vacate and set aside order of appointment is denied. Settle order.

Sec. 3.31 Provisions of Statutes and Rules

N.Y. Civil Practice Law and Rules (CPLR)

Article 22. Stay, Motions, Orders and Mandates

Sec. 2201 (omitted)
Sec. 2211 Application for order; when motion made. A motion is an application for an order. A motion on notice is made when a notice of the motion or an order to show cause is served.
Sec. 2212 Where motion made, in supreme court action (omitted)
Sec. 2213 Where motion made, in county court action. (omitted)
Sec. 2214 Motion papers; service; time. (a) Notice of motion. A notice of motion shall specify the time and place of the hearing on the motion, the supporting papers upon which the motion is based, the relief demanded and the grounds therefor. Relief in the alternative or of several different types may be demanded.

(b) Time for service of notice and affidavits. A notice of motion and supporting affidavits shall be served at least eight days before the time at which the motion is noticed to be heard. Answering affidavits shall be served at least two days before such time. Answering affidavits shall be served at least five days before such time if a notice of motion served at least ten days before such time so demands; whereupon any reply affidavits shall be served at least one day before such time.

(c) Furnishing papers to the court. Each party shall furnish to the court all papers served by him. The moving party shall furnish at the hearing all other papers not already in the possession of the court necessary to the consideration of the questions involved. Where such papers are in the possession of an adverse party, they shall be produced by him at the hearing on notice served with the motion papers. Only papers served in accordance with the provisions of this rule shall be read in support of, or in opposition to, the motion, unless the court for good cause shall otherwise direct.

(d) Order to show cause. The court in a proper case may grant an order to show cause, to be served in lieu of a notice of motion, at a time and in a manner specified therein....

Rule 2220 Entry and filing of order; service. (a) Entry and filing. An order determining a motion shall be entered and filed in the office of the clerk of the court where the action is triable, and all papers used on the motion and any opinion or memorandum in writing shall be filed with that clerk unless the order dispenses with such filing....

(b) Service. Service of an order shall be made by service of a certified copy of the order...

Article 30 Remedies and Pleading

Sec. 3001-3023 (omitted)

Rule 3024 Motion to correct pleadings. (a) Vague or ambiguous pleadings. If a pleading is so vague or ambiguous that a party cannot reasonably be required to frame response he may move for a more definite statement.

(b) Scandalous or prejudicial matter. A party may move to strike any scandalous or prejudicial matter unnecessarily inserted in a pleading....

Rule 3034 Motion procedure to settle statement terms. (omitted)....
Rule 3042 Procedure for bill of particulars. (a) Notice (omitted)

(b) Motion. Instead of proceeding by demand, the party may move for a bill of particulars, or copy of the items of account in the first instance....

Article 32 Accelerated Judgment

Sec. 3201 (omitted)

Rule 3211 Motion to dismiss. (a) Motion to dismiss cause of action. A party may move for judgment dismissing one or more causes of action asserted against him on the ground that:

1. a defense is founded upon documentary evidence; or
2. the court has not jurisdiction of the subject matter of the cause of action; or
3. the party asserting the cause of action has not legal capacity to sue; or

4. there is another action pending between the same parties for the same cause of action in a court of any state or the United States; the court need not dismiss upon this ground but may make such order as justice requires; or

5. the cause of action may not be maintained because of arbitration, collateral estoppel, discharge in bankruptcy, infancy or other disability of the moving party, payment, release, res judicata, statute of limitations, or statute of frauds; or

6. with respect to a counterclaim, it may not properly be interposed in the action ; or

7. the pleading fails to state a cause of action; or

8. the court has not jurisdiction of the person of the defendant; or

9. the court has not jurisdiction in an action where service was made under section 314 or 315; or

10. the court should not proceed in the absence of a person who should be a party.

(b) Motion to dismiss defense. A party may move for judgment dismissing one or more defenses, on the ground that a defense is not stated....

Rule 3212 Motion for summary judgment. (a) Time; kind of action. Except as provided in subdivision....

Article 44 Trial Motions

Sec. 4401 Motion for judgment during trial. (omitted)

Sec. 4402 Motion for continuance or new trial during trial. (omitted)

Sec. 4403 Motion for new trial or to confirm or reject or grant other relief after reference to report or verdict of advisory jury. (omitted)

Sec. 4404 Post-trial motion for judgment and new trial (omitted)

Sec. 4405 Time and judge before whom post-trial motion made. (omitted)

Sec. 4406 Single post-trial motion. In addition to motions made orally immediately ofter decision, verdict or discharge of the jury, there shall be only one motion under this article with respect to any decision by a verdict on issues triable of right by a jury; and each party shall raise by the motion under rule 2215 every ground for post-trial relief then available to him....

Examples of Motions or Demurrers

1. Motion to dismiss for lack of jurisdiction (N.Y. CPLR, Rule 3211)
   a. No delegation of jurisdiction territorially
   b. No delegation of jurisdiction of the party
   c. No delegation of jurisdiction of the cause of action
   d. No delegation of jurisdiction of the remedy
2. Motion to dismiss for improper venue.
3. Motion to dismiss for lack of jurisdiction of the defendant or of the respondent.
4. Motion to dismiss for failure to state facts sufficient to constitute a cause of action.
5. Motion for summary judgment.
6. Motion for nonsuit at close of plaintiff's evidence.
7. Motion for nonsuit at conclusion of all of the evidence.
8. Motion for a directed verdict.
9. Motion to set aside the verdict and for a new trial.
10. Motion for judgment notwithstanding the verdict.
11. Motion in arrest of judgment.
12. Motion to vacate a judgment.

Note on Demurrers

1. Definitions: A demurrer is the formal mode of disputing the sufficiency in law of the pleading of the other side. In effect it is an allegation that, even if the facts as stated in the pleading to which objection is taken be true, yet their legal consequences are not such as to put the demurring party to the necessity of answering them or proceeding further with the cause.... A general demurrer is a demurrer framed in general terms, without showing specifically the nature of the objection, and which is usually resorted to where the objection is to matter of substance.... A special demurrer is one which excepts to the sufficiency of the pleadings on the opposite side, and shows specifically the nature of the objection, and the particular ground of the exception. (Black, Law Dictionary)

2. N.Y. Civ. Prac. Act, Sec. 277: "The demurrer is abolished. An objection to a pleading in point of law may be taken by motion for judgment as the rules provide." This provision is omitted from CPLR but seems implied in Rule 3211, in authorizing a motion to dismiss on the ground that e.g. "7. a pleading fails to state a cause of action"; or e.g. that "A party may move for judgment dismissing one or more defenses, on the ground that a defense is not stated."

Federal Rules of Civil Procedure (FRCP)

I, II, Rules 1-6 (omitted)

III. Pleadings and Motions

Rule 7. Pleadings allowed; Forms of Motions.

(a) Pleadings (omitted)

(b) Motions and other papers (1) An application to the court for an order shall be by motion which, unless made during a hearing or trial, shall be made in writing, shall state with particularity the grounds therefor, and shall set forth the relief or order sought. The requirement of writing is fulfilled if the motion is stated in a written notice of the hearing of the motion.

(2) The rules applicable to captions, signing, and other matters of form of pleadings apply to all motions and other papers provided for by these rules.

(c) Demurrers, Pleas, etc., Abolished. Demurrers, pleas, and exceptions for insufficiency of a pleading shall not be used....

Rule 12 Defenses and Objections - When and How Presented - By Pleading or Motion - Motion for Judgment on Pleadings.

(a) When Presented. (omitted)

(b) How Presented. (omitted)

(c) Motion for Judgment on the Pleadings. After the pleadings are closed but within such time as not to delay the trial, any party may move for judgment on the pleadings. If, on a motion for judgment on the pleadings, matters outside the pleadings are presented to and not excluded by the court, the motion shall be treated as one for summary judgment and disposed of as provided in Rule 56, and all parties shall be given reasonable opportunity to present all material pertinent to such a motion by Rule 56.

(d) Preliminary Hearings. (omitted)

(e) Motion for More Definite Statement. If a pleading to which a responsive pleading is permitted is so vague or ambiguous that a party cannot reasonably be required to form a responsive pleading, he may move for a more definite statement before interposing his responsive pleading. The motion shall point out the defects complained of and the details desired...

(f) Motion to Strike. Upon motion made by a party before responding to a pleading or, if no responsive pleading is permitted by these rules, upon motion made by a party within 20 days after the service of the pleading upon him or upon the court's own initiative at any time, the court may order stricken from any pleading any insufficient defense or any redundant, immaterial, impertinent, or scandalous matter...

Sec. 3.4 Elements of a Remedy, Exercise of the
Sec. 3.41 Jurisdiction

COMMERCIAL CASUALTY INS. CO. v CONSOLIDATED S. CO. (1929) 278 US 177, 73 LEd 252

On certificate by the United States Circuit Court of Appeals for the sixth Circuit for the opinion of the Supreme Court of the United States of questions arising upon appeal by defendant from a judgment of the District Court for the District of Ohio refusing to vacate a default judgment on the ground that the venue was improper....

Mr. Justice VAN DEVANTER: The material facts are: A corporation of Indiana brought a transitory action at law against a corporation of New Jersey in a Federal district court in Ohio. That court's jurisdiction was invoked only on the ground that the parties were citizens of different states; and the value of the matter in controversy was in excess of the statutory requirement. The defendant was doing business in Ohio, and, in accord with the state law, had designated a local agent upon whom process against it might be served. Summons was duly served within the district upon that agent. The defendant neither appeared nor answered within the period limited therefor, and judgment went against it by default. Later in the same term the defendant moved that the judgment be vacated and the action dismissed because the action was brought in a district in which neither party resided. That motion was denied. The defendant then moved that the judgment be vacated, and leave to defend be granted, on the asserted ground that the summons, although forwarded by the agent to the defendant's home office, had been overlooked. That motion also was denied. The defendant then sued out a writ of error from the circuit court of appeals. The certificate--after eliminating the ruling on the second motion--says of the asserted basis of the first motion:

"Familiar cases say that this defect in the jurisdiction pertains to the venue, and defendant may either insist upon it or may waive it. In this case there was neither affirmative insistence nor affirmative waiver. Defendant allowed the time for effective objections to expire and did nothing."

Shortly stated, the question propounded is whether it was open to the defendant, after permitting the cause to proceed to judgment by default, to object that the action was not brought in the district of the residence of either party.

The pertinent statutes are Sec. 41 and 112, title 28 USC. One provides that district courts shall have "original jurisdiction" of certain classes of civil suits, including suits "between citizens of different states" where the value of the matter in controversy, exclusive of interest and costs, exceeds $3,000. The other provides that, "where the jurisdiction is founded only on the fact that the action is between citizens of different states, suit shall be brought only in the district of the residence of either the plaintiff or the defendant."

These provisions often have been examined and construed by this court. Summarized, the decisions are directly to the effect that the first provision invests each of the district courts with general jurisdiction of all civil suits between citizens of different states, where the matter in controversy is of the requisite pecuniary value; and that the other provision does not detract from that general jurisdiction, but merely accords to the defendant a personal privilege respecting the venue, or place of suit, which he may assert, or may waive, at his election.

The decisions also make it plain that the privilege must be "seasonably" asserted; else it is waived. Whether there was a seasonable assertion in the present case is the real question to be determined.

We are of the opinion that the privilege is of such a nature that it must be asserted at latest before the expiration of the period allotted for entering a general appearance and challenging the merits. In ordinary course, when that period expires the defendant either will have appeared generally for the purpose of contesting the merits or by suffering a default will have assented that his adversary's allegations be taken as confessed for the purposes of judgment. In either event the suit will have reached the stage where attention must be given to the merits. In common practice objections to venue are presented and acted upon at an earlier stage; and this, so far as we are advised, is true of the elective privilege here in question. No adjudged case is cited in which a different practice is either sustained or shown. To hold that such a privilege may be retained until after the suit has reached the stage for dealing with the merits and then be asserted would be in our opinion subversive of orderly procedure and make for harmful delay and confusion.

It was apparent on the face of the plaintiff's petition that jurisdiction was grounded solely on diversity of citizenship and that the suit was brought in a district of which neither party was a resident. The defendant, although duly served with a proper summons apprising it of the time within which it was required to appear and answer, permitted that time to elapse without making any objection to the venue, or place of suit, by motion, pleading or otherwise.

The Ohio practice statute prescribes that all objections thus appearing when so neglected shall be deemed to have been waived, "except only that the court has no jurisdiction of the subject-matter of the action and that the petition does not state facts which show a cause of action." Ohio Gen. Code, Sec. 11,311.

Here the objection was not that the court was without jurisdiction of the subject-matter of the suit, but that the suit was not brought in the district of the residence of either party--a waivable matter of venue only.

Our conclusion is that the objection was not seasonably made and therefore that under our decisions, as also the Ohio statute, it was waived. The question before stated must be answered in the negative. A second or alternative question is propounded in the certificate, but an answer to it is rendered unnecessary by the answer to the other:

Question No. 1, Answer No.

CHERNICK v RODRIGUEZ (SpCtKingsCo 1956) 150 S2d 149

Civil action. On defendant's motion to set aside alleged service of summons and complaint.

BRENNER, Justice. The named defendant appears specially to set aside the alleged service of summons and complaint. There appears to be no need for a reference because upon the facts admitted by the defendant the service is valid.

Defendant admits (1) that he had identified himself to the process server; (2) that he refused to open the door leading to his apartment, and (3) that after the process server dropped the summons and complaint in the vestibule entrance he secured possession of the papers and forwarded them to his lawyer. Thus, there were in this case the necessary elements of "delivery" pursuant to Section 225 of the Civil Practice Act and "leaving" in compliance with Rule 53 of the Rules of Civil Practice. Schenkman v Schenkman, 206 M 660, 136 S2d 405, affirmed 284 AD 1068, 137 S2d 628.

The closed window of a car separated the process server from the defendant in Levine v National Transportation Co. 204 M 202, 125 S2d 679, affirmed 282 AD 720, 122 S2d 901, where service was declared valid. I see no substantial difference between that case and the case at bar. Here a closed door separated the process server from the defendant; In each case the process server indicated his purpose; in each case the defendant identified himself and declined to accept the process; finally, in each case the process was left with the defendant who had both knowledge and possession thereof. Clearly, the defendant failed to perform the duty imposed upon "persons within the jurisdiction to submit to the service of process." Gumperz v Hofmann, 245 AD 622, 624, 283 S 823, 825, affirmed 271 NY 544, 2 NE2d 687.

Motion denied. Settle order on notice.

AVERY et al. v O'DWYER, Mayor, et al (SpCtNYCo 1952) 201 M 989, 110 S2d 569

Action by Joseph Avery and another against William O'Dwyer, individually, and as Mayor of the City of New York, and others...

HOFSTADTER, Justice. The individual defendants, sued both individually and in their respective capacities as officials of the City of New York, move to vacate the service of the summons in this action upon them on the ground that no personal jurisdiction over them was acquired. The purported service on these individuals was made by leaving a copy of the summons and complaint with a clerk in the office of the corporation counsel of the City of New York, in charge of a room bearing a sign which stated in substance that papers were to be served there. One of the photographs on a companion motion reproduces a photograph of a sign reading "Summons and Complaint v The City of New York. Please serve the summons and complaint only at the office of the corporation counsel (this office)". The clerk in charge requested the attorney making the service to wait until he called the chief clerk of the Corporation Counsel's office to the receiving desk; the chief clerk directed the clerk in charge to accept service. He did so and stamped on the cover of the original complaint

"A Copy of the Within Paper Has This Day Been Received
At the Office of the Corporation Counsel
Dec. 21, 1951
Denis M. Hurley
Corporation Counsel"

The foregoing attempted service cannot be sustained as valid personal service upon the individual defendants, either individually or officially, for the reason that no provision of law authorizes service upon them by delivery of the summons to the corporation counsel. Though the plaintiff argues that service on city official s is customarily made on the corporation counsel, in these instances the service is followed by a general appearance and jurisdiction is acquired by such appearance, rather that the service. Since the validity of the service is challenged in this case, the challenge must be upheld and the service on the individual defendants vacated.

There is at the same time before the court a motion by the plaintiff to correct the title in the summons and complaint to include the name of the City of New York inadvertently omitted from the title. The summons and complaint were stapled together and served at the same time. The summons names as defendants the individuals already mentioned, "individually & on behalf of the City of N.Y.", without separate designation of the official title of each of these individuals. In the title of the complaint, however, the official title of each is stated separately. The City of New York, as such, however, does not appear as defendant in the title of either the summons or the complaint.

The very first paragraph of the complaint alleges that the defendant, the City of New York, is a domestic municipal corporation. In another paragraph appear allegations of acts bearing on the cause of action imputed to "thedefendant City of New York." Another paragraph refers to a prior proceeding brought to enjoin "said defendant, the City of New York." It is, moreover, alleged that more than thirty days have elapsed since the filing of the claim sued on and that the Comptroller of the City of New York has refused to make an adjustment or payment therof and that less than a year has elapsed since the accrual of the cause of action -- allegations only appropriate and, indeed, required in a complaint against the City of New York. The plaintiff's affidavit also states that a hearing was held on the claim sued on after its filing with the Comptroller.

The City opposes the amendment on two grounds: (1) that it was not properly served and (2) that the omission of its name from the title is a jurisdictional defect which cannot be cured by amendment.

The question of the validity of the service on the City of New York depends on other considerations than those applicable to the individual defendants. CPA Sec. 228, provides that, if an action is brought against the City of New York, personal service of the summons must be made by delivering a copy within the state "to the mayor, comptroller or counsel to the corporation." It is thus clear that service on the corporation counsel is expressly authorized by law and constitutes a service on the city. Was there service on the corporation counsel in this case? I think there was unquestionably service on him. Service was made at the place and in the manner prescribed by him, presumably for his convenience and to enable him to administer his office in an orderly fashion. To treat such service as ineffectual because the summons was not handed to the corporation counsel himself would be inadmissible. The corporation counsel has set up a regular system and has invited litigants to abide by and rely on that system. To permit the corporation counsel at his whim to treat service made as directed by him as not being service on him would place the public at his mercy and lead to chaos. I therefore hold that the corporation counsel was served as required by Civil Practice Act, Sec. 228.*

In support of the motion to amend the title it is urged that the context of the complaint, served with the summons shows a clear purpose to designate the City of New York as a defendant in the action. Though the city had knowledge of the claim through its presentation to the Comptroller and the hearing on it, and though I am persuaded that the omission of the city's name from the title was a mere oversight, I feel constrained to deny the motion to amend the title. The summons is the process by which the court acquires jurisdiction over the defendant. Here, the city is not named as defendant in the title of either the summons or the complaint. The broad power of amendment conferred by Civil Practice Act, Sec. 105** is, of course, to be exercised liberally to prevent a miscarriage of justice through too rigid subservience to form. Nevertheless, under the guise of amendment basic jurisdictional requirements may not be wholly disregarded. That is, in my opinion, what the plaintiff seeks to attain by the proposed amendment. Though the plaintiff's plight may be unfortunate it cannot override the jurisdictional barrier. In the absence of authority --and none has been brought to the court's attention--the power to amend cannot be strained to that extent. The motion to amend the title is, therefore denied.
Settle order.

AVERY v O'DWYER (1st Dept 1952) 280 AD 766, 113 S2d 686

Action by Joseph Avery and another against Wm. O'Dwyer, and others, individually and on behalf of the City of New York. The Supreme Court, New York County, Special Term, Hofstader, J. (110 S2d 569), entered an order vacating and setting aside the summons and service of summons and denying plaintiffs' motion to correct title of summons and title of complaint, and plaintiffs appealed.

PER CURIAM. Special Term correctly held that the attempted service upon the individual defendants, either as individuals or as officials, cannot be sustained and that part of the order appealed from should be affirmed.

We think, however, that Special Term should have granted plaintiffs' motion to correct the title in the summons and complaint to include the name of the City of New York inadvertently omitted therefrom. The captions did not explicitly include the City formally as a defendant but joined the other defendants "individually and on behalf of the City of New York." The papers, however, served clearly and unmistakably gave notice to the City that it was a defendant in the action. This is deomonstrated by the whole context of the complaint. The City was not prejudiced as it fully understood and indeed acted on such notice.

Jurisdiction was acquired and the inadvertent defect in description can be and should be cured pursuant to the provisions of Civil Practice Act, Sec. 105. That section, inter alia, provides that if a substantial right of a party is not prejudiced, an omission or defect "must be disregarded." On this record a new party is not added; we hold that jurisdiction was acquired and that under the statute, the inadvertent formal omission may be corrected; otherwise form is exalted above substance. (The People ex rel Durham Realty Corporation v Cantor, as Commissioners, 234 NY 507, 138 NE 425, reversing 201 AD 834, 192 S 657, on the dissenting opinion of Clarke, P. J....)

---

*N.Y. Civil Practice Act (CPA):
"Sec. 228. Personal service of summons upon domestic corporation. Personal service of the summons upon a domestic corporation must be made by delivering a copy thereof, within the state, as follows:
1. I"If the action be against the City of New York, to the mayor, comptroller or counsel to the corporation." cf. N.Y. Civil Practice Law and Rules (CPLR), Rule 311.

**N.Y. Civil Practice Act (CPA):
"Sec. 105. Mistakes, omissions, defects and irregularites. At any stage of any action, special proceeding or appeal, a mistake, omission, irregularity or defect may be corrected or supplied, as the case may be, in the discretion of the court, with or without terms, or, if a substantial right of any party shall not be thereby prejudiced, such mistake, ommission, irregularity or defect must be disregarded." cf. N. Y. Civil Practice Law and Rules (CPLR), Rules 305 and 3025.

All concur except Peck, P.J., and Cohn, J., who dissent and vote to affirm.

Order modified by affirming the vacatur of the summons and complaint on the individuals named either individually or officially and by reversing that part of the order denying plaintiffs' motion to correct the title under section 105 and the said motion granted and, as so modified, affirmed with $20 costs and disbursements to appellants.

ZUCKERMAN v McCULLEY (DCtEdMo 1948) 7 FRD 739

HULEN, District Judge. Defendant moves to quash the return of service in this case because it was not served in accordance with Rule 4(d) (1), Federal Rules of Civil Procedure, 28 USCA following section 723c. Under Rule 4(d) (1) service on an individual may be obtained by delivering a copy of the summons and the complaint to the defendant personally, or by leaving copies thereof at his dwelling house or usual place of abode with some person of suitable age and discretion then residing therein, or by delivering copies to an agent authorized by appointment or by law to receive service of process.

The return in this case reads as follows:

"I hereby certify and return, that on the 15th day of October 1947, I received the within summons, and executed same by serving the defendant, Una McCulley by leaving a true copy of Summons, together with a copy of Complaint attached thereto, as furnished by the Clerk of the Court, with an elderly negro who answered the door and said that he was the janitor of the house but who would not give his name, at St. Louis, Missouri, on October 29, 1947."

At hearing on the motion it developed that the defendant lived at 95 Maple Place in St. Louis and operated a rooming house at 5097 Washington. Defendant was out of the City at the time of attempted service and the Deputy United States Marshall served the summons by leaving copy thereof, together with a copy of the complaint, at the Washington address with the janitor.

Certainly the manner of attempted service does not meet the terms of the Rule but the plaintiff urges that there was a substantial compliance with the Rule and since the defendant ultimately received copies of the summons and complaint, defendant's motion should be overruled. It has been held that the Rule on service should be construed liberally to effectuate service where actual notice of suit has been received by the defendant. (See Rovinsky v Rowe, 6C, 131 F2d 687, 689.) In the Rovinsky case service was obtained in Menominee, Michigan, which the defendant always considered his home, as the defendant kept some of his clothes and always had his bedroom ready for occupancy at that home of his widowed mother. Defendant was unmarried and his place of abode had been in different places in the United States for more than twelve years, particularly in the east, and finally at Duluth, Minnesota. It was held, however, that summons and complaint left at the home of defendant's mother was left at his usual place of abode under the Rules so as to give the court jurisdiction over defendant. This place had "been throughout his life the place of his legal residence, the place where his parents lived, where his mother lives now, the place called 'Home' and the one place to which he returns when he has the opportunity to do so***." The case of Skidmore v Green, (D.C. 33 FSupp. 529), appears to us to be more in line with the facts of the present case. In the Skidmore case the defendant spent most of his time traveling about the country in an automobile and trailer, but in his application for license plates he gave as his address a house owned by his brother in New York State where he had formerly resided and to which his pension checks were mailed. It was held that the New York address was the usual place of abode for the purpose of service under the Rule.

While these cases illustrate the liberality with which the Rule for service of summons is construed, yet in our opinion they fall short of authority of plaintiff's position that the service in this case meets the Rule.... The return of the Deputy Marshall states that the summons and complaint were left with "an elderly negro who answered the door and said that he was the janitor of the house", and the evidence developed that is exactly what did happen, but there is no evidence of the janitor "residing therein." On the contrary the evidence is undisputed that the janitor only spent part of the day at the Washington Avenue address, doing janitor work, and we are unable to find any authority as a basis for holding under these circumstances that the janitor was residing within the house.

Motion of the defendant to quash the return of service of summons is sustained and said return is quashed.

ROSS v KONOR (3d Dept 1888) 2 S169, 49 Hun 610 mem.

Action by George B. Ross against Valentine Konor for the recovery of $80, alleged to be due on contract. Defendant denied plaintiff's demand and alleged by way of counter-claim that plaintiff was indebted to him in the sum of $125 for services performed and merchandise furnished. There was judgment for plaintiff, and defendant appeals...

INGALLS, J. This action was commenced in the county court of Montgomery county by the service of a summons. No copy of the complaint accompanied it. The defendant, by his attorneys, appeared generally in the action, and a copy of the complaint was served, and an answer was interposed, wherein the defendant (1) denied each and every allegation of the complaint; (2) alleged, by way of counter-claim, "that within six years last past, at plaintiff's request, defendant performed services and furnished merchandise for benefit of said plaintiff to the value of one hundred and twenty-five dollars; that a demand has been made upon said plaintiff for payment of same, but that no part thereof has ever been paid."

That the county court possessed jurisdiction of the subject-matter is not questioned by the defendant. The only contention of the defendant, so far as the question of jurisdiction is involved, is that the complaint did not allege that the defendant was, at the time of the commencement of the action, a resident of the county of Montgomery, and therefore the county court did not acquire jurisdiction of his person. No motion was made to set aside the summons upon that ground. The defendant did not demur to the complaint upon that ground, which he could have done. (Code Civil Proc. Sec. 488, subsec. 2;) nor did he allege any such ground of defense in his answer. The jurisdiction of the court was in no manner questioned by the defendant until the trial. We conclude that the defendant submitted to such jurisdiction, and waived all objection thereto, and as, upon the trial, he was shown, by competent evidence to have been an actual resident of that county at the commencement of the action, the county court committed no error in entertaining the action. (McCormick v Railroad Co. 49 NY 303...) In McIntyre v Carriere, (17 Hun(NY) 65), the case of McDonald v Truesdail, which was decided in this court, is referred to, wherein the action was commenced by the service of a summons without the complaint, as in the present action; and this court held that jurisdiction was acquired by the service of the summons, and that the county court was justified in amending the complaint by reducing the claim of damages from $5,000 to $1,000. The decision in that case involved a much greater stretch of authority than is required to sustain the proceedings in the present action. We are referred by appellant's counsel to Gilbert v York, (41 Hun(NY) 595). In that case the defendant demurred to the complaint; thus raising the question of jurisdiction at the first opportunity. Again, the complaint in that case failed to show jurisdiction of the subject-matter, as well as of the person of the defendant. It will be seen that prominence was given to that circumstance in deciding the case referred to. In the case at bar, jurisdiction of the subject-matter is conceded, which we think distinguishes it from the case cited. The distinction referred to seems to be recognized in Wheelock v Lee, (74 NY 495). Judge Rapallo says, at page 498: "In a case in which the court had jurisdiction of the cause on some of the other grounds, as for instance, where the cause of action arose within the city of Brooklyn, the general rule would apply that a general appearance cures any defect in the service of process to bring the defendant into court, and even the total absence of any service." Reference to the complaint herein shows that the cause of action arose in the county of Montgomery, and that the claim of damages is within the jurisdiction of the county court. We also refer to the opinion in Dwyer v Rathbone, infra, which was argued in this court at the May term, 1888. We conclude that the court properly excluded evidence in support of the defendant's pretended counter-claim, as it affirmatively appeared that the articles were not claimed to have been furnished within the period limited by the defendant's counter-claim, and no motion was made to amend the pleading. The judgment must be affirmed, with costs.

Sec. 3.42 Pleadings
Sec. 3.421 Pleadings by Plaintiff

HAYWARD v HOOD (1stDept 1887) 44 Hun(NY) 128, 8 StR 457, aff'dnoop109 NY 643

Appeal from a judgment dismissing the complaint, and from an order sustaining a demurrer interposed by the defendants herein to a supplemental complaint.

The court, at General Term, said: "By an order of this court the defendants were granted leave to file a supplemental complaint, and by the order granting such leave the defendants were permitted to answer or demur. In pursuance of such leave, the plaintiff, in addition to the former complaint, theretofore served, made this supplemental complaint, alleging certain additional facts to those which were contained in the original complaint. The defendants demurred to this supplemental complaint upon the ground that it did not state facts sufficient to constitute a cause of action, which demurrer was sustained, and this appeal was taken from the order entered thereon.

"It is undoubtedly true that the supplemental complaint did not set up a cause of action as against the defendants. It was not intended so to do. It was the mere allegation of additional facts to those which had been alleged in the original complaint for the purpose of supplementing that complaint. It is also true that the order gave the defendants the right to answer or demur to said supplemental complaint. But as the supplemental complaint did not pretend to set out an independent or different cause of action from that contained in the original complaint, it was to be read as part and parcel of the complaint, and if the two contained a cause of action which was not demurrable an answer upon the part of the defendants was required. It would seem, therefore, that no issue whatever was raised by the demurrer to the supplemental complaint, that not being a complete complaint within itself, and that it was error to entertain such demurrer.

"The order and judgment appealed from must, therefore, be reversed and the defendant allowed to withdraw said demurrer and to answer upon payment of the costs of demurrer and of the appeal from the order sustaining the same."...

Opinion by VAN BRUNT, P. J.; Brady and Daniels, J. J., concurred.

Judgment reversed, with leave to defendant to withdraw demurrer and answer on payment of costs of demurrer, and of the appeal from the order sustaining the same.

BARBER v FARMERS & TRADERS LIFE INS. CO. (SpCtKingsCo 1951) 109 S2d 448

Marie Edna Barber nee Murphy filed two complaints against Farmers & Traders Life Insurance Co. seeking commissions due and earned prior to termination of contract between the parties and damages for breach of such contract. Defendant moved to dismiss....

KEOGH, Justice. Defendant moves to dismiss two complaints. Plaintiff alleges that in 1941 plaintiff and defendant were parties to a written contract under the terms of which plaintiff became "general agent" of defendant insurance company. Plaintiff continued in the employ of defendant until August 11, 1945, when the latter gave written notice of termination of said contract. Further alleging nonpayment by defendant of commissions due and earned by plaintiff for a period prior to termination of contract, amounts of which are unknown to plaintiff but believed to be at least a fixed sum stated, plaintiff prays that defendant be required to give an accounting, that the exact amount of the moneys due be ascertained and judgment had.

Plaintiff pleads an action in law and prays for equitable relief. Whether one or other is pleaded is determined from the factual presentation of the pleadings. (Model Building & Loan Ass's of Mott Haven v Reeves, 236 NY 331, 333, 140 NE 715, 716.) The prayer for relief is not determinative, although it may be considered in connection with the cause of action set forth. The pleadings should contain a demand for judgment to which plaintiff believes that she is entitled, Civil Practice Act, Sec. 255, and such demand should be warranted by the facts recited. A complaint which states no cause of action cognizable in equity but which prays for equitable relief should be dismissed upon motion made before answer is served. (Low v Swartout, 171 AD 725, 729, 157 S 1067, 1071.) Plaintiff may not improperly proceed in equity and thereby deprive defendant of the right to trial by jury.

Plaintiff herein has failed to plead any basis for relief "cognizable in equity." Her failure to allege "no adequate remedy at law" is noted but is not the sole basis for the determination. Alleging that defendant was plaintiff's agent as to moneys due her and that such created a quasi trusteeship, in connection with which she may have an accounting, does not state a cause of action in equity that is legally sufficient. (Sloane v United Features Syndicate, Inc., 135 M 365, 238 S 91.) Plaintiff should proceed at law even though she does not know the exact amount for which judgment should be demanded; (Block v Selectar Mfg. Co., Supp 56 S2d 845, 846; and cf. Lockwood v Bedell Co., 178 AD 695, 696, 165 S 850, 851.) Motion to dismiss complaint granted with leave to plead over.

Considering next the motion addressed to the complaint in Action No. 2, defendant seeks a dismissal thereof (1) as legally insufficient, or (2) alternatively, as barred by the Statute of Limitations; alternatively, defendant seeks an order (3) requiring plaintiff to serve an amended complaint separately stating and numbering causes of action, or making the cause of action attempted to be asserted against it more definite and certain.

Defendant claims that it is unable to determine from a reading of this complaint whether plaintiff seeks therein to recover (1) for commissions, (2) damages for breach of contract, or (3) damages for willful injury to plaintiff's property rights in the agency contract.

Plaintiff takes the position upon the argument herein that she has pleaded but a single cause of action at law for damages for breach of contract.

The written contract for the asserted breach of which plaintiff sues is not attached to and incorporated in the complaint, nor are specific parts thereof recited therein.

The complaint in action No. 2 is clearly at law and demands money damages. It pleads a hiring under a written contract and wanton and willful termination.

It is not alleged that the hiring was to become effective on the date the contract was executed, nor is the duration of the contract pleaded, nor whether it was for a stated term or at will. Again, it is not set forth whether or not the employment was terminated as of the date of the letter of termination or whether such termination was in violation of plaintiff's rights under the terms of a written contract other than is to be gathered from the use of words "thereby breaching its agreement," which is a legal conclusion. Plaintiff is under a statutory compulsion to make a showing of material ultimate facts, CPA Sec. 241; (Sherman v International Publications, Inc., 214 AD 437, 441, 212 S 478, 482). The words "wantonly and wilfully" do not add to such a cause of action as plaintiff says she has attempted to plead. If plaintiff is pleading merely a cause of action for breach of contract, such characterization should be omitted.

It may be that the contract gave the parties the right to terminate it with or without notice. If the hiring were at will, this also would follow. There are no factual recitals as to the nature of the breach, only the manner in which it was effected (Bender's Forms of Pleading, vol. 4, p. 5).

Plaintiff has sufficiently complied with Rules of Civil Practice, rule 92, as amended, but if she seeks to recover damages for the asserted breach, the manner in which such damage was sustained should be indicated. From the averments of the present complaint the damages sought would seem to be commissions earned. There is no averment that defendant denies this obligation, that it remains unpaid in whole or in part, or that defendant has in any way refused to meet it.

There is no showing wherein damages otherwise have been sustained. While a pleader is under no obligation to plead his measure of damages and pertinent details, if necessary, can be procured by way of a bill of particulars, there should be a showing of facts from which damages properly can be inferred. (Lurie v New Amsterdam Casualty Co., 270 NY 379, 382, 1 NE2d 472, 473.) Of course, if special damages are sought, these must be specifically shown.

Motion to dismiss complaint granted, with leave to plead over. Settle orders on notice.

KRAFT v RICE (1stDept 1899) 45 AD 569, 61 S 368

Appeal from special term, New York county.

Action by Benjamin F. Kraft against Samuel M. Rice. From an interlocutory judgment overruling a demurrer to the complaint, defendant appeals.

O'BRIEN, J. We agree with the court below in the statement of the rule relating to the sufficiency of a pleading on contract, that, if it clearly sets forth a contract and its breach, even though the theory of damages predicated thereon may be erroneous, it would be a statement of a good cause of action. The difficulty, however, with this complaint, is that there is no allegation of a breach. The whisky, having been pledged to the defendant, was rightfully in his possession, and was there to remain until a certain note was paid. Though the payment of the note is alleged, there is no allegation of a demand for the return of the whisky, which would be necessary to show a breach. If, in addition to the contract, a breach was alleged, then the plaintiff would be entitled to at least nominal damages, and the complaint would not be demurrable. The complaint, however, was not framed on that theory, but what is sought is the recovery of $500 paid out to secure a return of the whisky. What is therefore sought is special damages. If we construe the pleading as one for special damages, which was undoubtedly the theory in the pleader's mind, then complaint is clearly insufficient. As stated, what is here sought to be recovered is $500, claimed to have been expended by the plaintiff "to secure to himself the return of the said whisky." This is an allegation of special damage, which in the absence of any facts showing how such special damage arose, is insufficient. The rule on this subject is stated in 1 Rum, Prac. p. 325, as follows:

"Where special damages are sought to be recovered, they must be fully and accurately stated. Havemeyer v Fuller, 60 HowPrac (NY) 316. Facts must be set forth in the complaint from which the court can see that the plaintiff has sustained damage. A mere conclusion asserting damage is not sufficient. Thompson v Gould, 16 AbbPrac(NS)(NY) 424."

Apart, therefore, from the question of whether there is sufficient allegation to justify nominal damages, it is apparent that such were not sought in this action, but, on the contrary, that the plaintiff had assigned to him, not the cause of action for breach of the contract, but a cause of action for the special damages which Brintnall suffered by being obliged to pay to some one - for some purpose or for some reason undisclosed - $500 for the return of the whisky.

We think the demurrer was good, and that the judgment should be reversed, with costs, and the demurrer sustained, with costs, but with leave to the plaintiff, upon payment of costs, to serve an amended complaint. All concur.

BARRETT, J. (concurring). I do not think that the plaintiff here would have been entitled to nominal damages, even though he had distinctly averred a breach of the alleged contract. He is the assignee of but a particular demand, namely, his assignor's alleged right, title, and interest in the sum of $500, which the latter was compelled, in some undisclosed way, to pay to secure the return of the whisky. He is the assignee of no other demand. Consequently no cause of action for damages, nominal, ordinary, or special, resulting from a breach of the contract, is vested in him. The right to the $500, if there be any such right, cannot flow, even as special damages, from the nonfulfillment of the promise averred. If anything, it is an independent demand, in the nature of a special action on the case, growing out of insufficiently disclosed facts. The damages for the breach of the agreement to return the whisky upon the payment of the note would be the cost of replacing it in the market. Upon the other hand, if the refusal to then return it amounted in effect to a conversion, the damages would be its value at the time of conversion. In neither aspect of the case would the sum paid to secure its return have been the measure of damages. If in some other aspect that sum might have been recovered, the facts constituting the special case on that head would have been averred. It follows that, however the facts as pleaded be viewed, the plaintiff by his assignment took nothing relating to the damages appropriate either in an action for a breach of contract or for conversion. For these reasons, I agree that the demurrer was well taken.

Sec. 3.422 Pleadings by Defendant

INTERNATIONAL RY. CO. v JAGGARD (4thDept 1922) 204 AD 67, 197 S 384

Action by the International Railway Company against Ernest K. Jaggard, individually and as president of the Buffalo Jitney Owners' Association, a voluntary association of more than seven persons, and others. From an order denying the plaintiff's motion to strike out certain allegations contained in the answer of defendant Jaggard, plaintiff appeals....

DAVIS, J. The complaint alleges that plaintiff is engaged in operating a street surface railroad in the city of Buffalo, and in July, 1922, a large number of its employees struck, and for a time it was unable to operate its cars; that the defendants and others immediately, without lawful authority, under the provisions of sections 25 and 26 of the Transportation Corporations Law (Consol. Laws, c. 63), began to operate motor vehicles to carry passengers for hire on the streets served by the plaintiff, and have continued an unlawful competition with the plaintiff, who is without adequate remedy at law; and relief is asked that the defendants be restrained from operating such motor vehicles, unless lawfully authorized, and that the plaintiff have damages.

The defendant Jaggard, individually and as president, etc., interposed a somewhat lengthy and complicated answer. The plaintiff moved to have the affirmative allegations pleaded as defenses separately stated and numbered and divided into paragraphs, and to have certain parts of the answer struck out as "sham, frivolous, irrelevant, and unnecessary." Thirteen different parts of the answer are pointed out in the order to show cause as falling within these classifications.

At Special Term the court with commendable patience sought to assist the parties in reaching an agreement on these matters in controversy and in getting a pleading prepared that would be unobjectionable. At the end of these consultations an order was granted denying plaintiff's motion, and an amended answer was attached to the order, representing the joint labors of the court and counsel. Such efforts to prepare a pleading by general agreement rarely produce satisfactory results. (Day v Day, 95 AD 123, 125 88 S 504.) They did not here, and plaintiff has appealed.

A simpler and more summary method exists. Where a pleading contains a mass of irrelevancies and redundancies mingled together with admissions, denials, and defenses so inextricably that it is quite impossible to separate them and strike out the bad without completely redrafting the pleading, it is no part of the court's duty to attempt to eliminate the parts of the pleading that are not good, but the parts so mingled and objected to should be struck out entirely. Gutta-Percha & Rubber Mfg. Co. v Holman, 150 AD 678, 135 S 766.

The rule in the case just cited was applied to a complaint. The same rule may be applied to an answer. (Uggla v Brokaw, 77 AD 310, 79 S 244.) An answer should be so drafted as to disclose readily to the court what the issues are. Our system of pleading permits and requires this. It is not necessary to admit formally in the answer anything alleged in the complaint; only denials are provided for. (Civil Practice Act, Sec. 261; Stroock Plush Co. v Talcott, 129 AD 14, 113 S 214.) Following denials, the answer may next contain a statement of new matter constituting a defense or counter-claim, and it may set forth as many defenses or counter-claims, or both, as defendant has; but each should be separately stated, numbered, and divided into paragraphs, numbered consecutively, each as nearly as may be containing a separate allegation. Civil Practice Act, Sec. 261, 262; rule 90, Rules of Civil Practice.
mandatory. A defense may not be jumbled up with other defenses, nor with a denial or denials.
Marcuse, 119 AD 478, 103 S 1026.)

The answer as finally drafted and allowed by the order, in my opinion, still contains much irrelevant matter constituting no defense, and the numbering of the separate paragraphs has practically disappeared. In some respects it is an improvement on the original answer, for it has abandoned the improper method of interposing a denial by alleging that defendant has no knowledge or information sufficient to form a belief on certain subjects, and "therefore denies the same."

The answer alleges with much detail the events following the cessation of street car service as a result of the strike, and the overpowering necessity of furnishing some kind of transportation to take the place of that withdrawn. It is possible that an emergency may justify the performance of an act constituting an invasion of private rights, which the law has prohibted but is not malum in se. (38 Cyc. 525, 1066. See, alos, Brooklyn City RR Co. v Whalen, 191 AD 737, 742, 182 S 283, affd 229 NY 570, 128 NE 215.)

We do not need to determine that question now, but I think the defendant is entitled to set up briefly (without reciting evidence) in his answer any acts of himself or of the members of the association during what they regard was a public emergency. The allowance of such an allegation in the answer is not an adjudication as to its materiality, and does not constitute a decision that evidence under it would be competent. (Michigan Steam Ship Co. v American Bonding Co., 109 AD 55, 57, 95 S 1034.) A brief allegation as a defense that the defendants had applied through the regular channels, and were expecting shortly to be granted lawful authority to do business, while anticipatory may constitute a proper defense in an equity action, where injunctive relief is demanded.

I do not see how the question of the plaintiff's dealings and contracts with its employees can be a material issue in this action. Prolix allegations of that character in the answer were entirely irrelevant. If the plaintiff is not running its cars for any reason, it has no more interest in what the defendants are doing than any citizen. If it is running its cars, and the defendants are interfering with its business, then it is immaterial in this issue by what means its cars are being run. Likewise the transactions between the city and the plaintiff relative to the cause of the strike, as particularly illustrated by "Schedule A" attached to the answer, are immaterial and those allegations in the answer are both irrelevant and frivolous. The issue as to whether plaintiff's losses were caused by defendant, or resulted from its own acts, would ordinarily be raised by defendant's denial. But, if defendant wishes to plead as a defense that plaintiff's losses were due to its own fault, a simple statement of that fact is sufficient...

With these suggestions, I leave the drafting of any new answer to the defendant's attorney. The order appealed from should be reversed...

Order reversed, with $10 costs and disbursements, and motion granted, with $10 costs, with leave to the defendant to serve an amended answer within 20 days, upon payment of the costs of the motion and of this appeal. All concur.

Sec. 3.43 Trial (calendar, hearing, evidence, arguments)

PEOPLE v DAVIS (1951) 303 NY 235,

LEWIS, J. This appeal by the defendant, by permission of a member of this court (Code Crim. Pro., Sec. 519, subd. 1; Sec. 520, subd. 3), presents for our review a judgment of the County Court, Nassau County, affirming a judgment of the City Court of the City of Glen Cove, which convicted the defendant of assault in the third degree and disorderly conduct, the sentence in each case having been suspended (Penal Law, Sec. 244, 722).

By the original and superseding informations it was charged that on March 3, 1950, on a public street in the city of Glen Cove, the defendant assaulted a local police officer and then and there used profane, abusive and threatening language of such a character as to occasion a breach of the peace, and cause a crowd to collect.

There is evidence, adduced upon the trial, that while the complainant, a local police officer, was preparing a summons for the defendant's violation of a local parking ordinance, the defendant, on a public street in the city of Glen Cove, addressed the police officer in foul and abusive language and inflicted blows upon him, thereby causing a crowd to gather.

In that state of the record we cannot say as a matter of law that there was no substantial evidence which served as a basis for a finding, by the trier of the facts, of the defendant's guilt as charged. Concluded, as we are, by the circumstance and by the concurrent action of the courts below, from a consideration of the facts (People v Most, 171 NY 423, 427...) we pass to the remaining inquiry whether, on the trial, the defendant's rights were prejudiced by any ruling of the trial court to which an exception was taken.

Upon this appeal the argument is made that the City Court of the City of Glen Cove, as convened to conduct the defendant's trial, was without jurisdiction in the absence of an order by a County Court Judge--claimed to have been required by subdivision 2 of section 702-a of the Code of Criminal Procedure--designating the judicial officer who presided at the trial.

The circumstance of record which the defendant cites as the basis for his argument is that the Judge who presided at his trial was an Acting City Court Judge who, without designation by an order of a County Court Judge, took over the case following the disqualification of the City Court Judge before whom the case was called and before any evidence was taken. Further facts from the record will contribute to an understanding of the problem presented:

On March 4, 1950, when charges were filed against the defendant, an appearance in his behalf in the City Court of the City of Glen Cove was originally made by an attorney, at whose request Judge Joseph A. Suozzi, the City Court Judge then presiding, adjourned the defendant's formal arraignment until March 28, 1950. On the latter date, when the defendant appeared in City Court and charges previously filed with the court were read to him, a second attorney noted his appearance as counsel for the defendant. Thereupon Judge Suozzi permitted the withdrawal from the case by the attorney who originally appeared who stated that he "***had represented defendant Davis free of charge at his request and by request of the National Association for the Advancement of Colored People." After granting a "request" by the original attorney "***that all the defenses and challenges be made in writing", and having permitted him to "intervene", as he phrased it, "as a friend of the Court", Judge Suozzi--who did not preside at the trial--adjourned the case, upon the defendant's request, for trial on April 21, 1950.

It also appears that, following arraignment of the defendant the case--involving, as it did, the arrest of the defendant, a member of the Negro race--had aroused local interest and had been the subject of discussion during at least one local "conference" attended by Judge Suozzi. It was that circumstance which prompted Judge Suozzi on April 21, 1950--the adjourned date for the defendant's trial--to make the following statement:

"The Court: I wish to say that at the time I participated in the conference the only thing that transpired during my presence was a general discussion with respect to relations between white and colored people, and at that time my only declaration was that I would give the defendant in this case as fair a trial as I would give anyone. On the basis of the fact we have had an interval in between I want to ask you for the record: do you have any objection to my sitting on this case? Do you feel I can try this in a fair and impartial manner? As far as I am concerned, I have made no judgment on this case and I wish you to state for the record what your feelings are on this." In response to that inquiry, counsel for the defendant then voiced his objection to Judge Suozzi presiding at the trial, to which objection Judge Suozzi made the following statement:

"The Court: I want this case to proceed as impartially as I feel we can do it. If the feeling of the defendant is I cannot try this case, feeling his rights are being prejudiced, on that ground I think perhaps the best thing to do is to get somebody else to try this case." Thereupon Judge Suozzi disqualified himself and adjourned the case until April 28, 1950, when a trial was had before Acting City Court Judge William J. Cosgrove of the City Court of Glen Cove.

For reasons presently to be stated, we think the defendant's challenge to the jurisdiction of the trial court by which he was convicted--such challenge being based upon the lack of a County Court Judge's order designating the Acting City Court Judge to preside--is without merit. True it is that subdivision 2 of section 702-a of the Code of Criminal Procedure provides that, if a magistrate shall become disqualified pending final disposition of a case, a transfer of the cause for trial before another magistrate may be affected by an order of the County Judge. That statute, however, does not prescribe the exclusive procedure where, as in the present case, the Legislature has expressly provided for the City of Glen Cove an alternative method of substitution in the event the City Court Judge disqualifies himself. The Charter of the City of Glen Cove, as amended by chapter 380 of the Laws of 1942, provides "The mayor may, from time to time, designate a person with the same qualifications to act in the temporary absence or disqualification of the city judge, with the same jurisdiction." (Emphasis supplied). In the absence of any asserted claim by the defendant to the contrary, we take judicial notice of the fact that on April 28, 1950--the date when the evidence was taken upon which the defendant was convicted--Judge Cosgrove has been duly appointed and had qualified as an Acting City Court Judge under the statute last quoted above. Accordingly, we find in the record no basis for the defendant's claim that the City Court of the City of Glen Cove as convened with Acting City Court Judge Cosgrove presiding was without jurisdiction to render the judgment of conviction with which this appeal is concerned.

Nor does the record contain any evidentiary basis whatever for the suggestion that the attorney who originally appeared for the defendant was present at any time during the trial had on April 28, 1950, before Acting City Court Judge Cosgrove, and there is no evidence that any ruling or judicial act by that presiding officer was influenced by the displaced attorney.

Concluding, as we do, that the defendant's trial was conducted by a properly constituted court, and finding in the record no evidence from which an inference or prejudice to the defendant's rights may be drawn, the judgment should be affirmed.

FULD, J. (dissenting). When charges were first filed against him in the City Court of the City of Glen Cove, defendant was represented by an attorney. When arraigned several weeks later, he appeared by another attorney, and the first one was permitted to "withdraw". Then, after defendant's new counsel had attacked the regularity of the proceedings, the other asked the Judge presiding to allow him to "intervene as a friend of the Court", because, as he expressed it, "his conduct had been put in question by defendant. The court granted the request, despite the fact that it was clear from his statement that he wanted to remain in the case, not to assist defendant, but to vindicate some supposed right of his own, and despite the further fact that he had already taken a position, if not adverse to defendant, certainly not helpful to him, by insisting upon the burdensome and unusual requirement "that all the defenses and challenges (by defendant) be made in writing and sworn to." And while it is true, as the court notes in its opinion, that the record fails to show that the displaced attorney was present on April 28th, the day on which the trial proper was held, the fact seems to be asserted by defense counsel, and acknowledged by the assistant district attorney, on the argument before us upon this appeal--that he conferred with the prosecutor during the course of the trial.

One accused of crime has an absolute and unqualified right to have counsel of his own choosing, and that, of course, encompasses the right to relieve himself of an attorney formerly retained...

It may well be that there is no proof in this case that the displaced attorney violated any confidence of his former client or that his intervention in the case influenced any ruling or judicial act of the judge or affected the outcome of the trial. But that does not mean that we may disregard the asserted impropriety as technical or harmless...

The conviction should be reversed, and a new trial ordered.

Judgment affirmed.

WILLIAM H. WATERS, INC. v HATTERS' FUR EXCHANGE, INC.
(1stDept 1919) 185 AD 803, 174 S 90

Appeal from Trial Term, New York County

Action by William H. Waters, Incorporated, and another, against the Hatters' Fur Exchange, Incorporated. From an order of the Trial Term, Part 2, granting a preference of the trial of the issues and placing the cause on the calendar of Part 14 for trial, defendant appeals.

LAUGHLIN, J. The notice of motion for the order was not served with the notice of trial, as required by section 793 of the Code of Civil Procedure and rule 3 of the Trial Term, rules, and the application should have been denied on that ground. Marks v Murphy, 27 AD 160, 50 S 622; Eckhard v Jones, 45 AD 562, 61 S 257; Meyerson v Levy, 117 AD 475, 102 NY Supp. 704; McIntire v National Nassau Bank, 150 AD 668, 135 S 760. But, if the application had been timely made, it should not have been granted.

The order was granted solely on the ground that a material witness for the plaintiff was 73 years of age and ill, and it is claimed, although the evidence in support of the contention is not very satisfactory, that there is reasonable ground to believe that he will not be able to attend the trial unless it shall take place soon. The probable inability of the witness to attend the trial, owing to advanced age or illness, would warrant an order for his examination under subdivision 5 of section 872 of the Code of Civil Procedure, but does not constitute a statutory ground for the preference of the trial of the issue (see section 791, Cod. Civ. Proc.), nor is it ground for such a preference under the general rules or practice or the special rules of practice in this department (see Trial Term rule 3, and Special Term rule 8).

We are also of opinion that it does not afford a sufficient ground for granting a preference of the trial of the issues herein over other issues under the authority of subdivision 10 of section 791 of the Code of Civil Procedure or under the inherent power of the court to control the order of the trial of issues on the calendar, which must now be deemed to be finally established. Riglander v Star Co., 98 AD 101, 90 S 772, affirmed 181 NY 531, 73 NE 1131. Such an exercise of power would result in the time of the court being taken up with like applications in many cases, and would disorganize the calendars and impose great hardships on litigants, not only by preventing the trial of their causes in their order on the calendar, but by subjecting them to the expense of remaining prepared for trial, with no degree of certainty with respect to the time their causes would be reached for trial.

The order should therefore be reversed, with $10 costs and disbursements, and the motion denied, with $10 costs. Order filed. All concur.

OLEARCHICK v AMERICAL STEEL FOUNDRIES)

MARTIN v CARNEGIE-ILLINOIS STEEL CORPORATION) (DCWD Penn 1947) 73 FSupp 273

Actions by Anthony Olearchick, and others against American Steel Foundries, a corporation, and by Frank S. Martin and others against Carnegie-Illinois Steel Corporation, a corporation under the Fair Labor Standards Act of 1938, Sec. 16(b), 29 USC Sec. 216(b), to recover overtime compensation, liquidated damages, and attorney's fee. On motion to remove cases from jury trial list.

WALLACE S. GOURLEY, District Judge. These cases are similar in nature and raise the same problem, and as a result thereof are considered and determined in one opinion....

Two questions have been raised by the defendant in each of the proceedings

1. Under the law, should this case be tried by the Court, or should it be tried by the Court with a jury?

2. Regardless of how the case is to be tried, is it expedient to try at the May Term of Court, 1947?

The second question has now become moot for the reason that each of these cases has been continued by the Court pending disposition of the question raised in the motion to remove the cases from the Jury Trial List for the May Term, 1947.

It is first necessary to consider the existing law as to the right of trial by jury in cases brought under the Fair Labor Standards Act for overtime compensations, liquidated damages, and attorneys' fees. There does not appear to be any existing Act of Congress or (sic) is there any provision in the Fair Labor Standards Act, 29 U.S.C.A. Sec. 201 et seq., its supplements or amendments, which specifically states one way or the other as to whether or not a right to a trial by jury shall exist.

Rule 38 of the Federal Rules of Civil Procedure, 28 U.S.C.A. following sections 723c, provides as follows:

"Rule 38. Jury Trial of Right

"Right Preserved. The right of trial by jury as declared by the Seventh Amendment to the Constitution or as given by the statute of the United States shall be preserved to the parties inviolate.

"Demand. Any party may demand a trial by jury of any issue triable of right by a jury by serving upon the other parties a demand therefor in writing at any time after the commencement of the action and not later than 10 days after the service of the last pleading directed to such issue. Such demand may be indorsed upon a pleading of the party."

Although Section (b) of Rule 38 provides a time within which demands for a jury trial must be made, said provision of this rule does not enter into the argument since demand for jury trial in each of the cases was timely. The Fair Labor Standards Act under which these suits have been brought does not provide for a trial by jury as a matter of right, nor as hereinbefore mentioned does any other Act of Congress so provide. In order for the plaintiffs to show that they are entitled to a jury trial as a matter of right, they must show that the right is preserved by the Seventh Amendment to the Constitution. That Amendment provides that "In suits at common law, where the value in controversy shall exceed twenty dollars, the right of trial of trial by jury shall be preserved, and no fact tried by the jury shall be otherwise reexamined in any court of the United States, and then according to the rules of the common law."

It is further provided in Rule 39(a) of the Federal Rules of Civil Procedure:

"Rule 39. Trial by Jury or by the Court

"(a)
By Jury. When trial by jury has been demanded as provided in Rule 38, the action shall be designated upon the docket as a jury action. The trial of all issues so demanded shall be by jury, unless (1) the parties or their attorneys of record, by written stipulation filed with the court or by an oral stipulation made in open court and entered in the record, consent to trial by the court sitting without a jury or "(2) the court upon motion or of its own initiative finds that a right of trial by jury of some or all of those issues does not exist under the Constitution or statutes of the United States."

It is contended by the Defendants that an action brought under the provisions of section 16 (b) of the Fair Labor Standards Act is not a common law action, but is a very special and purely statutory right of action given to the employees only under the Act and exercisable only in the manner described by the Act.

It is the contention of the plaintiffs in each action that under the provisions of the Fair Labor Standards Act, the remedy which is invoked is not a public remedy, but is private in nature as it applies to each plaintiff who claims a right to recover for overtime compensation, liquidated damages and attorney's fees which the defendant in each instance has refused and neglected to pay in accordance with the provisions of existing law. It was set forth by Congress at the time of the enactment of the Fair Labor Standards Act, more particularly the Act of June 25, 1938, c. 676, Sec. 2, 52 Stat. 1060, 29 U.S.C.A. Sec. 202, as follows:

"Sec. 202. Congressional finding and declaration of policy,

"(a)
The Congress finds that the existence, in industries engaged in commerce or in the production of goods for commerce, of labor conditions detrimental to the maintenance of the minimum standard of living necessary for health, efficiency, and general well-being of workers (1) causes commerce and the channels and instrumentalities of commerce to be used to spread and perpetuate such labor conditions among the workers of the several States; (2) burdens commerce and the free flow of goods in commerce; (3) constitutes an unfair method of competition in commerce; (4) leads to labor disputes burdening and obstructing commerce and the free flow of goods in commerce; and (5) interferes with the orderly and fair marketing of goods in commerce.

"(b)
It is declared to be the policy of sections 201-219 of this title, through the exercise by Congress of its power to regulate commerce among the several States, to correct and as rapidly as practicable to eliminate the conditions above referred to in such industries without substantially curtailing employment or earning power. June 25, 1938, c. 676, Sec. 2, 52 Stat. 1060."

It is, therefore, the primary purpose of the Fair Labor Standards Act, through the exercise of legislative power, to prohibit the shipment of goods in interstate commerce if they are produced under substandard labor conditions and such prohibition has been held to be an appropriate exercise of the power of congress over interstate commerce. (Roland Electric Co. v Walling, 326, US 657, 66 SCt 413, 90 LEd 383.)

The Act was also a design to extend the frontiers of social progress by insuring all able-bodied working men and women a fair day's pay for a fair day's work, or to secure to workers the fruits of their toil and exertion. It was also primarily designed to aid the unprotected, the unorganized, and the lowest paid of the nation's working population, that is, those employees who lack sufficient bargaining power to secure for themselves a minimum subsistence wage. Congress also had in mind the intent to protect said groups of population from substandard wages and the excessive hours which endangered the national health, well-being and free flow of goods in interstate commerce. (cases)

In short, the main purpose of the Act was to maintain a decent standard of living and to establish and gradually raise minimum wages. The provisions for overtime compensation were inserted not to discourage or limit overtime work, but as a part of a plan to raise sub-standard wages by providing a definite pay for overtime work when such work was required. The Act is a "remedial statute" aimed at bettering the status of labor in the interest of humanity and, as such, is entitled to liberal construction. (Collins et al. v Kidd et al., D.C. 38 FSupp. 634.)

In a message to Congress proposing the Fair Labor Standards Act, the President of the United States outlined the purpose of the law "As we move resolutely to extend the frontier of social progress, we must be guided by practical reason and not by barren formula. We must ever bear in mind that our object is to improve and not to impair the standard of living of those now under-nourished, poorly clad and ill-housed."

I have been unable to find any decided cases on the point under the Fair Labor Standards Act, and counsel has been unable to draw any similar proceeding to the Court's attention.

The defendant contends that a similar question arose under the National Labor Relations Act in connection with an order reinstating employees and directing the payment of wages for time lost. In the case referred to, the National Labor Relations Board found that the Jones and Laughlin Steel Corporation had violated the National Labor Relations Act of 1935, 29 U.S.C.A. Sec. 151 et seq., by engaging in unfair labor practices affecting commerce. It was contended by the defendant company that since the National Labor Relations Board not only ordered reinstatement of the employee who had been dismissed from their employment, but directed the payment of wages for the time lost by the discharge, less amounts earned by the employees during that period, that the entry of the order for the payment of wages was equivalent to a money judgment and, as a result thereof, contravened the Seventh Amendment with respect to trial by jury. The Supreme Court held that the Seventh Amendment to the Constitution has no application to cases where recovery in money damages was an incident to equitable relief even though damages might have been recovered in an action at law, or that it does not apply where the proceeding is not in the nature of a suit at common law. It was further held that the contention under the Seventh Amendment was without merit for the reason that the reinstatement of an employee and payment for time lost were requirements imposed for violation of the statute, and are remedies appropriate to its enforcement. (National Labor Relations Board v Jones & Laughlin Steel Corp., 301 US 1, at page 48, 49, 57 SCt 615, 81 LEd 893, 108 ALR 1352).

The law seems to be definitely settled that in actions filed under section 16(b) of the Fair Labor Standards Act, in which claim for injunctive relief has been asked, that no right to trial by jury exists for the reason the relief claimed is equitable in nature. (cases)

In each of the cases now being considered by the Court there has been no claim for equitable or injunctive relief asked in any respect, and the claim for money damages is, therefore, not incident to equitable relief in any respect. In National Labor Relations Board v Jones and Laughlin Steel Corp., supra, the decision directed the reinstatement of the employees who had been dismissed since the company had been guilty of discrimination, and said order was in the nature of equitable relief. This is true for the reason that the purpose of the proceeding was to compel the employer to rehire the employees, or have issued a directive in which the defendant company became obligated to reinstate the discharged employees. The recovery of the wages lost during said period of discharge was purely incidental to the equitable relief, which in the first instance was demanded. I believe, therefore, that the decision of the Supreme Court of the United States in the proceeding before the National Labor Relations Board is distinguishable from the facts which are presented in the question now before this Court.

Section 7 of the Sherman Anti-Trust Act, 15 U.S.C.A. Secs 1 et seq., 15 note provides a remedy not dissimilar in nature to that proceeding by Section 16(b) of the Fair Labor Standards Act. There a right of action is given to any person who is injured in his business or property by reason of anything forbidden in the Anti-Trust Laws "And shall recover threefold the damages by him sustained, and the cost of suit, including a reasonable attorney's fee".

A long line of decisions hold that a suit in equity does not lie under this section; that an action thereunder is an action at law as to which the parties are entitled to a jury trial by virtue of the Seventh Amendment to the Constitution. (cases)

It is of the essence, in determining whether or not a jury trial should be granted, to make inquiry as to what the plaintiff's bill of complaint seeks and whether it is, in its nature, either equitable or legal. This is true for the right to a jury trial would depend upon the facts stated in the complaint. I think a fair examination of the pleadings will disclose that the only relief claimed is for a money judgment, together with liquidated damages and attorneys' fees, as provided by the Act. There is no equitable relief asked for in any way whatsoever.

If the issues tendered by the pleadings are purely legal, the parties are entitled to a jury trial as of right under Rule 38(a) and demanded under Rule 38(a) and (b). (Cases)

Rule 38 of the Federal Rules of Civil Procedure, 28 USCA following section 723c, abolishes any distinction between law and equity. (Conn. v Kohlemann, D.C., 2 FRD 514.)

The distinction between law and equity, abolished by the new rules, is in procedure and not one between remedies, and a distinction still remains between jury actions and nonjury actions. This remains in the same manner as existed before the adoption of the new rules and what was an action at law before their adoption under the provisions of the Seventh Amendment still remains a jury action. (Moore's Federal Practice, Vol. 3, p. 3004, et. seq.; Bellavance v Plastic-Craft Novelty Co. et al., D.C., 30 FSupp. 37.)

The right of a jury trial in civil cases at common law is the basic and fundamental feature of our system of federal jurisprudence which is protected by the Seventh Amendment to the United States Constitution. A right so fundamental and sacred to the citizen, whether guaranteed by the Constitution or provided by statute should be jealously guarded by the courts.

Thus, to determine the validity of the plaintiffs' demand for a jury trial, inquiry must be made into the status of the case had it arisen when the formal distinctions between an action at law and a suit in equity still existed. It has been often said that the trial by jury is a fundamental guarantee of the rights and liberty of the people, and subsequently every reasonable presumption should be indulged in against its waiver.

The guarantee under the Seventh Amendment applies only to suits of such character as may be maintainable under common law at the time the amendment was adopted, and under the Sixth Amendment only those proceedings technically criminal in character. (Cases)

The determination of the mode of trial, whether by jury or otherwise, must be pursuant to and in accordance with established principles of common law, and inquiry must be made into the nature of the cause of action and appropriate remedy as they existed under common law. If the cause of action is legal in nature and formerly remedial in a court of law, the right of trial by jury cannot be denied; but, if the cause of action is equitable in nature and formerly remedial in a court of equity, trial by jury should not be allowed. (Berman v Automobile Insurance Co. of Hartford, Conn., D.C., 2 FRD 94.)

No problem is presented in assimilating the computation of overtime for employees under contract on a fixed weekly wage whether the wages are fixed on an hourly or weekly wage. (Overnight Motor Transportation Co., Inc. v Missel, 316 US 572, 579 580, 62 SCT 1216, 86 LEd 1682.)

As result thereof, the mathematical calculations can be had through the means of a pre-trial conference or through invoking other applicable remedies provided by the Federal Rules of Civil Procedure. As a result thereof, no confusion of unnecessary burden would rest on the part of the jury. (O'Malley et al. v Chrysler Corporation, 7Cir, 160 F2d 35.)

The questions for adjudication in an act under the Fair Labor Standards Act are:

a. That each of plaintiffs was employed by the defendant.

b. That each of the plaintiffs was engaged in the production of goods for commerce.

c. That the labor or services rendered was concerned in the process or occupation necessary to the production of goods for commerce.

d. That each of the plaintiffs has not received compensation for overtime as provided by the Act. (Cases)

The reference to the court in Section 216 of the Fair Labor Standards Act that "The court in such action shall, in addition to any judgment awarded to the plaintiff or plaintiffs, allow reasonable attorney's fees to be paid by the defendant, and costs of the action," I believe includes and means the court and jury, if the case is tried before a jury. (Acme Lumber Co., Inc., v Shaw, 243 Ala 421, 10 So2d 285; Ashenford v Yukon & Sons, 237 MoApp 1241, 172 SW2d 881.)

The Court is, therefore, authorized, after verdict of the jury, to make an order allowing attorneys' fees pursuant to motion therefor and after hearing evidence on such motion. (Edwards v South Side Auto Parts Co., ______ MoApp., ______, 180 SW2d 1015.)

These cases disclose nothing more than a money judgment which is sought against each of the defendants based upon the provisions of the Fair Labor Standards Act. No equitable relief is sought. Notwithstanding that its virtue is now hidden behind the camouflage of a "Civil action"; still there it stands in the strength and dignity of pure logic, an action in assumpsit, on contract, at law.

Although neither the Fair Labor Standards Act nor any other law of the United States grants a right to a trial by jury, since this is a claim for money damages, I believe that under the provisions of the Seventh Amendment to the Constitution, the right to a trial by jury should not be denied, there being no claim for equitable relief in any respect in this proceeding.

Therefore, the motion to remove the above entitled cases from the jury trial list is refused.

ELWELL v CHAMBERLIN (1864) 31 NY 611

APPEAL from the general term of the Supreme Court of the city of New York, where a judgment entered upon a verdict in favor of the defendant has been affirmed.

This was an action by James W. Elwell and others against Moses Chamberlin, Jr., as the drawer of a check for $2215.20, to the order of Charles N. Mills, upon the Nassau Bank, dated the 14th October, 1856, indorsed to the plaintiffs by the drawers. Payment of the check having been refused, notice of non-payment was duly given to the defendant. The defence was usury. On the first trial of the cause, the plaintiffs had a verdict; but the judgment was reversed at general term, and a new trial awarded. (2Bosw. 230.) On a second trial, the jury were peremptorily instructed to find a verdict for the defendant, which, however, resulted in another reversal, and the award of a third trial. (4 Bosw. 520.)....

On a third trial, the defendant having the affirmative of the issues, the learned judge allowed his counsel the closing to the jury; to which an exception was taken....

The jury found a verdict in favor of the defendant, and the judgment entered thereon having been affirmed at general term, the plaintiffs took this appeal.

DAVIES, J.--The first point made by the counsel for the appellants is, that the judge erred in permitting the counsel for the defendant, at the trial, to have the closing address to the jury. In this, the learned judge was clearly correct. It appears from the case, that the defendant opened the case to the jury, by calling the first witness. He had the affirmative of all the issues made by the pleadings, and if he had offered no evidence to sustain them, the plaintiffs would have been entitled, without adducing any testimony, to have a verdict and judgment for the amount demanded in their complaint. The party having the affirmative issue upon the record, is always entitled to begin. It was conceded in this case, that the defendant had such affirmative, as he began, and, as it would appear, without objection. It generally follows, that the party entitled to commence his evidence, is entitled to the close; and under our present system of pleading, it very frequently occurs, that the defendant has the affirmative, and when he has, it has been also generally admitted, that he was entitled to open and close the case to the jury.

Under our former system of practice, if the defendant did not plead the general issue, but admitted upon the record the plaintiff's cause of action, and sought to avoid it, by some affirmative defence, the rule and practice of the courts in England prevailed in this state. (2 Dunlap Pr. 637; 1 Paine & Duer 522; Gra. Pr. 289.) That rule is announced in an authoritative and able work on the practice of the court of King's Bench, where the author observes: "It has been laid down, as a general rule, that the party who has to maintain the affirmative of the issue, must begin the evidence....

MULLIN, J. --(concurring opinion omitted)

IN RE FALABELLA'S WILL (SurrNYCo 1913) 139 S 1003

FOWLER, S. Contested probate proceeding.

The usual objections--testamentary incapacity and undue influence--were interposed to the probate of the will of Angelina Falabella by the husband of the testatrix. Husband and wife lived apart at the time the will was executed. The will is in favor of the mother of testatrix. There were no children of the marriage.

The allegation that the testatrix subscribed the will is contested, and the genuineness of her signature is challenged. But three respectable and unimpeached witnesses swear that they saw testatrix sign the will with her own hand. The husband, who was not present at the execution of the will, simply states that, in his opinion, the subscription to the will is not that of testatrix. No handwriting experts were called, and there was no other comparison of handwriting specimens conceded to be genuine. The husband was allowed to give his testimony without objection. Under this state of facts subscription of the paper propounded by testatrix is found. The other statutory requirements for the due execution of the will were established by the testimony of the subscribing witnesses.

As to the plea of undue influence, the burden of proof is on the contestant, and does not shift throughout a probate proceeding. Such is the statement of the Court of Appeals in a very late case, and it seems to complete a definitive doctrine of great importance in probate law. It may be expedient and proper, in view of this important decision of the Court of Appeals, for the surrogate to take this early occasion to make clear his appreciation of the gravity of such final determination on this important point, as this is the court of this state in which most contentious probates of importance are heard and determined in the first instance.

The burden of proof in contested probate proceedings is sometimes said "to rest ordinarily on proponent" throughout the cause. (Cases) But in other cases of equal authority it is stated that the burden of proof on a plea of undue influence, for example, is on contestants. If the burden then shifts from proponent, the burden of proof is not always on proponent. These two decisions are, on their face, types of adjudications of weight. I had hoped that I might give heed in this court of first instance to both doctrines by attributing the primary meaning of the term "onus probandi" to the first class of cases and the secondary sense of the ambiguous term to the second class of cases. "Burden of proof", onus probandi, is an equi vocal term. It refers, primarily to the obligation resting on a party who has the affirmative of an issue of fact to establish it by a preponderating weight of evidence, and, secondarily, to a duty to go forward with the evidence at a precise moment in a judicial proceeding. (Cases) If the different decisions on burden of proof in will contests could be reconciled, it would bring the modern law of this state into line with the former probate law of New York and England (Barry v Butlin, 1 Curt. 637; s.c., 2 Moo. P.C. 480...) as well as with that prevailing in the Commonwealth of Mass...; otherwise our law stands apart.

But a very plain intimation in the Matter of Will of Kindberg, 207 NY 220, 100 NE 789, very lately decided by the Court of Appeals, makes it, I think, impossible to reconcile the adjudications. A late writer, in his useful compendium of the case law of evidence, well states that it is "a hopeless task to undertake to reconcile the decisions which relate to the burden of proof in respect to the probate of wills." Jones, Ev. Sec. 189. Professor Thayer, in his most admirable of all modern treatises on the true bases of the law of evidence, points to the root of this difficulty. Thayer, Prelim. Dissertation on Ev. 354 et seq.; Thayer's Cases on Ev. 69.

In a proceeding to test the validity of the probate of a will, pursuant to section 2653a, Code of Civil Procedure, the statute regulates the burden of proof and the procedure. The statute prescribes that in that class of actions-- "the decree of the surrogate admitting the will or codicil to probate shall be prime facie evidence of the due attestation, execution and validity of such will or codicil."

It then proceeds to regulate the procedure on the trial of such actions. It has been generally supposed by the profession that the burden of proof in that class of actions rested on the contestant solely by virtue of the statute....

The reason why I was induced to think that the burden of proof, in its primary significance, in a probate cause rested always on the proponent I shall proceed to state.. These reasons were of three kinds: (1) Because statute and the state of the pleadings naturally placed the burden of proof on proponent. (2) Because the traditional practice in probate proceedings so placed it. (3) Because both reason and authority had sanctioned it.

The state of the pleadings in a proceeding for probate naturally placed the burden of proof, in its primary signification (or, in other words, the necessity of sustaining all the issues on the will by a preponderance of evidence), on a proponent. In order to entitle a proponent to a decree of probate, he must establish (1) due execution of a testamentary script, pursuant to the statute of wills; (2) testamentary capacity; (3) freedom from restraint. Now a plea of undue influence is a mere negation of an allegation of freedom from restraint. Dayton on Surrogate's Practice, 177. If we assume that it is the pleadings which always fix the burden of proof in the first instance, then, on the principle originally adopted by our courts from the Roman law, "Ei incumbit probatio qui dicit non qui neget," onus probandi rests always on the proponent in a proceeding for probate (Doheny v Lacy, 168 NY 213, 220, 61 NE 255), except in the exceptional instance of special pleas in bar, such as former judgment, when proponent is temporarily relieved of the burden....

That the common or traditional law regulating the proceedings in the courts of the surrogates, in the absence of statutes, placed the burden of proof or weight of evidence on all the issues in a proceeding for probate on the proponent, there can be no doubt. If any change has been made in this state in the common law, it is by reason of later adjudications of authority in this state. The burden of proving undue influence in probate was carefully considered in a leading case in England by the Privy Council on appeal (Barry v Butlin, 1 Curt. 637; s.c., 2 Moo. P.C. 480); and it was held that onus probandi in every case lies upon the party who propounds a will, and he must satisfy the conscience of the court that the instrument so propounded is the last will of a free and capable testator....

After careful consideration I am obliged, however, to conclude that the statement in the decision in Matter of Will of Kindberg, to the effect "that undue influence is an affirmative assault on the validity of a will, and that the burden of proof does not shift, but remains on the party asserting it," is deliberate and final; and that it is applicable to an original proceeding for probate in this court.... To this rule I must defer in this cause. I do so the more willingly because of the great excellence and deserved renown of the high court which has established the rule, no doubt with wisdom and deliberation. To the Court of Appeals the welfare, peace, and dignity of this state owe a great debt....

There is no presumption of fraud or undue influence in a probate cause from mere relations of confidence. Nor does the burden now shift on a plea of undue influence. The contestant has failed to support his plea of undue influence, and I must pronounce for the will.

Let the decree for probate be presented for my signature.

Sec. 3.44 Adjudgment: Verdict and Judgment; Findings of Fact, Decision, Order, Judgment, Decree; Opinion

HURWITZ v DUKAS (1stDept 1921) 195 AD 416, 186 S 276

Suit to foreclose a mechanic's lien by Joseph E. Hurwitz and another against Julius J. Dukas, as trustee, with Solomon Levin impleaded. From a judgment foreclosing the lien, defendant Levin appeals...

PAGE, J. The plaintiffs were subcontractors of the defendant Levin, who had a contract for restoration of a building partly destroyed by fire. The plaintiffs' notice of lien makes no mention of the contract, but states that the name of the person by whom the lienors were employed, and to whom they furnished materials, is Solomon Levin; that the labor performed was carpentry, glazing, and hanging hardware; the material furnished was hardware, lumber, trim, sash, doors, and glass; that the agreed price and value of such labor and materials is $3,861.25, and the amount unpaid is $2,062.03. We consider it doubtful whether this notice complied with the requirements of the Lien Law (Consol. Laws, c. 33). There is, however, a mere substantial defect in the plaintiff's case.

The complaint in the action was framed upon a contract, and also upon a quantum meruit; the plaintiffs stating at the trial that they did not claim under the contract. The evidence was entirely insufficient to support a judgment on that theory. It was necessary for the plaintiffs to prove what materials were furnished, and the reasonable value thereof, what labor was performed, and its reasonable value. One of the plaintiffs was allowed to testify, reading from the bill of particulars, which he had no part in preparing, and which was not made up of any book entries or memoranda he had prepared or ever seen, upon the theory that he was refreshing his recollection. The language of the bill of particulars was very general, and the testimony of the witness merely added to this general language, "We furnished," or "furnished and erected," or "installed." No testimony was given as to the details of any of the material, or the value thereof, or of the amount of labor. This evidence was accepted as proof of the performance of the contract, for which the contract price was $2,300. Some deduction was made for certain things that the plaintiffs admitted they had failed to furnish, which were called for by the contract. As to the extra labor performed and the materials furnished, the other plaintiff, who gave the information to the attorney to enable him to prepare the bill of particulars was allowed to testify from the bill of particulars in the same general manner. He, however, gave his estimate as to the amount of materials and the amount of labor that must have been furnished or employed, which gave a total of about $1,500. Not a book was produced, nor was any proof offered as to the actual amount of materials furnished, or the actual amount of labor performed.

The plaintiffs failed to prove any cause of action upon a quantum meruit. They admit that they did not perform the contract; in fact, in their reply they state:

"That all of the provisions of the contract were disregarded in respect to the work and material set forth in the contract."

The plaintiffs' attorney, realizing that, tested by the rules of evidence, he had failed to establish a case, claims in his brief that such rules are not to be invoked "in an action in equity triable before a court without a jury, where very frequently a good deal of testimony is permitted merely for the purpose of aiding the conscience of the court and enabling it to come to a just decision," while he states that he does not admit that incompetent testimony was allowed, but "that, if any of the testimony was not strictly in exact accord with the strict rules of evidence, such testimony did not in any way prejudice the rights of the appellant."

Plaintiffs in a court of equity must bear the same burden of proving their cause of action by legal and competent evidence as the plaintiff in any action; and in this case they failed to establish their cause of action, either upon a quantum meruit or upon contract. The motion made at the close of the plaintiffs' case should have been granted. The findings of the court, in so far as they relate to the plaintiffs' lien and the portion of the judgment entered thereon, should be reversed, with costs to the appellant, and the complaint dismissed, with costs to the defendant Solomon Levin.

Settle order on notice. All concur.

MAYONBERG v PENNSYLVANIA R. CO. (3dCir 1947) 165 F2d 50

O'CONNELL, Circuit Judge. Plaintiff appeals from a "judgment of non-suit" granted at the close of the presentation of his case. Plaintiff, the sole witness to testify, asserted that he was a passenger traveling from New York to Long Branch, N.J., on a train operated by defendant, a common carrier. Reading a newspaper, he was sitting in an aisle seat in the rear of the train. Across the aisle were four men playing cards. Three other men, subsequently joining the game, stood in the aisle between the seat of plaintiff and those of the four card players. Occasionally, one of these three standing men, hereinafter called the injurer, would bend over. Each time the injurer did so, he struck the plaintiff. Plaintiff objected, but the injurer paid no attention to him. Eventually the train stopped at a station. "When the train started up again," according to plaintiff, "this man landed in my eye with his elbow." It is the injury to plaintiff's eye for which recovery is here sought.

Plaintiff further testified that the second of the two cardboards, on which cardboards the game was being played, had been supplied by a member of the train crew at about the same time as the three men joined the game; and that the trainman, walking through the car several times during the course of the game, had had to "brush up" against him to get through that particular part of the car.

The theory upon which the court granted the nonsuit was that the playing of cards is not inherently dangerous, and that, regardless of the degree of care required of defendant, the burden of proof that the injury arose out of the negligence of defendant's servants lay with plaintiff. The court said, "I don't think I can spell out and leave to conjecture on the part of the jury what caused the elbow to strike the man in the eye. It is up to the plaintiff to prove that and he has not done it."

Jurisdiction in this case stems from diversity of citizenship. This being so, the substantive law to be applied is that of New Jersey, where the cause of action apparently arose. (Klaxon v Stentor, 1941, 313 US 487, 61 SCt 1020, 85 LEd 1477.)

We shall treat the motion for a nonsuit and the "judgment of nonsuit" as a motion for a directed verdict and a judgment entered upon a directed verdict respectively, in accordance with Rule 50(a) of the Federal Rules of Civil Procedure, 28 U.S.C.A. following section 723c. See Schad v Twentieth Century-Fox Film Corporation, (3 Cir., 1943, 136 F2d 991). As was stated in the Schad case, "Upon a motion by the defendant for a directed verdict at the close of the plaintiff's evidence it becomes the duty of the trial judge, after viewing the evidence and all inferences reasonably to be drawn therefrom in the light most favorable to the plaintiff, to determine whether, as a matter of law, his evidence makes out a case upon which the law will afford relief." 136 F2d at page 993.

Two questions, then, are presented: (1) Could the court below hold as a matter of law that plaintiff had not introduced evidence from which a jury might reasonable determine what caused the injurer's elbow to strike plaintiff in the eye? and (2) if plaintiff did meet the burden of proof as to the cause of the injury, was there a jury question whether defendant had failed to meet the standard of care defendant owed to plaintiff?

We believe that, in deeming conjectural what caused injurer's elbow to strike plantiff's eye, the court below inadvertently overlooked the testimony of plaintiff that he was struck "when the train started up again." On the basis of that statement alone, a jury might reasonably have inferred that it was the starting of the train which led to the injury. (See Dickinson v Erie R Co., 1914, 85 N.J.L. 586, 588, 90 A 305), in which the court reiterated the principle that, to warrant a nonsuit or a directed verdict, something more than the mere weight of the evidence must be involved; (and cf. Deschamps v L. Bamberger & Co., 1942, 128 NJL 527, 529, 27 A2d 3, 4, and Shipp v Thirty-Second Street Corporation, 1943, 130 NJL 518, 523, 33 A2d 852, 854).

There is no evidence that, on this particular occasion, the starting of the train was performed negligently. To prevail, therefore, plaintiff had to establish that a jury could have found defendant negligent, under all the circumstances, for the failure of defendant's agent to protect plaintiff adequately against the risk of being injured by the standing card players....

New Jersey lays upon a common carrier the duty of using a "high degree of care" for the safety of the carrier's passengers. (N Jersey cases)... With these principles in mind, we need not inquire whether there is any inherent danger in card playing which is unaccompanied by other factors; but rather we direct our analysis to whether there was a demonstrable risk created by three individuals playing cards while standing in the aisle and whose attention was so diverted as to raise substantial doubt whether, in the event that the train swayed or jerked, they would exercise due care to avoid physical contact with passengers in the vicinity. We are not prepared to say as a matter of law that no such risk existed, nor that a trainman aware of the game and compelled to inch his way through the congested area did not have reasonable notice of that risk to the plaintiff. "The rule supported by authority is that when a passenger shows that he was injured *** through some act or omission of the carrier's servant, which might have been prevented by due care, then the jury have the right to infer negligence, unless the carrier proves that due care was exercised." (New Jersey cases) We are impelled to the conclusion that foreseeability is left by New Jersey courts to the fact-finding body unless, as was the situation in Hoff v Public Service R Co. (1918, 91 NJL 641, 103 A 209, 211, 15 A L R 860), "nothing took place to indicate to any one that the plaintiff was in danger." In the case at bar, we deem untenable any argument that, as a matter of law, a trainman could not reasonably have anticipated that an injury like that concerning which the plaintiff testified might result from permitting the standing card players to remain where they were on the moving train. (Cf. Hansen v North Jersey St. Ry. Co., 1900, 64 NJL 686, 696, 697, 46 A 718, 721; and cf. Lillie v Thompson, 68 SCt 140.)

We conclude, therefore, that the judgment of the court below must be reversed and the cause remanded for a new trial.

GOODRICH, Circuit Judge (dissenting). The rule applied by the majority would seem to make a carrier responsible for any bumps suffered by sitting passengers from those standing in aisles. In other words, allowing people to stand in the aisle becomes liability creating conduct; at any rate, unless the train crew can ascertain constantly that the standing passengers are giving full attention to the maintaining of their equilibrium upon starts and stops. I do not suggest that the majority opinion would espouse such a doctrine as a matter of law, but it seems to me the practical effect of the ruling in this particular set of facts. I think the judgment of the District Court was correct and should be affirmed.

MODEC v CITY OF EVELETH (1947) 224 Minn 556, 29 NW2d 453

JULIUS J. OLSON, Justice. Plaintiff recovered a verdict for $2,000 in her negligence action against defendant. Upon defendant's alternative motion for judgment or a new trial, the court, by its order here for review, granted the motion for judgment. Plaintiff has appealed.

During the time here involved, defendant was the owner of a building known as the Hippodrome, constructed at least 20 years ago and used in large part during the winter for hockey games. It has a large arena, which during the winter months is covered with ice and is used by high-school, college, semi-professional, and independent teams for hockey games, and also by the general public for skating. During other seasons, it is used for various recreational and educational projects put on by the city. We are primarily concerned with the arena as it is used during the winter, which is also the hockey season.

The arena is surrounded by seats for the use of spectators. In front of the first row of seats there is a wooden wall which extends above the ice surface about four feet. The bottom row of seats is about two feet below the top of this wall. From there, the rows of seats rise in tiers, so that spectators occupying seats at the higher levels are afforded an unobstructed view of the games staged on the ice.

In the playing of hockey, goals are placed at the ends of the arena. Back of the goals are wire nets. These are of sufficient height to protect against possible injury to any spectator sitting behind the goals from a flying puck if it is raised off the ice by a player's stick. There is no such net along the sides of the rink.

At the time in question, the city had leased this building to a private concern, referred to in the record as the Eveleth Hockey Association. For that privilege or right, it paid the city $150 for the hockey season. As lessee, it was in full charge of the arena, and it charged and collected general admission fees. There were no reserved seats, and spectators who paid the admission fee had the right to select any seat they wished or could obtain. There is no evidence in the record that plaintiff could not have taken a seat back of the wire net behind one of the goals had she so desired.

The record does not show how often a puck actually leaves the ice, clears the side wall, and lands among the spectators, or the probability of its doing so. Hockey has been played in this arena for more than 20 years, and this was the first time, so far as the record discloses, that a puck shot by one of the players had struck a spectator.

Plaintiff was about 37 years of age at the time she suffered the injury for which this action was brought. She had lived in defendant city all her life and had attended several hockey games there. She also had a brother who played hockey. She knew how the game was scored, and she was generally familiar with such hockey terms as "net", "puck", and "end zones."

In granting the motion for judgment, the trial court recited the fact that the teams of many schools, universities, and other institutions play hockey extensively, and that this is especially true in the region of Eveleth and other Range towns. The court was of the view that in the situation here presented a person attending such a game was presumed to know and appreciate the risks of being hit by a puck during the playing of the game, and that the rule of law as applied by this and other courts in baseball games should apply here. Applying our holdings in baseball cases, the court concluded that defendant had not been proved negligent in any respect, and that plaintiff had assumed the risk of injury. In support of its view, the court cited Wells v Minneapolis Baseball & Athletic Ass'n (122 Minn 327, 142 NW 706, 46 LRA, NS 606 AnnCas 1914D, 922). It recognized the fact that there is a division of opinion among the courts as to whether the nonliability rule applied in baseball games should be applied to hockey. It cited cases from California, Nebraska, Massachusetts, and Rhode Island holding that spectators are not so familiar with hockey as they are with baseball, and for that reason assumption of risk becomes a fact issue for the jury to determine. These courts think that hockey is a comparatively new sport and little known to most people; hence, that the risks commonly known and appreciated by spectators in connection with baseball games do not apply to hockey games.

Hockey is played on the ice by two opposing teams of six persons each. The playing space, which is oblong in shape, is usually limited by marks on the ice or by barriers, such as the wooden walls in this case. At each end of the playing area, a short distance removed from the barrier, there are goals. These are fashioned of netting over a frame in the shape of a leanto, with the open side away from the barrier. The players use skates and are equipped with long-handled sticks or clubs. The striking end of the hockey stick forms about a 110-degree angle with the handle, is about 16 inches long, three to four inches high, a fraction of an inch wide at the top, and slightly wider at the bottom. The puck is the bone of contention in the game.

The object of the game is to place the puck in the goal of the opposing team either by pushing it or by striking it with such force from the playing area as to cause it to fly past the opposing player guarding the goal. Bodily contact is not barred, but is an accepted way for a player to stop his opponent. Thus, the ability to give and take is essential to a successful hockey player. Speed is also an important phase of the game. Sports authorities generally consider it to be the fastest game played in this country and Canada. Thus, the ability of these expert skaters to execute at high speed the difficult plays of the game and the strength required to withstand the crushing contacts inflicted by player upon player in an effort to get possession of the zealously guarded puck show that hockey is a game where speed, skill, and physical endurance are of the utmost importance. It is a man's game. When the puck is passed from player to player across the playing area, it often rises from the ice. Since the puck is round with a flat bottom and top, it is not always possible for a particular player to determine the direction the puck will take when in flight, nor how high it will rise. Any person of ordinary intelligence cannot watch a game of hockey for any length of time without realizing the risks involved to players and spectators alike.

That there are dangers involved in hockey games as well as in baseball games is apparent. As to baseball, two cases have come to us for review. But this is our first case involving hockey.

In the Wells case we said (122 Minn at page 331, 142 NW at page 708, 46 LRA, NS 606, AnnCas 1914D 922): "***Baseball is not free from danger to those witnessing the game. But the perils are not so imminent that due care on the part of the management requires all the spectators to be screened in. In fact, a large part of those who attend prefer to sit where no screen obscures the view. The defendant has a right to cater to their desires. We believe that as to all who, with full knowledge of the danger from thrown or batted balls, attend a baseball game the management cannot be held negligent when it provides a choice between a screened in and an open seat; the screen being reasonably sufficient as to extent and substance."

We approved what was said in the cited case in the Brisson case, where, speaking of defendant's duties to spectators, we said (185 Minn at page 508, 240 N.W. at page 904): "***We do not think that the management must, in order to free itself from the charge of negligence, provide screened seats for all who may possibly apply therefor. In our opinion they exercise the required care if they provide screen for the most dangerous part of the grandstand and for those who may be reasonably anticipated to desire protected seats, and that they need not provide such seats for an unusual crowd, such as the one in attendance at the game here involved."

And we concluded, 185 Minn at page 509, 240 NW at page 904: "***In our opinion no adult of reasonable intelligence, even with the limited experience of the plaintiff, could fail to realize that he would be injured if he was struck by a thrown or batted ball, such as are used in league games of the character which he was observing, nor could he fail to realize that foul balls were likely to be directed toward where he was sitting. No one of ordinary intelligence could see many innings of the ordinary league game without coming to a full realization that batters cannot, and do not, control the direction of the ball which they strike and that foul tips or liners may go in an entirely unexpected direction."....

We think, however, (after discussing contra Neb. case) that the baseball cases should be followed here. Hockey is played to such an extent in this region and its risks are so well known to the general public that as to the question before us there is no difference in fact between the two games so far as liability for flying baseballs and pucks is involved. We think the reason for so holding is found in such cases as Hammel v Madison Square Garden Corp. (156 M 311, 279 NYS 815, 816,) where the court said: "No case has been found which passes upon this exact situation. There are, however, a number of cases where spectators at baseball games have been injured by batted balls coming into the stand. The consensus of opinion in these cases is that there is no liability; that the proprietors of a baseball park are not obliged to screen all the seats; that the spectators occupying seats that are not screened assume the risk incident to such use." (Citing cases.)

To the same effect is Ingersoll v Onondaga Hockey Club, Inc., (245 AD 137, 281 S 505.) In the Canadian case of Elliott v Amphitheatre Limited (1934) (3 West. Wkly. 225) the court said; "The plaintiffs have to establish that there was negligence on the part of the defendant, and the question arises - what negligence have they proved? It is shown that the premises in which the game was played were constructed in the usual way, and *any danger through the playing is open and visible.* The defendant is bound only to keep the place in the same condition as other places of amusement of the like kind according to the best known mode of construction. There is no absolute duty to prevent danger, but only a duty to make the place as little dangerous as such a place could reasonably be having regard to the contrivances necessarily used in such a game." (Italics supplied).

In the light of our prior cases involving baseball games, we conclude that plaintiff assumed the risks incident to the playing of a hockey game at the time and place in question and that the trial court was right in granting the motion for judgment. Order affirmed.

ULINE ICE INC. v SULLIVAN (1950) 88 USAppDC 104, 187 F2d 82

WASHINGTON, Circuit Judge. This appeal raises the question of the liability or non-liability of the proprietor of a sports arena to a patron-spectator injured during the course of an ice hockey game.

Mr. and Mrs. Sullivan were asked to join a party of friends who planned to attend a professional ice hockey game on the evening of March 19, 1946, at the defendant's arena. One of the party, who had been a frequent spectator at ice hockey games, purchased the tickets, selecting seats in one of the more expensive sections of the arena. Mr. Sullivan reimbursed him for two of the tickets, and the group went to the arena together. The game had already started. They were conducted to their seats, which were in the front row, on the sideline near the end zone with an unobstructed view of the play near the goal. The seats directly behind the goal line, at the end of the playing area, were screened by a wire mesh. The seats occupied by the Sullivans and their party were the first group of seats in the unscreened open-view area adjacent to the screened section. It was the first time that Mr. and Mrs. Sullivan had seen a game of ice hockey. They are natives of Tennessee, where the sport is seldom played, and had recently moved to Washington.

During the course of the game -- apparently about halfway through -- the hockey puck came flying up and out of the playing area, and struck Mrs. Sullivan in the face. The lenses of her spectacles were crushed, pieces of glass being driven into her eyes. She was taken to a hospital for treatment. About 98 per cent of the vision of her right eye has been lost. Suit was brought by her and her husband against the defendant company, the husband seeking damages for medical expenses and loss of consortium. The verdict and judgment awarded $17,000 in damages to Mrs. Sullivan, and $3,000 to Mr. Sullivan. The defendant company appeals.

Appellant alleges that it was not negligent, and that in any event Mrs. Sullivan assumed the risk of injury. It assigns as error the denial by the trial court of appellant's motion for a directed verdict, the granting of certain instructions requested by appellees, the denial of certain instructions requested by appellant, and the charge in its entirety.

First, as to the question whether appellant was negligent. It is not disputed that during a typical game the hockey puck leaves the playing area several times, and that it may fly into the seats in the side area as well as into the screens at the end areas, although the latter is the more usual. There was testimony that, despite this possible danger to those sitting at the sides, in all areas in the country a portion of the side area is not screened; that approximately 60 per cent of the arenas have the same amount of screening as the Uline Arena, or less; and that the remaining arenas provide a larger screened area than does appellant (protecting seats comparable to those occupied by the Sullivans). Finally, there was testimony that no arena, by signs, or otherwise, warns patrons that by sitting in unscreened areas they are in possible danger of being hit by the puck.

Appellant argues that because it applied what it considered the customary amount of protection, it could not, as a matter of law, be negligent; that it was entitled to a directed verdict, or at least to a charge that if it provided the customary protection, it had exercised due care. The trial court, on the other hand, considered that what was customary and usual was merely persuasive as to what constituted due care, and that the matter was one for the jury. We think the trial court was correct. First, in view of the testimony that in 40 per cent of the arenas there was a greater screened area, it is questionable that appellant has established that the protection it provided was the customary amount. But apart from that, what is customary may very well be improvident. It is true that the exhibitor of a sports event is not an absolute insurer of the safety of the patron. But the mere fact that exhibitors generally provide a certain measure of protection to spectators does not preclude the possibility that reasonable men would have provided a greater measure. "What usually is done may be evidence of what ought to be done, but what ought to be done is fixed by a standard of reasonable prudence, whether it usually is complied with or not. * * * otherwise those promoting such forms of amusement could create a rule of law for their own exemption." Appellant argues, however, that additional screening was not feasible, because the spectators do not desire to have their vision blocked by wiring and the requisite supports. Appellant further contends that to post notices warning spectators of the danger of sitting in unscreened areas would be superfluous because the danger is common knowledge, or at least is obvious to anyone who sees the screening, and observes the game for a few moments. But the questions whether a reasonably prudent operator would have provided additional screening, despite the usual practice and the desires of the customers, and whether a reasonably prudent operator would have provided notices for the benefit of the unwary or uninformed, were for the jury. We think the instructions adequately presented these questions to the jury, and further, that the evidence supports the jury's finding that the appellant was negligent.

This brings us to the question of assumption of risk. There have been many decisions involving this question in cases where spectators were injured at sporting events, primarily in attending baseball games. In the baseball cases, with few exceptions, it generally has been held that, as a matter of law, the spectator assumes the risk of the normal hazards of watching such a game; and that, as a matter of law, the danger of being hit by a ball which flies into an unscreened area is a normal hazard, within the common knowledge possessed by reasonably prudent persons. There are also several decisions in cases involving an injury, similar to that which occured here, to spectators of hockey games. These decisions are conflicting. The courts of four states have held that the question of assumption of risk is one of fact for the jury, which must determine whether the game's dangers are common knowledge attributable to the plaintiff, and, if not, whether the particular spectator had knowledge of the hazards involved. The courts of three states follow the rule established in the baseball cases. Appellant contends that the latter rule is the one which should be applied here, and that appellee, by selecting unscreened seats, assumed the risk of the injury she incurred.

The trial court determined that the jury must decide the question of assumption of risk. The jury was charged that if Mrs. Sullivan knew of the danger, "or in the exercise of reasonable care and prudence should have known of the danger * * * she acquiesced and assumed the risk of injury in occupying * * * (unscreened) seats to view the game." We think that this was a proper charge, and that in view of the testimony the determination of the jury that the appellee did not assume the risk is amply supported by the evidence.

The exhibition of ice hockey, like the exhibition of baseball or any other sporting event, is a business. And ordinarily the exhibitor and not the spectator must bear the burdens and expenses to which the exhibition may give rise. The spectator is not a participant but a consumer, like the buyer of any other product. Usually, the onus is not on the spectator to know of all the dangers and to be aware of all the hazards, but on the exhibitor to provide all practicable protection and warn of all significant dangers. There may be, of course, situations where the danger is so patent or well known that, as a matter of law, the spectator assumes the risk. The baseball cases are decided on such a premise, though we need not here determine whether we agree with these decisions. We do not have such a case before us. Professional hockey is not now played in the District and the attempt at its establishment here was unsuccessful and shortlived. It was not shown to have achieved, like baseball, either a local or a nationwide acceptance. Under such circumstances, we believe that it is a jury question whether the dangers inherent in sitting in an unscreened, ring-side seat at a hockey match are common knowledge chargeable to the appellee.

Appellant further argues that, apart from common knowledge, the appellee here either was sufficiently well informed of the danger, or, after seeing the screens and the play for a short time, should have been aware of it, and that she thus assumed the risk. We do not agree. Here the appellee testified she did not know that the puck could leave the playing area, that she did not know that the zone she was sitting was dangerous, and that this was her first time at a hockey game. "Primarily the game was played upon the playing surface of the ice and not in the air. * * * The flying off of the 'puck' into the vicinity where the plaintiff sat seems to have been an occasional event which took place often enough so that the jury might find that the defendant with its familiarity with the game and the place ought to have anticipated it, but that the possibility of danger from that source would not naturally occur to * * * a patron who had never seen it happen."

Affirmed.

BERK v SCHENECTADY HOTEL CO., INC. (3dDept 1952) 110 S2d 69

Morris H. Berk sued the Schenectady Hotel Co., doing business under the name and style of Van Curler Hotel, for injuries sustained when hot water came out of shower faucet marked "cold. The Supreme Court, Schenectady County, Best, J., entered judgment for defendant on a verdict of no cause of action, and entered an order denying plaintiff's motion to set aside the verdict and for new trial, and plaintiff appealed....

COON, Justice. Plaintiff with a companion, one Rudolph, arrived at the Van Curler Hotel in Schenectady, N.Y., on September 29, 1946, at about eight thirty o'clock p.m. They were assigned to the same room as paying guests of the hotel. They had driven that day from their homes in Pennsylvania, where both were business men, to attend a meeting pertaining to their business, which was to occur the following day. Neither used the shower in the hotel room bath that evening. The following morning between seven and seven thirty o'clock, plaintiff wished to take a cold shower. His companion, Rudolph, remained in bed reading a newspaper. Plaintiff's testimony is that he stepped into the tub, fixed the shower curtain inside the tub, and turned a faucet marked "Cold." Instead of cold water, hot water came out. Plaintiff describes it as "a burst of hot water and scalding steam." Plaintiff stepped suddenly backward and fell across the edge of the tub. He shouted and his companion Rudolph, came to his rescue, and found the plaintiff with his body partly outside and partly inside the tub, with the hot water still running from the shower.

After carrying the plaintiff to the bed, Rudolph returned and found that both faucets in the bath were marked "Cold" in black letters upon white porcelain. Defendant concedes that such was the case. The events in the bathroom are entirely undisputed. The hot water faucet had been marked "Cold" for some time, and defendant's only excuse is that faucets had been difficult to obtain. However, they were obtainable at that time, and, of course, could have been relabeled in a number of ways. The only other defense offered by defendant was that the heat of the water was thermostatically controlled at 145 degrees, and could not have produced steam. Even so, water of 145 degrees is too hot, and its sudden application to the body, especially when cold water was expected, could produce a shock. An impulse to escape would be inevitable.

The plaintiff contends that the verdict is against the weight of the evidence. That is the sole question presented.

The only real conflict in the case portains to plaintiff's injuries. As to some of his injuries which developed some time later there is a real comflict. However, it is without dispute that plaintiff sustained some injuries which were immediately evident, and any finding to the contrary would be unsupported by evidence.

Thus there is presented a situation on undisputed testimony from which the question of negligence and contributory negligence must be determined. Defendant's duty of reasonable care was certainly not fulfilled when it knowingly mislabeled a hot water faucet. Such conduct amounted to an open invitation to a paying guest to rely upon the fact that turning that faucet would produce cold water. Defendant knowingly set up a situation which invited injury, foreseeable in the exercise of ordinary prudence. In Hansen v United Stores Realty Corp., (257 NY 584, 178 NE 805), a plaintiff's verdict was sustained in favor of a hotel guest because faulty construction resulted in scalding water emerging from a shower when plaintiff turned the handle on the shower mixer to a point between "cold" and "warm".

Defendant urges that plaintiff was guilty of contributory negligence in that he did not elect to take a shower in the "customary" manner, did not "test" the temperature of the water from outside the tub, and did not discover that both faucets were marked "Cold" and investigate. There was no need for plaintiff to "test" the water, because all he wanted was cold. He was under no legal duty to follow any particular procedure in taking a shower, nor was he bound to investigate beyond defendant's open invitation to be sure the water would be cold.

Precedents are of little value in cases involving the weight of evidence. Each case must depend upon its own particular facts. That a court may and should under proper circumstances, set aside the verdict of a jury as against the weight of evidence, is beyond question. An excellant discussion of the subject in general will be found in the opinion of Mr. Justice Bergan in Rapant v Ogsbury, (sup., 109 S2d 737). Here there is no conflict of testimony on the question of negligence, contributory negligence, and injuries of at least some degree. The jury was not weighing the credibility of witnesses. Upon undisputed evidence the verdict of the jury seems so grossly contrary to the evidence that it could not have been based upon the evidence. A new trial is necessary in the interest of justice.

Judgment and order reversed, on the law and facts, and a new trial ordered, with costs to abide the event.

RAPANT v OGSBURY et al. (3dDept 1952) 279 AD 298, 109 S2d 737

Joseph Rapant sued Edwin L. Ogsbury and another for damages resulting from an automobile collision. From a judgment of the Supreme Court, Schenectady County, Trial Term, Best, J., on a jury's verdict of no cause of action by any of the parties, plaintiff appealed...

BERGAN, Justice. In a curve-in-the-road collision occuring on a slippery winter's day and resulting in reciprocal claims the jury has found no cause of action all around. One of the parties appeals and urges upon us the adoption of his contention that as to him, at least, the verdict is against the weight of the evidence.

This kind of a case will serve rather well to illustrate how delicate that question is and how, in common with several other areas of law governed by judgment and discretion, there is no objective standard to apply.

Whatever the variation of the language in which it is expressed, decision always comes to rest on the sense of the judge addressed to the reasonableness of the jury's verdict; but this in turn is a subjective process strikingly similar to the jury's own kudgment of the facts in the first place.

Neither process stands on firmly staked off ground and neither has as its standard the benefit of that measured certainty which goes with mathematical solutions. On the very lack of tooled precision in this process lies its value as an instrument of adjudication. The most baffling conflicts are found in fields uncomprehended by the measurements of mathematics.

The power to review a jury's verdict concedes, in the first place, the premise that a "question of fact is for the jury" and, of course, this is required for most cases by the Constitution. This concession carries with it the established rule that the "weight of evidence" is the jury's own province and that a court will not interfere unless it can see that no reasonable man would solve the litigation in the way the jury has chosen to do.

It merely begs the question, therefore, to say that "only issues of fact" underlies a verdict, because if the power and the necessity for judicial supervision over verdicts is once admitted, there is a point where the power begins to be exercised.

It is easy to describe the point that has been acted upon in actual cases, but not to state it definitively so that it can serve as a guide to be followed with certainty in the next case. The point of interference is where the judge thinks the jury has gone much too far afield from the course the judge regards as proper, in the sense of his professional way of looking at facts.

All this is the description of a process and not the definition of a rule. It does not state just where a verdict will be regarded as against the weight of evidence and just where it will not be so regarded, because either that cannot be stated definitively or at least there has been no notable success achieved in the formulation of a statement.

Many written expressions can be found in reported cases where judges have grappled with exigencies in the process of decision. The industry of counsel for the appellant has, indeed, discovered some 88 cases which are cited in support of the point that the verdict here is against the weight of the evidence. From the opinions, language is liberally quoted to which most lawyers would subscribe at once.

All the language of decision leads ultimately to saying that the result depends on how the judge weighs what the jury has done. A few judicial expressions which are quoted by appellant for our benefit will illustrate this.

To justify setting aside a verdict there must be an "overwhelming preponderence" of evidence against it. (Franklin Coal Co. v Hicks, 46 AD 441, 442, 61 S 875, 876.) This preponderance must be so "great" that a jury could not have reached the verdict on "any fair interpretation of the evidence." (Jarchover v Dry Dock, E. B. & B. R. Co., 54 AD 238, 240, 66 S 575, 576.) The verdict will be set aside when it is such that it would "startle by its absurdity." (Hospital Supply Co. v O'Neill, 10 M 655, 657, 31 S 792, 793.) The court will interfere when the preponderance of evidence is "very great" against the verdict, (Suhrada v Third Avenue R. Co., 14 AD 361, 363, 43 S 904, 905), or where the evidence is "overwhelming" the other way. (Cheney v New York Cent. and HRR Co. 16 Hun (NY) 415, 420); or where it is "most clearly and manifestly" against the evidence, (Culver v Avery, 7 Wend(NY) 380, 384); or where the "undisputed evidence and the probabilities clearly indicate that it was contrary to the weight of the evidence" (Palisade Curtain Co., Inc. v Korn, 197 AD 88, 90, 188 S 497, 498). It is in cases of "excessively preponderating" evidence against the verdict that a new trial especially is justified, (Harris v Second Avenue R. Co., 48 AD 118, 120, 62 S 562, 563), and the expression "excessively preponderating" was used in Graham v New York City Railway Co., (54 M 566, 567, 104 S 869).

It would be possible to quote language of this sort at very great length from the reported cases; and while it was useful in expressing the rationale that guided the judges either in thinking that the jury was so wrong as to warrant interference or in thinking the other way that the jury was right, the language is helpful only in showing that the hard choice of decision always depends on what the judge thinks of the case at hand.

Here the appellant addresses to us a very strong and heavily documented argument that he ought to have won the case at the trial. The argument, although it seems very logical in its detailed and cumulative effect, does not carry us with it to the point of interference with the verdict.

We think the jury was not under the compulsion of reasonable necessity of rendering a verdict for appellant. Whatever the words may be that seem useful to describe our thinking, the product of our judgment is that we ought not in this case change what the jury has decided.

The accident occurred on a county road which had an area of 12 feet in which the snow had been plowed out. There was a very sharp curve at the place of collision. Appellant testified that he saw respondent driver when he was 75 feet away going 30 to 40 miles an hour; that appellant stopped his vehicle against the snowbank on the right and that respondent driver came skidding around the curve with unchecked speed and ran into him. There is proof by appellant and other witnesses that respondent driver said the accident was his fault.

But the respondent driver said he was traveling only 10 or 12 miles an hour around the curve and that he first saw appellant's car forty feet away and it was then in the middle of the road; that he applied his brakes; that appellant was not stopped but in motion and attempted to pull to the right, and as he did so the left front ends of the vehicles collided. He described his purported admission of fault after the collision in these words: "I said it was partially my fault inasmuch as neither of us could stop."

The jury did not have to be persuaded that there was any negligence in this kind of a collision on this kind of a road; and appellant first of all had the task of persuasion in this respect. Nor must the jury have taken the appellant's version of events entirely.

In short, he need not necessarily have persuaded them as he was bound to do if he were to prevail on the trial, that he had acted, and the respondent driver had not acted, in the situation with the prudence of the reasonably careful driver.

In deciding who is right and who is wrong, or if nobody is right or wrong, when vehicles come together on a plowed-out and slippery road the judgment of jurors is quite apt to be better than that of judges.

Judgment affirmed, with costs.

GETTINS v BOYLE (2dDept 1918) 184 AD 499, 171 S 711

Suit by Anthony Gettins and John Gettins against Catherine Boyle, individually and as executrix of Mary F. McCleary, deceased, and another. From that portion of the judgment adverse to them, plaintiffs appeal, and from that part of the judgment adverse to them, defendants appeal.

JAYCOX, J. The plaintiffs contributed $3,000 toward the purchase price of the real property, known as No. 235 Grand Avenue, Brooklyn, N. Y. The deed for the property was taken in the name of Mary F. McCleary. This money was advanced in accordance with an agreement between the plaintiffs and Mary F. McCleary, by which it was agreed that, if the plaintiffs would advance said sum of $3,000 toward the purchase price of said premises, Mary F. McCleary at her death would devise the premises to the plaintiffs--John Gettins to have a life estate therein and Anthony Gettins to have the remainder in fee. Pursuant to said agreement, said Mary F. McCleary made a will, three days after the purchase of said premises, in and by which she devised a life estate in said property to John Gettins and the remainder to Anthony Gettins. This will then recites:

"The above provision is so made pursuant to a verbal agreement entered into between John Gettins, Anthony Gettins, and myself at the time of the purchase of the above-described premises, and upon the payment by them of the sum of three thousand dollars, which sum constituted three-fifths of the price by (sic) for such property."

Thereafter, and on April 17, 1906, Mary F. McCleary purchased real property known as No. 96 Adams Street, Brooklym, N.Y. On the 23rd of November, 1917, she made another will, which revoked the earlier will, and in this will she devised the premises at 96 Adams Street to John Gettins; the said devise to him, as provided in said will, being free from all expenses and transfer tax. Mary F. McCleary died November 24, 1917. The plaintiff John Gettin was a brother-in-law of the testatrix. Anthony Gettins is a son of John Gettins, and a nephew of the testatrix. No provision was made for him in the new will, dated November 23, 1917. The other parties to the action, Catherine Boyle and Mary Ann Malcolm, are nieces of the testatrix. The estate of the testatrix consisted of $844.10 in the Brooklyn Savings Bank and the two parcels of property mentioned above.

This action was brought to compel specific performance of the agreement between the testatrix and the plaintiffs. The court below has found that the plaintiffs are entitled to the relief prayed for in the complaint, but it has also found that by bringing this action the plaintiffs have elected to insist upon the Grand Avenue property being conveyed to them, and that as a condition of relief herein John Gettins must relinquish the property devised to him by the will of said Mary F. McCleary. The complaint merely asked for the specific performance of the contract made by the testatrix with the plaintiffs. The answers of the defendants denied the allegations of the plaintiffs' complaint as to the agreement and interposed the defense of the statute of frauds. Both parties have appealed. The defendants, however, are satisfied with the judgment as entered. The plaintiffs do not find fault with the law as enunciated by the trial court, but they do say that this was not a time for the application of that law. The defendants did not by their pleadings present the issue, and the parties did not litigate it.

While the maxim that "he who seeks equity must do equity" meets with the universal approval of the courts, courts are not to determine arbitrarily what the equities are between the parties. The question as to what the equities are must be presented by proper pleadings, and the issue thus presented determined upon the evidence. Pleadings and a distinct issue are essential in every system of jurisprudence, and there can be no orderly administration of justice without them. Litigants are entitled to know in advance the precise questions that they are required to meet at the trial, and the office of the pleading is to apprise the adverse party of the facts upon which the pleader relies to sustain his cause of action or defense. Proof without allegation is as ineffective as allegation without proof. Both are necessary to a recovery. (Southwick v First Nat. Bank, Memphis, 84 NY 420; Crane v Powell, 139 NY 379, 34 NE 911; Wickenheiser v Colonial Bank, 168 AD 329, 153 S 1035.) The rule is the same in equity as at law. The relief afforded must conform to the case made out by the pleadings as well as the proofs. (16 Cyc 483, Campbell v Consalus, 25 NY 613; Bailey v Ryder, 10 NY 363...)

The fact that relief is given by way of condition does not change the rule. The facts upon which the condition rests must be definitely established, and must be pleaded. (16 Cyc. 483.) As in this action there was no allegation in the answers of the defendants presenting the claim of plaintiff's election, that issue was not litigated, and should not have been determined.

The judgment, in so far as the same directs a conveyance by the plaintiffs, should be reversed, and, as modified, affirmed with costs to the plaintiffs appellants, payable out of the estate of Mary F. McCleary, deceased. All concur.

Sec. 3.45 Enforcement of the Adjudication.

BELFER v LUDLOW (SpCtKingsCo 1910) 69 M 486, 126 S 130

Action by Lazarus Belfer against William W. Ludlow and others. On motion for leave to issue execution.

BLACKMAR, J. On June 3, 1890, plaintiff recovered judgment against the defendant Morgiana Ludlow and others, and the judgment roll was filed on that day in the office of the clerk. The action was brought to foreclose a mechanic's lien, and the judgment was not in the form in which judgments in foreclosure are usually issued, but adjudged that the plaintiff recover of the defendant Morgiana Ludlow the sum of $721.61, with interest thereon from May 15, 1888, amounting in all to the sum of $809.08, and that plaintiff have execution therefor. The judgment also contained a provision directing the sale of certain property and the application of the proceeds to the extent of $314.20 and costs to the payment of the plaintiff's claim. This judgment was not docketed until December 28, 1893, although as stated, the judgment roll was filed June 3, 1890. No execution has ever been issued thereon. The present motion is for leave to issue execution on said judgment. The judgment debtor opposes the motion, claiming that the judgment is conclusively presumed to be satisfied and discharged according to the provisions of section 376 of the Code of Civil Procedure.

This section provides that a final judgment for a sum of money is presumed to be paid and satisfied after the expiration of 20 years from the time when the party recovering it was first entitled to a mandate to enforce it. The judgment debtor claims that the judgment was a complete and final money judgment at the time when the judgment roll was filed on June 3, 1890, and that, therefore, it is presumed to be paid and discharged, and no execution should be permitted thereon. The judgment creditor claims that the judgment was not final and enforceable until it was docketed on December 28, 1893, and that, as 20 years have not elapsed since that time, it is not presumed to be paid. The moving affidavits allege that the judgment is wholly unpaid except as to the sum of $100, and, as the authority of the court in permitting an execution to be issued after five years has elapsed can only be exercised if the court is satisfied that the judgment is unpaid, the decision upon this motion depends upon the question whether the presumption of payment attaches from lapse of time. The 20-year period began to run from the time when the party recovering the judgment was first entitled to a mandate to enforce it. The controlling question, it seems to me, is whether the judgment creditor could have issued an execution upon the judgment on the 3d day of June, 1890, or whether such execution could not have been legally issued until December 28, 1893.

The judgment is not the ordinary one of foreclosure and sale where the amount of the indebtedness is uncertain until the coming in of the referee's report of sale. If it were, it would be controlled by the case of French v French, (107 AD 107, 94 S 1026). The judgment was in form a final money judgment against the defendant, and if it had been docketed when rendered, as it might have been, the plaintiff could have issued execution on it immediately. Its nature is not changed by the provision for the sale of the land in satisfaction of part of the claim. But the clerk failed in performing his duty in docketing the judgment. The question therefore, it seems to me, comes down to the proposition whether an execution can be issued upon a judgment before it is docketed. Docketing is a ministerial act, to be performed by the clerk, and could be enforced by a writ of mandamus if the clerk should refuse to perform his duty in this respect, and the clerk is also liable to a penalty for such failure. (Code, Sec. 1246-1248.) Section 1365, however, provides as follows:

"An execution against property can be issued only to a county in the Clerk's office of which the judgment is docketed."

As said by the Court of Appeals in the case of Dunham v Reilly, (110 NY 371, 18 NE 91):

"The language seems to involve both an authority and a prohibition, an authority where the judgment is docketed in any county to issue the execution to that county, and a prohibition, couched in the word 'only', against any such issue to a county in whose clerk's office there is no such docket."

This matter seems to have been passed upon directly in the case of Kupfer v Frank, (30 Hun (NY) 74), in which it is held that an execution cannot be issued upon a judgment until the judgment has been docketed. (See, also, Harris v Elliott, 163 NY 269, 57 NE 406). Therefore it seems to be established by the weight of authority that a valid execution cannot be issued upon a judgment until it is docketed in the county. No execution, therefore, could have been issued upon the judgment in question until December 28, 1893.

The presumption of payment attaches 20 years after the party recovering the judgment was first entitled to a mandate to enforce it. An execution is a mandate (Code, Sec. 3343), and it is the only mandate which the judgment creditor can issue. The conclusion seems to be that the 20 years did not begin to run until December 28, 1893. Therefore no legal presumption of payment and nothing to contradict the affidavit of the plaintiff that no part of the said judgment, except the sum of $100, has been paid.

I have not considered the question of partial payment, for I do not think the evidence is sufficiently definite to enable me to pass upon it. The affidavit simply alleges the payment of $100 on account. The opposing affidavit denies that the defendant paid or authorized any payment or that it was paid in his behalf. Although I have no evidence of it, it is probable that the $100 was collected by the sale of the property. If so, certain interesting questions might arise under the provisions of section 377 of the Code.

Motion granted, with $10 costs. Settle order on notice.

WALKER v WALKER (1880) 82 NY 260, a20 Hun 400

APPEAL from an order of the General Term of the Supreme Court first department, entered April 29, 1880, affirming two orders of the Special Term, one of which directed the payment of certain sums as alimony and counsel fees within five days, or in default of such payment that the answer of the defendant be stricken out, and the other of which struck out said answer.

This answer was for a divorce a mensa et thoro.

An order was made herein directing the payment of a sum of money for alimony and counsel fees. After it was entered, upon affidavits alleging that defendant had removed from this State and become a resident of the State of Massachusetts for the purpose of avoiding a compliance with said order, and showing that he had failed to pay the sum directed to be paid, and that no collection of them had been accomplished by a precept issued for that purpose, the plaintiff applied for and obtained an order that defendant pay the same within five days from the service thereof upon his attorney, or in default thereof that his answer be struck out, and the cause proceed as if no answer had been put in. This order not being complied with, plaintiff thereupon obtained an order striking out defendant's answer and directing a reference to take proof of the facts charged in the complaint, as if no answer had been put in.

FOLGER, Ch. J. The defendant, having refused or neglected to obey an important order of the court, was in contempt, and liable to punishment by reason thereof. The punishment inflicted by the court was by an order made in the cause, to strike out the answer that had been put in by him, and to direct a reference to take proof of the matters stated in the order; the reference to proceed as if there had been no answer put in.

It is claimed that the court had no power to make that order; that every defendant has a vested right to make a defense to any action or suit or legal proceeding begun against him, and that he cannot be deprived of it.

It is conceded by the defendant that the Supreme Court on its equity side, has all the power and authority that formerly existed in Chancery in England and was continuously exercised by it. "The rule there must be the rule here," says Chancellor Kent, "for I take this occasion to observe, that I consider myself bound by those principles which were known and established as law in the courts of equity in England at the time of the institution of this court." (Manning v Manning, 1 JohnsCh(NY) 527-9.) It is not to be denied that a court of equity may refuse to a defendant in contempt the benefit of proceedings in it, when asked by him as a favor, until he has purged himself of his contempt. (See Brinkley v Brinkley, 47 NY 40-9, and cases there cited). But the rule has been held broader than that and enforced with much vigor. Chief Baron Gilbert lays it down in his Forum Romanorum. . . (p. 71) that "the answer will not be received without clearing his contempt;" and at another (p. 211): "So it is where a man hath a bill depending in court and falls under the displeasure of the court, and is ordered to stand committed. Here, when his cause is called, if the other side insist he hath not cleared his contempt, nor actually surrendered his body to the warden of the Fleet, he must do both these things before his cause can be proceeded in ***." It is stated by Lord Eldon, that it is a general rule, that a party who has not cleared his contempt cannot be heard. Vowles v Young, 9 VesJr. 173; Anonymous, 15 id. 174)...It is well to say here that Rice v Phle (55 NY 518) does not condemn this. That case holds that the pleading may not be stricken out, save on notice to the party (p. 523); and that the exercise of this power was legitimate was recognized by Marcy, J., in Birdsall v Pixley, (4 Wend(NY) 196.) The power seems to have been exerted or recognized by the Supreme Court in several instances, without question made by appeal. ((Farnham v Farnham, 9 HowPr(NY) 231; Barker v Barker, 15 id. 568; Ford v Ford, 41 id. 169).

We are brought to the conclusion that there has long been exerted by the Court of Chancery in England the power to refuse to hear the defendant when he was in contempt of the court by disobeying its orders, and that that power was in the Courts of Chancery of this country.

We do not think the cases of Wayland v Tysen (45 NY 282) and Thompson v Erie Railway (id. 471) and others of like result, are in the way of this conclusion. They were not cases of contempt, nor were they equity cases. Besides, there the answer was stricken out, with no loophole left for relief to the defendant. It is always in the power of the defendant, in a case like this in hand, to apply to the court and show that the order was irregularly made, or for leave to purge himself of the contempt and be let in again to make his defense. (Brinkley v Brinkley, supra.)

Order affirmed.

Sec. 3.5 Appellate Jurisdiction delegated by Constitution and Statute
Sec. 3.50 Constitutional and Statutory provisions

N.Y. State Constitution, Art. VI, Judiciary.

Sec. 3. (Court of appeals; jurisdiction) a. The Jurisdiction of the court of appeals shall be limited to the review of questions of law except where the judgment is of death, or where the appellate division, on reversing or modifying a final or interlocutory judgment in an action or a final or interlocutory order in a special proceeding, finds new facts and a final judgment or a final order pursuant thereto is entered; but the right to appeal shall not depend upon the amount involved.

b. Appeals to the court of appeals may be taken in the classes of cases hereafter enumerated in this section;

In criminal cases, directly from a court of original jurisdiction where the judgment is of death, and in other criminal cases from an appellate division or otherwise as the legislature may from time to time provide.

In civil cases and proceedings as follows:

(1) As of right, from a judgment or order entered upon the decision of an appellate division of the supreme court which finally determines an action or special proceeding wherein is directly involved the construction of the constitution of the state or of the United States, or where one or more of the justices of the appellate division dissents from the decision of the court, or where the judgment or or order is one of reversal or modification...

Sec. 5. (Appeals from judgment or order; power of appellate court; transfer of appeals taken to unauthorized appellate court.) a. Upon an appeal from a judgment or an order, any appellate court to which the appeal is taken which is authorized to review such judgment or order may reverse or affirm, wholly or in part, or may modify the judgment or order appealed from, and each interlocutory judgment or intermediate or other order which it is authorized to review, and as to any or all of the parties. It shall thereupon render judgment of affirmance, judgment of reversal and final judgment upon the right of any or all of the parties, or judgment of modification thereon according to law, except where it may be necessary or proper to grant a new trial or hearing, when it may grant a new trial or hearing.

If any appeal is taken to an appellate court which is not authorized to review such judgment or order, the court shall transfer the appeal to an appellate court which is authorized to review such judgment or order.

Sec. 8. (Appellate terms; establishment; how constituted; jurisdiction.) a. The appellate division of the supreme court in each judicial department may establish an appellate term in and for such department or in and for a judicial district or districts or in and for a county or counties within the department and designate the place or places where such appellate term shall be held...

N.Y. CPLR; Article 55, Appeals Generally

Sec. 5501. Scope of review. (a) Generally from final judgment. An appeal from a final judgment brings up for review:

1. any non-final judgment or order which necessarily affects the final judgment, including any which was adverse to the respondent on the appeal from the final judgment and which, if reversed, would entitle the respondent to prevail in whole or in part on that appeal, provided that such non-final judgment or order has not previously been reviewed by the court to which the appeal is taken;

2. any order denying a new trial or hearing which has not previously been reviewed by the court to which the appeal is taken;

3. any ruling to which the appellant objected or had no opportunity to object or which was a refusal or failure to act as requested by the appellant, and any charge to the jury, or failure or refusal to charge as requested by the appellant, to which he objected;

4. any remark made by the judge to which the appellant objected; and

5. a verdict after a trial by jury as of right, when the final judgment was entered in a different amount pursuant to the respondent's stipulation on a motion to set aside the verdict as excessive or inadequate; the appellate court may increase such judgment to a sum not exceeding the verdict or reduce it to a sum not less than the verdict.

(b) Court of appeals. The court of appeals shall review questions of law only, except that it shall also review questions of fact where the appellate division, on reversing or modifying a final or interlocutory judgment, has expressly or impliedly found new facts and a final judgment pursuant thereto is entered. On an appeal pursuant to subdivision (d) of section fifty-six hundred one, or subparagraph (ii) of paragraph one of subdivision (a) of section fifty-six hundred two, or subparagraph (ii) of paragraph two of subdivision (b) of section fifty-six hundred two, only the non-final determination of the appellate division shall be reviewed.

(c) Appellate division. The appellate division shall review questions of law and questions of fact on an appeal from a judgment or order of a court of original instance and on an appeal from an order of the supreme court, a county court or an appellate term determining an appeal.

(d) Appellate term. The appellate term shall review questions of law and questions of fact.

Sec. 5511. Permissable appellant and respondent. An aggrieved party or a person substituted for him may appeal from any appealable judgment or order except one entered upon the default of the aggrieved party. He shall be designatied as the appellant and the adverse party as the respondent.

Sec. 5513. Time to take appeal, cross-appeal or move for permission to appeal. (a) Time to take appeal as of right. An appeal as of right must be taken within thirty days after service upon the appellant of a copy of the judgment or order appealed from and written notice of its entry, except... (c) Time to move for permission to appeal. The time within which a motion for permission to appeal must be made shall be computed from the date of service upon the party seeking permission of a copy of the judgment or order to be appealed from and written notice of its entry, or...

Sec. 5515 Taking an appeal; notice of appeal. An appeal shall be taken by serving on the adverse party a notice of appeal and filing it in the office where... (Sec. 5516 — Sec. 5531 omitted)

Article 56 Appeals to the court of appeals. (Sec. 5601-Sec. 5615 omitted)
Article 57 Appeals to the appellate division (Sec. 5701-Sec. 5713 omitted)

U.S. Constitution, Article III (Federal Courts and Jurisdiction)

Sec. 2.... In all cases affecting Ambassadors, other public Ministers and Consuls, and those in which a State shall be Party, the supreme Court shall have original Jurisdiction. In all other Cases before mentioned, the supreme Court shall have appellate Jurisdiction, both as to Law and Fact, with such Exceptions, and under such Regulations as the Congress shall make...

U.S. Code Annotated, Chapter 81, Supreme Court

Sec. 1252. Direct appeals from decisions invalidating Acts of Congress.

Any party may appeal to the Supreme Court from an interlocutory or final judgment, decree or order of any court of the United States, the District Court for the Territory of Alaska, the United States District Court for the District of the Canal Zone and the District Court of the Virgin Islands and any court of record of Alaska, Hawaii and Puerto Rico, holding an Act of Congress unconstitutional in any civil action, suit, or proceeding to which the United States or any of its agencies, or any officer or employee thereof, as such officer or employee, is a party.

A party who has received notice of appeal under this section shall take any subsequent appeal or cross appeal to the Supreme Court. All appeals or cross appeals taken to other courts prior to such notice shall be treated as taken directly to the Supreme Court. (June 25, 1948, c. 646, 62 Stat. 928.)

Sec. 1253. Direct appeals from decisions of three-judge courts.

Except as otherwise provided by law, any party may appeal to the Supreme Court from an order granting or denying, after notice and hearing, an interlocutory or permanent injunction in any civil action, suit or proceeding required by any Act of Congress to be heard and determined by a district court of three judges. (June 25, 1948, c. 646, Sec. 1, 62 Stat. 928.)

Sec. 1254. Courts of appeals — Certiorari — Appeal — Certified Questions.

Cases in courts of appeals may be reviewed by the Supreme Court by the following methods:

(1) By writ of certiorari granted upon the petition of any party to any civil or criminal case, before or after rendition of judgment or decree;

(2) By appeal by a party relying on a State statute held by a court of appeals to be invalid as repugnant to the Constitution, treaties or laws of the United States, but such appeal shall preclude review by writ of certiorari at the instance of such appellant, and the review on appeal shall be restricted to the Federal questions presented;

(3) By certification at any time by a court of appeals of any question of law in any civil or criminal case as to which instructions are desired, and upon such certification to the Supreme Court may give binding instructions or require the entire record to be sent up for decision of the entire matter in controversy. (June 25, 1948, c. 646. Sec. 1, 62 Stat. 928.)

Sec. 1255. Court of Claims — Certiorari — Certified Questions.

Cases in the Court of Claims may be reviewed by the Supreme Court by the following methods:

(1) By writ of certiorari granted on petition of the United States or the claimant;

(2) By certification of any question of law by the Court of Claims in any case as to which instructions are desired, and upon such certification the Supreme Court may give binding instructions on such question. (June 25, 1948, c. 646, Sec. 1, 62 Stat. 928.)

Sec. 1256. Court of Customs and Patent Appeals — Certiorari.

Cases in the Court of Customs and Patent Appeals may be reviewed by the Supreme Court by writ of certiorari. (June 25, 1948, c. 646, Sec. 1, 62 Stat. 928.)

Sec. 1257. State Courts — Appeal — Certiorari.

Final judgments or decrees rendered by the highest court of a State in which a decision could be had, may be reviewed by the Supreme Court as follows: (1) By appeal, where is drawn in question the validity of a treaty or statute of the United States and the decision is against its validity.

(2) By appeal, where is drawn in question the validity of a statute of any state on the ground of its being repugnant to the Constitution, treaties or laws of the United States, and the decision is in favor of its validity.

(3) By writ of certiorari, where the validity of a treaty or statute of the United States is drawn in question or where the validity of a State statute is drawn in question on the ground of its being repugnant to the Constitution, treaties or laws of the United States, or where any title, right, privilege or immunity is specially set up or claimed under the Constitution, treaties or statutes of, or commission held or authority exercised under, the United States. (June 25, 1948, c. 646, Sec. 1, 62 Stat. 929.)

U.S. Code Annotated, Title 28, Chapter 83, Courts of Appeals.

Sec. 1291. Final decisions of district courts.

The courts of appeals shall have jurisdiction of appeals from all final decisions of the district courts of the United States, the District Court for the Territory of Alaska, the United States District Court for the District of the Canal Zone, and the District Court of the Virgin Islands, except where a direct review may be had in the Supreme Court. (June 25, 1948, c. 646 Sec. 1, 62 Stat. 929.)

Sec. 1292. Interlocutory decisions.

The courts of appeals shall have jurisdiction of appeals from:

(1) Interlocutory orders of the district courts of the United States, the District Court of the Territory of Alaska, the United States District Court for the District of the Canal Zone, and the District Court of the Virgin Islands, or of the judges thereof, granting, continuing, modifying, refusing, or dissolving injunctions or refusing to dissolve or modify injunctions, except where a direct review may be had in the Supreme Court;

(2) Interlocutory orders appointing receivers, or refusing orders to wind up receiverships or to take steps to accomplish the purposes thereof, such as directing sales or other disposals of property;

(3) Interlocutory decrees of such district courts or the judges thereof determining the rights and liabilities of the parties to admiralty cases, in which appeals from final decrees are followed;

(4) Judgments in civil actions for patent infringement which are final except for accounting. (June 25, 1948, c. 646, Sec. 1, 62 Stat. 929.)

Sec. 1293. Final decisions of Puerto Rico and Hawaii Supreme Courts.

The courts of appeals for the First and Ninth Circuits shall have jurisdiction of appeals from all final decisions of the supreme courts of Puerto Rico and Hawaii, respectively, in all cases involving the Constitution, laws , or treaties of the United States or any authority exercised thereunder, in all habeas corpus proceedings, and in all other civil cases where the value in controversy exceeds $5,000, exclusive of interest and costs. (June 25, 1948, c. 646, Sec. 1, 62 Stat. 929.)

Sec. 1294. Circuits in which decisions reviewable.

Appeals from reviewable decisions of the district and territorial courts shall be taken to the courts of appeals as follows:

(1) From a district court of the United States to the court of appeals for the circuit embracing the district;

(2) From the District Court for the Territory of Alaska or any division thereof, to the Court of Appeals for the Ninth Circuit;

(3) From the United States District Court for the District of the Canal Zone, to the Court of Appeals for the Fifth Circuit;

(4) From the District Court of the Virgin Islands, to the Court of Appeals forthe Third Circuit;

(5) From the Supreme Court of Hawaii, to the Court of Appeals for the Ninth Circuit;

(6) From the Supreme Court of Puerto Rico, to the Court of Appeals for the First Circuit. (June 25, 1948, c. 646, Sec. 1, 62 Stat. 930.)

FEDERAL RULES OF CIVIL PROCEDURE. IX APPEALS

Rule 72 Appeal from a District Court to the Supreme Court.

When an appeal is permitted by law from a district court to the Supreme Court of the United States, an appeal shall be taken, perfected, and prosecuted pursuant to law and the Rules of the Supreme Court of the United States governing such an appeal.

Rule 73 Appeal to a Court of Appeals.

(a) When and How Taken. When an appeal is permitted by law from a district court to a court of appeals the time within which an appeal may be taken shall be 30 days from the entry of the judgment appealed from unless a shorter time is provided by law, except that in any action in which the United States or an officer or agency thereof is a party the time as to all parties shall be 60 days from such entry, and except....

(b) Notice of Appeal. The notice of appeal shall specify the parties taking the appeal; shall designate the judgment or part thereof appealed from; and shall name the court to which the appeal is taken. Notification of the filing of the notice of appeal shall be given....

(c) Bond of Appeal. Unless a party is exempted by law, a bond for costs on appeal shall be filed....

Rule 74 Joint or Several Appeals to the Supreme Court or to a Court of Appeals; Summons and Severance Abolished (omitted)

Rule 75 Record on Appeal to a Court of Appeals (omitted)

Rule 76 Record on Appeal to a Court of Appeals; Agreed Statement (omitted)

Sec. 3.5 Appellate Jurisdiction delegated by Constitution and Statute (Cont'd)
Sec. 3.51 Territorially including Venue
Sec. 3.52 Of Parties or Res
Sec. 3.53 Of Grounds for Appeal or Review
Sec. 3.54 Of Appellate Remedies and Their Elements

PEOPLE ex rel CURTIS v HARRY R. KIDNEY, as Agent and Warden of Auburn Prison (1919) 225 NY 299, appdis 183 AD 451

APPEAL from an order of the Appellate Division of the Supreme Court in the fourth judicial department, entered June 5, 1918, which unanimously affirmed an order of the Cayuga County Court dismissing a writ of habeas corpus and remanding the relator to custody.

COLLIN, J. Marquis Curtis, confined in the prison at Auburn under conviction and sentence, secured the writ of habeas corpus to inquire into the cause of his detention, returnable on April 1, 1918, before the county judge of Cayuga County. The County Court, after a hearing, by an order, dismissed the writ and remanded him. The Appellate Division, upon his appeal, by its order entered June 5, 1918, unanimously affirmed the order of the County Court. The appeal here is from the order of affirmance.

At the outset, we must determine whether or not we have the power or jurisdiction to review the unanimous order of the Appellate Division, or, in more direct statement, whether the proceeding by writ of habeas corpus is a civil proceeding or a criminal proceeding. If it is a civil proceeding we have not power to review the order, because of the restriction imposed by section one hundred and ninety of the Code of Civil Procedure in this language: "From and after the 31st day of May, 1917, the jurisdiction of the court of appeals shall, in civil actions and proceedings, be confined to the review upon appeal of an actual determination made by an appellate division of the supreme court in either of the following cases, and no others: 1. An appeal may be taken as of right to said court from a judgment or order entered upon the decision of an appellate division of the supreme court which finally determines an action or special proceeding where is directly involved the construction of the constitution of the state or of the United States, or where one or more of the justices of the appellate division dissents from the decision of the court, or where the judgment or order is one of reversal or modification." The section has three other subdivisions, not one of which has a relevancy to the order here. We have uniformly held that all proceedings in a criminal action or proceeding are, generally speaking, governed by the Code of Criminal Procedure. (People v Redmond, 225 NY 206.) The Code of Criminal Procedure does not contain an enactment like unto section one hundred and ninety of the Code of Civil Procedure. The appeal at bar does not involve the construction of the Constitution of the state or of the United States, nor did a justice of the Appellate Division dissent from its decision. Therefore, if the appeal is in a civil proceeding, it must, under the mandate of the statute, be dismissed.

It has been stated by text-writers and in judicial opinion that the courts of England have not declared the proceeding by the writ of habeas corpus to inquire into the cause of detention either civil or criminal in its nature. (Martin v District Court, 37 Colo 110. See, also People ex rel. Tweed v Liscomb, 60 NY 559; Simmons v Georgia Iron & Coal Co., 117 Ga 305.) The courts of our country, compelled by legislative enactments regulating appellate jurisdiction or other matters of procedure, have been constrained to be more bold. In Ex parte Tom Tong (108 US 556) is, unquestionably, the leading decision determining the nature of the proceeding. There, as here, the jurisdiction of the court depended on whether the proceeding was to be treated as civil or criminal; if civil, the court had not, if criminal, it had jurisdiction. The petitioner, Tom Tong, was restrained of his liberty, because of alleged violation of law, under criminal precess. The court said: "Proceedings to enforce civil rights are civil proceedings, and proceedings for the punishment of crimes are criminal proceedings. In the present case the petitioner is held under criminal process. The prosecution against him is a criminal prosecution, but the writ of habeas corpus which he has obtained is not a proceeding in that prosecution. On the contrary, it is a new suit brought by him to enforce a civil right, which he claims, as against those who are holding him in custody, under the criminal process. If he fails to establish his right to his liberty, he may be detained for trial for the offense; but if he succeeds he must be discharged from custody. The proceeding is one instituted by himself for his liberty, not by the government to punish him for his crime. This petitioner claims that the Constitution and a treaty of the United States give him the right to his liberty, notwithstanding the charge that has been made against him, and he has obtained judicial process to enforce that right. Such a proceeding on his part is, in our opinion, a civil proceeding, notwithstanding his object is, by means of it, to get released from custody under a criminal prosecution." (p. 559.) It refused to take jurisdiction. It has consistently followed the decision. (Kurtz v Moffitt, 115 US 487, 494; Cross v Burke, 146 US 82, 88; Matter of Frederich, 149 US 70,75; Fisher v Baker, 203 US 174, 181.) Its reasoning and conclusion have been adopted by the greater number of the states in which codes regulate procedure. (State ex rel. Durner v Huegin, 110 Wis 189, 220; Matter of Thompson, 85 NJ Eq 221, 248; Selicow v Dunn, 100 Neb 615; Henderson v James, 52 OhioSt 242, 259; State ex rel. Board of Education of St. Louis v Nast, 209 Mo 708, 731; State ex rel. Beekley v McDonald, 123 Minn 84; Orr v Jackson, 149 Iowa, 641; State ex rel. Brandegee v Clements, 52 Montana, 57.) A few of the states declare the doctrine that the cause of the restraint determines whether the proceeding be civil or criminal. If the applicant for the writ be restrained by reason of the commission of a crime or of a criminal charge it is criminal; if otherwise it is civil. (Legate v Legate, 87 Texas, 248; Gleason v Board of Commissioners of McPherson County, 30 Kan 53.)

The legislature of this state has classified the proceeding as a civil proceeding. The Code of Civil Procedure enumerates the writ as a state writ (Section 1991), and contains elaborate provisions regulating the exercise of the common-law power to issue and adjudge it (Sections 2015-2066), including those relating to rights of appealing (Sections 2058-2064; People ex rel. Hubert v Kaiser, 206 NY 46). It is a special proceeding (sections 3333, 3334). The title relating to state writs is designated, "Special Proceedings instituted by State writ," and sections within the title frequently refer to such proceedings as special. It is a civil special proceeding (Section 3343, subdiv. 20). The Code of Criminal Procedure defines "Special proceedings of a criminal nature." (Section 2; part VI.) The proceeding by writ of habeas corpus is not one of the special proceedings of a criminal nature, and, assuredly, it is not within the definition of a criminal action. (Code of Civil Procedures, sections, 3335, 3336, 3337; Code of Criminal Procedure, section 5.) The Code of Criminal Procedure does not contain a provision authorizing or permitting an appeal to the Appellate Division from the final order in the habeas corpus proceeding (Sections 515, 517, 749, 750), and it applies only to criminal actions, and all other proceedings in criminal cases which are therein provided for (Section 962). The proceeding by writ of habas corpus is not therein provided for and is not thereby classified as a special proceeding of a criminal nature. (People ex rel. Taylor v Forbes, 143 NY 219.)

While the legislative classification is not controlling, because the legislature cannot, in such manner, create or destroy the actual nature of an action or proceeding, it is very significant and is in accord with the highest judicial opinion. We hold that the proceeding by the writ of habeas corpus to inquire into the cause of the detention of a person is a civil special proceeding to enforce a civil right, although its purpose is to effect the release of the person from imprisonment or custody under a criminal prosecution.

Legislative enactments prescribing and defining the rights of appeal are with us imperative. We have no jurisdiction to hear an appeal unless it is conferred by statute. Courts which are created by written law, and whose jurisdiction is, as is ours, defined by written law, cannot transcend that jurisdiction. This is the established rule in all actions and proceedings, civil or criminal or of a criminal nature. (People ex rel. Commissioners of Charities v Cullen, 151 NY 54.) Section one hundred and ninety forbids us from reviewing the order here appealed from. There is no merit in the appellant's assertion and argument that this proceeding directly involved the construction of the Constitution of the state. He avers that he is held in imprisonment by virtue of a sentence and judgment which the court had not the power to render and, therefore, are void. Whether or not the court had the power is determinable only through the interpreting of statutes. The meaning and not the validity of the statutes is involved. In a certain sense, perhaps, each enforcement of a statute by a court involves its constitutionality or the construction of the Constitution of the state. That sense, however, was not within the legislative mind or intention in enacting the present restriction of our jurisdiction. An appeal, upon the ground the appellant here asserts, must present to us directly and primarily an issue determinable only by our construction of the Constitution of the state or of the United States. (People ex rel. Moss v Supervisors of Oneida Co., 221 NY 367; Matter of Haydorn v Carroll, 225 NY 84.)

The appeal should be dismissed but, as the costs are discretionary (Code of Civil Procedure, sections, 3240, 2007; Matter of Holden, 126 NY 589; Matter of Teese, 32 AD 46; Matter of Barnett, 11 Hun (NY) 468), without costs.

Appeal dismissed.

Sec. 3.6 Examples of Appellate Remedies
Sec. 3.61 At Common Law
a. Writ of Error
b. Writ of Certiorari

Sec. 3.62 In Equity
a. An Appeal
b. Bill of Certiorari
c. Bill of Review

Sec. 3.63 Under Statute
a. Writ of Review
b. Appeal
c. Certified question

STORM v UNITED STATES (1876) 94 US 76.

ERROR to the Circuit Court of the United States for the District of California.

MR. JUSTICE CLIFFORD delivered the opinion of the court.

Errors of the Circuit Court resting in parol cannot be re-examined in this court by writ of error. Instead of that, the writ of error addresses itself to the record; and the rule is, that, whenever the error is apparent in the record, whether it be made to appear by bill of exceptions, an agreed statement of facts, or by demurrer, the error is open to re-examination and correction.

Whatever error of the court is apparent in the record, whether it be in the foundation, proceedings, judgment, or execution of the suit, may be reexamined and corrected; but neither the rulings of the court in admitting or excluding evidence, nor the instructions given by the court to the jury, are a part of the record, unless made so by a proper bill of exceptions. Suydam v Williamson, 20 How (US) 433.

Enough has already been remarked to show that the action is an action of debt founded on the bond given by the defendants to secure the faithful performance of covenants contained in their previously described written agreement. Reference has already been made to all the exceptions taken by the defendants to the rulings of the court during the trial before the jury; but it is also objected in argument here that the bond described in the complaint was not produced at the trial, and that no copy of it was ever filed in the case. Such an objection, if it had been made in the court below, might have been available for the defendants, unless the plaintiffs had overcome it by producing the instrument, or by showing its loss and due search for it without success, and had offered secondary proof of its contents. Parol proof of the contents of a lost instrument of the kind is admissible, provided it appear that proper search has been made for it without success.

Had the defendants intended to insist that the bond should be given in evidence, they should have made that intention known at the trial; and, if not given in evidence, they might have requested the court to direct a verdict in their favor, and, in case their request had been refused, they would have had the right to except to the ruling of the court in refusing their request for instruction. Nothing of the kind was done; and, for aught that appears in the record, it may be that the bond was given in evidence, or, if not, that the defendants waived the right to require its production.

Errors apparent in the record, though not presented by a bill of exceptions, may be re-examined by writ of error in an appellate tribunal; but alleged errors, not presented by a bill of exceptions, nor apparent on the face of the record, are not the proper subjects of re-examination by writ of error in this court.

Parties dissatisfied with the ruling of a subordinate court, and intending to seek a revision of the same in the Appellate Court, must take care to raise the questions to be re-examined, and must see to it that the questions are made to appear in the record; for nothing is error in law except what is apparent on the face of the record by bill of exceptions, or an agreed statement of facts, or in some one of the methods known to the practice of courts of error for the accomplishment of that object. Suydam v Williamson, 20 How 433; Garland v Davis, 4 id. 131; Steph. on Plead. 121; Slacum v Pomeroy, 6 Cranch, 221; Strother v Hutchinson, 4 BingNC 83.

Judgment affirmed.

JACKSONVILLE, T. & K. W. RY CO. v BOY (1894) 34 Fla 389, 16 So 290.

Certiorari to circuit court, Putnam county; J. J. Finley, Judge.

To review a judgment of the circuit court of Putnam county affirming a judgment of the county judge of said county against the petitioner.

MABRY, J. On the petition of the Jacksonville, Tampa & Key West Railway Company, filed in this court in May, 1890, a writ of certiorari was issued to the circuit court for the Fifth judicial circuit for Putnam county, commanding the clerk of that court to transmit to this court a true copy of the record in the case wherein the said company was appellant, and Antone Boy was appellee, and in which judgment was rendered affirming the judgment of the court of the county judge of the said county of Putnam. From the record filed as a return to the writ by the clerk of the circuit court it is made to appear that a suit was instituted by the respondent, Boy, before the county judge of Putnam county against the Jacksonville, Tampa & Key West Railway Company to recover $100, the value of a cow of respondent alleged to have been negligently killed by the company.

The declaration filed in the case alleged the value of the cow to be $100, and that plaintiff's claim for recovery arose under chapter 3742, Laws 1887. A trial of the case in the court of the county judge resulted in a verdict by a jury in favor of plaintiff (respondent here) for $100, for the value of the cow killed, with interest from the date of the presentation of the claim for payment at the rate of 20 per cent per annum, and $70 attorney fees.

It is contended for petitioner that the county judge proceeded illegally in allowing attorney fees, and also exceeded his jurisdiction in entering judgment for more than $100; and further, that the action of the circuit court in affirming the judgment of the county judge was illegal, and beyond its jurisdictional powers.

Our decision under the present writ must affect the proceedings before the circuit court, as the writ was directed to that court, and not to the county judge. But as the proceedings in the circuit court were on appeal from proceedings before the county judge, the transcript of the record of such proceedings filed in the circuit court must be examined in order to determine the legality of the action of the latter court therein.

The power of this court to review and quash, on the common-law writ of certiorari, the proceedings of an inferior tribunal, when it proceeds in a cause without jurisdiction, or when its procedure is illegal, or is unknown to the law, or is essentially irregular, is, we think, clear; but, while such power does exist, it must be remembered that its exercise is not a matter of right, but rests in the sound legal discretion of the court, and when the writ is granted it will not serve the purpose of a writ of error or appeal with a bill of exceptions. (Basnett v City of Jacksonville, 18 Fla 523; Edgerton v Mayor, etc. Id. 528.)

Whenever an appeal lies from the proceedings sought to be reviewed, the general rule is to deny the writ of certiorari. The doctrine is generally stated that the functions of the writ of certiorari at common law, when addressed to inferior tribunals, are only to bring up for review on the record questions of jurisdiction, power, and authority of such tribunals, and that the appellate court is confined to the questions whether the inferior court had jurisdiction, and acted within its limits. It was said in Edgerton v Mayor, etc.: "We had occasion, in the case of Basnett v City of Jacksonville, decided at this term, to state our views in reference to a common-law certiorari. We there held that such a certiorari does not serve the purpose of a writ of error or appeal with a bill of exceptions as known to our practice, and that, if the circuit court has jurisdiction, and there is no irregularity or illegality in the procedure, the record of which is brought to this court, the certiorari must be quashed."

In McAllilley v Horton, (75 Ala 491), it was decided that the functions of the common-law writ of certiorari extend alike to questions touching the jurisdiction of the subordinate tribunal and the regularity of its proceedings, and by it errors of law apparent on the face of the record may be corrected, but, in the absence of statutory authority, conclusions of fact cannot be reviewed. (Vide, also, Town of Camden v Bloch, (65 Ala 236.) The office of the common-law certiorari, as declared by the Illinois court, is to have the entire record of the inferior court brought up for inspection, in order that the superior court may determine therefrom whether the inferior court had jurisdiction, or had exceeded its jurisdiction, or had failed to proceed according to the essential requirements of the law, where no appeal or other direct means of reviewing the proceeding is given. (Donahue v Will Co., 100 Ill. 94; Hyslop v Finch, 99 Ill. 171. See also, Wedel v Green, 70 Mich 642, 38 NW 638.)

A distinction is made by some courts between cases where the writ goes to inferior courts of record and cases where it goes to officers or boards exercising only quasi judicial powers in proceedings of a summary character out of the course of the common law. In the first class of cases it is held the record only can be examined to ascertain whether such courts have acted within the scope of their jurisdictional powers, while in the second the record will be examined not only to see whether such officers or boards have kept within their jurisdictional powers, but whether or not they have acted strictly according to law; and errors and irregularities committed by them will be corrected. (Iron Co. v Schubel, 29 Wis 444; State v Whitford, 54 Wis 150, 11 N.W. 424; Cunningham v Squires, 2 W Va 422.)

The presentation of the case here has relation to the authority of the county judge to allow attorney fees under the statute, and his jurisdictional power to render a judgment for more than $100, and also the power and authority of the circuit judge to affirm on appeal such a judgment. The failure to find in the record the judgment complained of makes it unnecessary for us to say anything in reference to the power and jurisdiction of the county judge in the premises. The declaration filed in the case before him claimed $100 damages, and until a final judgment was rendered there was nothing for the circuit court to review on appeal. In the absence of such judgment it is unnecessary to determine the power of the circuit court to affirm or reverse it on appeal. Without a final judgment in the court of the county judge, we are at a loss to understand how there can be any regular or legal affirmance in the appellate circuit court of a judgment not shown to exist, and as we find such a condition in the record we must deal with it as we find it. The judgment of affirmance in the record before the circuit court was such an essential irregularity and departure from prescribed rules of procedure in such cases as to require that it be quashed, and a judgment will therefore be entered accordingly.

JOHNSON v HARMON (1876) 94 US 371

APPEAL from the Supreme Court of the District of Columbia.

MR. JUSTICE BRADLEY delivered the opinion of the court.

This was a bill in equity, involving, amongst other questions, the validity of a trust deed given by the complainant (the appellee here) to secure certain notes. The complainant charges in his bill that he was so intoxicated when he executed the deed and notes as to be incapable of understanding what he was doing. The court below, after considerable testimony had been taken, directed an issue to try the question whether the complainant, at the time of the execution of the deed of trust and notes, was capable of executing a valid deed or contract. The issue so directed was tried, and resulted in a verdict for the complainant; namely, that he was not capable of executing a valid deed or contract. The defendants took a bill of exceptions to the charge given by the judge who tried the issue, which was allowed, and signed by him. The cause afterwards came on to be heard upon the exceptions, and they were overruled. Subsequently a final hearing was had upon the pleadings, evidence, and verdict, and a decree was rendered for the complainant, directing the trust deed and notes in question to be vacated and set aside. From that decree this appeal was taken, and the only errors assigned are to the charge given by the judge to the jury on the trial of the feigned issue.

This is totally inadmissible. A bill of exceptions cannot be taken on the trial of a feigned issue directed by a court of equity, or, if taken, can only be used on a motion for a new trial made to said court. (2 Dan. Ch. Pr. (3d Am. ed.) 1106; Armstrong v Armstrong, 3 Myl. & K. 52; Ex parte Story,

12 Pet(US)343.) See the cases on new trials on feigned issues collected in 3 Graham & Waterman on New Trials, 1553, & c. The issue is directed to be tried for the purpose of informing the conscience of the Chancellor, and aiding him to come to a proper conclusion. If he thinks the trial has not been a fair one, or for any other reason desires a new trial, it is in his discretion to order it. But he may proceed with the cause though dissatisfied with the verdict, and make a decree contrary thereto, if in his judgment the law and the evidence so requires. A decree in equity, therefore, when appealed from, does not stand or fall according to the legality or illegality of the proceedings on the trial of a feigned issue in the cause; for the verdict may or may not have been the ground of the decree. It is the duty of the court of first instance to decide (as was done here) upon the whole case, pleadings, evidence, and verdict, giving to the latter so much effect as it is worth. An appeal from the decree must be decided in the same way, namely, upon the whole case, and cannot be made to turn on the correctness or incorrectness of the judge's rulings at the trial of the feigned issue.

Decree affirmed.

Mr. Justice CLIFFORD concurred in the judgment of the court, and delivered the following opinion:—(omitted).

Sec. 3.7 Elements of an Appellate Remedy, Exercise of the
Sec. 3.71 Jurisdiction
Sec. 3.72 Grounds for Appeal or Review (record on appeal)
Sec. 3.73 Hearing (briefs, oral argument)
Sec. 3.74 Adjudgment: Decision, Order, Judgment, Decree; Opinion
Sec. 3.75 Remittitur or Mandate

Sec. 3.7 Elements of an Appellate Remedy, Exercise of the
Sec. 3.71 Jurisdiction

STEVENS v STATE (3dDept 1950) 277 AD 418, 100 S2d 826

Action by Nancy Stevens, claimant, as administratrix of the estate of George Stevens, deceased, against the State of New York for deceased's death while a patient at Manhattan State Hospital. The Court of Claims, Bernard Ryan, J., 92 S2d 732, 196 M 712, granted a recovery in part, and denied a recovery in part, and claimant moved to compel the State to accept her notice of appeal. The Court of Claims, George Sylvester, J. (94 S2d 355, 197 M 315), denied claimant's motion without prejudice, and claimant appealed and filed a motion in the Appellate Division to compel the State to accept the notice of appeal....

BERGAN, Justice. The Statute regulating appeals in this court from the Court of Claims provides two alternative methods for the service of the order or judgment which begins the running of time against the taking of an appeal. (Court of Claims Act, Sec. 25.)

One method is consonant with the usual practice in the Supreme Court, by the service upon the adverse party or his attorney of the judgment with notice of entry. (Cf. Civil Practice Act, Sec. 612.)

The alternative method is one peculiar to the Court of Claims. It is by the "service by the clerk" of a "certified copy" of the order or judgment. An appeal must be taken within thirty days of service made in either alternative manner. (Sec. 25.)

At the argument we were advised that for many years it has been uniform practice in the Court of Claims for the clerk to serve by mail certified copies of the judgments of the court upon the parties in interest.

Here a certified copy of a judgment in favor of the claimant enclosed in a post-paid wrapper was deposited by a messenger for the clerk in the Post Office in the Capitol at Albany on August 24, 1949. The judgment had been entered on that day. It was directed to the attorneys for claimant at an address designated by them.

Such a designation of address was required to be made by the attorneys appearing, in pursuance of Rule 11, Rules of Civil Practice. The Rules and the Civil Practice Act apply to the Court of Claims in the absence of contrary directions in the Court of Claims Act, or in its own rules. (Court of Claims Act, Sec. 9, subd. 9.)

A notice of appeal to this court was served on the Attorney General and the Clerk of the Court of Claims on September 27, 1949, by the claimant's attorneys seeking a review of the adequacy of the award in claimant's favor.

This service was 34 days after the mailing of the certified copy of the judgment. The attorneys for the claimant state in their brief that they had sent the notice of appeal to a process server in Albany on September 19, with instructions not to make service until September 27.

The Attorney General returned the notice of appeal on the ground that service was not timely. Claimant then moved in the Court of Claims for an order compelling acceptance of her notice of appeal. The motion was denied by that court without prejudice to its renewal here. Claimant has appealed from that order and has also moved here for an order to compel the State to accept the notice of appeal.

The claimant's main argument is that the mailing of the certified copy of the judgment by the clerk was ineffectual as service; that the time to appeal, therefore, has not expired.

Section 25 of the Court of Claims Act does not specify how service of the certified copy of the judgment shall be made by the clerk to start the running of time to appeal. A direction for the "service" of a paper ordinarily means personal service unless by statute or rule another method is allowed.

This is quite well settled in principle. Thus, in Rathbun v Acker, (18 Barb (NY) 393), the General Term of the Supreme Court held that where the provisions of a statutory charter allowed village trustees to give notice to an owner of land to construct a sidewalk and he neglected to do so the trustees could construct it and impose a tax on the owner, the "giving of notice" meant personal service, and mailing was not enough.

A requirement of "notice" of charges against a police officer was held by the Special Term to mean personal notice in McDermott v Board of Police for Metropolitan Police Dist., (25 Barb. (NY) 635, 646). A statute requiring "notice in writing" of an application to change a proposed railroad route to be given to the company and the owners of land affected was held by the General Term to require personal service where the statute did not prescribe the form of service. (People ex rel. Niagara Bridge & Canandaigua R. R. Co. v Lockport & B.R.R. Co., 13 Hun(NY) 211.)

The notice of justification of sureties of an undertaking to discharge a mechanic's lien must be served personally in the absence of a legislative prescription for other service. (Matter of Boland v Sokolski, 56 M 333, 106 S 766. Cf. Morris v Morange, 26 HowPrac(NY) 247.)

In the light of this general background of what is meant by "service" without the definitive implementation of statute or rule inquiry is to be directed to Rule 20 of the Rules of Civil Practice, which, on this subject applies to the procedure of the Court of Claims as well to the Supreme Court.

Its pertinent provisions are that "a paper in an action," with certain expressly stated exceptions, may be served on an attorney by mailing it. The place of mailing shall be "in the city, village or town of the party or attorney serving it." The clerk of the Court of Claims is not, of course, a "party" or an "attorney" in the sense that those terms are used in the rule.

But the words, in turn, are not words which delimit the service, and are merely a prescription of the place of mailing which is quite a secondary matter in the scheme of the rule. General authority is granted to serve an attorney by mailing a "paper in an action" to him at the address he has designated.

A certified copy of a judgment is the kind of a paper in an action which could be served by mail. The rule does not require the service be made by an attorney or a party. It merely says that the paper "may be served" by mail. A statutory authorization to a public officer to serve a "paper in an action" upon a "party or an attorney" would bring the officer within the general permissive authority of the language of the rule.

The place of mailing was a direction to attorneys and parties making such service. It is good enough that the public officer, who, having a statutory authority to do an act which may be done by mailing, mails the paper in the place of his official office. This, we think, is a sufficient compliance with the rule. We regard the judgment to have been properly served and to have started the running of the time to appeal.

It is interesting to note that in the judicial decisions that have been considered here, beginning with that at the General Term in Rathbun v Aker, supra, (18 Barb.(NY) at page 395), the exception to the rule of personal service is where another mode is "indicated" as well as "specified"—language which was later followed or quoted and which suggests that if there is reasonable authority for other means of service it ought to be applied liberally.

The further argument of the claimant that the time begins to run when the paper is received rather that when it is mailed is wrong on such elementary grounds as to merit no extensive treatment. The statute added three days for the service of the notice of appeal where the judgment was served by mail. (Civil Practic Act, Sec. 164.) This does not help the claimant. The calculation is from the day of mailing which is the "service" through the post office. The notice of appeal was not served until 34 days after. We have no power of extension or extenuation.

Order affirmed and motion denied, without costs.

ADAMS v FOX, Executor, et al (1863) 27 NY 640

Motion to dismiss appeal. The defendant, P. G. Fox, demurred to the complaint. The judge at the special term held the demurrer not well taken, and gave judgment for the plaintiff, with leave to the defendant to withdraw the demurrer and answer. On appeal to the general term, the order was reversed, and judgment on the demurrer was given for the defendant, with leave to the plaintiff to amend the complaint. The plaintiff appealed here from this order, no judgment in the action having been entered, so far as appeared.

The papers on which the motion to dismiss was made were the case made on the appeal from the special to the general term, the order of the general term and the notice of appeal to this court.

DENIO, Ch. J. It is objected that this motion cannot be entertained, because the return has not been filed, and it is urged that until this is done, this court is not possessed of the case. But we think that when a notice of appeal has been served, and the proper undertaking perfected, the case is so far removed from the subordinate court, that we can entertain any application, which the case, in its then condition, may render necessary. Our general rules are based upon that idea, for they allow an order to dismiss an appeal for a default in filing the return.

The appeal which was attempted to be made in this case was premature. The determination of the demurrer, no doubt, entitled the defendant to judgment, unless the plaintiff should amend; but until final judgment was entered, the case was not in a condition to be reviewed here. The appeal must, therefore, be dismissed.

Ordered accordingly.

Sec. 3.72 Grounds for Appeal or Review (record on appeal)

HODINA v BORDEWICK (3dDept 1952) 110 S2d 62

Action by Joseph Hodina against Hans Bordewick to recover for the price of a wire baler delivered to defendant. From a judgment of the Supreme Court, Columbia County, Hamm, J., entered upon a verdict of the jury in favor of plaintiff, the defendant appeals....

PER CURIAM. Plaintiff has had judgment on his action for goods sold and delivered. The principal question on the appeal is whether that part of the verdict based on the sale and delivery of a wire baler to defendant can be sustained.

Plaintiff testified that defendant agreed to buy from him a wire baler which plaintiff then had on order and that defendant further agreed thereafter to furnish the use of the baler he was buying to cut standing hay on plaintiff's farm on shares. Plaintiff further said that defendant took possession of the baler in June, 1948; kept and used it until September and partially performed the agreement to cut hay.

Defendant denied sale. He said the agreement between the parties was to use the plaintiff's baler to cut plaintiff's hay on a share basis, and that when this was done the baler was returned to plaintiff's farm and left there.

All of this seems to us to have presented a clear issue whether or not there was an agreement of purchase and sale, and that issue, and the contentions of the parties about it, were distinctly submitted to the jury in adequate instructions by the judge.

The answer pleaded the statute of frauds and the specific factual problems that would arise under this defense were not submitted to the jury in the judge's charge. There was no exception to the charge or request for amplification in this respect. Defendant moved to strike out the proof in respect of the wire baler on the ground that the purported sale came within the statute of frauds and because he felt plaintiff had "failed to sustain the burden of proof of delivery or acceptance of delivery." But there was proof in the record, if the jury accepted plaintiff's version, from which it could have been found that there was delivery and acceptance of delivery.

If that was an open question on the record, and we think it was, the testimony in relation to the baler agreement should not have been stricken out, but it became a factual issue in the case whether the agreement was partially executed and thus enforcible even though not in writing.

There was presented to the jury in general terms the question whether there was an agreement of sale and a delivery. The judge in his charge outlined the theory of events upon which plaintiff argued there was a contract of purchase and sale and the theory of events upon which defendant argued there was no contract. If the factual pattern contended for by plaintiff was true there was no need as a matter of law for a writing to make the contract enforcible.

To say that the attention of the jury should have been more specifically directed to the question of delivery and acceptance as proof of the agreement adds nothing to the appeal because appellant did not take the means that were open to him to have this done, or to have urged, as he also urges now, that another measure of damages than the one submitted would have been more appropriate....

Judgment affirmed, with costs

BRAUER v NEW YORK CITY INTERBORO RY. CO. (1stDept 1908) 129 AD 384, 113 S 705

INGRAGAM, J. This action was to recover damages for personal injuries resulting in the death of the plaintiff's intestate. Plaintiff had a verdict and the defendant appealed and served a case, to which the plaintiff served amendments. Upon the settlement of the case, the trial judge allowed certain of the plaintiff's amendments, striking out exceptions taken by the defendant to the summing up of the plaintiff's counsel. Subsequently the defendant made a motion to restore the summing up and the exceptions taken thereto. That motion was denied, and the defendant appeals.

These proposed amendments related solely to counsel's summing up. Some of this was improper; but, as the objections in most cases resulted in the instruction by the judge to the jury not to consider the statements, and no exception was taken, there was no question presented for review. Counsel did except in several instances to the ruling of the court in relation to the summing up, and those exceptions, I think, should be inserted in the case. In submitting the amendment striking out lines 23 to 31 on page 165 of the case to the trial judge counsel for respondent said that, while there was an exception, the matter was not worthy of consideration by the appellate court. It is hardly the province of the trial judge to determine what exception would or would not be proper to be presented to the appellate court, and I think that amendment should have been disallowed, as it was conceded that there was an exception, and the appellant was entitled to have the exception presented on his appeal. The same applies to amendment 122, which was to strike out lines 13 to 33, inclusive, on page 167 of the proposed case. The counsel for respondent said that, while there was an exception, it was purely argumentative. I think the defendant was entitled to have that exception appear in the record. The same applies to lines 13 to 24, inclusive, on page 171. There counsel took an exception.

I think the order should be reversed and the case remitted to the trial judge, with instructions to disallow those amendments where an exception was taken, with $10 costs and disbursements to the appellant to abide the result of the appeal. All concur.

Sec. 3.73 Hearing (calendars, briefs, oral argument)

MATTER OF L'HOMMEDIEU v BD. OF REGENTS OF U. OF STATE OF N.Y. (3rdDept 1950) 276 AD 283, 94 S2d 268

Motion to strike from calendar, or to adjourn to another term an appeal from an order of the Supreme Court at Special Term (Schirick, J.) entered December 9, 1949 in Albany County, in a proceeding under article 78 of the Civil Practice Act, which directed appellants to desist from taking any action pursuant to the Feinberg Law (L. 1949, ch. 360) and to treat it as a nullity, upon the ground that such law is unconstitutional. By the motion the Appellate Division was also asked to render a pro forma decision and direct that the appeal be heard in the Court of Appeals, and to make certain corrections in the record before Special Term.

PER CURIAM. The appeal is by the Board of Regents and others from a final order of the Albany Special Term which determined that chapter 360 of the Laws of 1949, known as the "Feinberg Law" is unconstitutional.

Respondents on appeal move to strike the appeal from the calendar on the ground that the record and notice of argument were not served in sufficient time before this term, or in the alternative, adjourning the appeal to the next term.

They also move to refer the record back to the Special Term for correction of errors in its opinion. They move, additionally, to affirm the Special Term in a "pro forma decision," which shall direct the appeal be heard in the Court of Appeals.

If the case is adjourned until the next term which commences March 6, 1950, the schedule of our terms is such that it cannot be decided before the May term, which would delay submission of the question to the Court of Appeals by one side or the other until the summer or fall. We think such a delay in decision should be avoided in the interest of an early and ultimate determination of an important constitutional question.

This leads us to direct that the provisions of rules 12 and 13 of the Appellate Division Third Department Rules as to the time of service of the record, notice of argument and brief be waived. The appeal is placed at the foot of the January, 1950 calendar and will be heard when reached. The respondents on appeal and other parties interested in the questions involved and desiring to file briefs amicus curiae may file and serve their briefs on or before February 1, 1950.

This court has jurisdiction of the merits of the appeal and has no election or choice in entertaining an appeal properly before it. It should not render a "pro forma decision." Its duty is to consider fully, adequately and independently questions properly before it.

It certainly is without any power to direct that "the appeal be heard in the Court of Appeals." Such a direction would not only be gratuitous; it would have no sanction under the appellate procedure provided by the Constitution and the statute. The record has been certified in accordance with law. If there are to be corrections in it they are to be made in the usual way by the Special Term, and if they do not go to the substance, as it is conceded they do not, such correction would not affect the course of the appeal.

The motion in each of its specifications should be denied.

FOSTER, P.J., HEFFERMAN, BREWSTER, BERGAN and COON, JJ., concur.

The motion in each of its specifications is denied.

SCHLEY v PULLMAN CAR CO. (1887) 120 US 575

EJECTMENT. Plea, general issue. Judgment for defendant. Plaintiff sued out this writ of error. The case is stated in the opinion of the court.

MR. JUSTICE HARLAN: This is an action of ejectment, in which the plaintiff in error claims title to certain real estate in Cook County, Illinois, of which Pullman's Palace Car Company is in possession. A jury having been waived, the case was tried by the court, pursuant to a stipulation between the parties, that judgment should be entered for the defendant if the court was of opinion that a certain deed was valid and binding as a conveyance by husband and wife of the real estate therein described.

The deed and the certificate of acknowledgment annexed thereto, referred to in the stipulation, is as follows:

"THIS INDENTURE, made this twenty-sixth day of May, in the year of our Lord one thousand eight hundred and fifty-six, witnesseth: That I, Christina Lynn, sister and heir-at-law of Henry Millspaugh, deceased, who was a recruit of Lieutenant T.W. Denton, of Thirteenth Regiment, United States Infantry, war of 1812, with Great Britain, of the county of St. Clair, and State of Michigan, party of the first part, in consideration of the sum of forty-three dollars in hand paid by Milton & Thomas C. McEwen, of county of Orange, and State of New York, party of the second part, the receipt of which is hereby acknowledged, do hereby release, grant, bargain, and quit-claim unto the said party of the second part, their heirs and assigns, forever, all her right, title, claim and interest in that certain tract of land granted by the United States unto David Millspaugh and Christine Lynn, the brother and sister and only heirs-at-law of Henry Millspaugh, deceased, as follows, to wit: (Here follows a description of the land)...; to have and to hold the said premises, with all the appurtenances thereunto belonging or in anywise appertaining, to their only proper use, benefit and behoof of said parties of the second part, their heirs and assigns, forever.

"In witness whereof the said grantor—have hereunto set our hands and seals the day and year first above written.

CHRISTINA LYNN. (Seal)
William Lynn. (Seal)

"Signed, sealed and acknowledged in presence of —

"MARY A. LYNN,

"OBED SMITH.

"STATE OF MICHIGAN, COUNTY OF ST. CLAIR, ss:

"On this twenty-seventh day of May, A.D. 1856, before me, a justice of the peace in and for said county of St. Clair, personally came Christina Lynn and William Lynn, her husband, known to me to be the persons who executed the foregoing instrument, and acknowledged the same to be their free act and deed; and the said Christina Lynn, having been by me privately examined separate and apart from the said husband, and fully understanding the contents of the foregoing instrument, acknowledged that she executed said deed freely and without any force or compulsion from her said husband or from any one.

"OBED SMITH,
Justice of the Peace."

The court being of opinion that the deed was valid to pass to grantees all the right, title, and interest of Christina Lynn and William Lynn, her husband, in the real estate therein described, entered judgment for the defendant on its plea of not guilty.

Before entering upon the consideration of the case it is proper to notice the motion made in behalf of the plaintiff in error, to strike out certain parts of the printed argument filed by the counsel for the defendant in error. Notwithstanding the agreement, that the case should be heard in the court below upon the single question referred to in the stipulation, the counsel for the defendant in error states many things, which he declares to be "incontrovertible facts," and within the knowledge of opposing counsel, but which are wholly unsustained by anything in the record. The motion to strike out relates to those matters. The excuse given for this breach of professional propriety is "the extreme brevity of the record." But it is the same record upon which counsel for the company succeeded for his client, and which, by agreement, contained all that was to be submitted to the court. The excuse given furnishes no apology whatever for his violation of the terms of the stipulation, much less does it palliate his attempt to influence the decision here, by reference to matters not in the record, and which, he must have known, could not be taken into consideration. It is only necessary to say that the facts dehors the record, which have been improperly introduced into the brief of the counsel for the defendant in error, have not in any degree influenced our determination of the case.

The plaintiff insists that the deed was void under the laws of Illinois, upon two grounds: 1. That the husband is not a party to the deed; 2. That the acknowledgement is defective.

(Opinion on merits omitted.)

The judgment below was right, and is

Affirmed.

Sec. 3.74 Adjudgment: Decision, Order, Judgment, Decree; Opinion

KRULIKOWSKI et al v THE POLYCAST CORP. (1966) 153 Conn 661, 220 A2d 444

Suit for an injunction to abate a manufacturer's nuisance and for damages for injuries sustained. Matter was referred to Samuel Mellitz, State Referee, and from a judgment of the Court of Common Pleas, LaMacchia, J., for plaintiffs on referee's report, the defendant appealed.

HOUSE, Associate Justice. The several plaintiffs own and occupy residences in an industrial zone in Stamford....

The plaintiffs have joined in this action, alleging that, by reason of the noise, vibration and fumes arising from the defendant's manufacturing process, they cannot occupy their residences with comfort or sleep at night, that their health has been affected and that the value of their premises has been impaired. It is alleged that the acts of the defendant constitute a nuisance and cause irreparable injury to the plaintiffs and that they have no adequate remedy at law. By way of relief, the plaintiffs seek an injunction, "an order under the statute for the discontinuance or abatement of such nuisance or for regulating the manner of conducting (the) defendant's business, as the court may deem proper," and, as to each plaintiff, $5,000 damages....

On a stipulation for reference, this case was referred for trial before a referee, who, with counsel, visited the defendant's premises and toured the defendant's plant. His 120-paragraph report is based on this inspection and on over 1300 pages of testimony. The trial court accepted the referee's report, overruling the defendant's objections and exceptions to it. The court rendered judgment for the plaintiffs for damages in the respective amounts found by the referee, and it found that the plaintiffs were entitled to an injunction restraining the defendant from conducting its business activities in such a fashion as to permit offensive fumes and odors to invade the plaintiffs' premises. Adapting the injunction to the equities of the situation, the judgment in effect gave the defendant a stay of execution on the injunction, not to exceed four months, to allow it to complete the construction, already commenced, of a fifty-foot stack and related ventilation system.

In our review of the defendant's assignments of error, we have confined ourselves to matters appearing of record and claims which the record discloses were raised at the trial and were ruled upon and decided by the court adversely to the defendant's claim. Practice Book Sec. 652; Stanley v M.H. Rhodes, Inc., 140 Conn 689, 695, 103 A2d 143; Maltbie, Conn., App. Proc.Sec. 305. Facts found by the referee from conflicting evidence and his inspection of the premises "cannot be disturbed if there was evidence before the referee to support them. Katz v Martin, 143 Conn 215, 217, 120 A2d 826. It is futile to assign error involving the weight of testimony or the credibility of witnesses. Hartford-Connecticut Trust Co. v Putnam Phalanx, 138 Conn 695,699, 88A2d 393. Those were matters for the referee to determine." West Hill Construction Corporation v Horwath, 149 Conn 608, 612, 182 aA2d 919. No correction of the report of the referee which would materially affect his findings or the judgment of the court can be justifiably made. We must disregard the many references in the defendant's brief to matters not appearing of record, and we do not condone the failure to support statements of fact in the case with supporting references to the record. Practice Book Sec. 713 (b); Maltbie, Conn. App. Proc. Sec. 325....

There is no error. In this opinion the other judges concurred.

ROBISON v LOCKRIDGE (two cases), (4thDept 1930) 230 AD 389, 244 S 663

Appeal from Monroe County Court.

Separate actions by Mary L. Robison and by Raymond Robison against David Lockridge. From judgments for respective plaintiffs, in sums of $118 and $32, plaintiffs appeal on grounds of inadequacy thereof.

EDGCOMB, J. While the plaintiff Mary L. Robison was crossing a public street in the city of Rochester on the evening of March 4, 1929, she was struck by a car driven by the defendant. She and her husband commenced separate actions to recover the damages which each claimed to have sustained by reason of the alleged negligence of the defendant on the occasion in question. Mrs. Robison has been awarded a verdict of $118 and Mr. Robison of $32. We are asked to set aside these verdicts as inadequate.

Mrs. Robison was entitled to recover, if she made out a cause of action against the defendant, such an amount as would fairly compensate her for the pain and suffering which she endured as the result of the accident, and for any resulting physical incapacity. Her husband's damage was confined to the consequential loss of his wife's society and services, and the actual expenses which he was put to on account of her injuries.

Mrs. Robison's injuries were not permanent, and it is not claimed that they were very serious or of long duration. She received an injury to her left ankle, which two doctors diagnosed as a sprain, and one as a muscle strain. One physician testified that the muscles of the left side of her neck were sprained, and that she was nervous, and suffered from shock. There was no disfigurement of her person. She was employed at the time of the accident, and was earning $25 per week. She was laid up and kept from her work for two weeks. A wife's earnings during coverture belong to her husband, unless he relinquishes such right in her favor. Here such loss was given to the wife. That seems to have been done by the consent of her husband. He testified that his wife was accustomed to keep the money which she earned, and the trial court charged, without objection or exception, that the jury should include in any verdict which they awarded Mrs. Robison the sum of $50 which she lost in wages during the two weeks she was incapacitated from work. We may therefore assume that $68, the balance of Mrs. Robison's verdict, was the jury's estimate of what she was entitled to for her pain and suffering.

No precise rule has ever been formulated by which pain and suffering can be accurately measured and compensated for in money. No two cases of injury are exactly alike. Such damages are of such a nature that it is peculiarly fitting that they should be determined and fixed by a jury. We think that the evidence warrants a finding that the harm done to Mrs. Robison on the occasion in question was trivial in its nature, and that the resulting pain and suffering were of minor consequence.

Mr. Robison was given a verdict for the exact amount which he expended for his wife's doctors' bills. It does not appear that he was compelled to expend any other sum because of her injury. Both he and his wife could not recover the wages which she lost. He relinquished his right to that item on the trial, and consented that such loss be included in his wife's verdict. He cannot, therefore, complain because they were not given to him. It is true that he was entitled to recover, if at all, for the loss of his wife's society, and that nothing was awarded for that item. While he was undoubtedly entitled to nominal damages, at least, for loss of consortium, the jury could easily have found that such loss was in name only when attempted to be measured by dollars and cents. Like pain and suffering, it is impossible to lay down any definite rule which will measure the extent of recovery for the loss by a husband of his wife's society. It is a matter which is addressed to the sound discretion of a jury. The court would not be justified in setting aside the verdict and granting a new trial simply to enable the plaintiff to recover nominal damages. Dunbar v Sweeney, 230 NY 609, 611, 130 NE 913; McConihe v New York & Erie R. Co., 20 NY 495, 75 AmDec 420; Nolan v Harris, 52 HowPrac 409; Chase v Bassett, 15 AbbPrac. (NS) 293; Hopkins v Grinnell, 28 Barb (NY) 533.

It is true that the judgment of reasonable men often differs as to the compensation which should be awarded to an injured party, but here a jury of the parties' own selection, after seeing the parties and hearing all the testimony, have fixed the amounts which they thought would compensate the plaintiffs for the damages they sustained by reason of Mrs. Robison's accident. There is nothing in the record to indicate that the plaintiffs did not have a fair trial, or that anything occurred which would prejudice them in any way, or cause the jury to decide these cases on any basis other than on the evidence. The court would have no right to substitute its judgment for that of the trier of the facts. Hogan v Franken, 221 AD 164, 223 S 1; Dashnau v City of Oswego, 204 AD 189, 198 S 226; appeal dismissed 236 NY 542, 142 NE 276.

Some weight should be accorded to the action of the trial judge in refusing to set aside these verdicts. He saw the witnesses, and heard them testify; he had a distinct advantage over us by the action of the jury.

While both verdicts are small, and while undoubtedly the jury would have been justified in granting a more liberal award to each plaintiff, we do not feel that we should disturb the discretion of the trial court.

Judgment and order affirmed, with costs. All concur except CROUCH, J., and THOMPSON, J., who dissent and vote for reversal on the facts.

Sec. 3.75 Remittitur or Mandate

DRESSER v BROOKS (1850) 2 NY 559, 1 S 352

APPEAL from a judgment of the supreme court, brought Sept. 1, 1848. The appellant did not serve printed copies of the case, and on the 14th of August, 1849, the respondent entered an order dismissing the appeal for want of prosecution with costs, pursuant to the 7th rule of the court; and the case was remitted to the court below where execution was issued on the judgment, with costs of the appeal, amounting to $85.31; of which $25 was for costs before argument, and $50 for argument. (Code, Sec. 307).

H. DRESSER, in person, moved to set aside all the respondent's proceedings for irregularity. The 7th rule was not applicable to this case; the appeal having been taken before the present rules were adopted. (See Rule 19). Second, as the judgment of the court below was neither reversed, affirmed, nor modified, this was not a case for a remittitur. There was no judgment of this court within the meaning of the 16th rule of the court, or within the 12th section of the code. (McFarlan v Watson, 4 How. P.R. 128.) Third, execution has been issued for too much costs.

C.H. DOOLITTLE, for the respondent.

BRONSON, Ch. J. The appeal was pending when the 7th rule was adopted, (*), and when it took effect; the respondent waited forty days after the rule took effect, and no copies of the case having been served within that time, he then proceeded, under the 7th rule, and entered an order dismissing the appeal. The first question is, whether the 7th rule applies to such a case, or whether it is governed by the former practice. (See Rule 19.) A majority of the judges are of opinion that the rule applies; and consequently, that the appeal was regularly dismissed.

2. After a return has been filed, we think a remittitur is proper whenever any order is made which finally disposes of the appeal, although it may not be an order on the merits. It is a mistake to suppose the court held otherwise in McFarlan v Watson (supra). There was an appeal in that case from a judgment and an order, and the appeal was dismissed so far as related to the order only; and yet the respondent took a remittitur, and sent back the judgment as well as the order. This was clearly irregular, and for that reason the respondent's proceedings were set aside.

3. Although the respondent has been regular, the appellant would be relieved on terms, if we had power to grant it; but as the cause has been regularly remitted to the supreme court, we no longer have jurisdiction, and cannot grant relief. The only remedy is a new appeal.

4. Although the respondent may have charged too much costs, the remedy for that is by motion in the court below.

Motion denied.

ZAPF v CARTER (4thDept 1904) 90 AD 407, 86 S 175

Action by Francis X. Zapf against Lulu N. Carter, in which an appeal was taken by plaintiff to the Court of Appeals and there dismissed, and remitted to the Supreme Court, where an order was entered at Special Term making the judgment of the Court of Appeals that of the Supreme Court. On motion by defendant for judgment absolute.

SPRING, J. The respondent presents a copy of the remittitur of the Court of Appeals, and asks that an order be granted for judgment absolute. The appeal in this case was dismissed by the Court of Appeals (68 NE 1126), and upon the coming down of the remittitur the respondent applied to the Special Term for an order making the judgment of the Court of Appeals the judgment of the Supreme Court. The Special Term granted the motion. The order was entered, but did not provide for judgment absolute in favor of the respondent.

The order is not appealed from, and we might well rest our denial of the motion upon the ground that the order granted is binding upon this court, as it was proper to make the application to the Special Term, and its order is valid until reversed. Waiving that question, however, there is an insurmountable barrier to the motion. The appeal was dismissed by the Court of Appeals, and its entry does not authorize the entry of judgment absolute. The remittitur contains the judgment of the court of Appeals, and is sent down to the court below as the authority for order of the lower court. The Court of Appeals determines by its remittitur when judgment absolute may be entered. Section 194, Code Civ. Proc.

If there is any error in its remittitur in failing to order judgment absolute when the respondent is entitled to that relief, or if erroneous in any respect, the court issuing it may amend it. The order of the Supreme Court must conform strictly to the remittitur. That court has no power to vary the terms of this judgment of the Court of Appeals. Matter of Protestant E. Public School, 86 N. Y. 396; Wilkins v Earle, 46 NY 358; Parish v Delafield, 87 AD 430, 84 S 506; Rumsey's Practice (2dEd.) vol. 2, p. 875.

The motion is denied, with $10 costs. All concur.

---

*Rules of the Court of Appeals, adopted May 25, 1849 (2 NY 574

"Rule VII. Within forty days after the appeal is preferred, the appellant shall serve three printed copies of the case on the attorney of the adverse party. If he fail to do so, he shall be deemed to have waived the appeal; and on an affidavit proving the default, the respondent may enter an order with the clerk dismissing the appeal for want of prosecution, with costs; and the court below may thereupon proceed as though there had been no appeal."

McSWAIN v COUNTY BD. OF ED. OF ANDERSON CO., TENN, et al (EDTenn 1956) 138 FSupp 570

Suit for a declaratory judgment and to enjoin racial discrimination in public high schools of county.

ROBERT L. TAYLOR, District Judge. This case is before the Court on two motions, one being that of defendants for summary judgment under Rule 56 of the Federal Rules of Civil Procedure, 28 U.S.C.A. Urged in support of this motion is the theory that the case has become moot, for the reason that the five students for whom the suit was originally instituted are shown by affidavit to be no longer enrolled either in the schools of Anderson County or in Austin High School at Knoxville.

In opposition to the motion, plaintiffs insist that the original suit was a class action, instituted by plaintiffs for themselves and for all other Negroes of high school grade in Anderson County, similarly situated as were the original named plaintiffs. It was Clinton High School that the five students who initiated the action desired to attend. They did not represent themselves, however, as being the only Negroes of high school grade who were denied admission to the schools attended by white students in Anderson County. At the hearing of the case on its merits, it appeared that there were other Negroes similarly situated, all of whom were transported to a high school outside that County.

This Court held that, although the suit was instituted by plaintiffs purportedly as a class suit, it was not such in reality. The Court, accordingly, adjudicated their rights as they related to the Clinton High School. Exception was taken by the defendants to this holding and an appeal was perfected to the Court of Appeals. The case was not decided by that Court until the opinion was rendered by the Supreme Court in the case of Brown v Board of Education, 347 US 483, 74 SCt 686, 98 LEd 873.

On June 30, 1954, a mandate was received by the Clerk of this Court from the Clerk of the Court of Appeals which reads in part as follows: "It is ordered, adjudged, and decreed that the judgment of the district court be and is hereby reversed and the case remanded to the district court for further proceedings upon the authority and in accordance with the decision of the Supreme Court in Brown v Board of Education. (347 US 483, 74 SCt 686, 98 LEd 873) (Decided May 17, 1954).

On July 29, 1954, an order was entered by this Court stating that the final decree in the case should await the final decision of the Supreme Court in the case of Brown v Board of Education, supra. The Brown case decision, among other things, sustains plaintiffs' theory that the suit here should properly have been treated as a class action.

On September 16, 1955, an order was entered by this Court referring to the final decision in the Brown case and its directive to school authorities to discontinue segregation practices with reasonable expedition. The order provided that jurisdiction of the case would be retained for the issuance of such other orders as might be necessary.

Plaintiffs themselves have moved for the entry of a final decree.

It is the duty of this Court to comply with the clear mandate of the Supreme Court. The holding of that Court, as applied to this case, requires adoption by school authorities of Anderson County of a program of integration that will expeditiously permit the enrollment of Negroes of high school grade to the high schools of that county. The Supreme Court stated in substance that the school authorities should make a "prompt and reasonable start" toward that objective. The record here indicates that Anderson County school authorities have had this problem under consideration from time to time, apparently in good faith, but have as yet taken no positive action in the way of discontinuing segregation.

It is the opinion of this Court that desegregation as to high school students in that county should be effected by a definite date and that a reasonable date should be fixed as one not later than the beginning of the fall term of the present year of 1956.

In due course orders will be entered, the one denying the motion for summary judgment, the other granting the motion for a final decree and providing that segregation as to high school students in Anderson County be discontinued as of the time above indicated.

CHAPTER IV

RES JUDICATA

OUTLINE OF CHAPTER IV:

Sec. 4.1 Direct Attack upon a Judgment
Sec. 4.2 Collateral Attack upon a Judgment
Sec. 4.3 Direct Estoppel by Judgment
Sec. 4.4 Collateral Estoppel by Judgment
Sec. 4.5 The Rule as to Law of the Case

SUGGESTED READINGS:

Cleary: "Res Judicata Reexamined" (1948) 57 Yale LJ 339
Fryer and Benson: Legal Method and System
  Ch. 5, Sec. 2 "Law of the Case", pp. 378-388
  Id. Sec. 3 "Res Judicata", pp. 389-404
Gavit: Introduction to the Study of Law
  Ch. V., Sec's. 63-67 (generally on Res Judicata) pp. 173-182
Schleider: "Law of the Case" (Note, 1940) 40 Col LR 268
Scott: "Collateral Estoppel by Judgment" (1940) 56 Har LR 1

Sec. 4.1 Direct Attack upon a Judgment

BOORAEM v GIBBONS (1st Dept 1942) 263 AD 665, 34 S2d 198

PER CURIAM. The default judgment entered against defendants in June, 1932, should not have been vacated. Defendants' excuse for the ten years' delay in moving to vacate is that the attorney who appeared for them, and who has since died, did not advise them of the default judgment. Even assuming this to be so, we think that in the exercise of ordinary care and diligence defendants could have ascertained all the necessary facts concerning the outcome of their litigation with plaintiff. It is quite clear that defendants, who suffered numerous other default judgments, were spurred to act in this case only when plaintiff's vigilance uncovered available assets for the payment of his judgment.

Where the judgment is the result not of a default, but of an abandonment, the judgment should not be vacated or set aside. (Demuth v Kemp (No. 3) 144 AD 287, 289, 129 S 249.) Parties seeking to be relieved from their defaults must show a reasonable excuse for their neglect. (Clews v Peper, 112 AD 430, 98 S 404.) Upon the papers submitted defendants have failed satisfactorily to account for their neglect....

Order entered October 18, 1941, and order entered January 22, 1942, so far as appealed from, reversed with $10 costs and disbursements and the motion to open the default and vacate the judgment and the order in supplementary proceedings, and for other relief, in all respects denied....

DORE, J. (dissenting). After a careful examination of the record, I think it can not reasonably be said on the papers before us that the Special Term abused its discretion in opening this default. Plaintiff's claim was an alleged oral agreement by defendants that if one Farrington failed to pay notes (representing rent due plaintiff from Farrington as tenant on plaintiff's estate in Greenwich, Connecticut), they would pay the notes in the total sum of $3,500. No writing is produced signed by defendants evincing their obligation on this unusual alleged contract.

Plaintiff and defendants are still living, and accordingly the lapse of time has not deprived plaintiff of the essential witness to his claim. As to other witnesses who it is claimed would testify to defendant's alleged interest in the so-called Choralcelo venture, defendants swear that these witnesses are available and that they will testify for defendants.

There is no proof in these papers that defendants knew of the judgment and abandoned it. Plaintiff vigorously opposed sending that issue of fact to a referee.

The Special Term properly found that defendants, as clients implicitly relied on their attorney, now deceased, and had no means of guarding against the default which occurred on the general call of the calendar. While the parties are still living and available, a trial on the merits should be had before this default judgment on this unusual claim is collected with interest on notes dated 1929; the interest amounts to about 72% of the original claim. I am convinced that we may do a grave injustice if this order is reversed.

Accordingly I dissent and vote to affirm the orders appealed from.

For the reasons stated in this dissenting opinion, I vote to affirm the order granting the motion of the judgment debtors to vacate the third party order herein and the order for the examination of the judgment debtors in supplementary proceedings.

MARTINE v LOWENSTEIN (1877) 68 NY 456, appdis6 Hun 225

Appeal from order of the General Term of the Supreme Court in the first judicial department, reversing an order of Special Term which denied a motion on the part of the defendants for leave to file exceptions to a referee's report of sale herein, and for leave to be heard upon such exceptions.

This was an action to foreclose a mortgage.

The defendants Lowenstein did not appear and judgment was entered against them by default on the 14th May, 1872. On the 31st May, 1872, said defendants served affidavits and notice of motion that the judgment be opened, and that they be let in to defend, which motion papers were indorsed "R. W. Townsend, attorney for defendants Lowenstein." No other notice of appearance was served. The motion was heard and denied on the 12th July, 1872, when the defendants, by their attorney, served notice of appeal from the judgment and from the order denying the motion. Afterward, and on the 25th of June, 1873, on the consent of R. W. Townsend, an order was entered, ex parte, substituting Samuel J. Crooks as attorney for said defendants. The mortgaged premises were sold by a referee appointed for that purpose, and said referee filed his report of a sale with the clerk on the 23d September, 1873. No notice of the filing of such report was given to the defendants or their attorney, and on the 27th October, 1873, said attorney filed with the clerk exceptions to the report of the referee and served upon him and upon the attorney for the plaintiff, copies thereof, which were returned on the 29th October following with the indorsement that they were served too late; that the report had been "filed" more than eight days. The motion that the exceptions be heard was denied on the ground, as it appears by the memorandum indorsed by the judge on papers, that the defendants did not appear in the action until after judgment had been rendered by default and were not entitled, under Rule 39 (now Rule 30) of this court, to file exceptions to the report of the referee.

The General Term held the appearance to be sufficient to entitle defendants to notice of filing the report, and that such notice not having been served the exceptions were filed in time.

EARL, J. Attorneys are a body of men licensed by the courts to appear for suitors therein. A party to any action or special proceeding pending in court may appear therein by attorney, at any stage of such action or special proceeding, unless some statute or the order or process of the court requires him to appear in person. There is nothing in the nature of an appearance by an attorney which limits the right of such an appearance to a time prior to a judgment in an action, and we know of no statute and our attention has been called to no authority which imposes such a limitation.

A party defendant in an action may appear at any time before judgment or at any time afterward, so long as there is any proceeding in which he has any rights or interests to protect.

In an action to foreclose a mortgage, a defendant may have no defence, and hence he may permit the case to proceed to judgment without any appearance; and after judgment, if he should conclude that it was essential to the protection of his rights, he may appear by attorney, and require that he receive through him such notices as the law entitles him to.

Assuming in this case, that in order to entitle the defendants to the notice of filing the report of sale mentioned in Rule 39 of the Supreme Court, they must have given some notice of appearance by attorney, that court has held that there was sufficient notice of appearance, and we cannot interfere with such holding. Whether there has been a sufficient appearance in that court, it must determine according to its own rules and practice, and its determination cannot, certainly under any ordinary circumstances, be the subject of review here. Hence the exceptions were filed in time.

But, suppose the defendants were required by the rules of the Supreme Court to file their exceptions within eight days after the report of sale was actually filed, an omission to do so did not forever absolutely deprive them of any right to do so. The rules of the Supreme Court are generally under its control and are to be enforced and administered by it. It can overlook or relieve against a violation of them or a non-compliance with them. It is not the province of this court to enforce them, they relate to practice and procedure in that court, and it can permit a party to do after the time prescribed by any rule what he should have done before.

So far as appears here no harm was done to any one by the delay in filing the exceptions. It was not an absolute right of the plaintiff to have the report of sale confirmed without the hearing of the exceptions, and no substantial right of the plaintiff was interfered with in giving the defendants an opportunity to have their exceptions heard.

Hence, there is nothing to review here and the appeal should be dismissed, with costs. All concur. Appeal dismissed.

FISHER v GOULD (1880) 81 NY 228, a9 Daly 144

A demurrer was interposed to the complaint herein, and upon trial of the issue of law thus raised, an order was made overruling the demurrer, and that the plaintiff recover, with leave to the defendant to answer within twenty days. The defendant came in default by not answering within the time given, nor at all, nor did he appeal from the order overruling the demurrer, and judgment absolute was entered. Defendant then appealed from judgment entered, to General Term, and from there, to this court, without appealing from or specifying the order overruling the demurrer. This court affirmed the judgments below, with leave to the defendant to apply to the court below for leave to withdraw the demurrer and to answer. Defendant thereupon moved for such leave at Special Term.

FOLGER, Ch. J. This was a motion to the court below to give leave to withdraw a demurrer and to put in an answer (which was denied)....

Doubtless all matters of practice are, in the first instance, in the discretion of the courts in which questions of practice arise, when there are no statutory provisions or provisions by general rules of court that govern the cases. Yet matters of practice come after a while to be governed absolutely by the custom of the courts; and what is found in any case to have been held by authoritative decisions to be the custom of the courts, becomes thus, the way in which discretion must go. Now a long series of decisions have laid down the rule that, as a general principle, in the exercise of discretion for or against the withdrawal of a demurrer with leave to plead to the merits, it is not to be done where there has been judgment upon the demurrer overruling it, without leave to answer or with leave to answer not availed of by the demurrant. Stricter than this has been the rule sometimes (Saxby v Kirkus, Sayer(NY) 11) where, even when there had not been a judgment, yet the cause had been argued, and the opinion of the court had become known, leave to withdraw was denied. And when the court had given judgment and ordered it entered, and a term has elapsed, the party comes too late (Seaman v Haskins, 2 Johns Cas(NY) 284...) This has, however, been subject to an exception, when good faith is shown in interposing the demurrer, and merits are sworn to, and the plaintiff had not lost a trial (Miller v Heath, 7 Cow(NY) 101). The case in hand does not fall within any exception to the general rule as long established.

The court below was right in refusing the order asked for, if it deemed it injudicious to do so, and we may not reverse its decision.

Appeal dismissed

DELAWARE, LACKAWANNA & WESTERN RR CO. v RELISTAB, Judge U. S. Dist. Ct. for N. J. (1928) 276 US 1, 72 LEd 439, r15 F2d 137

On Writ of Certiorari to the United States Circuit Court of Appeals for the Third Circuit to review a judgment refusing to issue a writ of mandamus to restore a judgment which had been set aside by the District Court for the District of New Jersey.

Mr. Justice HOLMES: In this case one Ginsberg, in December, 1921, recovered judgment in the district court against the petitioner for injuries to himself and a minor son and for the death of another son, caused by a collission, at a crossing, between the plaintiff's truck and one of the petitioner's trains. The judgment afterwards was set aside on the evidence of two important witnesses, husband and wife, that they had committed perjury at the trial. A new trial was had which resulted in a judgment for the defendant, the present petitioner. The judgment was entered on June 21, 1923. It was taken to the circuit court of appeals on writ of error and on March 21, 1924, a mandate from that Court affirmed the judgment with costs. See 296 Fed. 439. The witnesses who had testified for the plaintiff at the first trial testified for the defendant at the second, and after the term of the district court in which the foregoing steps had been taken had expired without being extended in any form, the husband made an afffidavit showing that his testimony at both trials was false and that in fact he knew nothing about the matter. The trial judge was applied to, and after hearing testimony in open court he made an order on May 9, 1925, purporting to set aside the judgment that had been affirmed by the circuit court of appeals during a previous unextended term. The petitioners thereupon applied to the circuit court of appeals for a writ of mandamus to reinstate the judgment, but the circuit court of appeals held that it had no jurisdiction to grant the writ. 15 F (2d) 137. A writ of certiorari was granted by this court. 273 US 685, 71 L Ed. 840, 47 S. Ct. 247.

However strong may have been the convictions of the district judge that injustice would be done by enforcing the judgment, he could not set it aside on the ground that the testimony of admitted perjurers was perjured also at the second trial. The power of the court to set aside its judgment on this ground ended with the term. Re Metropolitan Trust Co. 218 US 312, 320, 54 Led. 1051, 1054, 31 S. Ct. 18. As the court was without jurisdiction to vacate the judgment mandamus is the appropriate remedy unless to grant that writ is beyond the power of the circuit court of appeals. Re Metropolitan Trust Co. 218 US 312, 321, 54 Led. 1051, 1055, 31 S. Ct. 18. We perceive no reason to doubt the power of that court. It had affirmed the judgment of the court below. Brown v Alton Water Co. 222 US 325, 332, 56 Led. 221, 224, 32 S. Ct. 156. Like other appellate courts (Re Potts, 166 US 263, 41 Led. 994, 17 S. Ct. 520), the circuit court of appeals has power to require its judgment to be enforced as against any obstruction that the lower court, exceeding its jurisdiction, may interpose. McClellan v. Carland, 217 US 268, 54 Led. 762, 30 S. Ct. 501. The issue of a mandamus is closely enough connected with the appellate power.

But it is said that the granting of the writ of mandamus is discretionary and it is implied that if we are of opinion that the circuit court of appeals was mistaken in denying its power to grant the writ, that court still might deny it on the ground that injustice would be done if the judgment were allowed to stand. But neither court would be warranted in declaring the judgment unjust after it had become unassailable, — certainly not on a speculation as to which of three statements is true, when it was known at the trial that the witness was perjured, either at the first trial, as he said, or then, —not to speak of the further difficulties that the plaintiff might encounter in the recent decision of Baltimore & O. R. Co. v Goodman, October 31, 1927, (275 US 66, ante, 167, 56 ALR 645, 48 S. Ct. 24). It certainly would be unjust to leave the case in the air because the District Court had made an unwarranted attempt to set aside a judgment that it had no jurisdiction to touch.

It follows that the writ should issue.

Judgment reversed

CLARK v CLARK (1922) 6 Mont 386, 210 P 93

Action by H. W. Clark against Myrtle Clark. From an order granting a motion of the defendant to set aside a decree for the plaintiff, plaintiff appeals...

HOLLOWAY, J. In October, 1920, an action for divorce was instituted in the district court of Silver Bow county by H. W. Clark against Myrtle Clark. In his complaint plaintiff alleged that he was then, and for two years continuously prior thereto had been, a resident of Montana, and that allegation was followed by a recital of facts constituting the grounds for divorce. At the time the action was commenced the defendant was a resident of Salt Lake City, Utah, and service was made by publication and by mailing a copy of the complaint and a copy of the summons to her. She failed to appear within the time allowed by law, and on December 4 her default was entered and evidence was taken by the court (Judge Jackson presiding), from which it was found "that all of the material allegations of said complaint are true, and that plaintiff is entitled to the relief prayed for." On the same day a decree of divorce in favor of the plaintiff was rendered and entered. Thereafter plaintiff remarried. On February 3, 1921, the defendant moved the court to set aside the decree upon the ground alone that the allegation in the complaint to the effect that plaintiff was, and for two years prior to October 20, 1920, had been, a resident of Montana, was false, as was the testimony given by him in support of that allegation. The motion was made upon the affidavit of defendant and the affidavits of three other persons, all tending to prove that plaintiff never had been a resident of this state. Before the motion was heard, the proceeding was transferred to department No. 2, presided over by Judge Carroll. Timely objections were made by the plaintiff to the hearing and to the evidence offered by the defendant, but these objections were overruled. At the conclusion of the hearing the court (Judge Carroll presiding) annulled and set aside the decree, and plaintiff has appealed from the order.

Waiving aside the question whether the evidence heard upon the motion does not preponderate in favor of plaintiff's contention that at the time the divorce action was commenced he was, and for more than a year prior thereto had been, a resident of this state, and assuming, for the purpose of this appeal only, that the allegation relating to residence was untrue, and that plaintiff's testimony in support of it was false, and we are face to face with the fundamental question for solution, namely: May a court of this state, in a proceeding other than upon motion for a new trial, set aside a judgment upon the sole ground that an allegation in the complaint necessary to support the judgment was proved by false testimony? The question is not a new one, not even in this jurisdiction. It has been answered by the courts over and over again, and reference to a few of the leading authorities will suffice for a statement of the general rule and the reason which prompts it.

The power of a court of equity to grant relief from a judgment obtained by fraud is inherent, and the rule relates to decrees in equity as well as to judgments at law (15 RCL 760, 761), but not every fraud committed in the course of a judicial determination will furnish ground for such relief. The acts for which a judgment or decree may be set aside or annulled have reference only to fraud which is extrinsic or collateral to the matter tried by the court, and not to fraud in the matter on which the judgment was rendered (15 RCL 762). In 2 Freeman on Judgments, Sec. 489, the rule is stated as follows:

"It must be borne in mind that is is not fraud in the cause of action, but fraud in its management, which entitles a party to relief. The fraud for which a judgment may be vacated or enjoined in equity must be in the procurement of the judgment. If the cause of action is vitiated by fraud, this is a defense which must be interposed, and, unless its interposition is prevented by fraud, it cannot be asserted against the judgment; 'for judgments are impeachable for those frauds only which are extrinsic to the merits of the case, and by which the court has been imposed upon or misled into a false judgment. They are not impeachable for frauds relating to the merits between the parties.'

In United States v Throckmorton (98 US 61, 25 LEd 93), the court, after reviewing the authorities at length, concludes as follows:

"We think these decisions establish the doctrine on which we decide the present case, namely, that the acts for which a court of equity will on account of fraud set aside or annual a judgment or decree, between the same parties, rendered by a court of competent jurisdiction, have relation to frauds, extrinsic or collateral, to the matter tried by the court, and not to a fraud in the matter on which the decree was rendered. That the mischief of retrying every case in which the judgment or decree rendered on false testimony, given by perjured witnesses, or on contracts or documents whose genuineness or validity was in issue, and which are afterwards ascertained to be forged or fraudulent, would be greater, by reason of the endless nature of the strife, than any compensation arising from doing justice in individual cases."....

The authorities are quite uniform in holding that these rules apply equally whether the judgment is attacked by motion made in the case or by a separate suit.

What, then, is meant by the expression "fraud which is extrinsic or collateral to the matter tried by the court?" It is extrinsic or collateral within the meaning of the rule, when the effect of it is to prevent the unsuccessful party from having a trial or from presenting his case fully, as, for instance, keeping him away from court by false promise of compromise, or purposely keeping him in ignorance of the pendency of the action, or where an attorney fraudulently pretends to represent a party and connives at his defeat, or, being regularly employed, sells out his client's interest (15 RCL 763), or where a party residing without the jurisdiction of the court is induced by false pretenses or representations to come within the jurisdiction for the sole purpose of getting personal service of process upon him, or where, through the instrumentality of the successful party, the witnesses of his adversary are forcibly or illegally detained from court or bribed to disobey subpoena served upon them, or where a judgment is obtained in violation of an agreement between the parties (1 Bigelow on Frauds, c.6.Sec.2.)

The allegation that at the time the action was commenced plaintiff was, and for at least one year prior thereto had been, a resident of this state, was indispensable to the statement of a cause of action for divorce (Section 3674, Rev Codes 1907 (sec. 5766 Rev Codes 1921); Rumping v Rumping, 36 Mont

39, 91 P 1057, 12 LRA (NS) 1197, 12 AnnCas 1090), and it was equally indispensable that plaintiff prove that allegation to the satisfaction of the court which heard the divorce case. Section 5767, Revised Codes 1921, provides:

"No divorce can be granted upon the default of the defendant alone, but the cause must be heard in open court, and the court must require proof of all the facts alleged."

The sufficiency of the complaint is not attacked; neither is there any contention made that the proceeding to obtain jurisdiction of the defendant was not in strict accord with the statute, and defendant does not suggest that she did not receive the copy of the complaint and the copy of the summons in ample time to make defense. Indeed, she does not suggest that she has or ever had any defense upon the merits. Assuming that she had notice of the pendency of the action, that is to say, that the letter containing the copy of the summons and copy of the complaint was received by her (section 10606, subdiv. 24, Rev. Codes 1921), she was made aware of the fact that plaintiff was claiming the necessary residence in this state, and if that allegation of his complaint was not true, she knew that he could obtain a decree of divorce only by false testimony; hence the obligation devolved upon her to appear in the action and contest the truth of the testimony concerning that fact, and, having failed to do so, she was thereafter precluded from raising the question either by motion or by a separate suit to set aside the decree. She had the opportunity to appear at the trial, and her position now is not different from what it would have been if she had appeared and had presented the same evidence _ore tenus_ which she presents upon the motion by affidavit, and the court had nevertheless accepted plaintiff's testimony as true and rendered the same decree which was rendered.

When the plaintiff filed in the district court of Silver Bow county his complaint, stating a cause of action for divorce, including the necessary allegation respecting residence, the court acquired jurisdiction of the subject-matter and of the plaintiff, and when the statutory proceedings for substituted service of process were observed, it obtained jurisdiction of the defendant, and was then authorized to hear the cause (15 CJ 797) and render a decree in plaintiff's favor if sufficient evidence was introduced to prove the essential averments of the complaint. Since the court recited that evidence was heard, from which it appeared "that all of the material allegations of said complaint are true, and that plaintiff is entitled to the relief prayed for," that recital must be accepted as conclusive so far as this proceeding is concerned....

The order vacating the decree is reversed.

Reversed.

Sec. 4.2 Collateral Attack upon a Judgment

TROUTMAN v STATE (3dDept 1948) 273 AD 619, 79 S2d 709, r72 S2d 177

Proceeding in the matter of the claim of Ralph Troutman, also known as George Conklin, against the State of New York to recover damages for claimant's allegedly wrongful detention in State Hospital for the insane...

FOSTER, J. Claimant has appealed from a judgment of the Court of Claims dismissing upon the merits a claim filed by him against the State of New York. The essence of the claim was that claimant had been illegally detained and confined as an insane person in the Dannemora State Hospital.

On April 6, 1932, claimant was sentenced, upon a conviction of an attempt to commit burglary in the second degree, to a term of imprisonment for seven years and six months. He was first confined in the New York State Prison at Auburn. Later he was transferred to Great Meadow Prison and then to Attica Prison, and while at the latter institution, upon the certification of the prison psychiatrist, he was transferred to the Dannemora State Hospital. This was on October 25, 1935. His commuted sentence for the crime for which he was convicted would have expired in January, 1937. On January 28, 1937, on the application of the Superintendent of Dannemora State Hospital and after examination by two private physicians not associated with the hospital, he was committed as an insane person to the

Dannemora State Hospital by order of the County Judge of Clinton County. The order of commitment recited that notice to the relator was not required because it would serve no useful purpose.

Thereafter, and between January 28, 1937, and December 21, 1943, claimant obtained fourteen writs of habeas corpus to obtain his release upon the ground that he was not insane. Each of these writs was dismissed. Finally he took an appeal to this court from an order of the Clinton County Court, entered January 25, 1943, dismissing a writ of habeas corpus. The order dismissing the writ was reversed on the law; the writ sustained, and the relator discharged without prejudice to a new proceeding on notice to determine the issue of his sanity. (People ex rel Conklin v Webster, 267 AD 453, 47 S2d 744). After this decision and in a new proceeding before the County Court of Clinton County, it was determined that claimant was not insane and his discharge from the custody of the Superintendent of the Dannemora State Hospital was directed.

The claim herein was dismissed in the Court of Claims chiefly upon the ground that when claimant was originally committed by the County Court of Clinton County to the Dannemora State Hospital the court had jurisdiction both of the subject matter and the person of claimant. We are unable to agree with this conclusion. Undoubtedly the court had jurisdiction of the subject matter in an abstract sense but it had no jurisdiction of the person of the claimant because no notice had been given to him. True it is that the section of the Correction Law under which claimant was committed by the County Court contains no requirement for notice (Correction Law, Sec. 384). But in construing a similar section of the Correction Law (section 440) relating to retention of mental defectives after the expiration of their terms of imprisonment it was held that notice to a prisoner is required by implication. That is to say, that even though the statute does not expressly require that notice of the application for the retention of a prisoner after the expiration of his termshall be given to a prisoner, nevertheless he is entitled to such notice as a matter of due process. (People ex rel Morrialle v Branham, 291 NY 312, 52 NE2d 881). By all the principles of analogy the rule stated in the case cited must apply also to section 384 of the Correction Law, and by the same process of reasoning it must be held that the order committing claimant as an insane person was void because no notice was given.

The opinion of the court below cites several cases to the effect that where a court has acquired jurisdiction in a case or proceeding its order or judgment therein affords protection to all persons acting under it although it may be afterward set aside or reversed as erroneous. But in those cases the court had jurisdiction which was lacking in the present case. Also the court below cites the general rule that a judgment of a court which has jurisdiction of a person and subject matter is binding until reversed and cannot be attacked collaterally. That is true of course, but where jurisdiction is lacking any judgment or order may be attacked collaterally or otherwise, and the person injured thereby is not required to have it vacated or reversed on appeal. No one, we think, would dispute the proposition that a judgment or order entered without notice of any kind is completely void for lack of jurisdiction and may be attacked in any manner that a party sees fit. (German Savings & Loan Society v Dormitzer, 192 US 125, 24 SCt 221, 48 LEd 373....) The cases cited deal mostly with property rights but certainly the rule would not be less embracive in a case involving personal liberty.

The circumstances of this claim are entirely different from those passed upon in Douglas v State, (269 AD 521, 56 S2d 245). There it was held that a special surrogate had jurisdiction to make the commitment, and that the same being valid on its face did not subject the state and officers of a state hospital for the insane to an action for false imprisonment even if the order was erroneously and improvidently made. In this case, we repeat, the order was not merely erroneous or improvident, it was made without any jurisdiction whatever; and lack of notice appeared upon the face of the order itself.

The fact that after the original commitment was made a series of writs of habeas corpus, procured on the application of the claimant, were dismissed by courts which undoubtedly had jurisdiction does not alter the fundamental lack of jurisdiction in the first instance, and affords no protection to those who participated in procuring the original commitment. Undoubtedly the issue of jurisdiction was not raised in the proceedings relative to such writs, and the only issue presented in each instance was the sanity of the claimant.

Under the circumstances we think it was improper to dismiss claimant's claim insofar as it related to his detention and confinement under the order of the County Court of Clinton County made on January 28, 1937, and that the judgment of dismissal should be reversed and a new trial granted. In so doing we are mindful of the fact that the order of the County Court of Clinton County, made on March 14, 1944; adjudging claimant to be sane and directing his release, related only to his condition at that time. Whether he was sane during any of the period between the date of his original commitment and the date of his release is a matter of proof concerning which we express no opinion.

Judgment reversed on the law and the facts with costs, and the claim remitted to the Court of Claims for a new trial....

GODARD v GRAY (1870) L.R., 6 QB 139 5 EngRulCas 726, 24 LT 89.

This was an action on a foreign judgment; and the question before the Court was raised by demurrer to a plea the effect of which is sufficiently stated in the judgment of Blackburn and Mellor, JJ., delivered by

BLACKBURN, J. In this case the plaintiffs declare on a judgment of a French tribunal, averred to have jurisdiction in that behalf.

The question arises on a demurrer to the second plea, which sets out the whole proceedings in the French Court. By these it appears that the plaintiffs, who are Frenchmen, sued the defendants, who are Englishmen, on a charter-party made at Sunderland, which charter-party contained the following clause, "Penalty for non-performance of this agreement, estimated amount of freight." The French Court below, treating this clause as fixing the amount of liquidated damages, gave judgment against the defendants for the amount of freight on two voyages. On appeal, the superior Court reduced the amount to the estimated freight of one voyage, giving as their reason that the charter-party itself, "fixait l'indemnite a laquelle chacune des parties aurait droit pour inexecution de la convention par la faute de l'autre; que moyennant paiement de cette indemnite chacune des parties avait le droit de rompre la convention," and the tribunal proceeds to observe that the amount thus decreed was after all more than sufficient to cover all the plaintiff's loss.

All parties in France seem to have taken it for granted that the words in the charter-party were to be understood in their natural sense; but the English law is accurately expressed in Abbott on Shipping, part 3, c. 1, s. 6, 5th ed., p. 170, and had that passage been brought to the notice of the French tribunal, it would have known that in an English charter-party, as is there stated, "Such a clause is not the absolute limit of damages on either side; the party may, if he thinks fit, ground his action upon the other clauses or covenants, and may, in such action, recover damages beyond the amount of the penalty, if in justice they shall be found to exceed it. On the other hand, if the party sue on such a penal clause, he cannot, in effect, recover more than the damage actually sustained." But it was not brought to the notice of the French tribunal that, according to the interpretation put by the English law on such a contract, a penal clause of this sort was in fact idle and inoperative. If it had been, they would, probably, have interpreted the English contract made in England according to the English construction. No blame can be imputed to foreign lawyers for not conjecturing that the clause was merely a brutum fulmen. The fault, if any, was in the defendants, for not properly instructing their French counsel on this point.

Still the fact remains that we can see on the face of the proceedings that the foreign tribunal has made a mistake on the construction of an English contract, which is a question of English law; and that, in consequence of that mistake, judgment has been given for an amount probably greater than, or, at all events, different from that for which it would have been given if the tribunal had been correctly informed what construction the English contract bore according to English law.

The question raised by the plea is, whether this is a bar to the action brought in England to enforce that judgment, and we are all of opinion that it is not, and that the plaintiff is entitled to judgment......

It is not an admitted principle of the law of nations that a state is bound to enforce within its territories the judgment of a foreign tribunal. Several of the continental nations (including France) do not enforce the judgments of other countries unless where there are reciprocal treaties to that effect. But in England and in those States which are governed by the common law, such judgments are enforced, not by virtue of any treaty nor by virtue of any statute, but upon a principle very well stated by Parke, B., in Williams v Jones, 13 M. & W. 633; 14 L. J. Ex. 145; "Where a Court of competent jurisdiction has adjudicated a certain sum to be due from one person to another, a legal obligation arises to pay that sum, on which an action of debt to enforce the judgment may be maintained. It is in this way that the judgments of foreign and colonial courts are supported and enforced." And taking this as the principle, it seems to follow that anything which negatives the existence of that legal obligation, or excuses the defendant from the performance of it, must form a good defence to the action. It must be open, therefore, to the defendant to show that the Court which pronounced the judgment had no jurisdiction to pronounce it, either because they exceeded the jurisdiction given to them by the foreign law, or because he, the defendant, was not subject to that jurisdiction; and so far the foreign judgment must be examinable. Probably the defendant may show that the judgment was obtained by the fraud of the plaintiff, for that would show that the defendant was excused from the performance of an obligation thus obtained; and it may be that where the foreign Court has knowingly and perversely disregarded the rights given to an English subject by English law, that forms a valid excuse for disregarding the obligation thus imposed on him; but we prefer to imitate the caution of the present Lord Chancellor, in Castrique v Imrie, No. 14, post L. R., 4 H. L. 445; 39 L. J. C. P. 364, and to leave those questions to be decided when they arise....

There are a great many dicta and opinions of very eminent lawyers, tending to establish that the defendant in an action on a foreign judgment is at liberty to show that the judgment was founded on a mistake, and that the judgment is so far examinable. In Houlditch v Donegall, 2 Cl. & F. at p. 477, Lord Brougham goes so far as to say: "The language of the opinions on one side has been so strong, that we are not warranted in calling it merely the inclination of our lawyers; it is their decision that in this country a foreign judgment is only prima facie, not conclusive, evidence of a debt." But there certainly is no case decided on such a principle; and the opinions on the other side of the question are at least as strong as those to which Lord Brougham refers.

....But we think it unnecessary to discuss this point, as the decisions of the Court of Queen's Bench (cases) seems to us to leave it no longer open to contend, unless in a court of error, that a foreign judgment can be impeached on the ground that it was erroneous on the merits; or to set up as a defence to an action on it, that the tribunal mistook either the facts or the law.

But there still remains a question which has never, so far as we know, been expressly decided in any Court.

It is broadly laid down, by the very learned author of Smith's Leading Cases, in the original note to Doe v Oliver, 2 Sm. L. C. 2nd ed. at p. 448, that "it is clear that if the judgment appear on the face of the proceedings to be founded on a mistaken notion of the English law," it would not be conclusive. For this he cites Novelli v Rossi, 2 B. & Ad. 757, which does not decide that point, and no other authority; but the great learning and general accuracy of the writer makes his unsupported opinion an authority of weight; and accordingly it has been treated with respect. In Scott v Pilkington, 2 B. & S. at p. 42; 31 L. J. Q. B. at p. 89, the Court expressly declined to give any opinion on the point not then raised before them. But we cannot find that it has been acted upon; and it is worthy of note that the present very learned editors of Smith's Leading Cases have very materially qualified his position, and state it thus, if the judgment be founded on an incorrect view of the English law, knowingly or perversely acted on;" the doctrine thus qualified does not apply to the present case, and there is, therefore, no need to inquire how far it is accurate.

But the doctrine as laid down by Mr. Smith does apply here; and we must express an opinion on it, and we think it cannot be supported, and that the defendant can no more set up as an excuse, relieving him from the duty of paying the amount awarded by the judgment of a foreign tribunal having jurisdiction over him and the cause, that the judgment proceeded on a mistake as to English law, than he could set up as an excuse that there had been a mistake as to the law of some third country incidentally involved, or as to any other question of fact.

It can make no difference that the mistake appears on the face of the proceedings. That, no doubt, greatly facilitates the proof of the mistake;....

...but in no case that we know of is it ever said that a defence shall be admitted if it is easily proved and rejected if it would give the Court much trouble to investigage it. Yet what other principle can we admit as a defence that there is a mistake of English law apparent on the face of the proceedings, and reject a defence that there is a mistake of Spanish or even Scotch law apparent in the proceedings, or that there was a mistake of English law not apparent on the proceedings, but which the defendant avers that he can show did exist.

The whole law was much considered and discussed in Castrique v Imrie, No. 14, post, where the French tribunal has made a mistake as to the English law, and under that mistake had decreed the sale of the defendant's ship. The decision of the House of Lords was, that the defendant's title derived under that sale was good, notwithstanding that mistake, Lord Colonsay pithily saying, "It appears to me that we cannot enter into an inquiry as to whether the French Courts proceeded correctly, either as to their own course of procedure or their own law, nor whether under the circumstances they took the proper means of satisfying themselves with respect to the view they took of the English law. Nor can we inquire whether they were right in their views of the English law. The question is, whether under the circumstances of the case, dealing with it fairly, the original tribunal did proceed against the ship and did order the sale of the ship."

The question in Castrique v Imrie was as to the effect on the property of a judgment ordering a ship, locally situate in France, to be sold, and therefore was not the same as the question in this case as to what effect is to be given to a judgment against the person. But at least the decision in Castrique v Imrie establishes this, that a mistake as to English law on the part of a foreign tribunal does not operate in all cases so as to prevent the Courts of this country from giving effect to the judgment.

.... For these reasons we have come to the conclusion that judgment should be given for the plaintiffs.

Judgment for the plaintiffs.

Section 4.3 Direct Estoppel by Judgment

PERRY v DICKERSON (1881) 85 NY 345

Appeal from judgment of the General Term of the City Court of Brooklyn, in favor of plaintiff, entered upon an order made March 30, 1880, reversing an order of Special Term, which granted a motion for a new trial.

This action was brought to recover balance alleged to be due the plaintiff for salary and commissions. In June, 1878, the defendants engaged the plaintiff to sell their goods upon a salary to which was to be added certain commissions upon the articles sold under a contract that he should work one year. In February, 1879, the plaintiff was discharged, as he alleges, without cause, after his discharge and before the commencement of this action he brought an action in a justice's court setting up the above facts and recovered a judgment. That judgment was pleaded in bar of this action but it appeared that the judgment was rendered on the ground that the dismissal was wrongful. A verdict was rendered for the plaintiff.

ANDREWS, J. To sustain the plea of a former judgment in bar of a second action, it must appear that the cause of action in both suits is the same, or that some fact essential to the maintenance of the second action, was in issue and determined in the first action, adversely to the plaintiff. In order to establish an identity between the causes of action in the two suits, it is not necessary that the claim made in the first action, embraced the same items sought to be recovered in the second. It is sufficient to bring the second action within the estoppel of the former judgment, that the cause of action in the former suit was the same, and that the damages or right claimed in the second suit, were items or parts of the same single cause of action, upon which the first action was founded. The law, to prevent vexatious or oppressive litigations, forbids the splitting up of one single or entire cause of action into parts, and the bringing of separate actions for each; and neither in this way nor by withholding proof of particular items on the trial, or by formally withdrawing them from the consideration of the jury, can the effect of the judgment, as a complete adjudication of the entire cause of action, be prevented. There can be but one recovery for an injury from a single wrong, however numerous the items of damage may be, and but one action for a single breach of a contract. (Farrington v Payne, 15 Johns(NY) 432...) But while the general principle is undeniable, that a former judgment on the same cause of action, bars a second action between the same parties, it is not always easy to determine when the causes of action are identical, or what is to be deemed a single or entire demand within the authorities.

In Guernsey v Carver (8 Wend(NY) 492), it was held that all the items due on a running account for merchandise sold, constituted but one demand, and that a recovery in one action for a part of the items, is a bar to a subsequent action for the residue. The same rule was applied in Stevens v Lockwood (13 Wend(NY) 646). In Colvin v Corwin (15 Wend(NY) 557), a judgment in an action to recover the price of one lottery ticket, sold to the defendant by the plaintiff's agent, was held to be a bar to a second action to recover the price of another lottery ticket, purchased of another agent at a different time and place. The decision proceeded on the ground that the two sales constituted but a single demand or cause of action. This case was strongly disapproved in Secor v Sturgis (16 NY 548), the court saying that it rested on no sound principle, and that it was a plain case of distinct and independent causes of action. The case of Bendernagle v Cocks (19 Wend(NY) 207) also proceeded upon the doctrine established by the earlier decisions, that an entire demand could not be severed, and separate suits brought thereon. If the case is subject to any criticism, it is because of the application of the doctrine to the facts of the case. The action was for breaches of distinct covenants to pay for manure and for work and labor, contained in an indenture of lease. The defendant pleaded in abatement, that the plaintiff had brought a prior action upon the lease, for the breach by the defendant of certain covenants therein on his part, which was still pending. The plaintiff replied that the covenants upon which the first suit was brought were other, distinct, and different, from those sued upon in the second action. The court sustained the defendant's demurrer to the replication, and he had judgment. It may be inferred from the opinion of Judge Cowen, that all the covenants in the lease, were for the payment of different amounts of money by the lessee to the lessor; and the learned judge seemed to regard it like the case of a contract to pay money in installments, and in this way reached the conclusion that the different breaches constituted a single cause of action. "Looking," he says, "as I think we must, on the several defaults to pay items, as so many successive breaches of a single contract, we here have an authority for saying that all such breaches are but parts of one indivisible demand, so far as they were committed at the commencement of the suit."

The only question presented for our decision in this case, arises upon the defense, setting up in bar of the action, the judgment obtained by the plaintiff in a justice's court, in March, 1879, for $22, besides costs, in an action brought against the defendants subsequent to February 10, 1879, for having wrongfully dismissed him from their employment on that day, in violation of their contract to employ him for the period of a year from June 22, 1878. The present action is brought for wages stipulated to be paid by the contract of employment, and earned and due, at the time of the wrongful dismissal. The plaintiff neither in his complaint nor on the trial in the justice's action, claimed to recover the wages earned. The claim for wages was expressly excluded by the terms of the complaint. It was an action solely for damages for the wrongful dismissal. On the other hand, in this action, the complaint sets out the contract of employment, alleges the rendition of services thereunder, and that the sum of $155.55, was due and owing the plaintiff therefor, for which sum, judgment is demanded. There is no averment of a wrongful dismissal, and no claim for damages therefor.

The decision of the question whether the judgment in the justice's action, is a bar to this action, turns, we think, upon the point whether the claim for wages earned and due before the wrongful dismissal, and the claim for damages for such dismissal, constituted a single and indivisible demand, within the authorities or two separate and independent causes of action. It is doubtless true, that the plaintiff could have prosecuted in one action, the claims for wages, and for damages for the wrongful dismissal. But it is not a test of the right of a plaintiff to maintain separate actions, that all the claims might have been prosecuted in a single action. A plaintiff having separate demands against a defendant on contract, or arising from distinct trespasses or wrongs, is not required to combine them in one action, although in most cases he may do so at his election. He may prosecute them separately, subject to the power of the court, in furtherance of justice, and, to prevent undue vexation and costs, to order the actions to be consolidated. (Phillips v Berick, 16 Johns(NY) 136.) That the claim for wages was earned and due before the dismissal and for damages for the wrongful dismissal, constituted two separate and independent causes of action, is clear upon reason and authority. The right to recover the wages was complete and perfect, before the right to damages accrued. Upon the wrongful dismissal, a new cause of action arose, wholly disconnected, in its origin and nature, with the claim for wages....

In this case the causes of action for wages and for a wrongful dismissal in a sense arise out of the same general contract. But the right to the wages was given by the contract. The right to damages results from the wrongful termination of the employment, which, so far as the defendants could do so, put an end to the contract altogether. The right to recover the wages, and the amount the plaintiff was entitled to therefor, was definite or capable of being made so, at the very time they were due. The damages for the wrongful dismissal, were incapable of exact ascertainment until the period for which the plaintiff was hired had expired, as they might be mitigated by his procuring other employment. In such a case must a plaintiff postpone his action for wages until the period of employment has expired? Or if he sues for his wages immediately on the dismissal, must he join in that action his claim for damages? We are of opinion that this alternative is not presented to him, and that he may bring his action upon either of the causes of action, without being barred by judgment thereon from subsequently bringing an action on the other.

It is to be recollected, that the principle is, that a former judgment is a bar to a subsequent action, when it is for the same cause. It would, we think, be unwarrantable to hold, that the causes of action in the justice's suit, and in this, are the same, or to treat the two causes of action as one, for the purpose of bringing the claim for wages, within the estoppel of the judgment in the first action.

Judgment affirmed.

POTTER v EMEROL MFG. CO., INC. (1stDept 1949) 275 AD 265, 89 S2d 68

CALLAHAN, J. The principal question in this case is whether a prior judgment in favor of the defendant estops the plaintiffs from bringing this action under the principle of res judicata.

The plaintiffs were formerly employed by the defendant as sales managers and sue to recover a bonus or commissions in addition to fixed salary under an "incentive sales program". They assert a right to such commissions payable on the basis of a percentage of sales in excess of quotas established by the employer.

The complaint pleads alternative causes of action in contract and quantum meruit. The latter (except as to one plaintiff) are predicated on the same agreements alleged in the causes of action sounding in contract and seek recovery for the agreed and reasonable value of the services rendered by the plaintiffs over and above a fixed salary or wages at a prcentage commission of net sales beyond a certain quota.

The prior action resulting in judgment for the defendant was brought on a complaint alleging the same factual claims and relying on an oral contract between the parties. The defendant moved to dismiss the complaint in that action on the ground that the agreement violated the statute of frauds. The plaintiffs opposed the motion and asserted the existence of writings or letters in the files of the defendant sufficient to meet the requirements of the statute. The plaintiffs, however, failed to produce any proof as to the actual existence of such memoranda. The court accordingly dismissed the complaint on the merits, and a judgment to that effect was entered in the former suit. There was no appeal from such judgment, which stands in full force and effect.

The Special Term has held that this judgment on the merits is not a bar to the present action for the reason that it was entered on motion under rule 107 of the Rules of Civil Practice. We cannot agree with this conclusion. The dismissal of the earlier complaint was not for failure to state a cause of action. There was a factual determination of insufficient memoranda to satisfy the statute of frauds, and the complaint was dismissed on the ground that the causes of action on behalf of the several plaintiffs were not provable against the defense of the statute. Though the facts underlying such determination were supplied by affidavits instead of oral testimony, we think that a judgment on the merits entered on such motion would be a bar to a second suit if there is sufficient identity between the causes of action alleged in the two complaints. While a decision on a motion relating to an intermediate step in an action is not ordinarily a final adjudication of the issues, (Bannon v Bannon, 270 NY 484, 1 NE2d 975, 105 ALR 1401), the decision in respect to the first complaint did not simply determine an intermediate step in the action but directed judgment finally disposing of the case. This decision on the merits is a bar to a second suit. Its correctness must be conclusively assumed in the absence of appeal.

If the dismissal of the prior complaint had been ordered on a motion in the nature of a demurrer addressed to the sufficiency of the pleading, a different rule would apply. As the merits are not considered on such motion, a determination dismissing the complaint for insufficiency on its face would not bar a second suit based on a sufficient complaint. (Joannes Bros. Co. v Lamborn, 237 NY 207, 209, 142 NE 587, 588.)

In respect to the causes of action on contract the present complaint merely alleges that a method or basis of compensation was put into effect between the parties "by agreement and by letters in writing signed by the duly constituted agent of the defendant." The plaintiffs have produced copies of four such letters sent to two of their number and another person not a party to the action. The most that can be said for the defendant's letters is that they contain statements in the nature of admissions as to a plan for compensation on a bonus incentive basis and the making of such an arrangement with the recipients of the correspondence. They also indicate that this plan was to apply generally to all territorial sales managers. The letters, however, are not conclusive as to whether the plaintiffs' employment under the alleged bonus plan was pursuant to oral or written agreement. If the plaintiffs are proceeding on an oral contract, the prior judgment in favor of the defendant clearly constitutes an estoppel. The subject matter of both actions is identical; the same employment, the same breach, and the same damages are involved. If we assume that the plaintiffs intend to base the contract counts of the complaint on an agreement in writing with the defendant, it is enough to say that the letters do not admit the existence of a written contract with any of the plaintiffs and are themselves sufficient to constitute such agreement. There is nothing in this record to show a valid and enforcible contract in writing between the parties. This makes it unnecessary to determine whether the result would be the same if the contract causes of action as alleged in the complaint were supported by allegations or proof of a writing signed by the defendant sufficiently complete and definite in its terms to satisfy the statute of frauds.

There reamins for consideration the plaintiffs' causes of action in quantum meruit. The defendant concedes that the plaintiffs may resort to quantum meruit even after an unsuccessful suit in contract. (See Elsfelder v Cournand, 270 AD 162, 59 S2d 34.) The question, however, is whether these counts have been properly pleaded so as to withstand the defendant's motion to dismiss. They appear to be based on the idential agreement alleged under the contract causes of action. The allegations thereof replead the terms and conditions of the bonus or commission arrangement for a percentage of net sales based on a quota. It would seem that the quantum meruit counts in their present form are actually duplications and reiterations of the causes of action in contract. They are affected by the same considerations that serve to defeat the latter in this action and are improperly pleaded in any event as alleging a special contract between the parties. In this connection, too, it is well to point out that if the bonus or commission agreement were oral, the quantum meruit allegations of the complaint based on the provisions of such alleged contract must fall. An agreement that is void under the statute of frauds cannot be the foundation of an action. (See Dung v Parker, 52 NY 494...) The plaintiffs, however, may each have a cause of action in quantum meruit that can be established independently of any express agreement with the defendant. If so, they may plead the same in a proper manner by way of an amended complaint alleging the rendition of services at the request of the defendant and their reasonable value....

Order unanimously reversed with $20 costs and disbursements to the appellant and the complaint dismissed, with leave to the plaintiffs to serve an amended complaint within ten days after service of the order, with notice of entry thereof, on payment of said costs. Settle order on notice.

All concur.

BEECH v CRAIN (This case appears supra, p. 82)

PAKAS v HOLLINGSHEAD (This case appears supra, p. 84)

Sec. 4.4 Collateral Estoppel by Judgment

KREKELER v RITTER (1875) 62 NY 372

This action was brought to set aside the lien of a mortgage held by defendant upon premises of plaintiff, upon the ground that the same was procured by fraud. The answer was a general denial and a former suit pending.

Upon the trial defendant's counsel offered in evidence a judgment in the Superior Court of the city of New York wherein the defendant herein was plaintiff and the plaintiff herein and her husband were defendants, in which action the same issues presented in this action were tried and determined in favor of the defendant. Plaintiff objected on the ground that it had not been set up in the answer or by supplemental answer. The objection was overruled and plaintiff's counsel excepted. Plaintiff offered to prove that said judgment was recovered by fraud and perjury. The court rejected the offer and plaintiff's counsel excepted. The court dismissed the complaint....

ALLEN, J. The record of the Superior Court was not offered or received in evidence in bar of the action, but merely as evidence of the fact in issue. Had it been offered as constituting a bar, or as an estoppel to the action, it would have been inadmissible, not having been pleaded as a defence. (Brazill v Isham, 2 Ker(NY) 9, per Denio, J.; Denhy v Smith, 18 NY 567.) But as evidence of a fact in issue it was competent although not pleaded like any other evidence, whether documentary or oral. A party is never required to disclose his evidence by his pleadings. The evidence was competent to disprove a material allegation of the complaint traversed by the answer. As evidence it was conclusive as an adjudication of the same fact, in an action between the same parties. (Wright v Butler, 6 Wend(NY) 284...) The court properly held that "the matter adjudicated between the parties in another action might be given in evidence." The judgment could not be impeached collaterally, nor could the same facts be retried between the same parties. The offer of the plaintiff was in effect to retry the issues. Judgments may be impeached in equity for fraud, but for no other reason. (Davoue v Fanning, 4 Johnson Ch(NY) 199.) The remedy of the plaintiff was by application for a retrial in the Superior Court, or for other relief if the judgment had been procured by false or mistaken testimony, and other evidence had been discovered by which the truth could be established....

Judgment affirmed.

CROMWELL v SAC COUNTY (1877) 94 US 351, 24 LEd 195

Mr. Justice FIELD. This was an action on four bonds of the County of Sac, in the State of Iowa, each for $1,000, and four coupons for interest, attached to them, each for $100. The bonds were issued in 1860, and were made payable to bearer, in the City of New York, in the years 1868, 1869, 1870 and 1871, respectively, with annual interest at the rate of ten per cent a year.

To defeat this action, the defendant relied upon the estoppel of a judgment rendered in favor of the County in a prior action brought by one Samuel C. Smith upon certain earlier maturing coupons on the same bonds, accompanied with proof that the plaintiff, Cromwell, was at the time the owner of the coupons in that action, and that the action was prosecuted for his sole use and benefit.

The questions presented for our determination relate to the operation of this judgment as an estoppel against the prosecution of the present action, and the admissibility of the evidence to connect the present plaintiff with the former action as a real party in interest.

In considering the operation of this judgment, it should be borne in mind, as stated by counsel, that there is a difference between the effect of a judgment as a bar or estoppel against the prosecution of a second action upon the same claim or demand, and its effect as an estoppel in another action between the same parties upon a different claim or cause of action. In the former case, the judgment, if rendered upon the merits, constitutes an absolute bar to a subsequent action. It is a finality as to the claim or demand in controversy, concluding parties and those in privity with them, not only as to every matter which was offered and received to sustain or defeat the claim or demand, but as to any other admissible matter which might have been offered for that purpose. Thus, for example, a judgment rendered upon a promissory note is conclusive as to the validity of the instrument and the amount due upon it, although it be subsequently alleged that perfect defenses actually existed, of which no proof was offered, such as forgery, want of consideration or payment. If such defenses were not presented in the action, and established by competent evidence, the subsequent allegation of their existence is of no legal consequence. The judgment is as conclusive, so far as future proceedings at law are concerned, as though the defenses never existed. The language, therefore, which is so often used, that a judgment estops not only as to every ground of recovery or defense actually presented in the action, but also as to every ground which might have been presented, is strictly accurate, when applied to the demand or claim in controversy. Such demand or claim, having passed into judgment, cannot again be brought into litigation between the parties in proceedings at law, upon any ground whatever.

But where the second action between the same parties is upon a different claim or demand, the judgment in the prior action operates as an estoppel only as to those matters in issue or points controverted, upon the determination of which the finding or verdict was rendered. In all cases, therefore, where it is sought to apply the estoppel of a judgment rendered upon one cause of action to matters arising in a suit upon a different cause of action, the inquiry must always be as to the point or question actually litigated and determined in the original action; not what might have been thus litigated and determined. Only upon such matters is the judgment conclusive in another action....

It is not believed that there are any cases going to the extent that, because in the prior action a different question from that actually determined might have arisen and been litigated; therefore, such possible question is to be considered as excluded from consideration in a second action between the same parties on a different demand, although loose remarks looking in that direction may be found in some opinions. On principle, a point not in litigation in one action cannot be received as conclusively settled in any subsequent action upon a different cause, because it might have been determined in the first action.

Various considerations, other than the actual merits, may govern a party in bringing forward grounds of recovery or defense in one action, which may not exist in another action upon a different demand, such as the smallness of the amount or the value of the property in controversy, the difficulty of obtaining the necessary evidence, the expense of the litigation, and his own situation at the time. A party acting upon considerations like these ought not to be precluded from contesting, in a subsequent action, other demands arising out of the same transaction. A judgment by default only admits for the purpose of the action the legality of the demand or claim in suit; it does not make the allegations of the declaration or complain (sic) evidence in an action upon a different claim....

If, now, we consider the main question presented for our determination by the light of the views thus expressed and the authorities cited, its solution will not be difficult. It appears from the findings in the original action of Smith, that the County of Sac, by a vote of its people, authorized the issue of bonds to the amount of $10,000, for the erection of a courthouse; that bonds to that amount were issued by the County Judge, and delivered to one Meserey, with whom he had made a contract for the erection of the courthouse; that immediately upon receipt of the bonds the contractor gave one of them as a gratuity to the County Judge; and that the courthouse was never constructed by the contractor, or by any other person pursuant to the contract. It also appears that the plaintiff had become, before their maturity, the holder of twenty-five coupons, which had been attached to the bonds, but there was no finding that he had ever given any value for them. The court below held, upon these findings, that the bonds were void as against the County, and gave judgment accordingly. The case coming here on writ of error, this court held that the facts disclosed by the findings were sufficient evidence of fraud and illegality in the inception of the bonds to call upon the holder to show that he had given value for the coupons; and, not having done so, the judgment was affirmed. Reading the record of the lower court by the opinion and judgment of this court, it must be considered that the matters adjudged in that case were these;that the bonds were void as against the County in the hands of parties who did not acquire them before maturity and give value for them, and that the plaintiff, not having proved that he gave such value, was not entitled to recover upon the coupons. Whatever illegality or fraud there was in the issue and delivery to the contractor of the bonds affected equally the coupons for interest attached to them. The finding and judgment upon the invalidity of the bonds, as against the County, must be held to estop the plaintiff here from averring to the contrary. But as the bonds were negotiable instruments, and their issue was authorized by a vote of the County, and they recite on their face a compliance with the law providing for their issue, they would be held as valid obligations against the County in the hands of a bona fide holder taking them for value before maturity, according to repeated decisions of this court upon the character of such obligations. If, therefore, the plaintiff received the bond and coupons in suit before maturity for value, as he offered to prove, he should have been permitted to show that fact. There was nothing adjuged in the former action in the finding that the plaintiff had not made such proof in that case which can preclude the present plaintiff from making such proof here. The fact that a party may not have shown that he gave value for one bond or coupon is not even presumptive, much less conclusive, evidence that he may not have given value for another and different bond or coupon. The exclusion of the evidence offered by the plaintiff was erroneous, and for the ruling of the court in that respect the judgment must be reversed and a new trial had.

Upon the second question presented, we think the court below ruled correctly. Evidence showing that the action of Smith was brought for the sole use and benefit of the present plaintiff was, in our judgment, admissible. The finding that Smith was the holder and owner of the coupons in suit went only to this extent; that he held the legal title to them which was sufficient for the purpose of the action and was not inconsistent with an equitable and beneficial interest in another.

Judgment reversed and cause remanded, for a new trial.

Mr. Justice CLIFFORD, dissenting: ....it is clear that a former judgment is a bar in all cases where the matters put in issue in the first suit were the same as the matters in issue in the second suit. (Ricardo v Garcias, 12 Cl&F 401...) "It results from these authorities that an adjudication by competent tribunal is conclusive, not only in the proceeding in which it is pronounced, but in every other where the right or title is the same, although the cause of action may be different." (2 Smith, L Cas, 7th Am ed. 788, 789; Big, Estop., 2d ed. 45; Aurora v West, 7 Wall(US) 96, 19 LEd, 47...)

Grant that; and still it is suggested that the plaintiff in the suit on the coupons did not introduce evidence to prove that he paid value for the bonds with the coupons; but the answer to that is, that he might have done so. He alleged in the declaration that he paid value and, consequently he might have given evidence to prove it, which shows that the question was directly involved in the issue between the parties.

Doubtless the plaintiff neglected to give evidence in that behalf, for the reason that he and his counsel were of the opinion that the evidence introduced by the defendants was not sufficient to repel the prima facie presumption, arising from his possession of the instruments, that he paid value for the transfer, and I am still of that opinion; but the remedy of the plaintiff, if surprised, was to except to the ruling, or to submit a motion for new trial.

Suggestions of that sort are now too late, nor are they sufficient to modify the effect of the judgment. When once finally rendered, the judgment must be considered conclusive, else litigation will be endless. Litigants sometimes prefer not to bring forward their whole case or defense, in order to enjoy the opportunity to bring us a reserve in case of defeat in the first contest; but a rule which would sanction that practice would be against public policy, as it would enable a party to protract the litigation as long as he could find means or credit to compel the attendance of witnesses and to secure the services of counsel.

ZARAGOSA v CRAVEN (1949) 33 Cal2d 315, 202 P2d 73

SCHAUER, J. Plaintiff appeals from an adverse judgment in this action brought by her to recover for personal injuries suffered in a collision between an automobile operated by defendant and one operated by plaintiff's husband, in which plaintiff was riding. A prior action brought by the husband against the same defendant to recover for his own personal injuries suffered in the same accident resulted in a final judgment against the husband. The question for decision is whether the issues involved in this action brought by the wife are rendered res judicata by the prior judgment against her husband. We have concluded that the wife was in privity with her husband in the prior litigation and that inasmuch as the issues which she seeks to litigate are the same as those decided adversely to the husband in the earlier action, the determination there is binding on plaintiff here and the judgment in defendant's favor, so holding, must be affirmed.

The collision between the automobile operated by plaintiff's husband, in which plaintiff was riding, and the automobile driven by defendant occurred in May, 1946. On June 3, 1946, plaintiff's husband, Joe Zaragoas, filed an action against defendant to recover for his own personal injuries alleged to have been caused by the collision. Approximately three weeks later plaintiff filed the instant action, in which she seeks damages against defendant for personal injuries allegedly received by her in the same collision. Defendant answered in each action, denying negligence on his part and alleging contributory negligence on the part of the husband, Joe Zaragosa.

On October 29 and 30, 1946, the action first filed was tried before a jury; that trial resulted in a verdict and judgment for defendant. No appeal was taken, and the judgment became final. Thereafter, on March 12, 1947, defendant, with leave of court, filed a supplemental answer to plaintiff's complaint herein; in it he alleges that the judgment against the husband in the first action constitutes an estoppel and renders res judicata against plaintiff and in favor of defendant the issues of defendant's negligence, the husband's contributory negligence, and proximate cause, raised by the pleadings in each of the two actions. By stipulation, the plea of res judicata was tried as a special issue by the court sitting without a jury. Over plaintiff's objection the record in the action brought by the husband was introduced into evidence. The court found in defendant's favor, judgment was entered accordingly, and plaintiff appeals.

Section 1908 of the Code of Civil Procedure provides, so far as here material, that a judgment of a court or judge of this state having jurisdiction to pronounce it, is "in respect to the matter directly adjudged, conclusive between the parties and their successors in interest by title subsequent to the commencement of the action or special proceeding, litigating for the same thing under the same title and in the same capacity, provided they have notice, actual or constructive, of the pendency of the action or proceeding." This court has declared that "In determining the validity of a plea of res judicata three questions are pertinent: Was the issue decided in the prior adjudication idential with the one presented in the action in question? Was there a final judgment on the merits? Was the party against whom the plea is asserted a party or in privity with a party to the prior adjudication?" (Cases).

It is not disputed that the issues of defendant's negligence and of the husband's contributory negligence were directly involved in the first action and that one or both of such issues were by the jury determined in defendant's favor. Plaintiff's complaint in the instant case is, of course, predicated upon alleged negligence by defendant, and, further, plaintiff concedes that, unless her recovery would be her separate property (a suggestion of which proposition is hereinafter discussed), contributory negligence by her husband would under the community property law of this state bar her recovery of damages for her personal injuries. (Cases). It is therefore apparent that the issues of negligence and contributory negligence, at least one of which, it is shown, was decided in defendant's favor in the prior adjudication, are identical with those issues as presented in the instant action. (See Todhunter v Smith (1934), 219 Cal 690, 694-695, 28 P2d 916, and authorities there cited; Sutphin v Speik (1940), 15 Cal2d 195, 201-202, 99 P2d 652, 101 P2d 497.) It is likewise not disputed that there was a final judgment on the merits in the prior adjudication.

Thus the remaining question is whether the wife - the plaintiff in the present action, against whom the plea of res judicata is asserted - was a party or in privity with a party to the prior action. It is our view that under well established law the wife, although she was not named as a party in the action brought by her husband, was in privity with him and, hence, substantially in the legal position of a real party in interest in that litigation and she is bound by the judgment rendered therein in defendant's favor.

The term "privity" denotes mutual or successive relationship to the same rights or property. (Cases.) And in 30 American Jurisprudence at page 957 (Sec. 225), it is declared that "Who are privies requires careful examination into the circumstances of each case as it arises. In general, it may be that such privity involves a person so identified in interest with another that he represents the same legal right." The "legal right" here, to recover community property, depends in both cases on negligence of the defendant and lack of contributory negligence on the part of the husband in relation to the one accident....

... Hence, it must be considered as the present law of this state that the cause of action for personal injuries suffered by either spouse during marriage, to whatever extent such cause of action may constitute property (cases), as well as any recovery therefor, constitutes community property - at least in the absence of agreement otherwise between the spouses....

It is thus apparent that plaintiff was in privity with her husband, i.e., had a mutual relationship to the same right or property, in the prior litigation. The right, or cause of action, involved in such prior litigation was community in nature and the proceeds of any judgment that might have been recovered from defendant would have belonged to both husband and wife, as community property. Therefore, as in Cutting v Bryan (1929), supra, 206 Cal 254, 258, 274 P 326, the husband was representing the community, to which if judgment had gone against defendant the latter would have owed payment (see McElroy v McElroy (1948), 32 Cal 2d ___, 198 P2d 683), and consequently the wife was also represented as to her interest in the community and is bound by the judgment.

The fact that the cause of action for injuries to the wife is different from the cause of action for injuries to the husband is here immaterial. "By virture of the doctrine of res judicata, the final determination of a court of competent jurisdiction necessarily affirming the existence of any fact is conclusive evidence of the existence of that fact when it is again in issue in subsequent litigation between the same parties in the same or any other court. The facts decided in the first suit cannot be disputed or relitigated, although the later suit is upon a different cause of action. (Cases). The doctrine of res judicata has a double aspect. A former judgment operates as a bar against a second action upon the same cause, but, in a later action upon a different claim or cause of action, it operates as an estoppel or conclusive adjudication as to such issues in the second action as were actually litigated and determined in the first action." (Todhunter v Smith (1934), supra, 219 Cal 690, 694-695, 28 P2d 916, 918.) We are satisfied that upon the record here the legal right to recover the community judgment in both cases depends on an asserted obligation (arising, if at all, from negligence of the defendant and the husband's lack of contributory negligence, both in proximate relation to the accident in question) which, if it did not exist in the one case, cannot exist in the other.....

For the reasons stated the judgment is affirmed.

CARTER, J. I dissent. The holding of the majority in this case is reminiscent of the period when a wife was a mere chattel of her husband, possessing no rights or property not subject to his ownership or control. The majority ignore the fact that a married woman, when wrongfully injured by a third person, may recover damages for her disfigurement and pain and suffering, which are elements of damage personal to her, and by no reasonable construction of our statutes can be said to constitute community property. The majority likewise ignore the effect of our statutory provisions granting to a married woman the right to bring an action for her personal injury in her own name without joining her husband as indicative of a legislative intent to make such recovery her separate property.

The result reached here not only denies the wife any recovery, it denies her "her day in court". A doctrine which produces such a result should not be enunciated by any tribunal which deserves the label "Court of Justice."

For the foregoing reasons, I would reverse the judgment.

FLEISCHER v DETROIT CADILLAC MOTOR CAR CO. (SpCtSpTm 1917) 165 S 245

Action by Harry Fleischer against the Detroit Cadillac Motor Car Company. From an order permitting service of answer upon defendant's default, plaintiff appeals.

GUY, J. In this action to recover damages for personal injuries, defendant defaulted in pleading. Four days after the default, plaintiff's attorneys wrote to the defendant's attorney, calling his attention to the matter, and notifying him that, unless a verified answer was promptly served, plaintiff would proceed to take judgment. Seven days afterwards defendant presented an answer to plaintiff's attorneys for acceptance, but they refused to receive it. The court, on motion, permitted the service of the pleading, and plaintiff appeals from the order.

Plaintiff's alleged injuries were sustained in a collision between a motorcycle on which he was riding and one of defendant's automobiles, and it appears that in a prior action in the Municipal Court the plaintiff and another, owners of the motorcycle, recovered judgment against this same defendant for the injuries to their property caused by the collision. That judgment is therefore res adjudicata as to the negligence of the defendant (Cahnmann v Metropolitan St. Ry. Co., 37 M 475, 75 S 970), and it follows that there is no defense to the plaintiff's claim; the only question to be determined being the amount of plaintiff's damages.

Under the circumstances the plaintiff should not, in the enforcement of his rights, be subjected to the delay incident to the placing of the cause on the calendar to await trial in the regular order (Rothschild v Haviland, 172 AD 562, 158 S 661), and it was error to permit the service of the answer. Reilly v Sicillian Asphalt Paving Co., 170 NY 40, 62 NE 772, 57 LRA 176, 88 Am St Rep 636, and other cases cited by respondent, are not in point, because there the question was whether the prior suit barred the maintenance of the subsequent action, not whether the judgment in the first action was res adjudicata in subsequent litigation between the same parties.

Order reversed, with $10 costs and disbursements, and motion denied, with $10 costs. All concur.

SEALFON v US (1948) 332 US 575, 68 SCt 237, 92 LEd 180, r161, F2d 481

Mr. Justice DOUGLAS: This case presents the question whether an acquittal of conspiracy to defraud the United States precludes a subsequent prosecution for commission of the substantive offense, on the particular facts here involved.

Two indictments were returned against petitioner and others. One charged a conspiracy to defraud the United States of its governmental function of conserving and rationing sugar by presenting false invoices and making false representations to a ration board to the effect that certain sales of sugar products were made to exempt agencies. The other indictment charged petitioner and Greenberg with the commission of the substantive offense, viz., uttering and publishing as true the false invoices. The conspiracy indictment was tried first and the following facts were shown:

Defendant Greenberg manufactured syrup and approached Sanford Doctors, a salesman for a brokerage concern, to sell vanilla syrup. Doctors negotiated some sales to petitioner who did a wholesale business under the name of Sero Syrup Co. Thereafter Greenberg asked Doctors to get a list from petitioner showing the places where petitioner made sales and told him that if any sales were made to exempt agencies, Greenberg could sell to petitioner in larger quantities. Doctors so informed petitioner and some time thereafter petitioner wrote to Greenberg saying, "at the present time some of our syrups are being sold at the Brooklyn Navy Yard" and various defense plants. Petitioner did sell some of his syrup to a vending company which had machines at the Navy Yard but it was not vanilla syrup and no sales were made to the Navy Yard as such. Greenberg thereafter presented a series of false invoices to the ration board purporting to show sales to petitioner for delivery to the Navy Yard. Petitioner's letter was never shown to the Board. On the basis of these invoices Greenberg received replacement certificates for 21 million pounds of sugar, 10 million of which he sold to petitioner in the form of vanilla syrup, and which was by petitioner sold to non-exempt consumers, mostly the National

Biscuit Company. Petitioner at first made payments to Greenberg by check but thereafter gave checks to his trucker which the latter cashed, deducted his trucking fee, and paid Greenberg.

The jury returned a verdict of not guilty as to petitioner. Thereafter a trial was had on the other indictment which charged petitioner and Greenberg with uttering and publishing as true the false invoices introduced in the conspiracy trial. Greenberg pleaded guilty and the trial proceeded against petitioner on the theory that he aided and abetted Greenberg in the commission of the substantive offense. The false invoices, the letter from petitioner to Greenberg, and essentially the same testimony were again introduced against petitioner. In addition, it was brought out on cross-examination that petitioner had unsuccessfully sought replacement certificates from his ration board for sugar contained in syrups sold at the Navy Yard and defense plants. Greenberg gave testimony from which the jury could conclude that petitioner was a moving factor in the scheme to defraud which was constructed around petitioner's letter and that he was familiar with Greenberg's intention to submit false invoices. Greenberg further testified that petitioner received $500,000 in cash under the agreement as a rebate of two cents a pound on all replacement sugar which Greenburg received on Navy Yard invoices whether or not it was used in syrup sold to petitioner. This time the jury returned a verdict of guilty and petitioner was sentenced to five year's imprisonment and fined $12,000.

Petitioner moved to quash the second indictment on grounds of double jeopardy (abandoned in this Court) and res judicata, and also objected to the introduction of the evidence adduced at the first trial. The district judge ruled against petitioner, and the court below affirmed. (161 F2d 481.) We granted the petition for a writ of certiorari because of the importance of the question to the administration of the criminal law.

It has long been recognized that the commission of the substantive offense and a conspiracy to commit it are separate and distinct offenses. (Pinkerton v U.S. 328 US 640, 643, 90 LEd 1489, 1494, 66 SCt 1180.) Thus, with some exceptions, one may be prosecuted for both crimes. Ibid. But res judicata may be a defense in a second prosecution. That doctrine applies to criminal as well as civil proceedings (U. S. v Oppenheimer, 242 US 85, 87, 61 LEd 161, 164, 37 SCt 68, 3ALR 516 . . .) and operates to conclude those matters in issue which the verdict determined though the offenses be different. (See U. S. v Adams, 281 US 202, 205, 74 LEd 807, 808, 50 SCt 269.)

Thus the only question in this case is whether the jury's verdict in the conspiracy trial was a determination favorable to petitioner of the facts essential to conviction of the substantive offense. This depends upon the facts adduced at each trial and the instructions under which the jury arrived at its verdict at the first trial.

Respondent argues that the basis of the jury's verdict cannot be known with certainty; that the conspiracy trial was predicated on the theory that petitioner was a party to an over-all conspiracy ultimately involving petitioner, Greenberg, and the Baron Corporation. Thus, it is said that the verdict established with certainty only that petitioner was not a member of such conspiracy and that therefore the prosecution was not foreclosed from showing in the second trial that petitioner wrote the letter pursuant to an agreement with Greenberg to defraud the United States. The theory is that under the instructions given the jury might have found that petitioner conspired with Greenberg and yet refused to infer that he was a party to the overall conspiracy.

The instructions under which the verdict was rendered, however, must be set in a practical frame and viewed with an eye to all the circumstances of the proceedings. We look to them only for such light as they shed on the issues determined by the verdict. (Cf. DeSollar v Hanscome, 158 US 216, 222, 39 LEd 956, 959, 15 SCt 816.) Petitioner was the only one on trial under the conspiracy indictment. There was no evidence to connect him directly with anyone other than Greenberg. Only if an agreement with at least Greenberg was inferred by the jury could petitioner be convicted. And in the only instruction keyed to the particular facts of the case the jury was told that petitioner must be acquitted if there was reasonable doubt that he conspired with Greenberg. Nowhere was the jury told that to return a verdict of guilty it must be found that petitioner was a party to a conspiracy involving not only Greenberg but the Baron Corporation as well. Viewed in this setting, the verdict is a determination that petitioner, who concededly wrote and sent the letter, did not do so pursuant to an agreement with Greenberg to defraud.

So interpreted, the earlier verdict precludes a later conviction of the substantive offense. The basic facts in each trial were identical. As we read the records of the two trials, petitioner could be convicted of either offense only on proof that he wrote the letter pursuant to an agreement with Greenberg. Under the evidence introduced, petitioner could have aided and abetted Greenberg in no other way. Indeed, respondent does not urge that he could. Thus the core of the prosecutor's case was in each case the same: the letter, and the circumstances surrounding it and to be inferred from it, and the false invoices. There was, of course, additional evidence on the second trial adding detail to the circumstances leading up to the alleged agreement, petitioner's participation therein, and what he may have got out of it. But at most his evidence only made it more likely that petitioner had entered into the corrupt agreement. It was a second attempt to prove the agreement which at each trial was crucial to the prosecution's case and which was necessarily adjudicated in the former trial to be non-existent. That the prosecution may not do.

Reversed.

Section 4.5 The Rule as to Law of the Case

CLUFF v DAY (1894) 141 NY 580

Appeal from judgment of the General Term of the Superior Court of the city of New York, entered upon an order made January 3, 1893, which overruled defendant's exceptions and ordered judgment in favor of plaintiff upon a verdict directed by the court.

This action was brought by plaintiff on her own behalf and on behalf of all others interested in the estate of Burgess Cluff, late of New York City, deceased.

The nature of the action and the facts, so far as material, are set forth in the opinion, which is given in full.

"This is a suit to charge the sureties on a bond of a non-resident executor with the sum adjudged by a decree of the surrogate of the city and county of New York, made in 1886, on an accounting by the executor, to be due from him to the estate of the decedent. The case has been twice tried, and this is the second appeal to this court. On the first trial the defendants had judgment in their favor on the ground that a decree made by the surrogate on a former accounting in 1873 changed the character in which the executor had up to that time held the funds and property of the estate, and that he thereafter held them in his character as trustee, and that the devastavit by which the property of the estate was wasted and lost occurred after the decree of 1873, and was, therefore, not covered by the undertaking of the sureties, which related only to the acts of the executor as such. The judgment of the trial court on the first trial having been affirmed by the General Term, an appeal was taken to this court, and was heard before the Second Division, which reversed the judgment below, and ordered a new trial (124 NY 195). The judgment of the Second Division was placed on the ground that the accounting and decree in 1873 did not terminate the executorial duties of the executor or change the character in which he held the property, but that until the decree of 1886 he continued to hold it as executor and not as trustee, and that, therefore, the sureties were liable for a failure of their principal to pay the sum adjudged against him by the decree on the second accounting. On a new trial a verdict was directed for the plaintiff for the amount adjudged by the decree of 1886, with interest. The General Term, on appeal, affirmed the judgment entered pursuant to the verdict on the second trial, and this appeal is taken from the judgment of affirmance.

"We are asked to review and reverse the judgments so rendered by the courts below, although they were rendered in precise conformity with the principles upon which the former decision in this court proceeded. It is insisted that the Second Division of this court erred in its construction of the decree of 1873, and in adjudging that the character in which the property was held by the principal of the defendants was not thereby changed.

"The facts were not changed in any material respect on the second trial. All the material facts bearing upon the liability of the sureties, presented by the present record, were in the record on the former appeal. The law of the case was determined after full argument and consideration by the Second Division of this court. It would be contrary to the general rule and present an unseemly spectacle for this court in some case, between the same parties, upon substantially identical facts, to reverse a judgment rendered by a coordinate branch on this court upon a full understanding of the facts and of the question of law involved, even although if the case was res novo we might be of the opinion that the law of the case was erroneously adjudged.

"The state has constituted courts of different grades for the ascertainment of public and private rights, and to afford an opportunity for the correction of errors it has arranged a system of appellate courts, and has vested the final jurisdiction in this court. There is no exemption in any tribunal from the infirmities of human judgment. But the state has an interest that controversies in the courts should at some time come to an end, and, when submitted to the final arbitrament, that the judgment rendered should be accepted as the final determination of the right in controversy. The court may proceed upon erroneous views of the facts or the law. But to permit the parties to an action to re-open a discussion on the law or the facts once deliberately determined by the court of last resort, on a subsequent appeal in the same case, on a suggestion of error in the former decision, would encourage litigation and diminish respect for judicial tribunals, which it is of the highest importance should be maintained. There is no iron rule which precludes a court from correcting a manifest error in its former judgment, or which requires it to adhere to an unsound declaration of the law. It may, for cogent reasons, reverse or qualify a prior decision, even in the same case. But the cases in which this will be done are exceptional, and the power should be sparingly exercised. Where by inadvertence a settled principle of law is supposed to have been overlooked, or a rule of property violated, the court affords by its rules an opportunity to have its attention again called to the matter before final judgment is entered. If the party against whom the judgment is rendered omits to avail himself of this opportunity, or if, having applied for a re-argument, the application is denied and the case goes to a new trial on the law as declared, the circumstances must be very unusual which would justify the court in reversing its decision on a second appeal in the same case and upon the same facts. The decision is a precdent upon the point of law involved which the court may or may not follow in cases subsequently arising, but in the particular case it is 'more than authority-it is a final adjudication' between the parties.

"We are not to be understood as in any respect questioning the soundness of the decision on the former appeal. We decline to consider the question. It depended upon the construction to be given to certain acts and documents, all of which were before the court and taken into consideration. It affected no general public interest, nor did it establish any doctrine in hostility to the previous law as declared by this court. If there was any error at all, it was in the application of admitted principles to the circumstances of the particular case. This court, following the general trend of judicial authority, has frequently refused to re-consider in the particular case its prior decision, on the ground that the parties were concluded thereby, and this rule has been followed where the first decision was by the Commission of Appeals (Oakley v Aspinwall, 13 NY 500...)

"The new points raised are not well taken and do not require special reference.

"The judgment should be affirmed, with costs." ....

ANDREWS, Ch. J., reads for affirmance. All concur.

Judgment affirmed.

GRAVES v DORSEY (1stDept 1952) 109 S2d 793

PER CURIAM. Under the court's charge the plaintiff could not prevail without proof that the defendant accepted a bribe of $3,000 to repudiate the contract. In the absence of objection the charge became the law of the case in this respect. The evidence entirely failed to estabish the acceptance of such bribe. In fact, the plaintiff conceded that he has had no proof on that subject, except mere rumor in the trade. Accordingly, and because the evidence as a whole failed to establish any malicious interference with the plaintiff's contract on the part of the defendant, the judgment should be reversed...

Judgment reversed, with costs of this appeal to the appellant and the complaint dismissed, and judgment is directed to be entered dismissing the complaint herein, with costs.

Settle order on notice.

SCHIENTAG, J. (dissenting in part). I dissent in part and vote to reverse and to order a new trial. The plaintiff failed to make out the cause of action alleged in his complaint. Neither the granting of the "conventional" motion to conform the pleadings to the proof nor the Judge's charge purported to deal with any alleged willful, malicious conduct of the defendant other than that specifically charged in the complaint. In the interests of justice, however, the plaintiff should have the opportunity of amending his complaint properly and proceeding to a new trial in accordance therewith.

CHAPTER V

THE JUDICIAL SYSTEM

<u>OUTLINE OF CHAPTER V</u>

Sec. 5.1 The Nature of Judicial Power

Sec. 5.2 The State Judicial System

Sec. 5.3 The Federal Judicial System

Sec. 5.3 The World Judicial System

<u>SUGGESTED READINGS:</u>

Art. III, Constitution of the United States
Art. VI, Constitution of the United States
Art. VI, Constitution of New York State
New York Judiciary Law
United States Judiciary Law
Bowman: Elementary Law
  Ch. 15, "Courts and Their Jurisdiction", pp 217-238
Carmody-Wait: Cyclopedia of New York Practice
  Vol. I, Ch. 2, "Courts and Their Jurisdiction" pp 13-214
Fryer and Benson: Legal Methods and System
  Ch's. 8, 9 and 10, pp 561-798
Gavit, <u>Introduction to Study of Law</u>
  Ch. VI, The Court System...pp 219-253
Kinnane: <u>Anglo-American Law</u>
  Ch. XVI, "Modern English Law...English Courts..." pp 433-466
  Ch. XVII, "American Law-Federal Courts..." pp 467-492
  Ch. XVIII, "American Law-State Courts..." pp493-519
Morgan: <u>Study of Law</u>
  Ch. I "The Courts," pp 1-39
Plucknett: <u>Concise History of the Common Law</u>
  Book I, Part II, "The Courts and the Profession," pp 82-255
Radin: <u>Anglo-American Legal History</u>
  Ch. 6, "The Administrators," pp 81-87
  Ch. 7, "The Common Law Courts," pp 88-97
  Ch. 8, "The Struggle between the Courts," pp 98-110
Smith: <u>Elementary Law</u>
  Ch. 22, "Courts and Their Jurisdiction," pp 363-383

Sec. 5.1 The Nature of Judicial Power

MATTER OF RICHARDSON (1928) 247 NY 401, r222 AD 591

CARDOZO, Ch. J. On December 15, 1927, a citizen of the State filed with the Governor charges against Maurice E. Connolly with a view to his removal from office as President of the Borough of Queens. On the following day the Governor, by an instrument in writing, which recited the filing of these charges, addressed a direction to a justice of the Supreme Court to hear the charges, and make report to the Governor thereon. "Pursuant to section 34 of the Public Officers Law, I do hereby direct that Honorable Townsend Scudder, one of the justices of the Supreme Court in and for the second judicial district of the State of New York, within which said Maurice E. Connolly resides, take evidence as to said charges with all the powers as by law provided, and I hereby further direct said Justice to report to me said evidence taken in such proceedings with his findings of the material facts deemed by him to be established in connection with said charges, together with his conclusion thereon."

Mr. Justice Scudder gave notice to the accused officer on December 30, 1927, that he would take the evidence at the County Court House in Long Island City on February 1, 1928, and at such adjourned hearings as might be from time to time announced. He signed the notice with the addition of his official title as Justice of the Supreme Court....

The assumption of these powers evoked challenge and resistance. On January 9, 1928, divers witnesses, subpoenaed to attend a preliminary session, made application to the Supreme Court to vacate the subpoenas on the ground that they had been issued without warrant of law. On January 24, 1928, Connolly, the accused official, made application to the Appellate Division in the Second Judicial Department for an order of prohibition. Upon the first of these applications, the Supreme Court at Special Term upheld the validity of the subpoenas and denied the motion to vacate them.

The witnesses, giving notice that only constitutional questions would be raised, have appealed directly to this court (Constitution, art. VI, Sec. 7, subd. 3; Civil Practice Act, Sec. 588, subd. 3). Upon the second application, the Appellate Division, by its first decision, made an order dated February 6, 1928, commanding Mr. Justice Scudder to "desist and refrain from any further proceedings in the matter of the charges against the petitioner by way of taking and hearing the evidence of witnesses except at a hearing at which the petitioner is afforded an opportunity of being present." To the extent that the proceeding was public, prohibition was denied....

The ruling by the Appellate Division was swiftly followed by legislation enlarging the powers of the delegate of the Governor in the matter of such charges. By Laws of 1928, chapter 15, which became a law on February 8, 1928, section 34 of the Public Officers Law was amended so as to provide that in any proceeding for the removal of a public officer, the Governor may direct his delegate, whether a judge or a commissioner, to conduct an investigation into the charges, or to take evidence as to the truth thereof at a hearing for such purpose, or both. If such a direction is made, the Governor may require the Attorney-General or the district attorney of the county in which the officer resides to assist the person so appointed both in the conduct of the investigation and thereafter in the hearing. Neither the officer so proceeded against nor the counsel of such officer shall have any right to be present at the investigation unless expressly so permitted. The judge or commissioner is authorized to employ counsel in any case where the Attorney-General or district attorney has not been directed to assist, and to employ such other assistants as may be necessary for the performance of his duties. Whoever is named by the Governor to conduct the inquiry is to be paid the fair value of his services unless he is already employed by the State or by a county or city, in which case he is to serve gratuitously. The expenses are made a county or city charge where the proceeding is one for the removal of a county or city officer. All acts theretofore performed by one designated by the Governor in a pending proceeding are legalized and confirmed.

Upon the adoption of this statute a motion was made to the Appellate Division to vacate its order of prohibition which had been limited, as we have seen, to the inquiry in camera. The motion was granted, and prohibition was denied. There is a recital in the order that the denial was on the law and not in the exercise of any discretionary power.

The two appeals, one by the witnesses from the order upholding the subpoenas, and the other by Connolly from the refusal of the order of prohibition are here before us now.

We think there has been an attempt by section 34 of the Public Officers Law, both in its original and in its amended form, to charge a justice of the Supreme Court with the mandatory performance of duties non-judicial. He is made the delegate of the Governor in aid of an executive act, the removal of a public officer (Matter of Guden, 171 NY 529). At the word of command he is to give over the work of judging, and set himself to other work, the work of probing and advising. His findings when made will have none of the authority of a judgment. To borrow Bacon's phrase, they will not "give the rule or sentence." They will not be preliminary or ancillary to any rule or sentence to be pronounced by the judiciary in any of its branches. They will be mere advice to the Governor, who may adopt them, or modify them, or reject them altogether.

From the beginnings of our history, the principle has been enforced that there is no power in Executive or Legislature to charge the judiciary with administrative functions except when reasonably incidental to the fulfilment of judicial duties (People v Hall, 169 NY 184; Matter of State Indust. Comm., 224 NY 13, 16). The exigencies of government have made it necessary to relax a merely doctrinaire adherence to a principle so flexible and practical, so largely a matter of sensible approximation, as that of the separation of powers. Elasticity has not meant that what is of the essence of the judicial function may be destroyed by turning the power to decide into a pallid opportunity to consult and recommend (cf. Frankfurter and Landis, Power of Congress, etc.; a Study in the Separation of Powers, 37 Harvard Law Review, 1010, 1020).

The question arose as far back as 1792. An act of Congress required the Circuit Courts of the United States to examine into the pension claims of soldiers and seamen of the Revolution, and to certify their opinion to the Secretary of War with a view to corrective legislation. The judges of the several circuits concurred in a determination that the duty was not judicial (Hayburn's Case, 2 Dall. U.S. 409). In 1851 the Supreme Court of the United States considered that determination and approved it, declining jurisdiction under an act not widely different (U.S. v Ferreira, 13 How(US) 40, 44). There was an opinion by Taney, C.J., which has become a landmark of the law (Gordon v U.S., 117 US 697; Matter of Sanborn, 148 US 222; Int. Com. Comm. v Brimson, 154 US 447; 481; Muskrat v U.S. 219 US 346, 353; Tutun v U.S., 270 US 568, 576; Liberty Warehouse v Grannis, 273 US 70, 74).

Nowhere has the doctrine thus established been applied more steadily or forcefully than in the courts of New York. (Matter of Davies 168 NY 89; Matter of State Ind. Comm., supra). The function of the judges "Is to determine controversies between the litigants." (Matter of State Ind. Comm., supra). They are not adjuncts or advisers, much less investigating instrumentalities, of other agencies or government. Their pronouncements are not subject to review by Governor or Legislature (Dinan v Swig, 223 Mass 516). They speak "the rule or sentence".

The statute was thus an encroachment upon the independence of judicial power even in the form in which it stood until recently amended. Still more clearly is it such an encroachment in its form as now reframed. The judge is made a prosecutor. He is to have his counsel and assistant counsel and experts and detectives. He is to follow trails of suspicion, to uncover hidden wrongs, to build up a case as a prosecutor builds one. If he were the district attorney of the county, he would do no more and no less. What he learns is not committed to a record available to all the world. It is locked within his breast to be withheld or disclosed as his discretion shall determine. No doubt he is to act impartially, neither presenting from malice nor concealing from favor. One might say the same of any prosecutor. The outstanding fact remains that his conclusion is to be announced upon a case developed by himself. Centuries of common-law tradition warn us with echoing impressiveness that his is not a judge's work. We should be sorry to weaken that tradition by any judgment of this court....

The range of our decision will not be misapprehended. We deny the power of the Legislature to charge a justice of the Supreme Court with the duties of a prosecutor in aid of the Executive. We do not question its power to lay such duties on the Executive himself or on a commissioner appointed as his agent or adviser. Just as the Governor may investigate and afterwards remove, so his commissioner may investigate and later recommend removal. Neither the one nor the other is subject to the supervision of the courts (Matter of Guden supra). The argument is made that by a provision of the charter — (Greater NY Charter, Sec. 122, 382), a president of a borough is to be removed in the same manner as a sheriff, and a sheriff is not to be removed without "an opportunity of being heard in his defense" (Constitution, art. 10, Sec. 1). Nothing in that requirement amounts to a direction that in the performance of an executive act, the function of inquisition shall be divorced from that of hearing and decision. Other answers are available, but they do not have to be developed.

We reach the final stage in the course of the respondent's argument. Granting that functions non-judicial may not be cast upon a judge so as to impose a duty of acceptance, the privilege we are told, is his to assume the performance of the duty, not in his capacity of judge, but in his private or individual capacity as if named as a commissioner. The action of the circuit judges who refused to hold themselves bound by the act of Congress of 1792 is cited as a precedent. Some of the judges, declining to serve in the capacity of judges, "agreed to construe the power as conferred on them individually as commissioners," and as commissioners reported to the Secretary of War (U.S. v Ferreita, supra at p. 50; U.S. v Todd, 13 How(US)52; cf. Matter of Gans. 17 F 471).

The Constitution of New York provides (Art. VI, Sec. 19): "The judges of the Court of Appeals and the justices of the Supreme Court shall not hold any other public office or trust, except that they shall be eligible to serve as members of a constitutional convention." There is no equivalent provision in the Constitution of the United States. The appellants maintain that service as commissioner in removal proceedings under section 34 of the statute, if not the acceptance of an office, is the acceptance of a public trust.

The prohibition has an ancient history. It goes back for its origin to the Constitution of 1777. At that time it was limited to the acceptance of an "office." "That the Chancellor and judges of the Supreme Court shall not, at the same time, hold any other office, excepting that of Delegate to the general Congress, upon special occasions; and that the first judges of the County Courts, in the several Counties, shall not, at the same time, hold any other office, excepting that of Senator or Delegate to the general Congress" (Constitution of 1777, art. XXV.)

The next Constitution, that of 1821, broadened the prohibition, at least in terms, so as to include not only an office but any public trust. "Neither the chancellor nor justices of the Supreme Court, nor any circuit judge, shall hold any other office or public trust. All votes for any elective office, given by the legislature or the people, for the Chancellor or a Justice of the Supreme Court, or circuit judge, during his continuance in his judicial office, shall be void" (Constitution of 1821, art. V. Sec. 7).

The depth of feeling on the subject can be gathered from the form of the resolution as first proposed to the convention by the judiciary committee: "They (the Chancellor and the judges) shall not, on any pretence, hold any other office or public trust, whether created under this constitution, or otherwise; and their acceptance thereof, shall vacate their judicial offices: Nor shall they be eligible to the office of governor, or lieutenant governor, within two years after the expiration, or resignation of their judicial offices" (Journal of Convention of 1821, pp. 101, 108; see also, p. 296).

The Constitution of 1846 continued the prohibition without substantial change from that of 1821. "They (the judges of the Court of Appeals and the justices of the Supreme Court) shall not hold any other office or public trust" (Constitution of 1846, art. VI, Sec. 8). A new prohibition was added. "They shall not exercise any power of appointment to public office" (Const. of 1846, art. VI, Sec. 8). This latter prohibition was dropped in the amendment of 1874, very likely in the belief that it was sufficiently embodied in the clause prohibiting the acceptance of any other public trust (People v Hall, 169 NY 184). No change was made in respect of these provisions by the Constitution of 1894, and none of importance by the revision of the judiciary article of 1926....

The problem now before us must be viewed in the background of authority supplied by this summary of the precedents. So viewing it, we think that within the constitutional prohibition there was an acceptance of a "public trust."

The statute annexes or seeks to annex to the office of a judge, not a temporary power to be exhausted by a single act (as in the case of the Washington relics), but a continuing power to be exercised whenever occasion shall arise. As often as the Governor commands, the judge is to obey. As often as the need arises, the call is to be met. He is to be a standing commissioner whose function is to serve when summoned. In such circumstances, the public trust does not cease to be continuing and permanent because the judge may be willing to fulfill it on one occasion and unwilling on another. As well might one urge that a power conferred upon the judges to fill vacancies in office whenever they occurred would be something other than a public trust because the judges might act as to one office and refuse to act as to another.

As well might one say that the order reviewed by this court in Matter of Davies (supra) could be upheld, though the statute had been read as conferring administrative powers, on the theory that when separate applications are separately considered, there is involved in respect of each the acceptance of a separate trust. In determining the quality of the trust, regard must be had to the intention of the Legislature in directing its creation. If the intention was, as here, to annex a permanent duty as an incident to the judicial office, a public trust has been created though the occasions for discharging it may be irregular or fitful.

The policy at the root of the constitutional prohibition reinforces this conclusion. The policy is to conserve the time of the judges for the performance of their work as judges, and to save them from the entanglements, at times the partisan suspicions, so often the result of other and conflicting duties. Some of these possibilities find significant illustration in the very cases before us now. Here is an inquiry which has already separated the respondent for more than two months from the discharge of his judicial duties, and which is likely to continue for many weeks to come.

The charges as first submitted involved a scrutiny of the acts of the accused official in multifarious transactions for fifteen years or more. Supplemental charges have now been filed with the result that the issues are more involved than ever. The great staff of counsel and assistants engaged upon the work is a token of its complexity and its probable duration. Interference so prolonged with assignments to judicial duty is the very evil that was meant to be hit by the prohibitions of the Constitution directed against dual office. True indeed it is that there may be times when the duties of a commissioner will be less onerous and protracted. Even so, the nature of the trust must be measured by its reasonable possibilities. Not what has been done under a statute, but what may reasonably be done under it, is the test of its validity (Stuart v Palmer, 74 NY 183).

The content of the duties tends with as much significance as their duration to point to performance as the acceptance of a public trust. A commissioner in these proceedings is more than a referee or an arbitrator, whose duties touch the parties affected by his decision, and concern the public interests remotely if at all. Here the very subject or the inquiry is one distinctively public, the tenure of a public officer. In pursuing that inquiry, the commissioner is authorized from time to time, so long as he functions as commissioner, to incur bills for his expenses and the expenses of his staff. These bills, subject to audit, will be payable from the public purse. If the power to incur such expenses and charge them on the public treasury is not a public trust, one is at a loss to understand how such a trust can be created.

We hold that the respondent is disqualified, while retaining the office of judge, to act as the delegate of the Governor under one name or another. The prohibitions of the Constitution are not to be evaded through the form of accepting as an individual what the judge must reject. At least that is so when what is done is official and not personal in its quality and incidents. In this instance neither Legislature nor Executive nor Judge had any thought of evasion. The Legislature did not intend when a commission was directed to a judge that he should act as an individual, his title as judge being mere descriptio personae. It annexed the duty to the office (cf. U.S. v Todd, 13 How(US)52). The Governor, in issuing the commission did not intend to invite co-operation by a private citizen as an act of grace or favor. The language of the designation is not the language of request or of appointment. It is the language of command, addressed by the Executive to a member of the judiciary who is expected to obey.

Above all, the respondent himself had no thought to accept the designation in any new capacity. From first to last he has assumed to act as judge and nothing else. He has made his return and affidavits as a justice of the Supreme Court. He has issued his notices and subpoenas with recitals that describe him as a justice of the Supreme Court, and with the addition of his title as such justice he has signed his name thereto. We were informed by his counsel that in case of need he will exercise the power to punish a contumacious witness for a contempt of his authority, though such power does not exist unless the subpoena has been issued by a justice of the court (Civil Practices Act, Sec. 406). Equivocal acts will be so interpreted as to escape a violation of the constitutional command, and even the risk of violation, when conduct, though permissible, is close to the line of danger. Here the acts are not equivocal. Nothing has been said and nothing has been done with the will to serve in any other capacity than that of a justice of the court.

We are satisfied that in so holding we do not misread the respondent's thought and purpose. The Governor, in selecting a judge so distinguished and experienced, was animated by a high sense of public duty, the desire to name a delegate of unquestioned ability and character. Mr. Justice Scudder was animated by a like sense of public duty in responding to a call to service. He thought, beyond a doubt, that the effect of the statute was to annex the duty to the office. If he was uncertain of its validity, he preferred to wait to condemn it until invalidity had been adjudged after argument and deliberation in appropriate proceedings. He supposed that he was discharging his duty as a judge in assuming a heavy burden incidental to the office. There is no reason to believe that his choice would have been the same if he had supposed that he was abandoning, pro tanto, his duty as a judge. His conduct is misinterpreted if we read it as evincing an election to step aside from his judgeship and take upon himself, with all the chances of illegality, the duties of a commissioner. He has been the judge throughout.

Upon the appeal by Richardson and others, the order of the Special Term should be reversed, and the motion to vacate the subpoenas granted.

Upon the appeal by the petitioner Connolly, the order of the Appellate Division should be reversed, and an order of prohibition granted commanding the respondent to desist from further action as a justice of the Supreme Court in the investigation or hearing of the subject-matter of these charges.

Ordered accordingly.

Sec. 5.2 The State Judicial System.

HAGGERTY v CITY OF NEW YORK (1935) 267 NY 252, r153 M 841

Appeal, on constitutional grounds, from a judgment, entered December 11, 1934, upon an order of the Municipal Court of the City of New York granting a motion by plaintiff for summary judgment.

Plaintiff's intestate was, prior to his death on December 15, 1933, a justice of the Municipal Court of the City of New York, having been elected in November, 1929, and taking office on January 1, 1930, the salary of such office then being $12,000. per year. Thereafter, on January 6, 1933, upon the recommendation of the Board of Estimate and Apportionment and pursuant to the provisions of chapter 637 of the Laws of 1932, the Board of Aldermen of the City of New York by resolution, as of January 1, 1933, the salary of plaintiff's intestate as such justice at $10,840. per year. At the time of the decedent's death the amount of salary alleged to have been withheld from him, over has protest noted upon the payrolls, was $996.60, to recover which the action was brought....

CRANE, Ch. J. The Constitution of the State of New York recognizes two classes of courts—constitutional courts, and inferior local courts of civil or criminal jurisdiction. The constitutional courts are those which are created or continued by the Constitution and, as to these, the Constitution gives certain power and jurisdiction as well as defining the nature and extent of the office. The inferior local courts are left to the creation, control and regulation of and by the Legislature.

tain power and jurisdiction as well as defining the nature and extent of the office. The inferior local courts are left to the creation, control and regulation of and by the Legislature.

Beginning with judiciary article, in effect January 1, 1926, known as article VI of the Constitution, we find provision made for the continuance of the Supreme Court, with general jurisdiction in law and in equity, subject to such appellate jurisdiction of the Court of Appeals as may be prescribed by law.

The term of office of a Supreme Court justice is fourteen years.

The Court of Appeals is continued, and the term of the judge fixed at fourteen years. Its jurisdiction is specifically detailed.

The County Court is next provided for, as appears in section 11: "The existing county courts are continued, and the judges thereof now in office shall hold their offices until the expiration of their respective terms." Some are to be elected for six years, others for fourteen years. The Constitution in section 12 even provides for the special county judge.

Then comes the Surrogates' Courts, which are specifically provided for in section 13 of this article: "The existing surrogates' courts are continued, and the surrogates now in office shall hold their offices until the expiration of their respective present terms." Some are to be chosen for six years and others for fourteen years.

We find also this article of the Constitution covers the Courts of General Sessions and also the City Court as they are constituted in the city of New York. Section 14 reads: "The court of general sessions in and for the city and county of New York is continued with its present jurisdiction, under the name of the court of general sessions of the county of New York." The term shall be fourteen years.

Section 15: "The city court of the city of New York is continued, and, from and after the first day of January in the second year following the adoption of this article, it shall have the same jurisdiction and power throughout the city of New York, under the name of the city court of the city of New York, as it now possesses within the county of New York and the county of Bronx."

These are the judicial offices created or continued by the Constitution, and beyond the power of the Legislature to control or regulate, except as that power is given to it expressly or impliedly by the Constitution.

As to justices of the peace, the Constitution (Sec. 17) provides that: "The electors of the several towns shall, at their annual town meetings, or at such other time and in such manner as the legislature may direct, elect justices of the peace, whose term of office shall be four years." Every other judicial officer of this State is a creature of the Legislature, whose office may be abolished at any time, and whose duties, as well as his office, are under the regulation and control of the Legislature. Thus, by section 17 of this judiciary article, we have this provision, following the enumeration of the above judicial offices and courts: "All other judicial officers in cities, whose election or appointment is not otherwise provided for in this article, including all judicial officers holding courts of special sessions, magistrates' courts, or other inferior local courts of criminal jurisdiction in the city of New York, shall be chosen by the electors of such cities or appointed by some local authorities thereof as may be prescribed by law."

And again, in section 18 we have this: "Inferior local courts of civil and criminal jurisdiction may be established by the legislature, but no such inferior local court which has been created since the first day of January, one thousand eight hundred and ninety-five, or is hereafter created shall be a court of record. All inferior local courts now or hereafter established may be regulated or discontinued by the legislature.

The Municipal Court of the City of New York is thus an inferior local court of civil jurisdiction, created by the Legislature. Nowhere do we find in the Constitution any provision for its creation, continuance or even existence. The Legislature having created it, may abolish it at any time or transfer its jurisdiction to any other tribunal. To regulate it, both as to tenure of office as well as to any other circumstance and condition, is a power specifically given by the Constitution, and this power includes the right at any time to change or modify the compensation of its judges. Surely if the Legislature has power to abolish the court and is given specifically plenary power to regulate it, as the whole includes the part, so this power must permit of the decrease or increase in salary.

That the Legislature may do this thing, unless controlled or restricted by the Constitution, is conceded. Therefore, it is sought to make the Municipal Court of the City of New York a constitutional court. This cannot be done without thwarting the clear intent and purpose as well as the express phraseology of this fundamental charter of State government. That section 9 has in it these words: "All other judicial officers, except justices of the peace, justices of the municipal court of the city of New York, and judges or justices of inferior courts not of record, may be removed by the Senate, * * *" does not make the Municipal Court a constitutional court by this mere mention of it any more than it does all other inferior courts within the possibilities of propagation.

Having provided for vacancies in the offices of judges of the Court of Appeals and the Supreme Court, the Constitution, by section 16, provided for other vacancies created in the constitutional judicial office by saying: "Vacancies occurring in the office of county judge, special county judge, surrogate, special surrogate, judge of the Court of General Sessions of the city of New York, or justice of the City Court of the county of New York, shall be filled by appointment by the governor by and with the advice and consent of the Senate if the Senate be in session," etc. Clearly, the courts which this article VI created and continued by constitutional mandate were those which I have specified, and did not include the inferior local courts of civil and criminal jurisdiction created by the Legislature, of which the Municipal Court of the City of New York is one.

Therefore, when section 19 of article VI provided for the compensation of judges it had reference to those judges whose office had been created or continued by the article itself. Unnecessary was it to give such power in the Constitution to the Legislature as it had such power anyway. It could create such local courts as it desired unless restrained by the Constitution, and pay the judges any given compensation. The Constitution, moreover, in section 18 had recognized the power of the Legislature to create local courts, regulate or discontinue them. The compensation section, reading: "All judges, justices and surrogates shall receive for their services such compensation as is now or may hereafter be extablished by law, provided only that such compensation shall not be diminished during their respective terms of office," has reference to those judicial officers created and continued by the Constitution, for it is only such that this article of the Constitution is dealing with generally. All other judicial officers, both as to creation, continuance, regulation and compensation are left entirely to the control and power of the Legislature.

Does it not seem somewhat strained to say that the Legislature may abolish the Municipal Court, may reduce the term of office to a week or a day, may create another court in its place and end the term of every judge (Schieffelin v Goldsmith, 253 NY 243) and yet cannot reduce his compensation? I can find nothing in the Constitution that limits the Legislature in this respect. The same reasoning adopted for the Special Sessions judge applies to the judge of the Municipal Court and, as to the former, this court has held that the Legislature could reduce his salary during his term. (Matter of Gresser v O'Brien, 263 NY 622, a146 M 909.)

If the Municipal Court be a constitutional court beyond the power and control of the Legislature, then in no way can its jurisdiction be limited or controlled so as to take from it the functions which it now has. (See People ex rel Wogan v Rafferty, 208 NY 451.)

The line of cleavage between the constitutional and the Legislative courts is clearly drawn by the Constitution of 1925, and it should not become blurred or obliterated by judicial interpretation. Matter of Adler v Voorhis (254 NY 375) is not in point. The statement that the Constitution has now given place to inferior local courts refers to those courts refers to those courts provided for in the Constitution, as above stated—the General Sessions and the City Court, and not to the Municipal Court of the City of New York. This case dealt with the time for holding elections, which was very materially changed by the new judiciary article.

Reference should be made to the rulings of the United States Supreme Court regarding this matter of inferior local courts under the Federal Constitution. In Williams v United States (289 US 553) it was held that the judicial power of the Court of Claims is not vested in virtue of article III of the Constitution, so as to bring its judges within the protection of that article as to tenure of office and compensation.

For these reasons the judgment should be reversed and the complaint dismissed with costs in all courts.

CROUCH, J. (dissenting). (opinion omitted)

MATTER OF STEINWAY (1899) 159 NY 250, a 31 AD 70

VANN, J. Steinway & Sons, once a copartnership, became a corporation in 1876 under the General Manufacturing Act of 1848, and the relator has been a stockholder therein ever since. He now holds 1,440 shares of its stock of the par value of $144,000, out of a total of 20,000 shares of the value of $2,000,000, but with an actual value much in excess of that sum. He has not been an officer of the corporation since 1881, and he has had no means of knowing much about the management of its affairs since 1892, when he was given an opportunity to examine the books. Since then he has been substantially ignorant as to all the details of the management and has had no access to the books or records.

Learning of certain practices that he considered improper, on April 12th, 1894, and March 27th, 1895, he made protests in writing to the company, but no attention was paid to them. On the 6th of April, 1896, he made a written request for leave to examine the books, but receiving no reply, on the 15th of that month he wrote requesting information, proper in character, upon certain subjects, and to this communication he received an answer from the secretary, dated April 23rd, 1896, written in behalf of the board of trustees, virtually refusing the information asked for on the ground that the relator intended to use it in "hostility to the interest of the stockholders."

On the 5th of April, 1897, he endeavored to ascertain certain material facts at the annual meeting, but without success, and thereupon he requested the officers and directors to afford his accountants and attorneys access to the books of account, vouchers and records of the company for the years 1892 to 1896, inclusive, for the purpose of examining the same. Receiving no reply, on the 8th of May, 1897, he served a written request upon the treasurer for a statement in writing, under oath, of the affairs of the company, embracing a particular account of all its assets and liabilities for each of the several fiscal years from 1892 to 1896, inclusive, and in response to this he received a general statement placing the assets at more than three millions of dollars, but distributed into only fourteen items, eight of which were over $100,000 each. The liabilities included but eight items, three of which were the capital stock, the surplus and the profit of 1896.

This was the first information as to the company's affairs which the petitioner had been able to obtain in five years, except that he once saw the balance sheet and inventory of January, 1893. Since 1891 the dividends declared by the company have dwindled in amount. In 1896 the dividend was only five percent, but never before since 1883 had less than ten per cent, and sometimes as much as eighteen and twenty per cent, been divided in dividends.

The relator claimed in his petition for a writ of mandamus to permit inspection of the books, that the officers of the corporation were engaged in an attempt to form an English stock company for the control of its business, with the design of selling their shares of the capital stock, or exchanging them for a much greater amount of shares in the English company and that efforts had been made by the stockholders and officers to induce him to sell his stock at $250 a share; but, as he insisted, it was impossible for him to fix upon any price without an opportunity to investigate the condition of the company. He specified various acts which he alleged to be improper on the part of the officers, such as the payment of exorbitant rentals, carrying on a banking business, allowing unusual rates of interest, inventorying the assets too low and paying the trustees salaries with no equivalent in services.

The opposing affidavits contain a large amount of matter relating to aggravating conduct on the part of the relator in the past, and alleging improper motives and ulterior aims on his part. Many general allegations of the petition were denied in haec verba, without stating the real facts. The president and other officers of the corporation denied the allegations of improper conduct on their part and claimed that the relator wished to force them to buy him out at an extravagant price. As no alternative writ was issued and the relator proceeded to argument upon his petition and the opposing affidavits, his right to a peremptory writ depends upon the conceded facts, the same as if he had demurred to the allegations of the defendants. (People ex rel. City of Buffalo v N.Y.C. & H.R.R.Co., 156 NY 570; Matter of Haebler v New York Produce Exchange, 149 NY 414; People ex rel. Corrigan v Mayor, etc., 149 NY 215; People v R. W & O.R.R.Co., 103 NY 95; Code Civ. Pro. Sec. 2070.)

While many of the facts alleged in the petition were denied, enough were left undenied to present a case for the exercise of judgment and discretion on the part of the Supreme Court, provided it has power in any case not expressly covered by statute, to authorize the inspection, wholly or in part, of the books of a manufacturing corporation, upon the application of a stockholder.

The Special Term denied the application of the relator for a peremptory writ of mandamus commanding the officers of the corporation to exhibit certain of its books and papers to him, but upon appeal to the Appellate Division the order of the Special Term was reversed by a divided vote, and the prayer of the petition granted, with certain regulations as to time, place and manner of exhibiting the books and papers. The Appellate Division allowed an appeal to this court and certified the following question for decision: "Has the Supreme Court the power, upon the petition of a stockholder, to compel by mandamus the corporation to exhibit its books for his inspection?"

The relator does not claim that the power in question has been conferred upon the court by statute, but he insists that it is a part of its inherent power. This position involves an inquiry into the origin and extent of the authority of the Supreme Court and its power of visitation, or of examining into the affairs of corporations according to the common law.

The origin of the Supreme Court was through a statute passed by the legislature of the colony of New York on the 6th day of May, 1691, whereby, among other things, it was enacted "that there shall be held and kept a Supreme Court of Judicature, which shall be Duely & Constantly kept at the City of New Yorke and not Elsewhere, att the severall & Respective times hereafter mentioned. And that there be five Justices at Least appointed & Commissionated to hold the same court, two whereof together with one Chief Justice to be a Quorum. Which Supream Court are hereby fully Impowered and Authorized to have Cognizance of all pleas, Civill Criminall, and Mixt, as fully and amply to all Intents & Purposes whatsoever, as the Courts of Kings Bench, Comon Pleas & Exchequer within their Majestyes Kingdom of England, have or ought to have, * * * ."

This statute was to remain in force for only two years, but it was renewed, recognized and continued by colonial act or royal ordinance substantially in the words quoted until the adoption of our first Constitution. (1 Col. Laws, pp. 226-229, 303-306, 358-380; 2 id. 462, 639, 948; 3 id. 546, 780, 1007; 4 id. 1088; 5 id. 73.) As has been well said by a recent writer, "This act founded the Supreme Court. * * * Not only did this act erect the tribunal which still continues the great law court of the state, but it vested in it a jurisdiction which change of government and constant reforms and revolutions in procedure have been powerless to abridge in any material respect, for while its jurisdiction has been enlarged by its union with the Court of Chancery, its ancient jurisdiction still remains unimpaired. The Supreme Court of the province was the instrument by which the great body of the jurisprudence of the English common law was applied to New York." (Fowler's Organization of the Supreme Court, 19 A.L.J. 211.)

The Court of Chancery was created, or as some insist, continued, by the same act and was subsequently kept in force in the same way. (Hoffman's Chancery Practice, 14; Graham's Jurisdiction, 140.)

Aside from the colonial statutes, which created and continued such courts only for fixed terms, royal ordinances were resorted to when the legislature failed to act, upon the theory that such action was authorized by the charter of the colony. The most notable were those passed by the governor and council on the 15th of May, 1699, and the 3rd of April, 1704, which are referred to by the revisers in a note to 1 R. L. 213, and published in full in appendix No. 5 at the end of the second volume of the Revised Laws. These ordinances, which were questioned but never overthrown, are substantially the same as the original act of 1691. Chalm. Col. Op. 249; 5 Col. Doc. 952; 1 E.D. Smith, Introduction, 50.)

The Supreme Court as thus continued by Lord Bellamont's ordinance of 1699 and the Court of Chancery as continued by ordinance on the 20th of August, 1701, and the 7th of November, 1704, were the same tribunals and possessed the same powers as those organized by the colonial legislature. (Appendix No. 7, 2 R.L. 13.) They were still in existence and exercising their powers when the convention met to organize a state government.

"Such parts of the common law of England and of the statute law of England and Great Britain, and of the acts of the legislature of the Colony of New York, as together did form the law of the said Colony on the 19th of April, 1775," were made and continued the law of this state by its first Constitution. (Const. of 1777, Sec. 35.) While that instrument neither created nor continued the Supreme Court or the Court of Chancery, except as stated above, it treated both as existing tribunals, for it alluded to the chancellor and the justices of the Supreme Court, regulated their terms of office and conferred upon them the power of appointing clerks for their respective courts. They thus explicitly recognized them as continuing in power under the state government as they had previously existed under the colonial government. (Id. Sections 33-37, 41.)

The second Constitution contained similar provisions, as to what constituted the law of the state, except that it omitted "the statute law of England and Great Britain," and abrogated such parts of both common and statute law "as are repugnant to this Constitution." (Const. of 1821, art. 5, Sections 1 to 7; art. 7, section 13.)

The third Constitution abolished the Court of Chancery and enacted that there should "be a Supreme Court having general jurisdiction in law and equity." (Const. of 1846, art. 6, and section 8 of art. 14.) It repeated the provisions as to what should be the law of the state. (Id. art. 1, section 17.)

The Revised Constitution now in force continues the Supreme Court "with general jurisdiction in law and equity," and provides that "such parts of the common law, and of the acts of the legislature of the Colony of New York, as together did form the law of the said colony, on the nineteenth day of April, one thousand seven hundred and seventy-five, and the resolutions of the Congress of the said Colony, and of the convention of the state of New York, in force on the twentieth day of April, one thousand seven hundred and seventy-seven, which have not since expired, or been repealed or altered; and such acts of the legislature of this state as are now in force, shall be and continue the law of this state, subject to such alterations as the legislature shall make concerning the same." (Art. 1, section 16; art. 6, section 1; Koch v Mayor, etc., 152 NY 72, 76; Matter of Knowack, 158 NY 482, 487.)

It is provided by section 217 of the Code of Civil Procedure that "the general jurisdiction in law and equity, which the Supreme Court of the State possesses, under the provisions of the Constitution, includes all the jurisdiction, which was possessed and exercised by the Supreme Court of the Colony of New York, at any time, and by the Court of Chancery in England, on the 4th day of July, 1776; with the exceptions, additions, and limitations, created and imposed by the Constitution and laws of the state. Subject to those exceptions and limitations, the Supreme Court of the state has all the powers and authority of each of those courts, and exercises the same in like manner." See, also, 1 R.S. 173, Section 36; Id. 196, Sec. 1; L. 1847, ch. 280, Sec. 16.) Thus we have the powers of the Court of King's Bench and the Court of Chancery as they existed when the first Constitution was adopted, blended and continued in the Supreme Court of the state, except as modified by Constitution or statute.

The right of a corporator, who has an interest in common with the other corporators, to inspect the books and papers of the corporation, for a proper purpose and under reasonable circumstances, was recognized by the Courts of King's Bench and Chancery from an early day, and enforced by motion or mandamus, but always with caution so as to prevent abuse. (Cases.) Lord Kenyon, in rendering judgment in The King v Babb (3 D. & E. 579, 580) assumed "that in certain cases the members of a corporation may be permitted to inspect all papers relating to the corporation." In Gery v Hopkins 7 Mod. 129, Case 175) the court, on granting the order to produce, said, "There is great reason for it, for they are books in a public company and kept for public transactions, in which the public are concerned, and the books are the title of buyers of stock by act of Parliament." In Rex v Fraternity of Hostmen, (2 Str. 1223 and note) the reporter states that the court said: "Every member of the corporation had, as such, a right to look into the books for any matter that concerned himself, though it was in a dispute with others."

The following cases arose in this state, but the most of them are not strictly in point, as they rest mainly upon statutory authority, which does not extend to the case in hand. (Cases.)

The courts of other states compel the officers of corporations to allow stockholders to examine the books upon due application for a proper purpose,...

The elementary works unite in holding that a corporator has the right in question, and that mandamus is a proper remedy....

We think that, according to the decided weight of authority a stockholder has the right at common law to inspect the books of his corporation at a proper time and place, and for a proper purpose, and that if this right is refused by the officers in charge a writ of mandamus may issue, in the sound discretion of the court, with suitable safeguards to protect the interests of all concerned. It should not be issued to aid a blackmailer, nor withheld simply because the interest of the stockholder is small, but the court should proceed cautiously and discreetly, according to the facts of the particular case. To the extent, however, that an absolute right is conferred by statute, nothing is left to the discretion of the court, but the writ should issue as a matter of course, although even then, doubtless, due precautions may be taken as to time and place so as to prevent interruption of business, or other serious inconvenience.

The appellants, however, insist that certain statutory provisions relating to the subject are exclusive, and as they do not extend to the case under consideration, that the Appellate Division had no right to grant the writ. The history of legislation upon the subject in brief is as follows: By the General Manufacturing Act of 1848 it was made the duty of the trustees of corporations organized under it to deep a transfer book which was required to "be opened for the inspection of stockholders and creditors of the company," substantially every business day at the office of the corporation. (L. 1848, ch. 40, Sec. 25.) This section was subsequently amended so as to require the treasurer to make a statement of the affairs of the company upon the request of persons owning a specified percentage of the capital stock. (L. 1848, ch. 201, Sec. 1; L. 1862, ch. 472, Sec. 1.)

The Business Corporations Law of 1875 required the directors of corporations organized thereunder "to cause to be kept at its principal office or place of business, correct books of account of all its business and transactions, and every stockholder in such corporation shall have the right at all reasonable times by himself or his attorney to examine the records and books of accounts of such corporation." (L. 1875, ch. 611, Sec. 16.) These statutes were all repealed in 1892 by the General Corporation Law. (L. 1892, ch. 687, pp. 1816-1819.) During the same year the Stock Corporation Law was passed, which provides that every stock corporation shall keep a stock book, which "shall be open daily, during business hours, for the inspection of its stockholders and judgment creditors, who may make extracts therefrom." (L. 1892, ch. 688, Sec. 29.) It also requires the treasurer, upon the request of stockholders owning a fixed percentage of the capital stock, to furnish a statement of all its assets and liabilities. (Id. Sec. 52.)

We do not think that the statute now in force is exclusive, or that it has abridged the common-law right of stockholders with reference to the examination of corporate books. By enabling a stockholder to get some information in a new way, it did not impliedly repeal the common-law rule which enabled him to get other information in another way, for the courts do not hold the common law to be repealed by implication, unless the intention is obvious. By simply providing an additional remedy the existing remedy was not taken away.

The statute merely strengthened the common-law rule with reference to one part thereof, and left the remainder unaffected. It dealt with but a single book, and as to that it amplified the qualified right previously existing, by making it absolute and extending it to judgment creditors. The stock book has no relation to the business carried on by a corporation, and the change was doubtless made to enable stockholders to promptly learn who are entitled to vote for directors, and judgment creditors to learn who are liable as stockholders for a failure to comply with the provisions of the act. The statute is silent as to the other books, and provides no system of inspection as a substitute for the right of examination at common law. The provision for a report from the treasurer was not designed to take away an old right, but to give a new one, not as a substitute but as an addition.

We think that the common-law right of a stockholder with reference to the inspection of the books of his corporation still exests, unimpaired by legislation; that the Supreme Court has power, in its sound discretion, upon good cause shown, to enforce the right, and that such power is a part of its general jurisdiction as the successor of the courts of the colony of New York, which had the jurisdiction of the Court of King's Bench and the Court of Chancery in England.

It follows that the order appealed from should be affirmed, with costs, and that the question certified should be answered in the affirmative.

Order affirmed.

MATTER OF MALLOY (1938) 278 NY 429, a253 AD 30

APPEAL from a judgment, entered January 6, 1938, upon an order of the Appellate Division of the Supreme Court in the third judicial department reversing, on the law and facts, a judgment in favor of appellant entered upon a decision of the court at a Trial Term, without a jury, and directing judgment, on new findings, in favor of respondent. On or about December 24, 1936, the appellant herein, as executor of Joseph J. Malloy, deceased, instituted a proceeding in the Schenectady County Surrogate's Court for a construction of a paragraph of the will of the decedent and for a determination approving and confirming a written contract or agreement entered into between the residuary legatees under the will and the appellant as such executor.

On the return date of a citation issued in such proceeding, the respondent herein, being one of the parties to said contract, filed an answer denying its validity and objecting to its approval by the Surrogate, to which answer the appellant filed a reply. Thereafter, upon the issues so raised by the pleadings, a stipulation was entered into between the parties framing such issues and providing that the same be tried before a jury at a stated Trial Term of the Supreme Court. Upon such stipulation an order was made by the Surrogate directing that the issues as therein stated be tried before the court and a jury at a Trial Term of the Supreme Court in the county of Schenectady which began on January 12, 1937.

The issues were not so tried as provided in such order but were tried on May 22, 1937, before a justice of the Supreme Court without a jury at the chambers of said justice in the city of Saratoga Springs pursuant to an oral stipulation of the parties. Following such trial, upon a decision of the trial justice, judgment was directed in favor of appellant.

The contract or agreement involved herein stated in substnace that decedent had executed, prior to his death, numerous deeds of real property owned by him which deeds had not been delivered to the grantees named therein but had been found by the executor in a safe deposit box of the decedent; that the property mentioned in the deeds constituted a part of the residuary estate of the decedent and that the parties to the contract desired that the wishes of the decedent in respect of such deeds should be carried out. It then authorized the appellant as such executor to deliver the deeds to the grantees named therein on certain conditions not here material and further provided that the said contract should not be in force until confirmed by the Surrogate.

The judgment in favor of the appellant entered upon the decision of the trial court determined that the decedent had, prior to his death, "delivered the title of the premises" described in the deeds, and that the grantees named therein had legal title to such premises; that the said contract or agreement was valid; that there was no legal reason why the same should not be confirmed but that, as the deeds had been delivered by the decedent, it was not necessary that the agreement should be confirmed.

In reversing such judgment, the Appellate Division found that there had been "no legal delivery of the title of the premises" described in the deeds and that such title was in the decedent at his death and became a part of his estate; that the contract or agreement was voidable for lack of consideration; that when respondent executed the same she was not fully informed of her rights thereunder and had signed the agreement by reason of material misrepresentations and because all the facts relative thereto were not disclosed to her before execution; and that she had received no benefit but had suffered a detriment by the execution of the contract. The portions of the judgment of the trial court and of the Appellate Division construing a paragraph of the will disposing of the residuary estate of the testator were not questioned on the appeal herein.

PER CURIAM. While we do not feel that the executor was guilty of any intentional wrong, we are in accord with the conclusion reached by the Appellate Division in this case and would be content to affirm without opinion were it not for the fact that a question has been raised as to the jurisdiction of the Supreme Court to grant the judgment which was granted.

The Supreme Court is a court of general jurisdiction. It may take the account of a trustee, probate a will, and exercise jurisdiction in many other matters where the Surrogate's Court also has jurisdiction. The Legislature cannot by statute deprive it of one particle of its jurisdiction, derived from the Constitution (Art. VI), although it may grant concurrent jurisdiction to some other court, as it has done to the Surrogate's Court.

When the parties appeared in the Supreme Court they stipulated or acquiesced in the proceedings which took place in that court and they became bound by the judgment entered. The fact that other proceedings had taken place in the Surrogate's Court and that the matter had been referred to the Supreme Court does not result in making everything done in the Supreme Court void and of no effect.

The parties, being of full age, could enter into a stipulation or bind themselves by acquiescence. They could waive a jury trial, consent to try the case at chambers, or in some other county. All those things they did. They also submitted proposed findings of fact and the attorney for the appellant here prepared the judgment and entered it. He also appeared and argued the case in the Appellate Division and never raised the question of jurisdiction. "Parties by their stipulations may in many ways make the law for any legal proceeding to which they are parties, which not only binds them, but which the courts are bound to enforce. They may stipulate away statutory, and even constitutional rights." (Matter of N.Y., L. & W.R.R.Co., 98 NY 448, 453.)

In Barone v Aetna Life Ins. Co. (260 NY 410) Chief Judge Pound wrote: "Giving additional jurisdiction to other tribunals does not take general jurisdiction away from the Supreme Court" (p. 414). In that case it was contended that the Industrial Board had exclusive jurisdiction to reform a workmen's compensation policy; therefore, that an action to reform the policy could not be maintained in the Supreme Court as it did not have jurisdiction. In that case it was also said: "To raise the point that the Board had first obtained jurisdiction, it should have pleaded another proceeding pending. This it failed to do and thus it waived the only point which was open to it to make" (p. 414). In the case at bar no one raised the question that there was a proceeding pending in the Surrogate's Court which prevented the Supreme Court from exercising its general jurisdiction.

From all that was done it appears just the same as though the parties had personally appeared in the Supreme Court and asked the court to proceed as it did. Such a proceeding would be informal and irregular and not to be approved. Nevertheless a judgment entered under such circumstances is binding.

The case of Robinson v Oceanic Steam Navigation Co. (112 NY 315) is not in point. The court was there dealing with the statute regulating actions against foreign corporations. In respect of such actions the Supreme Court has only such power as is conferred by statute. (See Ladenburg v Commercial Bank, 87 Hun(NY)269; Barker v Cunard S.S.Co., 91 Hun(NY)495.

Judgment affirmed.

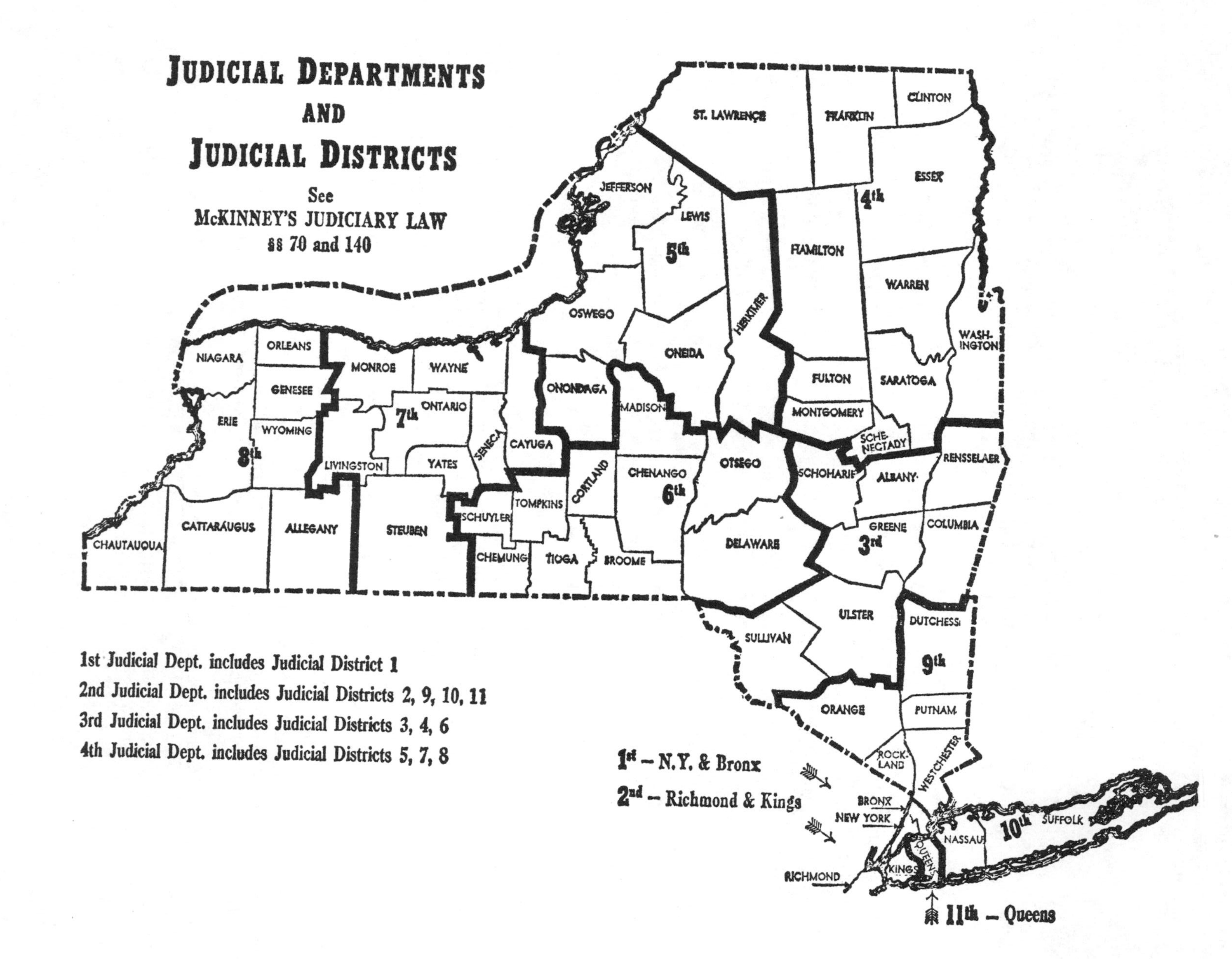
JUDICIAL DEPARTMENTS
AND
JUDICIAL DISTRICTS
See
McKINNEY'S JUDICIARY LAW
§§ 70 and 140
1st Judicial Dept. includes Judicial District 1
2nd Judicial Dept. includes Judicial Districts 2, 9, 10, 11
3rd Judicial Dept. includes Judicial Districts 3, 4, 6
4th Judicial Dept. includes Judicial Districts 5, 7, 8
1st – N.Y. & Bronx
2nd – Richmond & Kings
11th – Queens
ST. LAWRENCE
FRANKLIN
CLINTON
ESSEX
4th
JEFFERSON
LEWIS
5th
HAMILTON
WARREN
OSWEGO
ONEIDA
HERKIMER
WASH-INGTON
NIAGARA
ORLEANS
MONROE
WAYNE
FULTON
SARATOGA
GENESEE
ONONDAGA
MADISON
MONTGOMERY
ERIE
WYOMING
7th
ONTARIO
SENECA
CAYUGA
SCHE-NECTADY
8th
LIVINGSTON
YATES
CORTLAND
CHENANGO
6th
OTSEGO
SCHOHARIE
ALBANY
RENSSELAER
TOMPKINS
SCHUYLER
GREENE
3rd
COLUMBIA
CHAUTAUQUA
CATTARAUGUS
ALLEGANY
STEUBEN
DELAWARE
CHEMUNG
TIOGA
BROOME
ULSTER
DUTCHESS
SULLIVAN
9th
ORANGE
PUTNAM
ROCK-LAND
WESTCHESTER
BRONX
NEW YORK
10th
SUFFOLK
NASSAU
QUEENS
KINGS
RICHMOND

The Eleven Federal Judicial Circuits

See 28 U.S.C.A. § 41

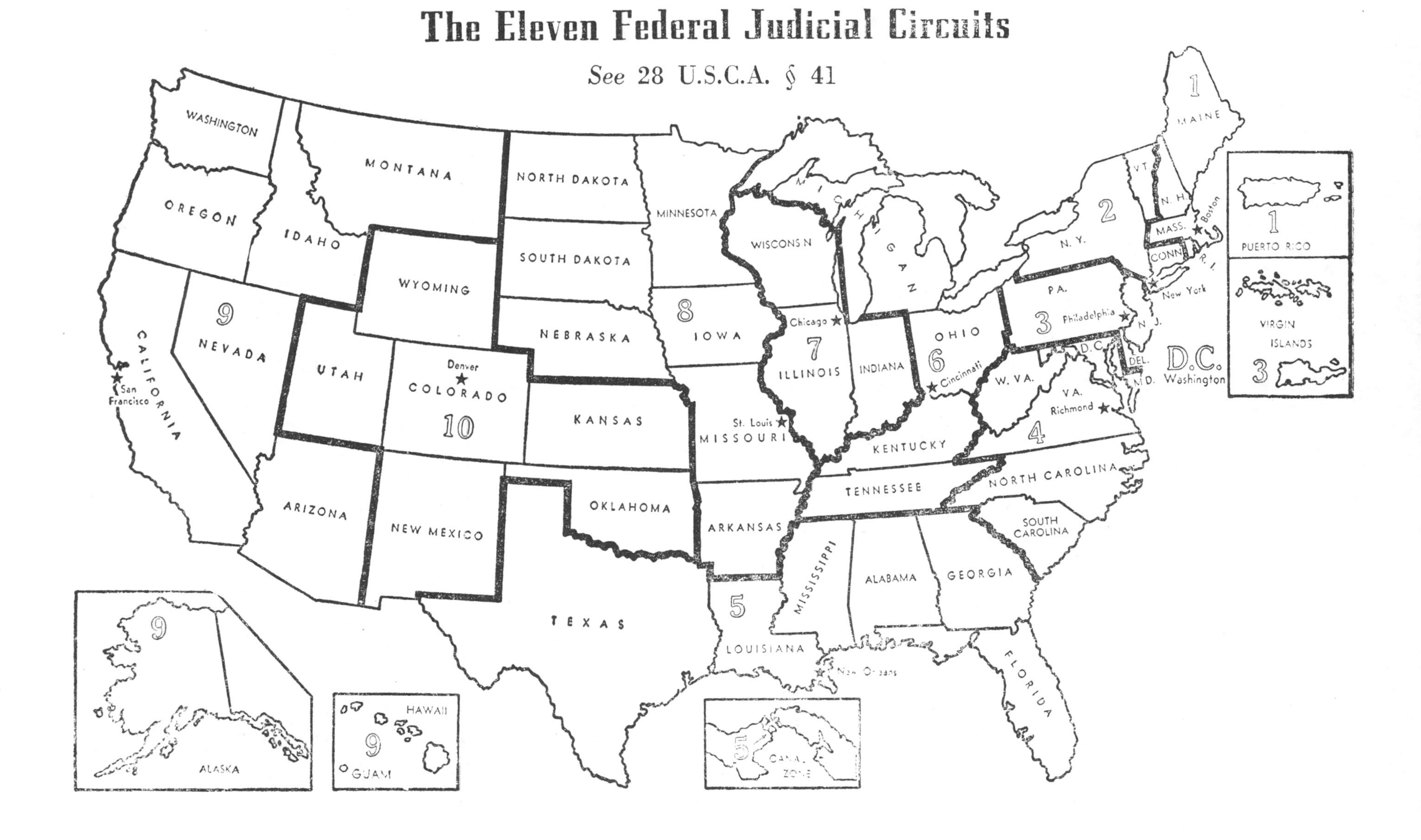

Reproduced with permission of West Publishing Company

Sec. 5.3 The Federal Judicial System

O'DONOGHUE v UNITED STATES) (1933) 289 US 516, 77 LEd 1356
HITZ v UNITED STATES)

Mr. Justice SUTHERLAND: These cases are here on certificates from the Court of Claims. They involve the same questions, were argued together at the bar, and may well be disposed of by the same opinion.

Daniel W. O'Donoghue is an associate justice of the Supreme Court of the District of Columbia, having been duly appointed to that position by the President, by and with the advice and consent of the Senate. He duly qualified as such justice on February 29, 1932, and has ever since been engaged in the performance of the duties of the office. At the time of his appointment and entry upon his duties, his salary was fixed by act of Congress (December 11, 1927), chap. 6, 44 Stat. at L.919) at the rate of $10,000 per year, which was paid to him until June 30, 1932.

William Hitz is an associate justice of the Court of Appeals of the District of Columbia, having been appointed on December 5, 1930, by the President, and later confirmed by the Senate. On February 13, 1931, he duly qualified as such associate justice and has ever since been engaged in performing the duties of his office. By the act of Congress already referred to, his salary was fixed at the rate of $12,500 per year. This amount he received until June 30, 1932.

By the Legislative Appropriation Act of June 30, 1932,....the disbursing officer of the Department of Justice, pursuant to the ruling of the Comptroller General, reduced the annual compensation by 10 per cent, in the case of Justice O'Donoghue, and by 20 per cent in the case of Justice Hitz, and over their protest paid to them for the months of July to December 1932, inclusive their compensation at this reduced rate.

On January 19, 1933, suits were brought in the Court of Claims to recover the amount of the deductions which had been made and enforced up to that time....

Upon this state of the record the Court of Claims certified the following questions upon which it desires instructions, under Sec. 3 (a) of the Act of February 13, 1925, chap. 229, 43 Stat. at L. 936, 939:

"I. Does Sec. 1, Article 3 of the Constitution of the United States apply to the Supreme Court (and to the Court of Appeals) of the District of Columbia and forbid a reduction of the compensation of the Justices thereof during their continuance in office?"

"II. Can the compensation of a Justice of the Supreme Court (or of the Court of Appeals) of the District of Columbia be lawfully diminished during his continuance in office?"....

The questions propounded by the court below, find no answer in any conclusive adjudication of this court; and it will materially assist us in arriving at a correct determination if we shall first consider the great underlying purpose which the framers of the Constitution had in mind and which led them to incorporate in that instrument the provision in respect of the permanent tenure of office and the undiminishable character of the compensation of the judges.

The Constitution, in distributing the powers of government, creates three distinct and separate departments—the legislative, the executive, and the judicial. This separation is not merely a matter of convenience or of governmental mechanism. Its object is basic and vital, Springer v Philippine Islands, 277 US 189, 201, 72 LEd 845, 849, 48 SCt. 480, namely, to preclude a commingling of these essentially different powers of government in the same hands. And this object is none the less apparent and controlling because there is to be found in the Constitution an occasional specific provision conferring upon a given department certain functions, which, by their nature, would otherwise fall within the general scope of the powers of another. Such exceptions serve rather to emphasize the generally involate character of the plan.

If it be important thus to separate the several departments of government and restrict them to the exercise of their appointed powers, it follows, as a logical corollary, equally important, that each department should be kept completely independent of the other—independent not in the sense that they shall not cooperate to the common end of carrying into effect the purposes of the Constitution, but in the sense that the acts of each shall never be controlled by or subjected, directly or indirectly, to, the coercive influence of either of the other departments. James Wilson, one of the framers of the Constitution and a justice of this court, in one of his law lectures said that the independence of each department required that its proceedings "Should be free from the remotest influence, direct or indirect, of either of the other two powers." 1 Andrews, Works of James Wilson (1896) p. 367....

The anxiety of the framers of the Constitution to preserve the independence especially of the judicial department is manifested by the provision now under review, forbidding the diminution of the compensation of the judges of courts exercising the judicial power of the United States. This requirement was foreshadowed, and its vital character attested, by the Declaration of Independence, which, among the injuries and usurpations recited against the King of Great Britain, declared that he had "made judges dependent on his will alone, for the tenure of their offices, and the amount and payment of their salaries."

In framing the Constitution, therefore, the power to diminish the compensation of the federal judges was explicity denied, in order, inter alia, that their judgment or action might never be swayed in the slightest degree by the temptation to cultivate the favor or avoid the displeasure of that department which, as master of the purse, would otherwise hold the power to reduce their means of support. The high importance of the provision, as the contemporary history shows, was definitely pointed out by the leading statesmen of the time. Thus, in The Federalist, No. 78, Hamilton said—"The complete independence of the courts of justice is peculiarly essential in a limited Constitution." And, in No. 79 —"Next to permanency in office, nothing can contribute more to the independence of the judges than a fixed provision for their support. . . .In the general course of human nature, a power over a man's subsistence amounts to a power over his will." (The italics are in the original.)....

The judges of the Supreme Court and of the Court of Appeals of the District of Columbia are of equal rank and power with those of other inferior courts of the federal system, and plainly within the spirit and reason of the compensation provision; and also within its intent, unless there be something in the Constitution, or in the character or organization of the District, or its relations to the general government, or in the character of the courts themselves which precludes that conclusion. Indeed, the reasons which have been set forth, and which impelled the adoption of the constitutional limitations, apply with even greater force to the courts of the District than to the inferior courts of the United States located elsewhere, because the judges of the former courts are in closer contact with, and more immediately open to the influences of the legislative department, and exercise a more extensive jurisdiction in cases affecting the operations of the general government and its various departments.

This court has repeatedly held that the territorial courts are "legislative" courts, created in virtue of the national sovereignty or under Art. 4, Sec. 3, cl. 2, of the Constitution, vesting in Congress the power "to dispose of and make all needful rules and regulations respecting the territory or other property belonging to the United States;" and that they are not invested with any part of the judicial power defined in the third article of the Constitution. And this rule, as it affects the territories, is no longer open to question. Do the courts of the District of Columbia occupy a like situation in virtue of the plenary power of Congress, under Art. 1 Sec. 8, cl. 17, "To exercise exclusive legislation in all cases whatsoever, over such district (not exceeding ten miles square) as may, by cession of particular States, and the acceptance of Congress, become the seat of the government of the United States?. . ." This inquiry requires a consideration, first, of the reasons upon which rest the decisions in respect of the territorial courts.

The authority upon which all the later cases rest is American Inst. Co. v 356 Bales of Cotton, 1 Pet. 511, 546, 7 LEd 243, 256, where the opinion was delivered by Chief Justice Marshall. The pertinent question there was whether the judicial power of the United States described in Art. 3 of the Constitution vested in the superior courts of the Territory of Florida; and it was answered in the negative. "The Judges of the Superior Courts of Florida," the court said, "hold their offices for four years. These Courts, then, are not constitutional Courts in which the judicial power conferred by the Constitution on the general government, can be deposited. They are incapable of receiving it. They are legislative Courts, created in virtue of the general right of sovereignty which exists in the government, or in virtue of that clause which enables Congress to make all needful rules and regulations, respecting the territory belonging to the United States. The jurisdiction with which they are invested, is not a part of that judicial power which is defined in the 3d article of the Constitution, but is conferred by Congress, in the execution of those general powers which that body possesses over the territories of the United States."....

A sufficient foundation for these decisions in respect of the territorial courts is to be found in the transitory character of the territorial governments....

How different are the status and characteristics of the District of Columbia! The pertinent clause of the Constitution (Art. 1, Sec. 8, cl. 17) confers the power on Congress to "exercise exclusive legislation. . .over such district. . .as may. . .become the seat of the government of the United States." These are words of permanent governmental power. The District, as the seat of the national government, is as lasting as the states from which it was carved or the union whose permanent capital it became....

The fact that Congress, under another and plenary grant of power, has conferred upon these courts jurisdiction over non-federal causes of action, or over quasi-judicial or administrative matters, does not affect the question. In dealing with the District, Congress possesses the powers which belong to it in respect of territory within a state, and also the powers of a state. Keller v Potomac Electric Power Co. 261 US 428, 442, 443, 67 LEd 731, 736, 43 SCt 445. "In other words," this court there said, "it possesses a dual authority over the District and may clothe the courts of the District not only with the jurisdiction and powers of federal courts in the several States but with such authority as a State may confer on her courts....

The government relies almost entirely upon the decision of this court in Ex Parte Bakelite Corp. 279 US 438, 73 LEd 789, 49 SCt 411. In that case we held that the Court of Customs Appeals was a legislative court, not a constitutional court under Art. 3 of the Constitution. In the course of the opinion attention was called to the decisions in respect of the territorial courts, and it was said that a like view had been taken in respect of the status and jurisdiction of the courts provided by Congress for the District of Columbia. This observation, made incidentally, by way of illustration merely and without discussion or elaboration, was not necessary to the decision, and it is not in harmony with the views expressed in the present opinion. "It is a maxim not to be disregarded," said Chief Justice Marshall in Cohen v Virginia, 6 Wheat. (US) 264, 399, 5 LEd 257, 290, "that general expressions, in every opinion, are to be taken in connection with the case in which those expressions are used. If they go beyond the case, they may be respected, but ought not to control the judgment in a subsequent suit when the very point is presented for decision. The reason of this maxim is obvious. The question actually before the Court is investigated with care, and considered in its full extent. Other principles which may serve to illustrate it, are considered in their relation to the case decided, but their possible bearing on all other cases is seldom completely investigated."....

We hold that the Supreme Court and the Court of Appeals of the District of Columbia are constitutional courts of the United States, ordained and established under Art. 3 of the Constitution; that the judges of these courts hold their offices during good behavior, and that their compensation cannot, under the Constitution, be diminished during their continuance in office.

In accordance with that view the questions propounded are answered.

Question No. 1, Yes.

Question No. 2, No.

The Chief Justice, HUGHES, Mr. Justice VAN DEVANTER, and Mr. Justice CARDOZO, dissenting:

We are of the opinion that the courts of the District of Columbia, as this court has repeatedly declared, are not courts established under Sec. 1 of Article 3 of the Constitution, but are established under the broad authority conferred upon the Congress for the government of the District of Columbia by p. 17 of Sec. 8 of Article 1. Hence, the limitations imposed by Sec. 1 of Article 3, with respect to tenure and compensation, are not applicable to judges of these courts.

ERIE R. CO. v TOMPKINS (1935) 304 US 64, 82 LEd 1188

On writ of Certiorari to the United States Circuit Court of Appeals for the Second Circuit to review a judgment affirming a judgment of the District Court of the United States for the Southern District of the New York in favor of plaintiff....

Mr. Justice Brandeis: The question for decision is whether the oft-challenged doctrine of Swift v Tyson shall not be disapproved.

Tompkins, a citizen of Pennsylvania, was injured on a dark night by a passing freight train of the Erie Railroad Company while walking along its right of way at Hughestown in that State. He claimed that the accident occurred through negligence in the operation, or maintenance of the train; that he was rightfully on the premises as licensee because on a commonly used beaten footpath which ran for a short distance alongside the tracks; and that he was struck by something which looked like a door projecting from one of the moving cars. To enforce that claim he brought an action in the federal court for southern New York, which had jurisdiction because the company is a corporation of that State. It denied liability; and the case was tried by a jury.

The Erie insisted that its duty to Tompkins was no greater than that owed to a trespasser. It contended, among other things, that its duty to Tompkins, and hence its liability, should be determined in accordance with the Pennsylvania law; that under the law of Pennsylvania, as declared by its highest court, persons who use pathways along the railroad right of way—that is a longitudinal pathway as distinguished from a crossing—are to be deemed trespassers; and that the railroad is not liable for injuries to undiscovered trespassers resulting from its negligence, unless it be wanton or wilful. Tompkins denied that any such rule had been established by the decisions of the Pennsylvania courts; and contended that, since there was no statute of the State on the subject, the railroad's duty and liability is to be determined in federal courts as a matter of general law.

The trial judge refused to rule that the applicable law precluded recovery. The jury brought in a verdict of $30,000; and the judgment entered thereon was affirmed by the Circuit Court of Appeals, which held (90 F2d 604) that it was unnecessary to consider whether the law of Pennsylvania was as contended, because the question was one not of local, but of general, law and that "upon questions of general law the federal courts are free, in absence of a local statute, to exercise their independent judgment as to what the law is; and it is well settled that the question of the responsibility of a railroad for injuries caused by its servants is one of general law.... Where the public has made open and notorious use of a railroad right of way for a long period of time and without objection, the company owes to persons on such permissive pathway a duty of care in the operation of its trains.... It is likewise generally recognized law that a jury may find that negligence exists toward a pedestrian using a permissive path on the railroad right of way if he is hit by some object projecting from the side of the train."

The Erie had contended that application of the Pennsylvania rule was required, among other things, by Sec. 34 of the Federal Judiciary Act of September 24, 1789 (Stat. at L. 73, 928, chap. 20, 28 USCA Sec. 725, which provides:

"The laws of the several States, except where the Constitution, treaties, or statutes of the United States otherwise require or provide, shall be regarded as rules of decision in trials at common law, in the courts of the United States, in cases where they apply."

Because of the importance of the question whether the federal court was free to disregard the alleged rule of the Pennsylvania common law, we granted certiorari. (302 US 671, ante, 518, 58 SCt50.)

First. Swift v Tyson (16 Pet. 1,18, 10 LEd 865, 871), held that federal courts exercising jurisdiction on the ground of diversity of citizenship need not, in matters of general jurisprudence, apply the unwritten law of the State as declared by its highest court; that they are free to exercise an independent judgment as to what the common law of the State is—or should be; and that, as there stated by Mr. Justice Story: "The true interpretation of the thirty-fourth section limited its application to State laws strictly local, that is to say, to the positive statutes of the state, and the construction thereof adopted by the local tribunals, and to rights and titles to things having a permanent locality, such as the rights and titles to real estate, and other matters immovable and intraterritorial in their nature and character. It never has been supposed by us, that the section ded a
us, that the section did apply, or was designed to apply, to questions of a more general nature, not at all dependent upon local statutes or local usages of a fixed and permanent operation, as, for example, to the construction of ordinary contracts or other written instruments, and especially to questions of general commercial law, where the State tribunals are called upon to perform the like functions as ourselves, that is, to ascertain upon general reasoning and legal analogies, what is the true exposition of the contract or instrument, or what is the just rule furnished by the principles of commercial law to govern the case."

The Court in applying the rule of Sec. 34 to equity cases, in Mason v United States (260 US 545, 559, 67 LEd 396, 401, 43 SCt200), said: "The statute, however, is merely declarative of the rule which would exist in the absence of the statute." The federal courts assumed, in the broad field of "general law," the power to declare rules of decision which Congress was confessedly without power to enact as statutes. Doubt was repeatedly expressed as to the correctness of the construction given Sec. 34, and as to the soundness of the rule which it introduced. But it was the more recent research of a competent scholar, who examined the original document, which established that the construction given to it by the Court was erroneous; and that the purpose of the section was merely to make certain that, in all matters except those in which some federal law is controlling, the federal courts exercising jurisdiction in diversity of citizenship cases would apply as their rules of decision the law of the State, unwritten as well as written.

Criticism of the doctrine became widespread after the decision of Black & W. Taxicab & Transfer Co. v Brown & Y. Taxicab & Transfer Co. (276 US 518,72 LEd 681, 48 SCt 404, 57 ALR 426). There, Brown and Yellow, a Kentucky corporation owned by Kentuckians, and the Louisville and Nashville Railroad, also a Kentucky corporation, wished that the former should have the exclusive privilege of soliciting passenger and baggage transportation at the Bowling Green, Kentucky, railroad station; and that the Black and White, a competing Kentucky corporation, should be prevented from interfering with that privilege. Knowing that such a contract would be void under the common law of Kentucky, it was arranged that the Brown and Yellow reincorporate under the law of Tennessee, and that the contract with the railroad should be executed there. The suit was then brought by the Tennessee corporation in the federal court for western Kentucky to enjoin competition by the Black and White; an injunction issued by the district court was sustained by the Court of Appeals; and this Court, citing many decisions in which the doctrine of Swift v Tyson had been applied, affirmed the decree.

Second. Experience in applying the doctrine of Swift v Tyson had revealed its defects, political and social; and the benefits expected to flow from the rule did not accrue. Persistence of state courts in their own opinions on questions of common law prevented uniformity; and the impossibility of discovering a satisfactory line of demarcation between the province of general law and that of local law developed a new well of uncertainties.

On the other hand, the mischievous results of the doctrine had become apparent. Diversity of citizenship jurisdiction was conferred in order to prevent apprehended discrimination in state courts against those not citizens of the State. Swift v Tyson introduced grave discrimination by non-citizen against citizens. It made rights enjoyed under the unwritten "general law" vary according to whether enforcement was sought in the state or in the federal court; and the privilege of selecting the court in which the right should be determined was conferred upon the non-citizen. Thus, the doctrine rendered impossible equal protection of the law. In attempting to promote uniformity of law throughout the United States, the doctrine had prevented uniformity in the administration of the law of the State.

The discrimination resulting became in practice farreaching. This resulted in part from the broad province accorded to the so-called "general law" as to which federal courts exercised an independent judgment. In addition to questions of purely commercial law, "general law" was held to include the obligations under contracts entered into and to be performed within the State, the extent to which a carrier operating within a State may stipulate for exemption from liability for his own negligence or that of his employee; the liability for torts committed within the State upon persons resident or property located there, even where the question of liability depended upon the scope of a property right conferred by the State; and the right to exemplary or punitive damages. Furthermore, state decisions construing local deeds, mineral conveyances, and even devises of real estate were disregarded.

In part the discrimination resulted from the wide range of persons held entitled to avail themselves of the federal rule by resort to the diversity of citizenship jurisdiction. Through this jurisdiction individual citizens willing to remove from their own State and become citizens of another might avail themselves of the federal rule. And, without even change of residence, a corporate citizen of the State could avail itself of the federal rule by re-incorporating under the laws of another state, as was done in the Taxicab Case.

The injustice and confusion incident to the doctrine of Swift v Tyson have been repeatedly urged as reasons for abolishing or limiting diversity of citizenship jurisdiction. Other legislative relief has been proposed. If only a question of statutory construction were involved, we should not be prepared to abandon a doctrine so widely applied throughout nearly a century. But the unconstitutionality of the course pursued has now been made clear and compels us to do so.

Third. Except in matters governed by the Federal Constitution or by Acts of Congress, the law to be applied in any case is the law of the State. And whether the law of the State shall be declared by its Legislature in a statute or by its highest court in a decision is not a matter of federal concern. There is no federal general common law. Congress has no power to declare substantive rules of common law applicable in a State whether they be local in their nature or "general," be they commercial law or a part of the law of torts. And no clause in the Constitution purports to confer such a power upon the federal courts.

As stated by Mr. Justice Field when protesting in Baltimore & O.R. Co. v Baugh (149 US 268, 401, 37 LEd 772, 786, 13 SCt 914), against ignoring the Ohio common law of fellow servant liability: "I am aware that what has been termed the general law of the country—which is often little less than what the judge advancing the doctrine thinks at the time should be the general law on a particular subject—has been often advanced in judicial opinions of this court to control a conflicting law of a state. I admit that learned judges have fallen into the habit of repeating this doctrine as a convenient mode of brushing aside the law of a State in conflict with their views. And I confess that, moved and governed by the authority of the great names of those judges, I have, myself, in many instances, unhesitatingly and confidently, but I think now erroneously, repeated the same doctrine. But, notwithstanding the great names which may be cited in favor of the doctrine and notwithstanding the frequency with which the doctrine has been reiterated, there stands, as a perpetual protest against its repetition, the Constitution of the United States, which recognizes and preserves the autonomy and independence of the States—independence in their legislative and independence in their judicial departments. Supervision over either the legislative or the judicial action of the States is in no case permissable except as to matters by the Constitution specially authorized or delegated to the United States. Any interference with either, except as thus permitted is an invasion of the authority of the State, and, to that extent, a denial of its independence."

The fallacy underlying the rule declared in Swift v Tyson is made clear by Mr. Justice Holmes. The doctrine rests upon the assumption that there is "a transcendental body of law outside of any particular State but obligatory within it unless and until changed by statute," that federal courts have the power to use their judgment as to what the rules of common law are; and that in the federal courts "the parties are entitled to an independent judgment on matters of general law: "but law in the sense in which courts speak of it today does not exist without some definite authority behind it. The common law so far as it is enforced in a State, whether called common law or not, is not the common law generally but the law of that State existing by the authority of that State without regard to what it may have been in England or anywhere else. . . . "the authority and only authority is the state, and if that be so, the voice adopted by the State as its own (whether it be of its Legislature or of its Supreme Court) should utter the last word."

Thus the doctrine of Swift v Tyson, is, as Mr. Justice Holmes said, "an unconstitutional assumption of powers by courts of the United States which no lapse of time or respectable array of opinion should make us hesitate to correct." In disapproving that doctrine we do not hold unconstitutional Sec. 34 of the Federal Judiciary Act of 1789, or any other Act of Congress. We merely declare that in applying the doctrine this Court and the lower courts have invaded rights which in our opinion are reserved by the Constitution to the several States.

Fourth. The defendant contended that by the common law of Pennsylvania as declared by its highest court in Falchetti v Pennsylvania R. Co. 307 Pa. 203, 160 A 859, the only duty owed to the plaintiff was to refrain from wilful or wanton injury. The plaintiff denied that such is the Pennsylvania law. In support of their respective contentions the parties discussed and cited many decisions of the Supreme Court of the State. The Circuit Court of Appeals ruled that the question of liability is one of general law; and on that ground declined to decide the issue of state law. As we hold this was error, the judgment is reversed and the case remanded to it for further proceedings in conformity with our opinion.

Reversed.

UNITED STATES v STANDARD OIL CO. (1947) 332 US 301, 91 LEd 2067

On writ of Certiorari to the United States Circuit Court of Appeals for the Ninth Circuit to review a judgment reversing a judgment of the District Court of the United States for the Southern District of California, Central Division, in favor of the United States....

Mr. Justice RUTLEDGE delivered the opinion of the Court.

Not often, since the decision in Erie R. Co. v Tompkins (304 US 64, 82 LEd 1188, 58 SCt 817, 114 ALR 1487), is this Court asked to create a new substantive legal liability without legislative aid and as at the common law. This case of first impression here seeks such a result. It arises from the following circumstances.

Early one morning in February, 1944, John Etzel, a soldier was hit and injured by a truck of the Standard Oil Company of California at a street intersection in Los Angeles. The vehicle was driven by Boone, an employee of the company. At the Government's expense of $123.45 Etzel was hospitalized, and his soldier's pay of $69.31 was continued during his disability. Upon the payment of $300 Etzel released the company and Boone "from any and all claims and demands which I now have or may hereafter have on account of or arising out of "the accident."

From these facts the novel question springs whether the Government is entitled to recover from the respondents as tort-feasors the amounts expended for hospitalization and soldier's pay, as for loss of Etzel's services. A jury being waived, the District Court made findings of fact and conclusions of law in the Government's favor upon all the issues, including those of negligence and contributory negligence. Judgment was rendered accordingly. (6 F Supp 807.) This the Circuit Court of Appeals reversed, (153 F2d 958), and we granted certiorari because of the novelty, and importance of the principal question. (329 US 696, ante, 608, 67 SCT 67).

As the case reaches us, a number of issues contested in the District Court and the Circuit Court of Appeals have been eliminated. Remainingis the basic question of respondents' liability for interference with the government-soldier relation and consequent loss to the United States, together with questions whether this issue is to be determined by federal or state law and concerning the effect of the release. In the view we take of the case it is not necessary to consider the questions relating to the release, for we have reached the conclusion that respondents are not liable for the injuries inflicted upon the Government.

We agree with the Government's view that the creation or negation of such a liability is not a matter to be determined by state law. The case in this aspect is governed by the rule of Clearfield Trust Co. v United States (318 US 363, 87 LEd, 838, 63 SCt 573), and National Metropolitan Bank v United States (323US 454, 89 LEd 383, 65 SCt 354), rather than that of Erie R. Co. v Tompkins (304 US 64, 82 LEd 1188, 58 SCt 817, 114 ALR 1487, supra). In the Clearfield case, involving liabilities arising out of a forged endorsement of a check issued by the United States, the Court said: "The authority to issue the check had its origin in the Constitution and the statutes of the United States and was in no way dependent on the laws of Pennsylvania or of any other state...The duties imposed upon the United States and the rights acquired by it as a result of the issuance find their roots in the same federal sources... In the absence of an applicable Act of Congress it is for the federal courts to fashion the governing rule of law according to their own standards."

Although the Clearfield case applied these principles to a situation involving contractual relations of the Government, they are equally applicable in the facts of this case where the relations affected are non-contractual or tortious in character.

Perhaps no relation between the Government and a citizen is more distinctively federal in character than that between it and members of its armed forces. To whatever extent state law may apply to govern the relations between soldiers or others in the armed forces and persons outside them or nonfederal governmental agencies, the scope, nature, legal incidents and consequences of the relation between persons in service and the Government are fundamentally derived from federal sources and governed by federal authority. (See Tarble's case (United States v Tarble) 13 Wall(US) 397, 20 LEd 597; Kurtz v Moffitt, 115 US 487, 29 LEd 458, 6 SCt 148.) So also we think are interferences with that relationship such as the facts of this case involve. For, as the Federal Government has the exclusive power to establish and define the relationship by virtue of its military and other powers, equally clearly it has power in execution of the same functions to protect the relation once formed from harms inflicted by others.

Since also the Government's purse is affected, as well as its power to protect the relationship, its fiscal powers, to the extent that they are available to protect it against financial injury, add their weight to the military basis for excluding state intrusion. Indeed, in this aspect the case is not greatly different from the Clearfield case or from one involving the Government's paramount power of control over its own property, both to prevent its unauthorized use or destruction and to secure indemnity for those injuries.

As in the Clearfield case moreover, quite apart from any positive action by Congress, the matter in issue is neither primarily one of state interest nor exclusively for determination by state law within the spirit and purpose of the Erie decision. The great object of the Erie case was to secure in the federal courts, in diversity cases, the application of the same substantive law as would control if the suit were brought in the courts of the state where the federal court sits. It was the so-called "federal common law" utilized as a substitute for state power, to create and enforce legal relationships in the area set apart in our scheme for state rather than for federal control that the Erie decision threw out. Its object and effect were thus to bring federal judicial power under subjection to state authority in matters essentially of local interest and state control.

Conversely there was no purpose or effect for broadening state power over matters essentially of federal character or for determining whether issues are of that nature. The diversity jurisdiction had not created special problems of that sort. Accordingly the Erie decision, which related only to the law to be applied in exercise of that jurisdiction, had no effect, and was intended to have none, to bring within the governance of state law matters exclusively federal, because made so by constitutional or valid congressional command, or others so vitally affecting interests, powers and relations of the Federal Government as to require uniform national disposition rather than diversified state rulings...

In this sense therefore there remains what may be termed, for want of a better label, an area of "federal common law" or perhaps more accurately "law of independent federal judicial decision," outside the constitutional realm, untouched by the Erie decision...

It is true, of course, that in many situations, and apart from any supposed influence of the Erie decision, rights, interests and legal relations of the United States are determined by application of state law, where Congress has not acted specifically... The Government, for instance, may place itself in a position where its rights necessarily are determinable by state law, as when it purchases real estate from one whose title is invalid by that law in relation to another's claim...

But we do not undertake to delimit or categorize the instances where it is properly to be applied outside the Erie aegis. It is enough for present purposes to point out that they exist, cover a variety of situations...

Whether or not, therefore, state law is to control in such a case as this is not at all a matter to be decided by application of the Erie rule. For, except where the Government has simply substituted itself for others as successor to rights governed by state law, the question is one of federal policy...

We would not deny the Government's basic premise of the law's capacity for growth, or that it must include the creative work of judges. Soon all law would become antiquated strait jacket and then dead letter, if that power were lacking. And the judicial hand would stiffen in mortmain if it had no part in the work of creation. But in the federal scheme our part in that work, and the part of the other federal courts, outside the constitutional area is more modest than that of state courts, particularly in the freedom to create new common-law liabilities....

Congress, not this Court or the other federal courts, is the custodian of the national purse. By the same token it is the primary and most often the exclusive arbiter of federal fiscal affairs. And these comprehend, as we have said, securing the treasury or the government against financial losses however inflicted, including requiring reimbursement for injuries creating them as well as filling the treasury itself....

When Congress has thought it necessary to take steps to prevent interference with federal funds, property or relations, it has taken positive action to that end. We think it would have done so here, if that had been its desire. This it still may do, if or when it so wishes....

Finally, if the common-law precedents relied on were more pertinent than they are to the total problem, particularly in view of its federal and especially its fiscal aspects, in none of the situations to which they apply was the question of liability or no liability within the power of one of the parties to the litigation to determine. In them the courts stood as arbiters between citizens, neither of whom could determine the outcome or the policy properly to be followed. Here the United States is the party plaintiff to the suit. And the United States has power at any time to create the liability. The only question is which organ of the Government is to make the determination that liability exists. That decision, for the reasons we have stated, is in this instance for the Congress, not for the courts. Until it acts to establish the liability, this Court and others should withhold creative touch.

The judgment is affirmed.

Mr. Justice JACKSON, dissenting...

As a matter of justice, I see no reason why taxpayers of the United States should relieve a wrongdoer of part of his normal liability for personal injury when the victim of negligence happens to be a soldier. And I cannot see why the principles of tort law that allow a husband or parent to recover do not logically sustain the right of the United States to recover in this case...

The courts of England, whose scruples against legislating are at least as sensitive as ours normally are, have not hesitated to say that His Majesty's Treasury may recover outlay to cure a British soldier from injury by a negligent wrongdoer and the wages he was meanwhile paid. Atty.-Gen. v Valle-Jones (1935) 2 KB (Eng) 209. I think we could hold as much without being suspected of trying to usurp legislative function.

JACOBSON v NEW YORK, N.H. & H. R. Co. (DCt Mass, 1953) 109 FSupp 513

ACTION to recover for death of passenger as result of injuries received when she was thrown from her seat onto the floor of a car in defendant's train.

FORD, District Judge. This is an action to recover for the death of plaintiff's decedent, alleged to have resulted from injuries received when she was thrown from her seat onto the floor of a car in defendant's train in which she was traveling as a passenger from Lake Worth, Florida, to Boston. Defendant moves to dismiss for lack of jurisdiction.

There is no diversity of citizenship, and the sole question is whether the allegations in the complaint of violation by the defendant of the Safety Appliances Acts, 45 USCA Sec. 1 et seq., make the cause of action one arising under the laws of the United States, 28 USCA Sec. 1331.

To make a case one arising under the laws of the United States, the right sought to be enforced should be a federal one. People of Puerto Rico v Russell & Co., 288 US 476, 483, 53 SCt 447, 77 LEd 903. It is not enough that in an action to enforce a right arising under state law or statute, a question of federal law is involved. Gully v First National Bank in Meridian, 299 US 109, 115, 57 SCt 96, 81 LEd 70.

The Safety Appliances Acts make violation of their prohibitations unlawful, and provide a penalty for such violations, but they nowhere confer any right of action for injuries or death caused by such violations. Urie v Thompson, 337 US 163, 188, 69 SCt 1018, 93 LEd 1282. While the Acts thus prescribe a duty, the right to recover for injuries suffered through a breach of such duty springs either from the common law or, in the case of a death action, from the applicable statute. Moore v Chesapeake & Ohio Railway Co., 291 US 205, 215, 54 SCt 402, 78 LEd 755. Thus, as the Moore case points out, an employee of a railroad suffering injury while employed in interstate commerce can rely on a violation of the Safety Appliances Act in an action in a federal court under the Federal Employers' Liability Act, 45 USCA Sec. 51 et seq. But it is the latter Acts, and not the Safety Appliances Acts which create the right of action and make the case one arising under the laws of the United States. Where the employee is injured in intrastate commerce the Employers' Liability Acts are no longer applicable, and while he may still rely on the breach of the duty imposed by the Safety Appleances Acts, his only right of action is that which is conferred by the applicable state statute or law. Gilvary v Cuyahoga Valley Railway Co. 292 US 57, 61, 54 SCt 573, 78 LEd 1123; Tipton v Atchison, Topeka & Santa Fe Railway Co., 9 Cir 78 F2d 450.

It is true that the Safety Appliances Acts were intended for the protection of passengers as well as employees of the railroads. Fairport, Painesville & Eastern Railroad Co. v Meredith, 292 US 589, 594, 54 SCt 826, 78 LEd 1446. But no federal statute confers any right of action for the death of a passenger resulting from a violation of the Acts. Any right of plaintiff to recover arises under the applicable death statute of the appropriate state (the state in which injuries causing the death were sustained is not stated in the complaint), and the fact that plaintiff may be entitled in an action brought under such a statute to rely on the violation of the duty imposed by the safety appliances Acts does not make this a case arising under the laws of the United States. Moore v Chesapeake & Ohio Railway Co., supra, 291 US at page 214, 54 SCt 402.

Defendant's motion to dismiss is allowed.

Sec. 5.4	THE WORLD JUDICIAL SYSTEM
Sec. 5.41	PRIVATE INTERNATIONAL LAW
Sec. 5.411	Regional Courts
Sec. 5.4111	The Privy Council of British Commonwealth of Nations
Sec. 5.4112	The Supreme Court of the United States
Sec. 5.4113	The Court of the European Communities
Sec. 5.4114	The European Court of Human Rights
Sec. 5.412	Private Organizations Promoting World Law
Sec. 5.4121	World Peace Through Law
Sec. 5.4122	International Commission of Jurists
Sec. 5.4123	
Sec. 5.42	PUBLIC INTERNATIONAL LAW
Sec. 5.421	The International Court of Justice (The World Court)
Sec. 5.422	The United Nations Organization (UNO)
Sec. 5.423	Hague Permanent Court of Arbitration
Sec. 5.424	Regional Authorities and Organizations
Sec. 5.4241	European Coal and Steel Community (ECSC)
Sec. 5.4242	European Economic Community (EEC)
Sec. 5.4243	European Atomic Energy Community (Euratom)
Sec. 5.4244	Organization of American States
Sec. 5.4245	North Atlantic Treaty Organization (NATO)
Sec. 5.4246	Warsaw Treaty Organization (WTO)
Sec. 5.4247	South East Asia Treaty Organization (SEATO)
Sec. 5.4248	Colombo Plan Council for Technical Cooperation in South and South-East Asia

CHAPTER VI

STARE DECISIS

OUTLINE OF CHAPTER VI

SUGGESTED READINGS:

Cornell Faculty: Introduction to the Study of Law
 Ch. VI, "The Judicial Process," pp 167-234
Dowling, P and P. Legal Method
 Ch. 3, "The Study of Law via the Study of Decisions," pp 113-238
Fryer and Benson: Legal Method and System
 Ch. 5, Sec. "Stare Decisis," pp 357-378
Gavit: Introduction to the Study of Law
 Ch. 5, Sections 68-92 (generally on Stare Decisis) pp 182-218
Hicks: Materials and Methods of Legal Research
 Ch. VI, "Case Law ..." pp 97-109
Kinnane, Anglo-American Law
 Ch. IV, Sec. 37 (b), "Judicial Decision," pp 71-85
Radin, Anglo-American Legal History
 Ch. 24, "The Rule of Precedents," pp 343-358
Read and MacDonald: Legislation
 Ch. 1, Sec. 2, "The Nature and Limitations of Judicial Law Making," pp 17-95
Smith: Elementary Law
 Ch. VII, Sec., "The Authority...of Judicial Decisions," pp 87-94
Spelling: Briefer and Law Finder
 Ch. II, "Characteristics of Decisions" pp 13-20

Sec. 6.1 Precedent Contrasted with Opinion

MOORE etal v CITY OF ALBANY (1885) 98 NY 396, a34 Hun 629

Appeal from a judgment of the General Term of the Supreme Court, third department, in favor of defendant, rendered on the submission of a controversy without process under section 1279 of the Code of Civil Procedure. . . .

EARL, J. The total assessment (for street improvement) upon the property of plaintiffs' testator was $2,164.62, in which was included $690.73, his proportionate share of the expense of extra filling above the required grade within the street lines, and the work done outside of street lines as above specified. The testator paid the assessment against his property under protest, and subsequently his executors commenced this action upon an agreed state of facts to recover back the money thus paid, as they claimed, under coercion, on the ground that the entire assessment was rendered void by the inclusion therein of the expenses of raising the grade, and of the work outside of the street lines on private property as above specified.

The learned brief submitted to us on behalf of the appellants has failed to convince us that the assessment assailed is invalid....

There is one fact to which the appellants attach much importance, which has not yet been noticed. After the assessment had been laid, Edward Clowry and another, whose lands had been assessed, commenced an action in the Supreme Court against the city, to vacate and remove the assessment as a cloud upon their title, and they recovered a judgment in February, 1881, which declared the assessment null and void for the same reasons now urged by these appellants, and vacated the same as to the lands of those plaintiffs. William Moore, the deceased testator, was not a party to that action, and yet his executors claim the benefit of that adjudication.

We know of no principle which will enable these appellants to claim the benefit of that judgment as res adjudicata in their favor. It is a general rule that estoppels by judgment must be mutual, that a party cannot claim the benefit of a judgment favorable to him unless he would be bound by a judgment in the same matter if adverse to him. If the judgment in that action had been adverse to the plaintiffs, then it certainly would not have bound William Moore, and he would still have been at liberty to assail the assessment and try all the questions relating thereto de novo upon their merits. A judgment as to all matters decided thereby, and as to all matters necessarily involved in the litigation leading thereto, binds and estops all the parties thereto, and their privies in all cases where the same matters are again brought in question. Such is the doctrine of res adjudicata.

There is also the doctrine of stare decisis, which is of a different nature. When a court has once laid down a principle of law as applicable to a certain state of facts, it will adhere to that principle and apply it to all future cases where the facts are substantially the same, and this it does for the stability and certainty of the law. It was the latter doctrine that was illustrated and enforced by the cases cited by the learned counsel for the appellants. In Chase v Chase (95 NY 373) we decided that an assessment which in another action had been held to be invalid, did not constitute such a defect in title to land as would justify a purchaser on account thereof to refuse to complete his purchase. We held so not because the purchaser was bound by the former adjudication to which he was not a party under the doctrine of res adjudicata, but because under the doctrine of stare decisis, the assessment which upon all the facts the court of last resort had held to be invalid, could not constitute a dangerous cloud upon title, as that court would adhere to its decision which would also be binding upon inferior courts whenever the same assessment again came in question.

So here, if these appellants, instead of invoking the support of a decision rendered at the Special Term of the Supreme Court, had cited a decision of this court condemning this assessment upon the same facts now produced they would have had a controlling authority in their favor. In the case of Bruecher v Village of Port Chester (31 Hun (NY) 550), the same doctrine was also appled. This court, in a prior case (71 NY 309), had held that the assessment there considered was void, and the Supreme Court in the case cited simply followed and applied the law thus laid down. If, therefore, the case of Clowery v The City was based upon the same facts existing here we think it was erroneously decided, and we do not feel called upon to yield to it as authority. Neither the doctrine of res adjudicata nor that of stare decisis applies.

It may be said, however, that subsequently to the rendition of that judgment, the act chapter

459 of the Laws of 1881, for the confirmation of this assessment, was passed, and thereafter the plaintiffs in that action paid fifty per cent of the assessment against them under the provisions of that act, and thus waived their objections to the assessment, and acquiesced in the occupancy of their lands by the embankments forming the slopes of the streets if such embankments were, as now claimed, upon their lands.

In holding this assessment to be valid we do not come in conflict with any authority in this court.

In People ex rel. Williams v Haines (49 NY 587), drainage commissioners appointed under an act of the legislature made drains through lands without obtaining the title to the lands taken, and made an assessment upon lands supposed to be benefited for the expense of the drains, and the assessment was held to be invalid because the drains were laid through the lands without first obtaining grants of the right to make them from the owners. We held that there was no power in the commissioners to construct the drains and assess the cost upon the property benefited without having first acquired the title to the lands used, and we further held that commissioners had no power subsequently to the assessment to acquire the title; and thus there was in that case no certainty that the benefit for which the assessment was imposed would be enjoyed.

In the Rhinelander case (68 NY 105) and the Cheesebrough case (78 id. 232), sewers were constructed through private property without the consent of the owners. In those cases there was no law under which the title to the lands used could be obtained and the assessments were assailed by the owners of the land wrongfully invaded.

The Ingraham case (64 NY 310) was much considered in this court; and there, where a sewer was constructed upon private property, we held that mere permission from the owners would be sufficient to authorize the construction of the sewer, and that because it did not appear that such permission was not given, or that the owners objected, the legal presumption was that permission was given; and that if no consent was given it was not a valid ground of objection that a trespass had been committed upon the lands of another. In that case the court said: "It is not enough to establish that in carrying out the improvement they have committed a trespass upon the lands of another party. That is a matter which rests between the city authorities and the person affected, and is not a valid ground of objection by a party assessed who had no interest in the land upon which the same is laid." The general language quoted may need qualification in its application to some cases to bring it into entire harmony with other authorities above cited. But the rule laid down and the language quoted is quite applicable to a case like this where it does not appear that the owners of the land invaded object, and where there is ample authority, if they should object, to acquire the title, and where also in any event the street will remain and the persons assessed for benefits will have the benefit of the same....

Judgment affirmed.

CRANE v BENNETT (1904) 177 NY 106, a77 AD 102

Appeal from a judgment of the Appellate Division of the Supreme Court in the first judicial department, entered December 23, 1902, modifying and affirming as modified a judgment in favor of plaintiff entered upon a verdict and or order denying a motion for a new trial. . . .

MARTIN, J. This action was for libel. It was based upon four articles published in the New York Herald, a newspaper owned by the defendant who resides in France but whose paper is published in the city of New York. Its management was confided solely to persons in his employ who had practical control of the entire business.

The plaintiff was a magistrate in the city of New York. The matter complained of was published in four issues of the defendant's newspaper, and related to alleged flagrant misconduct imputed to the plaintiff in the discharge of his official duties.... That each of the articles published was proved to be false and was libelous per se is not denied. . . .

Upon the trial the counsel for the defendant submitted to the court a great number of requests to charge, some of which were charged, others modified and charged as modified, while others the court refused. To such rulings exceptions were taken by the defendant. Although many of these exceptions were discussed by counsel upon the argument and in their briefs, still the exception to that portion of the charge by which the court instructed the jury "that the falsity of the libel is sufficient evidence of malice to uphold exemplary damages, but the plaintiff's right to recover exemplary damages is in the discretion of the jury," fully presents the only other question we deem it necessary to discuss or decide upon this appeal.

Indeed, we should not have regarded it necessary to discuss that question at all but for the fact that there seems to be a misapprehension among some of the members of the profession, and existing uncertainty on the part of the courts as to the effect of the decisions of this court relating to the existing rule upon that subject. The situation seems to have chiefly arisen from our decision in Krug v Pitass (162 NY 154), or from considering what was said in the opinion in that case without limiting it to the facts involved, rather than what was decided by the court.

That was an action against several defendants for the publication of an article libelous per se. Each of the defendants testified he had no malice or ill-will toward the plaintiff, when the latter, in order to show express malice, was permitted to prove against all the defendants that, several years before the publication, one of them, who knew nothing about the article until after it had been published, had made statements expressing ill-will and contempt for the plaintiff, which were never heard by or communicated to the other defendants before the publication complained of, and this court held that a judgment recovered against all must be reversed, as the general malice proved neither caused nor prompted the publication, and that the admission of such evidence presumably affected the verdict.

That case was properly decided. In the opinion, however, there are some expressions that may perhaps be regarded as not absolutely accurate because not including certain exceptions or added principles which would be applicable to a case where the circumstances were essentially different.

As was said by the learned writer of that opinion in Colonial City Traction Co. v Kingston City R.R. Co. (154 NY 493-495): "It was not our intention to decide any case but the one before us, * * * and our opinion should be read in the light of that purpose. If, as sometimes happens, broader statements were made, by way of argument or otherwise, than were essential to the decision of the questions presented, they are the dicta of the writer of the opinion and not the decision of the court. A judicial opinion, like evidence, is only binding so far as it is relevant, and when it wanders from the point at issue it no longer has force as an official utterance." (Stokes v Stokes, 155 NY 581, 594; Roberson v Rochester Folding Box Co., 171 NY 538, 551.)

It cannot be reasonably expected that every word, phrase or sentence contained in a judicial opinion will be so perfect and compliete in comprehension and limitation that it may not be improperly employed by wresting from its surroundings, disregarding its context and the change of facts to which it is sought to be applied, as nothing short of an infinite mind could possibly accomplish such a result.

Therefore, in applying cases which have been decided, what may have been said in an opinion should be confined to and limited by the facts of the case under consideration when the expressions relied upon were made, and should not be extended to cases where the facts are essentially different. When this rule is followed, much of the misapprehension and uncertainity that often arises as to the effect of a decision will be practically avoided.

Construing the Krug case in accordance with the foregoing rule and giving it only the effect suggested, it is manifest that it has in no way affected the doctrine that the proof of the falsity of a libel, of its character and of the circumstances under which it was published, is sufficient to present a question for the jury whether the malice was of such a character as to call for exemplary or punitive damages, and that that question rests with the jury alone...

Judgment affirmed.

Sec. 6.2 Binding and Persuasive Precedents

BUSSING v CITY OF MT. VERNON (2dDept 1907) 121 AD 502, 106 S 195

Action by John Bussing, Jr., against the city of Mt. Vernon. From a judgment entered on a referee's report, defendant appeals....

PER CURIAM. The judgment vacates an assessment on the plaintiff's property for the opening of a street in the city of Mt. Vernon, the defendant, on the ground that, whereas, the charter of the city required "a unanimous vote" of all of the members of the common council to allow the improvement, there was unanimous vote of only eight of such members, all that were present: the whole number being ten. That this did not make the proceeding and the assessment void was decided and affirmed in this court. (Matter of the Application of the City of Mt. Vernon, etc., 34 M 225, 68 S 823; 64 AD 619, 72 S 1097.)

Nevertheless another justice thereafter, in case of one of the landowners assessed, decided to the contrary, and no appeal was taken from this judgment by the city. This was all irregular. Our decision should have been followed. The learned referee in the present case felt constrained to follow this later decision; but he was under no such constraint. He should have followed our decision. We also deem it strange that, when the appeal was before us in the matter of the writ of mandamus to compel the cancellation of the assessment in accordance with this later judgment. (People ex rel Jardine v Brush, 115 AD 688, 101 S 312), we were not informed that the proceeding and assessments were the same that we had formerly upheld in the said case first tried. The square decision there given in favor of the city should not be permitted to be frittered away.

The judgment should be reversed, with costs, and the complaint dismissed.

WHITELY v TERRY (1stDept 1903) 83 AD 197, 82 S 89

Action by John W. Whiteley against Seth S. Terry to recover broker's commissions. From an order setting aside a verdict for plaintiff and granting a new trial, plaintiff appeals....

PATTERSON, J. The plaintiff sues, as the assignee of one Anspacher, to recover commissions claimed to have been earned by his assignor, as a real estate broker, upon the employment of the defendant. The allegations of the complaint are that the employment was made, and that Anspacher procured a purchaser for the property. The answer of the defendant denies generally these allegations, and sets up as an affirmative defense that he never have a written authority to Anspacher to sell the real property, as required by chapter 128, p 312, of the Laws of the State of New York, enacted in 1901 (section 640d, Pen Code). The cause came on for trial, and the plaintiff had a verdict, after which a motion was made for a new trial, which was granted; the order of the court being "that the verdict herein in favor of the plaintiff be, and hereby is, set aside, as being contrary to law, and a new trial granted."

The trial judge appears to have granted this motion on the ground that the plaintiff was not entitled to recover, because of the provision of the act of 1901 (section 640d, Pen Code). But irrespective of that enactment, the verdict was contrary to law, and the complaint should have been dismissed upon the motion made when the plaintiff rested, and which was renewed at the close of the whole proofs.

There was no evidence that the defendant employed Anspacher to sell the property, nor was there evidence that he was the procuring cause of the sale. Anspacher's own testimony disposes of the first proposition. He admits that he, by letter dated January 16, 1902, introduced himself to the defendant, and made a proposition with respect to a sale of the property, with a building loan. He testifies that at that time he was acting for Mr. Wandell, of Buffalo. At that point he does not claim to have been acting for, or to have been employed by, the defendant. Mr. Wandell seems to have dropped out of the transaction, as Mr. Terry would not make the building loan.

The plaintiff's assignor then testified that he told Terry that a broker had brought to him a party who thought of buying the lot, to which Mr. Terry replied that, if the party were "all right", he was perfectly satisfied to sell it upon certain terms. The party, the plaintiff's assignor says, was John W.

Stevens, or the John W. Stevens Building Company; but he also testifies he told Terry that Stevens, or the Stevens Company, was his (Anspacher's) customer. Anspacher seems to have had a talk with a Mr. Hellman about a sale of the property, but the proof does not show either that Terry employed Anspacher to make a sale, or that Hellman was authorized by Terry to employ him. There is nothing in the evidence which justifies the conclusion that Terry, either personally or through Hellman, employed the plaintiff's assignor, or that the defendant had reason to believe otherwise than that Anspacher was acting for other customers.

Nor does it appear that Anspacher procured the sale to be made. The proof shows, on the contrary, that he did not. The sale was effected by one Hilton, who never heard of Anspacher in the transaction. Mr. Finn, the purchaser, never met Anspacher until a week before the execution of his contract with Terry. The submission of the case to the jury under such circumstances, was error in law. The question as to whether there is evidence to support a finding is one of law. (Healy v Clark, 120 NY 642, 24 NE 316.)

If the above considerations are correct, then this order must be affirmed without regard to the question of the constitutionality of the act of 1901. In the 2d Dept, in Grossman v Gaminez, 79 AD 15, 79 S 900, it has been decided that the law is unconstitutional. The opinion of the court proceeds upon two grounds, viz., that the act is invalid because of the descrimination made between persons engaged in a legitimate business in different communities in the state, making it unlawful to engage in that business in cities of the first and second classes, unless under certain conditions, while it remains lawful to do so in other parts of the state without such conditions, and that it interferes unreasonably with the liberty of the citizen.

The learned court says that it has been unable to find any case which holds that the Legislature can make an act innocent and harmless in itself—a necessary or commonly used instrumentality of carrying on the ordinary vocations of life—a crime in one portion of the state, and not in another. But that is exactly what was held in the Havnor Case (149 NY 195, 43, NE 541, 31 LRA 689, 52 AmStRep 707). By the act of 1865, p 649, c. 823, it was made a misdemeanor for any person to work at the trade of a barber on Sunday, except in the city of New York and at Saratoga Springs, where business might be carried on until 1 o'clock in the afternoon of Sunday, and that was held to be a valid exercise of police legislation, and worked no deprivation of liberty or property, within the meaning of the Constitution. Criminal laws are not necessarily unconstitutional if they bear unequally upon persons in different parts of the state. The same offense punishable under a general law may be differently punished in different parts of the state. (Williams v People, 24 NY 405; Matter of Bayard, 25 Hun(NY) 546.)

We have no criticisms to make upon the general views expressed in the opinion of the court in the Grossman Case with respect to the police power, its extent, its purpose, or its circumscriptions, but that the Legislature may control and regulate, for the benefit of the public, methods by which business shall be transacted, cannot be disputed...Here there is nothing in the statute which interferes with a real estate broker conducting his business legitimately. He may negotiate contracts for real estate when he is authorized in writing to do so. We agree with what is said by the court in the Grossman case—that "we are at liberty to consider the established usages, customs and traditions of the people, and to have in view the promotion of their comfort, and the preservation of the peace and good order."

We discover in this statute that which the learned court in the Grossman case failed to find—that it is intended to correct the evil, which has time and time again been exemplified in the courts, of the oppressive litigation forced upon real estate owners by reason of unfounded claims made by real estate brokers that they had been employed to negotiate sales of property for such owners. The real estate broker is not as much controlled or trammeled in his business as was the barber in the Havnor case, who, by exercising his trade in one part of the state on an interdicted day, becomes a criminal, while in another part of the state he may work with impunity on that day.

If, as we apprehend, this statute was within the power of the Legislature to enact, although operating as it does, unequally in different parts of the state, we can see no reason why obedience to it cannot be compelled by making it a misdemeanor to violate it. If the state had power to issue the command, and those affected by the statute are required to obey, it was within the competency of the Legislature, if it saw fit, to add the sanction of punishment for disobedience. We are of opinion that the act is constitutional, and a reasonable exercise of police power.

The order appealed from must be affirmed, with costs. All concur.

DUNHAM v HASTINGS PAVEMENT CO. (1stDept 1907) 118 AD 127, 105 S 48

Action by Edward R. Dunham against the Hastings Pavement Company. From a judgment overruling defendant's demurrer to plaintiff's amended complaint, defendant appeals....

LAUGHLIN, J. This action is based upon a contract in writing which the defendant has insisted from the commencement of the litigation was void upon grounds of public policy. On two former appeals, after trials on the merits wherein the record, not only presented the contract, but proof of the nature and extent of the services rendered thereunder, this court adjudged that the contract was valid (56 AD 244, 67 S 632, 57 AD 426, 68 S 221, and 95 AD 360, 88 S 835), basing its decision mainly upon the authority of Cheseborough v Conover, 140 NY 384, 35 NE 633.

We are now asked on the face of the contract alone, which is set forth in the complaint in haec verba, to reconsider the former decisions of this court and declare the contract void upon the authority of Veazey v Allen, 173 NY 359, 66 NE 103, 62 LRA 362, which was drawn to the attention of this court on the second appeal, and on the authority of Hazleton v Sheckells, 202 US 71, 26 SCt 567, 50 LEd 939, and Sussman v Porter (C.C.) 137 Fed 161, and cases therein cited.

The views expressed in the opinion in Veazy v Allen, supra, which in this regard were not essential to the decision, incline toward the doctrine subsequently announced by the Supreme Court of the United States in Hazleton v Sheckells, supra, that the validity of a contract with respect to services concerning legislation or the action of public bodies or officials in awarding contracts is to be determined not by what is expressly contracted to be done, but upon what may be done thereunder and the tendency of the agreement, where the compensation is contingent upon success, to induce improper solicitation or the unlawful and corrupt use of money.

The Court of Appeals, however, in the Veazey case, supra neither expressly modified nor overruled the Cheseborough case, but, on the contrary, reaffirmed its doctrine. Under the broad doctrine announced in Hazleton v Sheckells, supra, it is clear that this contract could not be enforced. However, whether the contract be void upon grounds of public policy is not a federal question, but one for the exclusive jurisdiction of our own courts.

The majority of the court, as now constituted, would favor the adoption by the state courts of the doctrine enunciated by Hazleton v Sheckells, supra; but, since it apparently goes beyond any doctrine enunciated by the Court of Appeals and essential to the decision of the case before the court, and since the former decisions of this court under which this litigation has been continued were based upon a former decision of the Court of Appeals, we think it should be left to that court to decide whether it was intended by the Veazey Case, or is now the judgment of that court, that the doctrine of Hazleton v Scheckells, supra, should be fully adopted in this state.

The interlocutory judgment should therefore be affirmed on the authority of the decisions of this court on the former appeals herein.

SCOTT, J. (dissenting). I feel constrained to dissent from the affirmance of this judgment.

It is not strictly accurate to say that the legality of the contract was determined on the first appeal. All that was then decided was that the question of its legality should have been submitted to the jury. (56 AD 244, 67 S 632). Even this result was arrived at with reluctance, and under what was supposed to be a relaxation of the strict rule of Mills v Mills, 40 NY 543, 100 AmDec 535, embodied in the opinion in Cheseborough v Conover, 140 NY 382, 35 NE 633.

Since the first appeal the Court of Appeals in Veazey v Allen, 173 NY 359, 6 NE 103, 62 LRA 362, have expressly reaffirmed the rule of Mills v Mills in all its stringency, and have again held that the test to be applied to what is claimed to be a lobbying contract is not that the parties actually stipulated for corrupt action, or intended that secret and improper resorts should be made, but that it is enough to condemn such a contract that it tends directly to these results, and furnishes a temptation to plaintiff to resort to corrupt means or improper devices to influence legislative action. The Court of Appeals in discussing its decision of Cheseborough v Conover makes it quite clear that it had no intention in that case to relax the strict rule above stated.

It seems to me to be quite apparent, therefore, that the first appeal in this was decided upon a misapprehension as to the force and effect of Cheseborough v Conover. Upon the second appeal (95 AD 360, 88 S 835), although Veazey v Allen may have been cited by counsel, it is not referred to in the opinion, and was apparently not considered with reference to its explanation of Cheseborough v Conover.

It seems to me, therefore, that we are at liberty to consider de novo the question of the validity of the contract upon which plaintiff sues. As to its invalidity, tested by the rule stated in Mills v Mills and Veazey v Allen, I entertain no doubt.

In my opinion, therefore, the judgment should be reversed and the demurrer sustained.

Sec. 6.3 Effect of Overruling a Precedent

PEOPLE ex rel RICE v GRAVES (3dDept 1934) 242 AD 128, 273 S 583

Certiorari proceeding by the People of the State of New York, on the relation of Elmer L. Rice, to review the action of Mark Graves and others, as Tax Commissioners of the State of New York, in assessing an additional income tax against relator....

HEFFERNAN, Justice. This is a certiorari proceeding under the provisions of the Personal Income Tax Law (Tax Law, Sections 199,375) and the Civil Practice Act, to review a determination of the state tax commission in connection with the assessment of additional income tax against the relator for the calender years 1929, 1930, and 1931.

The parties are in accord as to the facts and only questions of law are involved.

During the years in question relator was the author and owner of plays known by the title, "The Left Bank," "Counselor at Law," "See Naples and Die," "Street Scene," "A Voyage to Purilia," "The Lady Next Door," "The Passing of Chow Chow," "On Trial," and "The Adding Machine." He was also the United States copyright proprietor thereof and had duly copyrighted the same in his own name in Washington, D.C., under the United States copyright law.

From the time of the enactment of the Personal Income Tax Law in this state in 1919 until 1928, the tax commission imposed and collected taxes upon income derived from copyrights in the form of royalties.

On May 14, 1928, the United States Supreme Court by a vote of five to four of its members in Long v Rockwood, (277 US 142, 48 SCt 463, 464, 72 LEd 824), affirmed the decision of the Massachusetts Supreme Court in the case of Rockwood v Commissioner of Corporations and Taxation, (257, Mass 573, 154 NE 182, 55 ALR 928), in which the court of last resort of that commonwealth held that the state had no right to impose an income tax upon royalties from patents or copyrights. Long v Rockwood held definitely: "A State may not tax the income received by one of her citizens as royalties for the use of patents issued to him by the United States * * * The courts of last resort in Pennsylvania and New York have held that a State may not tax patents granted by the United States (citing cases) and no opinion to the contrary has been cited."

In deference to the ruling in Long v Rockwood, the state tax commission conformed thereto and altered its regulations and the administration of the law to provide that income in the form of royalties from patents and copyrights issued by the United States government was not required to be included in gross returns.

On his state income tax returns for the years 1929, 1930 and 1931, relator entered in the schedule on the state income tax blanks, under "Nontaxable Income," the following sums derived by him from royalties from his United States copyrights received him as follows: 1929, $37,432.98; 1930, $29,498.27; 1931, $54,887.13. The above amounts, although stated in his return, were not included in gross income on returns filed for those years, and no tax was paid thereon upon the filing of the returns, nor was any tax demanded by the state. During this period the state made no attempt to assess any tax against relator on such income. In fact, it regarded his copyright royalties exempt and so instructed him.

On May 16, 1932, the United States Supreme Court, in the case of Fox Film Corporation v Doyal, (286 US 123, 131, 52 SCt 546, 548, 76 LEd 1010, by a unanimous decision overruled its own decision in Long v Rockwood. The case of Fox Film Corporation v Doyal, supra, involved the imposition of the gross receipts tax of the state of Georgia on the gross receipts of royalties from copyrights. The judges of Georgia's highest court were equally divided in opinion on the question presented. (172 Ga 403, 157 SE 664.) The United States Supreme Court held that copyright were not federal instrumentalities and that the income derived from them was not immune from state taxation, and further that nondiscriminatory tax upon such royalties does not in the slightest degree hamper the execution of the policy of the federal copyright statute (17 USCA Sec. 1 et seq.). In concluding its opinion the court said: "The affirmance of the judgment in the instant case cannot be reconciled with the decision in Long v Rockwood (277 US 142, 48 SCt 463, 72 LEd 824), upon which appellant relies, and in view of the conclusions now reached upon a reexamination of the question, that case is definitely overruled." Thereupon the tax commission again amended its regulations to provide that all royalties from patents or copyrights must be included in gross income.

On November 10, 1932, pursuant to the provisions of section 373 of the Tax Law, the tax commission effected a revision of the income tax returns of the relator filed within three years then past, and made assessments against the relator for the calendar years 1929, 1930, 1931 of additional income tax aggregating $3,231.85. upon the amounts of income received by the relator in those years, as royalties from his copyrights. No question is here involved as to the statutory authority for such assessments, but only the question as to the legality of exercising such authority.

The relator, under protest, in order to avoid the penalties threatened to be imposed, paid the additional assessment and then instituted the present proceeding to compel the state to refund the same. On this appeal relator contends that the state has no legal right to impose, retroactively, a tax upon income which was regarded as exempt during the three years prior to such imposition. The only question for determination is whether or not the state tax commission erred in applying the principle laid down in the Fox Film Case, holding that income derived from United States copyrights was not immune from state taxation, to such income received in the years 1929 to 1931, inclusive.

The effect to be given to the action of a court of last resort, when it reverses itself, is a subject which has given rise to prolific litigation and has for centuries furnished a theme for philosophical discussion by jurists and text-writers. Our of the age-old discussion there have been developed two fundamentally opposing theories. According to one theory the decisions of the courts are always conclusive evidence of what the law is. Followers of the other school assent that the decisions are evidence, but not conclusive evidence, of the law. Mr. Justice Cardozo, in his lectures entitled "The Growth of the Law," in connection with this subject said (pp 31, 32): "What are the rights of litigants who have acted upon a judgment of the highest court of a state to the effect that a statute is invalid, if a controversy between them comes before the same court after the earlier judgment has been overruled? You will find it hard to reach a solution of such a problem without wandering into a philosophical dissertation upon the nature of law in general." Again quoting (pp 121, 122) from that eminent jurist: "No doubt there are many rules of property or conduct which could not be changed retroactively without hardship or oppression, and this whether wise or unwise in their origin. So far as I am aware, no judge ever thinks of changing them. The picture of the bewildered litigant lured into a course of action by the false light of a decision, only to meet ruin when the light is extinguished and the decision overruled, is for the most part a figment of excited brains."

A natural desire for stability in the law gave rise to a reliance on decided cases as far back as Bracton and the early Year Books of the fourteenth century. According to the orthodox theory of Blackstone, which still claims at least the nominal allegiance of most courts, a judicial decision is merely evidence of the law, not law itself; and when a decision is overruled, it does not become bad law; it never was the law, and the discredited decision will be viewed as if it had never been and the reconsidered pronouncement regarded as law from the beginning. Despite the expressed disapproval of some courts of repute and certain eminent writers, the prevailing doctrine is not that the law is changed by the overruling decision, but that the court was mistaken in its former decision, and that the law is, and always was, as expounded in the later decision. It should be said, however, that many leading English and American writers on jurisprudence characterize this theory of law as childish fiction and champion the doctrine that the rules which the judicial organs of the state lay down in deciding cases constitute law. However, according to the great weight of authority the theory that courts make law is unsound. The courts do not make law, but simply declare law. A judicial decision is but evidence of the law. An overruling decision does not change law, but impeaches the overruled decision as evidence of law. Adopting the theory that courts merely declare preexisting law, it logically follows that an overruling decision operates retroactively. Courts have generally given retroactive effect to decisions which have overruled earlier precedents.

Where, in reliance on the earlier decision, a person has acquired contract or property rights which are valid under the law as then declared by the highest court of the state, or has done some act which according to that law is innocent, the logical outcome of this doctrine would often cause hardship and injustice. When confronted by this situation the great majority of the courts, at the call of justice, have refused to go the whole length of the doctrine and have held that though in general a change in judicial decision had a retrospective effect they would not apply it so as to impair vested rights such as property rights or those resting on contracts.

The United States Supreme Court, in Great Northern Railway v Sunburst Oil & Refining Co. (287 US 358, 364, 53 SCt 145, 148, 77 LEd 360, 85 ALR 254), speaking through Mr. Justice Cardozo said: "A state in defining the limits of adherence to precedent may make a choice for itself between the principle of forward operation and that of relation backward. It may say that decisions of its highest court, though later overruled, are law none the less for intermediate transactions. Indeed there are cases intimating too broadly (cf. Tidal Oil Co. v Flanagan (263 US 444, 44 SCt 197, 68 LEd 382)), that it must give them that effect; but never has doubt been expressed that it may so treat them if it pleases, whenever injustices or hardship will thereby be averted."

Salmond, in his work on Jurisprudence (8th Ed.) p 197, in discussing the retrospective effect of a later decision said: "The overruling of a precedent is not the abolition of an established rule of law; it is an authoritative denial that the supposed rule of law has ever existed. The precedent is so treated not because it has made bad law, but because it has never in reality made any law at all. It has not conformed to the requirements of legal efficacy. Hence it is that the overruling of a precedent, unlike the repeal of a statute, has retrospective operation. The decision is pronounced to have been bad ab initio. A repealed statute, on the contrary remains valid and applicable as to matters arising before the date of its repeal. The overruling of a precedent is analogous not to the repeal of a statute, but to the judicial rejection of a custom as unreasonable or as otherwise failing to conform to the requirements of customary law."

The effect of overruling a decision and refusing to abide by the precedent there laid down is retrospective and makes the law at the time of the overruled decision as it is declared to be in the last decision, except in so far as the construction last given would impair the obligations of contracts entered into, or injuriously affect vested rights acquired in reliance on the earlier decision. (15 C.J. 960 and cases there cited.)

The general principle is that a decision of a court of supreme jurisdiction overruling a former decision is retrospective in its operation, and the effect is not that the former decision is bad law, but that it never was the law. To this the courts have established the exception that where a constitutional or statute law has received a given construction by the courts of last resort, and contracts have been made and rights acquired under and in accordance with such construction, such contracts may not be invalidated nor vested rights acquired under them impaired by a change of construction made by a subsequent decision. Thus, for instance, the construction of a statute of descents established by the decisions of the courts at the time of a quitclaim deed by heirs claiming under the statute becomes a part of the contract and must govern the rights of the parties as against a different construction thereafter adopted by overruling the former decisions. The true rule in such cases is held to be to give a change of judicial construction in respect to a statute the same effect in its operation on contracts and existing contract rights that would be given to a legislative repeal or amendment; that is to say, make it prospective but not retroactive.

While there is high authority for the position that this is the only exception that should be allowed, yet some courts, in a case of unusual hardship, have extended the principle of this exception to criminal causes, and to cases where a title to real estate had vested. It has been held, however, that the principle should certainly not be further extended and applied to an erroneous decision on general mercantile law which is contrary to accepted doctrine and recognized business methods.

While the exception above noted, in respect to contracts made and rights acquired under a previous construction of a constitutional or statute law, is almost universally observed, yet in at least one jurisdiction it has been held that a decision by the highest court of the state holding a given statute constitutional will not be left in force, after a subsequent decision of the same court overruling the former decision and holding the statute unconstitutional, as to contracts entered into before the latter decision was rendered. According to this view a decision overruling a prior decision and holding unconstitutional a statute held to be constitutional by such decision does not impair the obligations of a contract entered into before the latter decision was rendered, as a decision of the court is not in fact a law, and if erroneously made cannot make a law. (7 RCL 1010 and cases there cited.)

Under the well-settled rules of jurisprudence of this state, it must be held that the law as pronounced by the United States Supreme Court in Fox Film Corporation v Doyal, retroacts to the date of overruled decision of Long v Rockwood, and that the law of this state is and always was that copyrights granted by the United States may be subject to the New York personal income tax.

Courts are bound in their very nature, to declare what the law is and has been, and not what it shall be in the future; if the courts were absolutely bound by their prior decisions, they would be without power to correct their own errors. (Wood v Brady, 150 US 18, 14 SCt 6, 37 LEd 981.) Contract rights cannot be impaired by a subsequent court decision altering the construction of the law. In Woodruff v Woodruff (52 NY 53, 58), the court said: "The counsel for the appellant is quite correct in saying that a decision of a court overruling a prior decision is a legal adjudication that the prior decision was not the law at the time it was made, although there may be rights of contract acquired under the first which the last decision will not affect."

Relator relies on Mercantile National Bank of Cleveland, Ohio, v Lander (C.C.) 109 F 21, affirmed in Lander v Mercantile National Bank of Cleveland, Ohio (CCA) 118 F 785, as a controlling precedent in the case at bar. In our view of the matter the Lander case is of most doubtful persuasive force. The Lander case involved an Ohio tax statute, and by a decision of the Ohio state courts in 1888, stockholders in national banks had been held entitled to deduct from the valuation of their shares, for tax purposes, the amount of their indebtedness; in 1897, the state court reversed itself. (Chapman v First Nat. Bank 56 Ohio St 310, 47 NE 54.) Thereupon the defendant county treasurer sought to collect taxes, based upon the decision in 1897, upon the stock of the plaintiff bank for years 1894, 1895 and 1896. Suit was brought in the United States Circuit Court in Ohio to enjoin such collection. The district judge held that the later decision was not retroactive and did not authorize the collection of taxes on the basis of the later decision, with respect to assessments before that time. On appeal to the Circuit Court of Appeals (118 F. 785) the decision of the lower court was affirmed, but upon an entirely different ground, namely, that the state statute under which the taxing officer sought to impose taxes for the years 1894, 1895 and 1896 did not authorize such action. The Circuit Court of Appeals' opinion is completely silent with respect to the question as to whether the later decision of the Ohio state court would have retrospective operation, provided statutory authority therefore existed.

In case such as the instant case, not involving the construction of the Constitution or laws of the federal government, the state courts are not bound by decisions of the District Judge for the Northern District of Ohio, in 109 F. 21, so strongly relied on by relator, could have only persuasive force. As a precedent it is valueless, but such persuasive force as that decision might carry is entirely dissipated by the fact that, though the decision was affirmed, the Circuit Court of Appeals did not adopt the reasoning upon which the decision was based. Opposed to this single descordant decision of a single judge is the well-settled principle of law on the subject in this state, as laid down by our Court of Appeals and adhered to over a long period of time. Thus in Butler v Van Wyck (1841) 1 Hill 438, at page 462, the court said:

to over a lon

"It is going quite too far to say that a single decision of any court is absolutely conclusive as a precedent. It is an elementary principle that an erroneous decision is not bad law—it is no law at all. It may be final upon the parties then before the court, but it does not conclude other parties having rights depending on the same question." This quotation was cited with approval in Leavitt v Blatchford, 17 NY 521.

Relator urges that the matter before us comes within the doctrine of stare decisis. As has already been pointed out, the decision in Long v Rockwood was never the law of the land and hence the doctrine of stare decisis does not cover the case. The obligation imposed upon the courts by the doctrine of stare decisis is a moral obligation only. Thsi doctrine has for its objects the salutary effect of uniformity, certainty, and stability of the law. The doctrine of stare decisis, like almost every other legal rule, is not without its exceptions. It does not apply to a case where it can be shown that the law has been misunderstood or misapplied, or where the former determination is evidently contrary to reason. (Rumsey et al v New York & N.E.R.R. Co., 133 NY 79, 30 NE 654, 15 LRA 618, 28 Am St Rep 600.) Chancellor Kent (1 Kent's Com (13th Ed.) 477), in commenting upon the rule of stare decisis, said that: "It is probable that the records of many of the courts of this country are replete with hasty and crude decisions; and in such cases ought to be examined without fear, and revised without reluctance, rather than have the character of our law impaired, and the beauty and harmony of the system destroyed by the perpetuity of error."

From what has been said we are convinced that the decision of the United States Supreme Court in the Fox Film case is to be given a retrospective effect, except as to any possible tested (vested) rights or contracts made or entered into in reliance upon the overthrown decision of Long v Rockwood. No well-founded claim can be made that the relator acquired any vested right or entered into any contract under the former decision. No such claim in fact is made, nor are there any property rights involved.

We have not overlooked the relator's contention that retrospective application of the decision of the Fox Film case works an apparent hardship as to him. We concede as much. The answer to that argument, however, is that the hardship in question is no greater on the relator than was that suffered by the state by the erroneous decision in Long v Rockwood. The ruling in that case deprived the state of revenue to which it was justly entitled. The construction in the instant case involves no hardship upon the relator beyond the payment of those taxes which he would have been required to pay in any event had the discredited decision in Long v Rockwood never have been made.

Courts have repeatedly said that an income tax, apportioned to the ability of the taxpayer to bear it, is founded upon the protection afforded to the recipient of the income by the state, in his person, in his right to receive the income and in his enjoyment of it when received. The state gives to the taxpayer security to life, liberty, and property, and it exacts in return a contribution to the support of that government, measured by and based upon the income, in the fruition of which it defends him from unjust interference....

Determination confirmed, with $50 costs and disbursements. All concur.

KENYON v WELTY (1862) 20 Cal. 637.

NORTON, J. The controlling facts in this case are these: The defendant Welty purchased a piece of land in the City of Sacramento at Sheriff's sale, under an execution issued upon a judgment rendered by the Superior Court of the City of San Francisco against one C.L. Ross, who was owner of the land. Welty conveyed a portion of the land so purchased to one Morris Nolan, who executed a mortgage upon it to the plaintiff Kenyon, as security for a loan of one thousand dollars. Afterwards, Welty procured a conveyance from Ross of all his title to the premises so bought at the Sheriff's sale, and including the portion sold to Nolan, and by him mortgaged to Kenyon. Shortly after the purchase, the decision of the Supreme Court of this State was made, in the case of Meyer v Kalkmann, that the Superior Court of the City of San Francisco had no jurisdiction to issue process to run outside the limits of the City of San Francisco.

After this decision, an agreement was entered into between Kenyon and Welty, in pursuance of which Kenyon transferred to Welty the mortgage of Nolan, in consideration of Welty's procuring a deed from his brother, in whom the title from Ross had become vested, to Kenyon, of a portion of the premises covered by the mortgage, and which portion was to be discharged from the lien of the mortgage. Some time after this agreement was carried into effect, the Supreme Court, in the case of Hickman v O'Neil overruled the former decision in the case of Meyer v Kalkmann. This action is brought to have this agreement set aside, upon the ground that it was made under a mutual mistake of the parties.

In the case of Goodenow v Ewer (16 Cal 461) this Court, speaking of mistakes of law, says: "Indeed, the weight of authority in the United States is, that the mistake, unless accompanied with special circumstances, such as misrepresentation, undue influence or misplaced confidence, constitutes no ground of relief." The Court then quotes: "It may be safely affirmed," says Mr. Justice Story, "upon the highest authority, as a well established doctrine, that a mere mistake of law, unattended with any such special circumstances as have been above suggested, will furnish no ground for the interposition of a Court of Equity; and the present disposition of Courts of Equity is to narrow, rather than to enlarge, the operation of exceptions."

The only mistake that existed in this case, if there was any mistake, was one of law. The parties supposed that the Nolan mortgage was invalid, and that the title derived through the conveyance from Ross was valid. But this supposition rested wholly upon their supposition as to the condition of the law. They knew what the law was before the decision in the case of Meyer v Kalkmann, and they knew of that decision, and they exercised their judgment as to the effect of that decision. There was no mistake or want of knowledge as to any fact that now appears in the case. Under the rule laid down in the case of Goodman v Ewer, this is therefore not a case in which relief can be granted, unless it be characterized by some special circumstance of the nature above suggested as constituting an exception.

The plaintiff insists that such circumstances are found in the fact that the title on which the Nolan mortgage rests was derived from the defendant Welty, and that he informed Kenyon, through the latter's agent, that the title was good when Kenyon was about to take the mortgage.

We should have great difficulty in saying, from anything we find in the facts of this case, that Welty would be under any obligation, legal or equitable, to make good the Nolan mortgage, if even the title had not been good. But, in fact, the title on which the Nolan mortgage rests, it appears, was good then and is now. The loss that the plaintiff has sustained is the result of the mistake as to the condition of the law, and, as a consequence, as to the condition of the title at a subsequent period, and depending upon a matter which subsequently arose, to wit: the decision in the case of Meyer v Kalkmann. The agreement which is now sought to be annulled was not induced by anything said or done by Welty; but on the contrary was, in some degree, extorted from him against his will. It was the result of a speculation upon, that is, the opinion of the parties as to the effect of a decision of this Court—in short, a pure mistake of law.

To establish the doctrine that all contracts made under a condition of the law, as expounded by the Supreme Court of the State, can be set aside if the court subsequently changes its opinions or corrects its errors, would be attended with very serious evils. What amount of confusion and litigation would arise in the City of San Francisco alone, if all contracts and conveyances, and transfers of possession, which were made under the supposed effect of decisions of this court as to titles in that city could now be repudiated and set aside, in consequence of those decisions having been overruled or modified! Upon this subject Chancellor Kent, in the case of Lyon v Richmond (2 John'sCh(NY) 59) says: "Every man is to be charged at his peril with a knowledge of the law. There is no other principle which is safe and practicable in the common intercourse of mankind; and to permit a subsequent judicial decision in any one given case on a point of law to open or annul everything that has been done in other cases of the like kind for years before under a different understanding of the law, would lead to the most mischievous consequences."

It is insisted that the Court below has found as a fact that the contract in question was made under a mutual mistake of fact as to the title; and as there was no motion for a new trial, it must be taken that the mistake in this case was one of fact and not of law. But the meaning of a particular expression in a finding must be considered in reference to the whole finding; and in this case there is no doubt that the meaning here is that the mistake as to the title was not as to any fact affecting the title, but as to the law affecting the title.

We have assumed in the consideration of this case, that it was a mistake to suppose the law to be as decided in the case of Meyer v Kalkmann, during the period that elapsed before that decision was overruled, because, for the purpose of this decision, it was not necessary to take a different view; but we do not intend to express any views upon the point.

The judgment must be reversed, and the Court below directed to dismiss the complaint.

CHAPTER VII

THE NATURE OF JUSTICE

OUTLINE OF CHAPTER VII:
(Lecture)

SUGGESTED READINGS:

Kinnane: Anglo-American Law
Ch. II, "The Need for Social Order and the Means for Securing it" pp. 11-21
Ch. III, "Regulated Order and Legal Justice" pp. 22-42
Pound and Plucknett: Readings on the History and System of the Common Law
Ch. I, "Fundamental Conceptions" pp. 1-42
Smith: Elementary Law
Ch. 8, "Persons and Rights" pp. 95-104

Cahn: The Sense of Injustice
"Justice and Power": I-IV, pp. 3-50

CHAPTER VIII

THE NATURE OF LAW

OUTLINE OF CHAPTER VIII:
(Lecture)

SUGGESTED READINGS:

Bowman: Elementary Law
Ch. 1, "The Nature of Law" pp. 1-20
Chs. 4-7 (generally on the Law) pp. 53-124
Dowling, P. and P.: Legal Method
Ch. 1, Sec. 1, "The Forms of the Law" pp. 2-15
Fryer and Benson: Legal Method and System
Ch. 1, Sec. 3, "Some Concepts of Law" pp. 122-142
Gavit: Study of Law
Ch. 1, "What is Law?" pp. 1-23
Gavit, F. and P.: Introduction to Law and the Judicial Process
Ch. VI, "The Nature of Law" pp. 601-608
Griffith: Outlines of the Law
Ch. I, Introductory, pp. 1-3
Hicks: "Legal Research"
Ch. 1-3 (generally on the Law) pp. 23-59
Kinnane: Anglo-American Law
Chs. I and IV-VI, (generally on the Law) pp. 1-10 and 43-165
Morgan: Study of Law
Ch. 2, "Nature and Sources of Law" pp. 40-49
Patterson: Jurisprudence
(generally on the nature of the Law)
Pollock: Essays in Jurisprudence and Ethics
Essay I, "The Nature of Jurisprudence" pp. 1-41
Essay II, "Laws of Nature and Laws of Men" pp. 42-59
Smith: Elementary Law
Ch. 1, "Nature of Law" pp. 1-11
Ch. 7, "The Rank & Interpretation of Laws" pp. 78-94
Ch. 10, "Divisions of Law" pp. 124-133
Woodruff: Introduction to Study of Law
Ch. 1, "Scope of Law" pp. 1-7

CHAPTER IX

LEGISLATION

OUTLINE OF CHAPTER IX

Sec. 9.1 The Nature of Legislation
Sec. 9.2 Legislative Jurisdiction (local, state, national, and world)
Sec. 9.3 Forms of Legislative Action
Sec. 9.4 Evolution of Legislative Action
Sec. 9.5 Construction and Interpretation of Legislative Action
Sec. 9.6 Enforcement of Legislation

SUGGESTED READINGS:

Article I, U. S. Constitution
Article III, N. Y. Constitution
Cohen: Materials and Problems on Legislation
(generally on Legislation)
Cornell Faculty: Introduction to the Study of Law
Ch. VI, Sec. C, D, E, F (generally on Legislation) pp. 175-191, 218-234
Dowling, P. and P.: Legal Method
Ch. VI, "Interpretation of Statutes" pp. 296-460
Ch. VII, "Coordination of Judge-Made and Statute Law" pp. 461-510
Gavit: Introduction to the Study of Law
Ch. III, Sec. 30 "The Legislative Function" pp. 80-82
Hicks: ----- Legal Research
Ch. V, "Statute Law and Statute Books" pp. 72-96
Horack: Legislation (generally on Legislation)
Patterson: Jurisprudence
Ch. 9, Sec. 3.11 "Legislation as a Form of Law" pp. 197-205
Plucknett: Concise History of the Common Law
Book I, Pt. III, Ch. 4 "Legislation" pp. 280-304
Read and MacDonald: -----Legislation (generally on Legislation)
Riesenfeld and Maxwell: Modern Social Legislation
(on recent legislative policies)
Smith: Elementary Law
Ch. 6, "Enacted Law" pp. 69-77
Ch. 7, Sec. 32-34 (generally on Legislation) pp. 78-86

Sec. 9.1 The Nature of Legislation

MATTER OF GREENE, Petition for the Appointment of a Referee to Pass upon His Claim against County of Niagara, Resp. (1901) 166 NY 485

Appeal from an order of the Appellate Division of the Supreme Court in the fourth judicial department, entered December 4, 1900, reversing an order of Special Term appointing a referee under chapter 614 of the Laws of 1900.

This appeal involves the validity of chapter 614 of the Laws of 1900, entitled "An act for the relief of William C. Greene, as receiver of the Merchants' Bank of Lockport."

Section 1 of this act authorized an application by Greene as receiver to a Special Term of the Supreme Court for the appointment of a referee to ascertain and report the amount of moneys advanced by the bank to Arnold as county treasurer in excess of the amount on deposit to his credit in said bank, for the purpose of paying, and which was used to pay, obligations of the county, and whether there existed any equities which should be considered by way of reduction of such amount and to report thereon...

In June, 1894, William C. Greene, as receiver of the Merchants Bank of Lockport, brought an action in the Supreme Court against the county of Niagara, Timothy E. Ellsworth, Josiah H. Helmer and Joshua S. Helmer to recover from said Ellsworth $7,399.45, the amount of alleged overdrafts from said bank as of date October 11, 1893, by John J. Arnold as county treasurer of the county of Niagara...

The defendant Ellsworth answered, disclaiming any interest other than as custodian of the fund, with the consent of the parties, subject to the order of the court. The Helmers did not answer.

The final judgment as affirmed by the Court of Appeals awarded the fund to the county. (8 AD 409; 31 AD 634; 161 NY 651.)...

LANDON J. The issue in the action of the receiver against the county of Niagara was whether the bank or the county was equitably entitled to the proceeds of the note and draft which Arnold, the defaulting treasurer, had deposited with Ellsworth. The receiver was defeated because he was not, as against the county equitably entitled to recover the overdraft. Whatever his rights were against Arnold, he had none against the county. The referee found in substance that the alleged overdraft was a fiction. It was produced by charging Arnold's account as county treasurer with $4,400 and $5,150 which Arnold, in 1891, to the knowledge of the bank, wrongfully advanced to it from the county funds. Thus the bank appropriated the very money it conspired with the treasurer to abstract from the county, and the amount appropriated was used to swell the total of his indebtedness to the bank. The more the bank could induce the treasurer to abstract for its use, the greater would be his overdraft on its books. If the bank had refunded the money and taken back its note and draft, and credited the treasurer's account with the same, there would have been no overdraft. By the judgment of the court the proceeds of the note and draft were used for the purpose for which they were originally intended, namely, to restore to the county the money that the bank had wrongfully obtained from it; and, continuing the method of bookkeeping employed by the bank, when the bank, under the judgment of the court, paid the note and draft through Ellsworth to the county, the treasurer's account should have been credited with the amount, and thus the overdraft would have disappeared. The assignment by Arnold of the note and draft to the bank could have no rightful purpose except to restore to the county the funds misappropriated on the pledge of these securities. That Arnold used the proceeds of his alleged overdraft to pay the obligations of the county does not aid the bank or its receiver. In equity there was no overdraft, and the judgment in the former action concludes the receiver upon that issue. (Young v Farwell, 165 NY 341.)

After the final judgment against the receiver, chapter 614, Laws of 1900, was passed. Its letter and purpose are to vacate the judgment obtained by the county and to grant a new trial to the receiver before a referee to be specially appointed for the purpose. In an action between private parties, it is well settled that after the litigation is closed by final judgment, the legislature cannot grant a new trial. To do so would be to deprive the successful party of his established rights and vested property, and for the legislative department to nullify the accomplished acts of the judicial department. The legislature has control of remedies by which final judgments may be obtained, but cannot confiscate, recall or put again in jeopardy the rights and property established by judgments already obtained. (Germania Savings Bank v Village of Suspension Bridge, 159 NY 362....

....Whether in a given case the legislature has kept within its power or has exceeded it, is of course, a judicial question. (Weisner v Village of Douglas, 64 NY 91.) Tested by this rule this act must fail, for the judgment which it aims to relieve against, passed against the receiver upon a full examination of the merits and not because of any disability of the county to do right, or lack of liability to respond, as the merits might require. If the receiver had recovered final judgment against the county in the former action, it is plain that the legislature could not have reopened the case in favor of the county; the judgment awarded the county affirmative relief because of its rights, not negative relief because of its disability, and, therefore, the judgment in its favor is as much above legislative invasion as if it had been in favor of the receiver.

The order should be affirmed, with costs.

Order affirmed.

Sec. 9.2 Legislative Jurisdiction (local, state, national, and world)
Sec. 9.21 Substantive Jurisdiction
Sec. 9.22 Adjective Jurisdiction

LAWTON v STEELE (1890) 119 NY 226, aff'd152 US 133; a6 S 15

Appeal from judgment of the General Term of the Supreme Court in the fourth judicial department, entered upon an order made February 12, 1889, which reversed a judgment in favor of plaintiffs entered upon a verdict, and ordered a new trial.

This action was brought to recover the value of sixteen hoop or fike nets belonging to plaintiffs, which were destroyed by defendant; twelve of the nets were found by defendant set in the waters of Black River bay, an inlet of Lake Ontario, for the purpose of catching fish, the four others were on shore. Defendant was a state fish and game protector and justified as such....

ANDREWS, J. The conclusions of the trial judge that Black River Bay is a part of Lake Ontario, within the meaning of chapter 146 of the Laws of 1886, and that the nets set therein were set in violation of the act chapter 591 of the Laws of 1880, as amended by chapter 317 of the Laws of 1883, were affirmed by the General Term. The trial judge, in his careful opinion, demonstrated the correctness of these conclusions, ahd nothing can be added to reinforce the argument by which they were sustained.

The point of difference between the trial court and the General Term relates to the constitutionality of the second section of the act of 1880, as amended in 1883. That section is as follows: "Sec. 2. Any net found, or other means or device for taking or capturing fish, or whereby they may be taken or captured set, put, floated, had, found or maintained in or upon any of the waters of this state, or upon the shores or islands in any waters of this state, in violation of any existing or hereafter enacted statutes or laws for the protection of fish, is hereby declared to be, and is a public nuisance, and may be abated and summarily destroyed by any person, and it shall be the duty of each and every (game and fish) protector aforesaid and of every game constable, to seize and remove and destroy the same, *** and no action for damages shall be maintained against any person for or on account of any such seizure or destruction." The defendant justified the seizure and destruction of the nets of plaintiff, as a game protector, under this statute, and established the justification, if the legislature had the constitutional power to authorize the summary remedy proveded by the section in question. The trial judge held the act in this respect to be unconstitutional and ordered judgment in favor of the plaintiffs for the value of the nets. The General Term sustained the constitutionality of the statute and reversed the judgment. We concur with the General Term for reasons which will now be stated.

The legislative power of the state which by the Constitution is vested in the senate and assembly (Sec. 1, art.3), covers every subject which in the distribution of the powers of government between the legislative, executive and judicial departments, belong by practice or usage, in England or in this country, to the legislative department, except in so far as such power has been withheld or limited by the Constitution itself, and subject also to such restrictions upon its exercise as may be found in the Constitution of the United States. From this grant of legislative power springs the right of the legislature to enact a criminal code, to define what acts shall constitute a criminal offense, what penalty shall be inflicted upon offenders, and generally to enact all laws which the legislature shall deem expedient for the protection of public and private rights, and the prevention and punishment of public wrongs. The legislature may not declare that to be a crime which in its nature is and must be under all circumstances innocent, nor can it in defining crimes, or in declaring their punishment, take away or impair any inalienable right secured by the Constitution. But it may, acting within these limits, make acts criminal which before were innocent, and ordain punishment in future cases where before none could have been inflicted. This, in its nature, is a legislative power, which, by the Constitution of the state, is committed to the discretion of the legislative body. (Barker v People, 3 Cow(NY) 686, People v West, 106 NY 293.) The act in question declares that nets set in certain waters are public nuisances, and authorizes their summary destruction. The statute declares and defines a new species of public nuisance, not known to the common law, nor declared to be such by any prior statute. But we know of no limitation of legislative power which precludes the legislature from enlarging the catagory of public nuisances, or from declaring places or property used in the detriment of public interests or to the injury of the health, morals or welfare of the community, public nuisances, although not such at common law. There are, of course, limitations upon the exercise of this power. The legislature cannot use it as a cover for withdrawing property from the protection of the law, or arbitrarily, where no public right of interest is involved, declare property a nuisance for the purpose of devoting it to destruction. If the court can judicially see that the statute is a mere evasion, or was framed for the purpose of individual oppression, it will set it aside as unconstitutional, but not otherwise. (In re Jacobs, 98 NY 98...)

The legislature in the act in question, acting upon the theory and upon the fact (for so it must be assumed) that fishing with nets in prohibited waters is a public injury, have applied the doctrine of the common law to a case new in instance, but not in principle, and made the doing of the prohibited act a nuisance. This we think it could lawfully do.

The more difficult question arises upon the provision in the second section of the act of 1883, which authorizes any person, and makes it the duty of the game protector to abate the nuisance caused by nets set in violation of law, by their summary destruction. It is insisted that the destruction of nets by an individual, or by an executive officer so authorized, without any judicial proceeding, is a deprivation of the owner of the nets of his property, without due process of law, in contravention of the Constitution. The right of summary abatement of nuisances without judicial process or proceeding, was an established principle of the common law long before the adoption of our Constitution, and it has never been supposed that this common-law principle was abrogated by the provision for the protection of life, liberty and property in our state Constitution, although the exercise of the right might result in the destruction of property...In Rockwell v Hearing (35 NY 308), Porter, J., speaking of the constitutional provision, said "there were many examples of summary proceedings which were recognized as due process of law at the date of the Constitution, and to them the prohibition has no application." Quarantine and health laws have been enacted from time to time from the organization of our state government, authorizing the summary destruction of infected cargo, clothing or other articles, by officers designated, and no doubt has been suggested as to their constitutionality. In Hart v Mayor, etc. (supra), a question was raised as to the validity of a city ordinance, subjecting a float moored in the Albany basin to summary seizure and sale upon failure of the owner to remove the same after notice. The court held the ordinance to be void as not within the power conferred upon the city by its charter, but it was held that the common law right of abatement existed, although the removal of the float in question involved its destruction. Van Wormer v Mayor, etc. (15 Wend(NY) 263), sustained the right of a municipal corporation to dig down a lot in the city, to abate a nuisance although in the process of abatement buildings thereon were pulled down. In Meeker v Van Rensselaer (15 Wend(NY) 397), the court justified the act of the defendant as an individual citizen, in tearing down a filthy tenement house which was a nuisance, to prevent the spread of the Asiatic cholera.

These authorities sufficiently establish the proposition that the constitutional guaranty does not take away the common law right of abatement of nuisances by summary proceedings, without judicial trial or process. But in the process of abating a nuisance there are limitations both in respect of the agencies which may be employed, and as to what may be done in execution of the remedy. The general proposition has been asserted in text-books and repeated in judicial opinions, that any person may abate a public nuisance. But the best considered authorities in this country and England now hold that a public nuisance can only be abated by an individual where it obstructs his private right, or interferes at the time with his enjoyment of a right common to many, as the right of passage upon the public highway, and he thereby sustains a special injury. (...(Fort Plain Bridge Co. v Smith, 30 NY 44; Harrower v Ritson, 37 Barb(NY) 301).

The public remedy is ordinarily by indictment for the punishment of the offender, wherein on judgment of conviction the removal or destruction of the thing constituting the nuisance, if physical and tangible, may be adjudged, or by bill in equity filed in behalf of the people. Bur the remedy by judicial prosecution, in rem or in personam, is not, we conceive, exclusive, where the statute in a particular case gives a remedy by summary abatement, and the remedy is apporpriate to the object to be accomplished. There are nuisances arising from conduct, which can only be abated by the arrest and punishment of the offender, and in such cases, it is obvious that the legislature could not directly direct the sheriff or other officer to seize and flog or imprison the culprit. The infliction of punishment for crime is the prerogative of the court and cannot be usurped by the legislature. The legislature can only define the offense and prescribe the measure of punishment, where guilt shall have been judicially ascertained. But as the legislature may declare nuisances, it may also, where the nuisance is physical and tangible, direct its summary abatement by executive officers, without the intervention of judicial proceedings, in cases analogous to those where the remedy by summary abatement existed at common-law...

But the remedy by summary abatement cannot be extended beyond the purpose implied in the words, and must be confined to doing what is necessary to accomplish it. And here lies, we think, the stress of the question now presented. It cannot be denied that in many cases a nuisance can only be abated by the destruction of the property in which it consists. The cases of infected cargo or clothing and of impure and unwholesome food are plainly of this description. They are nuisances per se, and their abatement is their destruction. So, also, there can be little doubt, as we conceive, that obscene books or pictures, or implements only capable of an illegal use, may be destroyed as a part of the process of abating the nuisance they create, if so directed by statute. The keeping of a bawdy house, or a house for the resort of lewd and dissolute people, is a nuisance at common law. But the tearing down of the building so kept, would not be justified as the exercise of the power of summary abatement and it would add nothing, we think, to the justification that a statute was produced authorizing the destruction of the building summarily as a part of the remedy. The nuisance consists in the case supposed in the conduct of the owner or occupants of the house, in using or allowing it to be used for the immoral purpose, and the remedy would be to stop the use. This would be the only mode of abatement in such case known to the common law, and the destruction of the building for this purpose would have no sanction in common law or precedent. (See Babcock v City of Buffalo, 56 NY 268; Barclay v Commonwealth, 25 Penn. St. 503; Ely v Board of Supervisors, 36 NY 297.)

But where a public nuisance consists in the location or use of tangible personal property, so as to interfere with or obstruct a public right or regulation, as in the case of the float in the Albany basin (9 Wend (NY) 571) or the nets in the present case, the legislature may, we think, authorize its summary abatement by executive agencies without resort to judicial proceedings, and any injury or destruction of the property necessarily incident to the exercise of the summary jurisdiction, interferes with no legal right of the owner. But the legislature cannot go further. It cannot decree the destruction or forfeiture of property used so as to constitute a nuisance as a punishment of the wrong, nor even, we think, to prevent a future illegal use of the property, it not being a nuisance per se, and appoint officers to execute its mandate. The plain reason is that due process of law requires a hearing and trial before punishment, or before forfeiture of property can be adjudged for the owner's misconduct. Such legislation would be a plain usurption by the legislature of judicial powers, and under guise of exercising the power of summary abatement of nuisances, the legislature cannot take into its own hands the enforcement of the criminal or quasi criminal law. (See opinion of Shaw, Ch. J., in Fisher v McGirr, supra, and in Brown v Perkins, 12 Gray(Mass) 89.)

The inquiry in the present case comes to this: Whether the destruction of the nets set in violation of law, authorized and required by the act of 1883, is simply a proper, reasonable and necessary regulation for the abatement of the nuisance, or transcends that purpose, and is to be regarded as the imposition and infliction of a forfeiture of the owners' right of property in the nets, in the nature of a punishment. We regard the case as very near the border line, but we think the legislation may be fairly sustained on the ground that the destruction of nets so placed is a reasonable incident of the power to abate the nuisance. The owner of the nets is deprived of his property, but not as the direct object of the law, but as an incident to the abatement of the nuisance. Where a private person is authorizedto abate apublic nuisance, as in case of a house built in a highway, or a gate across it, which obstructs and prevents his passage thereon, it was long ago held he was not required to observe particular care in abating the nuisance, and that although the gate might have been opened without cutting it down, yet the cutting down would be lawful. (Lodie v Arnold, 2 Salk. 458, and cases cited). But the general rule undoubtedly is that the abatement must be limited by necessity, and no wanton and unnecessary injury must be committed (3 Bl. 6, note.) It is conceivable that nets illegally set could, with the use of care, be removed without destroying them. But in view of their position, the difficulty attending their removal, the liability to injury in the process, their comparatively small value, we think the legislature could adjudge their destruction as a reasonable means of abating a nuisance.

These views lead to an affirmance of the order of the General Term...

It is insisted that the provisions in the act of 1883, authorizes the destruction of nets found on the land, on shores or islands adjacent to waters, where taking of fish by nets is prohibited, and that this part of the statute is in any view unconstitutional. Assuming this premise it is claimed that the whole section must fall, as the statute, if unconstitutional as to one provision, is unconstitutional as a whole. This is not, we think, the general rule of law, where provisions of a statute are separable, one of which only is void. On the contrary the general rule requires the court to sustain the valid provisions, while rejecting the others. Where the void matter is so blended with the good that they cannot be separated, or where the court can judicially see that the legislature only intended the statute to be enforced in its entirety, and that by rejecting part the general purpose of the statute would be defeated, the court, if compelled to defeat the main purpose of the statute, will not strive to save any part. (See Fisher v McGirr, supra.)

The order granting a new trial should be affirmed and judgment absolute ordered for the defendant on the stipulation, with costs.

Order affirmed and judgment accordingly.

PEOPLE v DEVLIN (1865) 33 NY 269

This was an action brought by the Attorney General against Daniel Devlin, chamberlain of the city and county of New York, to recover certain moneys in the hands of the defendant, which, it was claimed, he ought to have paid over to the state treasurer. The defendant claimed the right to retain the same as his commissions and fees.

The case was tried before a referee, who....found, either as a matter of fact or of law, as it might appear to the court, that there was of record in the office of the secretary of state of the state of New York, an act of the legislature, of which chapter 393, of the Laws of 1863, in the printed laws of that year, was a copy, on which record was an indorsement, signed by the secretary of state, who held that office during the year 1863, in the words following:

"State of New York)
Office of the Secretary of State.)

This act having been approved and signed by the Governor, on the 4th day of May 1863, I hereby certify, that the same became a law, on that day.

HORATIO BALLARD,
Secretary of State."

That from the journals of the senate and assembly for the year 1863, it appeared, that a bill, in terms agreeing with the said chap. 393, was, on the 17th day of April 1863, read a third time in the assembly, and passed, three-fifths of all the members being present, and ordered to be sent to the senate. That in the senate, on the 22d day of April, the said bill from the assembly was passed, without amendment, three-fifths of all the senators being present, and was ordered to be returned to the assembly, and the same was so returned; and that, thereupon, on the same day, the said bill was sent by the assembly to the governor. That, on the 23d day of April, the assembly requested the governor to return the said bill to the assembly; and, on the same day, the governor returned the said bill to the assembly, with a message stating that it was so returned, upon the request of the assembly.

That upon the return of the said bill, the assembly resolved that the 5th section of the said bill be stricken out...

But no further action was had...in respect to the said bill or act, so far as was proven by the journals of the senate and assembly.

And upon these facts, the referee decided as matter of law, that the defendant had no right to retain for his compensation, or otherwise, a greater sum than $2000, and that he ought to pay to the plaintiffs the balance of the amount retained by him, with lawful interest thereon, from the 1st May, 1864 (after deducting $2000), amounting in the aggregate to $20,600.99; for which sum he directed a judgment against the defendant.

Judgment was, accordingly, entered upon the referee's report, in favor of the People, for $20,600.99; and the same having been affirmed at general term, the defendant took this appeal.

POTTER, J.... The act of the legislature of May 4th, 1863, ch. 393, requires county treasurers, on or before the first day of April in each year, to pay the treasurer of the state the amount of state tax raised and paid over to them... The 5th section of the act of 1863, in terms, authorized county treasurers to retain the compensation allowed by law, at the time this act took effect, but restricted them to a sum not, in any case, to exceed the sum of $2000...

If, then, the 5th section of the act of 1863 was a law of the state of New York, when the funds in question came into the hands of the defendant, and when he paid over the amount which he did pay to the state treasurer, then the judgment below is right; otherwise, it should be reversed. This is the only and single question that remains.

As evidence that the act in question, including the said 5th section, is a law of the state, there was produced, on the trial, the record of such an act, from the office of the sceretary of state of 'the state of New York, on which record is an indorsement, signed by the secretary of state who held the office during the year 1863, in the usual form, certifying that the act had been approved and signed by the governor on the 4th day of May 1863, and the further certificate of said secretary, that the same became a law on that day. In the printed volume of the laws of that year, is a copy of the said act; the volume from which the statute was read is certified in like manner by the secretary of state. By the statute of this state of 1846, ch. 24, it is provided, that "all laws passed by the legislature may be read in evidence, from the volumes printed under the direction of the secretary of state. The evidence, therefore, of the existence of such a statute, was produced on the part of the people. By the revised statutes, vol, 1, p. 157 (marg. paging), Sec. 10 requires that the secretary of state shall receive every bill which shall have passed the senate and assembly, and been approved and signed by the governor, &c., and shall deposit such laws in his office. By Sec. 11, he is required to certify and indorse upon every such bill, the day, month and year when the same so became a law, and such certificate shall be conclusive evidence of the facts therein declared.

To impeach this record, the journals of the senate and assembly were introduced, which showed the action had upon the said bill, in those two houses, to be as contained in the report of the referee. And the question that first arises upon this showing is, can a legislative act, so certified, be impeached by the journals of the two houses? To determine this, we may resort to the constitution, the statute, and to the common or parliamentary law.

By the provisions of the present constitution, the common law of the colony of New York and acts of its legislatire as they existed on the 19th April 1775, and the acts of the legislature in force at the making the constitution, were made the law of the state. (Art. i., Sec. 17, Const. 1846). "The legislative power of the state shall be vested in a senate and assembly." (Art. iii., Sec. 1.) "A majority of each house shall constitute a quorum to do business, and each house shall determine the rules of its own proceedings." (Art. iii., Sec. 10.) "Each house shall keep a journal of its proceedings and publish the same, except such parts as may require secrecy." (Art. iii., Sec. 11). "Any bill may originate in either house of the legislature, and all bills passed by one house may be amended by the other." (Art. iii., Sec. 13.) "No law shall be enacted, except by bill." (Art. iii., Sec. 14). "No bill shall be passed, unless by the assent of a majority of all the members elected to each branch of the legislature, and the question upon the final passage shall be taken immediately upon its last reading, and the yeas and nays entered on the journal." (Art. iii., Sec. 16.) "Every bill which shall have passed the senate and assembly shall before it becomes a law, be presented to the governor, if he approve of it, he shall sign it, but if not, he shall return it, with his objections, to that house in which it shall have originated, who shall enter the objections at large on their hournal, and proceed to reconsider it," &c. (Art. iv.,

Sec. 9.) "On the final passage, in either house, of the legislature, of every act which imposes; continues or revives a tax, or creates a debt or charge, or makes continues or revives any appropriation of public or trust money, or property, or releases, discharges or commutes any claim or demand of the state, the question shall be taken by ayes and noes, which shall be duly entered on the journals, and three-fifths of all the members elected to either house, shall in all such cases, be necessary to constitute a quorum therein." (Art. vii., Sec. 14.)

The foregoing are all the constitutional provisions in regard to the performance of duties by the legislature, necessary to the passage of acts, in order to constitute them valid laws....

After the passage of a bill, in the legal and constitutional form, by both houses of the legislature, and the same has been transmitted by them to the governor, in the manner provided by the constitution, have the two houses exhausted their power over it, or can they, or can either of the said houses, without the consent of the other, recall the bill, by resolution, and revest themselves with power further to act upon it? If they do possess the power, it is not found in the constitution; it is not found in the statute; it is not shown to be the custom or usage. Although "each house shall determine the rules of its own proceedings," no rule for such a proceeding as that of sending for a bill in the possession of the governor, has been shown to exist; besides, the bill at that time, had become the act of both houses, and neither had then any further control over it.

The act of courtesy of the governor, in returning to the assembly the bill, at their request, conferred no power upon the house of assembly to act further upon it. Even if the governor had intended to allow them so to act (as by his subsequently signing the bill in the form he first received it, it seems, he did not), it is still a question of power. No authority is shown to be possessed by the governor, to perform such an act, as a part of the law-making power.

If the assembly possessed the power of recalling bills from the governor, after being passed by both houses and sent to him, it is not found in parliamentary law, and no custom of that kind is shown. If we may take judicial notice of parliamentary law, as contained in the rules of the assembly, made under the constitutional provision for that purpose, and published by them in the session of 1863, no such rule, or custom, or law is found. According to those rules (rule 43), the question upon the final passage of a bill shall be immediately after the third reading; so the vote was taken in this case. There can be but one third reading of a bill, and but one "final passage" in either house; this bill had received such third reading, and has its final passage in both houses before being sent to the governor. It having passed the senate, without amendment, the assembly then had no power to amend it, by any rule or custom of legislation. When both houses have thus finally passed a bill, and sent it to the governor, they have exhausted their powers upon it, except the power of sending it to the governor, by the house in which it originated, according to parliamentary law...

There is no doubt, that each house of the legislature, by virtue of the constitutional provisions we have cited, and perhaps inherently, have power to determine for itself rules and orders to govern them in the various stages of legislation, and in relation to all matters relating to the exercise of their rights, powers and privileges. When such rules or laws have been established by them, as they were in this instance, they become the law of that body for such purpose, and are binding upon them as the law to govern them in such proceedings; and this is called parliamentary law. (2 Salk. 503; 2 Ld. Raym. 1105.) And when they have established such rules, and they thus become the law, for such purpose, they cannot themselves arbitrarily depart from such law, and conduct their proceedings by other rules, not known to or adopted by such body. And, though acts of the legislature, signed by the governor, not in conflict with the constitution, may be omnipotent in this regard, to overcome violations of parliamentary law, in producing their passage, it is quite clear, that anything short of an act of the legislature can work no such effect as to legalize a breach of their rules.

I am of opinion, that the legislative journals were not legitimate evidence, to impeach the statute produced. They are not made evidence by the constitution; they are not made so by the statute; they were never made so, at common law. They are, doubtless, evidence, from the necessity of the case, on grounds of public convenience, and from the public character of the facts they contain, to prove the proceedings of the body whose records they are, because the constitution requires them to be kept. Whenever any act or proceeding of such body becomes necessary to be shown as evidence, such journals may be received; but to impeach the force and effect of a solemn statute, duly certified, no authority can be found, within the limits of my research, to admit them to be legitimate evidence, but much authority may be found to the contrary...

It would be destructive not only to all public confidence, but would open a wide door for litigation, if our statutes, published by publuc authority, were liable to be annuled or impeached by issues of fact, to be raised either of fraud in procuring their passage, or in lack of conformity to rule, by either house in the usual forms of enactment. If the defence interposed in this case, that no such statute exists, can be make available, and such questions, as questions of fact, can be brought into the courts for trial, an intolerable condition of legal uncertainity would result. Such a case is unheard of; it is too dangerous in its consequences, to be entertained as an experiment; it is without authority as a precedent. I have not been able to find any error in the judgment that demands a reversal. I think, the judgment should be affirmed.

Judgment affirmed.

Sec. 9.3 Forms of Legislative Action

A. Form of a Statute:

STATE OF NEW YORK

S. 1992

Intro. A. 2885
Print A. 2950

SENATE — ASSEMBLY

January 25, 1967

IN SENATE—Introduced by Mr. DONOVAN—read twice and ordered printed, and when printed to be committed to the Committee on Corporations

IN ASSEMBLY—Introduced by Mr. BUCKLEY—read once and referred to the Committee on Cities

AN ACT

To amend chapter eighty-eight of the laws of eighteen hundred seventy-three, entitled "An act to incorporate the Faxton Hospital in the city of Utica," in relation to the board of managers of such hospital

The People of the State of New York, represented in Senate and Assembly, do enact as follows:

Section 1. Section six of chapter eighty-eight of the laws of eighteen hundred seventy-three, entitled "An act to incorporate the Faxton Hospital in the city of Utica," as amended by chapter five hundred eighty-nine of the laws of nineteen hundred sixty-six, is hereby amended to read as follows:

§ 6. At each annual meeting the council shall elect five managers for the term of three years, to succeed the five managers whose terms of office shall expire at said annual meeting. Men and women shall be eligible to the office of manager(, but no member of the professional staff of the hospital shall be eligible to such office). If the managers shall not be elected on the day fixed by law every manager shall continue to hold his office and discharge his duties until his successor has been elected. Whenever any vacancy shall occur in the office of manager by death, removal, resignation, or otherwise, the vacancy shall be filled by the remaining managers. The board of managers, at its discretion, may elect up to three additional managers-at-large to be elected for a term of one year.

§ 2. This act shall take effect immediately.

EXPLANATION—Matter in *italics* is new; matter in brackets [ ] is old law to be omitted.

B. Form of a Resolution

STATE OF NEW YORK
IN SENATE
Albany

January 30, 1967
Resolution No. 46

By: MR. BRYDGES

SENATE RESOLUTION expressing the sympathy of the Senate of the State of New York to the family of Lt. Col. Edward H. White II, U.S. Air Force, and directing the appointment of a committee of the Senate to attend his funeral.

Whereas, The nation was shocked to learn of the tragic deaths of three of our great astronauts; and

Whereas, These men who became national heroes and carried with them the hope and aspirations of our people in opening up the field of space exploration were intrepid, brave officers who gave their lives that our nation might contribute new knowledge to the world in the field of science; now, therefore, be it

RESOLVED, That the Senate does hereby express to the families of the deceased its deepest sympathy in their great loss; and be it further

RESOLVED, That the Temporary President of the Senate shall appoint a committee of four Senators to attend the funeral, on Tuesday, January thirty-first, nineteen hundred sixty-seven, of Lt. Col. Edward H. White II, U. S. Air Force, at the West Point Cemetery, one of the hallowed locations of our Empire State, where many notable heroes of our nation lie; and be it further

RESOLVED, That a copy of this resolution be transmitted to the family of Lt. Col. White.

By order of the Senate,

____

Secretary

C. Form of a Concurrent.Resolution

LBDC 11:AYB 12/6/66

By Ferraro

40 State of New York
Jan 24, 1967
in Senate

Finance

CONCURRENT RESOLUTION requesting the Governor to issue a proclamation designating March twenty-fifth of this year as Hellenic Day

Whereas, on March twenty-fifth, eighteen hundred twenty-one the Greece of modern times once again became an independent Nation through the never ceasing faith, hope and courage of her people; and

Whereas, in the century that followed Greece has struggled unceasingly to preserve her freedom and the freedom of the world with the same indomitable spirit of the ancient Lacedaemonians at Thermopylae; and

Whereas, even today Greece is in the forefront of the fight for freedom and democracy and engaged in a momentous struggle to resist aggression and to stem the tide of communism which threatens to engulf the World and impose its slavery upon all people, everywhere; and

Whereas, Persons of Greek origin and descent have greatly contributed to the progress of the United States and are loyal, industrious and law abiding, as is eminently befitting an ancient cultured race; and have settled throughout our Country entering various phases of American life, and contributed greatly thereto, and are noted for their community spirit in matters of charity and humane consideration; now, therefore, be it

Resolved (if the Assembly concur), that the Legislature of the state of New York acknowledges the contribution made to our Nation by persons of Hellenic origin by endorsing the celebration of the anniversary of the Greek Independence on March twenty-fifth, nineteen hundred sixty-seven; and be it further

Resolved (if the Assembly concur), that the Governor, of New York shall issue, publish, and declare an appropriate proclamation to the people of New York state designating for observance this year the twenty-fifth day of March as Hellenic Day.

D. Form of a Memorial

LBDC 1/23/67 6:3b 50

State of New York
Jan. 31, 1967
in Senate

FINANCE

By Mr. Liebowitz

CONCURRENT RESOLUTION OF THE LEGISLATURE OF THE STATE OF NEW YORK memorializing the Congress of the United States to make a study of the feasibility of subsidizing part of the cost of the installation of air pollution devices or systems on all motor vehicles and to enact legislation pertaining thereto

Whereas, The Legislature finds that a national emergency exists because of air pollution; and

Whereas, Motor vehicles are the most potent factor in causing this contamination, causing more than forty per cent of the air pollution in cities; and

Whereas, The dangerous chemicals emitted by motor vehicles each day when inhaled is equivalent to smoking two and one-half packs of cigarettes per day; and

Whereas, A simple solution to alleviate this dangerous condition would require every used car to be equipped with an air pollution device or system; and

Whereas, A bill now pending before this Legislature would require used car dealers to install such equipment before re-sale but it would impose too great a financial burden to require all cars to be so equipped without some subsidy; now, therefore, be it

Resolved (if the Assembly concur), That the Congress of the United States be and hereby is memorialized to make a study of the feasibility of subsidizing part of the cost of the installation of air pollution devices or systems on all motor vehicles and to enact, with all convenient speed, legislation to implement its findings; and be it further

Resolved (if the Assembly concur), That copies of this resolution be transmitted to the House of Representatives of the Congress of the United States by forwarding one copy thereof to the Clerk of the House of Representatives and one copy to each member of the House of Representatives from the state of New York.

Sec. 9.4 Evolution of Legislative Action
Sec. 9.41 Legislative Investigations
Sec. 9.42 Lobbying

PEOPLE ex rel. McDONALD v KEELER, As Sheriff, etc. (1885) 99 NY 469, r32 Hun 563.

APPEAL from order of the General Term of the Supreme Court, third department, made May 6, 1884, which reversed an order of the Court of Oyer and Terminer in and for the county of Albany, denying application of relator for release from Albany County jail on habeas corpus from imprisonment, and directed his discharge...

RAPALLO, J. The return to the writ of habeas corpus in this case showed that the realtor was held by the sheriff in his custody by virtue of a commitment issued by the president and clerk of the senate of this State on the 28th of February, 1884, a copy of which committment was annexed to the return....

From the return and traverse and the recitals contained in the resolutions therein set out, it appears in substance that charges of fraud and irregularity having been made by the public press and others against the commissioner of public works in the city of New York, the senate on the 14th of January, 1884, adopted a resolution directing and empowering its standing committee on the affairs of the cities to investigate the department of public works in said city, with power to send for persons and papers and to report the result of such investigation and its recommendations concerning the same to the senate; that the relator being summoned to appear and testify before such committee, attended, and, after having been examined at considerable length, declined to answer certain question propounded to him by the committee and refused to be further examined and retired from the presence of the committee without their permission.

These facts having been reported by the committee to the senate, that body, on the 25th of February, 1884, directed its president to issue his warrant to the sergeant at arms, commanding him to arrest the relator and bring him before the bar of the senate to answer why he should not be punished as guilty of a contempt of its dignity and authority. A warrant having been accordingly issued, the relator was, on the 27th of February, 1884, brought before the bar of the senate and there arraigned, by its order, for a breach of its privileges, in disobeying a subpoena issued by its committee on cities to appear before said committee and give testimony upon an investigation then pending before it, and in refusing to answer proper questions put by said committee and in refusing to be further examined before said committee and he was thereupon called upon for his answer to the charge. He requested to answer by counsel, which request was granted, and, after counsel had been heard in his behalf, a resolution was adopted requiring the committee on cities to report all the testimony and proceedings had by the committee in relation to the relator, on the following day.

On the 28th of February the report was presented and was afterward, by resolution, made a part of the record in the further consideration of the case. From this report it appears that the relator was allowed to be attended and advised by counsel, during his examination before the committee; that on various questions being propounded to him he was instructed by his counsel not to answer, and being required by the committee to answer them, he declined to do so on the ground of the advice of his counsel. After numerous refusals to answer, of this description, the committee, on motion, directed that its chairman no longer recognize the right of the witness to have any counsel present. Thereupon the counsel instructed the witness to withdraw from the committee and leave with him. The chairman stated to the witness that if he did, it would be at his peril, and he replied that he took the peril of it. He was informed that his examination was not concluded, and was advised by the chairman not to leave, and the witness replied that he would take the consequences...

... the Senate adopted the following resolution: "that William McDonald having been declared to be guilty of a contempt of the senate, and being convicted thereof for refusing to answer, as a witness, pertinent questions propounded by the standing committee on the affairs of cities of the senate, in the investigation of the department of public works in the city of New York, and being summoned as a witness and appearing before the committee, for refusing to submit to an examination, as a witness, before such committee, on the subject of said investigation, and quitting the presence of said committee, be and he hereby is remanded into the custody of the sergeant-at-arms, and is hereby sentenced to be, by said sergeant, imprisoned in the county jail of Albany county, there to remain until he shall consent to appear before the standing committee on the affairs of cities, as a witness, and answer the questions put to him by the said committee, in the matter of said investigation, said imprisonment, however, not to extend beyond the final adjournment of the present legislature; and the keeper of the said common jail of the county of Albany is hereby commanded to receive said William McDonald and him safely keep and imprison in said jail until the adjournment of the present legislature, unless sooner discharged by order of the senate."

In pursuance of this resolution the commitment in question was issued by the president and clerk of the senate and directed to the sergeant-at-arms and the sheriff of the county of Albany, and the relator was accordingly imprisoned in the county jail.

The broad ground is now taken on the part of the relator that the senate had no jurisdiction or power to adjudge him guilty of the contempt with which he was charged or to imprison him therefor...

Title 2, chapter 7, part 1 of the Revised Statutes, entitled "of the powers, duties and privileges of the two houses and their members and officers" provides as follows (Sec. 13): "Each house has the power to punish as a contempt and by imprisonment, a breach of its privileges, or of the privileges of its members, but such power shall not hereafter be exercised except against persons guilty of one or more of the following offenses:

1. The offense of arresting a member or officer of the house in violation of his privilege from arrest as hereinbefore declared.
2. That of disorderly conduct in the immediate view and presence of the house, and directly tending to interrupt its proceedings.
3. That of publishing any false and malicious report of the proceedings of the house, or of the conduct of a member in his legislative capacity.
4. That of refusing to attend or be examined as a witness either before the house or by a committee to take testimony in legislative proceedings.
5. That of giving or offering a bribe to a member, or of attempting by menace or any other corrupt means or device, directly or indirectly, to control or influence a member in giving his vote, or to prevent him from giving the same.

The five enumerated offenses are the only ones which either house is authorized to punish as contempts, and they take the place of the numerous offenses and acts which were treated by Parliament as contempts.

In the...case of Kilbourn v Thompson (103 US 168), which was a similar action, the plaintiff had on proceedings similar to those taken in the present case, been convicted of a contempt and sentenced by the house of representatives to imprisonment. It appeared on the face of the proceedings that the contempt consisted of his refusal to answer a question propounded by the committee of the house appointed by a resolution, which was set forth. This resolution directed the committee to investigate certain business transactions in which the United States government was interested simply as a creditor of one of the parties; and the Supreme Court held that the preamble and resolution under which the committee was appointed showed upon their face that the investigation ordered did not have for its object any legislative action, or the impeachment of any officer of the government, but the collection of a debt owing to the government, a power which Congress could not exercise, but which was vested only in courts of justice; that in ordering such an investigation the house of representatives exceeded the limits of its powers and consequently the committee had no authority to require the plaintiff to testify before it.

The only express provision of the State Constitution which is claimed to be violated, is that which declares that no person shall be deprived of life, liberty or property without due process of law. If the statute in question was within the power of the legislature to enact, the proceedings against the relator were due process of law. He was imprisoned by virtue of a pre-existing law, informed of the charge made against him, and was heard in person and by counsel in his defense. The proceedings need not be according to the course of the common law (Happy v Mosher 48 NY 313...) and we necessarily come back to the question whether the legislature had power to enact the law.

But the main ground upon which the statute is assailed is, that it confers upon each of the two houses a power, which is in its nature judicial, to hear, adjudge and condemn; that no such power can be conferred by statute upon the legislature itself or either branch thereof; that the Constitution gives the senate and assembly only legislative power, and that judicial power is vested in the courts named in the Constitution and in such inferior courts as may be created, and that the grant of judicial power to the courts is an implied prohibition of its assumption by the legislature, except as authorized by the Constitution...

The power of obtaining information for the purpose of framing laws to meet supposed or apprehended evils, is one which has from time immemorial been deemed necessary and has been exercised by legislative bodies. In this State it does not rest upon precedent merely, but is expressly conferred by statute (1 RS 158 Sec 1, 2) which provides that every chairman of a committee, either of the senate or assembly, or of any joint committee, is authorized to administer oaths to witnesses; and when the committee is by the terms of the resolution appointing it authorized to send for persons and papers, the chairman has the power, under the direction of the committee, to issue compulsory process for the attendance of any witness within the State whom the committee may wish to examine, and to issue commissions for the examination of witnesses out of the State. To subject a witness to punishment as for a contempt, the testimony sought must, as has already been shown, relate to a legislative proceeding. (1 RS 154, Sec. 13, subd. 4).

It is difficult to conceive any constitutional objection which can be raised to the provisions authorizing legislative committees to take testimony and to summon witnesses. In many cases it may be indispensable to intelligent and effectual legislation to ascertain the facts which are claimed to give rise to the necessity for such legislation, and the remedy required and irrespective of the question whether in the absence of a statute to that effect either house would have the power to imprison a reluctant witness, I cannot yield to the claim that a statute authorizing it to enforce its process in that manner is in excess of the legislative power. To await the slow process of indictment and prosecution for a misdemeanor, might prove quite ineffectual and necessary legislation might be obstructed, and perhaps defeated, if the legislative body had no other and more summary means of enforcing its right to obtain the required information. That the power may be abused, is no ground for denying its existence. It is a limited power, and should be kept within its proper bounds; and when these are exceeded, a jurisdictional question is presented which is cognizable in the courts. My conclusion is that subdivision 4 of section 13, 1 Revised Statutes, is constitutional and valid.

Two other points are presented on this appeal. One is that the investigation on which the relator was sought to be examined was one which the house was not authorized to institute, and that the case, therefore, falls within the decision in Kilbourn v Thompson, and the other, that the questions which the relator refused to answer were not pertinent or proper. This second point we do not deem it necessary to discuss, because the contempt charge consisted, not merely of the relator refusing to answer those questions, but of his refusing to be further examined, or to remain in attendance upon the committee, though informed that his examination was not concluded and warned not to leave, and that if he left he did so at his peril. Assuming that the statute (subd. 4 of Sec. 13) is valid and that the investigation was a legislative proceeding which the house had authority to institute, we think that by refusing to be further examined, and withdrawing from the presence of the committee without its consent, he brought himself within the terms of subdivision 4 defining as an offense "refusing to attend or be examined as a witness either before the house or a committee to take testimony in legislative proceedings".

His refusal to be further examined, or to remain in attendance, was placed upon the ground that the committee refused to recognize his right to be attended by counsel and act under his advice in answering questions, but we are of opinion that he had no constitutional or legal right to the aid of counsel on such examination. The constitutional provision on the subject is that "in any trial in any court whatever the party accused shall be allowed to appear and defend in person and with counsel as in civil actions." (Const. art. 1, Sec. 6). This provision has been very liberally construed and held to apply to trials before any authority having jurisdiction to try, and in People ex rel. Mayor, etc. v Nichols (79 NY 582), this court held that a police commissioner, appearing before the Mayor of the city of New York to show cause why he should not be removed for cause, pursuant to the statute, was entitled to defend by cousel.

But here the relator was not on trial, nor was he a party, but he was a mere witness called upon to testify in relation to charges against another person, and there was no trial pending against any one. As well might a witness, examined before a grand jury conducting an investigation of a charge against anotner person, with a view to his indictment, claim the right to be attended by counsel. We do not think that a mere witness has that right.

Sec. 9.6 Enforcement of Legislation

THE BOARD OF COMMISSIONERS OF EXCISE, Respondent, v GURDON F. MERCHANT, Appellant. (1886) 103 NY 143 a34 Hun 19.

AN APPEAL from judgment of General Term, affirming a judgment in favor of plaintiff for damages and costs, and an order denying motion for a new trial upon judge's minutes.

The action was one for penalties incurred by defendant in selling liquors, etc., without a license.

EARL, J. ....Upon the trial of this action the judge charged the jury that "the law provides in such case as this, that upon proof being made of the fact that liquor was seen to be drank on the premises, that is prima facie evidence that it was sold with intent that it was to be drank on the premises." To this portion of the charge defendant's counsel excepted, and the exception is now relied upon as pointing out error fatal to the judgment.

In section 11 of the Excise Act (Chap. 628, Laws of 1857), provision is made for licenses to storekeepers, and shop-keepers, authorizing them to sell spirituous liquors in quantities less than five gallons not to be drank upon their premises. Then in section 12 it is provided as follows: Such licenses shall not be granted unless the commissioners are satisfied that the applicant is of good moral character, nor until such applicant shall have executed a bond to the people of this State *** conditioned that*** he will not sell, or suffer to be sold, any strong or spirituous liquors or wines to be drank in his shop or house, or in any out-house, yard or garden appertaining thereto, and that he will not suffer any such liquor sold by virtue of such license to be drank in his shop or house or in any out-house, yard or garden belonging thereto; and whenever any person is seen to drink in such shop or house, out-house, yard or garden belonging thereto, any spirituous liquors or wines forbidden to be drank therein, it shall be prima facie evidence that such spirituous liquors or wines were sold by the occupant of such premises or his agent with the intent that the same should be drank therein. On any trial for the offense last aforesaid, such occupant or agent may be allowed to testify respecting such sale." It was undoubtedly this law to which the judge referred in his charge.

All the provisions of section 12 have reference to licenses to sell liquor in quantities less than five gallons not to be drank on the premises, and the rule of evidence prescribed applies only to cases where such licenses have been granted. The defendant had such a license from September 6, 1880, to May 1, 1881 when it was revoked.

Upon the trial the plaintiff gave evidence tending to show violations of the license by the defendant by the sale of liquor to be drank upon his premises between September 1, 1880, and June, 1881, and the proof of sales was limited to that period. The charge of the Judge was authorized by the statute if applied to drinking liquor upon defendant's premises during the time he had the license. But it was not authorized if applied to the drinking of liquor there before September sixth, or after May first. There was no specific, definite evidence that any of the drinking took place before the first or after the latter date, and if the defendant desired to have the charge so qualified as to apply only to drinking which took place while the license was in force, he should have called the attention of the Judge to the facts, and have requested the qualification; and now the charge must be treated as if it applied only to the period covered by defendant's license.

Thus, the charge was authorized by the words of the statute. But the learned counsel for the appellant claims that this provision of the statute is unconstitutional on the ground that it violates the constitutional guaranties of due process of law and trial by jury. We think the claim unfounded. The general power of the legislature to prescribe rules of evidence and methods of proof is undoubted. While the power has its constitutional limitations, it is not easy to define precisely what they are. A law which would practically shut out the evidence of a party and thus deny him the opportunity for a trial would substantially deprive him of due process of law. It would not be possible to uphold a law which made an act prima facie evidence of crime over which the party charged had no control and with which he had no connection, or which made that prima facie evidence of crime which had no relation to a criminal act and no tendency whatever by itself to prove a criminal act.

But so long as the legislature, in prescribing rules of evidence, in either civil or criminal cases, leaves a party a fair opportunity to make his defense and to submit all the facts to the jury to be weighed by them, upon evidence legitimately bearing upon them, it is difficult to perceive how its acts can be assailed upon constitutional grounds.

Affidavits in town bounding acts and tax deeds have been declared to be prima facie evidence of regularity and validity, and numerous statutes of similar character are to be found in this and other states. In Comm. v Williams (6 Gray 1) it was held in a criminal prosecution for a violation of an excise law, that a statute which provided that the delivering of any spirituous and intoxicating liquors in or from any building or place other than a dwelling house, "shall be deemed prima facie evidence of a sale," was constitutional and valid. In State v Hurley (54 Me 562), it was held that an act which provided that "whenever an unlawful sale" of intoxicating liquors "is alleged and a delivery proved, it shall not be necessary to prove payment, but such delivery shall be sufficient evidence of sale" was constitutional.

In Howard v Mott (64 NY 261), ALLEN, J., said: "The rules of evidence are not an exception to the doctrine that all rules and regulations affecting remedies are, at all times, subject to modification and control by the legislature. ***It may be conceded, for all the purposes of this appeal, that a law that should make evidence conclusive which was not so necessarily in and of itself, and thus preclude the adverse party from showing the truth, would be void, as indirectly working a confiscation of property or a destruction of vested rights. But such is not the effect of declaring any circumstance or any evidence, however slight, prima facie proof of a fact to be established, leaving the adverse party at liberty to rebut and overcome it by contradictory and better evidence."

Here the act which is made prima facie evidence of an illegal sale takes place upon the premises of the person charged, has some relation to and furnishes some evidence of the alleged illegal sale, and occurs in a place where liquors are authorized to be kept and sold. To make drinking the liquor in such a place and under such circumstances prima facie evidence of an illegal sale to the person drinking, violates no constitutional guaranty. It leaves a party ample opportunity to make his defense. It is specially provided, what is now the general law, that the party can be a witness in his own behalf, and thus it can never be difficult for him to show what the facts really are. The burden of proof is not even really changed. The statute enables the prosecutor to make a prima facie case by proof of the drinking. But the defendant can show the circumstances attending the drinking, his relation thereto and any other facts tending to absolve him from liability, and then on the whole case, the burden still rests upon the prosecution to establish the alleged sale. The defendant has the full benefit of jury trial and due process of law and a full and fair opportunity free from any undue hindrance or embarrassment to make his justification and defense. Hence the charge resting upon the statute was not erroneous.

But the statute need not be invoked to uphold the charge. Under the circumstances of this case, the drinking was good common law evidence of a sale in violation of the statute. The defendant kept liquor for sale, and was shown to be engaged in selling it to be drunk upon his premises quite indiscriminately to persons calling for it. It is against all experience that he gave it away or that persons came there to drink liquor bought elsewhere. It was in his power to prevent the drinking which took place from glasses presumably furnished by him. Evidence of the drinking under such circumstances was certainly prima facie proof that the liquor was bought to be drunk there, and sufficient to justify the charge.

We are, therefore, of opinion that the judgment should be affirmed with costs. All concur.

Judgment affirmed.

References are to chapter and page number for 49 pages of Chapters I and II and thereafter only to page numbers.

References are to chapter and page number for 49 pages of Chapters I and II and thereafter only to page numbers.

References are to chapter and page number for 49 pages of Chapters I and II and thereafter only to page numbers.

References are to chapter and page number for 49 pages of Chapters I and II and thereafter only to page numbers.

References are to chapter and page number for 49 pages of Chapters I and II and thereafter only to page numbers.

SUPPLEMENT NO. I

[Each item herein is to be studied as a part of the Section in this book on the page indicated at the left margin.]

p 5, Sec. 1.1 Affidavit of Personal Service [not in Record on Appeal]

STATE OF NEW YORK COURT, COUNTY OF

Plaintiff

against

Defendant

AFFIDAVIT OF PERSONAL SERVICE OF SUMMONS

State of New York } ss.:
County of

....

being duly sworn, deposes and says that he served the summons in the above entitled action upon the following named defendant at the following place and time , viz.:

NAME STREET, CITY & STATE TIME & DATE

by delivering to and leaving with defendant, personally, a true copy thereof, and deponent further says that he knew person so served to be the same person mentioned and described in the said summons as defendant therein, and that at the times of making such service, deponent was over eighteen years of age and not a party to this action. That he asked defendant whether defendant was in the military service of the United States Government, in any capacity whatever, and defendant replied he was not. Defendant was clad in ordinary civilian clothes and wore no military uniform of any kind.

Deponent further states that he describes the person actually served as follows:

Sex	Skin Color	Hair Color	Age (Approx.)	Height (Approx.)	Weight (Approx.)
☐ Male	☐ Black	☐ Light	☐	☐	lbs.
☐ Female	☐ White	☐ Med.			
	☐	☐ Dark			
		☐			

Other Identifying Features:

Sworn to before me, this

day of , 19

(Print Name Below Signature)

Notary Public – Commissioner of Deeds

p 2, Sec. 2.1 Elements of a Cause of Action
[compare with p iii of Table of Contents]
p 16-24, Sec. 2.11 Legal Interest of Plaintiff (contract)
p 16-17 a. Unilateral Contract [1 case]
p 18-21 b. Bilateral Contract [3 cases]
p 21-24 c. Quasi Contract [3 cases]

p 24 Sec. 2.11 Common Counts

The Common Counts

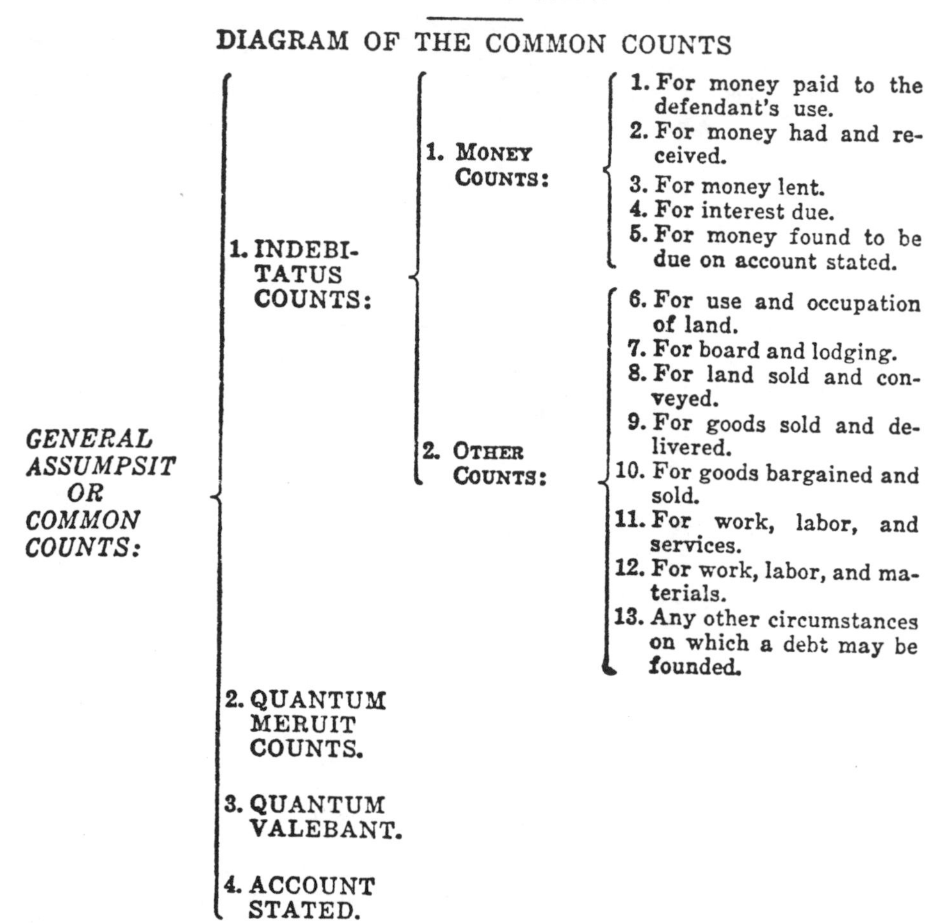

MCKELVEY, Common Law Pleading, § 39 (St. Paul, 1944).

362. *Origin of the Common Counts:* "In declaring in debt, except possibly upon an account stated, the plaintiff was required to set forth his cause of action with great particularity. Thus, the count in debt must state the quantity and description of goods sold, with the details of the price, all the particulars of a loan, the names of the persons to whom the money was paid with the amounts of each payment, the names of the persons from whom money was received to the use of the plaintiff with the amounts of each receipt, the precise nature and amount of the services rendered. In *Indebitatus Assumpsit,* on the other hand, the debt being laid as an inducement or conveyance to the assumpsit, it was not necessary to set forth all the details of the transaction from which it arose. It was enough to allege the general nature of the indebtedness, as for goods sold, money lent, money paid at the defendant's request, money had and received to the plaintiff's use, work and labor at the defendant's request, or upon an account stated, and that the defendant being so indebted promised to pay. This was the origin of the common counts." AMES, *Implied Assumpsit,* 2 HARV. L. REV. 53 (1888); AMES, LECTURES ON LEGAL HISTORY, c. XIV, pp. 153, 154 (Cambridge, 1913).

See, article by KING, *The Use of the Common Counts in California,* 14 So. CALIF. L. REV. 288 (1941).

See Reppy — "Introduction to Civil Procedure" page 489

REGINA RABB, Plaintiff, v BOWERY SAVINGS BANK, Defendant.

Civil Court of the City of New York, New York County, May 20, 1974.

IRA J. RABB for plaintiff. CADWALADER WICKERSHAM & TAFT (W. Mowry Connelly of counsel) for defendant.

Irving Younger, J. In 1965, plaintiff and her husband bought a house. Defendant is their mortgagee.

The mortgage says that the mortgagors shall make certain monthly payments "to be held in trust by the mortgagee." Plaintiff has made the payments. Defendant enters them in an "escrow account" out of which it pays taxes and other assessments on the house. The amount received has exceeded the amount expended for at least the last six years. In 1968, the average monthly balance in plaintiff's favor was $346.76; in 1969, $351.09; in 1970, $485; in 1971, $456.56; in 1972, $604.05; and in 1973, $731.87.

In January, 1974, plaintiff commenced this small claims action "for interest on tax excrow money given to defendant from January, 1968. Breach of fiduciary relationship." Defendant has not objected to the failure to join plaintiff's husband as a party, CPLR 1001, and the facts are stipulated.

In *Tierney v Whitestone Sav. & Loan Assn.,* N.Y.L.J., Jan. 16, 1974, p. 21, col. 2, and 77 Misc 2d 284) a case indistinguishable from this case, Judge Margulies found for the plaintiff. With all diffidence, I decline to follow him.

Plaintiff must establish some basis for holding defendant liable. Since the mortgage contains no promise by the bank to pay interest on the escrow balances, there has been no breach of an express contract. Since plaintiff has offered no evidence of an unstated agreement to pay interest, there has been no breach of an implied contract. Since the Legislature had not spoken, there has been no breach of a statutory obligation. (But, see, L. 1974, ch. 119, providing henceforth for payment of interest on escrow accounts.)

Not seriously disputing any of these conclusions, plaintiff argues that "the rule of just compensation," derived from dicta in *Bevier v Covell* (87 N.Y. 50); *Boston Road Shopping Center v Teachers Ins. & Annuity Assn. of America* (13 AD 2d 106, affd. 11 NY 2d 831); *Fleschner Bros. v Consolidated Edison Co. of N.Y.* (279 App. Div. 69, affd. 304 N.Y. 815) requires a decision in her favor. Although it would be rash to quarrel with the idea that people should be compensated where it is just that they be compensated, I can hardly accept it as a basis for liability. Alas, litigants must do something more than demand justice: ***they must demonstrate a cause of action.***
[emphasis added]

So plaintiff urges that her claim is for money had and received, a theory which usually avails when a plaintiff has given money to a defendant who should, for whatever reason, be made to return it. Here, plaintiff does not sue for the return of anything she gave defendant. Her contention is a more subtle one.

Defendant took plaintiff's escrow payments and commingled them with its general funds. It invested its general funds in the money market - commercial paper, certificates of deposit, treasury bills, etc. - earning whatever interest the money market was then paying. Plaintiff argues that these earnings rightly belong to her, and hence that she has a cause of action for money had and received.

When plaintiff says that the bank's earnings on her escrow payments rightly belong to her, she speaks words of equity. We are taught, however, that this does not convert an action for money and received into an equity action.

"That an action is of an equitable nature does not make it an action in equity.

"When, in an action for money had and received, all the facts show that the plaintiff is *ex aequo at bono* entitled to recover, his right to recover is a legal one and maintainable in a court of law." *(Chapman v Forbes,* 123 N.Y. 532, 537.)

We must go further. In *Chapman,* the allegation was that defendant refused to pay to plaintiff money which defendant had been given by a third person who had received it as the agent of plaintiff's testatrix. There was no fiduciary relationship between plaintiff's testatrix and defendant, a circumstance which limits the Court of Appeals' holding. "And in the particular case before the court there is no such relation of trust between the parties as would render the cause of action cognizable in equity. Equitable relief is not demanded, nor is a case made by the complaint for granting any relief of an equitable nature." *(Chapman, supra,* p. 537.) Here, by contrast, there was a relation of trust between the parties: defendant agreed in the mortgage to hold plaintiff's escrow payments "in trust" for the purposes specified. The complaint alleges "breach of fiduciary relationship," which, allowing for the succinctness customary in small claims cases, sounds in equity. And the transactions at issue, looked at closely, show an equitable cause of action. Defendant was to hold plaintiff's escrow payments in trust. Defendant was thus obliged not to commingle them and not to use them for its own gain. Defendant did both. It follows that, although none of the escrow payments have been dissipated, defendant may be made to disgorge to plaintiff the fruits of its breach of fiduciary obligation.

Plaintiff's remedy, in short, is an accounting of defendant's gain, that is, the interest defendant earned by investing plaintiff's escrow payments in the money market. This may be more or less than the sum obtained by computing interest on the escrow balances, but whatever the amount, the cause of action is equitable. I am therefore obliged to dismiss the complaint for lack of subject-matter jurisdiction (CCA, §§ 202, 1801), and I do.

p 43, Sec. 2.14 — Substantive Right to Relief

a. to be paid damages; or
b. to be given possession of a chattel; or
c. to be given possession real property; or
d. to have specific performance of a contract;
e. and others

p 50, Sec. 2.2 — Examples of Causes of Action

I. Examples of Causes of Action *at Common Law*

A. *Criminal* Offenses [cf Causes of Action]

1. Arson	7. Manslaughter
2. Assault	8. Mayhem
3. Bigamy	9. Murder
4. Burglary	10. Rape
5. Forgery	11. Suicide
6. Larceny	12. (and others)

B. *Contractual* Causes of Action (ex contractu)

1. to be paid damages for breach of a covenant or contract under deal (Covenant)
2. to be paid a certain sum of money (debt)
3. to be paid damages for non-performance of a special contract not under seal (Special Assumpsit)
4. to be paid damages (1) for a breach of contract express or implied-in-fact (common counts); or for non-performance of a duty implied-in-law to pay for a benefit conferred - quasi-contract (General Assumpsit)

C. *Tortious* Causes of Action (ex Delicto)

1. Assault, to be paid damages for (Trespass vi et armis)
2. Unlawfully carrying away goods or property, to be paid damages for (Trespass de bonas asportatis)
3. Unlawful entry upon land, to paid damages for (Trespass quare clausum fregit)
4. Conversion by an unlawful use, to be paid damages for (Trover)
5. Spoil or destruction as to real property, to be paid damages for (waste)
6. To be given possession of real property (Ejectment)
7. To be given possession of goods unlawfully taken (Replevin)
8. To be given possession of chattels unlawfully detained (Detinue)
9. To be paid damages for (Trespass on the Case)

a. Abuse of Process	f. Malpractice
b. Alienation of Affections	g. Negligence
c. Deceit	h. Nuisance
d. Libel	i. Slander
e. Malicious Prosecution	j. and others

p. 74, Sec. 2.4 — Types, Aspects, Facets, Features, of a Cause of Action

a. Unitary Nature and Differentiation 74, 76, 78, 79, 81, 88
b. In Personam vis-a-vis in Rem, Cause of Action 102, 116, 134
c. Transitory vis-a-vis Local, Cause of Action 102, 134
d. Continuing Cause of Action 82, 84, 88
e. Divisible Cause of Action 84, 81, 87, 88, 104
f. Ancillary, Dependent, Derivative, Causes of Action 2, 48, 223
g. Co-Owners or a Class of Persons vis-a-vis a Cause of Action 91
h. Administrative Causes of Action 12, 53 Supp. p 5
i. Accrual of a Cause of Action 90
j. Termination of a Cause of Action: abatement, lapse, moot, extinguishment, barring, merger, of a Cause of Action 92, 93
k. Survival and Revival, of a Cause of Action 93
l. and others

p 91, Sec. 2.4h. ADMINISTRATIVE CAUSES OF ACTION

Worker's Compensation Claim under Workers' Compensation Statute in New York State

WHAT EVERY WORKER SHOULD KNOW IN CASE OF ON-THE-JOB INJURY

The law requires the employer:—

1. To provide workers' compensation so that you may properly be taken care of in case of an on-the-job injury.
2. To post a notice,
   a. If he carries insurance, giving the name of the insurance carrier;
   b. If he is self-insured, stating that he is self-insured. Look for this notice in your place of employment. Advise the Board if it is not posted in a conspicuous place.

YOUR RIGHTS:

1. The Workers' Compensation Board will on its own initiative schedule such hearings as appear to be necessary. In addition, the Board will schedule your case for hearing if you so request. YOU ARE ENTITLED TO A HEARING.

2. You have the right to choose the doctor to treat you, if he is authorized by the Chairman of the Workers' Compensation Board to treat your type of injury. Your doctor can let you know whether he is so authorized. If you are unable to select a doctor, or if you do not desire to do so and so advise your employer in writing, your employer is obliged to provide the necessary medical attention. Your doctor's bills (and bills for hospital and other services of a medical nature) will be paid for directly by your employer or his insurance company, if your case is not disputed. If your case *is* disputed, hearings will be held to determine who is responsible for them. Do not pay these bills yourself pending such a determination.

3. In addition, you are entitled to be reimbursed for drugs, crutches or any apparatus such as belts, if they are properly prescribed by your doctor and if you have paid for them yourself; also for carfares and other necessary expenses going to and from your doctor's office or a hospital. You should secure a receipt for such expenses (or prepare a bill in the case of carfares), and present it to your employer or his insurance carrier for payment. If payment is refused, the bill or receipt should be sent to the Workers' Compensation Board with a statement of the fact that payment has been refused by the employer or his carrier.

4. You are entitled to compensation if your injury keeps you from work more than one week, compels you to work at lower wages, or leaves you with permanently injured eyesight or hearing, serious facial scars, or any permanent injury or stiffness of a finger, hand, toe, foot, leg or arm.

Workers' Compensation is payable directly and without waiting for an award, except when the claim is disputed. Duly licensed representatives of organizations may assist their members with claims and at hearings. You may consult the nearest office of the Workers' Compensation Board for advice. While a claimant usually needs no one to represent him, you have the right to be represented by an attorney or a duly licensed claimant's representative. However, do not pay for such services directly. Their fee will be fixed by the W. C. Law Judge and deducted from your award.

WHAT YOU MUST DO:

1. Tell your employer or foreman at once of your injury no matter how slight it is. Tell him where and how you were injured. If this notice is not given to your employer within 30 days after the injury, you may lose your right to compensation.

2. You should secure medical attention promptly from a doctor authorized by the Chairman of the Workers' Compensation Board to treat workers' compensation injuries, and request your doctor to file the proper medical reports with the Board and with your employer or his insurance carrier, without delay.

3. Make out this claim for compensation and send it to the nearest office of the Workers' Compensation Board as soon as possible. If this is not done within two years after the date the injury occurred you may lose your right to compensation.

4. If you need additional copies of this form and cannot obtain them from your employer, write for them to the nearest office of the Workers' Compensation Board.

5. Attend the hearings on your case when you are notified to appear.

6. Go back to work as soon as you are able.

Compensation is never as high as your wage. The law limits it to two-thirds of your weekly wage and not more than the maximum per week stated in the law effective on the date of injury.

* * *

IT IS A MISDEMEANOR TO MAKE A WILLFUL FALSE STATEMENT OR REPRESENTATION FOR THE PURPOSE OF OBTAINING BENEFITS UNDER THE PROVISIONS OF THE WORKERS' COMPENSATION LAW.

BOARD RULES

Rule 12 [12 NYCRR 300.12]. **Certification of Question to the Board:**

When a claim presents a novel or important question of law or a question of public policy, a Referee [Worker's Compensation Law Judge] before rendering his decision thereon may certify such question to the Board. In such a case the Referee shall develop the record on the question involved and submit to the Board for determination his findings of fact and the question presented by the record for decision.

Rule 13 [12 NYCRR 300.13]. **Application for Review:**

An application to the Board to review any decision of a Referee shall be in writing and shall specify the grounds thereof. It may be accompanied by a reference to or excerpt from the offical minutes or such part thereof as is relevant to the issue raised. Such application shall be filed within thirty days after notice of filing of the decision.

The Board shall either act upon said application for review without further hearing or direct that a hearing be held before the Board for argument on the application. Upon such review and upon the evidence in the record, the Board may affirm, reverse, or modify any decision or award as the law and the facts may require, or take any other action as may be in the interest of justice. *[As amended, March 1, 1965.]*

Rule 14 [12 NYCRR 300.14]. **Application for Rehearing:**

Application may be made by any party in interest for rehearing or reopening of a claim. Such application must indicate that: [omitted]

p. 134, Sec. 3.121 [insert these two paragraphs before opionion of Mr. Justice Field:]

On the trial, the defendants, to show title out of the plaintiffs, offered in evidence the judgment for the costs, the execution issued thereon, and the sheriff's deed; to the introduction of which the plaintiffs objected, on the ground that the judgment for costs was a judgment **in personam** and **in rem,** and was rendered against the defendant, who was a nonresident of the State, without his appearance in the action or personal service of citation upon him, but upon a citation by publication only, and therefore constituted no basis of title in the purchaser under the execution.

The court sustained the objection and excluded the document from the jury; and the defendants excepted to the ruling. No other evidence of title being produced by the defendants, a verdict was found for the plaintiffs, and judgment in their favor was entered thereon; to review which the case is brought to this court on a writ of error.

p 154, Sec. 3.41 JURISDICTION
Sec. 3.412 AFFIDAVIT OF PERSONAL SERVICE [See supra Supp. p 1, Sec. 1.1]

p. 163, Sec. 3.422 NOTE OF ISSUE [See Supp. p 7 & 8 infra

p 198-199 GROUNDS FOR APPEAL OR REVIEW [pp refer to Ch. I Record of Case on Appeal]
Plaintiff's Grounds for Appeal: pp 10, 13, 22, 23, 28

Defendant's Grounds for Appeal: pp 12, 18-19, 27, 30, 33

No grounds for Appeal: pp. 11, 12, 13, 17, 23, 24, 25, 26, 29

VIVIEN DOYLE, Resp. v GEORGE STREIFER, et al., Apellants (3d Dept. 1970) 34 A D 2d 183, S2d

APPEAL from a judgment of the Supreme Court, entered December 2, 1968, in Sullivan County, upon a verdict rendered at a Trial Term (Arthur A. Davis, Jr., J.), in favor of plaintiff..

REYNOLDS, J. This is an appeal from a judgment of the Supreme Court, Sullivan County, entered upon a jury verdict in favor of respondent and a denial of appellants' motion to set aside the verdict.

The judgment in this case must be reversed and a new trial granted. The plaintiff, a tenant, alleges a fall on an areaway which formed a portion of the way of ingress and egress to her apartment. It was claimed that the areaway or court was covered with a sheet of mirror-like ice.

The negligence in this case was that there was no snow or ice removal in the areaway involved between November, 1966 and February 24, 1967, the alleged date of the accident. Such proof was offered and received over obligation. On this record such evidence was remote, irrelevant, and constituted prejudicial error. The defendant has testified to the maintenance and snow removal and the use of ashes and salt when necessary and where he got these materials. A business establishment, an employment agency, was located on the same areaway as the house in which plaintiff resided and there was testimony that many people went in and out every day.

The landlord is under a duty to use reasonable care to keep the walks and areaways which constitute the ingress and egress of the tenant reasonably safe, but cannot be held liable for a defect in his property unless he has notice of the defect or in the exercise of due care should have had such notice. In these snow and ice situations he may know that snow has fallen and thus realize that a dangerous condition exists but he is entitled to remedy the condition. Where he has not had a sufficient time to remedy the condition caused by the elements liability will not result (*Hoffman v. Bachrach,* 20 A D 2d 790; *Preuschoff v. Wank,* 16 A D 2d 690; *Falina v. Hollis Diner,* 281 App. Div. 711, affd. 306 N.Y. 586). Where as here, the defendants were confronted with a claim that the areaway was covered with a sheet of mirror-like ice, it is apparent that the correct date and the condition existing on that date and just prior thereto become most important and not a condition existing in November, December or January.

There was an error in the charge which constituted serious prejudice to the defendant. The court charged the jury that the sanitation and health section (Multiple Residence Law, § 174) applied to snow and ice. This section reads: "The owner shall keep all and every part of a dwelling and the lot on which it is situated in good repair, clean and free from

[Continued on Supplement page 9]

This space for Clerk's file stamp

NOTE OF ISSUE
(TYPE OR PRINT)

ourt Case No..........................

.................................Court,...County, N. Y.

NOTICE FOR.............................., 19.......

..................................Term of Court.

Trial } Jury demanded ☐
Without jury ☐

Filed by Attorney for.................................

Date summons served...............................

Date issue joined.....................................

NATURE AND OBJECT OF ACTION (Specify for *each* cause of Action)

Negligence	M.V.	R.R.	Bldg. & Sidewalk	Other
Personal Injury	☐	☐	☐	☐
Property Damage	☐	☐	☐	☐
Both	☐	☐	☐	☐

Other Tort (specify)..

Contract (specify)..

Other Law (specify) ....

Matrimonial (specify)...

Other Equity (specify) ....

Amount Demanded $...........................

Other Relief ....

....

Preference claimed under ....

n the ground that..

....

ttorney(s) for Plaintiff(s)
ffice and P.O. Address
hone

Attorney(s) for Defendant(s)
Office and P.O. Address
Phone

Note: Clerk will not accept this note of issue unless reverse side is completed

ORM 809 - Note of Issue

TUTBLANX - Tuttle Law Print, Publishers, Rutland, Vt.

Affidavit of Service

State of New York, County of ss.:

being duly sworn, deposes and says, that on the day of , 19 , he served the within note of issue on Esq., the attorney for the plaintiff / defendant in the within entitled action, at his office at during his absence from said office by then and there leaving a true copy of the same with , his partner; his clerk; therein: a person having charge of said office. That deponent is years of age.

....

Sworn to before me this day of , 19

....

State of New York, County of ss.:

being duly sworn, deposes and says, that he served the within note of issue on Esq., the attorney for the plaintiff / defendant in the within entitled action, on the day of , 19 , through the Post Office, by depositing a true and correct copy of the same properly enclosed in a postpaid wrapper, in: a Branch Post Office; a Post Office Box; regularly maintained by the government of the United States at

and under the care of the General Post Office, in the

that being then the post office of the attorney for the plaintiff, / defendant, Directed to the said attorney for the plaintiff / defendant, at No.

that being the address designated by he for that purpose upon the preceding papers in this action. That deponent is years of age.

....

Sworn to before me this day of , 19

....

Admission of Service

Due service of a note of issue, of which the within is a copy, admitted this day of , 19 .

....

Attorney for

Statement of Readiness

Required under special rule respecting calendar practice

	[Mark one] Complete	Waived	Not required
1. All pleadings served	....	....	....
2. Bill of Particulars served	....	....	....
3. Physical examinations had	....	....	....
4. Examinations before trial completed	....	....	....
5. All depositions now known to be necessary completed	....	....	....

6. There has been a reasonable opportunity to complete the above proceedings.

7. The case is ready for trial.

Dated:..

(Signature)..

Attorney for
Office and P.O. Address:

Stipulated that the above enumerated proceedings have been completed or waived.

Dated:..

....

Attorney for Plaintiff

....

Attorney for Defendant

vermin, rodents, dirt, filth, garbage or other thing or matter dangerous to life or health''. There is nothing in the legislative history of this section which would indicate that it was intended to apply to snow and ice cases which arise as a result of precipitation from the sky, and such a construction, it seems obvious, was not the intention of the Legislature and is improper. The court charged that this defendant had a statutory duty under this section and that ice and snow was a thing or matter dangerous to life or health within the meaning of the statute and that if the defendant violated this section and it was a proximate cause of plaintiff's injury they *must find* that defendant was negligent. Although no exception was taken to the charge, the error was a fundamental one and we should take cognizance of it in the exercise of our power to reverse and to grant a new trial in the interests of justice. *(De Joseph v. Gutekunst,* 13 A D 2d 223; *Bulat v. O'Brien,* 13 A D 2d 904; *Cohen v Gilbert,* 12 A D 2d 301; *Molnar v Slattery Contr. Co.,* 8 A D 2d 95.)

Injection of insurance coverage into the trial was improper. No motion for a mistrial, however, was made in this case.

Some of the statements in the summations were definitely improper. The statements by plaintiff's counsel that the plaintiff and the other tenants were being discriminated against because of race and color and that defendants' customers were drunkards went beyond the bounds of propriety and were prejudicial. Defendants' counsel also made some remarks which were improper. Upon a retrial counsel should act with propriety.

The judgment should be reversed, on the law and the facts and the interests of justice, and a new trial ordered, without costs.

HERLIHY, P.J., STALEY, JR. GREENBLOTT and SWEENEY, J.J., concur.

Judgment reversed, on the law and the facts and in the interests of justice, and a new trial ordered, without costs.

p 205, Scc. 3.75 Remittitur or Mandate

ALEXANDER v HOLMES COUNTY Bd. of Education (1969) 396 US 20, 90 S.Ct. 29

PER CURIAM.

This case comes to the Court on a petition for certiorari to the Court of Appeals for the Fifth Circuit. The petition was granted on October 9, 1969, and the case set down for early argument. The question presented is one of paramount importance, involving as it does the denial of fundamental rights to many thousands of school children, who are presently attending Mississippi schools under segregated conditions contrary to the applicable decisions of this Court. Against this background the Court of Appeals should have denied all motions for additonal time because continued operation of segregated schools under a standard of allowing "all deliberate speed" for desegregation is no longer consitutionally permissible. Under explicit holdings of this Court the obligation of every school district is to terminate dual school systems at once and to operate now and hereafter only unitary schools. Griffin v. County School Board, 377 U.S. 218, 234, 84 S.Ct. 1226, 1235, 12 L.Ed2d 256 (1964); Green v. County School Board of New Kent County, 391 US 430, 438-439, 442, 88 S.Ct. 1689, 1694-1695, 1696, 20 L.Ed.2d 716 (1968). Accordingly,

It is hereby adjudged, ordered, and decreed:

1. The Court of Appeals' order of August 28, 1969, is vacated, and the case is remanded to that court to issue its decree and order, effective immediately, declaring that each of the school districts here involved may no longer operate a dual school system based on race or color, and directing that they begin immediately to operate as unitary school systems within which no person is to be effectively excluded from any school because of race or color.

2. The Court of Appeals may in its discretion direct the schools here involved to accept all or any part of the August 11, 1969, recommendations of the Department of Health, Education, and Welfare, with any modifications which that court deems proper insofar as those recommendations insure a totally unitary school system for all eligible pupils without regard to race or color.

The Court of Appeals may make its determination and enter its order without further arguments or submissions.

3. While each of these school systems is being operated as a unitary system under the order of the Court of Appeals, the District Court may hear and consider objections thereto or proposed amendments thereof, provided, however, that the Court of Appeals' order shall be complied with in all respects while the District Court considers such objections or amendments, if any are made. No amendment shall become effective before being passed upon by the Court of Appeals.

4. The Court of Appeals shall retain jurisdiction to insure prompt and faithful compliance with its order, and

may modify or amend the same as may be deemed necessary or desirable for the operation of a unitary school system.

5. The order of the Court of Appeals dated August 28, 1969, having been vacated and the case remanded for proceedings in conformity with this order, the judgment shall issue forthwith and the Court of Appeals is requested to give priority to the execution of this judgment as far as possible and necessary.